Systems Development

HANDBOOK

4th EDITION

Systems Development HANDBOOK

4th EDITION

Paul C. Tinnirello
EDITOR

AUERBACH

Boca Raton London New York Washington, D.C.

Library of Congress Cataloging-in-Publication Data

Systems development handbook / edited by Paul C. Tinnirello. — 4th ed.
p. cm.
Includes bibliographical references.
ISBN 0-8493-9822-3 (alk. paper)
1. Application software—Development Handbooks, manuals, etc.
I. Tinnirello, Paul C.
QA76.76.D47S955 1999
005.1—dc21 98-34563
CIP

This book contains information obtained from authentic and highly regarded sources. Reprinted material is quoted with permission, and sources are indicated. A wide variety of references are listed. Reasonable efforts have been made to publish reliable data and information, but the author and the publisher cannot assume responsibility for the validity of all materials or for the consequences of their use.

Direct all inquiries to CRC Press LLC, 2000 Corporate Blvd., N.W., Boca Raton, Florida 33431.

No claim to original U.S. Government works
International Standard Book Number 0-8493-9822-3
Library of Congress Card Number 98-34563
2 3 4 5 6 7 8 9 0

Contributors

RICHARD BELLAVER, *Professor of Computer and Information Science, Cleveland State University, Cleveland, OH*

BEN A. BLAKE, *Professor of Computer and Information Science, Cleveland State University, Cleveland, OH*

SCOTT C. BLANCHETTE, *Senior Associate, c. w. Costello & Associates, Inc., Middletown, CT*

BIJOY BORDOLOI, *Assistant Professor of Information Systems and Management Sciences, University of Texas, Arlington, TX*

JOHN G. BURCH, *Professor, Accounting and Computer Information Systems, University of Nevada, Reno, NV*

JANET BUTLER, *Independent Consultant, Ranchos de Taos, NM*

PATRICIA L. CARBONE, *Principal Staff Member, Mitretek Systems, McLean, VA*

JOHN CARE, *Regional Technical Manager, Vantive Corporation, Yardley, PA*

DALE COHEN, *Electronic Messaging Team Project Manager, R.R. Donnelley & Sons Co., Chicago, IL*

JAMES R. COLEMAN, *President, Yazoo Enterprises, Lawrenceville, GA*

KEN DOUGHTY, *Principal Consultant, O'Driscoll & Doughty Associates, Brisbane, Australia*

SHARI DOVE, *Andersen Consulting Group, Lake Forest, IL*

RICHARD T. DUÉ, *President, Thomsen Dué and Associates, Ltd., Edmonton, Alberta, Canada*

LEN DVORKIN, *President, Italex Consulting, Inc., Thornhill, Ontario, Canada*

ADAM FADLALLA, PhD, *Assistant Professor of Computer and Information Science, Cleveland State University, Cleveland, OH*

DAN FOBES, *Software Architect, Yardley, PA*

FREDERICK GALLEGOS, *IS Audit Advisor and Faculty Member, Computer Information Systems, California State Polytechnic University, Pomona, CA*

JAMES E. GASKIN, *Consultant and Author, Dallas, TX*

MICHAEL L. GIBSON, *Professor of Management, Auburn University, Auburn, AL*

IDO GILEADI, *Manager, Deloitte & Touche Consulting Group and Lecturer, Ryerson Polytechnic University, Toronto, Ontario, Canada*

Mike Glassey, *Computer Auditor, Department of Social Services, England*
Donald Golden, PhD, *Professor of Computer and Information Science, Cleveland State University, Cleveland, OH*
Hal H. Green, *Director, Manufacturing Systems Division, SETPOINT Inc., Houston, TX*
Franke Grieco, *Manager of Information Systems Audit, Brisbane City Council, Brisbane, Australia*
Fritz H. Grupe, *Associate Professor, Computer Information Systems, University of Nevada, Reno, NV*
Carl Stephen Guynes, PhD, *Professor, College of Business Administration, University of North Texas, Denton, TX*
Linda G. Hayes, *Chief Executive Officer, WorkSoft, Inc., Dallas, TX*
Gilbert Held, *Director, 4-Degree Consulting, Macon, GA*
David K. Holthaus, *Software Specialist, Nationwide Insurance Enterprise, Columbus, OH*
Ashvin Iyengar, *Consultant, Object Technologies Group, Deloitte & Touche Consulting Group, Toronto, Ontario, Canada*
Paul J. Jalics, PhD, *Professor of Computer and Information Science, Cleveland State University, Cleveland, OH*
Lee Janke, *Consulting Manager, Unidata Professional Services, Denver, CO*
Brian Jeffrey, *Managing Director, International Technology Group, Mountain View, CA*
Leon A. Kappelman, *Department of Business Computer Information Systems, College of Business Administration, University of North Texas, Denton, TX*
James A. Larson, *Senior Software Engineer, Intel Architecture Lab, Hillsboro, OR*
Carol L. Larson, *Freelance Desktop Publisher, Hillsboro, OR*
William N. Ledbetter, PhD, *Professor of Management, Tuskegee University, Tuskegee, AL*
William F. Lenihan, *Senior Manager, Deloitte & Touche Management Consulting, Stamford, CT*
Richard J. Lewis, Jr., *eCom Connections and Miami University, Oxford, OH*
David Litwack, *President, dml Associates, Fairfax, VA*
Joe Luchetski, *University of Texas, Arlington, TX*
Victor Matos, PhD, *Associate Professor of Computer and Information Science, College of Business Administration, Cleveland State University, Cleveland, OH*
Gordon E. McCray, *Assistant Professor, Information Systems and Technology, Wake Forest University, Winston-Salem, NC*
John McMullen, *Technical Writer, Mortice Kern Systems Inc., Waterloo, Ontario, Canada*
Ulla Merz, PhD, *Principal Consultant, P2E, Boulder, CO*
Santosh K. Misra, PhD, *Associate Professor of Computer and Information Science, Cleveland State University, Cleveland, OH*
J.P. Morgenthal, *Java Computing Analyst, nc.focus, New York, NY*
Nathan J. Muller, *Independent Consultant, Huntsville, AL*

JOHN P. MURRAY, *IT Consultant, Madison, WI*
DOUG NICKERSON, *Software Engineer, Cape Cod, MA*
POLLY PERRYMAN, *Independent Consultant, Stoughton, MA*
KENNETH P. PRAGER, *Principal, Riverton Management Consulting Group, Inc., Palmyra, NJ*
RUSSELL L. PURVIS, *Assistant Professor, Management Information Systems, University of Central Florida, Orlando, FL*
STEVE RABIN, *American Software, Atlanta, GA*
T.M. RAJKUMAR, *Associate Professor, Department of Decision Sciences and Management Information Systems, Miami University, Oxford, OH*
TOM L. ROBERTS, JR., *Assistant Professor, College of Business Administration, Middle Tennessee University, Murfreesboro, TN*
PATRICIA L. SEYMOUR, *Principal and Founder of Technology Innovations, Danville, CA*
DUANE E. SHARP, *President, SharpTech Associates, Mississauga, Ontario, Canada*
JOANNA S.P. SHUM, *Programmer, Hong Kong, China*
MICHAEL SIMONYI, *Systems Architect, Etobicoke, Ontario, Canada*
LOUISE SOE, PhD, *Associate Professor, Computer Information Systems, California State Polytechnic University, Pomona, CA*
MARTIN D. SOLOMON, *Senior Associate, c. w. Costello & Associates, Inc., Middletown, CT*
J. WAYNE SPENCE, *Business Computer Information Systems Department, College of Business Administration, University of North Texas, Denton, TX*
ANDREW J. SWADENER, *Consulting Manager, Unidata Professional Services, Denver, CO*
RAY WALKER, *Senior Consultant, Process Control Initiative, DuPont Engineering, Houston, TX*
BRYAN WILKINSON, *Director of Information Systems Audit, Teledyne, Inc., Los Angeles, CA*
EVA Y.W. WONG, *Assistant Professor, Department of Information Systems, City University of Hong Kong, Hong Kong, China*
LEO A. WROBEL, *President and Chief Executive Officer, Premiere Network Services, Inc., DeSoto, TX*

Contents

Introduction

System development remains as one of the most demanding and challenging activities in the computing industry. Continuous advancements in technology, compounded with aggressive business competitiveness have fueled an extremely difficult and often overwhelming development atmosphere. Rapidly evolving technologies, such as e-Commerce or Component Objects, exemplify both the opportunities and complexities for building tomorrow's advanced systems. Adding to this challenge has been the serious shortage of skilled workers who can competently fulfill the system development mission.

IT professionals, who work in the system development environment, are struggling with the pace of such change as well as the stress of integrating new applications within the framework of existing systems. Concurrently, there is continuous demand for better control and accountability of IT expenditures. Furthermore, there has been more pressure for software professionals to acquire business related knowledge without sacrificing technical savvy. Clearly, accomplishing the diverse challenges of application development requires maturity, adaptability, and perseverance.

This edition of the handbook has been updated to reflect the latest information and proven strategies involved with system development. It builds on the strengths of earlier editions by providing a vast array of real world and practical knowledge from development experts. I have endeavored to preserve continuity with the experiences that many development managers share about system development, including my own experiences. Thus, the collective set of chapters offers a compelling portfolio of all facets of the application development process, including post-development issues.

Software development technology trends in this past year continue to emphasize critical and urgent need of reducing the overall time to bring applications to production. The exploding growth of the Internet and Web-based applications have further emphasized this need. Section I,

"Management and Planning," Section II, "Development Strategies," and Section IV "Programming Techniques," each review the practical and realistic aspects of new development methods including multi-tiered client server, object oriented development, and Internet based systems. Although these newer development methods are gaining widespread acceptance, there are significant risks to those organizations who are not prepared to examine the technology from all sides. Thus, the opportunities that may be gained from a new type of technical advancement can be lost due to misunderstanding or poor strategy.

Exploiting the massive amount of accumulated data within an organization's information framework has also been a serious business challenge to development managers. Section V, "Database Functionality and Design," Section VI, "Operating Platforms," and Section VII, "Networking and Connectivity" provide numerous procedures for capitalizing on the vast amount of stored information. Organizations that aggressively pursue methods for effective information extraction will be better prepared to meet the economic challenges of the revolutionary e-business world.

The past efforts toward Year 2000 date compliancy has brought much attention on the issues that surround deployed application systems. Going forward, there will be more changes as organizations try to leverage as much life out of existing systems. Section VIII, "Testing Software Applications," Section XI, "Supporting Existing Software," and, Section XII, "Post Development Administration," cover important details regarding applications that migrate from development to the production environment. Given the accelerated pace of development, many systems are quickly transferred into production mode without rigorous testing or control mechanisms.

Regardless of the numerous challenges that surround development, there is always an abundant array of new and exciting opportunities that are enabled via new technology. Section III, "Tools, Tips and Practices" and Section IX, "Quality and Productivity Initiatives" offer valuable information about leveraging new technology to help meet business goals and objectives. This includes breakthrough tools that take advantage of code reuse and component based technology.

Sustaining the necessary awareness of business and technology events is becoming more burdensome each day. Finding the time to investigate and explore various development paths is often compromised by the hectic stride of today's IT environment. Section X, "Leveraging Staff Resources," provides useful guidelines for those who manage or lead development teams. Isolating oneself from business and technology trends is extremely risky. While it is often important to maintain the stability of existing applications, it is equally, if not more important, to stay near the edge of new opportunities.

The factors that lead to successful system development are not happenstance. Accomplishment requires the maturity of experience, a keen sense of adaptability, and the commitment to perseverance. Possessing these talents does not guarantee success, but without such skills the development effort is even more arduous. Unfortunately there are no exact blueprints for the development process nor is there a singular style or procedure. Despite what may be published or taught, application development also requires a broad spectrum of technical and managerial wisdom, as well as the ability to seek out new methods and alternatives. Furthermore, these skills must be synchronized with the business climate of a given organizational environment.

Managing the system development process is a delicate balancing act of people, technology, and corporate culture. Achieving the necessary skills for this challenge is an unceasing process. Perhaps this may explain the high failure rate of many development projects or the burn out rate of many software managers. I recognize the difficulty of mastering the various demands that these three segments impose on the application development function. Fortunately, many of the chapters in this handbook provide insights that can ease the burdens associated with development.

Keeping pace with needs of programming staff has become more formidable, especially in a tight labor marketplace. Career uncertainty seems to loom about as result of new and specialized software technologies. Satisfying the interests of highly qualified professionals, and concurrently motivating those who lumber in older technologies is no easy task. Yet, without the necessary development talent, organizations risk loss of business opportunities. While outsourcing techniques can assist some application needs, it cannot accommodate all of the issues that face today's development requirements.

Determining the value of technological advancements is more complicated as each year passes. The continuous flurry of predictions and expectations about hardware and software trends is often confusing, if not misleading. It is important to maintain the status quo without losing an edge on the future. But at what cost? Not all new technology is ready for rigorous production demands. And many development managers are thrust into decisions regarding new tools and techniques without the benefit of benchmarks or pilot projects.

Development managers are no longer isolated programming servants in hiding. In fact, the trend for closer integration of business and technical expertise is an accepted prerequisite for IT professionals. However, recent shifts in economic conditions have forced many software managers to rethink application development strategies based on business survival and corporate mood. Making the appropriate decision could be more "politically correct" than "technically correct." This can be especially true as business departments take more responsibility for their own application development.

Although the aforementioned conditions have existed for decades, there is greater intensity and acceleration in today's development environment. Each good decision is a function of quicker responsiveness with the potential of greater return on investment. Likewise, poor decisions can be more perilous. Regardless of the adversities, software development still holds the promise of using technology for the furtherance of business goals. And many IT managers are eager to continue the pursuit of fulfilling such goals via successful development techniques.

Effective use of this handbook can best be accomplished if the reader previews the chapters by reading each section introduction. Most sections are organized around the various components and phases of application development. In some instances, the section may represent a subdiscipline, such as database technology, to the overall development structure. Numerous chapters make reference to ideas found in other sections. Some chapters could easily fit into other section areas, so the reader is advised to look at all material when searching for a particular topic or concept. Unlike other books, which have limited scope, the handbook is an ideal tool that encompasses an extensive range of development material. In many ways it can be used as both an encyclopedia and guidebook. For the reader, this provides a concise source for easy reference.

The daily challenges of system development will remain as long as business needs exist. For those of us who strive to earnestly improve the process, it is never boring or dull. From my own experiences as an application development manager and now as a senior level IT executive, I am cautious about predictions that suggest quantum improvements to the development process will occur overnight. While some technical advancements may provide significant improvements, it is still likely that strong and steady incremental steps for development are supported by commitment and determination. Utilizing the information in this book can leverage the ability not only to survive, but succeed amidst an environment of ongoing change. I am encouraged by the new material in this edition and hopeful it will strengthen your determination, offer opportunity for insight, and generate enthusiasm for development challenges that lie ahead.

Section I

Management and Planning

Management and planning are necessary prerequisites to the complexities associated with application development. Yet, meeting the demands to fulfill projects expeditiously can compromise the most stringent plans. As a result project management and planning practices are being observed more carefully in both large and small corporations. Numerous organizations are assessing the value of all department levels, including the IS area, for productivity, quality, and return-on-investment. Driving this mission has been the increased demand of business competition fueled by globalization of the economy. IS environments are particularly prone to scrutiny due to the increasing expenses associated with development initiatives. Development managers must continually justify the cost of existing technology, while assessing the value of new solutions. The dynamics of today's IS climate may not allow for the traditional techniques used in management and planning. In response, some organizations are revamping current management and planning procedures while other organizations are pursuing alternate methods to manage application development activities.

Chapter 1, "Project Meetings: A Communication and Coordination Tool," explains how to structure meetings so that they are effective tools for managing systems development projects.

One of the ways for improving the management of software projects is described in Chapter 2, "Project Assessment: A Tool for Improving Project Management." This chapter describes a practical guide for analyzing projects that can be used as a benchmark for determining the appropriate course of action needed. Since each development project has unique characteristics, it makes sense to evaluate the project from various standpoints, rather than from just the programming effort typically involved. Understanding the dynamics of such issues will help strengthen the role that project management plays in the implementation of new technology.

Application development challenges will remain as organizations get beyond the difficulties of millennium date conversions. As such, it is important to remember that the basic issues for managing system development are still critical for success, including the capture of system requirements. Chapter 3, "Managing Systems Requirements," describes four major activities: capturing, organizing, reviewing and controlling that are part of the system requirement process. Perhaps the most common issue for project failure may be the result of misunderstood or misstated system requirements. Development managers are well aware of the changing specifications associated with project implementation. The information contained in this chapter can minimize unnecessary changes and help ensure the timely delivery of applications that meet user needs.

Outsourcing continues to gain the interest of those organizations who seek an alternative to internally developed application systems. Development managers are often unprepared, and sometimes unwilling, to objectively evaluate the various outsourcing options available. Recent surveys indicate that reckless outsourcing practices can be volatile to an organization's technology endeavors. Likewise, ignoring outsourcing can be just as dangerous, especially with the shortage of skilled IS professionals. These issues only emphasize the need to carefully assess all sides of the outsourcing marketplace. Chapter 4, "Managing The Risks of Outsourcing Systems Development," the authors challenge the reader's knowledge about outsourcing alternatives. Although outsourcing alleviates some of the resource issues required for development, there is still a need for project management as a means of ensuring implementation success.

Chapter 1
Project Meetings: A Communication and Coordination Tool

Ulla Merz

Good coordination is an important factor in project success. In turn, coordination success is based on interpersonal networks and informed project members, as reported in the survey study "Coordination in Software Development" by Robert E. Kraut and Lynn A. Streeter.[1]

Data from that same survey of 65 software projects suggests that personal communication is important for successful coordination in software development projects. The drawbacks are the high cost of one-on-one interaction and the lack of tangible results. The same survey also found that project members do not find formal impersonal communication, such as written requirements documents, source code, and data dictionaries, very valuable.

Project meetings are an opportunity to combine the benefits from personal communication and formal impersonal communication. Meetings are a place for personal interactions. Documenting the outcome of a meeting by writing meeting minutes or updating a design document realizes the benefits of the work accomplished in the meeting.

WHAT IS WRONG WITH MEETINGS

Review the following questions and check the ones that can be answered with a "yes."

- Have you attended meetings where you did not get the information you needed?
- Have you attended meetings where the atmosphere was hostile or abusive?
- Have you attended meetings where most of the decisions were postponed?
- Have you attended meetings where the purpose was unclear?

0-8493-9822-3/00/$0.00+$.50

In all the cases where the answer was a yes, the meeting was not an effective coordination tool.

MAKING MEETINGS A VALUABLE COMMUNICATION TOOL

What do meetings that one experienced as valuable to attend — meetings one keeps going back to — have in common? Here are some responses people gave in a survey for a project post-mortem:

- The meetings address issues of concern.
- It is important to get everyone face to face, but also limit the time spent doing so.
- Everyone gets the same information.
- Everyone is made aware of the changes.

Personally, the Sunday church meetings and the weekly toastmaster's meetings are meetings the author keeps going back to, because they seem valuable. Effective meetings have several things in common:

1. The needs of each participant are met.
2. Concerns important to the group as a whole are addressed.
3. The purpose is clear.
4. The atmosphere is comfortable.

The following sections discuss what can be done to make meetings an effective communication tool:

- identify the purpose of the meeting
- define the deliverables or work products of meetings
- create the atmosphere/context for success

Define the Purpose of the Meeting

There are mainly three types of meetings:

1. meetings for exchanging information
2. meetings for making decisions
3. meetings for solving problems

Examples for each are (1) the project status meeting, which has the purpose of exchanging information; (2) scope/issue meetings, which have the purpose of making decisions; and (3) design meetings, which have the purpose of producing a quality product design.

An information exchange meeting achieves its purpose if all team members get the information they need to proceed with their work. Information exchange meetings are the place to disseminate product requirement changes, raise technical issues, announce changes in the lives of project team members, and report on risks that have either increased or decreased. Information exchange meetings are great forums for team members to use each other as sounding boards for their upcoming decisions.

An important part of a decision-making meeting is to provide participants with the facts they need to make decisions. A decision-making meeting does not achieve its purpose if the decisions are postponed. The purpose is to arrive at decisions that all participants agree to and can support.

The purpose of a problem-solving meeting is not only to develop a solution, but also to formulate jointly a common problem definition. It is important that all meeting participants have a chance to make a contribution. Just as with decision-making meetings, the purpose of problem-solving meetings is to decide on a solution.

Once the purpose in general has been defined, the next step is to prepare a specific agenda. An agenda is an outline of the content for the meeting. What needs to be on the agenda depends on the task at hand. For example, the agenda for a change control board meeting will list the specific cases to be discussed. It also may contain a discussion and vote on procedural changes and an announcement of a personnel appointment. An agenda for a status meeting will list important milestones, such as the documentation freeze, the beta release, and the version of the upcoming software build.

When preparing a meeting agenda, ask questions that will help identify the topics to be addressed. For example, when preparing an agenda for a status meeting, ask the following questions:

- Which information is needed to begin work on upcoming tasks and who needs it?
- Which external information and decisions have an effect on the project?
- Which deliverables require coordination between several team members?
- Are there any concerns that were brought up?
- Which activities and tasks have been worked on?

Define the Work Products That Result from Meetings

No matter what the kind of meeting, it is necessary to record the information shared and the outcome of the meeting in meeting minutes. Without meeting minutes, all work accomplished in the meeting is lost. Having a person record the information shared, the decisions made, and the problems solved relieves other participants from keeping records themselves and allows them to participate in the meeting.

Exhibit 1.1. Template for Status Meeting Minutes

Who attended?

General Information:

Issues and Decisions:

  Issue

  Action Plan

  Owner

  Due Date

  Comments

Summary of accomplishments and outlook for each area

Using a template for the meeting minutes makes them fast to prepare, easy to read, and assures that nothing is forgotten. Exhibit 1.1 presents a template for status meeting minutes.

There are additional work products, depending on the particular purpose of a meeting. Information exchange meetings usually have a list of action items as a result.

The work products of decision-making meetings are the alternatives that have been evaluated, the decisions made, and their supporting reasons. The resulting decisions are recorded in a permanent repository, preferably accessible to all team members now and in the future.

The work product of a problem-solving meeting varies and depends on the problem. It can be a design document, a project schedule, or a budget. Just as with the meeting minutes, it is important to assign ownership to a participant who is responsible for recording the work product and for distributing it to all participants. For example, the purpose of a meeting may be to define a documentation plan consisting of templates for all internal documentation. The recorder/owner is responsible for creating the final electronic form of the templates and for sharing them with all interested parties.

Create an Atmosphere for Success

The atmosphere or context of a meeting is an important factor that allows people to share information, make decisions, and solve problems jointly. Knowing the purpose and work products of a meeting are necessary, but if meeting participants do not feel comfortable to share information or opinions, the meeting will not achieve its objective. People need to feel comfortable so they can focus on the task at hand. Participants need to feel and know that they can communicate openly, that their perspectives are respected, and that they can express their creativity.

HOW TO MAKE PEOPLE FEEL COMFORTABLE

Meeting participants will feel more comfortable, if

- a meeting adheres to a common format
- the facilitator provides guidance
- the facilitator uses context-free questions to solicit needs and feelings

People feel comfortable if they know what they can expect. Think of that recent Sunday church meeting. How is it different from the one before? It is the content that is different, but not the format. A common format makes people feel comfortable that they can participate and that they know how. This is also the secret formula of toastmaster's meetings. Every meeting has the same format, an invocation, a joke, two speeches, and table topics followed by evaluations. The content is what is different. One can think of the familiar format as a ritual that makes participants feel at ease.

A standard format for the different types of meetings will provide comfort, as people know what to expect and how to participate. Exhibit 1.2 presents formats that may serve as suggestions for particular meetings.

Even if meeting participants are familiar with the format of the meeting, they still appreciate some guidance through the meeting. Just as written overviews, summaries, and transitions are included to help a reader understand the written word better, spoken transitions, summaries and overviews help meeting participants to follow along better. By suggesting an agenda, the facilitator can provide an overview of the meeting. Articulating a transition will remind participants to move on to the next topic. The facilitator can bring closure to a discussion by summarizing the items of agreement.

Gerald Weinberg and Donald Gause in *Exploring Requirements — Quality before Design*[2] point out the importance of context-free questions in requirements gathering. There is also a place for context-free questions in meetings. The purpose of context-free questions is to clarify and define the process. Example questions are

- How long should be spent discussing a particular item?
- How should decisions made in meetings be documented?
- How should decisions be made?

The facilitator can use context-free questions to solicit and comment on the perceived mood, to verify a common understanding, and to inquire whether or not the needs of individual participants are met. Example questions are

Exhibit 1.2. Suggested Meeting Formats

Information Exchange Meeting
- Share general information
- Follow up on decisions and action items from previous status meetings
- Summary of accomplishments
- Outlook of upcoming work and decisions in the different functional areas
- Summary of action items

Decision-Making Meetings
- Presentation of facts
- Input and comments from stakeholders
- Discussion and evaluation
- Decision making
- Summary of decisions made and postponed

Problem-Solving Meeting
- Share problem perception
- Joint problem definition
- Joint problem analysis
- Joint development of alternative solutions
- Evaluation of solution
- Decision making
- Summary of solution

- Did people get all the information they needed?
- Is the meeting moving too slowly?
- Does this summary express it clearly?

OPEN COMMUNICATION ALLOWS INFORMATION EXCHANGE

Making participants feel comfortable is the first step to open communication. Open communication is based on trust and trust can be earned by maintaining neutrality in all work products that result from meetings, especially the meeting minutes. For meeting minutes that means no editing, no omissions, and no additions to what was said and decided in the meeting. Open communication means not holding back information, not judging information or opinions, and includes respectful listening. Open communication is absolutely essential in status meetings, because without quality data, the wrong picture is painted.

ADVOCACY AND INQUIRY IMPROVE DECISION MAKING

When it comes to decision making, it is important to hear all sides that have a stake in the decision. Project scope meetings that discuss changes in the product requirements depend on input from all stakeholders, especially those that are not present, such as the customer. The technical architect needs to advocate the integrity of the product, technical support may represent the customer's view, and marketing may argue the position of the company compared with the competition. As much as each view needs to be communicated assertively, there also needs to be inquiry to learn more about the different perspectives. As the different views are presented, the assumptions, reasons, and facts behind them need to be questioned. A balance between advocacy and inquiry will contribute to better decisions.

CREATIVITY AND PROBLEM SOLVING

Meeting participants need to be ready to solve problems jointly. Creating a comfortable environment goes a long way toward making participants ready. It is true for training that more learning happens if people take ownership in the learning process. It is also true for meetings that participants need to have ownership in the problem to be solved. People feel ownership if they receive confirmation that their contributions are appreciated and important. The facilitator can emphasize the ownership by acknowledging each contribution.

Brainstorming is still the best-known and best-understood technique for stimulating creativity. Its ground rule is — *no judgment of the different contributions.* To make sure everyone gets a chance to contribute, the facilitator can give each person the floor by going around the room and asking each person for his or her input.

USING PROJECT MEETINGS AS SUCCESSFUL COORDINATION TOOLS

For project meetings to serve as communication and coordination tools they have to achieve the following goals:

- inform project members
- provide opportunities to contribute expertise and knowledge
- achieve agreement and support for the outcome

To attain these goals this article has focused on three aspects of meetings:

1. A well-defined purpose
2. A tangible outcome
3. A comfortable and supportive atmosphere

All three are important for successful and effective communication. Defining the purpose of a meeting and the work products that result from it will sharpen the content. Creating the right atmosphere for the meeting helps participants to focus their attention. No matter whether the purpose of the meeting is to exchange information, make decisions, or solve a problem, people need to feel comfortable to participate.

Once the purpose of the meeting has been identified, the deliverables have been defined, and the atmosphere for getting work done in meetings has been created, one can watch for indicators that signify it is happening.

One can look for tangible evidence that work is coordinated, decisions are carried out, and solutions are implemented. It will also be noticed that people are on time for meetings, that they are fully engaged during meetings and that they ask to hold meetings, to get their work done.

References

1. Robert E. Kraut and Lynn A. Streeter, "Coordination in Software Development," Communication of the ACM, Vol. 38, No. 3, March 1995.
2. Donald C. Gause and Gerald M. Weinberg, *Exploring Requirements — Quality before Design*, Dorset House, ISBN 0-9322633-13-7.
3. Larry L. Constantine, "Work Organization: Paradigms for Project Managment and Organization," *Communications of the ACM*, Vol. 36, No. 10, October 1993.
4. Michael Doyle and David Straus, *How to Make Meetings Work*, Jove Books, ISBN 0-515-09048-4.
5. Peter Senge et al., *The Fifth Discipline Field Book*, Currency Book, ISBN 0-385-47256-0.

Chapter 2

Project Assessment: A Tool for Improving Project Management

Russell L. Purvis and Gordon E. McCray

The long-term viability of any IT organization is dependent upon the success of its systems development activities. New development projects hold the promise of expanding services and increasing the productivity and efficiency of established work processes. Yet, few development projects deliver on this potential, instead falling victim to any of a collection of pitfalls. Project managers are all too familiar with technological or business evolution that renders the project obsolete before its completion, project escalation and costs that spiral out of control, and deterioration of communication among system designers and developers. Furthermore, as the complexity and importance of applications increase, the implications of failed development efforts are magnified. An effective project management process, therefore, is critical to the successful completion of development work.

Project assessments are an essential component of the project management process that often are forgone or neglected. Performed regularly, assessments foster early problem detection and correction by enhancing feedback and generating continuous improvement in the project management process. The benefits of project assessments are significant and include

- maintaining open communication between project team members and stakeholders
- protecting the investment of the organization by promoting more thorough planning, thereby improving performance and identifying problems before they threaten project success
- encouraging the project manager to maintain and produce timely records and reports, providing an appropriately ordered and controlled development environment
- detecting ineffective management activities or practices that often are invisible when regularly scheduled reviews are not undertaken

0-8493-9822-3/00/$0.00+$.50

- applying evaluative information gleaned from assessments toward continuously improving the systems development methods and execution on future projects
- providing a mechanism by which team members may voice their concerns and observations regarding the project or methodology
- providing a training and learning opportunity for current and prospective project managers as they participate as members of review teams

As with all control processes, the breadth and depth of project assessments should be commensurate with the risk associated with the project.

THE PROJECT ASSESSMENT PROCESS

The guidelines presented herein are based upon the *Project Management Body of Knowledge* published by the Project Management Institute. The *PMBOK* (pronounced "pim-bok") identifies and describes the generally accepted and proven practices associated with project management. These practices are grouped into nine categories referred to as knowledge areas, each with associated subprocesses: integration, scope, time, cost, quality, human resources, communication, risk, and procurement management. The subprocesses are executed over time, with the output of one subprocess serving as input to another. The result is a chronological progression through a series of related activities, each with associated tools, techniques, and practices.

Project assessments are undertaken within the context of these activities as they unfold over time, typically grouped into five overarching processes: initiation, planning, execution, control and close-out (Exhibit 2.1). Iteration frequently occurs between project execution and planning as actual project work proves some aspect of the project plans intractable. Iteration also occurs between the project control and close-out procedures when it is determined that all project deliverables have yet to be met satisfactorily. Three of these processes (planning, control, and close-out) can be decomposed further into a collection of subprocesses, referred to as core processes within the PMBOK. As depicted in Exhibit 2.1, all five overarching processes necessarily rely upon a set of facilitating processes.

INITIAL ASSESSMENTS

Once begun, systems development projects can prove extremely difficult to abandon. It is imperative then that a clear scope be defined for development projects. Early project assessment, therefore, is essential. The purpose of the initial project assessment is to assure management that each new project is feasible, has a viable plan, and has achievable targets. The initial assessment

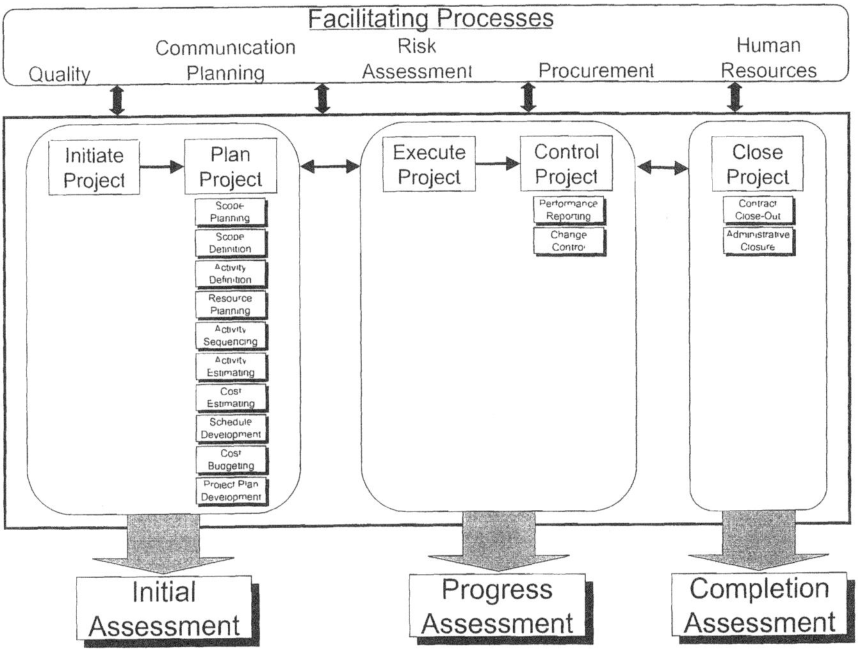

Exhibit 2.1. Project Assessments

- provides an assurance that the project is starting with defined objectives and goals
- determines whether project plans are complete, defining all deliverables as well as tasks and needed resources to develop those deliverables
- establishes a discipline for the project manager, requiring an overall demonstration of effective planning

This assessment establishes an initial project baseline against which future changes in project scope or system functionality can be gauged.

The initial assessment provides an evaluation of the deliverables associated with the project initiation and project planning processes (Exhibit 2.2). Deliverables for these processes include the product description, project charter, constraints and assumptions, statement of scope, work allocation structure, project work plan, and supporting detail information. Project reviewers should concern themselves with several issues during this assessment:

- Structure: Is the project team structure compatible with the organization type (functional, weak matrix, balanced matrix, strong matrix, or projectized)? Is the project manager's authority and role consistent with the team structure?

Exhibit 2.2. Processes and Associated Deliverables

Process	Deliverables
Initiate and Plan	• Project charter • A description of the management approach to be used • Scope statement that defines the project deliverables and project objectives • Work breakdown structure decomposed to the appropriate level of control • Cost estimates • Work plans defining task start and finish dates and responsible resources • Baselines for cost and schedule • Major milestones • Key staff • Key risks including constraints and assumptions • Open issues and pending decisions
Execution and Control	• Work results — deliverables that have been completed fully or partially • Product documentation developed to describe the project's deliverables • Approvals verifying acceptance of project products • Rework of defective deliverables • Completed checklists used to assure quality • Performance appraisals • Performance or status reports organizaing and summarizing project progress • Change requests and change request log • Proposals and contracts defining seller's ability to provide the requested product
Close-out	• Project archives • Formal acceptance • Lessons learned • Contract file

- Project scope: Does the project support the strategic plan of the organization? Is the project scope specific in defining what is included in and excluded from the project?
- Project deliverables, objectives and completion criteria: Is there a natural progression between the business need or other impetus for which the project was begun, the objectives of the project, the product description, project deliverables, and work allocation structure? Are these thoroughly specified? Are the completion criteria specific and acceptable to all stakeholders, particularly to the sponsor, the client, and IT operations?
- Feasibility: Is the project technically, operationally, and financially feasible? How reasonable is the project schedule?
- Assumptions and constraints: Are assumptions and constraints written and communicated to all stakeholders? Do the stakeholders understand the inherent risk associated with each?

- Time, cost, and quality estimates: Are time, cost, and quality estimates realistic? Are these estimates acceptable to stakeholders?
- Client and project team responsibilities: Are client and team responsibilities well defined? Have they been communicated to stakeholders, and do the stakeholders support them?

PROGRESS ASSESSMENTS

Progress assessments are performed at predetermined intervals during the execution of the project. Assessment intervals depend upon (1) the size of the project, (2) the duration of the project, (3) the phase of the project, (4) risk assessment outcomes, (5) project team experience, (6) the level of participation by the project manager, and (7) project manager experience. A critical element of success in conducting progress assessments is knowing what to assess and what problems to anticipate in the project. Only then can problems be addressed early, prior to impacting severely the project effort. Progress assessments focus upon the deliverables in the execution and control processes (Exhibit 2.2).

Progress assessments focus on comparing actual versus planned activities and outcomes in an effort to identify deviations that may indicate a project in trouble. Deviations, however, only signal potential problems. Project reviewers then must identify the root cause of any deviations and determine the size and potential impact of the problems. Additionally, gauging the criticality of the problem, the project manager must prescribe an action plan to address the deviations. Deviations may evolve in several project areas:

- Project plans: Do the project plans define what must occur to allow the project to achieve its predetermined objectives? If plans are inadequate, they are likely to misdirect the project. A series of related issues must be addressed:
  - Do the plans exist? Plans must be in written form and conform to standards.
  - Are the plans complete, consistent, and practical? Are there review, rework, and approval tasks? Are there tasks for external dependencies such as hardware and software delivery and installation? Are tasks defined in detail, with each task having completion criteria and a detailed description?
  - Are the work plans working documents? Look for indications that the plans are used to execute and control the project.
- Change control: Are change control procedures being used? Is the final disposition of a change request communicated to the project team within an appropriate time frame? Does the original work plan include time for investigating project change requests? Is time spent investigating project change requests being reported and recorded? Is

change activity consistently reported to management? Are change decisions being made within an appropriate time frame? Are approved changes reflected in the documentation, training, and other implementation processes? If so, how? Have there been too many changes? If so, why?

- Products: Do all work products have quality assurance checks to ensure that the products conform to approved format, content, level of detail, and quality? Do the products reflect the current baseline?
- Client participation: Does the client share accountability for the success or failure of the project? Are client obligations being fulfilled? Is the user approving deliverables? Are approvals performed in an appropriate time frame?
- Development environment: Is the current environment undergoing any significant changes? Have new environmental design constraints been imposed late in the project? Are operation and change management procedures reflected in the schedule?
- Resources: Is project staffing adequate? Are the skills of the project team being used effectively? Is the project manager's span of control too narrow or too broad? Are the contributions of part-time project team members acceptable? Are people continually being added to the project team? Is there a high turnover rate on the project team? Have any key team members been replaced and, if so, what is the impact on the schedule? Is overtime being tracked by the project manager? Is overtime excessive? Has overtime become a ready solution to the underestimation of time required to perform project-related work? Has the efficiency of overtime been demonstrated? How is it measured? Is overtime work contributing to morale problems?
- Communications: Is communication with all stakeholders being performed in a timely manner? Are important decisions and approvals being documented? Is an audit trail available? Are there open communication channels between the sponsor, clients, and project team? Are status-reporting methods and formats consistent, or are new performance measures frequently introduced? Do progress reports contain quantitative measures? Do team members submit written status reports consistently? Is the project manager completing status reports consistently, and are they consistent with the team member reports?
- Morale: What are the stakeholders' perceptions of the project manager? Does there appear to be a personality conflict between any of the project team members? Does there appear to be a conflict between project team members and clients? Are there constant changes in project direction?
- Lessons learned: Is new knowledge being accumulated in an organized manner as the project progresses? Common practice is for such knowledge to be considered at the conclusion of the project when typ-

ically it is too vague and removed from the actual experience from which it arose to be of significant value.

- Assumptions and constraints: Are the assumptions and constraints elucidated at the outset of the project still valid? Is there a formal means of updating assumptions and constraints and communicating these changes to all stakeholders?
- Project scope: Is the scope of the project still consistent with the strategic plan of the organization? Has the scope of the project been creeping unchecked? If so, are mechanisms available to halt this trend?
- Time, cost, and quality: Have time, cost, and quality estimates proven reliable? If not, what is the cause of their inaccuracy? Are time spent, costs, and quality within acceptable limits?
- Relationship management: Are vendors, outsourcers, and contractors meeting their commitments relative to the project? Is the project manager providing to outside constituents the necessary information to allow them to perform adequately their responsibilities?

PROJECT COMPLETION ASSESSMENTS

Project completion assessments are used to determine whether project objectives were met through the completion and implementation of project deliverables. It further verifies that contractor obligations were met and formal acceptance of the project was secured. The assessment provides a particularly rich composition of historical information that can benefit future projects. This assessment can complement, but is not a replacement for, the postinstallation review. The assessment should evaluate planned versus actual outcomes for the project and should determine

- the extent to which the envisioned benefits of the project were realized
- the extent to which budgeted costs were met for the individual phases of the project and the overall project
- the extent to which the project met its specified schedule and milestones
- the extent to which the project met specified quality standards

Consistent with the use of historical information in the *PMBOK*, this information contributes to a historical knowledge base from which are gleaned valuable lessons to be applied to future project management efforts. In this manner, the project management process is improved continually.

ASSESSMENT RESULTS

Preliminary findings resulting from any of the three project assessments are brought before the project manager for review and consideration. Performed correctly, the project manager is made to feel involved in the articulation of the findings and recommendations emerging from the review. The project manager then should use the assessment findings to develop a detailed action plan.

Naturally, the project manager may not agree completely with the findings and conclusions of the assessment, the severity rating assigned to problems, or final recommendations; reasonable differences of opinion will occur. Working toward an agreement that will prove acceptable to all stakeholders, both reviewers and the project manager therefore should be granted an opportunity to present to upper management their opinions, concerns, and suggestions.

Following resolution of conflicts within a prespecified period of time (typically within one week), the project manager should develop an action plan. Quick response times are important to preserve project momentum. The action plan should address systematically each problem identified in the project assessment. In addition, the action plan should identify required resources and specify a schedule for resolving the problems. This plan then is folded into the revised and realistic overall project work plan. Problems and progress toward their resolution then should be tracked and reported upon within management status reports until resolved.

CONCLUSION

Project failure usually results from a breakdown in the project management process. Project assessments can provide an objective evaluation of a project by

1. assisting the project manager in recognizing and confronting existing or potential problems
2. suggesting appropriate solutions
3. providing management with sufficient information to take early corrective action, if required
4. offering a mechanism for continuing communication between and amongst senior and information technology management

To be successful, however, project assessments are dependent upon several factors. First, the organization must have instituted a formalized project management process. Assessments require a benchmark of deliverables and processes such as that offered by the *PMBOK*. Second, the intent of the assessment must be to assist the project manager rather than critiquing that manager. Project assessments can be an important vehicle for learning, providing necessary support to project managers as they develop their skills. Third, project assessment team members must have the appropriate skills and characteristics. Team members must possess an in-depth understanding of the project management process and application development. Team members also should be mature and experienced, with the ability to analyze problems objectively and quickly, identifying important underlying trends.

The complexity, capriciousness, and conceptual nature of systems development projects point to the need for a systematic approach to such efforts. For many organizations, formal project management is the strategy of choice. Often, however, project management fosters conflict. Senior management wants detailed planning and progress reporting on projects. Conversely, project teams often view time spent on formal project management activities as time wasted — time better spent performing the countless tasks associated with the project itself. Project assessments can bridge this void effectively. They provide requisite feedback to upper managers and project managers while simultaneously enhancing the efforts of project team members.

Recommended Reading

1. Keil, M., Pulling the plug: Software project management and the problem of project escalation, *MIS Quarterly*, 19, 421, 1995.
2. Pinto, J. and Slevin, D., Critical success factors in successful project implementation, *IEEE Transactions on Engineering Management*, 34, 22, 1987.
3. Duncan, W.R., *A Guide to the Project Management Body of Knowledge*, Project Management Institute, Upper Darby, PA, 1996.

Chapter 3

Managing Systems Requirements

Polly Perryman

Requirements management is composed of four major activities: capturing the requirements, organizing them, reviewing them, and controlling them. Each of these activities provides benefits to both the customer and developer in ensuring the project is moving in the right direction. All of these activities occur in conjunction with the requirement definition and analysis phase of the software development life cycle (SDLC). This includes establishing and implementing a process for maintaining control of the requirements for the remainder of the SDLC.

The working definition of each of the four activities in this section provides a starting place for understanding requirements management. Further sections of this article present a more detailed discussion of each of the activities.

CAPTURING REQUIREMENTS

To take a product from concept to reality, the expertise and desires of the client are conveyed to the system analyst. The system analyst in turn must assess the information in relationship to the desired technology and then prepare a feasible customer and developer plan for product development. The feasibility plan is used as the basis for discussions. The requirements are the output product from these discussions wherein the customer and development experts expose the must have vs. the it would be nice to have items while considering the available schedule and budget.

ORGANIZING REQUIREMENTS

Organizing the requirements by project, system, and subsystem gives both the customer and the developer clear requirements that should be tracked during the development effort. Organizing the requirements in this manner supports simultaneous development work in multiple functional areas, which increases productivity and improves quality. Organizing requirements within these classifications additionally ensures that potential risks to the project can be identified and assigned more easily to the

0-8493-9822-3/00/$0.00+$.50

right people ensuring that viable mitigation of the risks are planned. Organizing the requirements by project, system, and subsystem also helps control change, provides a better definition of what must be tested, and makes sure necessary functionality does not fall through the cracks.

REVIEWING REQUIREMENTS

It is important that the requirements be reviewed by the right personnel to ensure that all of the necessary items have been included and planned for development. When the requirements are organized, the selection of review groups is easier and the review will be better because the right people are assigned to evaluate and approve the requirements. It is during the review of the requirements that the customer gains significant insight as to the developer's true understanding of the properties the product must possess to ensure success in the marketplace. Skewed perceptions can be corrected at minimal cost at this point in the project.

CONTROLLING REQUIREMENTS

Once the initial set of requirements has been evaluated and approved, the course of action for moving the project to completion can be planned meaningfully. Impacts to the project plan are minimized by controlling changes to the requirements. The value in controlling changes to the requirements is that the project stays on course, thereby reducing or eliminating cost overruns and schedule delays. The other significant benefit occurs as the system is tested because everyone who has been involved in the project has been able to understand what requirements will be tested and what the product will have, do, and use. In other words, the boundaries established by the requirements can be used to measure the success of the development effort.

CAPTURING REQUIREMENTS

In March 1996, Frank McGrath addressed the problem of capturing requirements at a meeting of the Project Management Association in Tysons Corner, Virginia. In summary, McGrath pointed to the software community as being simply arrogant in starting development work without having requirements nailed. By example, he pointed to the building trades. What general contractor would start construction of a building with a requirement that states, "It will be a big building with offices inside?" What does that mean? What is the requirement for a manufacturing plant in which airplanes will be made or a skyscraper where many businesses will reside?

McGrath continued using the general contractor example, pointing to the fact that the general contractor finds out not only what type of building, but also what materials need to be used in the construction of the building. The general contractor then finds out what tolerances are needed in the materials and so on and so forth. Given some thought, it is easy to see how important clarifications are in defining requirements in the building trades. They are no less important in the software business, but all too often software developers wrongly feel that they deal in the creative zone where it is far more difficult to articulate and capture requirements effectively.

It may not be as hard as it seems. Software developers must first remember that they are capturing people's dreams, not what they need — though they may need it — not what they want — though they may want it. Software developers are capturing their dreams, their true desires. In this respect it is very personal for each person participating in the requirements definition process. They may argue over minor points and fail to communicate what is going on in their mind. A leader of the requirements definition process can overcome this by:

1. Conducting regularly scheduled meetings with a previously distributed agenda so that the right people attend and the attendees know what will be covered and what is expected of them.
2. Structuring each meeting to ensure that previously identified requirements are documented for review and analysis, allowing new requirements to be submitted and recorded for review at a future meeting and making sure that requirements that are out-of-scope for a specific project or release of a project are identified and tabled.
3. Making sure that each person at the meeting has an opportunity to speak and be heard without criticism or fear of being laughed at or made to feel dumb or stupid.
4. Spending time to make certain the information communicated as a requirement is meaningful; that is, make sure everyone understands that the big building is a tall skyscraper and not a warehouse or a manufacturing plant.

Although it may appear that a significant effort is being spent to capture and review requirements, there is a big pay-back if the requirements are identified correctly up front. The cost of correcting software for missing or incorrect requirements goes up significantly the later in the development process the error is found.

These unattractive and very costly statistics can be brought down significantly when the ambiguities common enough to everyday conversation and exaggerated by the separate areas of expertise brought to the table by the customer and the developers are eliminated. Use the helpful hints and techniques proven over time by software professionals such as Donald Gause and Gerald Weinberg, who are noted in the field of requirements definition. The result will be a negotiated understanding of the customer's desire and a certainty that everyone involved in the project is working toward completion of the same system. Start by removing ambiguities at the statement level.

Clarifying Ambiguous Requirements

Ambiguity at the statement level is tested through verbalization of visualizations. For example, if the requirement is to build a structure to protect a human against wind and rain and snow and ice is given to five people, each of the five people may have a different visualization. One might visualize a kiosk at a bus station, another a three-bedroom ranch house, and someone else a nice shiny Rolls Royce. As people at the meeting explain their visual image of what has been stated, clarification can be made, and agreement can be reached.

So, how does one visualize the following requirement statement: The user will be able to store one or more windows in a scrapbook, and how does one express that vision. The visualization here may not be as obvious, but one certainly would want to know if anyone around the conference table is getting the impression that they will be able to store windows into a scrapbook the way files can be stored in directories for indefinite periods of time. So, test the statement:

- What is the customer interpreting the statement to mean?
- What does the developer intend the capability to be, i.e., a brief functional description of what will be implemented to satisfy the requirement?
- What are the system requirements, i.e., How many windows will be stored? How long are they required to be stored? What are the retrieval time requirements for different types of storage?

Document the negotiated understanding that is reached between the customer and the developers regarding the requirement(s) and how it (they) will be implemented.

At the word level, use synonyms and comparisons to clarify and ensure the correct interpretation of what is being said. For example, if the requirement is initially stated as:

A big clock will be displayed ...

It should be restated as:

A large clock will be displayed ...

Start by using the synonym large for the word big. Then, clarify the use of the word large again using a specific comparison, i.e., does large mean it fills the entire screen or just half of the screen? Finally, restate the requirement to spell out the specific size or range of sizes to which the customer and the developers have agreed. In this way, the understanding by both the customer and the developer are consistent. There will be no surprises when the product is presented as complete. More importantly, the incidents of on-the-spot fixes that add up so quickly at the end of a project will be reduced significantly.

Determining Scope

The value of eliminating compound requirements can be seen at all levels, from upper management to project developers and from the customer to the quality assurance team. Only after compound requirements are eliminated can the true scope of the project be assessed, change control applied, testing be correctly managed, and meaningful metrics be collected.

A simple example of a compound requirement is: The user must be able to add, delete, and modify a row. What causes this to be a compound requirement are the multiple things that the user must be able to do. In determining the scope of the work, the compound requirement will be considered as one unit of work, when in fact to provide this capability within the system it may take three separate programs to make it happen. Additionally, if any portion of a compound requirement encounters a problem during testing, the entire requirement is shown as not satisfied. This can skew test result metrics.

To rid a project of compound requirements, identify the statements within each requirement, then make each statement a standalone requirement. This action not only helps to clarify the requirement, but it also provides a more accurate view of the size and scope of the project. The other thing that eliminating compound requirements does is allow requirement dependencies to be identified and tied together in a database.

ORGANIZING REQUIREMENTS

Now that the requirements are single-statement directives, it becomes easy to classify them by type. The three major types of requirements are:

- Project requirements.
- System requirements.
- Subsystem requirements (also referred to as application, module, or functional requirements).

Project Requirements

Project requirements are the customer-imposed schedules, deliverables, and resources under which the project will operate. One example of a project requirement is "Each project will have an ABC company representative assigned to the production team." Another might be: "The product will be delivered not later than (NLT) July 10, 199N." Still another might be "Monthly Status Reviews will be conducted."

System Requirements

System requirements are the performance, storage, protocols, standards, and conventions that must be met by the product. These requirements guide the development effort. Being able to reference easily the Requirements List for system requirements ensures that decisions made by developers always will consider the goals for the product in setting down the development direction and methods.

Subsystem Requirements

Subsystem requirements are the product-specific content, capabilities, limitations, and look and feel of the planned end product. It is advisable to classify further functional requirements into logical groups of requirements, for example, purchasing and forecasting. Still further organizations may desire to ensure that art requirements, text requirements, and action requirements are identified and then arranged together in the flow of the logical grouping selected.

By classifying requirements, three very important things are accomplished. The first of these is staff composition because it should be clear what skill sets are needed. The second is that it becomes easier to see what test scenarios need to be developed and when the test scenarios provide many (requirements) to one (test) opportunities and when multiple tests may be required to demonstrate the full capability of one requirement. This type of information helps in planning the overall testing effort because the scope of the effort can be predicted more accurately thus ensuring the machines, networks, and people needed for testing are in place when the system is ready to be tested.

The third thing classifying requirements is to simplify the change controls essential to managing requirements. The value in this is that during the course of the project should technology shift or requirements change, the total impact of the change can be assessed because all components of the change will be identified early in the process. Neither the customer nor the developer will get to the end of the project thinking all is well only to find out that something fell through the cracks. The requirement list becomes easy to reference, maintain, and use when the requirements are classified by type.

Documenting Requirements

Documenting for maximum benefits means less work later. For example, when the different types of requirements are gathered and a numbering scheme ensuring distinction between the types of requirements is used, tracking and impact analysis is more easily performed. This distinction is important in tracking the requirements for compliance, gathering data related to the various types of requirements for analysis of performance and quality. Being able to gather this information means developers readily and consistently can offer customers documented quality improvement on both technical and business fronts. Measurable data will become available from which determinations can be made regarding the size and scope of projects and the impact of technology issues.

Whether the classified requirements list is stored in a database, word processing tables, or a spreadsheet, it is important that it is located and formatted in such a way that it is accessible and useable to the majority of people on the team. The requirements list is a project asset and should be thought of as such. Management, the development team, and the customer have a ready tool for determining what is within the scope of the project and what is not.

REVIEWING REQUIREMENTS

When the requirements analysis has been completed and the requirements have been organized, then three types of reviews need to be conducted:

- Peer reviews.
- Management reviews.
- Customer reviews.

Peer Review

Peer review is made up of senior-level system designers and testers, preferably those who have had little or no involvement in the definition and analysis of the requirements for this project. They bring the objectivity needed at this point to identify ambiguous requirements, nontestable requirements and potential risks, and to make recommendations for improvement in the documentation of the requirements. Using the insight gained from the peer review, the system development team should get additional information from the customer as needed to develop corrections. When the proposed corrections have been developed, a management review should be conducted.

Management Review

Management review is the formal presentation of the requirements in terms of budget, schedule, and risks for the project. Executives, senior managers, marketing and account representatives and quality assurance specialists need to participate in this review. The review itself should be structured to ensure that the output from it results in firm commitments to the creation and implementation of the detailed project plan for meeting the requirements. If this commitment is not strong at this point, it is an indication that one or more of the requirements need to be further assessed for feasibility within the defined scope of the project budget and schedule. This assessment must be made with the customer to achieve consensus on the requirements that will be met by the proposed system. When management has reviewed the requirements list and all modifications and adjustments have been made, a formal customer review should be scheduled and conducted.

Customer Review

Customer review should include the management review counterparts on the customer side, the customer project team, the development project team, and full quality assurance representation. The purpose of this review is to finalize the requirements list. This is accomplished by presenting the fully analyzed requirements list, presenting and explaining the differences between the requirements list and the initial wish list the customer presented, and providing the documentation that supports the information presented. The customer review should result in a requirements list that clearly states what the system will do, how it basically will operate, and what users can expect in terms of usability, ergonomics, and learning curves. At the conclusion of the customer review, all of the players who have a stake in the system development effort should be in agreement about what the project, system, and subsystem requirements are. The requirements list thus is finalized and baselined to ensure control of the requirements throughout the life of the project.

CONTROLLING REQUIREMENTS

Controlling the requirements may be the most important aspect of achieving success on a project and ensuring the full usability of the developed system. Control does not mean that there are never any changes to the original baselined requirements. It does mean that all of the stakeholders in the project are informed of and involved in a requirements control process that eliminates the single greatest threat to any system development project — requirements creeping.

Requirements creeping can and probably should be viewed as a villainous saboteur who, like a chameleon, takes on many different colors. This villain strikes out with only one purpose: get someone, anyone on the project, to make a change in the baselined requirements without assessing the impact and logical disposition of the change and informing all parties of the need for the change. To eliminate requirements creeping:

- Baseline requirements.
- Have a change control method in place for handling any type of modification to baselined requirements.

- Make certain that all people involved in the project, both on the publishing side and on the development side, understand the process and methods used to baseline requirements and to affect change to the baselined requirements.

The requirements list baseline is established following the customer review meeting and should be given a unique identifier at that time. It must be distributed to all participants as the only requirements list to be used as design work commences. The identifier should have provisions for indicating the version or edition or release. If an approved change is made to the requirements list, the identifier must be updated and the revised requirements list distributed to all participants.

Controlling the Change of Requirements

For example, say that as the design of the Graphical User Interface (GUI) gets underway, the designer realizes that there is no requirement for the GUI to provide transportation to the query subsystem, a function the designer thinks will be essential to the user. Using the requirements control process, the designer does not add the function (which would creep the requirements). Instead, the designer prepares an incident/problem report that notes the fact that there is not a requirement for the GUI to query transportation and notifies the keeper of the requirements list, who may be the quality assurance manager, the engineering manager, the project manager or someone in configuration management.

The information provided by the designer is assessed for project impact and disposed of in one of the following ways:

1. The change is approved as a necessary component of the current system development effort. In this case, the schedule and budget will be assessed for impact. If the schedule must be maintained, a management decision will need to be made regarding adding a resource to do the programming, increasing hours for one or more existing programmers, or contracting out that piece of work. If the budget is already at bare bones and the schedule must be met, then the increased hours most likely will be included in the nonpaid exempt employee overtime category, but management must realize that they are increasing the project risk.
2. The change is approved as a modification to the current system to be implemented in the first software release subsequent to the initial delivery of the system. A work-around may or may not need to be developed for the initial implementation. The point is to make sure that there is agreement with the customer as to who is going to develop the work-around should it be needed. The other critical point to be made here is that the change control records and the process for using them must be implemented so that items such as this do not

fall through the cracks as development for the next release gets underway.

3. The change is approved as a potential future enhancement to the current system without a specific schedule for implementation. Similar to the change approved as a modification, the change control records must be precise to ensure that the decision specific to this change is not lost. Because this change will not become part of the next release, it will go back to wish list status and be carried through the entire requirements process. The reason for this is to make certain that the development of this enhancement is scheduled for work and delivery within the context of all other existing work.
4. The change is rejected. This closes out the incident report. No work is scheduled now or for the future. There may be many reasons for this type of a response. Whatever the reason, the rejection action and the reason for rejection should be recorded within the change control process. A record of all closed changes is maintained to ensure accurate project history and to provide the rationale on why the change was rejected.

Whenever any software is released to the customer, the release should follow a defined release management process that includes the specific identification of all of the components that are included in the software release as well as the components that are assumed to be present (i.e., system software). This identification also should include the specific incident/problem reports that were corrected by the release and any work-arounds that were developed for the known problems that exist in the software.

Chapter 4

Managing the Risks of Outsourcing Systems Development

Ken Doughty and Franke Grieco

The Information Technology (IT) outsourcing strategy is usually associated with the contracting out of an organization's entire Information Services (IS) function to an external service provider. There are a number of organizations that are not outsourcing the whole IT function, but only those functions considered to be not "core" competencies. System development is a function often considered to be non-core and therefore outsourced.

Arguably, the decision to outsource should be based on a detailed analysis of the organization's Strategic IT Plan and Corporate Plan. From this analysis it can be determined whether outsourcing conforms with the organization's strategic direction or if it is required to facilitate the organization's IT strategies. The main arguments for outsourcing are the minimization of the risks associated with system development and the maximization of return on investment in information technology (more value for money). Therefore, outsourcing the system development function is considered by many a risk reduction and cost minimization strategy.

The more sobering argument is that outsourcing system development does not eliminate the risks associated with it. However, it transfers some risks to the contractor and exposes the outsourcing organization to new risks.

The factors that may contribute to an outsourcing decision include:

- The development of the Strategic IT Plan, resulting in identification of the system development function as no longer being a "core competency"
- The dramatic increase in the availability of "off-the-shelf" parameter-driven software (e.g., SAP, Oracle Financials, People Soft, BAAN, MAN/MAN/X)

0-8493-9822-3/00/$0.00+$.50

- Previous system development experience by the organization (especially failures)
- Access to "best practice" software development organizations (ISO9000 certification)
- Lack of credibility in the organization's Information Systems (IS) Department
- Accelerated realization of reengineering benefits
- The rising cost of in-house system development
- Reduction in and better control of system development costs
- Lack of adequate infrastructure or resources and skills to develop systems to meet the organization's requirements on time and within budget
- The opportunity to free the organizations resources for other purposes
- Business venture with developers in marketing a product

Executive management are demanding that systems development managers, as part of their mandate, ensure that the risks associated with system development are being minimized. To facilitate this the Information Systems Audit and Control Association (ISACA) recently released a document titled "Control Objectives for Information and Related Technology (COBiT)."[1] This document replaces the Control Objectives, which was the ISACA standard for auditing information technology. COBiT has been developed with a business orientation as the main theme and designed not only to be utilized by auditors, but also, and more importantly, as a comprehensive checklist for business process owners.

COBiT provides a framework for ensuring that an organization has a strong internal control environment for its information technology business processes. COBiT Section Planning and Organization PO9–Assess Risks states that:

> Control over the IT process of assessing risk that satisfies the business requirement of ensuring the achievement of IT objectives and responding to threats to the provision of IT services is enabled by the organization engaging itself in IT risk-identification and impact analysis, and taking cost-effective measures to mitigate risks....

COBiT clearly details the requirement for reviewing the risk management of any information technology project, including systems development. However, limited audit resources and other business related priorities can restrict the ability to adequately cover the development process (i.e., when systems development is outsourced). Therefore, a framework is required to ensure compliance with the professional association's requirements and assists the organization in the risk management of its system development. This includes managing the risks associated with outsourcing system development.

This chapter defines risk management and how it should be applied to system development. Additionally, a detailed risk model and IS audit approach for the risk management of outsourcing software development, utilizing COBiT, is demonstrated.

The model discussed in this chapter provides a control approach that identifies system development risk, risk factors, risk rating, and risk reduction strategies in outsourcing the system development process.

RISK MANAGEMENT

To develop the COBiT approach and its application requires a sound understanding of risk management concepts. Ideally, a systems development manager should use a proven and documented methodology in the application of risk management techniques. For example, the Australian/New Zealand Standard AS4360[2] defines the first generic standard on risk management in the world. The standard defines the following terms:

Risk. The chance of something happening that will have an impact upon objectives. It is measured in terms of likelihood and consequences.

Risk Management. The systematic application of management policies, procedures, and practices to the tasks of identifying, analyzing, assessing, treating, and monitoring risk.

Risk Treatment. The selection and implementation of appropriate options for dealing with risk.

The standard also provides guidelines in its appendices for the following areas:

- Application of Risk Management
- Steps in Developing and Implementing a Risk Management Program
- Generic Sources of Risk and Their Areas of Impact
- Examples of Risk Definition and Classification
- Examples of Quantitative Risk Expressions
- Risk Management Documentation
- Identifying Options of Risk Treatment

Systems development managers can utilize this standard not only in gaining a sound understanding of the risk management concepts, but also in its application.

Systems development managers should also be aware of the other tangible risks associated with project management that may contribute to the failure of the outsourcing software development project. The following risks are project risks irrespective of whether outsourcing is utilized or not; they are included here to provide a checklist of issues to consider during the contract negotiation phase with the preferred outsourcing contractor and during the planning for, and initial setup of any project.

1. Failure to have a clear business objective for the project that is well understood by all participants and stakeholders in the project.
2. Having too large a scope for the project or not having the scope of the project clearly defined.
3. Ineffective project management, which is demonstrated through factors such as:
   - Either no or poor project management methodology or procedures
   - No project management charter or unclear specifying of the role, duties, and responsibilities of the project manager or project team members
   - Multiple project managers, with responsibility for the management of the project not clearly defined
   - Lack of a formal, and regularly updated, project plan
   - Failure to adhere to the project plan
   - The project plan not covering all stages of the project from its initiation through to the postimplementation review
   - Irregular project progress reporting or progress reporting that imparts little real information to the project sponsor and steering committee
   - Authority of the project manager may be implied rather than stated and communicated to all the stakeholders by executive management
   - Project team members may be working independently without any overall coordination, resulting in wasted resources and contributing to the failure of the project
   - Project reporting lines may either be not established, not clear or be to inappropriate management
   - Project monitoring systems may not have been established or developed at the outset of the project
   - Monitoring standards or benchmarks to measure the performance of project management may not be established or may be inappropriate
   - Project reports may not be sufficiently detailed to assist executive management to monitor the progress of the project in terms of work completed against milestones and budgets
   - Insufficient knowledge of project management software to effectively use the software
4. Not having a clearly defined project structure:
   - No clearly defined sponsor/owner for the project at the senior management level
   - Not having the right mix of IT and user staff (stakeholders) on the project team
   - Project team members not having appropriate levels of technical skills and experience

5. The Project Manager and or project team may not have the skills or training to undertake the role. Often the Project Manager is user appointed because he "knows" the current system.
6. Long lead times between project deliverables
7. Uncontrolled or high levels of requests for modifications to the design specifications during the development and implementation phases of the project
8. Failure to control the change management aspects of the project such as:
   - Maintaining user involvement and commitment
   - Redesign of business processes and work practices
   - Changes in the organization structure
   - Training
   - Post implementation support

SYSTEM DEVELOPMENT METHODOLOGY

For the purposes of this chapter it is assumed that the executive management of the organization has made a strategic decision that system development is no longer a core competency. This decision was based on a detailed analysis in developing the organization's strategic IT model.

The strategic IT plan details the IS department's strategic direction from being a system developer and maintenance provider to adopting a "caretaker role" with regard to the organization's current legacy systems. This means that system development of new systems, including the purchase of off-the-shelf software solutions, will be outsourced.

It is important that the organization's executive management "manage" this change in strategic direction from internal system development to outsourced development. A key point to note is: an organization's processes have a greater influence on the culture of the organization than behavior. Therefore, a competent change management process must be undertaken to ensure that there is a cultural and business change that will be accepted by the organization as a whole. If the executive management does not manage the process competently, it may result in the rejection of the outsourcing concept and also cause dysfunctional activities by stakeholders (e.g., System Owners, Users, and the IS department).

Today, systems development methodologies address the issue of risk management, whereas previously risk management in system development was often implied in the process rather than a project task item that had to be addressed, actioned, and signed off. Previously IS management was recommending to executive management to develop or redevelop systems without the support of a risk analysis being undertaken. This exposed the organization to unidentified and unmanaged risk that may have lead to business objectives not being attained.

System development methodologies, for example, APT3 address risk management in the following terms:

Project Initiation

- Responsibilities of all parties involved in the project.
- Deliverables and delivery schedule.
- Acceptance criteria.
- Risk, problem, and change management.
- Standards and procedures to be used.

Identify System Risks. Document the risks at the system level. These risks include loss of systems and/or data caused by hardware malfunctions, human errors, malicious damage, fraud, viruses, unauthorized use, hacking, theft or sabotage.

Assess Probability of Risk Occurring. Examine each identified risk and estimate the potential for its occurrence.

Determine the compounded probability of risks identified occurring. (For example, if there are 200 risks with a possible 1 in 100 chance of occurrence per annum, then there is a probability of 2 risks per annum.)

Assess Risks

- Identify the critical system consequences of each of the risks occurring and place monetary values on them.
- Assess strategic risks and consequences for the business.
- Review the results of the exercise with management and rank the risks.
- Document damage potential, the costs associated with the occurrence of the risks and the overall probability.
- Document the risk management strategies and the likely costs.

Review Current Risk Management Processes

- For each risk, identify the countermeasures currently in place and their annual costs.
- Examine each risk and estimate its probability.
- Examine the effectiveness of the countermeasures.
- Document the current countermeasures, their costs, the risk probability, and the potential costs to the organization.

Determine Overall Risk Management Strategies. Document potential risk management techniques that could be used in place of current practices.

Systems development managers should ensure that the organization's system development methodology addresses not only the risk management process, but also the consistent application of the process throughout the system development life cycle. Further, they have to ensure that the results of the Risk Analysis is complete and accurate and they are to be conveyed to the organization's executive management before the outsourcing of System Development is approved.

MANAGING RISK

Inadequate risk assessment and management may lead to software development projects going "off-the-rails" due to unidentified risks eventuating and being poorly managed. The associated extra costs and time escalations can:

- Detrimentally impact the viability of a software development project
- Lead to failure in achieving strategic business objectives
- In a worst case scenario cause an organization to go out of business

The systems development manager can assist the organization in developing a risk framework by utilizing the COBiT[1] PO9 "Assess Risk Guidelines. By adopting and appropriately applying the COBiT PO9 Guidelines, the systems development manager ensures that a comprehensive coverage of the risks associated with outsourcing software development.

A risk assessment framework should be an intrinsic part of a business continuity plan. The framework would require an assessment of risks that could impact on the organization reaching its business objectives on a regular basis. The assessment should also identify the residual risk (the risk the organization s management is willing to accept). Ideally, it should provide risk assessments for the organization as a whole and for the separate processes including major projects.

The COBiT PO9 Assess Risk Guideline refers to a number of control objectives that need to be addressed in its application. The control objectives are:

1. Business Risk Assessment
2. Risk Assessment Approach
3. Risk Identification
4. Risk Measurement
5. Risk Action Plan
6. Risk Acceptance

Business Risk Assessment

The organization's management needs to identify its role in contributing to the organization's objectives, policies, and strategies when making decisions about risk. These must be clearly understood as they help to define the criteria as to whether a risk is acceptable or not, and the basis of control.

COBiT states that management should establish a systematic risk assessment framework.

The organization needs to have policies and standards in place to provide guidance to the staff responsible for risk management. Responsible staff need to be aware of the instances where risk assessment needs to occur and the desirable criteria that should be used.

For example, the size (i.e., monetarily, time frame, impact on the business) a project must be for a risk assessment to be mandatory. Guidelines for the context that should be used, (e.g., strategic context, organizational context or project/process context). In some instances, it may be necessary to assess risk at both the global and project levels).

Risk-Assessment Approach

To ensure a consistent and acceptable standard of risk assessment an approved approach needs to be in place. It should outline the process for determining the scope, boundaries, methodology, responsibilities, and required skills.

There has been a considerable amount of research performed in the area of risk management and assessment. Therefore, management does not need to reinvent the wheel in establishing an approach. In many instances, management only needs to determine what approach is best suited for the business. For example, in developing a risk measurement approach the Australian/New Zealand Standard AS/NZS 4360:1995 "Risk Management" can be utilized.

Exhibit 4.1 outlines the steps to be followed in developing the risk action plan template for outsourced system acquisition/development projects. It is at a high level and simply follows the COBiT control objective steps.

The AS/NZS 4360:1995 "Risk Management" standard was used as the basis for developing the risk action plan template found later in this chapter. A matrix approach was utilized, as shown in Exhibit 4.2.

Exhibit 4.3 is an example extracted from the template.

Risk Identification

There are number of methods of identifying risks, for example:

- Surveys, questionnaires, interviews
- Workshops, discussion groups
- Past history failure analysis
- S.W.O.T analysis
- Documentation and analysis of flows (data, physical etc.)
- Modeling
- Analysis of local and overseas experiences, etc.

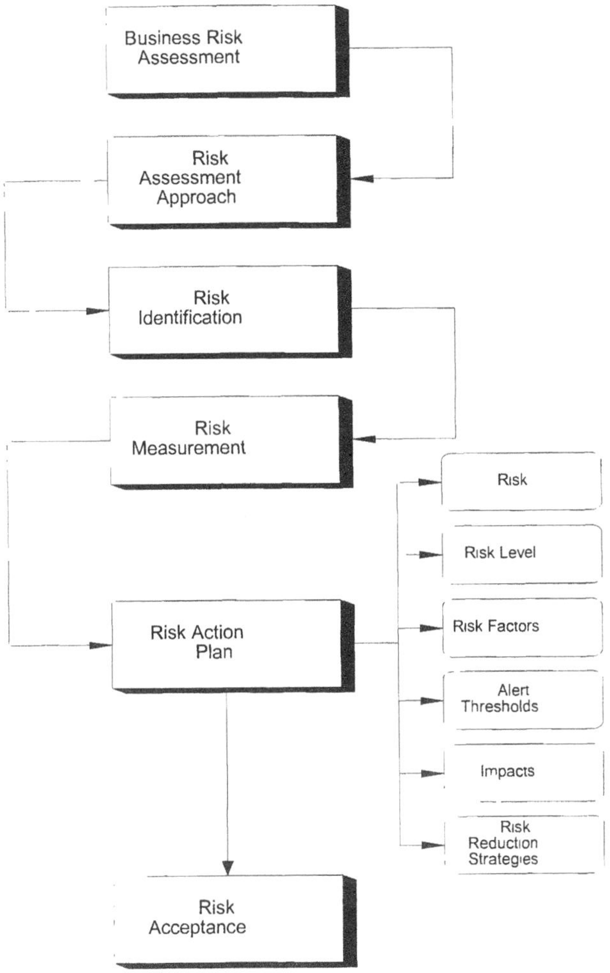

Exhibit 4.1. IS Risk Approach.

Exhibit 4.2. Excerpt from the Risk Action Plan Template

Title	Description
Risk	The risk being addressed.
Risk level	A measure of likelihood and seriousness of a risk's impact. It is calculated using the A/NZS 4360 Risk Management Standard.
Risk factors	A list of the elements that collectively contribute to the risk.
Alert thresholds	The symptoms or events that indicate the risk is likely to occur.
Impacts	The specific effects if the risk occurs.
Risk treatments	The strategies that can be implemented to minimize the likelihood or impact of the risk.

Exhibit 4.3. An Example Extracted from the Risk Action Plan Template

Title	Description
Risk	Inability of Outsourcing Contractor to fulfill contract requirements
Risk level	H (High)
Risk factors	Outsourcing Contractor loses the capability to continue satisfying contract requirements due to excessive demands placed on its resources (e.g., Customer base grows too fast or the Company loses key resources).
Alert thresholds	Expanding client base. (Winning new project contracts and soliciting large new clients.)
Impacts	The organization's requirements become low priorities for the Outsourcing Contractor.
Risk treatment	Monitor contract schedule/contract performance. Link incremental payments with successful completion of project milestones within a set timeframe.

If a workshop method is used, then the attendees should consist of the project team representatives, project stakeholders, and, if possible, individuals who had previous experience in developing a risk framework.

The auditor's role in the workshop is one of a facilitator. The facilitator's role is to ensure that all workshop participants clearly understand the project's strategic business objectives, and requirements and that a comprehensive list of risks are identified. The attached template provides a good basis for the list. However, it is only a basis and not a complete list suited for every type of outsourced system development project. The risks, risk measurement, and risk treatments will vary depending on the type of project, type of organization, and type of industry.

The risk identification workshop should attempt to identify as many risks associated with the project both within and outside the control of the organization. Areas to be included are

- Threats
- Vulnerabilities
- Strategic directions
- Relationships

Risk Measurement

This risk measurement phase requires the analysis of the likelihood and consequences of each risk identified. The guidelines provided by AS 4360 suggest that the risk level is a function of the likelihood of a risk occurring and the possible impact of the risk if it eventuates. Once the likelihood and impact of a risk are estimated the results are incorporated into a matrix to give the final risk level a value.

The rankings for the likelihood of a risk occurring are detailed in Exhibit 4.4.

Exhibit 4.4. A Ranking of the Likelihood of a Risk Occurring

Level	Description	Description
A	Almost certain	The event is expected to occur in most circumstances.
B	Likely	The event will probably occur in most circumstances.
C	Moderate	The event should occur at some time.
D	Unlikely	The event could occur at some time.
E	Rare	The event may occur only in exceptional circumstances.

Exhibit 4.5. An Example of Likely Events

Level	Description	Description
A	Almost certain	Unauthorized entry through use of poor passwords.
B	Likely	Corruption of backup media due to poor storage conditions
C	Moderate	Theft of equipment due to visitors being unsupervised.
D	Unlikely	Flooding on the top floor of a high rise building.
E	Rare	Physical damage to facilities due to terrorist attack.

Exhibit 4.6. Ranking of the Consequences of a Risk Occurring

Level	Description	Description
1	Insignificant	Low financial loss; minimal reduction in customer service, staff morale, or operational efficiency; minor impact on cash flow or ability to plan business activities; no or low political impact.
2	Minor	Medium financial loss; medium reduction in customer service, staff morale, or operational efficiency; medium impact on cash flow or ability to plan business activities; medium political impact.
3	Moderate	High financial loss; high reduction in customer service, staff morale, or operational efficiency; high impact on cash flow or ability to plan business activities; high political impact.
4	Major	Major financial loss; major reduction in customer service, staff morale, or operational efficiency; major impact on cash flow or ability to plan business activities; major political impact.
5	Catastrophic	Total financial loss; huge reduction in customer service, staff morale, or operational efficiency; catastrophic impact on cash flow or ability to plan business activities; total political impact.

Exhibit 4.5 is an example of likely events.

The rankings for magnitude/impact of consequences if a risk occurs are described in Exhibit 4.6.

Exhibit 4.7 exemplifies the different categories of risk impact.

Combining the estimated rankings for likelihood and impact from the above tables into another matrix provides a measurement of risk. The final risk measurement rankings are depicted in Exhibit 4.8.

Exhibit 4.7. Categories of Risk Impact

Level	Description	Description
1	Insignificant	Nonstakeholders protesting their lack of involvement in the project.
2	Minor	High staff turnover in project teams requiring an increase in training expenditure and lost productive time due to new project team members familiarizing themselves with the project requirements.
3	Moderate	Failure to reach milestones within planned time frame causing overruns in expenditure and key strategic objectives not being achieved
4	Major	Failure of a major IT project to provide the expected results (i.e., the project not yielding expected returns on investment).
5	Catastrophic	Halfway through the project the outsourcing contractor goes into receivership, bringing the project to a halt until all legal issues are resolved and expertise and resources are again organized to continue the project.

Exhibit 4.8. Measurements of Risk

	Consequences				
Likelihood	Insignificant 1	Minor 2	Moderate 3	Major 4	Catastrophic 5
A (almost certain)	S	S	H	H	H
B (likely)	M	S	S	H	H
C (moderate)	L	M	S	H	H
D (unlikely)	L	L	M	S	H
E (rare)	L	L	M	S	S

H = High risk: detailed research and management planning required at senior levels
S = Significant risk: senior management attention needed.
M = Moderate risk: management responsibility must be specified.
L = Low risk: manage by routine procedures.

Therefore, if a risk is likely to occur and the possible impacts are considered major, then the risk level is regarded as High (H).

Risk Action Plan

In developing a risk action plan the following categories should be covered.

Risk Factors. Risk factors are the basic elements that collectively contribute to the risk. These can be identified, for each risk, during the risk identification phase (e.g., during the workshop).

For example, Risk — the selected outsourced software developer may lose the ability to satisfy its contractual obligations.

The risk factors that may contribute to this risk include:

- Financial difficulties
- Takeover by another company, broken up, and sold off
- Change in the outsourced software developer's strategic direction
- Outsourced software developer decides that there are no longer any benefits to be obtained in continuing with the outsourcing contract arrangement

Alert Thresholds. Alert thresholds, which include events or trends that indicate the probability of a risk occurring, is becoming more likely.

For example, for the risk identified above, rumors of cash flow problems could be an indication of financial difficulties. A ratio analysis of the outsourced software developer's financial statements could indicate possible financial difficulties.

Impacts. The impacts represent the likely result if a risk eventuates.

For the risk identified above, if the outsourced software developer is bankrupted, then the organization has the task of picking up the pieces (i.e., continuing the software development of the strategic business system). This would require either building in-house teams to continue with the project or finding another suitable contractor. Either way the organization would incur losses in time and money.

Risk Treatments/Risk Action Plan. The risk treatments are risk management strategies for minimizing the likelihood of occurrence or the impact on the organization if the risk eventuates.

For example, to minimize the impact of the outsourcing contractor going into liquidation, the outsourcing firm can ensure that an escrow agreement is entered into by all relevant parties. This will provide the outsourcing firm with access to all source code and documentation if such an event occurs.

Alternatively, the outsourcing firm could foster a partnership working relationship. Depending on how critical the system development is, it could provide financial support to the outsourcing contractor, if required.

Risk Acceptance

Once the risk management strategies have been identified, a number of steps are required.

The first being an identification of what risks executive management are prepared to accept (i.e., residual risk). The residual risks are usually those events that have a very low likelihood of occurrence or very low material impact. For example, there is a very low likelihood that the earth will be struck by asteroid one cubic kilometer in size and the impact on the operations of the organization if the petty cash float of $20.00 being stolen is very low.

The remainder of the risks need to be addressed. The implementation of the relevant risk strategies need to planned and costed. If viable (i.e., cost-effective), then the strategies should be implemented. However, if not, alternative strategies need to be developed.

Most important, the responsibility for the implementation of the risk reduction strategies need to be assigned to a manager with the appropriate skills, commitment, and authority.

USING THE TEMPLATE

The successful contractor's responsibilities include:

- The selection of the development tools
- The development of a fully functional system that meets the user's requirements and complies with the strategic IT architecture
- The effective management of the change management process
- The acquisition and installation of the hardware platform and operating system

The hardware and software maintenance was not included within the scope of the development project.

The following is a list of definitions relevant to the template (see Exhibit 4.9).

- **Developer:** The organization acquiring the product or service
- **Outsourcing Contractor:** The prime contractor, the organization responsible for delivering the product or service
- **Application Developer:** The organization providing the skill and resources to design the application, write the code, and build the database
- **Hardware Provider:** The organization that will provide the computer equipment
- **DBMS Provider:** The organization that provides the database development products
- **Change Management:** The organization responsible for the change
- **Contractor:** Management required to make the implementation of the new system a success
- **Middleware Provider:** The organization that provides the software tool products for the development of the application

1. COBiT — Control Objectives for Information and Related Technology (COBiT); Systems Audit and Control Association (ISACA) — 1996.
2. AS4360 — Risk Management — Standards Association of Australia.
3. APT — APT Methodology. EXECOM, Perth. Western Australia, 1993.

Exhibit 4.9. The Risk Audit Assessment Template

Risk	Risk Level	Risk Factors	Alert Thresholds	Impact	Risk Treatment
Inability of Outsourcing Contractor to fulfill contract requirements.	H	Outsourcing Contractor loses the capability to continue adequately satisfying contract requirements due to excessive demands placed on its resources (e.g., Customer base grows too fast or the Company loses key resources).	Expanding client base. (Winning new projects and soliciting new customers.)	The organization's requirements become low priorities for the Outsourcing Contractor.	Monitor schedule/contract performance. Monitor acceptance criteria compliance. Prioritize the Developer business with vendor.
		Outsourcing Contractor is no longer commercially viable (e.g., Goes into receivership or liquidation.)	Analysis of financial performance indicates that Outsourcing Contractor will go or goes into receivership.	Restricted access to hardware, source code, and documentation, which has been paid for but is still in the possession of the contractor.	Ensure that the Developer has the ability to take over or acquire critical Outsourcing Contractor's resources in order to keep the project going.
		Outsourcing Contractor changes ownership. The new owners break up and sell off the Contractor's assets and it ceases to exist. The new owner may take action that would relinquish its contractual obligations to the Developer.	News of takeover threats by a corporate raider.	Loss of contractor for system development, maintenance, support, and enhancement	Contract condition that contractor supplied equipment becomes the Developer property on payment and that transfer of ownership is confirmed by the subcontractor. View software acquisition documentation to determine extent of license/copyright ownership by Outsourcing Contractor to see if it may have a detrimental effect.

Exhibit 4.9 (Continued). The Risk Audit Assessment Template

Risk	Risk Level	Risk Factors	Alert Thresholds	Impact	Risk Treatment
		Outsourcing Contractor is or becomes fundamentally incapable of delivering (e.g., they lied about their ability).	Deliverables are constantly not met.	Incur costs associated with finding replacement contractors or organizing resources internally.	Contract condition requiring contractor to provide certified financial information on a regular basis for the purposes of evaluating financial performance.
				If Outsourcing Contractor goes into receivership ownership of hardware and software license may revert to subcontractors (This is sometimes a contract condition between prime contractors and subcontractors).	Ensure that Outsourcing Contractor indemnifies the Developer over any action that may arise between Outsourcing Contractor and its subcontractors (e.g., Copyright ownership claims, etc.).
Risk of Outsourcing Contractor losing interest in meeting contractual obligations.	H	Outsourcing Contractor decides to change its strategic direction and no longer wishes to support, maintain, or enhance the product the Developer acquired.	Outsourcing Contractor is sold/taken over.	Loss of contractor for system development or diminished service.	Ensure that the Developer has the ability to veto the transfer of software copyright ownership to a third party (i.e., the Developer should have the ability to stop the sale of copyright ownership to a small unknown company). This should also apply to the transfer of support and service contracts.

			Change in profile of contractor's client base.	Loss of contractor for system maintenance, support and enhancement or diminished service.	Retender or complete project with internal resources.
					Details of personnel involved in developing and maintaining system.
					The Developer has access to Outsourcing Contractor's marketing strategy and market research material for assessment purposes.
					Ensure that the Developer has the ability to approve key personnel for the project including those employed by subcontractors as well as Outsourcing Contractor.
Risk of Outsourcing Contractor losing interest in meeting contractual obligations.	H	The product provided matures to a point that it would no longer be financially viable for the contractor to continue enhancing it.	Sunset clause of facilities support/maintenance .	Incur costs associated with finding replacement contractors or organizing resources internally.	Ensure that the Developer has the ability to veto the transfer of software copyright ownership to a third party.
		The product fails in the marketplace and Outsourcing Contractor loses interest.	Relationship deterioration between Developer and Contractor.	Loss of contractor for system development or diminished service.	Ensure that contracts between Outsourcing Contractor and subcontractors are in place and the Developer has access to the contracts.

Exhibit 4.9 (Continued). The Risk Audit Assessment Template

Risk	Risk Level	Risk Factors	Alert Thresholds	Impact	Risk Treatment
Risk of Outsourcing Contractor losing interest in meeting contractual obligations.					Outsourcing Contractor should commit to providing support for the product for a minimum of five years. (The Developer should not be committed to acquiring Outsourcing Contractor's support for more than one year at a time.) Performance guarantees from contractor signed by a guarantor. Ensure that the Developer has the ability to veto the transfer of software copyright ownership to a third party.
Risk of Application Developer losing capacity or interest for meeting contractual obligations.	H	Application Developer is no longer commercially viable (e.g., Goes into receivership.)	Analysis of financial performance indicates that Application Developer will go into receivership.	Time blowouts, increased costs and loss of expertise.	Outsourcing Contractor must have the ability to acquire ownership of source code copyright in the event that Application Developer go out of business. This should be evidenced by the Developer.

		Application Developer decides to change its strategic direction and no longer wishes to support, maintain, or enhance the product.	Application Developer goes into receivership.	Increased costs in product maintenance and support.	Contract condition that permits the Developer unencumbered access to source code and related documentation if Outsourcing Contractor goes out of business.
		Application Developer changes ownership. The new owners break up and sell off the Contractor's assets and it ceases to exist.	Change in management or ownership.	Increased costs in maintenance and support and a possible loss of access to expertise.	Ensure that there are no legal restrictions preventing the Developer from employing key personnel that worked for the outsourcing contractor.
			Application Developer is sold/taken over.		*(The above three treatments apply to all three risk factors listed in this section.)*
Risk of Hardware Provider losing capacity or interest for meeting contractual obligations.	L	Hardware Supplier is no longer commercially viable (e.g., Goes into receivership.)	Hardware Supplier goes into receivership.	Hardware no longer supported.	Provide support internally.
		Hardware Provider decides to change its strategic direction and no longer wishes to support, maintain or enhance the hardware the Developer acquired.	Change in management or ownership.	Increased costs in supporting and maintaining.	Port system to a new platform.
		Hardware Provider changes ownership. The new owners break up and sell off the Contractor's assets and it ceases to exist.	Hardware Supplier is sold/taken over.	Costs associated in porting to another platform.	Ensure that hardware satisfies open systems standards.

Exhibit 4.9 (Continued). The Risk Audit Assessment Template

Risk	Risk Level	Risk Factors	Alert Thresholds	Impact	Risk Treatment
				(The above three impacts may apply to all or some of the risk factors listed in this section.)	*(The above three treatments apply to all three risk factors listed in this section.)*
Risk of DBMS Provider losing capacity or interest for meeting contractual obligations.	L	DBMS Provider is no longer commercially viable (e.g., Goes into receivership.)	DBMS Provider goes into receivership.	DBMS Provider no longer supported.	Port to another DBMS.
		DBMS Provider decides to change its strategic direction and no longer wishes to support, maintain or enhance the product the Developer acquired.	There is a change in management or ownership.	Costs associated in porting to another DBMS.	Ensure that DBMS satisfies open systems standards.
		DBMS Provider changes ownership. The new owners break up and sell off the Contractor's assets and it ceases to exist.	DBMS Provider is sold/taken over.	*(The above impacts may apply to all or some of the risk factors listed in this section.)*	*(The above treatments apply to all three risk factors listed in this section.)*
Risk of Change Management Contractor (Change Management Contractors) losing capacity or interest for meeting contractual obligations.	H	Change Management Contractor is no longer commercially viable (e.g., Goes into receivership.)	Change Management Contractor goes into receivership.	Time loss.	Find some one to replace Change Management Contractor.

		Change Management Contractor loses the capacity to provide.	Analysis of financial performance indicates that Change Management Contractor will go into receivership.	Time loss.	Perform change management function internally. Select a change management contractor with sound financial and performance backgrounds. *(The above treatments apply to all risk factors listed in this section.)*
Risk of Middleware Provider losing capacity or interest in meeting contractual obligations.	L	Middleware Provider is no longer commercially viable (e.g., Goes into receivership.)	Middleware Provider goes into receivership.	Middleware Provider product no longer supported.	Replace Middleware Provider with alternative product.
		Middleware Provider decides to change its strategic direction and no longer wishes to support, maintain or enhance the product the Developer acquired.	Change of management or ownership.	Cost of changing product.	Ensure that product satisfies open systems standards.
		Middleware Provider changes ownership. The new owners break up and sell off the Contractor's assets and it ceases to exist.	Middleware Provider is sold/taken over.	*(The above impacts may apply to all or some of the risk factors listed in this section.)*	*(The above treatments apply to all three risk factors listed in this section.)*
The risk of relationship deterioration between the Developer and Outsourcing Contractor.	H	A dispute between the Developer and Outsourcing Contractor.	A high degree of disputes/unresolved disputes.	Extended delivery times.	Ensure that relationship is built on basis of partnering not an adversarial contract. Neither party should be too restrictive in its demands or lack flexibility in accepting solutions.

Exhibit 4.9 (Continued). The Risk Audit Assessment Template

Risk	Risk Level	Risk Factors	Alert Thresholds	Impact	Risk Treatment
The risk of relationship deterioration between the Developer and Outsourcing Contractor.			Disputes can occur while trying to reach a compromise over a system functionality; payments; and product/service quality.	Cost overruns.	Good project planning can contribute to a healthy relationship between vendor and purchaser. The project plan should clearly stipulate: - The roles and responsibilities of all parties; - Who the key personnel are for both the Developer and Outsourcing Contractor; - Project time plan; - Channels of communication; - Risk management approach; and quality planning.
				Diminished deliverable quality.	Dispute resolution procedures in contract (i.e., escalation, arbitration, etc.). Nominate an independent mediator, agreeable to both parties, to decide on unresolved disputes.

The risk of having to pay for modifications to the application.	L	Outsourcing Contractor maintains that all modification requests are Developer specific. Therefore the Developer must pay. This may be the case early on in the project life as the Developer will be one of a few customers if not the only one.	Being billed by the contractor for any modifications requested.	Cost overruns and disputes.	Commitment from Outsourcing Contractor that they will provide software version support for at least 18 months for each release. To have access to support, the Developer should not be committed to upgrade each time there is a new release of the product. Hourly rates should be stipulated in a contract schedule to cover requested services that are outside the contract. Rate increases should be negotiated and specified in the contract. Ensure that there is a formal process for handling modification requests. The process should ensure that quotes are provided, in accordance with schedule rates, and that the request is formally approved by the Developer before Outsourcing Contractor performs any work on the request. Dispute resolution clause in contract.

Exhibit 4.9 (Continued). The Risk Audit Assessment Template

Risk	Risk Level	Risk Factors	Alert Thresholds	Impact	Risk Treatment
The risk of having to pay for modifications to the application.					Nominate an independent arbitrator to decide on unresolved disputes. Contract conditions and monitoring.
The risk of there being misinterpretation of system specifications.	S	Outsourcing Contractor's interpretation of functional specifications may differ from the Developer's.	Disputes between the Developer and Outsourcing Contractor. Outsourcing Contractor wishing to renegotiate Contract requirements.	Cost overruns and disputes	Ensure that the specifications are adequately defined (use an accepted methodology. etc.) Adequate planning and partnership fostering, as for previous risk, to ensure that issues never escalate to a dispute stage. Dispute resolution clause in contract. Nominate an independent arbitrator to decide on unresolved disputes.

Lack of control over deliverable quality.	S	Outsourcing Contractor loses its QA accreditation.	Lack of QA accreditation proof.	Diminished deliverable quality.	The Developer agent should be appointed to evaluate contractor quality assurance systems.
		Inadequate QA acceptance criteria is specified in the contract.	Constant failure of deliverables to meet design review or acceptance criteria.		The contract or project plan should detail quality requirements and acceptance standards.
		Lack of escape clauses in the Contract.			Acceptance criteria should be clearly defined and based on the detailed design specifications.
		Detailed design specifications are inadequate.			Payments should be tied to performance.
					The Contract should contain dispute resolution procedures.
					Contract condition that Outsourcing Contractor maintains its quality accreditation.
					Contract condition to rectify faults "bugs" in system that were not found during the course of reasonable testing.
					(The above treatments may apply to all risk factors listed in this section.)

Exhibit 4.9 (Continued). The Risk Audit Assessment Template

Risk	Risk Level	Risk Factors	Alert Thresholds	Impact	Risk Treatment
Product licenses restricting the Developer's use of facilities.	S	Changes in legal structure and relationships of the Developer entities.	Business Units become independent corporations. The Developer Units establishing one-stop shops or similar. The Developer extending its network through agents and other facilities. Separate the Developer Entities (Developer gets broken up into more than one Developer).	Facilities licenses restrain use of facilities by other entities. Business or organizational development opportunities constrained.	Contract condition that will allow for the Developer entities and agencies to utilize systems. Contract to indicate that the Developer does not pay for additional costs for extra site licenses or user licenses. Alternatively, the contract could contain formulae for calculating costs associated with obtaining site licenses and user licenses.
Ongoing availability of key contractor personnel (HR plan for key project personnel succession).	H	Outsourcing Contractor may have an inadequate staff training and replacement strategy. Outsourcing Contractor's knowledge base may be sensitive to staff loss.	High staff turnover for contractor. Inability of contractor to meet deadlines.	Time blowouts. Inability to obtain product support, etc.	Identify key resources and implement strategies to maintain their availability (e.g., Ensure that Outsourcing Contractor plan to train and maintain at least four people that are adequately familiar with the product).

		Inadequate system documentation maintained by Outsourcing Contractor.			Outsourcing Contractor to provide information, on a regular basis, of their key project personnel detailing their skills, experience, and background. Ensure that the contract does not restrict the Developer from employing key staff that leave Outsourcing Contractor. *(The above treatments may apply to all three risk factors listed in this section.)*
Risk of adequate performance criteria and KPIs not clearly specified in contract.	H	Inability to define KPIs.	Lack of Contractor accountability.	Detrimental impact on deliverable quality.	Base KPIs on detailed system specifications.
		KPIs artificially set too high or too low.	Software deficiencies diminished data integrity.	(The above impact applies to both of the risk factors listed in this section.)	Use industry standards for setting KPIs. Expert assistance in defining KPIs. Mutually agreed KPIs.
			Disputes with Contractor.		Ability to modify KPIs during course of project. *(The above treatments may apply to all risk factors listed in this section.)*

Exhibit 4.9 (Continued). The Risk Audit Assessment Template

Risk	Risk Level	Risk Factors	Alert Thresholds	Impact	Risk Treatment
Viability of equity interests (funding the development but not owning the product).	S	No intellectual property rights.		No royalty streams for the Developer and potential loss of revenue. Competitors can easily negate any competitive advantage provided by the technology via acquisition.	Informed executive or policy decision on whether to partake in royalties or not. An affirmative decision could result in a long-term relationship between the developer and the outsourcing contractor.
No apparent risk sharing arrangement with contractor.	S	The contract price does not adequately account for the risks taken and the returns forgone by the Developer.		Contract price too high	Competitive tenders.
Outsourcing Contractor may demonstrate the product to prospective customers and use the Developer as a demonstration site.	M	The Developer becomes a Beta site.	Testing Beta releases of the product on a frequent basis.	Down time due to failure of Beta software.	Restrictions on Beta testing. Stringent testing before allowing any Beta versions into the Developer production environment.

Therefore, there is a risk that a business partnership agreement with the Outsourcing Contractor may cause too much disruption in the Developer.		There are frequent new releases of the product (every six months).	Too many visits from prospective customers.	Costs associated with staff time taken up demonstrating the product.	Restrictions on product demonstrations.
			Staff complain that they cannot complete their own work due to customer visits.	Overtime costs associated with catching up on work backlogs.	Contract condition indicating that liabilities to rest with Outsourcing Contractor for any costs or losses incurred by the Developer during testing or product demonstrations.
Risk of inaction or delay in making decision on project supply contract.	S	Long periods for decisions to be made.	Evaluation and decision to appoint a contractor takes too long.	Damage to the Developer Image.	Streamline process for future decisions.
				On cost factor added into tenders by any party tendering for jobs in the Developer.	Improve process for briefing tenderers.
			Complaints received from tenderers.	Tenders withdrawn.	
				Tender price may be revised upward.	

Exhibit 4.9 (Continued). The Risk Audit Assessment Template

Risk	Risk Level	Risk Factors	Alert Thresholds	Impact	Risk Treatment
Risk of developing Project in-house.	H	The Developer not currently geared up for developing a system for project type project (inadequate internal skills base and resources).	No suitable Contractors. Inability to reach agreement with tenderers.	Schedule and budget overruns. Requirements unsatisfied. High costs	Detailed performance measures for all contract deliverables. Detailed planning and an adequately skilled project team. Follow recognized methodology. QA and audit reviews. Employ or contract into the organization the required skill base and expertise. Performance based payment.
The risk of failure in the change management processes	H	System not meeting stakeholder expectations. System not being used to its fullest potential. System considered a failure and a hindrance to business processes. Decreased level of service.	Inadequate stakeholder involvement or ownership. Poor promotion and selling of new system to users/stakeholders. Lack of adequate staff training and documentation.	Nonacceptance of the system	Ensure adequate stakeholder involvement and encourage ownership of system. Monitoring processes. QA acceptance of change management. Develop a change management plan that includes communication of issues to all stakeholders and training.

		No realized productivity or performance gains. Increase customer complaints.	Poor redeployment and retraining planning. Change Management Contractor becomes unavailable.		*(The above treatments may apply to all or some of the risk factors listed in this section.)*
Risk of overcontrol by the Developer.	S	Relationship between the Developer and Contractor is not one of partnership but confrontational.	The contract is too restrictive. The Developer's organizational culture is not conducive to a partnership with the Outsourcing Contractor.	Diminished quality in service and deliverables.	Obtain expert advice to ensure that the contract is not too restrictive. Ensure that undue pressure is not placed on the outsourcing contractor (i.e., it is not the Developer's main objective to force the Outsourcing Contractor into receivership).
		Multiple project managers.	Too many groups established to review contractor progress and performance. No formal communication channels established between the Contractor and the Developer.		Ensure that communications with the tenderer are through one point. Ensure that a charter contains the explicit authorities defined. It should also contain procedures on how the Developer will deal with Outsourcing Contractor during modifications and after the contract is set. *(The above treatments may apply to all the risk factors listed in this section.)*

Exhibit 4.9 (Continued). The Risk Audit Assessment Template

Risk	Risk Level	Risk Factors	Alert Thresholds	Impact	Risk Treatment
The Developer's inability to address changing customer needs across a wide range of business processes.	S	Contractor cannot address modification requests quickly so that Developer processes can adjust to meet customers changing needs.	Modifications requests are not addressed in a timely fashion by the contractor.	Cost increases. Time blowouts.	The project functional specifications require that many parameter changes can be performed by the user. This will minimize dependency on the Outsourcing Contractor for implementing system modifications.
					Adequate acceptance testing to ensure functionality.
Security Risks					
• Unauthorized access to the Developer data and equipment.	H	Poor security culture.	Poor access controls at Outsourcing Contractor premises.	Cost overruns.	Outsourcing Contractor must have a disaster recovery capability. It should have insurance to cover Developer equipment on their premises. Back-up processes should be in place with at least one set of copies going off site to Developer-designated premises.
• Malicious intent to undermine project.	H		Poor access controls on the Developer premises.	Time deadlines not met.	Evidence of above requirements must be provided on demand during course of contract.

• Disaster recovery planning and risk management during development and implementation phases.	H		Poor Industrial Relations policies or their poor implementation. Lack of Business Continuity Planning and risk minimization strategies by Outsourcing Contractor.	Project failure or termination.	
Risk that the Developer's data provided for development and test purposes or even residing in the production environment could be accessed and used for unauthorized purposes.	H	The Developer not having access to or control over its own data leading to unauthorized access or usage of the data.	Ownership clauses not included in contract.	Damage to the Developer's image. Possibility of missed income. Costs incurred to access data or use data in different ways.	Contract to indicate ownership of all data and its usage. Independent audit review of Outsourcing Contractor's logical and physical security.
The risk of functionality changes during the course of the project.	H	Initiation of change requests.	The Developer decides on new types of fees, taxes, and rebates. Payment requests from Outsourcing Contractor for unauthorized change requests.	Increases in contract cost. Time blowout for project completion.	Ensure that there is a formal process for handling modification requests. The process should ensure that quotes are provided, in accordance with schedule rates, and that the request is formally approved by the Developer before Outsourcing Contractor performs any work on the request.

Exhibit 4.9 (Continued). The Risk Audit Assessment Template

Risk	Risk Level	Risk Factors	Alert Thresholds	Impact	Risk Treatment
The risk of functionality changes during the course of the project.					The project functional specifications require that many parameter changes can be performed by the user. This will minimize dependency on the Outsourcing Contractor for implementing system modifications. Acceptance testing to ensure functionality.

Section I Checklist

1. Does your organization use a formal project management methodology for all programming activities? If not, what determines the need for using a formal approach?
2. Is project management a necessity in your environment or an optional part of development and support activities?
3. Are you confident about the benefits of project management or are you reluctant to embrace all aspects of the process?
4. When, if ever, should project management procedures be abandoned to meet project deadlines? Does this happen often in your organization?
5. How are project management practices conveyed to IS staff and end users in your organization? Is there formal training?
6. Does your organization periodically review project management procedures for effectiveness? If so, is it done before or after a crisis takes place?
7. Have you ever engaged in nontraditional project management procedures so as to advert difficulties with traditional methods? Does it work?
8. How are system requirements managed in your organization? Is this done by committee or via some other method?
9. From your experience, do user requirements change more or less often during implementation?
10. When does the user requirement phase end in your environment? Is it before the project begins or during the development phase?
11. Has your organization identified legacy systems for replacement or re-engineering? Which is more appropriate?
12. What is your organizations' experience in re-engineering older application systems? Is it more difficult or less difficult than expected?
13. In your opinion, how should outsourcing be used effectively? Is it best suited for new development or ongoing support tasks?
14. What pitfalls have you identified with outsourcing IS projects?
15. What analysis methods are used in your organization to determine the appropriate need for or against outsourcing. Is cost always a factor?

Section II
Development Strategies

Diverse advancements in all forms of computing technology have not changed the lure and attraction that application development generates for the IS professional. This perception has been justified by the amount of interest that software development receives from the computing industry. Most notable are in the growing number of vendors who provide hardware and software technology, consulting and outsourcing services, as well as advancements in academic research. However, this overwhelming level of attention can have a formidable price. In the past, development expenditures have been warranted by the creation of new application systems that improve or enhance business processes. Currently there is concern over the cost to maintain a state-of-the-art development environment. Some organizations are questioning the return on investment for expensive development technology. Since many of the fundamental business systems have already been automated, it may be more difficult to warrant further expense on new applications. Surprisingly, the trend for introducing new development technology continues to escalate, and this in turn can drive the desire to build newer business applications that exploit the advancements in system development. Consequently, development mangers are now faced with the additional challenge of justifying new applications, and the technology needed to build systems. Without a doubt, today's application development is still exciting, but more demanding and with little room for errors.

Chapter 5, "Six Myths about Managing Software Development in the New Millenium," begins this section with a factual look about the nature of development activities. Even though opinions vary about the manner in which software development exists, it is hard to ignore the truths that many development managers have experienced throughout the years. This includes the fact that requirements do not always exist, programming specifications are not a substitute for system description, and development is not always a linear function. Recognizing the basic temperament of software development may not change the needed effort to build actual new systems. But it can help expose the challenges that must be met to realistically implement applications that utilize new technology.

The need for exploiting alternative development methods is examined in Chapter 6, "Rapid Application Development and Management." Rapid Application Development (RAD) has been an excellent choice for building new systems in comparison to proprietary methodologies of the past. But it is often accompanied by other methodologies or techniques that are tailored for a given project or development environment. RAD is not a panacea, nor can it be the only technique available for software developers. By understanding its strengths and weaknesses, there can be an improved advantage in accomplishing implementation tasks that have usually taken significant more time in the past.

Organizations that have repeatedly developed software application systems over the last several decades are now seeking more return on the investment in software code. Evolving and shifting technologies often made this goal hard to achieve, but recently the use of components and object-oriented techniques have aided in getting closer to the objective. Even so, there are still numerous challenges in assessing where to apply the use of existing code to enterprise systems. Chapter 7, "Leveraging Developed Software," offers insight to the realization of software reusability and portability. This includes the need to appropriately identify target business areas for reuse and benefit analysis. It can be difficult for some user departments to accept the functionality of an existing system as it is applied to a new business solution. This issue is further discussed in Chapter 8, "Developing Workstation-Based Client/Server Applications." Beyond the use of existing code is the issue of utilizing existing skills of developers. Many organizations fail to capitalize on skill sets of software developers due to perceived opportunities with newer technologies requiring newer skilled professionals. But leveraging development assets can only be accomplished by examining the software and the skills needed for further expansion.

The introduction of the graphical user interface (GUI) almost two decades ago has been a radical departure from menu screens found in earlier application systems. Since its inception, the GUI has continued to evolve as a critical component to desktop application, especially in client/server and Internet based systems. Perhaps the great interest in GUI programming is due to the perception that it casts on the application as a whole. If the interface is too busy, the application may be viewed as too complicated. However, if the interface helps users identify business functions, then the application is viewed positively. Chapter 9, "The Influence of Software Design on Human-Computer Interaction," provides meaningful insight that details the process of building strong, well-defined and meaningful interfaces to applications. Many business users appreciate the graphical user interface because it can provide powerful access to an application without being too computer cryptic. At the same time, it can offer greater enhancements to productivity. But graphical development is not as easy as it may appear. Despite the numerous software products available for GUI development, there remain important issues that managers must recognize as part of the overall application development process.

Formal methodologies and procedures are frequently targeted as areas in which to improve software development. Unlike software tools, it is still unclear if development methodologies are best described as art or science. This uncertainty has created much controversy among software vendors, consultants and professional developers. Chapter 10, "Effective Systems Development Management: The Experts Advise," provides an informative perspective on the value of development methodologies. This chapter offers various opinions from leading experts about those project phases that can influence the success or failure of application development. Managers will find these opinions helpful in forging a strategy for development in their own environment.

Chapter 5
Six Myths about Managing Software Development in the New Millennium

Linda G. Hayes

MYTH 1: REQUIREMENTS EXIST

That requirements exist is the fundamental assumption of all software development projects. At first they exist in the minds of the users, in documented form from which the design proceeds, and then form the basis for acceptance of the finished project.

As logical and hopeful as this may sound, it is generally not proven true. Although users know what they want, it is not unlike the Supreme Court's understanding of pornography: they know it when they see it. Until then, requirements are inchoate: inarticulate needs that do not, of themselves, describe the features and functions that would satisfy them.

What is widely attributed to scope creep, or the continuous expansion of the project requirements, is really just the natural process of distilling user needs into objective expression. For example, a requirement for a banking application might be to maximize the profitability of each customer. Once understood, this requirement spawns new requirements: the need to maximize the number of services sold to a single customer, which leads to the need for a unified database of all customers and services, and relational access among them.

Once the implementation begins, these requirements metamorphose into yet more: users realize that what appear to be many separate customers and accounts are often managed by a single individual, such as a parent creating trust accounts for children, and the requirement arises to define and associate subaccounts, followed by the need to present consolidated statements and reports ... and so forth, and so on.

0-8493-9822-3/00/$0.00+$.50

Therefore, if the project manager assumes the requirements can be expressed coherently and completely before development commences, and the entire project plan and schedule is based on that assumption, subsequent changes wreak havoc. Scope creep, then, is really the inevitable realization that requirements are living, growing things that are discovered instead of defined.

Reality: Seek Problems, Not Solutions

Instead of asking users to describe requirements and solutions, ask them to describe their problems. If this is a new system, find out why it is being created — what is being done today and how will it change with the system? If this is a rewrite of an existing system, ask what is wrong with the old one. What problems will be solved?

This is a radically different approach than asking for requirements. A commonly told illustration of this involves the building manager whose tenants complained about slow elevators. After rejecting a series of costly elevator upgrade or replacement scenarios, the manager hired a problem-solving expert.

This expert interrogated the manager. What was wrong with the elevators? The tenants, he said, were complaining about waiting for them. Why did that matter, the expert asked? Because if they are unhappy they may move out, the manager responded, and I may lose my job. The expert promised a solution.

The next day, mirrors were installed outside the elevators on all floors. The tenant complaints subsided. The expert explained: the tenants were complaining about waiting, not about the elevators. The solution was to make the wait more pleasant, and mirrors offer the most popular pastime of all: admiring ourselves. This solution, of course, cost a tiny fraction of the time and money to speed up the elevators.

The point is, if one focuses on the real problem, one will arrive at the best solution. If starting with a solution, the wrong problem may be solved.

MYTH 2: DESIGNS ARE DOCUMENTS

The next assumption proceeds from the first. If requirements can be captured and subdued into a static state, then the design can be based upon them and reduced to a written document from which development flows. This assumption fails not only because the first is flawed, but also for an independent reason. It is difficult, if not impossible, to adequately express functionality in words and pictures. Software is interactive; documents are not.

There are at least two levels of interactivity of a design. The first is external, at the user interface level: what the user sees and does. A perfectly plausible screen design on paper may prove to be impractical when created. What appear to be trivial matters, such as using the mouse to position focus on a field or object, may render the application awkward and unworkable to a high-speed data entry clerk, trained in touch-typing, whose fingers never leave the keyboard.

The second level of interactivity is internal: the hardware platform, operating system, development language, database, network topology, and other decisions that affect how processing occurs and data is managed. An otherwise elegant database design may fail due to response time of the underlying network access protocol, or sheer volume demands.

Reality: Go with the Flow

Instead of expressing the design as a series of static artifacts — data elements, screens, files, reports — describe it in terms of business processes. What will the user do with it?

Users do not think about customer information databases or order entry screens. They think about adding a new customer as the result of an order, answering customer questions about their orders, shipping the orders and sending out invoices, and making sure invoices are paid. They think in terms of processes, information, and workflow: they know their job.

Understanding the system as a set of processes as a user experiences it, beginning to end, will lead to a much different design than approaching the subject as a set of disparate entities. It forces the consideration of the flow and purpose of information — not how it is stored, but when and why it is used.

Another important aspect of what is done is, how many and how often? Will there be 100 customers or one million? What happens most frequently — entering new customers or checking on orders? Are dozens of orders received daily, or thousands? These numbers will greatly influence the internal design of the system, including not just the amount of storage but the throughput rates. The external design is also affected: screens are designed to support the way they will be needed. Frequently needed information will be readily accessible, and high volume transactions streamlined for heads-down entry instead of heads-up aesthetics.

Do not ask the users what they want to see. Ask them what they need to do.

MYTH 3: DEVELOPMENT IS LINEAR

If the foundation of requirements was coherent and complete, and the structure of the design solid and stable, development would indeed be a simple, predictable matter. In the traditional, linear development life cycle, coding is a segment that begins after design and ends with test.

Yet everyone knows this is not how it is. Our budgets tell us so. Sixty to 80 percent of corporate IT budgets are consumed by maintenance, which is a euphemism for development on existing systems — systems that have already been "released," sometimes decades ago. There is not an application alive — that is, being used — that does not experience constant development. Whether called modifications or enhancements, the fact is that 25 percent of even a so-called stable application undergoes revision each year.

This indicates that software systems reflect the business, and successful businesses are in a state of continuous change and improvement. Change can be a good thing, but only if it is planned.

Reality: The Schedule Rules

Once ready to start creating the system, set a schedule that provides for the earliest possible release of the least possible amount of functionality. In other words, deliver the system before it is ready. Do not come up with the design and then the schedule: come up with the schedule first and design as you go. Do not target for error-free completion; attempt to have something that does something.

Sometimes called "time-boxing," this approach focuses on rapid-fire releases where the amount of functionality in a given release is based on the amount of time, not the other way around. One can think of this as rapid prototyping — it is and it is not. Rapid prototyping usually means throwing together a mock-up that is used as a model for the real thing. Instead, this is the real thing, it is just successively refined. Today's development technologies make it only incrementally more difficult to create a screen that works than one that does not.

In the early stages one might use a "toy" or personal database while nailing down the actual contents, then later shift to an industrial strength version when the tables settle down. The point is to get users to use it right away. The sooner they use it, the faster will be their feedback. Make sure everyone knows this is a moving target, and do not get painted into any corners until necessary. Stay out of the critical path at first, and let the users report when it is ready for prime time.

Expect changes and problems and plan for them, which means not only releasing early but repeatedly.

MYTH 4: DEVELOPERS DEVELOP AND TESTERS TEST

The mere fact that there is a title or job description of tester does not mean that testing is only done by testers. Quite the contrary: a major component of the test effort occurs in development.

The fact is, only the development organization has the knowledge and information essential for unit, integration, and system testing: testing the individual units, their interaction with each other, and their behavior as a whole. Developers are responsible for creating the software, and they not only *should* test it — they *must*.

The assumption that only testers test is especially insidious, because it shifts responsibility for software quality to those least able to affect it. The testers are not there to check up on development; they are there to protect the business. When development operates under the assumption that they have a safety net, the odds are higher that the system will crash.

The real and only reason for having an independent test organization is to represent the users: not to assure that the software does not break, but that it does what the business needs.

Reality: From the End of the Line to the Front

In this new paradigm, testing moves from the last line of defense for development to the front line of defense for the business users. It changes from testing to make sure the software runs to making sure the business does. Developers test software; testers test business processes.

This means the test cases and conditions are derived from the processes that have replaced the requirements. Testers do not verify that the order entry screen pull-down list of items is sorted alphabetically; they try to enter 100 orders in an hour. Granted, the sorting of the list may dramatically affect productivity if it is not alphabetized, but the focus is on how well the job gets done, not how well the development was done. The design has no meaning outside of its purpose: to support the process.

In this scenario, testers are not baby programmers hoping to graduate to real development. They are expert users, making sure that the business needs are served. Developers are not creative, temperamental artistes; they are professionals delivering a working product. The purpose of testing is not to break the system, it is to prove it.

MYTH 5: TESTERS DETERMINE QUALITY

Test organizations generally find themselves in an impossible position. They are asked to determine when or whether the software is "ready." This is impossible because the testers usually cannot control the quality of the software provided by development or the rate at which problems are corrected. They cannot control what end users expect of it or will do with it. To say that the schedule is out of their hands ... well, that should go without saying.

The uncomfortable truth is that testers are often approached as impediments to release, as though they somehow stand in the way of getting the software out the door. This is a dangerous idea, because it puts testing in a no-win situation. If they find too many problems, the release to production is delayed; but if they do not find enough, the release fails in production.

Reality: Ask, Do Not Tell

In the millennium, the business decides when the software is ready, based on what the test group discovers. The rolling release strategy provides for a constant flow of functionality, and the test organization's role is to constantly measure and report the level of capability and stability of the software. However, it is the business user's decision when it is acceptable. In other words, the user may elect to accept or waive known problems in order to obtain proven functions. This is a business decision, not a test criteria.

This does not absolve development from creating working product or test from performing a thorough analysis. It does mean that it is not up to them to decide when it is ready. This can work either way; the developers may be satisfied with a design that the users reject, or the users may decide they can live with some bugs that drive the testers up the wall.

The key is to remember that the system belongs to those who use it, not those who create it.

MYTH 6: RELEASES ARE FINAL

The initial release of an application is only the first of many, perhaps over decades. Mission-critical applications are frequently revised monthly, if not more often, throughout their entire lives. The idea that everything the system will ever do must be in the first release is patently untrue.

This belief drives schedule slip: that one must hold up or delay the system because it does not do one thing or another, or because it has bugs. The truth is that it will never do everything and it will always be imperfect. The real question is whether it can provide value to the business today and, especially, in the future.

Thus, a software release is not an event, it is a process. It is not a wall — it is a step.

Reality: The Rolling Release

The concept of a release as a singular, monolithic and, often, monster event is an anachronism. Software that truly serves the business is flexible and responsive, supporting competitive agility and rapid problem resolution. Releases are like heartbeats: if they are not happening regularly, the system is dying.

Therefore, instead of a one-year development project with a vacuum after that, plan for four quarterly releases followed by monthly ones. During test, make weekly builds available. While this may sound like a pressure cooker, and using traditional methods it would be, it can be properly positioned as a safety valve.

Design defects are more easily corrected the earlier they are identified. Additionally, errors or inconsistencies are less annoying if they will be corrected in weeks instead of months. Emotion over missed requirements subsides considerably if they will be coming sooner rather than later. Value is perceived faster, and the potential for runaways is all but eliminated.

All of this, of course, drastically changes the nature of testing.

RECOMMENDATIONS

With a development process based on assumptions that are consistently demonstrated to be untrue, it is no wonder one misses schedules and budgets. The answer, of course, is to throw out the existing process and define a new one based on reality

The accelerating rate of new technology and techniques aimed at improving the development process can address the technical hurdles but not the organizational ones. In order for this rapid-fire, rolling release strategy to work, several things have to happen.

Code Speed

Although it sounds good to say that developers need to slow down and get it right, the fact is they need to speed up and get it perfect.

A case in point is the no longer simple process of creating a build, or executable. The build process involves assembling all of the individual components of an application and compiling them into a single, working whole that can be reproduced and installed as a unit. With the advent of component-based development, this is no mean feat. The build may encompass dozens, if not hundreds, of discrete modules, libraries, and files. As a result, the build can take days ... if not weeks, or even months, to get it right.

In the time-box, rolling release world, builds are done no less than weekly. The only way for this to work, and work consistently, is for the code to be under tight management and control and for the build process to be strict and streamlined. Speed has a way of burning off fat, and sloppy coding practices cannot survive the friction of this new model.

Standard Standards

Many development shops have adopted, documented, and published development standards, only to find them in useless repose, stored in binders, never to be referenced again. Without constant training, consistent code inspections, and other oversight practices, standards quickly fall by the wayside. To a developer, standards are straightjackets to be worn only unwillingly.

The new millennium will not tolerate nonstandard practices for the simple reason that they will not work. Delivering increments of functionality means that each succeeding layer must fit smoothly with the others: it is like trying to build a brick wall — the bricks must be of uniform size and shape to keep it from falling over.

Not to be overly harsh, but maverick programmers will not cause the organization to step up enforcement procedures; they will cause the organization to cull them out. When running a tight train schedule, one does not coddle late passengers ... one leaves them behind.

Owning Responsibility

Users, on the other hand, must step up to the plate and own the system being developed for them. No longer can the test organization serve as a staging area for new hires or misfits, following a random, spontaneous agenda that shifts with time and turnover. It must be an elite corps of experts who bring their professionalism to bear.

Nor can users hide behind the excuse that they are not technical and must rely on development to tell them how and what to do when. Nonsense. They must take the responsibility for articulating what they need, assuring that they get it, and deciding when to release it. They pay the price to have it developed; they will pay the price if it cannot be used.

SUMMARY

While no one questions that development technology is taking quantum leaps almost every day, few question the fact that our process for applying that technology can still be found in a 1950s textbook. This anomaly is crippling our ability to move into the next millennium, and must be exposed and removed. If something quits working, it needs to be fixed ... or replaced.

Chapter 6

Rapid Application Development and Management

Mike Glassey

This article is based on the author's personal knowledge and experience of rapid application development (RAD) as operated through the dynamic systems development method (DSDM). Although there may be other methodologies used in conjunction with RAD, it is believed that the principles contained within this guidance will be applicable to most RAD-style projects, but may need to be adapted accordingly. This guidance should not be perceived as definitive, but may be used for education and for the formulation of audit workplans for RAD projects.

BACKGROUND TO RAD

Rapid application development (RAD) was developed as an alternative development methodology to traditional sequential methods of application development, which many developers were beginning to perceive as unsuitable for the high rate of business change prevalent in today's environment. Change is endemic in the business world and has become a fact of life for many of today's organizations. With the advent of business process re-engineering, downsizing, outsourcing, and the opportunities made possible through the advent of electronic commerce, it is likely that the days of stable environments may be gone forever, soon to be followed by companies who attempt to stand still against the tidal wave of change.

Given this increasingly dynamic environment, organizations not only require faster and better solutions, but require them as soon as possible. As a result of this requirement, RAD is perceived in some areas as a possible solution to this problem.

Perceived benefits of using a RAD approach include:

- A reduced development time, with a product typically being delivered within months, rather than years.

0-8493-9822-3/00/$0.00+$.50

- An increased sense of user ownership, through active user involvement in application development, and accordingly the production of a system that supports real business requirements.
- A reduced need for user training, through early exposure to the developing system (and hopefully through development of a more instinctive system through inclusion of user preferences).
- The delivery of systems at the specified time. (Within the DSDM methodology, slippage of dates is strictly prohibited.)

Risks of RAD

There is also a widely held perception of RAD as a quick and dirty solution that allows systems to evolve in an uncontrolled and haphazard fashion. This has led to accusations of RAD being an acronym for Really Awful Designs or Rapid Approach to Disaster.

In this sense, both views are true. While RAD does offer significant benefits for adopters, there are also pitfalls to be traversed, ideally through the application of a suitable methodology, such as DSDM. However, even traditional projects are not without their problems, and many surveys have shown that there is generally a high rate of failure in projects, including those established with accepted tools and techniques and managed through tried and tested project management methodologies. This suggests that there is a generic problem to be addressed, rather than one caused by, for example, a RAD approach, and that is the failure of organizations to manage projects that are allowed to spiral out of control.

Given this background, consider that the adoption of a RAD project involves not only an opportunity, but an element of risk. However, as with all projects, there is an inherent risk in need of management, and risky solutions such as RAD to compensate for a lack of control in our environments should not be ignored.

THE BASIS OF RAD

In addition to the perception that traditional methods of development do not meet the needs of today's customer, there is also the argument that these methods have failings in their assumptions, namely:

- That user requirements can be defined accurately;
- That user needs at the point of delivery will not have changed since the time of the specification, which may well have taken place over 18 months previously; and
- That the users really know what they want.

The adoption of these assumptions has contributed to a history of misunderstandings and failed relationships between developer and user and a lack of respect or appreciation for the skills of the other. This has led to the underlying perception that customers do not know what they want and that developers take too long and do not understand the needs of the business.

RAD uses a different set of assumptions:

- That the design process is iterative;
- That active user involvement is imperative; and
- That testing is not a separate activity, but an integrated part of the development process.

Timeboxing and Slippage

The DSDM approach takes a very firm stance regarding time scales for delivery in that there will be no slippage whatsoever allowed for delivery of products. However, in the knowledge that something has to give, it is functionality that is allowed to slip. While at first this may seem an unsatisfactory approach, the success rests firmly on the management of the process through time boxes, which are aimed at regular small releases and should result in the following:

- The slippage in functionality will be dictated and managed by user requirements. In this way, the users will see firsthand the results of requests for enhanced functionality or unexpected changes and the knock-on effect for expected work. By adopting this approach, users are encouraged to manage their own expectations, with the effect of any unreasonable demands becoming apparent and hard decisions falling to the users themselves to make.
- There will be regular releases of product, as the RAD approach is based on release being small and often rather than large releases arriving perhaps yearly (and late!). In this way, there will be a joint sense of achievement for user and developer alike, rather than the perceived failure of late delivery.
- When bugs or gaps in essential functionalities are identified, there will be more opportunity to get the situation rectified at the next release, as this will be around the corner.

However, this approach may not be applicable for all systems, and careful consideration should be given to health and safety systems, where slippage of functionality may not be an option.

RAD EXPECTATIONS

Care should be taken not to rely too much on preconceived ideas and expectations based on experience of traditional projects, but instead to concentrate on ensuring that:

- There is agreed criteria for the selection of projects as being suitable for RAD (i.e., that there is a RAD policy within the organization).
- RAD roles within the organization are fully defined, ideally at project initiation.
- There is a methodology in place.
- Management is involved from the top down.
- There is full commitment.
- Users and developers have a strong working relationship.
- There is strong configuration management of releases.
- Users sign up to prototypes and products (although this may be the visual representation of the system rather than a specification of the system based on paper).

In this sense, the RAD approach is participatory, as day-to-day working with the project will be the best way to establish a gut feeling for the success of the working environment.

PROJECT STARTUP

RAD projects are viewed as risky, and perhaps the first task is to decide whether the project is indeed suitable for a RAD approach. This should be considered at both the feasibility study and business study stages.

The key to determining this suitability is ensuring that all key personnel have received training in RAD principles and practices. Ideally, the first workshop would commence with a joint training session on RAD and JAD (joint application development) to ensure that all parties agree and sign up to use the methodology and have a common understanding of their roles and responsibilities within the project.

Key personnel need to be identified and involved as soon as possible to ensure buy-in from all parties. This is particularly important with RAD as key products appear early in the life cycle, and it is imperative that these are seen as having been developed jointly and agreed to by all parties. It is necessary to ensure that users are empowered to allow all decisions to be made within the workshop. It is acceptable that an element of consultation may be required with action points being allocated to take away from the meeting, but generally it is expected that users should be in a position to state their requirements for the proposed system within the workshop environment and effectively sign up to the prototype developed within that workshop.

Further training may be required for the facilitator, who will need additional skills. The role of the facilitator is key to the process as he or she is responsible for driving the workshops. It is important that the facilitator role is seen as being independent, and not linked to any of the groups involved in the JAD sessions. The facilitator should have the power and

Exhibit 6.1. The Five Stages of a RAD Project

Stages	Key Products
Feasibility Study	Feasibility report Feasibility prototype (optional) First cut estimates Outline plan
Business Study	Business area definition (defined users, defined business processes, defined information requirements) Prioritized functions Outline prototyping plan System architecture definition
Functional Model Iteration	Functional prototype Nonfunctional requirements Implementation plan Review documents Risk analysis
System Design and Build Iterations	Tested system to meet functional and nonfunctional requirements Design review documents Design prototypes
Implementation	Delivered systems Trained users User manual Project review document

confidence to be able to drive through the workshop without imposing his or her own view on the discussion.

THE MAIN STAGES OF A RAD PROJECT

There are five main stages to a RAD project, with key outputs expected at each stage (Exhibit 6.1); however, some stages may have been combined. For example, the feasibility and business stages may have been completed together. Alternatively, the functional and design/build stages may have been completed in the case of working prototypes being adopted.

Testing

Testing is integrated into the RAD life cycle and should not be considered as a separate activity. This is particularly true of user testing, as users get very early exposure to the new system. There will be a need for user expectations to be managed, as it may not be apparent to users why there will be a delay in producing a working system once prototypes have been created. Similarly, there will be a need to ensure that performance issues are handled in a similar manner, although it may be possible to emulate performance limitations through the prototyping process (see Exhibit 6.2).

Exhibit 6.2. How Testing Fits into RAD

RAD Stages	Products for Dynamic Testing	Test Stages
Feasibility Study	Feasibility Prototype	Prototype Testing
Business Study	None	None
Functional Model Iterations	Functional Prototype	Prototype Testing
System Design and Build Iterations	Design Prototype, Tested System	Prototype Testing, Unit/Integration/System Testing
Implementation	Delivered System	Acceptance Tests, Field Tests for Software Products

JOINT APPLICATION DEVELOPMENT

Joint application development (JAD) is a workshop technique that is mandatory for RAD projects, although JAD also can be used as a standalone technique. In its true sense, JAD should be viewed as an intensive prototyping environment, where users and designers can produce a front-end system in flight.

Suitable modelling techniques should be identified for use in JAD workshops. Typically, they might involve a programmer sitting at a keyboard, connected to an overhead screen, displaying changes to the proposed front-end system dynamically. There should also be some mechanism for recording nonfunctional requirements, (e.g., security, audit, performance, capacity).

Within the prototyping process consideration may be given to producing prototypes for:

- Business.
- Usability.
- Performance and capacity.
- Capability and techniques.

JAD Sessions

Key personnel in these sessions typically include:

- Executive sponsor.
- Workshop owner.
- Facilitator.
- Scribe.
- Representative users (business areas, policy, legal).
- Project manager.
- Project sponsor (visionary).
- Technical coordinator.

Due to the nature of JAD, it is important to ensure that a suitable environment exists, away from the workplace and free from distractions. Consideration should be given to:

- Room layout.
- Equipment.
- Amenities.

It is important to get full attendance at a JAD session, as invitations will only be sent to key personnel, who will be required to sign up for products produced within the workshop. If key personnel are not present at a JAD session, it may be that the workshop should not proceed, as the amount of product that can be produced and agreed will be limited.

There also should be a clear understanding of the reason for the JAD. This may be achieved by a mixture of pre-JAD reading and an introduction to the JAD by the facilitator, explaining the purpose of the JAD and specification of the JAD rules for that session (e.g., active participation; silence is seen as agreement).

FUTURE OF RAD

With the increasing use of Internet technologies and Java, there are more opportunities for a RAD approach to be adopted, even when dealing with legacy systems that may have the capacity for a browser interface to be bolted on. This creates danger as well as opportunity, mainly due to the immediacy of roll-out and availability. Mistakes may become immediately apparent and high-profile (truly World Wide).

However, this immediacy lends itself well to the use of prototyping and the creation of immediate front-end systems designed in workshop sessions with full user involvement. Of course, prototyping may lead to the appearance of a final product when there is little or no underlying code or possibly even no actual functionality. Only by combining new techniques and tools with traditional controls such as input validation checks, logic checks, integrity checks, and testing for performance and reliability can one ensure that high quality systems are produced that enable organizations to move forward securely.

Chapter 7

Leveraging Developed Software: Organizational Implications

Hal H. Green and Ray Walker

Leveraging is the reusability or portability of application software across multiple business sites. The extent to which an application can remain unchanged as it is installed and made operational at each location is referred to as leveragability.

Leveraging can reduce the cost of acquiring and maintaining application software. However, the ultimate measure of leveraging is the resulting business benefit — the cost of delivering a working capability from site to site across an enterprise.

Whether a manufacturer chooses an off-the-shelf or custom software solution, achieving leveraging requires the cooperation of multiple sites, beginning with the initial phases of the process. In downsized companies and companies with greater decentralization of decision making, this type of businesswide effort can become difficult. This is especially true when the application is not necessarily a supply-chain level application but one affecting more directly the manufacturing process.

ASSESSING PREPAREDNESS FOR LEVERAGING

Where a leveraging opportunity exists, limiting the scope of the target sites to a common business, product type/configuration, or other shared interest may mitigate some of the management challenges to leveraging. This strategy contains the leveraging activity to sites that are likely to benefit most. These sites are likely to be willing to compromise on functional requirements to realize the reduced costs of acquiring and supporting the leveraged application.

Analysis Team Responsibilities

Leveragability of software is affected by the initial choice of platforms. Ideally, the application should result from a rigorous data and function

0-8493-9822-3/00/$0.00+$.50

modeling phase that clearly depicts the natural systems of the sites. All too often hardware, operating systems, and data base platforms are the decisions that precede, shape, and limit the follow-on choices. As is the case for all good design practice, business requirements should drive technical architecture, not the other way around.

If a solid data and function model exists for each site, the choice of acquiring or developing software becomes clearer. When an off-the-shelf application exists serving most of the business needs, then the choice becomes a selection between vendors' offerings relative to the specification. When no commercial offering exists on the market that satisfies the site's information model, then new development or modification of some existing software are the obvious choices. In either case, the following questions are germane to understanding the number of sites that can apply the application to be acquired or developed:

- Will changes in product or the manufacturing differences affect the applications?
- How do manufacturing business practices change from site to site?
- What type of process control or I/O systems exist at each site?
- What hardware, system software, and networking protocols exist at each site?
- Do the user communities differ at each site with respect to their information needs?
- What user communities should be interviewed to assess requirements?
- What type of training or follow-on consulting must be provided to make the application effective at each site?
- Who will be responsible for first-line support at each site once the application is commissioned?

Answers to these and a host of other questions should be captured as part of the deliverables that result from the analysis process. Once the architecture vis-á-vis the applications are known, the quality and location of sites to be included in the analysis can be selected.

Exhibit 7.1 presents an overview of the process of requirements analysis or documenting the common specification across the target business. In Exhibit 7.1, leveraged resources represent the analysis team responsible for designing and delivering the application across multiple sites. Site resources consist of two groups:

- *The user community.* Users provide the business objectives and needs.
- *The IS community.* IS maps the effect of systems on manufacturing operations.

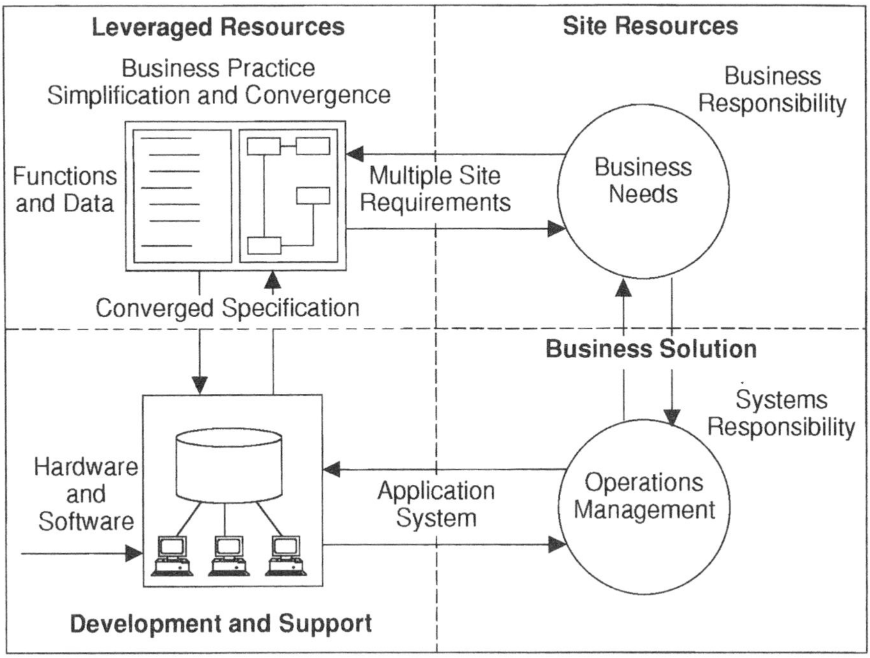

Exhibit 7.1. Roles and Responsibilities Model for Leveraged Software Development Support

The analysis team captures information needs across multiple sites. In a manufacturing context, information needs may be similar to these examples:

- Amount of product waste on yield on each line by shift.
- Statistics of key process/quality parameters.
- Recipe or formulary for each product.
- Trend of selected process values over time.

A successful modeling effort results in a shared specification that enjoys system independence in that it describes what the business does, not simply "how" it does it. The use of a shared data and functional model is an effective means of creating a living specification that reflects the information needs of the business.

Data and functional models resulting from analysis can also be used to complete development. Whether the design team elects to purchase an off-the-shelf application components or to develop custom software, the model-based specification is useful. Whether full life cycle Computer-Aided Software Engineering tools or 4GL tools are employed, the data and functional specification are foundational to the applications. Fourth-generation client/server tools that allow decoupling of client processes from the data base server can be effectively used to capture user screen requirements during prototyping.

ORGANIZING FOR LEVERAGING

Leveraging is a business objective, originating from a purposeful decision to provide common solutions across numerous manufacturing sites. Leveraging begins, therefore, with the affected organizations sharing this business objective.

Businesses that enjoy a culture where ideas germinate at the lower levels of the organization can offer some of the greatest challenges to leveraging. These businesses often build strong IS capabilities at the plant and manufacturing sites to support and build new manufacturing software applications. For such organizations, their strength is also their weakness when it comes to leveraging applications software. Overcoming the cultural and organizational barriers at a site to a businesswide or corporatewide convergence effort or solution can become a serious hurdle to the planner and analyst. One means of mitigating this problem is the use of a leveraged application work group that represents the various sites.

Leveraged Application Work Groups

The leveraged application work group is responsible for capturing the business benefits that accrue across multiple manufacturing sites during the definition, development, and deployment of an application. The work group is composed of representatives from each business or site that derives benefit from the application, as well as a project engineer or analyst and a sponsor from the corporate staff function that is held accountable for the program's success.

The work group is formed soon after an individual business unit or site requests development of a new manufacturing application. Additional sites and business units are solicited for membership in the work group by distributing a brief description of the application and anticipated benefits from deployment across multiple sites. A project engineer or analyst is assigned to draft a detailed specification that is then reviewed and upgraded by the work group. Upon reconciliation of all the requested modifications to the specification, the document is reviewed with the application supplier. The supplier provides a proposal for developing the application (functional design concepts, cost, and schedule).

Funding from each site and business unit for the development of the application is a key component in the success of leveraging software. Funding from multiple sources reduces the cost for each individual site.

Upon delivery of the application analysis and detailed design documents from the supplier, the application work group reviews the design and decides what modifications or scope changes are required. The work group is responsible for making certain that the final design will bring the maximum benefit across the different sites.

The application work group decides which site is appropriate for piloting the application. Selection of the first site is important because this site's learnings will be the basis for deployment at additional sites. After installation at several sites, the work group compiles all the installation learnings and benefits information. A best practices/implementation guide is compiled for rollout at multiple sites.

A communications bulletin is distributed to all the business units and sites for potential reuse of the application. This communication alerts sites considering development of a similar or redundant application.

DELIVERING LEVERAGED APPLICATIONS

If as a result of the analysis and design it is determined that an off-the-shelf package exists to provide the desired solution, the construction phase assumes the characteristics of a rollout. Key considerations revolve not around code development but around applying the packaged software in the target sites. Key concerns are:

- Integration with existing systems (if necessary).
- Data base population plans.
- Interfaces with I/O devices.
- Any necessary modifications of the off-the-shelf software.
- User training.
- Ongoing support.

The use of pilot or prototype systems is encouraged as a means of continuing to align user expectations for leveraging the application. Working pilots in plants are an excellent means of identifying potential benefits of the application if a solid base case is first established for comparison. Pilots serve as a platform for technical and performance evaluations while at the same time providing a test bed for the user community before full implementation or rollout.

Planning the Applications Platform

The analyst and designers must plan for leveraging from the initial phases of the project. Common data base platforms, common user interfaces, and even common I/O drivers are not sufficient to realize the full benefits from leveraging. Exhibit 7.2 presents an overview of an applications platform and illustrates delivery of leveraged applications.

Beginning with the data base, standards should be set around data base configuration. If the data base engine is relational, then the data model

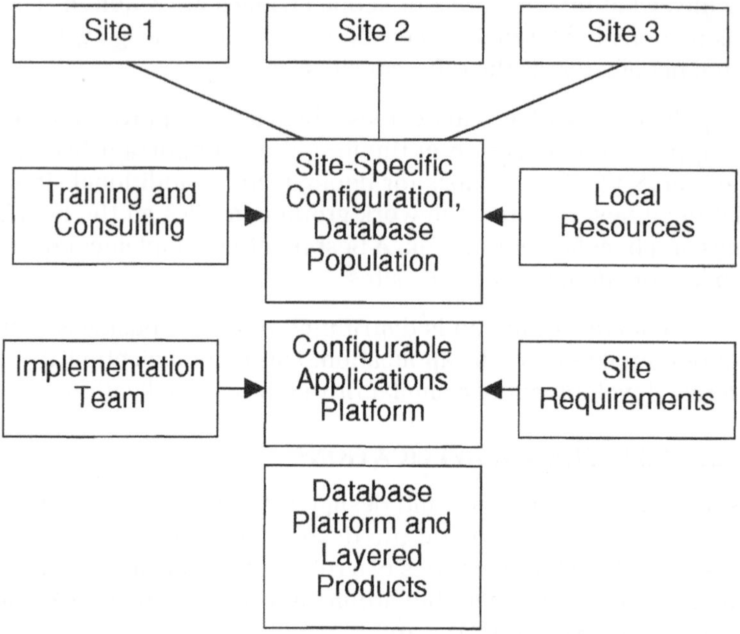

Exhibit 7.2. Rollout Concept

becomes the common basis of configuration. If the data base is part of a real-time process control system, then standards could include tag naming conventions, data types, screens, process icons, trends, and SPC charts.

Layered over the data base engine are the applications that will operate on data in the data base. The applications should be sufficiently complete such that only data base population need occur once the systems are delivered to the site. This means meta data is known and fixed. Likewise, user screens are complete and ready to work out of the box. Process control systems that use configurable GUI are a convenience and a luxury if uniquely configured for each site.

Common GUIs screens with generic capabilities from site to site offer greater economy to create and less cost to support. Where graphical screens are being leveraged across multiple sites, there is usually sufficient economy created by the leveraging approach to produce higher quality graphics. The quality of the delivered applications should go up with leveraging.

Ideally, applications can be made operational quickly once hardware and system-level software is operational. A factory acceptance test should be performed where the complete system is staged, integrated, and checked out before rollout.

CONCLUSION

There are organizational implications in any effort to effectively leverage software. Leveraged software development and support requires the cooperation of multiple sites beginning with the initial phases of the process.

It is also appropriate to point out that the business model for leveraging software, reviewed in this chapter, implies fewer contributors to the effort. The need to have a different system integrator provide development or application programming per site is diminished, if not eliminated. The leveraged application work group is likely to find that the applications can be made operational with a small dedicated team systematically moving from site to site.

Chapter 8
Developing Workstation-Based Client/Server Applications

Steve Rabin

Advances in workstation technology have historically outpaced corresponding software improvements. Sophisticated computer processing chips have, in general, been available years before the operating system software was able to exploit them (e.g., 32-bit processing technology was available on workstations well before any 32-bit software came out of the development laboratories). Application and corresponding systems support software has also lagged.

The introduction of stable operating systems and environments has changed this situation, providing database and network vendors with the opportunity to integrate their products with distributed platforms. In addition, a variety of software development tools are available that allow developers to create new applications that effectively use distributed environments. These environments are usually open or network-oriented systems using a GUI and distributed RDBMS.

To successfully shift development to these workstation-based environments, it is critical that an organization:

- Understand what tasks must be performed.
- Have the right mix of people (and skills) to perform the given tasks.
- Agree on and stick to a common method of performing these tasks.
- Use effective, productive tools.
- Develop a distributed model.
- Implement a transformation strategy.
- Anticipate people, training, management, hardware, and software issues.

0-8493-9822-3/00/$0.00+$.50

OBJECTIVE: EFFICIENT USE OF RESOURCES

Distributed applications need to be as portable as possible to maximize the long- and short-term investment being made to the application. This investment includes its technological underpinnings, the planned production environment, and future production environments.

Within the constraints of current business realities, for an organization to achieve competitive advantage with information technology it must efficiently use available resources. Two key IS resources are current production applications and the employees who developed and are maintaining them.

Distributed applications (where applicable) can be created by combining code that currently exists (possibly from a host system or even simpler workstation application) with new code. This combination makes the best use of existing(and still valuable) application code while allowing new code and its underlying technology to be efficiently integrated. The resulting new application code should therefore meet the organization's design criteria in a most productive and cost-efficient way.

The blending together of old and new code involves the redevelopment of current application code. A determination must be made as to which portions of the code are still relevant and what, if anything, must be done to this code. This analysis process also lends itself to the creation of true platform-independent code — that is, a single set of source code that can be operated on a variety of platforms and environments with some recompilation.

This is a critical concept because no one can foresee all future production/development environments. As new users are introduced to the software, it is quite likely that the software will be required to operate on platforms that were not originally envisioned. All issues involving operating systems, diverse communications, databases, graphical (and nongraphical) interfaces, and client/server technologies need be examined in terms of portability.

INITIAL WORKSTATION DEVELOPMENT CONSIDERATIONS

Applications used to operate the business and provide competitiveness are a valuable resource. In addition, IS professionals have acquired a wealth of information about those systems and underlying business principles. Any distributed workstation development project must consider techniques and methodologies that use current application assets in a cost-effective way. This approach allows IS management to combat several existing development dilemmas, including backlog of work, containing or reducing IS costs, incorporating new technologies to increase competitiveness, and using the large amount of existing application code and the expert knowledge that was developed along with it.

Although this concept is not a new one, the idea of redeveloping older, outdated systems into new strategic systems is often overlooked. Because the concepts incorporate many of the best ideas of the past and present, this strategy can be successfully implemented in a wide variety of IS shops. It is not geared to any one particular methodology or environment and can be implemented in small, manageable, goal-oriented steps.

Initially, an application is selected that requires modernization, either technically or functionally. For the purposes of this discussion, this means an application that is being developed to operate in an environment that includes:

- Distributed cross-platform operating systems, most likely DOS, Windows, OS/2, or UNIX.
- Client/server modeling to disperse application functions across the network.
- GUI front ends, most likely Windows, Presentation Manager, or Motif.
- Data modeling to distribute the data using a RDBMS.
- Communication facilities to handle multiple platform protocols (e.g., TCP/IP, APPC, or IPX).

Although the goal may be to turn an existing application into a next generation, state-of-the-art solution, this is not likely to happen all at once. It is better, especially for organizations new to distributed solutions, to phase the development of the system. This allows new tools and technologies to be assimilated into the organization while still providing ever-increasing benefits to the system's users.

For example, the base functions of an existing CICS application may be redeveloped for a graphically based client/server environment. The first phase of this project might be to port the front end of the CICS system to a graphical workstation environment. This benefits the user and starts the development of graphical code and expertise that can be used throughout the remainder of the project. Later phases would include converting to a distributed relational database, client/server functional modeling, and eventually incorporating support for all of the required communication interfaces (including host interfaces, proprietary systems, and currently popular platform protocols).

SCOPE AND GOALS OF DISTRIBUTED APPLICATIONS DEVELOPMENT

Once the application is selected and the business design issues are resolved, a variety of decisions must be made. The first of these concerns the target environment. It is always desirable to develop and execute the application in the most productive architecture possible. This may be a host, but distributed client/server or a combination of environments is the most likely architecture. Related user interface and communication issues must be examined. One decision will be whether a text-based or a GUI makes the most sense. Similarly, will the system be CICS-based or will another communications protocol provide a better solution?

The distributed model also needs to be considered. This model is concerned with both the physical aspects of the application (and the enterprise it operates within) along with the conceptual aspects of how the business processes (and associated data) are to be split. Issues to be examined include whether key business processes will be performed on the client, server, or both, and where the data resides and how its integrity is to be ensured.

Although there are several standard distributed models in use, it is easier to build and manage an application that only distributes data (and to a much lesser extent business processes) when it is an absolute necessity. Building a distributed application must be done in stages, and the last stage is data distribution. This facility requires close coordination between the program, database, network, and associated middleware facilities.

In addition, plans need to be made for the testing and maintenance of these distributed and potentially platform-independent applications. Cataloged test scripts help, as does development that follows a single source code strategy. An automated method of delivering and possible implementing the software may also be required. A method of delivering upgrades and fixes for distributed applications needs to be devised.

Testing is an area that requires careful attention when processes and possibly data are being distributed and the platforms/environments are not homogeneous. Distributed processes include business logic and the GUI presentation. The logic needs to be tested on both the client and server, although the presentation may reside on multiple desktops. Distributed client/server testing tools are becoming available to help execute testing procedures, but they are not a replacement for a sound testing methodology. A simple example illustrates this point. An error is found in the Windows program of a user data entry screen. This screen is also displayed to Presentation Manager and Motif users. Does the error also exist in these environments? Is the correction made to the Windows program the correct one for the other environments? Assuming that it is, is the correction made carefully so as not to introduce new errors? These are all critical issues in distributed testing that a tool can help with but not solve.

REDEVELOPMENT STRATEGY

Open environments offer a variety of benefits, but they require careful planning, a sound methodology, and a suite of integrated design, development, and maintenance tools. A single set of source code that can operate on multiple environments is the answer to many of these issues. It solves the problem of multiple sets of source code for specific environments and code integrity.

All of the distributed applications development work described in this article can be accomplished using COBOL. This is true of all of the operating environments and all aspects of the code, including communications and GUI interfaces. This approach is recommended because many existing systems that are critical to the success of their businesses are mainframe and COBOL based. In addition, most of the systems people are trained in COBOL and its host environments (e.g., CICS, IMS, DB/2). IS organizations need to understand that their COBOL investment can fit in with strategic efforts for future systems.

This approach does not exclude other or mixed technology solutions; in fact, in certain instances they make sense. It does, however, emphasize that the mass of older application code can be profitably used across a variety of platforms and environments.

Because the changes implied throughout this article have an impact on many business disciplines, organizations are having to recruit the support required to complete what is usually a multiyear effort. IS can offer short-term deliverables within the longer-term strategic goals using certain fundamental principles and tools.

FUNDAMENTAL DEVELOPMENT GUIDELINES

Many questions come to mind when examining distributed development, usually pertaining to learning a new language, understanding multiple GUI APIs, data acquisition, and communicating between platforms. There is no reason to switch languages. Tools are available to handle the multiple GUI environments, and distributed DBMSs are accessible with Structured Query Language. Even platform-to-platform communications issues are simplified by several high-level tools.

When developing applications in and for a new platform, several basic development guidelines still apply. These include:

- Developing a conceptual development strategy.
- Determining technical and functional development guidelines.
- Determining technical and functional application guidelines.
- Converting the conceptual development strategy into a logical transformation strategy.

This analysis is usually performed by a combination of automated analysis and old-fashioned desk work. People from the business and data processing sides of the application work together as a team. The organization, not IS, is creating a strategic system capable of taking the business through the end of the century.

Experience has repeatedly shown that certain fundamental practices must be in place before beginning a distributed development project (or any development project for that matter). First, a software development life cycle and methodology must exist. Second, policies and procedures for accepting and controlling deliverables must be implemented. This situation is equally true for a developer completing a program change or the project team completing the entire distributed system. Programs in the system will be expected to operate in different environments and must be tested accordingly. Finally, these points must be well defined and understood by all concerned. The organization must believe in and see the benefit of these methodologies and procedures if it is going to use them.

EXTENDING THE EXISTING DEVELOPMENT STRATEGY

Although training is going to be a requirement, because developers need to understand the new platform and environment in order to be productive and design an application that makes significant use of its facilities, the bottom line is that a project can and should be implemented using a methodology and techniques that are similar to those currently in place.

In areas where the methodology needs to be revised — GUI design, for example — it is an extension to the existing development strategy. Similarly, a new tool is an extension to the tool set and not a new development workbench. The point is not to minimize potential changes being made to the code but to explain that these changes are evolutionary and must be integrated into the existing environment and organization design strategies. As shown in Exhibit 8.1, the time and tasks required to complete client/server projects are closely related to traditional applications development.

TRANSFORMATION METHODOLOGIES

The heart of the distributed development process is the transformation methodology, which combines the business and technology visions into a coherent whole. This method is actually the coalescence of top-down (business vision)and bottom-up (technical vision) approaches. The result is the overall organization transformation policy: a strategic statement or contract defining what the system will be and what it will take to get there.

The top-down strategic input is required to understand the business vision. This input determines what the requirements of the new application are, or if it is an existing application, what needs to be revised. The prospective users of the new system and the environments in which the system is to be employed are also part of the business vision.

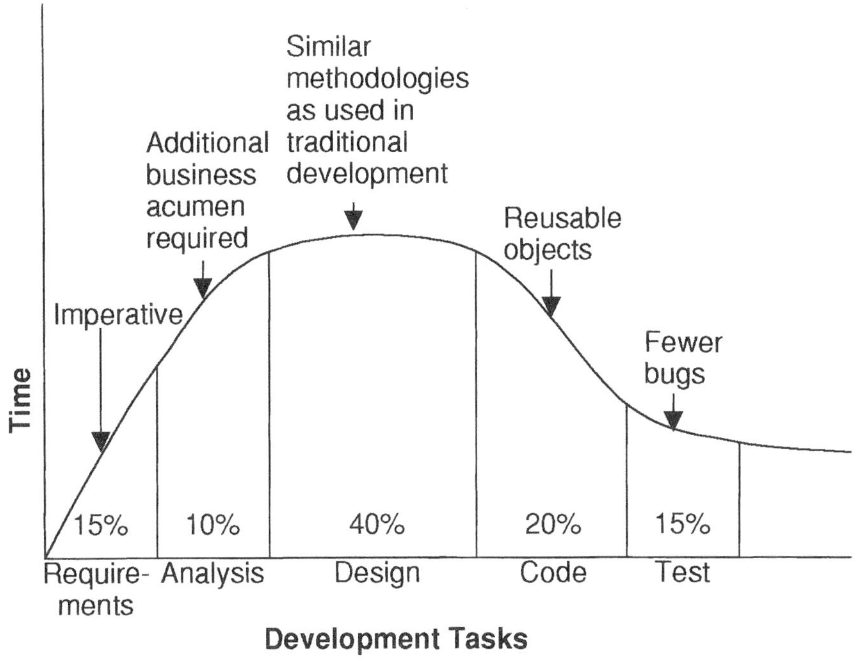

Exhibit 8.1. Client/Server Development

The bottom-up tactical input is required in order to understand the platform, environment, and technical issues of the new system, and to analyze the composition of the existing system, including data, program, process relationships, and associated software/hardware requirements. From this input, short-term deliverables can be identified under the long-term transformation strategy.

The last part of this phase is to determine feasibility and conformance to the vision. This takes participation from the business and IS sides, preferably in face-to-face meetings. It must be technically feasible and reasonable to develop and implement the business vision. If, for example, the business vision requires a palm-size, pen-based color computer with distributed networking capabilities, an evolutionary implementation may be required until the technology is both workable and available.

By no means should the business vision be cut short or revised by the IS organization, but it is the responsibility of IS to explain to corporate executives what it takes to meet the business vision. A technical compromise may be necessary in order that the business functions can be properly implemented within a reasonable time frame and the design of the system meets the target audience's needs in a meaningful way.

CODE DEVELOPMENT

Functional Analysis

Once the plan is formalized and in place, the business of developing the system can begin in earnest. An analysis of the existing base of application code should be done to identify overlapping functions — that is, functions the target system and currently existing systems have in common.

There are many application-specific functions that can be used in the new system without change (e.g., date routines, calculations, and report formats). It is important to use this existing base of code because it is both proven and understood by the professionals developing the new application. Leveraging existing assets, both code and people, is one of the keys to successfully developing in new environments.

Because these functions may be used repeatedly during the development process, reusable code libraries or repositories should be developed. In addition to determining functional code that already exists, all other functions should be identified and cataloged. It may be that some of the target functions are excellent candidates for code generation (if that is available).

Once the functional analysis is complete, a wealth of information should also be available about existing code and new system processes (i.e., how the system is to accomplish its functions). This information is critical when existing processes and underlying code are to be used as much as possible(in one form or another).

Data Requirements

Functions, processes, and the application code comprise only half of the equation. Data relationships and requirements must also be defined. Distributed data models for the target system need to be analyzed and cataloged. A data repository is an excellent means of tracking the data requirements of the system and ensuring the data is not duplicated. Equally important, data residence needs to be established if the data is to be truly distributed. The host, servers, and local workstations may each contain information critical to the application as a whole.

The analysis of data representations in the system often indicates where improvements can be made. Common problems include redundant data and inconsistent data use. It is not unusual to discover that some of the required data remains undocumented, a situation that must be corrected.

Modernizing data representations involves careful review of the design and (where applicable) the code. This involves identifying key data structures and where and how they are manipulated, as well as standardizing data names and definitions and propagating them throughout the system.

Finally, data access methods should be reviewed to determine the means by which data will be acquired in the target environments.

ASSEMBLING PLATFORM-INDEPENDENT CODE

Once the processes are isolated so that the platform-independent nature of the code can be formed, the application code can begin to be reassembled. To take advantage of specific environments, it may be necessary to symbolize the code.

Symbolization is simply a process of adding code that is assembled at compile time, most likely using a precompiler. Although this is not a requirement of distributed applications or platform independence, it provides certain advantages. A simple example is taking advantage of a monitor that displays 44 lines of data rather than the more traditional 25 lines.

THE PROBLEM OF DIVERSE INTERFACES

One of the major issues of coding for diverse environments is the many APIs that are encountered. This is especially true for data acquisition, GUI presentation, and communication protocols. Standardizing around SQL and databases that support distributed data access provides a solution to the data issue. GUI presentation is not as easily solved without the use of a tool. Several sophisticated tools are available that provide a common interface to many of the prevalent GUI.

A more detailed look at the communication issue helps explain how a single set of source code handles diverse interfaces. The use of tools that support a CCI or AAI allows the same code to execute across platforms, regardless of the protocol. APPC, Named Pipes, NetBIOS, and IPX are several of the communication protocols that can be used to provide distributed services. An application can have access to both individual environments and distributed open environments in this manner. This allows the same source code to elegantly handle the complexities of distributed communications. Exhibit 8.2 illustrates this concept.

In a distributed applications environment, each of the isolated functions must be tested as a coordinated whole under all target environments. The same code may be required to operate under DOS, OS/2, Windows, or UNIX. Similarly, the integrity of the code must never be compromised. Regardless of the platform, the code operating on a single, secure version must be maintained.

DISTRIBUTED DEVELOPMENT TOOLS

There are many COBOL-oriented development and maintenance tools that allow developers of distributed, workstation applications to take advantage of the techniques described in this article, including tools that

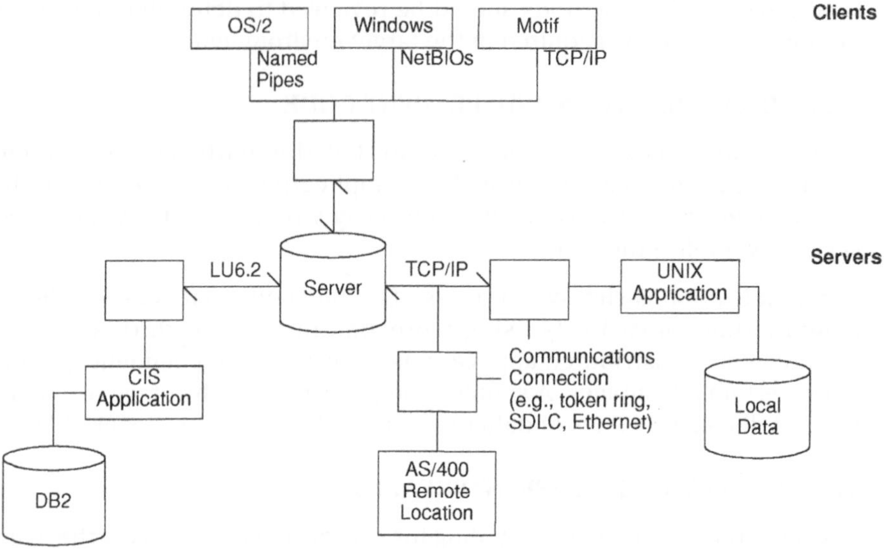

Exhibit 8.2. Communication Facilities for Distributed Services

provide cross-platform support and are compatible with code initially developed for other environments. Workstation-based tools are available that support development for DOS, Windows, OS/2 Presentation Manager, UNIX, and UNIX Motif. These tools use a variety of platform-specific runtime environments so that the code need not be developed to that level of detail.

When the application code is developed at a higher level, it is possible for the same source to execute in diverse environments. For example, the Micro Focus Operating Systems Extensions (OSX) environment provides COBOL programs (and thus COBOL developers) with the same services and the same interfaces for all target operating environments. Applications developed on one system can be ported to another with minimal, if any, code modification. Other tools enable developers to prototype and create graphical and character-oriented user interfaces that can be ported across all target operating environments.

A set of communication and Structured Query Language database services tools support high-performance application interfaces to a variety of networks and databases. SQL services provide support for Gupta, Microsoft SQL Server, NetWare SQL, Oracle, OS/2 Database Manager, Informix, Sybase, XDB, and others. AAI and CCI provide network and client/server support. AAI (AAI) allows program-to-program communication between platforms — that is, one program can call another program as if it were a localized routine. CCI supports network (and internetwork) application communications.

Distributed testing tools must operate on multiple platforms and have the ability to visually analyze the program logic and determine how much of the code is actually being executed during the test. A tool that provides the developer with a common interface across platforms is critical because developers may encounter a situation requiring them to test a function in an unfamiliar environment.

Because less specific skills are needed for distributed applications development, selecting the definitive computing environment is a much smaller issue because applications can be moved to other platforms. Most important, scarce development resources can be used where they will have the greatest impact, developing business application code.

CONCLUSION

Distributed applications provide many benefits to the organization. They allow both business and systems professionals to solve problems while positioning their companies for the future. In many cases, code from existing systems can be salvaged and turned into high-quality, next-generation applications. Development staff members are already familiar with the code and, to a certain extent, the basic methodology and tools. It is not necessary to reinvent the wheel.

The key design criteria to be taken into account before moving applications development to a distributed client/server environment include:

- Process models.
- Data models.
- Object distribution.
- Repositories.
- Stored procedures.
- Language.
- Program modules.
- Communications.
- Desktop presentation (GUI).
- Distributed platform testing.
- Application distribution.

These criteria should be assimilated into the development process using the transformation strategies described in this article. In some respects, distributed applications development is different from other systems development efforts for mainframes, midranges, and standalone workstations, but there are similarities in the way the project should be approached. Data modeling, process design, function analysis, and prototype acceptance are examples of tasks that are performed in all structured applications development projects. It is not necessary or even advisable to get wrapped up in the technology. The ultimate tool, methodology, or environment is always going to be out there waiting to be discovered. A better approach is to take small, measurable steps with definable goals and allow the project to generate momentum with initial successes toward the organization's ultimate goals.

Chapter 9
The Influence of Software Design on Human-Computer Interaction

Joanna S.P. Shum and Eva Y.W. Wong

The widespread use of computers in organizations places increasing demands on the effectiveness and efficiency of computer systems in performing users' tasks. Research has shown that there is a direct relation between human-computer interaction (HCI) and user productivity; therefore, computer-based systems should be comprehensible, consistent, and easy to use.

However, some systems designers, analysts, and managers are still unaware of the importance of user interfaces. Many current systems are poorly designed, and users become innocent victims of a "user-hostile" system. Ideally, there should be a body of knowledge that can be consulted by systems designers who are seeking to apply sound HCI principles to the design of their products. This chapter discusses the primary issues related to HCI.

DEFINING USER INTERFACE

Very often, the first point of contact a person makes with a computer system is at the user interface. The user interface is the point where the person and the computer system exchange inputs and outputs; that is, the human and the computer communicate with each other through the interface. A well-designed user interface is of primary importance in the effective use of the system, because to many users, the interface is the system. Generally accepted wisdom is that a quality user interface must be flexible, learnable, consistent, transparent to the user, and perceived as being under the user's control, all characteristics that are often used to evaluate the usability of an interface.

In spite of this, however, quality user interfaces are not a common part of the user's experience in computing. Instead, frustration and anxiety are a part of daily life for many users of computerized information systems. Some even develop cases of computer shock and terminal terror. This is

0-8493-9822 3/00/$0 00+$.50

because the programmers can tend to be insensitive to the relationship between the computer and the human being. Users put a lot of effort into learning command languages or menu selection systems that they expect to help them, but the failure of systems analysts and designers to make systems easily and comfortably usable by laymen is the most significant inhibiting factor in the future progress of IT. Obstacles in ineffective interfaces include inconsistent command languages, confusing operation sequences, chaotic display formats, inconsistent terminology, incomplete instructions, complex error recovery procedures, and misleading or threatening error messages.

The study of HCI concerns the efficiency and quality of computer-based systems as perceived by the people who use them, whether for necessity or enjoyment. Increasingly, systems managers are realizing that major improvements in productivity can be brought on by the thoughtful application of HCI principles, including a substantial difference in lowering learning time and error rates and increasing performance speed and user satisfaction. Whereas commercial designers already recognize that systems that are easier to use have a competitive edge in information retrieval, office automation, and personal computing, corporate systems designers and software engineers, programmers, and managers have as yet to step forward and fight for the user.

Analysis and Modeling

HCI is a system that consists of users, software, and hardware. The purpose of the system's design is to enable work and other activities to be performed more effectively, efficiently and, when performed by people, with more enjoyment and satisfaction. Because work consists of tasks, task modeling and task analysis form a central part of HCI design, and a disciplined, iterative approach and a thorough study of human performance in the use of interactive systems are important steps toward successful HCI. An increasing number of systems developers, systems analysts, and managers are collecting performance data from users, carrying out subjective satisfaction surveys, and inviting users to participate in systems design.

Moreover, messages and feedback, conveyed to users in the form of system messages, are critical. In the past, many system messages were unfriendly and uninformative; positive messages, however, convey the genuine concern a designer has for the users, and these are the type of messages that should be sent. If users feel competent in using the system, believe they can easily correct errors, and have confidence that they can accomplish their tasks, they will pass on the message of quality to the people with whom they come into contact. In this way, the cycle of seeking information, incorporating it, and providing positive feedback is beneficial to systems developers, end users, and corporate clients and customers.

INTERFACE DESIGN GOALS

Human-computer interaction encompasses a wide variety of issues concerning the point of contact between the user and the computer. Some of these issues are device or hardware specific, for example, the choice of screen resolution, keyboard and mouse interaction, response time, and display rate. Others, such as the use of various dialogue types, system messages and semantic/syntactic models are software-specific HCI issues.

The topics and choices to be made in the design of the HCI are many and varied. In general, the trend has been to move away from computer-oriented designs, in which the user puts forth a great deal of effort to accommodate the needs of the machines, toward a user-oriented design, where the burden is placed on the machine rather than the user. Sophisticated tools have been developed for the systems analyst/programmer to aid them in the development of user-oriented interfaces and interactions.

Every designer wants to build a high-quality interactive system that is respected by colleagues, popularly used by users, and circulated widely. Appreciation comes, however, not from flamboyant promises or stylish advertising brochures, but from inherent quality features that are achieved by thoughtful planning, sensitivity to user needs, careful attention to detail in design and development, and diligent testing. One of the keys to HCI design success is the understanding of human diversity and user characteristics: Users learn, users differ, and users reflect on their knowledge. Designers, therefore, must know their users, the task that the users are trying to accomplish, and the users' attitudes toward computers. The software designer must take into account the specific user type for a particular software application to develop a user interface that meets the users' needs.

Designers must keep in mind that the computer is merely a tool to aid users to accomplish their tasks, and the interface between the user and any tool should be natural and intuitive and should not take attention away from the task at hand. As systems with inadequate functionality frustrate the user and are often rejected or underutilized, and excessive functionality probably causes more mistakes, it is important to strike a proper balance.

Another design goal is to ensure system reliability, availability, security, and integrity. The software architecture and hardware support must ensure high availability, ease of maintenance, and correct performance. Attention must also be paid to privacy, security, and information integrity matters. Protection must be provided against unwarranted access, inadvertent destruction of data, or malicious tampering.

USER CHARACTERISTICS' EFFECT ON DESIGN

Computer systems are designed to aid people in performing their tasks. An effective interaction design is one in which a user carries out his work with minimal conscious attention to his tools and maximal effectiveness. It is free of distractions and is reasonably "friendly." Ideally, the design of an interface should model the cooperative person-to-person conversation. Thus, certain psychological blocks, particularly boredom, panic, frustration, confusion, and discomfort, should be minimized.

To maximize the benefits brought by an application system, the interactive system designers should understand the remarkable diversity of human abilities, backgrounds, motivations, personalities, and work styles. Proper attention to human factors often leads to reductions in the cost and time for development. A carefully tested design generates fewer changes during implementation and after release of new systems.

In addition to the attention to human factors, design theories and principles provide a way to organize the design process and weight alternatives. In fact, the user interface of many contemporary systems can be improved. The cluttered and multiple displays, complex and tedious procedures, inconsistent sequences of actions, and insufficient informative feedback can generate unnecessary stress and anxiety that reduce the efficiency and increase error rates and job dissatisfaction.

Measurable Human Factors

As mentioned earlier, designers should be aware of the user community and the set of user tasks. For each user and each task, precise measurable objectives guide the designer, evaluator, purchaser, or manager. The following five measurable human factors are central to evaluation: time to learn, speed of performance, rate of user errors, subjective satisfaction, and retention over time.

Every designer would like to succeed in every aspect, but there are often forced trade-offs. If the rate of errors is to be kept at a minimum, the speed of performance may have to be sacrificed. In some applications, subjective satisfaction is the key success factor, while in others short learning times or rapid performance may be paramount. Project managers and designers must be aware of the trade-offs and make their choices according to requirements documents that detail which goals are primary.

Several design alternatives should be raised and reviewed by designers and users. On-line prototype versions of the system create a more realistic environment for review. After detailed examination of the design goals, the selected choice should be written down. The user manual and technical reference manual can be written before the implementation to provide another review and perspective on the design. Then the implementation can be carried out. Finally, acceptance testing should be carried out to certify that the implemented system meets the goals of the designers and users.

The Impact of Motivation

The study of motivation has been a major field of activity within psychology. Herzberg's motivation-hygiene theory and Vroom's expectancy theory have often been used to explain the effect of motivation on system acceptance or rejection. In practice, the computer user is typically gaining mastery over the computer in an occupational and organizational context. Thus, the extent to which each of these motivation theories can be applied to the HCI domain needs to be carefully considered.

If Herzberg's theory is adopted, the implications for HCI are that users' interactions must promote feelings of achievement, recognition, responsibility, and advancement. In addition, the work itself must continue to interest the individual. According to Vroom's expectancy theory, the primary relevance is in terms of the "expectancy" attribute, that is, effort will result in performance. When individuals approach the computer, they must have some perceptions that they will gain mastery over the task. Otherwise, they will be demotivated and give up.

Interacting with a computer, like person-to-person interaction, involves three types of basic human processes: perception, cognition and motor activity. The systems designer is required to design human-computer interaction techniques which minimize the work required by these processes, both individually and in combination. Human factors relate most to the perceptual and motor processes, concerned as they are with the application of psychological and physiological knowledge to human performance. The field of cognitive psychology provides insight into memory and learning processes.

SYNTACTIC/SEMANTIC MODEL OF USER KNOWLEDGE

In outline, this explanatory model suggests that users have syntactic knowledge about device-dependent details and semantic knowledge about concepts. The syntactic and semantic knowledge are two kinds of knowledge in long-term memory.

Syntactic Knowledge

This deals with the details of command syntax. For example, in a text editor, syntactic details would include the knowledge of what command inserts a new line after the third line of a text file, which icon to click on to scroll text forward, which abbreviations are permissible, and which of the numbered function keys activates the previous screen. This knowledge is arbitrary and therefore acquired by memorization. A user who switches from one machine to another may face different keyboard layouts, commands, function key usage, and sequences of actions. Syntactic knowledge is system-dependent, with some possible overlap among systems. This kind of knowledge is volatile in memory and easily forgotten unless it is regularly used.

Semantic Knowledge

This deals with concepts or functions. Semantic knowledge is hierarchically structured from low-level functions to higher-level concepts. The lower-level functions are close to the syntax of the command language. In a text editor, lower-level functions may include cursor movement, insertion, and deletion, whereas in the higher-level concepts, the expert user decomposes the problem domain from the top down into several lower-level concepts closer to the program. This presentation accommodates the two most common forms of expertness: Task experts who may be novice computer users and computer user experts who may be new to a task. Task experts are people who clearly understand the user tasks and task flow, and computer user experts are people who are familiar with the computer systems.

Semantic knowledge is hierarchically organized, acquired by meaningful learning or analogy, independent of the syntactic details, usually transferable across different computer systems, and relatively stable in memory. Designers of interactive systems can apply the syntactic/semantic model to systematize their efforts. The model suggests that the semantics of the task objects should be made explicit, with the user's task actions laid out clearly. The computer objects and actions can be identified and the actual syntax is shown.

The underlying principles that are applicable in most interactive systems are as follows:

- Strive for consistency.
- Enable frequent/expert users to use shortcuts.
- Offer informative feedback.
- Design dialogues to yield closure.
- Offer simple error handling.
- Permit easy reversal of actions.
- Support internal locus of control.
- Reduce short-term memory load.

These principles should be refined, extended, and interpreted to fit different environments. The principles focus on increasing the users' productivity by providing comprehensible displays, simplified operations, and informative feedback that increase the sense of mastery, competence, and control over the system.

DESIGN ISSUES AND CONSIDERATIONS

By analyzing the relationship between user characteristics and design theories and principles, certain design issues should be taken into consideration by the designers to let people communicate effectively and efficiently with the computers.

These highlighted design issues can be treated as references by system designers. They should carefully consider the design philosophy to meet the user's requirements so as to reduce training and errors, increase efficiency of users, and increase user satisfaction. By taking care of the human factors in the design process, the designer can increase user acceptance and this can indirectly improve the productivity of the users.

Mental Processing Requirements

One of the most useful design philosophies for developing user-oriented HCI considers the computer system simply as a tool to aid the user in performing tasks. Thus, the designer should ensure that the computer system simplifies, rather than complicates, the user's tasks. A system that requires a lot of time, effort, and training to use is not likely to be a successful product. In HCI design, the "computer-as-a-tool" philosophy implies that designers must actively pursue techniques to reduce the mental processing operations required just to be able to use the tool. Mental processing operations include requirements for the user to learn complex commands and syntax, memorize encrypted codes and abbreviations, or translate data into other units or formats before they can be applied to the problem at hand. A well-designed computer system reduces task-specific mental processing, especially those types of processing that are performed more effectively by computers than by people, such as calculations and accurate storage and recall of large amounts of prespecified information.

Allocation of Functions

To design an effective HCI, an understanding of the capabilities and limitations of both the system and the users is critical to the allocation of functions to be performed by either the user or the system: The computer should perform tasks that computers do better, and the user should perform tasks that people do better. In general, people are better suited to control, monitor, act as decision maker, and respond to unexpected events. The computer is better suited to store and recall data, process information using prespecified procedures, and present options and supporting data to the user. Human memory is flexible but slow, unreliable, and imprecise. Computer memory is fast, reliable, and accurate but is limited to what has been programmed.

In routine interface design situations, several rules of thumb for allocation of functions seem useful.

- *Reducing the amount of memorization of commands, codes, syntax, and rules required of the user.* For example, the interface should permit users to select from a list of displayed options rather than entering memorized command strings.
- *Reducing the amount of mental manipulation of data required of the user.* The interface should present data, messages, and prompts in clear and directly usable form.
- *Reducing requirements for the user to enter data.* If information is available to the system, or if the design can make this information available to the system, the interface should not require the user to enter it manually. Dialogues should be structured so that user entries are minimized. Selecting from displayed lists instead of entering choices manually is also an effective technique to reduce input requirements.
- *Providing computer aids, such as online checklists, summary displays, and online problem diagnosis.* This reduces the amount of mental processing required of the user.
- *Using computer algorithm to preprocess complex, multisource data.* Information can be presented as a composite, integrated view of complex patterns or relationships among many variables.

Developing Mental Models

A mental model is a cognitive representation or conceptualization of a system's internal mechanics developed by a user. The user's mental model of the system's parts and their operations permits the user to predict the appropriate procedure for a desired outcome, even if he or she has forgotten the procedure or never encountered it before. The mental models developed by different users can vary considerably in sophistication, accuracy, and usefulness. As users become more experienced in using computers, they develop models that may prove effective to some degree when learning a new computer system.

Decisions made by the designer of an HCI can have a major impact on the ease or difficulty with which a typical user is able to develop an effective mental model of the system. Design issues that can help users in building effective mental models include: consistency, physical analogies, expectations, and stereotypes.

Ease of Learning, Ease of Use, and Functionality

A critical step in defining the design philosophy for the user interface is to establish the appropriate balance of ease of learning, ease of use, and functionality. Ease of learning is the extent to which a novice user can become proficient in using a system with minimal training and practice. Ease of use is the extent to which the system allows a knowledgeable user to perform tasks with minimal effort, for example, less time, fewer key strokes, or fewer transactions. Functionality is the number and kind of different functions the system can perform.

To provide system features that are easy to learn and easy to use and that support all functionality requires careful attention to HCI design. To optimize ease of learning, ease of use, and functionality, designers have to furnish different designs for novice, expert, and intermittent users. They should avoid excessive functionality yet provide multiple path capabilities, such as menu bypass, type-ahead, and user-defined macros. The design approach should encourage and support the gradual evolution of a user from a novice to an expert; therefore, such features as using default options, allowing reversible actions for error recovery, and making frequently used functions easy to evoke should be employed. Thus permitting system functions to be progressively disclosed and encouraging users to evolve gracefully.

The development of the user interface of a system is usually part of the system development cycle. In this sense, most system development methodologies can be used for interface development. As the user interface is very important in terms of helping users to form positive impressions of the system, prototyping is often used as its development methodology. With prototyping, users can participate directly in the design of the interface. They can also try out the prototypes and give feedback and suggestions to the system developers to further refine the interface. When the system is finally delivered, user acceptance will almost be guaranteed, and part of the training may even have already been done.

As user interface design becomes more sophisticated and complex, tools and techniques become available to aid the design and development process. Two of the more popular tools are user interface management systems (UIMS) and user interface tool kits.

UIMS

An integrated set of tools, UIMSs help programmers create and manage many aspects of interface. Just as a DBMS is used to provide data independence, a UIMS provides for user-interface independence from the rest of the system's applications. When the communication between the user interfaces and the other applications in a system is handled by the UIMS, the user interfaces can be modified independently, without affecting the logic and functioning of the other applications.

User Interface Tool Kits

On the other hand, a tool kit is a library of routines used for user interface implementation. Routines in a user interface tool kit can be used to implement low-level interface features, such as menus and buttons, into a interface. However, these routines have to be invoked within applications, making them intricately integrated into the applications. Furthermore, UIMSs are comparatively simpler to use and can be learned fairly quickly, whereas a user interface tool kit provides little or no support for a nonprogramming interface design.

CONCLUSION

As mentioned earlier, this chapter aims to investigate the importance of comprehensive, consistent, and user-friendly software design, such that improvement can be made to the HCI. To this end, the chapter has covered the following areas:

- The primary design goals.
- The human factor design considerations including the measurable human factors goals, the impact of motivation and the incorporation of human diversities.
- The HCI theories and principles, including the syntactic/semantic model of user knowledge.
- The design issues and considerations, including the mental processing requirements, the suggested ways in the allocation of functions and helping user to develop effective mental models, the importance in balancing the ease of learning, ease of use, and functionality issues.

In addition, the appendix at the end of this chapter provides a questionnaire that can be used by programmers to determine user requirements.

Advancements in the areas of input devices, voice processing, and virtual reality could lead to fundamental changes in the way humans and computers interact. The key element in the evolution of the interface is the integration of different input modalities. Rapid progress and development in input devices and speech technology mean that these devices may replace the keyboard as the input device of choice in the near future.

Windows is becoming and will continue to be the predominant PC operating environment. This change from the DOS command-driven way of working to the menu- and icon-driven method of Windows has been relatively easy. This confirms theories and principles on user-friendly software interfaces, and opens up new areas of interest into GUI.

With the cost of hardware going down and the capabilities and features of hardware increasing, the multimedia interface is becoming popular. Thus, research efforts have to be expended in this area in order for the benefits to quickly reach the end users.

Successful HCI seems to be a universal request; race and geographical differences do not alter this fundamental requirement of system design and development. Since HCI is becoming more and more critical, designers are increasingly placing effort into building effective HCI systems. This area, however, provides various rich new opportunities for further research.

APPENDIX

Questionnaire

This questionnaire is aimed at collecting your opinion about the user interface of the applications you use. This questionnaire is divided into three parts. Part I concerns your personal details. Part II is designed to determine your opinion about different interface modes. Finally, Part III asks about your practices and habits in using computer systems. Please answer all questions in this questionnaire and in as much detail as possible in case of open-ended questions.

PART I: PERSONAL DETAILS

1. What is your age?
   - ☐ Under 21
   - ☐ 21 - 25
   - ☐ 26 - 30
   - ☐ 31 - 35
   - ☐ Over 35
2. What is your sex?
   - ☐ Male
   - ☐ Female
3. What is your level of education?
   - ☐ Secondary
   - ☐ Postsecondary
   - ☐ Other, please specify ______________________
4. What is your current occupation?______________________
5. What is your area of occupation (e.g., banking, manufacturing, etc.)?

   ____

PART II: OPINIONS ABOUT THE INTERFACE MODE

6. Please rate the following interface modes according to your frequencies of use. Please circle the most appropriate answer.

a) Menu interaction	Unusual	1	2	3	4	5	Usual
b) Fill in the blanks (forms)	Unusual	1	2	3	4	5	Usual
c) Command languages	Unusual	1	2	3	4	5	Usual
d) Direct manipulation (e.g., window, icon)	Unusual	1	2	3	4	5	Usual
e) Natural language	Unusual	1	2	3	4	5	Usual
f) Questions and answers	Unusual	1	2	3	4	5	Usual

7. Please specify other interface modes, if any, that are not mentioned in question 6 above. ______________________
8. Please rate the interface mode according to following criteria. Circle the most appropriate answer. If the interface mode is not applicable, leave it blank.

a) Speed

(i) Menu interaction	Slow	1	2	3	4	5	Fast
(ii) Fill in the blanks (forms)	Slow	1	2	3	4	5	Fast
(iii) Command languages	Slow	1	2	3	4	5	Fast
(iv) Direct manipulation	Slow	1	2	3	4	5	Fast
(v) Natural language	Slow	1	2	3	4	5	Fast
(vi) Questions and answers	Slow	1	2	3	4	5	Fast

b) Accuracy

(i) Menu interaction	Error free	1	2	3	4	5	Many errors

(ii)	Fill in the blanks (forms)	Error free	1	2	3	4	5	Many errors
(iii)	Command languages	Error free	1	2	3	4	5	Many errors
(iv)	Direct manipulation	Error free	1	2	3	4	5	Many errors
(v)	Natural language	Error free	1	2	3	4	5	Many errors
(vi)	Questions and answers	Error free	1	2	3	4	5	Many errors

c) Training time

(i)	Menu interaction	Long	1	2	3	4	5	Short
(ii)	Fill in the blanks (forms)	Long	1	2	3	4	5	Short
(iii)	Command languages	Long	1	2	3	4	5	Short
(iv)	Direct manipulation	Long	1	2	3	4	5	Short
(v)	Natural language	Long	1	2	3	4	5	Short
(vi)	Questions and answers	Long	1	2	3	4	5	Short

d) Your preference

(i)	Menu interaction	Very low	1	2	3	4	5	Very high
(ii)	Fill in the blanks (forms)	Very low	1	2	3	4	5	Very high
(iii)	Command languages	Very low	1	2	3	4	5	Very high
(iv)	Direct manipulation	Very low	1	2	3	4	5	Very high
(v)	Natural language	Very low	1	2	3	4	5	Very high
(vi)	Questions and answers	Very low	1	2	3	4	5	Very high

e) Flexibility

(i)	Menu interaction	Very limited	1	2	3	4	5	Very high
(ii)	Fill in the blanks (forms)	Very limited	1	2	3	4	5	Very high
(iii)	Command languages	Very limited	1	2	3	4	5	Very high
(iv)	Direct manipulation	Very limited	1	2	3	4	5	Very high
(v)	Natural language	Very limited	1	2	3	4	5	Very high
(vi)	Questions and answers	Very limited	1	2	3	4	5	Very high

9. Please indicate the input devices you have used before.
   - ☐ Keyboard
   - ☐ Mouse/trackball
   - ☐ Joystick
   - ☐ Touch screen
   - ☐ Other, please specify________________________________

10. Please rate the input devices according to following criteria. Circle the most appropriate answer. If the input device is not applicable, leave it blank.

a) Speed

(i)	Keyboard	Slow	1	2	3	4	5	Fast
(ii)	Mouse/trackball	Slow	1	2	3	4	5	Fast
(iii)	Joystick	Slow	1	2	3	4	5	Fast
(iv)	Touch screen	Slow	1	2	3	4	5	Fast
(v)	Other, please specify __________	Slow	1	2	3	4	5	Fast

b) Ease of use

(i)	Keyboard	Very hard	1	2	3	4	5	Very easy
(ii)	Mouse/trackball	Very hard	1	2	3	4	5	Very easy
(iii)	Joystick	Very hard	1	2	3	4	5	Very easy
(iv)	Touch screen	Very hard	1	2	3	4	5	Very easy
(v)	Other, please specify __________	Very hard	1	2	3	4	5	Very easy

c) Your preference

(i)	Keyboard	Very low	1	2	3	4	5	Very high
(ii)	Mouse/trackball	Very low	1	2	3	4	5	Very high
(iii)	Joystick	Very low	1	2	3	4	5	Very high
(iv)	Touch screen	Very low	1	2	3	4	5	Very high
(v)	Other, please specify __________	Very low	1	2	3	4	5	Very high

11. Please rate the usefulness of the following information interface tools. If the interface tool is inapplicable, please just leave it blank.

a) Graphics	Very limited	1	2	3	4	5	Very useful
b) Color	Very limited	1	2	3	4	5	Very useful
c) Animation	Very limited	1	2	3	4	5	Very useful
d) Feedback (e.g., sound)	Very limited	1	2	3	4	5	Very useful
e) Other, please specify ________	Very limited	1	2	3	4	5	Very useful

PART III: PRACTICES AND HABITS

12. How long have you been using a computer?
    - ❑ Under 1 year
    - ❑ 1 - 2 years
    - ❑ 3 - 4 years
    - ❑ 5 - 6 years
    - ❑ More than 6 years, please specify: _____ years
13. Do you have a PC at home?
    - ❑ Yes
    - ❑ No
14. Which of the following application types do you use most often? (Choose one.)
    - ❑ Windows applications (e.g., Microsoft Word, Excel)
    - ❑ DOS applications (e.g., Wordstar, Lotus 1-2-3)
15. Please indicate the learning medium of the above applications. (Select all that apply.)
    - ❑ Company
    - ❑ Computer literacy program
    - ❑ Academic institution
    - ❑ Self-study
    - ❑ Online tutorial/training course
    - ❑ Other, please specify ________
16. Please indicate the problems you encountered when using computer systems.
    - ❑ Inconsistent command language
    - ❑ Confusing operation sequences
    - ❑ Chaotic display formats
    - ❑ Inconsistent terminology
    - ❑ Incomplete instructions
    - ❑ Complex error recovery procedures
    - ❑ Misleading or threatening error messages
    - ❑ Inadequate/unavailable reference books
    - ❑ Online help not available
    - ❑ Other, please specify ________
17. Please indicate your reasons in selecting the above application type (specified in question 14).
    - ❑ Comprehensive
    - ❑ Systemwide consistency
    - ❑ User-friendly
    - ❑ Popular
    - ❑ Speed
    - ❑ Habit
    - ❑ Other, please specify ________
18. Please comment on the user interface design. ________

    ____
19. Please rate the following factors in order of importance for a good user interface:

a) Reliability	Least important	1	2	3	4	5	Most important
b) Accuracy	Least important	1	2	3	4	5	Most important
c) Flexibility	Least important	1	2	3	4	5	Most important
d) Speed	Least important	1	2	3	4	5	Most important

e) Training time	Least important	1	2	3	4	5	Most important
f) Systemwide consistency	Least important	1	2	3	4	5	Most important
g) Ease of use	Least important	1	2	3	4	5	Most important
h) Help facilities	Least important	1	2	3	4	5	Most important
i) User-centered feedback (e.g., messages)	Least important	1	2	3	4	5	Most important
j) Other, please specify	Least important	1	2	3	4	5	Most important

Thank you for your valuable time. Your opinion is important to us.

Chapter 10

Effective Systems Development Management: The Experts Advise

Tom L. Roberts, Jr., Michael L. Gibson, and William N. Ledbetter

The effective management of systems development projects is an elusive goal for all systems development professionals. The industry has a poor track record in bringing projects in on schedule, within budget, and with full performance characteristics and capabilities. Many factors contribute to the success or failure of a systems development project. A systems development project is often a complex interplay of project management tools, systems development methodology, and CASE tools.

Every system development project has individual characteristics and priority that makes management of the project unique. For every project, systems development managers must adapt their management skills to the unique aspects of the project to maintain quality and the project schedule. Because this task is complex, it is no surprise that effective systems development can be so elusive.

To help systems development mangers better understand the complexities of systems development project management, twelve leading systems development experts were interviewed to give insight to systems development management. They were interviewed to help systems development managers identify the project management skills and areas needed to bring a project to a successful conclusion. Among the topics discussed in these interviews were: roles and responsibilities, the development process, and the use of automated tools.

THE INTERVIEWS

The authors selected the twelve experts by using citation lists, leading consultants mentioned in IS literature, and consultants who were members

0-8493-9822-3/00/$0.00+$.50

of a large nonprofit organization of systems professionals. All the individuals selected are very knowledgeable in systems development methodologies. The mix of experts includes external consultants and practicing systems professionals, who may not be as well-known but have extensive experience in practical IS projects. The experts interviewed are:

- *Ed Yourdon.* Yourdon & Associates; Consultant, Author, Methodologist.
- *Garland Favorito.* Consultant.
- *Ken Orr.* Ken Orr & Associates; Consultant, Author, Methodologist.
- *Vaughan Merlyn.* Ernst & Young; Consulting Partner, Author.
- *Dr. Sami Albanna.* Yourdon & Associates; Consulting Manager.
- *Donna Wicks.* Consultant.
- *Mike Rice.* Coopers & Lybrand; Managing Associate.
- *Dennis Minnium.* Texas Instruments; IEF Developer.
- *John Riley.* Texas Instruments; National Consulting Practices Manager, IEF
- *Rick Bastidas.* Consultant.
- *Susan Ball.* IDE Director, Educational and Consulting Services.
- *Mariann Manzi.* Dun & Bradstreet Software; Software Development Manager.

The structured interview given to each expert was developed on the basis of reviewing system development methodologies, CASE, and IS projects in existing MIS and computer science literature concerning systems development methodologies. The structured interview questions were open-ended and intended to prompt the experts to freely and more completely offer insight on their perspectives and experience in developing and using methodologies, using CASE, and participating in IS projects.

The interviews were either conducted in person or by telephone and lasted one to two hours. Each interviewer followed the same structured interview guide with little variation. All interviews were taped and transcribed to assure complete reconstruction of answers to each question.

The content of each interview was analyzed. The interviewers separately identified and extracted items of importance from each expert's interview. They then combined the set of extracted items from each interview into a single set for that interview. A second content analysis was performed across the twelve different combined sets of extracted items to derive the final set of combined items across all expert interviews. The results of the second content analysis were compiled and collectively evaluated.

The rest of this chapter examines the most important points from the interviews.

THE IMPORTANCE OF UNDERSTANDING LIFE CYCLE PHASES

Valuable Points from Experts

- One must understand the phases to use a methodology.
- The methodology will guide you through the life cycle phases.
- Preceding phases build products for succeeding phases.
- Knowing the deliverables of each phase is crucial.
- You must understand the phases to assure proper utilization of the methodology not in terms of fixed deliverables.

Discussion

A vital point of the experts is that a methodology cannot be used unless its life cycle phases are defined and understood. The organization should have some individuals who understand all of the phases. However, many specialists involved in the process may not necessarily need to know all of the details. Many of these specialists may only need to know methodology phase deliverables (i.e., the output of each phase). Understanding a methodology's deliverables is crucial to its use.

Knowledge of the life cycle phases should be a major focus in training of personnel using the process. Training programs phase should possess segments that provide explanations of each life cycle phase to personnel involved with the phase. The use of experienced personnel and expert consultants can also help in making sure that the individuals involved in the process understand the methodology.

UNDERSTANDING WHEN SOME LIFE CYCLE PHASES MAY BE SHORTENED

Valuable Points from Experts

- Lay out the project plan at the beginning of the project.
- Recognize that there are a variety of different factors for particular projects.
- Realize that alternative life cycles enable you to customize the life cycle to a particular project.
- Train everyone on the overall life cycle and life cycle phases.
- Understand what happens if certain activities are deleted.
- Know the dangers of making everything optional.
- Realize that typically the entire universal set of a methodology is not used on every project.
- Make the life cycle phases flexible.

Discussion

The project plan should be laid out at the beginning. This plan should put together the schedule and identify and allocate the resources necessary to complete the project. The methodology provides the basis for carrying out a project. It can be customized to an environment for new system development, enhancements, maintenance, or packaged software acquisition. Adaptability of any life cycle-based methodology is critical at the project level. In training, everyone involved needs to know the overall life cycle and individual life cycle phases and must pay particular attention to what happens if certain activities are deleted. An inherent danger exists in making too many of these activities optional.

For efficient use of a methodology, a systems development manager plans each individual project and customizes the portions of the methodology to be used for the project. The realization that every project has its own characteristics should be taken into account. The key is coordination between methodology and project specifics.

UNDERSTANDING WHO SHOULD BE INVOLVED IN CERTAIN PHASES

Valuable Points from Experts

- Key players are needed for required activities.
- Roles and responsibilities are keys to phases.
- Specialists with particular skills are needed for each phase.
- Understanding who is involved in changes over the life cycle of a project.
- Identifying who should be involved in specific phases provides ownership of a particular deliverable and identifies roles and accountability.
- Not having the right people reduces system quality.

Discussion

Roles and responsibilities should be clearly defined for the project. Project success is based on having the right people with the proper skills at the appropriate time and place in the life cycle. Projects lacking people with the proper expertise are vulnerable to mistakes.

Coordination and efficient use of personnel by systems development managers is vital to successful project management. IS managers must decide upon the exact personnel needed to complete each phase of the project. These personnel decisions must be made before the start of the project during the project planning phase. Matching knowledge and expertise with methodology phases is essential to every project.

UNDERSTANDING THE REUSABILITY BETWEEN LIFE CYCLE PHASES

Valuable Points from Experts

- Realize that the basis for any phase needs to be the deliverables from the previous phase.
- Make sure that one phase's deliverable is a clear communication document to the next phase.
- Understand the transition between phases.
- Identify reusable components.
- Make sure the life cycle used has full integration from phase to phase.
- Understand that a full life cycle methodology is cumulative.
- Realize that it is difficult to implement and control reusability.
- Have requirements traceable through the project to make sure original requirements are met.

Discussion

A full life cycle methodology should be integrated from stage to stage. The results of one stage should be used to start the next stage; without such integration some type of bridge must be built. The only real reason to have a full life cycle methodology is its cumulative nature.

The successful IS project manager will realize the capabilities of a methodology and use them as adeptly as possible. Virtually every methodology contains components that may be reused from one life cycle phase to the next. It is the challenge of systems development managers to reuse as many components as possible to streamline a project. However, systems development managers should exhibit some measure of caution to control reusability to ensure quality. Requirements traceability is a must for satisfying this need.

MANAGEMENT INVOLVEMENT IN LIFE CYCLE PHASE

Valuable Points from Experts

- Have project champions from the business.
- Project management and management involvement all the way through project and methodology implementation.
- Each management level understands their project roles.
- Upper management understands that their role is to force the use of the methodology.
- Management keeps track of the deliverables.
- Management knows what types of people from their organization are needed in the project.
- Create an overall plan, a schedule, and a resource plan for the project.
- Management knows what resources are needed from phase to phase.

- Management trains on the methodology.
- Provide feedback to managers on projects.

Discussion

Project management is the critical role. Project management and management involvement must begin at the outset and stay current all the way through the project. Management's role is to force the use of the methodology. Management must believe in the life cycle-based methodology; otherwise, people will abandon it.

Additionally, the project will need a champion from the business user group to sell the project to end users. The champion should know what types of people from their organization are needed as the project progresses through the life cycle.

Management must realize the importance of its role for successful projects. The only way for a manager to guarantee project success is to get directly involved with the project. IS managers should make an effort to understand the technology involved with the methodology being used and an effort to sell the benefits of this technology to IS personnel.

MANAGEMENT'S TIME COMMITMENT FOR IMPLEMENTING THE METHODOLOGY

Valuable Points from Experts

- Management allows enough time to implement the methodology.
- Management provides enough financial funding to implement the methodology.
- Management understands the learning curve, decreased productivity, and limited benefits before a methodology takes hold.
- Management commits time, resources, and money as well as the process changes.
- Realize that shortcuts will lead to lower quality.
- IS personnel realize that management cannot wait too long.
- Management commits to retraining personnel for the new methodology.

Discussion

Management must understand that they are tooling and retooling an IS factory. Commitment of learning curve time and resources is essential to implementing the methodology. Management must realize that the first few projects may increase in overall project completion time by several months. Adequate time to complete the project must be allowed, or shortcuts will be taken that cause problems for the whole process. The flip side is for management to not have to wait too long for project completion. If the methodology adds too much time to the process, the project will probably never be started. As a result, it is best to have the first projects that are completed with the new methodology to be important projects that have a relatively short duration time.

Patience is the key to using new technology and methodologies. Systems development managers must focus on the project process. They must understand that the benefits from using the new methodology will be realized once the learning curve concerning the technology has been reached by IS personnel.

DEVOTING ENOUGH TIME TO PERFORMING THE MODELING ACTIVITIES

Valuable Points from Experts

- Understand that enough time must be allocated or it is not worth attempting.
- Realize that modeling takes a lot of time.
- Know that enough time must be devoted to analyzing the area of study to determine what is necessary.
- Understand that methodologies emphasize where to spend time.

Discussion

A methodology should place emphasis on where systems personnel should spend time as opposed to where they would naturally spend the time. The process is going to take a lot of time, especially if staff members are going through classroom training. The learning curve on using the methodology for modeling will take a considerable amount of time.

Systems development managers should recognize that very few projects offer shortcuts to the systems development process. Business and systems modeling are vital components to system project success and performance. Many times project schedules attempt to circumvent modeling activities to simply get a system completed. Every effort should be made by systems development managers to resist any attempts to take shortcuts to just simply get the system out of the door.

MANAGEMENT'S RESOURCE COMMITMENT TO IMPLEMENTING THE METHODOLOGY

Valuable Points from Experts

- Have a methodology coordinator to develop in-house training.
- Have a champion for the methodology.
- Have management plan for the methodology implementation.
- Have management bring in consultants to help with the paradigm shift.
- Be sure management understands what resources are necessary.

Discussion

If IS does not commit time, people, and dollars, then it really does not have a commitment to the methodology. There must be a methodology coordinator, who among other activities will develop in-house training. If there is no champion in an organization, methodology implementation will not be successful.

Systems development managers should focus their efforts upon getting resources for the IS project. They should have an understanding of what resources are necessary for each particular project from the initial project planning phase. Once project specifics are known, managers should act as project champions in an attempt to sell it to senior management. This championing of a project is an essential part of getting the resources needed for a successful project.

MANAGEMENT FOLLOW THROUGH WITH THE PROCESSES

Valuable Points from Experts

- Upper management requires that the methodology be followed.
- Management provides a method of measurement to show some measurable observable benefits to the developers.
- Management commits to the methodology.
- Management follows through with the implementation process.
- Management creates an implementation plan.
- Management understands the need for investing in retraining and modernization.
- Project managers and IS personnel take operational responsibility.
- Management realizes that a cultural change is not completed unless it is mandated, enforced, watched, and measured.

Discussion

False starts kill business; if management does not assume the responsibility for the process of implementing the methodology, then it will not be done. A cultural change is not completed unless it is mandated, enforced, watched, and measured. It is important that managers measure across the implementation process just as they do elsewhere. You just do not take a methodology and dump it into an organization and expect it to grow by itself; you need an implementation plan. If management forgets about it, then people will also forget about it. Management must show commitment throughout the implementation and use of the methodology, not just at the beginning.

Following through with new technology is important. The key is involvement with the processes. Systems development managers must continually illustrate to their staff how important the process is to each project.

THE VALUE OF USING LIFE CYCLE SUPPORT TOOLS

Valuable Points from Experts

- Promote integration between different life cycle phases.
- Realize that if the tools are poorly integrated, the gains made during one phase may be dissipated in another phase.
- Use tools to implement techniques.
- Integrate code with models.
- Maintain diagrams from which the code gets generated.
- Automate the system development process.

Discussion

In the paper-based methodologies of the 1970s, problems were fixed directly in the code and not the specifications. Today, it is critical that a methodology be supported by automation and that the coding is eliminated. Diagrams from which the code is generated are maintained rather than the code itself.

Systems development managers should understand that automation supporting most information system development techniques exists in today's computing environment. Managers should make every effort to take advantage of these automated tools to assist with the development process.

THE VALUE OF SHARING FRONT AND BACK END CASE SPECIFICATIONS

Valuable Points from Experts

- Ensure accuracy of specifications.
- Make sure application systems reflect the business requirements.
- Allow models to help generate code.
- Create traceability.
- Reduce the need for documenting code and speeding up the maintenance process.

Discussion

Specifications should waterfall. The bottom line is that one should be able to take an attribute and not have to enter it again later in the physical design. Models should help generate the code. They should be tied together; otherwise, the whole reason for doing the modeling is lost.

THE VALUE OF USING OTHER WORKSTATION TOOLS

Valuable Points from Experts

- Measure a project's progress.
- Provide automated means for documenting work.

- Support presentations.
- Produce high-quality, better-looking documents.
- Provide error checking capabilities.
- Help to control the software development process.

Discussion

Online methodologies of the future will tie together workstation tools (project management, estimating tools, and CASE). The organization should have a project management-based methodology and graphics support. It is clear that some automated means of documenting the results of work is needed. Graphics on one life cycle phase should feed the next phase.

ACTUALLY USING TOOLS THE WAY THEY ARE DESIGNED TO BE USED

Valuable Points from Experts

- Understand which tools are flexible.
- Use tools the way your goals and objectives are set up.
- Find innovative ways to use tools within the process.
- Realize when innovations can impact the next phase of the life cycle.
- Realize that tools assist the methodology.
- Follow standards when using tools.

Discussion

In today's environment, the use of automated tools is essential. Many of the processes cannot be done by hand. Tools must be used the way they are designed to gain the greatest benefit from them. Some tools can be used to make the end deliverable look different than the original intent. These changes are not necessarily bad as long as they do not affect the next life cycle stage. Tools should be used consistent with the goals and objectives and every organization is going to be different. However, one should not get carried away with using the tools for special purposes for which they are not designed.

OTHER POINTS ABOUT PROJECT MANAGEMENT

The experts made supplementary statements that were not prompted by specific questions but are additional points of importance to project management.

Valuable Points from Experts

- Use estimating tools to estimate throughout the project.
- Provide greater productivity.

- Ensure quality and information integrity.
- Realize that initially there will not be productivity gains.
- Keep people on track with the methodology.
- Eliminate redundant activities.
- Realize that tools do not solve the problem.
- Guide the process.

Discussion

Project management tools are essential to successful projects. In general, project management tools keep people on track and guide the process. Estimating tools are important in producing guidelines for the life cycle. The combination of these tools provides a more complete set of workstation tools in support of using a methodology and completing IS projects on time, within budgets, and with a satisfactory final product.

CONCLUSION

The experts leave little doubt as to the need for managing the life cycle phases of the methodology. Knowing the phases and what goes into each phase is vital to successful projects. However, this knowledge does not guarantee success. The use of automated life cycle support tools is a necessary extension to the methodology in successfully completing IS projects. These tools should span the project management activities, project estimation, and actual performance of systems development tasks. Their integration is a prerequisite of a reliable project completion process.

The most important issues about systems development according to the panel of experts are

- The importance of understanding life cycle phases
- Understanding when some life cycle phases may be shortened
- Understanding who should be involved in certain phases
- Understanding the reusability between life cycle phases
- Management's involvement in life cycle phases
- Management's time commitment for implementing the methodology
- Devoting enough time to performing the modeling activities
- Management's resource commitment to implementing the methodology
- Management's follow through with the process
- The value of using life cycle support tools
- The value of sharing front and back-end CASE specifications
- The value of using other workstation tools
- Actually using tools the way they are designed to be used

Section II Checklist

1. What strategies does your organization promote in an effort to improve the application development process? Has this strategy been successful?
2. Does your IS organization embrace every new development methodology in an effort to find the perfect development process? If not, does it shy away from newer techniques altogether?
3. How would you compare your knowledge of new development techniques over those that have been successful for you in the past? Are new techniques worth studying?
4. Could your IS environment prove the use of newer development techniques as successful? If so, what means would it use (i.e., cost, time, staff, quality, etc.)?
5. Do you anticipate another paradigm change regarding application development? How will this affect decisions about changes to current practices in your organization?
6. What is your organization's position on embracing code reuse? Is it cautious or too optimistic?
7. Is reusability viewed as another trendy "panacea" or "silver bullet" within your organization? If so, is this opinion based on cursory evaluation or an in-depth analysis?
8. What steps have you taken to understand leveraging existing code for further development?
9. Do you have a development strategy for GUIs? If not, do you follow vendor recommended guidelines for GUI development?
10. In your opinion, should programmers or end users design GUIs? How is this done in your environment?
11. Do end users in your organization judge the value of an application based on the GUI or the entire functionality of the system?
12. What myths about software development still exist in your organization? Who holds them, users or developers?
13. How are development projects started in your organization? Is this based on business need or is it driven by the capabilities of new technology?
14. Do you hold meetings with your development staff to discuss new methods to improve development?
15. Based on your experience, is application development an art or science? What development strategy would be more suitable to your opinion? Could you develop your own strategy for developing quality applications?

Section III
Tools, Tips, and Practices

Identifying the most effective tool or methodology for improving the application development process has been an evasive goal for many organizations. The multitude of products and techniques provide an unusual level of opportunity and at the same time can create confusion and uncertainty amidst ongoing technical change. Caution should be exercised when struggling to find the single most important tool or the next "silver bullet" solution. It is doubtful that any one tool or procedure will satisfy the diverse demands of the development and support process.

For many organizations, the routine of selecting appropriate tools is often time consuming and difficult. Techniques that work in some organizations may not work in others. Furthermore, not every tool or technique will perform well in all development and support situations. Development managers must be aware that choosing the best suite of tools or techniques should be based on matching key factors that surround the unique characteristics of a given development environment. These factors may include organizational size, corporate culture, application development maturity, budget, and resource availability. As application tools and techniques continue to evolve, there will be an ongoing need to balance the use of tools and their overall contribution to development and support objectives.

Current appeal of object-oriented technology is founded on a long standing idea of reusable software procedures. This concept has been implemented in early forms through functions, subroutines, and common code libraries. Despite the name, the premise of reusing code is often harder to exploit due to misunderstanding about the basic mechanics of the process. Chapter 11, "Ten Steps to Realizing Application Code Reuse," offers a general overview for implementing and administrating a workable reuse strategy. As a follow up, Chapter 12, "Components: Reuse in Action," provides guidelines for implementing component technology. Although components themselves are low risk technology, implementing requires a high level of software engineering discipline and cooperation among all participants in the development environment.

Chapter 13, "Managing Object Libraries," provides an excellent discussion on methods and practices to improve the success of software objects. The benefits of reusable software are not often fully achieved due to poor management of code libraries and the inventory mechanism to track existing modules, including appropriate identification of module functionality. By establishing early guidelines, reusable code or objects can be utilized by a greater number of software developers and thus improve development projects. Avoiding the effort to organize reusable code will eventually waste the promise of newer techniques such as object-oriented development.

The use of desktop computing throughout an organization has yielded many opportunities that may have otherwise required more formal programming efforts. In particular, business professionals have many extensive of spreadsheet applications that provide vast capabilities and information needed for day to day decisions. Unfortunately, many of the user developed spreadsheet programs escaped the discipline of IS practices and the result has been somewhat alarming. Chapter 14, "Converting Spreadsheets to Tiered Enterprise Applications," examines the issues surrounding the use of spreadsheet programs in the typical organization. As technology platforms advance, the need to update the spreadsheet application also exists. And in some instances forces a difficult choice in supporting the spreadsheet program. This chapter offers guidelines for creating enterprise applications that capitalize on the existing spreadsheet logic and thus preserves the original effort used in its development.

Spreadsheets are only one form of packaged software that can boost development productivity. The advent of more sophisticated computing platforms and richer quality off the shelf products have seriously challenged the "make vs. buy" decision. In Chapter 15, "Management Skills Needed in a Packaged Software Environment," a discussion on the pros and cons of purchased software is given. There is little doubt that more organizations are acquiring software as a means of deploying systems more rapidly and with less specific staff resources. However, this may not always be true, especially with larger applications such as ERP. Development managers should recognize all issues with packaged software before embarking on an acquisition that could require significantly more expense than the initial cost of the software itself.

Support for deployed software applications remains an important task for all organizations that rely on computing systems. Regardless of the origin, either purchased, developed, or a combination of both, the need to meet user changes and updates is important. In planning the system, thought should be given to post-implementation support as part of the development process. Chapter 16, "Web-Based Customer Self Service," offers an enlightening overview of the benefits of using Internet technology to support deployed systems. The use of these techniques can be applied in both Internet and Intranet environments on a 24 × 7 basis. Many IS professionals are already familiar with, not to mention dependent on, Web-based support techniques as a means for improving maintenance on hardware and software used within the IS environment. This same method can provide a significant saving in staff effort, as well as, satisfying end users' need in a timely manner.

Software metrics are still a popular technique as a means of evaluating software development efforts. Metrics can provide valuable information to IS organizations when analyzing software support tasks and assessment of enterprise software portfolio management. There is also an added benefit to improve development by applying well-defined metric measures. However, establishing meaningful metric indicators is not an easy task. Chapter 17, "Software Metrics: Quantifying and Analyzing Software for Total Quality Management," reviews the basics requirements of a comprehensive metric program. Once established, development managers can adjust and tune metric measurements to further improve software development productivity and quality.

Chapter 11
Ten Steps to Realizing Application Code Reuse

Richard T. Dué

The overwhelmingly favorable economics of software reuse have been apparent for over 30 years. Unfortunately, the systematic reuse of application software has been elusive. Most organizations have no planned approach to the identification, evaluation, storage, and dissemination of proven application code. Highly productive individual programmers do reuse their own code, but often just in a "cut and paste" manner within their own programs. Interestingly, however, most programmers willingly reuse operating system, compiler, telecommunication, database, and system utilities code.

EIGHT REASONS WHY REUSE FAILS

It is the reuse of application program code that has, for the most part, been a failure. Time after time application programmers start with a blank sheet of paper, or an empty computer screen, and write code that essentially has already been developed hundreds of thousands of times before. The following eight reasons are among the causes for the failure to reuse application code:

- *"I didn't know the modules existed."* Because there are no inventories of existing code, nor any easy way to access these inventories, reuse of code is only accidental. Programmers only informally exchange modules of code based on chance meetings in hallways or on computer bulletin boards.
- *"I cannot trust code developed by other people."* Certainly, a lot of substandard, poorly documented code exists. Complex systems designs can result in unforeseen results as programs interact with each other, or with new hardware and software environments. However, writing

0-8493-9822-3/00/$0.00+$.50

more code that no one else can trust is obviously not an effective solution.

- *"This application calls for unique code."* Certainly, there are situations (applications with critical hardware or time constraints, for example) that sometimes justify heroic programming efforts. Most new application code, however, is just repetition of typical information processing functions that have been already produced hundreds of thousand of times.
- *"It will be faster for me to write the code myself."* Paradoxically, programmers who make this argument are only willing to spend a few minutes looking for existing code before starting to write new programs that they expect will take them up to several weeks to develop.
- *"I was never taught about reuse."* Software engineering textbooks and university and technical school courses teach new practitioners to build systems from first principles. Reuse is not promoted or even discussed. Students are evaluated on the basis of their individual effort. Few attempts are made to teach students teamwork or to demonstrate the benefits of specialization and component-based systems assembly.
- *"I'm not reusing software that was built in that way."* The intellectual challenge of solving an interesting software problem in one's own unique way mitigates against reusing someone else's software components. Reuse initiatives are often attacked by the majority of programmers as stifling their creativity.
- *"I've never heard of any good experiences with reuse."* Efforts at creating reusable application code libraries have failed since the 1960s. Since reuse seems to be unobtainable, few organizations are willing to spend more time and money pursuing it.
- *"Why should I reuse software if I do not see the pay back?"* Less than 5 percent of organizations in North America measure the productivity of their investment in information technology. In the few organizations that even bother to measure the productivity of their application development resources, productivity is only measured and rewarded in terms of lines of new code written. In my opinion, it is this lack of appropriate productivity measurement that allows the preceding seven, largely spurious, arguments against reuse to prevail. There can be no movement to large-scale application code reuse until organizations institute effective information technology productivity metrics programs.

THE CASE FOR REUSE

Capers Jones, at Software Productivity Research, suggests that organizations will see a 30:1 return for every dollar invested in an appropriate reuse approach. There is no other greater information technology investment opportunity today. He points out that while the average cost to build a function point (a language-independent measurement of the functions or services provided by a computer program) in the United States is $1,000, an equivalent commercial package can be obtained for about $0.25 per function point. The equivalent shareware package would cost about $0.01 per function point.

Of course, despite their current popularity, commercial and shareware packages cannot always meet the unique needs of every organization. The effective reuse of packaged code will probably only occur at a much smaller level of granularity than an entire application. Unique systems can be assembled from well-tested and documented components and subsystems. Java and ActiveX components distributed on the Internet will certainly be a major step in the reuse of small, cost-effective packages of code that can be used to assemble systems.

The real benefits of reuse, however, are not to be found merely by the reuse of code. The cost of writing code is only about 15 percent to 20 percent of the total cost of developing and implementing a system. Even 100 percent code reuse is thus unlikely to have a major impact on the true costs and duration of an application development project.

EFFECTIVE STRATEGIES FOR REUSE

The significant difference, in my opinion, between the successful reuse of operating systems, compilers, telecommunication software, databases, and system utilities code and the failure to reuse application software is that system software is viewed as a given infrastructure that provides services that help develop applications. Most application programmers are happy to rely on this infrastructure.

The Application Code Infrastructure

In contrast, application development is viewed as an end in itself that always requires the development of unique code. It is time to stop viewing applications as unique projects. Instead, systems development managers must extend the scope of the concept of infrastructure to include the reuse of standard components and proven patterns of requirements specification, analysis, design, documentation, testing, training, and project management.

This infrastructure approach to reuse will require a fundamentally different systems development life cycle approach. Instead of analyzing (literally loosening up or pulling apart a thing into its constituent parts) and designing (arranging parts according to a plan), application developers are going to have to start focusing on the assembly of proven, reusable components. This component assembly, or object-oriented, approach requires developers to concentrate on "discovering" (observing and learning about) the application domain, assembling "real world" simulation models of the domain from proven components or objects, and then synthesizing the required information services from these collections of components. The benefits of this new "reuse-in-the-large" approach include:

- Proven solutions can be applied to similar problems.
- Less time need be spent on development.
- Existing documentation can be reused.
- People without theoretical systems engineering training and experience can follow patterns and guidelines to assemble applications from the existing infrastructure.
- Organizations can concentrate on the information services they require instead of worrying about how to implement systems.
- Management will be able to plan and control their organization's systems against standard frameworks.
- Auditors will be able to used established patterns to assess the economy, efficiency, and the effectiveness of the organization's information systems.

A TEN-STEP APPROACH TO CODE REUSE

The introduction of a successful code reuse initiative will require at least the following ten steps discussed in the following paragraphs.

Identify and Commit a Champion. A champion is the most senior manager who has the most to gain from the success of the reuse project. In most cases this will be a senior user department manager whose success will be directly attributable to the operation of competitive, flexible, and low-cost information systems.

Perform a Maturity Assessment. Paradoxically, reuse of application code is unlikely in organizations that consider information technology as a cost center rather than an investment center. As organizations move along the information technology management learning curve, they begin to identify, plan, control, document, measure, and manage their investments in information systems. Relatively immature companies that only consider the short-term costs of their information systems are unlikely to commit to the expense of the reuse-in-the-large approach. Companies that have successfully moved along the information technology management learning curve start to understand the long-term payoff of the reuse culture investment. There are several maturity assessment programs such as those offered by the Carnegie Mellon University's Software Engineering Institute, which can be used to measure an organization's information technology management maturity.

Establish and Use Productivity Metrics. A successful reuse program most be evaluated with an appropriate set of productivity metrics. Almost unbelievably, over 95% of North American organizations have no measures of the productivity of their investment in information technology. The following — rather unorthodox — set of productivity metrics should be used to measure the business success (as opposed to the technical success) of the reuse initiative:

- *Profitability.* What is the direct effect of the organization's investment in the reuse-in-the large approach and the organization's profitability?
- *Customer Satisfaction.* What is the effect of the organization's investment in the reuse-in-the-large approach on the satisfaction of the organization's ultimate customers? Ultimate customers are the final end users of the organization's products and services. They are not clients or users within the organization.
- *Time to Value.* How long does it take to turn Information Technology investments into profits?
- *IT Value Added.* How much value is added by Information Technology to the organization? Is this value increasing over time?
- *Business Alignment.* Are the organization's investments in Information Technology understood and supported by the managers in the main functional areas of the business?
- *Employee Satisfaction.* What are the cross-industry comparative rates of employee turnover and compensation? What is the rate of increase in the intellectual capital of the organization?
- *Productivity and Quality.* What is the actual level of productivity and quality of the organization's Information Technology personnel when compared to the best industry practices? Productivity measurement must be done using technology neutral measures such as function points.
- *Improvement Rate.* How quickly are all of the productivity metrics showing improvement?
- *SDLC Shape Change.* How is the organization changing the shape of its system development life cycle? Ideally the length of the cycle should be decreasing while an increasing percentage of the cycle is spent on planning and modeling compared to a decreasing percentage spent on coding, documentation, and testing.
- *Learning Rate.* How long does it take to introduce new technologies into the organization? What is the participation rate, how long does it take to reach a critical mass of users?
- *Rework Change Rate.* What is the rate of improvement in finding and fixing errors? Is there a shift in error identification and elimination of errors from the end of the system development life cycle to the beginning of the cycle?

Institute a Quality Assurance Function. The purpose of a quality assurance function is to ensure that the organization is adequately undertaking all of these ten steps.

Institute Project Management. The introduction of a reuse initiative is a project that will require effective project management. This means that a full-time project management expert will be required to plan, estimate, schedule, develop a risk analysis and contingency plan, and monitor the success of the reuse-in-the-large approach.

Select and Adhere to an Appropriate Reuse-Oriented Methodology. An appropriate methodology concentrates on identifying and employing proven component frameworks, design patterns, and best practices. In contrast, an inappropriate methodology is concerned with developing each individual application in isolation.

Institute Training. As with any new development technique, programmers needed to be trained in reuse. This is even true for beginning programmers, who have probably received no educational training on reuse.

Hiring Practices. A reuse-in-the-large program will require employees who are capable of working at high levels of abstraction, who feel comfortable with understanding and modeling the domain, who are able to work directly with users, and who are able to work in teams. There is no place for heroic "cowboy" coders in mainstream application development.

Acquire Tools. Appropriate reuse tools include groupware and repository-based CASE tools. These tools must be used to facilitate communication of proven frameworks, patterns, and best practices among all members of the organization.

Monitor Ongoing Benchmark Testing. The final step in the reuse program is to monitor the success of the reuse initiative against industry benchmarks and best practices.

CONCLUSION

Reuse-in-the-large requires that organizations establish and support a culture of reuse. This culture must include the use of appropriate systems development methodologies, the establishment of repositories of components, design patterns, and best practices, and the installation of rational productivity metrics. In the absence of a culture of reuse, the only alternative systems developers have to write their own code. The consequence is inefficient, uneconomical, and largely ineffective additions to the program maintenance headaches already facing most organizations.

The 10 steps toward establishing a culture of code reuse will help systems development managers to overcome the eight roadblocks to reuse in the following ways:

- By acquiring development tools and adopting a methodology that promotes reuse, application developers will be able to find code they can reuse. They will also better understand how the code was created and be more receptive to reusing it.
- By instituting a quality assurance function for reuse, developers will be able to better trust code's reliability and should have more confidence about reusing it.
- A code reuse champion will help dissuade developers' doubts about reuse raised by past negative experiences.
- By hiring developers who are capable of working with high levels of abstraction, systems development managers should find their developers will be less likely to find the need for creating unique code.
- A training program will also help developers to overcome the practices that were fostered by past education and training and that encouraged developers to write code instead of reuse it.
- Most important, the rewards of reuse have to be demonstrated to upper management as well as to developers. Benchmarking reuse, the companion step of performing a maturity assessment, and using productivity metrics as well as using project management techniques to roll out the reuse program will all help to buy the backing of the entire organization needed to realize the rewards of code reuse.

Chapter 12

Components: Reuse in Action

Janet Butler

Component-based development is the latest hot topic in the application development world. Once again, industry analysts are touting a way to improve developer productivity, speed the development process, deliver applications at lower cost, and produce applications that are flexible to business needs, while providing customers with high-quality service.

While all this rhetoric has a familiar ring, causing immediate skepticism, most previous solutions to development issues have related to magic, new, easy, silver-bullet technologies. Examples are the many tool-driven solutions tried, such as fourth-generation languages and computer-aided software engineering, or the platform-related solutions attempted, such as the three-tier client/server environment and the Internet.

By contrast, an interesting aspect of component-based development is that it utilizes not new, but older, more traditional technologies: modularity and reusability. In addition, component-based development is not easy; rather, it requires a high degree of software engineering discipline to implement at an enterprisewide level. Finally, component-based development differs from other approaches in one other major way. Enterprise-level component advocates are concerned with integrating legacy applications into component development projects, rather than delivering spanking new applications that ignore legacy assets — or liabilities.

HISTORY AND CONTEXT OF COMPONENTS

Components are not a new concept; instead, they embody modularity, a useful programming technique that is among the long-term, fundamental concepts of software engineering.[1] While the notion of modularity has remained a constant, however, it keeps coming back in different guises; in this case, as components.

Because modularity plays a major role in determining the quality and maintainability of a system, a well-designed software system is structured into modules. In such a system, each module has a well-defined interface to other modules, performs a well-defined function, hides design decisions,

0-8493-9822-3/00/$0.00+$.50

and can be independently tested and/or verified. In this way design issues are localized. Because design decisions are isolated from one another, there is only a minimal effect when changes occur. And design experience from these systems is being codified into component libraries, patterns, and predefined frameworks, offering reuse capabilities.[2]

For its part, reusability is the process of building software systems from components (or artifacts) designed for reuse. In fact, some analysts see reuse as the only technology that allows a company to simultaneously address software cost, time-to-market pressures, flexibility, and quality. By contrast, other software development approaches trade these requirements against one another.[3]

In addition to these substantial benefits to be gained, reuse also offers substantial opportunities. Because software systems are typically composed of similar parts, the majority of each software system can be built from an assembly of existing reusable components.

The reuse of existing software development assets can then become an essential part the software development process of an organization. The amount of new code that must be written for a system is reduced by using proven components, which have either been acquired or been previously built and tested in-house. Reusability can extend to source and object code, design patterns, document templates, test scripts, user interface layouts, and software process definitions.

However, it is hard to build high-quality reusable components. In this effort, developers might have to build similar systems several times before they can identify and define reusable items. Furthermore, deliverables that were built for a specific project typically require substantial work before they can be of more general use. In addition, it takes more time and discipline to write a piece of code to be reusable, and package it so that it is usable. This might involve generalizing a component, standardizing documentation, and/or storing the code in a controlled repository.

Given the difficulties associated with reuse, a major key to success is a dedicated organizational effort, with specifically allocated resources. However, time-to-market pressures or project time constraints seldom permit the extra work required, so there has been little institutionalization of reuse. Still, there have been recent gains regarding components, reuse frameworks to develop applications quickly, patterns, and libraries.

THE LEGO MODEL OF DEVELOPMENT

It has been said that, "Components are the implementation of reuse, so all the rules that pertain to reuse transfer directly to componentry."[4] Component-based development is the assembly of applications from prebuilt, pretested, reusable software pieces or components, which some industry analysts have compared to Legos.[5] Thus, components are basic, discrete building blocks which, when assembled into applications, offer a new paradigm for application development.

Components can be further defined as modules within larger systems, which are often object oriented or based on object technology, and are defined by well-documented interfaces. Components are usually developed and executed independently, and are able to communicate with one another.

The component concept generally comes out of object technology, and both may be described as small code modules that execute certain actions. In distinguishing objects from components, however, whereas components are self-contained, independent units that can communicate and interact with other components, objects can interact with other objects only within a hierarchy of other objects.

Furthermore, while components can be composed of objects, the reverse is not true. Both programming techniques produce modular code, but component-based development need not be object oriented.

Components are useful largely because of their Lego-like nature. With object-oriented programming, one small change can ripple through an application, creating havoc.

This results from the inheritance of object-oriented systems. When an inherited attribute is changed in the "parent" object, the change is also seen in all the "child" objects that contain the inherited attribute. Some see the dependencies created by inheritance as a major reason object-oriented development has failed to deliver on the reuse promise.

Object-oriented development with strict inheritance is extremely complex, and the resulting applications are difficult to model and test. Furthermore, because developers cannot clearly understand all the objects, they seldom recognize the potential value of the object in other applications.

Components differ from objects because of the higher level of abstraction of what some have called "large-grained" components. The latter focus on the component interface, allowing application builders to concentrate on business processes. They need no longer address the inner workings of fine-grained components or objects, which entails knowledge of the underlying technology, a proper method of implementing the components, and complex dependencies among the various components.

Such large-grained components can be easily removed or added, typically requiring only a local effort. So components can be added to enhance functionality or change features or taken away to reduce requirements, without completely breaking the whole application.[1]

REUSE, NOT FREE USE

Why develop with components? The many benefits to components include not only reuse, but also ease of maintenance and scalability. In addition, projects can be completed more quickly with component use.

Some analysts predict that the trend toward components will quickly escalate, because the applications are more easily implemented, more scalable, more adaptable, and more easily maintained. In addition, component development lends itself to iterative, ongoing development and maintenance.

Indeed, many see a marriage of component-based development and rapid application development (RAD) in the future, based on libraries of reusable components. However, others believe that a major disadvantage of current component technology comes directly from its appeal. For them, RAD is a flaw in component development, because of its reduced emphasis on design. While this problem is not unique to components, they say, RAD components make it worse, discouraging design.[6]

RAD was conceived as an answer to problems of top-heavy development practices, which often resulted in project failure. And RAD spawned such useful techniques as joint application design/development and prototyping. With RAD there is also less documentation, an emphasis on collaborative user involvement, and a focus on iterative and incremental development.

However, as noted above, RAD can also mean no modeling. In addition, because RAD solutions answer immediate needs, they often result in inconsistent interfaces, redundant information, and an increase in maintenance. Therefore, some warn that, "Reuse is not free use," explaining that RAD is a high-risk approach for the component development of large, complex software projects. In fact, they say, the level of rigor and detail should be much *greater* with components.[7]

LEVERAGING LEGACY SYSTEMS

Component-based development is among only a handful of methods that offer a way to leverage legacy systems. Thus, the component approach to application development may be seen as a practical way to reuse the logic, data, and application services of existing legacy applications. A variety of techniques can be used to "wrap" legacy applications, including use of an existing application programming interface (API), using "screen scraper" technology, or interfacing to legacy middleware such as CICS.

Another viewpoint describes two ways of integrating components and legacy systems. The first is to physically break the application into functional, modular units, to be wrapped and packaged for reusability. The second way is to build application programming interfaces for the functions of the application, which can then be called when needed. And, although the first method is more difficult, it works best in a distributed environment. When legacy applications are wrapped as components, they can be expanded with new functions, migrated to different platforms, or integrated with new technologies such as the Internet.[5]

However, not everyone agrees, instead recommending that companies distinguish legacy assets from legacy liabilities, and not use component terminology to "purify" legacy liabilities. From this perspective, organizations should not cleanse obsolete, nonstandard technology with the label of "component." While some legacy systems can be wrapped and used for a while as is, they should not be called components. Instead, developers should build components specifically as such, and adhere to a standard.[4]

AN ALPHABET SOUP OF STANDARDS

To date, components have been most commonly associated with the desktop space. The two component "flavors" that operate at this level are the Sun Java Beans and the Microsoft ActiveX/Component Object Model (COM).

In addition, two dominant players are coming to the fore regarding distributed component standards. The first, considered an open standard, is the Common Object Request Broker Architecture (CORBA), from the Object Management Group (OMG), Framingham, MA. OMG, a marketing arm for standards in object technology, has approximately 700 company members, and offers meetings every two months.

The second player moving into distributed component standards is Microsoft, with its COM/ActiveX/DCOM (distributed COM). This *de facto* standard describes conventions, rules, and notations for defining interfaces to components.

MOVING TOWARD SUCCESS

Components and distributed applications make for a good marriage, say industry analysts. In fact, some see component-based development as a critical element in the evolution of distributed applications. Thus, components are considered more suitable to a distributed architecture than traditional applications, because of the independent nature of components. These self-contained yet interoperable components offer scalability in a distributed, multitier environment.

Components are easily combined into an application that is deployable on the Internet, for example. In this environment, component-based applications can be called from any client, whether it be a Web browser, a Java applet, or a laptop computer. In fact, components are particularly useful where the desktop computing environment is largely unknown.

However, to date, much of the existing component work has concentrated on connecting independent pieces of system functionality. Developers are just beginning to consider component use when developing and deploying large, distributed, mission-critical applications. But component use for large systems requires several critical success factors.

Four essential ingredients have been defined in the large-scale use of component-based approaches for enterprise-level application domains. These are methods for designing component-based solutions that focus on functions and their interaction; tools that support specification of business components; implementation techniques that offer systems management support; and a component management and assembly infrastructure.[8]

Some analysts see the need for a practical, integrated, component-based software process for enterprise systems. They recommend four project roles that are integral to the success of a component-based process:

- *Reuse manager* — Plans and manages the activities of the component team, and sets reuse policy.
- *Reuse librarian* — Uses administrative and technical skills to manage and publicize the component models and repository.
- *Reuse assessor* — Uses a knowledge of existing systems, packages, databases, generic models, and available components to evaluate reuse requirements, opportunities, and improvements both within and across projects.
- *Reuse architect* — Provides the reuse "vision" via architectural scoping and modeling, identifying/acquiring reusable components, and promoting reuse.[7]

For others, a component development strategy for the enterprise requires tools for building business components; a model for building components and enabling communication between them; and a plan for moving from existing applications to systems based on components. Here, the techniques for construction of an enterprise component architecture include constructing, assembling, and managing enterprise components; wrapping legacy applications; aiming tools at the Internet and network computing; and acquiring components from external sources.

One key to success is a development tool that enables development teams to build and assemble components, preferably based on a repository. A second success factor is to build component applications for a distributed, three-tier architecture, separating client applications from server-centric application services, and from Web services. And organizations should not use new, unknown languages and technologies to build components.[5]

According to one systems integrator, the successful use of components requires preparation in three areas: technology, process, and organization. Regarding technology, organizations should investigate such component architectures as the Microsoft COM/ActiveX or the Sun Java Beans. Companies should also invest in framework development. This is especially necessary if its enterprise software is becoming more complex, or if it is becoming too expensive to rebuild custom solutions from scratch.

In terms of process, successful component use requires iterative development cycles, which include generalization phases, in order to refine designs and implementation. After the software is built, another generalization phase will ensure that the software can be reused on other projects. Such generalization should become part of the life cycle. However, organizations should consider buying components before building them.

Finally, component success requires organizational change, so components become a way of life. In this effort, architectural teams can be made responsible for creating and publicizing reusable solutions. And the organization should look beyond current system requirements, motivating shared solutions across projects, and rewarding contributions to component and framework use.[6]

THE EVOLVING USE OF COMPONENTS: NOT ALL CREATED EQUAL

As component use evolves, it is changing the face of application development. The latter is moving away from the paradigm of creating and integrating developed software, and toward a new model, where components are selected that support business functions, and then assembled into applications. However, such evolution requires the building of component libraries and repositories, the institutionalization of component use, and a redefinition of components to fit the enterprise level.

As noted above, the component world may be divided into categories of fine-grained and large-grained components. The former, like objects, produce a small piece of functionality. These fine-grained components must work together with others to deliver a complete, recognizable function. Examples are the individual elements, such as buttons or dialog screens, that comprise a graphical user interface (GUI) screen.

By contrast, large-grained components perform a complete business function. Examples are a general ledger, a letter of credit, or even an entire legacy application.

Similarly, a distinction may be made between technical and business components. The former, similar to fine-grained components, are the "under-the-covers" type of component, which support many business areas, and can be commonly bought.

Business components, however, requiring specific business knowledge for their creation, must often be built by the particular organization. Issues at this level include storing components in repositories, transitioning the organization to do component-based development, and changing the "not invented here" mind-set of developers.[9]

Some companies are already building component repositories, in which they store reusable software for use across projects. To date, these are most successful for nondomain components, such as user interfaces.

Thus, today, most component-based development consists of wiring together simple graphical controls like those of ActiveX, Java applets, or Java Beans, to create a user interface. This generally means downloading the component from the Internet, and determining its suitability.

In addition, organizations are finding desktop components to be ideal for simple applications, with two-tier and Web-based clients. Desktop components also work well for such mainstream applications as form-based data entry. Other candidates for desktop components are well-understood applications with stable requirements and applications with a single life span that will not be upgraded.

However, complex, sophisticated, enterprise-level applications require algorithms and directions to capture and codify design. One viewpoint sees software frameworks as "the scaffolding" needed for component assembly, and a good way to embody design.[6]

Most component-based work so far has addressed infrastructure and middleware for connecting independent pieces of system functionality. Now, however, organizations are starting to evaluate component-based development for large, distributed mission-critical applications, with their needs for robust operations and high transaction rates, and other requirements of multiple simultaneous users.

To create robust, flexible, large-scale business applications, components must provide core business functionality. To support the range and functionality of business rules and database access, a clear, unambiguous specification is needed, separating the component specification from its design and implementation. This allows multiple, alternate component implementations for the same specification. In addition, the method must specifically support an interface-focused design approach.

Well-designed, abstract component interfaces have been suggested as a critical success factor in developing enterprise-level component applications. To this end, users must model their work flow (business processes), use cases, and sequences to identify the requirements of the applications.

Unfortunately, today's modeling tools seldom address work flow, use case, and sequence modeling. This disconnect between the modeling of business processes and modeling of the software that implements them makes it hard for software designers to achieve the abstraction they need to create well-designed interfaces.

Other key elements have been identified that are missing in component-based architectures. While current component products target modeling, design, and coding, this is not the case with established automated testing, configuration management, and application management products. However, successful component-based projects require release management support from configuration management tools, as well as testing of component interaction from quality assurance testing tools.[11]

For industry analysts, components offer great flexibility and productivity to application developers in a changing environment, providing the means through which organizations can respond rapidly to new business processes and needs, take advantage of new technology, and meet the demands of end users. They range from low-level components like ActiveX and Java applets, to high-level business components. Therefore, some have predicted that component-based development will be a key new programming technique for the next two to three years.[5]

Eventually, analysts anticipate that information technology (IT) organizations will be able to build or buy a suite of components which, when assembled, will provide complete applications. They predict that developers will be able to build applications from a repository of components that are developed in-house, created by third parties, or produced by other organizations. While this is not yet possible, many development and provider organizations are moving in that direction. Ultimately, the promise of reuse will be realized, as components are continually recycled, and nothing of value is lost.

GETTING STARTED

Many IT organizations comprise different, isolated development groups, which do not trust one another. These various groups may build systems based on competing, incompatible component models. In addition, IT organizations tend to offer positive recognition and incentives for developers who build new, custom systems, rather than those who assemble applications from reused code and components. Finally, it is difficult for developers to understand the value and best use of components.

Therefore, to successfully implement and leverage components, companies can start the process right now by

- *Standardizing the different groups in the IT organization* — Standardizing process support across different, isolated development groups;

- *Supporting component management* — Establishing a centralized repository available to all development groups; this includes locating, storing, and controlling component access and promotion;
- *Creating incentives for reusing code and components* — Versus building custom applications;
- *Providing a clear definition of components* — To help developers understand their value and best use;
- *Implementing a standard design framework;*
- *Designating reuse advocates* — Who help developers implement components, from both technical and organizational perspectives;
- *Making the new technology and processes compatible with natural human process patterns* — So there is less resistance to change.

Sources

1. "Component road map," *Managing System Development*, December 1997, pp. 1–4 ff.
2. "Software engineering: Practice, process, product, and progress," by Janet Butler, *Managing System Development*, March 1998, pp. 1–6.
3. "Value-added year 2000: Harvesting components for reuse," White Paper by Carma McClure, 1997, p. 3.
4. "What is a component?" editorial by Marie A. Lenzi, *Distributed Computing*, January/February 1998, p. 7.
5. "The real-world enterprise: Where do components fit?" by Karen D. Moser, *Uniface Magazine*, February 1998, pp. 18–21.
6. "The promise of composable software," *Managing System Development*, pp. 6–7.
7. "An integrated component-based process," by Paul Allen and Stuart Frost, *Object Magazine*, February 1998, pp. 36–8 ff.
8. "Toward component-based development for the enterprise," by Alan Brown, *Designing the Future: Enabling the Global Enterprise*, Hewlett-Packard, 1998, p. 12.
9. "The component conumdrum," by Viktor Ohnjec, *Application Development Trends*, December 1996, pp. 55–56 ff.
10. "Inside Microsoft's component strategy," by David Wihl, *Application Development Trends*, February 1998, pp. 47–51.
11. "Using component technology," *Managing System Development*, December 1997, pp. 4–5.
12. "Middleware — the essential component for enterprise client/server applications," White Paper prepared by International Systems Group, Inc., 1997.

Chapter 13

Managing Object Libraries

Polly Perryman

Software reuse is a concept that has been bounced around in the industry for years and years, still information systems developers are searching for ways to master its implementation. The principles of object-oriented design and development have shown themselves to be a starting point for developing reusable software. Application of the principles, however, only offers a partial solution since compliance with the principles and the development of objects does not automatically result in reusability. It requires a great deal of planning and effective management of object libraries. This is because until the commonality of the object types is defined and effectively managed the value of software reuse cannot be realized.

Many companies miss out on valuable opportunities to streamline processes while improving product because they do not have a cohesive plan to implement object library management. Other companies lose out because they think object library management is a practice limited to documented object-oriented design methodologies. Still other companies use clumsy procedures intending to promote software reuse without ever realizing the importance of planning for software reuse, which is itself a form of object library management. When the essential components of object library management are understood and implemented, these missed opportunities can knock again.

One of the biggest mistakes companies make is "throwing" objects into a library without a scheme for making sure the team benefits from them. For example, a company had a practice of telling coders if they develop a routine that others can use to put it in Library X. This was so everyone could access and use the code. This had a major impact on one project. Several developers faithfully added routines to a common library that indeed saved development time for database access, output, and a number of other common functions. A young fellow we will refer to as Sam contributed a particularly well-used routine. The problem was that while Sam's common object executed beautifully, it was unfortunately a resource hog, and when it was used by other developers it created problems. The impact of modifying the object to correct and improve the performance issues and retest the

0-8493-9822-3/00/$0.00+$.50

fifty-plus programs using the object was significant. The schedule delay was unacceptable to the customer. Funding for the project was withdrawn.

On another project where the "throw-it-in" approach to object library management was used without a master plan coders duplicated efforts by individually creating their own renditions of routines for common use. The object library became so convoluted with multiple objects for the similar types of functions that no one was able to use it. The benefits gained by the concept were preempted entirely by the approach.

So how can object library management be implemented effectively without impinging on the creativity of talented staff. It basically depends on three things to be successful. The first is appointment of a design authority. The designated design authority assumes full responsibility for establishing the highest classification for objects, the characteristics for base objects within the classification, and determining which objects possess commonality to the system for potential reuse within the application, upgrades, and related products. The person who takes on the role of the design authority must communicate beyond the structure of the objects, making certain that the development team understands the standards and methods used to structure, document, build, and subsequently maintain the object library.

The second area for success lies in the effective use of basic configuration management functions, such as version control and release management. The implementation of the configuration management functions may use any of the configuration management tools in the market today, such as Rational-Atria ClearCase or Intersolv's PVCS, that have been upgraded to work with large objects. The configuration management functions may also be implemented using internally developed tools and methods when purchase of these tools would strain the budget.

The third area for success is quality control and testing. The quality control and testing that must be performed covers more than the demonstration the coded object works to specifications. It also must ensure that development personnel are complying with the structure established for object management that allows for improvement in the processes used by development personnel using the object library.

Object library management can and should be practiced regardless of the development methodology being used because it offers direct benefits to developers and customers alike. The most direct benefit of object library management is better product at lower cost. While this may sound like a television commercial for every imaginable product on the market from baby diapers to automobiles, the positive effects of object library management can demonstrate improved productivity through team-focused procedures and higher quality through uniformity, consistency, and, most importantly, meaningful design controls.

With the components of success identified, it is important to note that as languages, systems, and user applications become increasingly complex to program, the need for object management takes on greater implications in the life of a product. As many companies are finding out, the effects of poor object library management impacts not only initial development of a product but results in spiraling chaos with the maintenance and upgrade of the product.

THE DESIGN AUTHORITY

The design authority is a role rather than a position. The role may be filled by a single individual, such as the engineering manager, the lead design engineer, the system architect, or by a group of people who work together to satisfy the goals of object library management. The critical point is to define the role and fill it. It is important not to confuse the design authority role with the responsibilities of a configuration control board whose function is quite different.

Once the design authority role has been assigned, the work of managing object libraries can begin in earnest. Using input from the users, a rudimentary framework for objects can be set up. It is here that the design authority may elect to use the Unified Modeling Language (UML). Whether UML or some other method is used, it is of particular importance that the system requirements are clearly defined, analyzed, and documented. They are the basis upon which all of the design and system testing are based and they must be clearly understood by all parties. The initial object framework can and probably will be a hodgepodge of objects and classifications both at the highest level and at base levels. The reason for this is that the users will be providing their input at different levels. For instance, one or two of the users may be listing specific types of reports they need to generate on a cyclical basis, while other users may be stating their desire to employ animation and sound without specifying what type of animation or sound. The result is that input will be provided on various levels and the design authority must be able to determine the value to place on the information.

This may be better explained by referring to some of the early discussions about object-oriented programming (see the **Recommended Reading** list at the end of this chapter) in which a classic shape example was used for clarification. In the example, shapes became the classification for managing objects that performed functions on a shape, such as changing the shape's size or moving it. The type of shapes, circles, squares, and triangles, inherit the capabilities of the objects. This allows functions to be performed on any type of shape, thus setting up the ability for reuse of the functions on shape types added to the system at later dates.

It is the design authority who begins to set up a framework for new and continuing development. Decisions will need to be made as to whether the input falls into the circle/square category, the perform-on category, or the shapes category. If it is a shape category it will hold objects. If it is an object it will do something. It is the objects then that need to be constructed. It is the classification and management of these objects that takes the design authority to the next critical work effort.

In order for an object to do it is something, it needs to possess both the data and function qualities necessary to perform. Peter Coad and Edward Yourdon expressed these qualities as an equation: Object-oriented = Objects + Classification + Inheritance + Communication with Messages.[1] The design authority, in maximizing the potential of solid object library management, must be able to cross reference and promote the use and reuse of these qualities in the development environment. For instance, objects in an edit classification may include copy, move, and delete. The construction of the object must permit these functions to be performed on any designateded text or graphic unit. As such, the design authority can, within the object library management structure, ensure the reuse of these objects from one product to another and from one upgrade to the next. In planning the object libraries, the design authority must also consider those types of objects that will more likely be upgraded in the short and long terms. While the quickness of advancing technology may make this step seem like crystal ball engineering, the design authority will have responsibility for working with management to minimize technological risks and keep development moving in a forward rather than circular direction.

It is not the role of the design authority to determine how the defined object structure is implemented within the configuration system. That function is performed by specialists in configuration management.

CONFIGURATION MANAGEMENT

Configuration management is a function best performed by a specialist who has three principal tasks. The first is making certain the version control mechanisms sustain the object classifications and hierarchy structure laid out by the design authority. The second is ensuring that the version control mechanisms put into place support the application development staff in easy retrieval and storage of objects. The third is tracking the correct object versions and building them into defined releases of the product. Whether your organization has a configuration management tool in place or not, when the decision to implement an object library management plan is made, a serious comparative capability evaluation of the existing tool and those available in today's market must be made.

Most of the recognized configuration management tools available today will at a minimum provide version control and support release builds.

Nearly all of the tools allow text, graphic, and multimedia object storage. The trick in selecting and using a tool for object library management is in evaluating the available tools in relationship to the scope of the efforts it will be supporting and the manpower investment the company is willing to make to ensure the successful implementation of the tool. It is critical that during this evaluation focus is maintained on the design structure and intended reuse capabilities desired. This means it needs to be evaluated not only for what it will do today, but whether it will meet the needs of your organization in terms of future growth. For example, current plans for your product over the next five year are to support both Windows and Macintosh users. The tool that best fits the design structure and size requirements for the projects only runs in a UNIX environment today. The question as to how the developers will effectively be able to take advantage of the version control features of the tool must be addressed, as does how clean the build feature of the tool really stays.

A similar dilemma presents itself when an organization uses off-site developers for various pieces of the system. One example can be taken from a company whose off-site animation staff developed their product, which was eventually embedded within the company's primary product. It turned out that the operating system used by the off-site developers was not compatible with the configuration management tool being evaluated. A number of work-arounds were drafted and discussed, but the bottom line was that each of them made the version control and build processes cumbersome and less reliable. A lesser known configuration management tool offered the necessary interface for this off-site work and provided all of the other features in a somewhat diminished capacity. The question that had to be asked and answered was which tool was going to best meet the goals of the organization now and in the future. If the organization was willing to fumble through for a while and gamble that the interface for off-site programming was going to constructed or the off-site programmers could be transitioned to a different compatible operating system, then perhaps the more well known tool would be a good choice. If the need for better object management was immediate and the organization was willing to gamble on the eventual expansion of the lesser known tool's capabilities, then the less sophisticated tool would be a good choice.

These examples are merely representative of the types of questions that must be part and parcel of a configuration management tool evaluation. Other important questions include, but are not limited to:

- What support does the vendor supply in configuring the tool in your organization's environment?
- If interfaces are going to be constructed by the tool vendor, will they become part of the configuration management tool product line or

stay a customized piece of software your organization will become responsible for maintaining?
- What training is required by your organization's staff to set up and operate the tool effectively?
- How many man-hours must be devoted to maintaining the tool in order to ensure successful use of it?

Even when the current in-house tool meets the technical specifications for object library management and object development, there are still set-up factors to be considered in assessing the planned design authority structure in relationship to the current configuration of the tool. New areas may need to be prepared and a different hierarchy may need to be defined to support the build features of the tool. This work cannot be overlooked during the evaluation process.

Another stumbling block to successful object library management is in the planning of releases. Here the design authority and configuration management specialists need to work closely to define the contents and status of each release. It is not sufficient for the design authority to send an e-mail that says include x, y, and z. Success is based on knowing not only that x, y, and z are in the release, but also knowing the problem state of x, y, and z within the overall scheme of the object library management plan. In other words, the plan for release A will include version 2.2 of x, version 2.3 of y, and version 4 of z, and we know that version 2.3 of y includes a few glitches that should be fixed before the release date but will not crash the software if they are not fixed. However, version 4 of z may cause some problems, in which case the fallback plan is to use version 2.8 of z because version 3 of z had to be recalled. This is the type of information that becomes part of the release plan composed by the design authority and the configuration management specialist. This, of course, brings us right to the third component needed for successful object library management, quality control and testing.

QUALITY CONTROL AND TESTING

How did the design authority and configuration management specialist make the decision on which version of z to use if the possible problems with z surfaced during the release build. The answer is that version 2.8 was a thoroughly tested and proven object within the system and it did not have a relationship with either x or y. It would not need to be retested. It could just be used because the quality control supporting solid object library management includes traceability, predictability, and uniformity, which are achieved by testing the design, the constructed objects, the object relationships, and the object system. Keep in mind that objects that have been tested can be used and used and used without having to test and test and test. New development will occur in a more orderly manner, because the structure laid out within the object library management plan will lend itself to a clearer and more logical next step. The quality controls are essential in taking the management of objects from basic reuse in the initial product to a viable expanded product vision.

Working with the design authority, quality control personnel complement the object library management plan while imposing and enforcing these controls, because the structure of the objects and the communication from the design authority to the development staff ensures that everyone is working toward the same goal. The quality group does the testing of the object and ensures that it meets the construction and use guidelines established. Quality control accomplishes this by being a part of the development rather than an appendage to development, validating the object structure and conducting walkthroughs where questions and issues can be raised and resolved. The quality group should work closely with the configuration management specialists to ensure the integrity of the released product by validating both the configuration of the tool being used for version control and release management and verification of the product release plan.

SUMMARY

The goal is to maximize an organization's competitive edge in the marketplace. The components for successful object library management presented in this chapter can be raised to whatever level of sophistication best fits your organization. The important thing is to plan and manage the objects constructed.

On a small project the biggest problem may appear to be people resources. Keep in mind that there are three roles that need to be played for success. This may mean that the lead designer is also the design authority and a developer and the configuration management specialist. The quality control and testing role, however, must be performed by someone other than this person. If necessary, even a nontechnical project manager can perform the quality control and testing role as long as the concepts and goals of the project are clearly stated and the basics of object library management are understood. The greatest benefit to the small project is that communication between the design authority and developers is stronger and the set-up of the configuration management tool generally much easier.

On a large project there are larger problems. There the design authority may be a team of people in which some protocol and tie-breaking mechanisms need to be laid out from the start in order to keep the design moving. Communication between the design authority and the developers is more difficult to maintain. The set-up of the configuration management tool may take several weeks and training sessions may need to be conducted to ensure that developers fully understand what is expected of them. And quality control and testing is more involved and necessary. The biggest benefit in a large project is the value of being able to gain a greater long-range vision for the application or product and in being able to cross-train personnel in many areas.

The point is to take action. Whether the project is the conversion of a legacy system to the new technology or the development of new systems with existing and future technology. Begin by committing in black and white what your organization needs to accomplish. Then establish an organization to assess and plan for that accomplishment. Once the plan is formulated, provide training whether it is vendor supplied, seminars, or in-house group sessions. Success can be repeated over and over again when there is a plan to implement and an understanding of the technology. Then appoint the design authority, start evaluating configuration management tools, and prepare a testing strategy that will meet your organization's goals for object management.

Notes

1. Coad, Peter, and Yourdon, Edward, *Object-oriented Analysis*, Englewood Cliffs, NJ: Prentice-Hall, Inc., 1990.

Recommended Reading

Jacobson, Ivar, Griss Martin, and Jonsson Patrik, *Software Reuse*, ACM Press, 1997, pp 60-61, 117, 356 and 436.

Entsminger, Gary, *The Tao of Objects, A Beginner's Guide To Object Oriented Programming*, M & T Publishing, Inc., 1990.

Chapter 14
Converting Spreadsheets to Tiered Enterprise Applications

Dan Fobes

At a time when companies are discussing their distributed computing plans, it may be alarming to find that many of these same companies are running critical business processes within a spreadsheet. It is not uncommon to see a PC off in the corner running a DOS version of Lotus 123, where Lotus macros generate data for users or other systems. With the year 2000 approaching, and no future versions of DOS or DOS-based spreadsheets on the horizon, these companies are faced with a decision: either upgrade to the latest spreadsheets, or reengineer them as enterprise applications. There is a cost associated with both; however, the results are very different. Upgrading the spreadsheet simply maintains status quo, with data, and the business rules for how to operate on that data, isolated to the desktop PC. However, converting a spreadsheet to a tiered enterprise application results in centralized data and distributed processing that can be shared by many clients across the enterprise, including spreadsheets. This article proposes a solution for companies that choose to move spreadsheets to an enterprise application using a tiered approach.

DEFINITIONS

Before rewriting the spreadsheet-based system, a definition of application tiers is required. All applications, even a spreadsheet, can be broken down into three tiers:

1. data tier: physical data storage and management
2. presentation tier: user input/output
3. business tier: code for processing "business rules"

Data Tier

The data tier of a spreadsheet is simply the raw data contained within the cells. Today, relational database management systems (RDBMS) such as Oracle are commonly used as data repositories. Database architects

0-8493-9822-3/00/$0.00+$.50

(DBAs) manage the logical design of the RDBMS such as the layout of tables that hold data, while database administrators (also referred to as DBAs) manage the physical design of an RDBMS such as the location of tables on a disk, cache size, controllers, etc. Similar to spreadsheets, the fundamental storage structure in an RDBMS is a two-dimensional grid of data called a table. Moving the data from a spreadsheet into an RDBMS is feasible because a spreadsheet's limitations rarely exceed those of an RDBMS. Staff should include at least one database architect and one database administrator. The database architect should balance an understanding of the business requirements with the technology of RDBMS design. The database administrator will not require a large understanding of the business processing, but will require an understanding of the internals of the RDBMS, the hardware it is implemented on, and be responsible for implementing disaster recovery procedures such as backups.

Presentation Tier

The presentation tier of a spreadsheet is the spreadsheet application itself. Certainly, the goal is NOT to rewrite the spreadsheet interface. Defining the user-interface requirements for the target application is going to be specific to each business, and will likely be a significant subset of what a spreadsheet provides. When choosing a tool to rewrite the presentation tier, it is important that the choice support the target desktop's object technology (e.g., ActiveX objects should one's clients be running a form of Microsoft Windows). Some choices are:

1. Microsoft's Visual Basic
2. C++/Java
3. Object COBOL

The programmer for the presentation tier should be someone with a strong technical background in event-driven application development and experience with object-oriented design and analysis.

Business Tier

The business tier of a spreadsheet, similar to the data, is contained within the spreadsheet, but is represented by cell formulas or macros. Moving to a distributed model requires macros to be rewritten, and choosing WHAT to code the macros in is not as important as HOW it should be done. The minimum technical requirement for the business development tool is support of distributed objects (e.g., Microsoft's DCOM). Exhibit 14.1 can be used to select a tool. The choice depends on many factors, with internal expertise being the major factor to consider. The programmer for the business tier should be someone who has a good understanding of the business objectives of the application. This programmer will work closely with the presentation programmer and database architect; and between

Exhibit 14.1. Summary Sheet

Summary	My Calculations	Bank Statement
Start Balance	1,000,000	1,000,000
Activity Summary	XXXX	XXXX
Interest	XXXX	XXXX
Fees	XXXX	XXXX
Final Balance	XXXXX	XXXX

the three, the business objectives of the application and the technology required for its implementation will be covered.

DESIGN

Data Tier

Once the tiers of the existing spreadsheet environment have been defined, work can begin on moving them to a more appropriate technology — one tier at a time. The simplest tier to port will be the data tier. First, the database administrator will create a database for the project, and the database architect will create a table per spreadsheet. The design of each table should follow the design of the spreadsheet. For example, Exhibit 14.1 illustrates a spreadsheet that tracks data between two sources, such as that between a person and a bank for a specific account. There are two ways to implement this: one maps the spreadsheets rows and columns directly into table rows and columns (see Exhibit 14.2), while the other approach maps spreadsheet rows and columns to table columns (see Exhibit 14.3).

In Exhibit 14.2, an attempt is made to preserve the spreadsheet design as closely as possible; but because each row has a different meaning, a rowID is required. An additional table of rowIDs and their meanings, effectively a data dictionary, must be added as well. One advantage to this approach is that it closely resembles the source spreadsheet. Also, the design is extremely flexible because new fields, changes to existing fields, etc., can be done by adding/updating rows in the data dictionary table. A disadvantage is that a column can only contain one data type. If rows in the summary spreadsheet change data types — for example, from type money to type float — additional pairs of columns have to be added to account for them. As a result, each row will have some blank columns. Another approach, illustrated in Exhibit 14.3, sees the rows of a spreadsheet converted to columns

Exhibit 14.2. Table Design 1

Column 1	Column 2	Column 3
RowID Type: Integer	MyCalcs Type: Money	BankCalcs Type: Money

Exhibit 14.3. Table Design 2

Column 1	Column 2	Column 3	Column 4	Column 5
StartBalance Type: Money	ActivitySummary Type: Money	Interest Type: Float	Fees Type: Money	MyCalcs Type: Boolean

and an additional column made to account for the two columns (if MyCalc is false, this row of data is from the bank). Although structurally different from the spreadsheet, it requires no extra tables and is very readable. It is also very efficient on space — no row will have blank columns. However, modifications such as additional fields or changes to existing fields will likely require the creation of a new table based on the new design, and code to move the data from the older to the new version.

There are two obstacles to consider that might affect the design of the data tier:

1. When using the design in Exhibit 14.3, one spreadsheet may contain a large number of rows, and exceed the limitations of a RDBMS (e.g., more than 255 rows is at least a 255-column table).
2. One spreadsheet may contain many logical grids of data.

Both have the same solution: the spreadsheet must be broken down into more than one table. For example, the Activity Summary in Exhibit 14.4 can be displayed on the same spreadsheet as Exhibit 14.1, but its data should be stored in a separate table.

Interfacing to the Data Tier

With the database tables designed, how does application code get to it? The most common way an external tool communicates with an RDBMS is by issuing commands written in a 4th Generation Language (4GL) called structured query language (SQL) through a standardized interface such as the open database connectivity (ODBC). To access data in tables, a client application issues an SQL statement such as "Select startBalance from SummaryTable." Additionally, most RDBMSs support the concept of stored procedures: modules of SQL code stored within the RDBMS server. Stored procedures can take parameters and are accessible through ODBC.

A DBA cannot write the presentation code in SQL; however, the stored procedure feature does give the architect an option for business logic —

Exhibit 14.4. Activity Sheet

Date	Withdrawal/Deposit	Source	Amount
9/1/98	W	Bank	1,000,000
9/8/98	D	Bank	1,000,000
9/8/98	W	Foodstore	1,000,000

code it completely within the RDBMS server engine as stored procedures. With an SQL-based business tier, code is compiled and executed within the RDBMS, typically yielding much better performance than a 3GL implementation. However, 3GLs such as C++ are more powerful to develop with than SQL (e.g., SQL modules are limited in size and complexity). Also, 3GL development tools that integrate an editor, compiler, and debugger far exceed the capabilities of SQL-based tools. Finally, different RDBMSs have different "extensions" to SQL — not all SQLs are equal. Moving stored procedures from one RDBMS to another is rarely trivial, requiring updates to take advantage of each engine's "extensions."

The optimal solution is a combination of both: implement the business tier in a 3GL, but do not issue any SQL — called predefined stored procedures. To do this requires generic operations such as retrieveXXX, updateXXX, and deleteXXX, to be coded as stored procedures where XXX represents a logical entity (e.g., a table or user grid). By creating an API of stored procedures within the RDBMS, the 3GL is insulated from both the variations of SQL code and changes to the database schema. The task of moving from one RDBMS to another becomes a DBA task to port the stored procedures, not a business programmer's task.

Presentation Tier

The code for the presentation tier serves two purposes:

1. to present information (data)
2. to provide an ability to act on that information (inquire button)

The presentation tier is responsible for receiving requests from the user or system, passing those requests on to appropriate modules for processing, and then displaying the results. This can be accomplished by creating an application that displays a grid in a window, something easily accomplished with a tool such as Visual Basic. The design of the grid, columns, and rows should be visually similar to the spreadsheet being reengineered. One "feature" of many grids is that they can be data-aware, meaning they can be "pointed" to an RDBMS table or stored procedure for data. Besides the simplicity of hooking into an RDBMS, one benefit of data-aware grids is that they can be configured to bring results over the network one page at a time. That is, given a query that returns a large result set (e.g., thousands of rows), the grid can be set up to bring back subsets of data (e.g., 100 rows) as the user scrolls the results. However, data-aware grids are effectively "tied" to the database through some intermediate object that holds connection information. The main problem with data-aware grids is that they are always "connected" to the database, taking up valuable resources on the RDBMS server. This approach simply does not scale well; and, more importantly, it ties the presentation tier implementation to the data tier design. Tying the design of the presentation tier to the data tier should be avoided given the differences in their design. A disconnected grid is the better approach. The problem of queries with large result sets still exists, but advances in RDBMS access technology, driven by the demand to access data residing on servers over the Internet (a connectionless protocol), are beginning to address this.

Business Tier

There must exist code with intelligence about the data (i.e., data relationships and dependencies). Typically, a spreadsheet has many inter-cell calculations, such as the Activity Summary calculation in Exhibit 14.4. The temptation is to place this logic in either the presentation tier or the data tier. In examining this option when designing the data tier, it was concluded that the lack of powerful development tools, combined with the various "extensions" to SQL across RDBMS, discourages this approach. This was also examined in the presentation tier and it was concluded that this would tie the presentation tier design to the data tier design, resulting in rigid application that would be difficult to port to other presentation platforms (e.g., from a Windows client to a browser). By placing the code that manages the calculations and dependencies in a separate tier, and having the presentation tier query it for data, the flexibility of the application is increased. It will be seen later that the business tier can be extended to enhance performance by reducing database connections.

As observed in Exhibit 14.3, the design of the data tier can look very different from the presentation tier. Having the design of the business tier follow the design of the data tier (e.g., an object per table) offers no benefit because the data tier will have stored procedures that insulate the business tier from the details of the design. Therefore, the design of the business objects should closely follow that of the presentation tier, simplifying presentation tier ports, and resulting in a design that is more user oriented than programmer oriented.

PUTTING IT TOGETHER

As illustrated in Exhibit 14.5, the spreadsheets of Exhibits 14.1 and 14.4 are broken down into two forms for input, two objects for business processing, and two tables for storage. The two tables are the Summary table and the Activity table. The Summary table will follow the design of the table in Exhibit 14.3 because rows change data types and there are a small number of rows. The Activity table can be designed identical to the spreadsheet (see Exhibit 14.6).

The Withdrawal/Deposit field could be of type Boolean, but was left as a character field to account for other types of transactions such as transfers. Stored procedures will be created that read and write Activity table records and Summary table records.

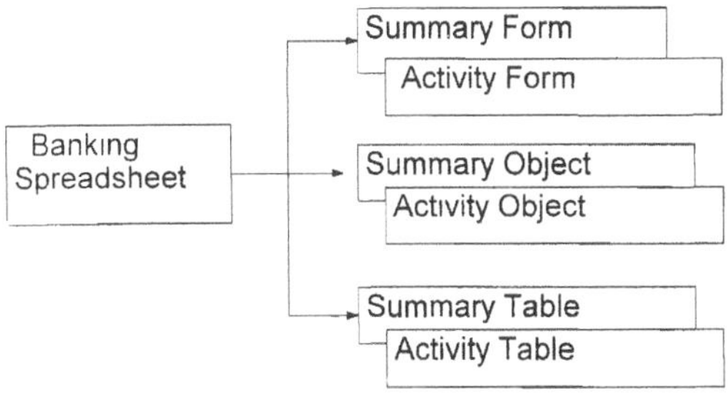

Exhibit 14.5. Architectural Overview

The design of display objects (e.g., forms, HTML pages) within the presentation tier simply follows the design of the spreadsheet, except in the case where one spreadsheet has multiple grids of data. Specifically, an application will be created that allows the user to select one grid of data with which to work. For purposes of simplicity, there will be one grid per display object. Although the original design might have been a spreadsheet with the Summary and Activity grids on the same worksheet, display objects with large amounts of data are difficult to comprehend if the user has to scroll through many rows. One grid per display object also takes advantage of events that fire when the user switches from one view to another. For example, if the presentation is running on a Windows client, each grid would be on a form, and a double-click within row 2 of the Summary form's grid could fire an event, which causes the Activity form to be displayed. The Activity form now has "focus." The user can enter rows of data into the Activity form, and upon closing the form, another event can be set up to fire, which flushes the Activity data to the database and instructs the Summary form to "refresh" itself.

Each display object will have an associated business object that interfaces to the data tier and incorporates some business rules. When the display objects lose and regain focus, events can be set up for them to interface with the database, apply business rules, and communicate with other business objects. For example, using the previous Windows client example, when the user creates the Activity form by double-clicking on row 2 of the Summary form, an Activity object can be created and the Activity form displayed. The Summary object can create the Activity object upon that event, then register itself with the Activity object via a pointer. Once the Activity form is closed, the Activity object can determine if data was

Exhibit 14.6. Activity Table

Date	Withdrawal/Deposit	Source	Amount
Type: date	Type: char Size: 1	Type: char Size: 16	Type: Money

Exhibit 14.7. Summary Object

Properties	Methods
.StartBalance	InquireStartBalance()
.ActivitySummary	InquireActivitySummary()
.Interest	InquireInterest()
.Fees	InquireFees()
.FinalBalance	CalcFinalBalance()

changed, perform some internal calculations such as calculating the balance (previously a macro), call a stored procedure to write its data, and then indicate this update to the Summary object. The Summary object can gather the new data from the Activity object and execute business rules that apply to this update, such as recalculating its final balance (again, this was likely a macro in the spreadsheet). Once the Summary form gets focus again, it can refresh itself from the Summary object, effectively pulling in the updated results.

There are two things to note in this approach.

1. It duplicates data across tiers. This duplication results in tier independence, which is more flexible.
2. The business objects perform the macro calculations, not the forms. If the presentation tier performed the calculations, changes in presentation tier would have to include these, complicating the port. It is better to duplicate data than the code that operates on it.

Exhibits 14.7 and 14.8 present tables of both objects, along with some properties and methods for each. Note that most methods of the business objects will simply call equivalent stored procedures, which read and write tables within the RDBMS. The exceptions are the totals, which the objects calculate based on business rules (previously macros).

An extension to this design is a database object in the business tier. To call stored procedures, each business object will have to connect to the database and login. An alternative is to have one database object manage this connection, and the business objects use it whenever a stored procedure needs to be called. This reduces the number of connections, and provides

Exhibit 14.8. Activity Object

Properties	Methods
.Date	WriteDate()
.TransactionType	WriterTransType()
.Source	WriteSource()
.Amount	WriteAmount()
	.CalcActivityTotal()
.SummaryObj	

scalability for applications requiring many business objects that need to interface to the database.

DEPLOYING THE APPLICATION

At the least, this application will be deployed in a two-tier configuration: each user will run the presentation tier on a desktop computer while accessing data that resides on a server. A decision has to be made as to where the business tier should be placed. The easiest place to put the business tier is on the client, especially if one's target is a Windows client. With Microsoft's ActiveX, COM, and ODBC technologies, business objects are easily connected to the presentation tier, then pointed to the data tier. However, the network must be considered when making this decision. If the business tier is working with large amounts of data stored in the data tier, the network will be saturated. Also, if the business objects need to perform complex calculations, the desktop PC might not have the horsepower required to do so in an acceptable amount of time. Finally, business objects cannot be deployed on the same machine as the presentation tier when the target presentation is a browser. These instances argue for a server-based business tier, which is significantly more complicated to deploy, but more scalable. It also brings up another decision: should the business tier be placed on the same server as the data tier? The answer to that lies in the complexity of the business objects. If they are compute intensive, the answer is no; if they are I/O intensive, yes.

CONCLUSION

The most important factor to consider when writing an application is the architecture; an application should be based on a three-tier design, even if it will be deployed in a two-tier environment. The second most important consideration is staff. The staff surrounding each tier should have varying business and technical expertise. When moving a spreadsheet application to a tiered application for the enterprise, the following steps should be considered.

1. Define the application tiers of the existing spreadsheet.
2. Identify the staff, and then tools, for the target distributed application that will replace it.
3. Design each tier with the goal of tier independence (e.g., do not use data-aware grids because this ties the presentation design to the data tier design). This will result in duplication, but enhances the flexibility of the result.
4. First implement the design, and then optimize it by considering some central objects in the business tier (e.g., a database object that contains the connections to the database) and various deployment strategies (e.g., move the business tier to the data server).

It is important to note that the process outlined above is not intended to replace spreadsheets altogether. With the data centralized, and processing distributed, spreadsheets become a valuable analytic tool, customizable per desktop, with access to both.

Notes

Rumbaugh, J. et al., *Object Oriented Modeling and Design*, Prentice-Hall, 1991.
Lippman, Stanley, Lajoie, Josee, *C++ Primer*, Addison-Wesley 1998.
Appleman, Dan, *Developing ActiveX Components with Visual Basic 5.0*, Ziff-Davis Press, 1997.

Chapter 15
Management Skills Needed in a Packaged Software Environment

Janet Butler

Traditional, customized development has in many cases become too expensive, and protracted development times may cause organizations to miss business windows of opportunity. The purchase of packages and off-the-shelf components, as well as contracted development, can offer major payoffs in cost reduction and speed of delivery. Due to the competition in every quarter, organizations would be far more vulnerable to major business risk if they did not seek alternatives to traditional development. However, the new approaches themselves pose many dangers.

WHY PACKAGES?

There is little doubt that organizations are increasingly moving to packaged software for major applications. The term coined for packages in industry is enterprise resource planning (ERP) software; that in government is commercial off-the-shelf (COTS) software, which may, however, simply refer to purchased components.

A recent study reported a 50/50 ratio of applications bought, versus those built in-house. Those conducting the study predict an imminent change in that ratio to three to one in favor of purchased software.[1]

Government Computer News also conducted a recent survey of 127 managers who agreed that commercial software is the wave of the present and the future. Of the respondents, 58.3 percent said that they use commercial software for one or more of these purposes: financial accounting, human resources, procurement, and electronic commerce. In addition, 85.7 percent of 42 respondents said that customizing commercial software has saved them money.[2]

Many analysts have attributed the "feverish" pace of package purchases to the Year 2000 (Y2K) crisis. By this view, users running out of time to fix Y2K problems have chosen instead to install packaged software that is

0-8493-9822-3/00/$0.00+$.50

already Y2K compliant. If this assessment is accurate, purchases of ERP applications should soon slow down as the Y2K market reaches saturation.

Recently, however, this premise has been refuted. While few doubt that avoiding year 2000 fixes on home-grown applications has fueled the package market, users are voicing many other business reasons for buying packaged software.

In fact, year 2000 fixes were not even mentioned in a recent survey asking "Why buy?" by Forrester Research Inc., Cambridge, MA. Instead, the 50 information technology executives surveyed gave the following business reasons for replacing an application with packaged software: for more flexibility as business needs change (26 percent), to use common technology across business units (24 percent), to facilitate business process reengineering (18 percent), for tighter integration among applications (8 percent), to standardize applications after acquisitions (6 percent), and other (18 percent).[3]

It appears that purchased software is here to stay, and the market will continue to grow, unabated. Packages allow an organization to deliver a complex system in a relatively short time. In addition, common applications are available in many languages and for many platforms. There is also a large installed base of users, accompanied by a proven track record of success, and purchased software provides extensive documentation. Furthermore, once the purchased software is installed, the organization spends far less money, time, and effort for ongoing maintenance than it would for in-house-developed software. And the organization need not redefine requirements for legal or other new requirements. Instead, this is the vendor's job.

The benefits of purchased software derive largely from economies of scale. The vendor need only develop the software once, and can then distribute the cost of development and ongoing maintenance over a large installed base.

However, there are downsides to purchased software. For one, it is just as difficult for a software supplier to develop software as it is for an in-house organization. In addition, commercial software is generally developed for the most widely accepted/installed technology. So it might not run efficiently on a particular computer or operating system. In fact, commercial software might use obsolete technology.

Additionally, purchased software is slow to evolve. It is very expensive for a vendor to make major functional changes to commercial software. By a kind of "reverse economy of scale," just as the cost of development and maintenance decreases because it is spread across a large installed base, so does the cost of implementing major improvements increase.

Another negative of purchased software is the use of multiple programming languages. In order to reduce maintenance and improve flexibility, vendors tend to write all or part of their software using home-grown report writers or fourth generation languages (4GL). This might work well for the first package an organization buys, but it becomes a linguistic nightmare with subsequent purchases.

Say that each vendor provides at least one language, which may, however, differ from package to package; and the in-house development group also purchases one or more general-purpose 4GLs. The multiple languages generally do not talk to one another. The languages present a major overhead-ache, given their learning curves, requirements for cross training, and dependence on trained personnel.

Databases have also become an issue when an organization purchases software. Since packages are seldom designed for a specific database management system, an organization might have to make a choice in selecting software based either on functionality or database compatibility. It therefore becomes difficult for an organization purchasing software to have a single-image corporate database of information. In turn, this limits the organization's ability to fit its software to the business's changing requirements.

Risks associated with purchased software also include such vendor-related issues as vendor stability, mergers, acquisitions, and nonperformance. Organizational issues include software modifications, training requirements, budgeting considerations, and installation standards.

Despite its downsides, purchased software is being hailed as among the few viable solutions to meeting an organization's market needs. Given its productivity benefits, packaged software enables companies to deliver complex systems in a relatively short time.

A new skill for the development function, then, is the effective selection of purchased software. This means that the organization must thoroughly understand its requirements, both functional and technical.

HOW TO DEFINE REQUIREMENTS-PLUS

The traditional software development life cycle consists of requirements analysis, software design, code, test/implementation, and maintenance/enhancement. Of these phases, the first and last, requirements and maintenance, respectively, are the stages most relevant to the purchase of packaged software. However, the concerns here are somewhat different than with in-house software.

As noted above, the key to successful software selection is establishing requirements. Although requirement definition has always been a critical phase in the software development life cycle, the steps must be expanded. Of course, functionality remains number one on an organization's checklist of requirements, whether it is developing its own software, buying a packaged application, or contracting with a supplier to have a custom system built. However, an organization purchasing a package must not only determine its functional requirements, it must analyze available software, and compare and weight the functional characteristics of each product to the requirements.

In this process, similar requirements can be grouped into these general classifications[4]:

- product capabilities — functional requirements for the type of software required, be it operating system or application software
- technical support information — including product documentation and operating systems supported
- implementation information — including report set-up, hardware requirements, software prerequisites, implementation effort, and complexity to change
- miscellaneous — including pricing and maintenance schedules, discounts, the installed base of users, vendor information, and user group information

As many companies are well aware, the major software vendors are formidable negotiators. Thus, software purchasers must understand both their opponents' and their own requirements. They must know, for example, the type of software needed, how it will be used, how many users will access it, and how frequently. They must also know whether the software will be deployed locally or globally, how soon it might be migrated to a different hardware platform, and if an outsourcer will at some point take charge of the software.

To date, few companies have much experience in replacing applications developed in-house with integrated commercial packages, so they rarely agree on the percentage of requirements that must be met out of the box. However, if users customize commercial software to any significant degree, they will suffer the consequences when they upgrade to the vendor's next release. Customization should never be undertaken lightly because customized functions might no longer work after a patch or a new system release. In addition, those purchasing software must realize that choice of a package involves many compromises. Some required functions might be only partially met, while others will be entirely missing. Unfortunately, software purchasers often do not understand their own requirements. So they select software based on specifications presented by a single vendor.

HOW TO NEGOTIATE A SOFTWARE LICENSE

Compared to those who bought technology in the past, today's software purchasers are far more sophisticated, possessing both financial and legal knowledge about software licensing issues. In addition, software is now becoming more of a buyer's than a seller's market, due to the competitive nature of the software market and the growing rate of technology change.

Information technology buyers must still anticipate difficult negotiations with vendors, however, due to the growing marketplace complexity. When mainframes and minicomputers were the only existing platforms, applications were licensed based on the box terminals. While this changed dramatically with client/server computing, traditional licensing models completely broke down with the advent of World Wide Web-based computing.

Software is generally licensed rather than sold because the product consists of intellectual property, plus the media it is printed on. Because the developing vendor technically retains ownership of the application, it negotiates a license governing its use with the purchaser. When IBM unbundled software from computer hardware in 1969, it became common practice for software vendors to explicitly price software licenses. However, both maintenance costs and license prices were based primarily on vendor experience with computer hardware maintenance, or the cost of the original software development.

By the 1980s, the major software pricing method had become tiered pricing, which was done in two ways. In the first, users paid a fixed price to start, and a monthly or annual maintenance fee for license renewal and support, usually between five and ten percent annually of the original fee. By the second tiered-pricing method, users paid a fixed initial fee for a specified term of use, and a subsequent monthly or annual maintenance fee for support.

Support in tiered pricing usually referred to corrections or bug fixes, as well as upgrades. These new versions included perfective and adaptive changes. If little or no maintenance fee was charged, bug fixes were generally free, installable patches; and upgrades were handled separately. Installation of the upgraded or corrected software was seldom included.

Beginning in the early 1990s, the primary software licensing model became 99-year or perpetual right-to-use licenses for a user or organization. However, there are many types of software licensing plans in use today. While software is sometimes licensed for use by a particular user, client/server applications that operate on a network might be priced on the number of PCs that have access. Purchasers might pay for software based on concurrent or named users, or on site-specific or global use. Alternatively, licenses might be based on servers, networks, or even on the customer's annual revenue. In general, organizations use a transaction-oriented approach in buying software licenses.[5]

Software buyers will have an edge if they know the vendor's motivations and the industry environment where it competes. Such an understanding can prevent miscommunications and misunderstandings. In addition, buyers can attempt to leverage volume by licensing software on a corporate-wide basis, rather than by divisions or business units.

In purchasing software, buyers would be wise to:

- obtain competitive bids from several vendors, which helps determine a market price to use in negotiations
- deal with a vendor executive
- understand the vendor's business model
- use a professional arbitrator
- demand clauses for maintenance and support
- try to use their own standard contract
- create a standard licensing process within their organization

Although obtaining the best price for software is important for the purchasing organization, flexibility should take precedence. After all, there are many organizational changes taking place that might in turn change the way the software is used. As examples, the organization might undergo a merger, an acquisition, data center consolidation, or centralization. When such an organizational change takes place, users might have to buy a new license, unless the contract specifies otherwise. In fact, some analysts have estimated a 70 percent probability that corporations that do not so specify, will have to repurchase their software license within three years.[1] In addition, an initial software license fee may account for only 10 to 15 percent of the total cost of ownership of software over five years. Thus, the purchasing organization might have opportunities for savings in usage rights, audit clauses, maintenance, and the rights to new versions.

In selling or licensing software, vendors initially try to sell the product for the highest price; they then attempt to earn more money on the sale over time. Because it gains them the most money, they try to make the license as restrictive as possible, giving them more control. Conversely, it is the purchasing organization's goal to obtain a less restrictive license.

The software license is the first product the vendor sells, but software maintenance is often a separate issue. Thus, in software maintenance, as in new development, there are classic choices of "do" or "buy." The choices might apply differently, depending if the maintenance is corrective, perfective, or adaptive. Most vendors offer a contract for maintenance or service, or a warranty. In this way, maintenance can become a marketable product and a source of revenue.[5]

HOW TO EVALUATE SOFTWARE VENDORS

Mergers, competition, and falling software prices are corroding standard software support and services. In this marketplace, purchasing organizations should add new requirements when evaluating software vendors. They should consider:

- Human factors — before purchasing packages, organizations should judge the vendor's quality of interaction with human beings for software support and customer service. They might even call the technical support line, timing how long it takes to get through and assessing how difficult questions are handled.
- Corporate structure — purchasing organizations should determine if the vendor is a publicly or privately held corporation. If the former, the vendor might aim at maximizing shareholders' investments. If the latter, its goal might be customer satisfaction. In addition, the buyer should determine if the software being evaluated is the vendor's primary offering or only one of many products, how much the vendor has invested in development, how often it issues new releases, how committed it is to the product, and what the effect would be if support were lost.
- Size in relation to customer focus — smaller companies tend to place more emphasis on customer care than larger ones.
- User input into product development — if the software is strategic to the purchaser's business, the buying organization should determine what impact it can have on future product development. For example, it should ascertain how the vendor responds to customer input, if it can take part in beta programs, and how the vendor handles customer feedback on enhancements and improvements. After all, the buying organization can best protect its software investment if it can influence product development.[6]

CONCLUSION

For whatever reason users are buying packaged software, the fact remains that commercial software has great and growing appeal. There are several trends in software purchasing that call for action on the part of purchasing organizations.

For starters, ERP package solutions will continue to replace user-developed applications, so buyers should develop flexible enterprise agreements to meet their business needs. In addition, software vendors are increasingly dependent on maintenance revenue, and buyers should see it as a strategic imperative to negotiate maintenance terms as part of the initial license agreement. Furthermore, buyers should be wary of the increased risk in software contracts resulting from the continued consolidation of vendors. Enterprises should also seek multinational software agreements to address global requirements. Finally, with the Internet accelerating the rate of change in technology, purchasers should aim at increased flexibility in their software license agreements.[1]

Packaged applications are becoming strategic to many businesses. Therefore, software buyers should attempt to form strategic relationships with these types of suppliers, versus those who sell commodity-type products, such as Netscape and Microsoft. It pays dividends for an organization to have a good rapport with a package supplier because the buyer is dependent on the vendor for products.

In short, today's software development environment has new skill requirements, including the selection of computer software, the negotiation of licenses, and the choice of and partnership with vendors. Savvy developers would be wise to buff and enhance their skills to deal with these new needs posed by package acquisition, deployment, customization, and maintenance.

To ensure job security in a changing environment, developers would be wise to take immediate action. Since requirements are so critical in successful package and vendor selection, their first step should be to **become proficient at establishing requirements.** In this effort, a spreadsheet might be a helpful tool in spelling out the functional requirements, listing the available software, and comparing and weighting the functional characteristics of each product in terms of requirements.

Next, because license negotiation is so critical, developers should **learn negotiation skills.** To this end, developers can take a class in negotiation, given by a business school, an adult education provider, or a private organization.

For the best outcome in negotiations, developers should also **develop a standard contract** for their company, which includes a maintenance clause. Finally, because so much effort is generally involved in "reinventing the wheel," they should help to **create a standard licensing process** within their organization.

Notes

1. Don't be a licensing lightweight! by Rick Whiting. *Software Magazine*, January 1998, pp. 20–2+.
2. Agencies want their apps off the shelf, survey reveals, by Florence Olsen, *Government Computer News*, September 29, 1997, p. 1, 8.
3. ERP more than a 2000 fix, by Craig Stedman, *Computerworld*, August 3, 1998, p. 1, 84.
4. Selecting computer center software, by Howard Miller, *Enterprise Management Issues*, September/October 1997, pp. 19–21+.
5. Software licensing models amid market turbulence, by Cris Wendt and Nicholas Imparato, *Journal of Software Maintenance*, 9, 1997, pp. 271–80.
6. Does size really matter? by John Lipsey, *AS/400*, February 1998, pp. 19–20+.

Chapter 16

Web-Based Customer Self Service: Justifying And Planning Applications

John Care

Leading companies use the World Wide Web to gain powerful competitive advantages in sales, support, marketing, customer service, and product delivery. Strategic use of the Web enhances communication and enables companies to attract new customers, decrease costs, and increase long-term customer loyalty. Yet the *Wall Street Journal* reported in late 1997 that 80 percent of the Fortune 500 sites it contacted via the Internet requesting product information or service failed to respond.

A Forrester Research survey of 40 companies with active Internet service sites released in December 1997 showed that 13 percent of calls were being handled across the Web. Respondents expected this number to rise to 31 percent over the next two years.

CUSTOMER SELF-SERVICE

Call center directors report that between 80 and 90 percent of incoming calls to their customer support organization involve issues and questions that have been previously reported by and solved for other customers. A common heuristic is that 85 percent of calls relate to usability and functionality ("How do I"), 10 percent are administrative, and only 5 percent truly deal with new errors and faults.

Given that at least four calls out of five should be able to be solved with some minimal research, three obvious categories for productivity improvements suggest themselves. First, the use of a search engine to perform keyword searches; second, utilizing a knowledge base to solve problems via a question and answer session; and thirdly — let the customer solve their own problem.

Based on the current technology infrastructure, use of the World Wide Web is rapidly becoming the accepted mechanism for self-service support. However, before embarking on the path of simply posting some Web pages

0-8493-9822-3/00/$0.00+$.50

containing Frequently Asked Questions (FAQs), there are many other considerations to note.

This article addresses each of these points below and provides some practical insights for organizations looking to justify, build, and deploy a Web-based self-service solution:

- technology set
- return on investment
- user interface
- 24 by 7 uptime
- customer management
- sales and marketing
- implementation
- vision

The Technology Set

The technology choice is actually one of the lesser issues of basic self-service support. As long as a standard Web browser is utilized, with no special software or security requirements, virtually any Web development environment tied to any open support system can be used. A more major test of technology is that of scalability, as most initial estimates of Web site hits are woefully inaccurate. To design a scaleable architecture, it is worth reviewing a brief history of Web page technologies.

Static HTML. Static HTML can be considered the original Web access approach. A user navigates to a URL, the browser looks for the server machine on the Internet, and having found it, requests the specific page. The page is then sent to the browser, which interprets the HTML tags and converts it to a neatly formatted page.

CGI and Forms. Static HTML is a one-way connection as there is no means to send data back to the server. The use of forms allowed designers to place edits and check boxes on their pages. CGI (Common Gateway Interface) makes it possible for the server to pass form data to another application. Typically, CGI functions well for smaller sites, but runs into scalability problems for larger applications. Each person submitting form information requires his or her own copy of the CGI application to run on the server. Often this process has to load a large program such as the Perl interpreter. Many early interactive Web sites fell into this trap and responded by adding more and hardware.

The APIs. As a result of the scaling issues, server side APIs were developed. Microsoft produced ISAPI and Netscape the ISAPI. Either API provides similar functionality by not starting another program for every form to server communication. However, the APIs are fairly complex and still require programs to manage the interfaces to the Web server. Once written, NS/ISAPI programs (usually coded in C or Perl) require regular maintenance, assuming a site is keeping its content fresh.

The ASP. Active Server Pages provide the efficiencies of API access without all the complexity and programming. In an ASP system, code is written, using a scripting language, within the HTML page along with the tags themselves. When a Web server locates an ASP page (annotated with an .asp extension), the code is executed on the server itself, generating, in effect, a pure HTML page. An often quoted security advantage is that the ASP code is stripped out before the page is sent to a browser, preventing access to the source of proprietary applications.

ASP is a feature of the Microsoft Internet Information Server (IIS), but pages can be delivered to both Microsoft Internet Explorer and Netscape Navigator. It is important to note that ASP is different from client-side scripting. Although client-side and server-side scripting share many similarities, and can be used concurrently, client-side scripts:

- are downloaded as part of the page and are visible to the user; therefore, one's code could be modified and/or stolen
- can only run on browsers that support the language being used
- are run by the browser only after the page has been downloaded from the server

The majority of ASP pages are created using either VBScript or Jscript. Generally, VBScript is considered easier to learn for those with minimal scripting or programming background, while Jscript is positioned as a language for the more experienced programmer. From personal experience, those familiar with VBScript or even Visual Basic will discover that there are common functions, such as InputBox or MsgBox, which are not supported in the ASP environment. Another hard-learned lesson is that Jscript is case-sensitive, while VBScript is not.

Return on Investment (ROI)

The economics of self-service support can be truly compelling. However, be warned that even conducting a rudimentary ROI analysis can reveal some significant gaps in the cost structure of a call center. The example shown in Exhibit 16.1 shows a simple breakdown of cost savings using extremely conservative cost numbers.[1]

However, numerous other factors will materialize once the system is released.

1. Call center volume will actually increase after Web access is in use for several months. This strange phenomenon is explained by the fact that the better support one provides, the more often customers

Exhibit 16.1. Breakdown of Cost Savings

Calls handled per month		10,000
Average cost of first call		$12
Average cost of Web response		$1
Percent of calls handled via Web		23%
Status calls		12%
Maint/patch/collateral		5%
New cases		6%
Cost of sending CD or literature		$8
Cost Savings	=	10,000 calls * 23% *($10 – $1) + (10,000 * 5% * $8)
	=	$26,300 + $4000
	=	$30,300 per month

will call. Customers are also more likely to hit a Web site for an update rather than call in for an update. The huge success of the Federal Express online package tracker (http://www.fedex.com/us/tracker) is a testimonial to this effect.

2. Average call length will tend to slowly increase, as 'easy' questions will be siphoned off to the Web. Some callers will have exhausted all self-help possibilities before picking up the phone.
3. The competition will regard one's support Web site as a source of useful information.
4. Storage and postage charges for CDs, diskettes, and other hard collateral will diminish.
5. Within a few months, most corporations re-examine their support cost structures with a view to driving/incenting customers to the Web.

In fact, a recent study[2] showed that a full Internet customer service rollout for a hypothetical $650 million company could save 43 percent of the labor cost per customer contact by the year 2000. The full savings came to $780,000 or more.

User Interface

The user interface of a self-service site is of equal importance to the content itself. In order to continue to drive usage after the first few visits, a site needs to provide a user-customized option for the interface as well as the content similar to a "My Yahoo" style of front page (see Error! Bookmark not defined.). The more a customer feels he owns and has control of the page, the more it will be used. Although frame technology has recently been in vogue, there seems to be movement away from this metaphor back to standard buttons and pseudo drop-down menus.[3]

As a general guide, pages should provide a "home," a "next," and a "restart" button. On any page on the Web site, it should be intuitively obvious, or obviously labeled, as to what is the next expected step. Error messages should be user oriented — "You failed to fill in a required field" is a distant second to "We need your zip code, please press the back button and type it in."

Avoid animated GIFS or multimedia-intensive pages. For a business to consumer self-service site, it is a reasonable assumption that access will be at 28.8kbps. This should therefore be the speed your QA group uses to test the site.

Lights-Out (24×7) Support

Self-service support does allow for "cheap" 24 by 7 support. A typical 12 by 5 support center should expect a minor surge of activity every morning, based on the prior evening, and a larger peak awaiting them on a Monday morning from weekend access. Although initially a significant number of companies priced 24 by 7 Web access into their basic support services, there is a growing initiative for Web support to be the standard package, and make 1-800 "live" access the premium service. Either way, one is in a position of offering better service outside of classic business hours.

The 24 by 7 support option will require that the Web server, resolution, and support databases, plus any other back-end systems be monitored for uptime and failures. This will usually necessitate automated pager support for these services from the IT organization.

Customer Management

The perception of giving away support makes it difficult to manage customer expectations. Some demanding customers will want the provider to solve all their problems, while others may not use the service as it is free and one "gets what one pays for."

Word of mouth in the marketplace can also be a predictor of customer management. Research originally conducted for the Coca-Cola Company's Consumer Affairs Department shows that customers who are dissatisfied with a company's products tell twice as many people about their experiences as those who are satisfied.

Multiple TARP surveys[4] have shown that, on average, 50 percent of consumers and 25 percent of business customers who have problems never complain to anyone. Furthermore, problem experiences reduce customer loyalty by 10 to 30 percent. For every five customers who have an unpleasant experience, a corporation is at risk of losing some or all future revenue from at least one of them. An oft-quoted article, "Learning from Customer Defections" by Frederick F. Reicheld,[5] states: "On average, the CEOs of U.S. corporations lose half their customers every five years."

The message behind these statistics is that although self-service support is an excellent way of increasing customer service and potentially decreasing customer defections, it must be done with a purpose. Technology-aware customers will have great expectations of a Web site and will assume that all posted information is current and that any interactions will be conducted as fast as, if not faster than, person-to-person over the telephone. Should a corporation not be willing to commit to this, it is simply offering its customers yet another item to complain about.

Sales and Marketing

Approximately 70 percent of customer contacts a typical United States corporation has with its customers are through its support services. Any customer contact is a selling opportunity; a satisfied customer is likely to give a company more business. The support features of a Web site should always provide some means of selling to those satisfied customers.

To satisfy the sales and marketing organizations, self-service customers should be able to:

- ask for a sales representative to contact them
- request literature on any product or service
- upgrade or renew any of their existing products or services
- purchase a product

Organizations sophisticated enough to have segmented their customers based on profitability can at least prioritize service based on these rankings. Common business sense dictates that it is better to keep the most profitable customers happy and offer premium services rather than provide a one-size-fits-all approach. Applying the infamous Pareto Principle, which states that 20 percent of customers generate 80 percent of profit, is an excellent start. This ratio can vary widely: in the car rental industry the top 0.5 percent of customers account for 25 percent of rentals. At one midwestern bank, the top 27 percent of customers accounted for 100 percent of profit and covered the losses incurred by the 31 percent of customers on whom the bank was losing money.[6]

Implementation

For the development manager charged with building and deploying a self-service site, the most important piece of advice is plan. Despite the fact that this is a Web project, and tasks are measured in days instead of weeks, an outline project plan is still a requirement. However, a good plan executed well this week is better than a perfect plan started next quarter.

Having gathered the basic requirements, it is essential to prioritize the scope — just like any other project. The Help Desk Institute suggests that the project team focus on two or three big wins for both the support center and the customers — such as online case submission, status checks, or knowledge base searches. Once phase I has been rolled out, stop and monitor the site, actively seek customer feedback for improvement, and build on that feedback. Then market the site, educate the customers on its use, and, above all, focus on the fact that the customer just wants to get the answer as quickly as possible.

Introduction of the tools and technologies to create the site frequently leads to the realization that support processes have to be re-examined. For example, encouraging customers to use the site to check problem status means that statuses need to be updated regularly and accurately. As soon as a CSR takes any action on a call, it should be noted; and if workflow in the package does not support this automatically then the CSRs need to be retrained. SLAs (Service Level Agreements) need to be enforced to measure response time, escalations, and callback metrics.

One other important process in an online support center is the creation of a knowledge expert who has the authority to publish resolutions and other materials to the site (in conjunction with the Web master). This prevents multiple solutions to a problem being posted and has also saved many organizations the embarrassment of having internal documents published to their customers. The knowledge expert also has a responsibility for consistency as well as content. As soon as a user searches for a resolution and the engine brings up more than one hit, he becomes less confident that it will work. If the Web site brings back a screenful of solutions, the user will pick up the phone and call anyway.

From the tools and technology viewpoint, there are two approaches. First, many enterprise support packages, such as Clarify, Remedy, and Vantive, already offer "out-of-the-box" self service products that integrate with their current offerings. These modules can then be customized using standard tools such as Microsoft Interdev or Frontpage. Second is the use of an in-place homegrown system with a customized Web user interface. Irrespective of the approach, there is a broad list of hardware and software prerequisites, including:

- high-speed Internet access
- a corporate network supporting an intranet
- hardware for the Web server delivering pages
- Web server software
- An e-mail server (based on the expected volume of incoming e-mails)
- a database server and software for storing customer data
- (optional) a middle-tier application server
- Internet browsers (Netscape and Microsoft)
- a test environment
- HTML development editor and source control software (most RDBMS vendors supply their own JDBC interfaces)
- (optional) CTI/telephony integration

Vision

Providing online access to problem resolutions, patches, FAQs, and case submission should be viewed as just the first phase of this new paradigm. As more and more consumers are driven to the Web, incremental services added to the support site could serve to differentiate competitive product offerings. Forward-thinking corporations already building their third generation sites are looking to incorporate a plethora of new technologies.

Education. IDC surveyed 200 representative businesses and determined that the United States will spend nearly $13 billion on training programs in the year 2001 for IT training alone. Technology-based training (i.e., non-classroom instructor led) will account for one third of that market. For corporations delivering technology products — notably software vendors — the capability to cheaply and efficiently deliver Web-based education will be key. Companies such as Asymetrix and Docent already have 1.0 products in the marketplace to meet this need.

E-mail. The volume of e-mail, notably from end-user consumers, is already rapidly rising and widely regarded as an instant-turnaround form of rapid communication. Failure to acknowledge and respond to customer e-mail is as large a breach of the relationship as a 30-minute hold time. Incorporating a rules-based e-mail tracking and response system will ensure that these messages do not slip through the cracks. Products such as eGain from eGain Communications and @Once Express from BEI are already serving these needs.

Call Passthru. No matter how well designed the site and the system, some users will experience difficulties or will require assistance after they have exhausted online services. Providing a "Call Me" button either linked to the phone number from their profile — via Internet telephony or standard AT&T style — or associated with the initiation of an Internet chat session gives the customer a last resort action. Once a customer has transferred into a phone queue from the Web site, they should be placed at or near the front of queue and not at the back.

Data Passthru. Self-service Web sites should be paired with self-help applications. In short, an application should be able to self-diagnose and provide data across a Web link to an intelligent agent within a self-service system. Applications of this kind for the diagnosis of PC problems are already proving to highly successful. Add-on products such as Rescue are transforming the face of high-tech support.

CONCLUSION

In summary, just as AOL has brought the Internet to the general public, the increasing costs of personal telephone support are bringing the Internet to the customers of U.S. corporations. Numerous research surveys and case studies have all shown that the early adopters of Web-based self-service support have gained economic and competitive advantages. However, as in any other major undertaking, a careful amount of planning, involving not only the support and IT organizations, but also sales and marketing, is necessary before embarking on the creation of self-service Web sites. These are not soft dollars; the COO of a financial services company recently stated to this author that the revenue impact of service improvements were an order of magnitude greater than the cost impact. After all, customers are responsible for 100 percent of your revenue.

Notes

1. The SSPA (Software Support Professionals Association) reports that a member survey indicated the cost per call ranged from $9 to $200, with $53 being the industry average.
2. Forrester Research available at www.forrester.com.
3. Creative Good (http://www.creativegood.com), a usability consulting company, provides a free e-mail letter that includes usability news, site design tips, and reviews of Internet commerce sites.
4. An overview of these surveys can be found in the September 1998 issue of *Teleprofessional Magazine* (Technology Access Research Programs).
5. *Harvard Business Review*, March/April 1996. Reprint #96210.
6. An excellent treatment of customer value is provided by Don Peppers and Martha Rogers (http://www.1to1.com/-) *CIO Magazine*, Sept. 15th, (http://www.cio.com/archive/enterprise/091598_hs_content.html).

Companies cited in this article

Asymetrix	http://www.asymetrix.com/
Docent	http://www.docent.com/
Egain Communications	http://www.egain.com/
BEI	http://www.businessevolution.com/
Rescue	http://www.rescueme.net/
Clarify	http://www.clarify.com/
Siebel	http://www.siebel.com/
Vantive	http://www.vantive.com/

Chapter 17

Software Metrics: Quantifying and Analyzing Software for Total Quality Management

Bijoy Bordoloi and Joe Luchetski

ONCE AN IS DEPARTMENT HAS ESTABLISHED A SOFTWARE DEVELOPMENT PROCESS, it must quantitatively determine the parameters associated with that process and its products. A quantitative approach allows the organization to compare its performance with that of its competitors. Weaknesses and areas requiring management's attention are highlighted, and benchmarks are established to measure the organization's future improvement. These quantitative measurements are performed using software metrics.

Today, software metrics are enjoying widespread interest as mainstream IS organizations adopt the Total Quality Management (TQM) strategy and its emphasis on quantitative measurement. This renewed inquisitiveness is generating new and increasingly powerful metrics.

Software metrics are quantifiable measures used to determine various characteristics of a software system or a software development process. Software system characteristics are typically size, complexity, and reliability, whereas the software development process is characterized by cost and allocation of resources. The product versus process classification is the most common method of differentiating software metrics. However, other metric classifications have been suggested, including:

- Predictor versus result
- Direct versus indirect
- Subjective versus objective
- Quality versus productivity

0-8493-9822-3/00/$0.00+$.50

None of these classifications are mutually exclusive. They serve to characterize the point of view of the metric user rather than the metric itself.

PROCESS METRICS

Process metrics are also known as resource or global metrics. Their objective is to quantify characteristics for the overall software development process, as opposed to the characteristics for a specific life cycle phase. Typically, process metrics predict overall cost, total development time, work effort, or the staffing levels and durations required to implement a software development project. Most process metrics are based on empirical data and employ a series of adjustments to tailor their predictions to the specific product and development process. They are designed to be used very early in the development process, usually by the end of the requirements analysis phase or early in the system design phase. Often, they are constructed to allow metric users to revise and refine their predictions as the software development process progresses.

FUNCTION POINT METRICS

The function-oriented approach allows the function points for a particular project to be calculated very early in the development process, usually in the requirements analysis phase and no later than the system design phase.

The number of function points for a particular project is calculated as follows. First, five product parameters are counted:

- Number of external inputs
- Number of external outputs
- Number of logical internal files (i.e., master files)
- Number of external interface files
- Number of external inquiries

Each parameter is assigned a complexity rating based on a three-level scale, simple (i.e., low complexity), average, or complex (i.e., high complexity), as shown in Exhibit 17.1. Each parameter count is multiplied by its

Exhibit 17.1. Complexity Rating

	Complexity Rating				
Parameter	**Count**	**Low**	**Average**	**High**	**Total**
Inputs	x3	x4	x6	=	
Outputs	x4	x5	x7	=	
Logical Internal Files	x7	x10	x15	=	
External Interface Files	x5	x7	x10	=	
External Inquiries	x3	x4	x6	=	
	Total Unadjusted Function Points (FC)				____

assigned complexity rating, and the resulting values are summed to obtain the total unadjusted function points (FC).

Next, the Degree of Influence is determined for each of the project's 14 general characteristics. The Degree of Influence is based on the following six-level scale:

- Not present/no influence = 0
- Insignificant influence = 1
- Moderate influence = 2
- Average influence = 3
- Significant influence = 4
- Strong influence = 5

The 14 general characteristics are as follows:

- Data communications
- Distributed functions
- Performance
- Heavy use configuration
- Transaction rate
- On-line data entry
- End-user efficiency
- On-line update
- Complex processing
- Reusability
- Installation ease
- Operational ease
- Multiple sites
- Facilitated change

The degrees of influence for all 14 characteristics are summed together to yield the total degree of influence (DI). The Processing Complexity Adjustment (PCA) is calculated using the formula PCA = 0.65 * 0.01 DI. Finally, the number of function points for the project is calculated by the formula:

$$\text{Function points} = FC(PCA)$$

To determine the size, cost, or work effort required for a particular project, its calculated function point value is compared to historical data for projects with the same or relatively similar values.

With the size and availability of historical data increasing rapidly, the function point method is probably the most widely used metric; however, it is not without its critics. The popularity and widespread use of function points has spurred the development of a number of variations.[1] These alternate methods and the subjectivity required to determine complexity ratings and degree of influence have caused a number of experts to question function point reliability. The International Function Point User Group (IFPUG) has attempted to address these concerns by publishing the *IFPUG Function Point Counting Practices Manual,* offering training and certification in function point methodology and by funding a study with the Massachusetts Institute of Technology to evaluate function point reliability.

This study, by Chris F. Kemerer, examined interrater and intermethod reliabilities using more than 100 different function point totals from 27 actual commercial systems. Interrater reliability attempted to determine whether evaluation of the same system by two different individuals would result in the same value. Intermethod reliability attempted to determine whether evaluation of the same system using the IFPUG methodology versus one of the variations would result in significantly different function point values. The study's findings indicate that function point raters and methods are robust and reliable. The median interrater variation was approximately 12 percent, whereas the correlation across two methods was as high as 95 percent.[2]

THE CONSTRUCTIVE COST MODEL

Barry Boehm developed the Constructive Cost Model (CoCoMo) to predict the work effort and development time required for the management and technical staffs in a software development project. The formulas do not include support staff, such as secretaries. In addition, CoCoMo covers only the development phases, not the full software life cycle. CoCoMo estimates begin with the system design phase (i.e., after the system requirements have been analyzed) and conclude with the integration and system test phase. CoCoMo does not include installation of the product or maintenance. However, the model can be used for maintenance predictions by adjusting the parameters and drivers to reflect the maintenance task, environment, and reuse of design and code.

CoCoMo is size-oriented. Its estimates are based on the number of lines of source code delivered in thousands. The model is designed to provide predictions at three levels, basic, intermediate, or detailed, depending on the information known about the product. The model is also constructed to allow the user to adjust the prediction to compensate for the project's complexity and the development environment. This is accomplished using three modes (i.e., organic, semidetached, or embedded), 15 cost drivers, phase-sensitive effort multipliers, and a three-level product hierarchy.

The basic CoCoMo formulas take the general form:

$$\text{Effort (in person months)} = K_d = a(\text{KDSI})^b \text{ and}$$

$$\text{Development Time (in months)} = t_d = a(K_d)^b$$

where:

KDSI = thousands of delivered source instructions.

The values of the parameters a and b are determined by the project mode and the model's prediction level. For effort (K_d), a equals:

Prediction Level Mode	Basic	Intermediate	Detailed
Organic	2.4	3.2	3.2
Semidetached	3.0	3.0	3.0
Embedded	3.6	2.8	2.8

Also, b varies with mode only:

Mode	For All Prediction Levels
Organic	1.05
Semidetached	1.12
Embedded	1.20

For development time (t_d), a equals 2.5 for all three modes and prediction levels, and b varies with the mode only:

Mode	For All Prediction Levels
Organic	0.38
Semidetached	0.35
Embedded	0.32

Mode is used to categorize the project type. Organic mode projects are typically developed by a small team, highly experienced with this type of application and the language used for implementation. Organic projects have fairly loose requirements.

Embedded projects exist at the other end of the spectrum. They are unique and technologically challenging, with stringent requirements. The project team is large and has very little experience with this type of application and language.

The semidetached mode falls somewhere between the easy organic and the difficult embedded projects. Semidetached projects are moderately complex, and the development team has a degree of familiarity with this type of project and the language.

The basic prediction level is used to obtain a quick-and-dirty estimate of the overall project's effort (i.e., K_d) and development time (i.e., t_d). This level is intended for use early in the development process, either at the end of the requirements analysis phase, or as soon as a reasonable estimate of the lines of source code is available. The predictions at this level can be adjusted for mode only.

Intermediate CoCoMo

This is the most commonly used prediction model. To the mode adjustment, intermediate CoCoMo adds 15 cost drivers to tailor the effort estimate to the complexity and development environment for the specific project. The data required to use intermediate CoCoMo should be available in the system design phase and definitely by the detailed design phase. This allows the metric user to refine and to update the estimates calculated using basic CoCoMo. In fact, CoCoMo estimates can be modified whenever development parameters change, the estimate of the KDSI improves, or new information becomes available.

The intermediate CoCoMo cost drivers are grouped into four attributes, as follows:

- Product attributes:
  - Required software reliability (RELY)
  - Database size (DATA)
  - Product complexity (CPLX)
- Computer attributes:
  - Execution time constraints (TIME)
  - Main storage constraints (STOR)
  - Virtual machine volatility (VIRT)
  - Computer turnaround time (TURN)
- Personnel attributes:
  - Analyst capability (ACAP)
  - Applications experience (AEXP)
  - Programmer capability (PCAP)
  - Machine familiarity and experience (VEXP)
  - Programming language experience (LEXP)
- Project attributes:
  - Modern programming practices (MODP)
  - Use of software (CASE) tools (TOOL)
  - Development schedule (SCED)

The effect of each cost driver is rated on a six-level scale: very low, low, normal, high, very high, or extra high. For most cost drivers, a numerical value is given for each rating level, with nominal always corresponding to a rating of 1.00. The appropriate rating for each driver is selected, and all selected values are multiplied together to yield the effort adjustment factor (EAF). The EAF adjusts the effort estimate as follows:

$$K_{dADJ} = EAF(K_d)$$

Intermediate CoCoMo also allows the total effort estimate to be partitioned into several life cycle phases, including product design (i.e., analogous to system design), detailed design, code and unit test, and integration and test. The partitioning is accomplished by project size (e.g., small [2 KD-SI], intermediate [8 KDSI], or medium [32 KDSI]) using a series of tables that provides an estimate of the total effort (by percentage) expended in each life cycle phase. Separate tables are provided for each project mode.

Detailed CoCoMo

This model adds two more enhancements to intermediate CoCoMo. The first enhancement provides separate cost driver ratings for each of the four life cycle phases covered by the model. The other enhancement allows the metric user to track the product through a three-level development hierarchy. These levels are module, subsystem, and system. Most authors agree that the increased complexity of the detailed level does not significantly improve the accuracy of CoCoMo estimates.

The effort and development time estimates are used to calculate productivity in KDSI/per month, full-time staffing levels (FSP), and peak FSP. These values can be obtained for the overall project and for individual phases, depending on the CoCoMo level used. Most other authors find the accuracy of CoCoMo estimates to be highly dependent on the selection of the cost driver ratings, which is a fairly subjective selection process. It is recommended that IS departments develop a database of CoCoMo estimates and the corresponding actual project data to allow future CoCoMo estimates to be calibrated to the organizations' specific development processes.

THE PUTNAM CURVE

Lawrence H. Putnam, in his characterization of the software development process, took a theoretical approach and validated it with empirical data. Putnam's theoretical approach is based on the work of Norden, who based his work on Lord Rayleigh's.[3]

Lord Rayleigh developed Rayleigh curves to explain the behavior of surface disturbances or waves. He observed that these waves are governed by two forces: one force acts on the rising edge of the disturbance, and the other acts on the decaying edge. He postulated that the overall shape of the wave could be modeled as a function of the relative changes in the magnitudes of the two forces over time. Exhibit 17.2 illustrates Rayleigh curves.

Norden postulated that the effort and time duration for research and development projects could be characterized using Rayleigh curves. Norden hypothesized that Rayleigh curves also describe the way people

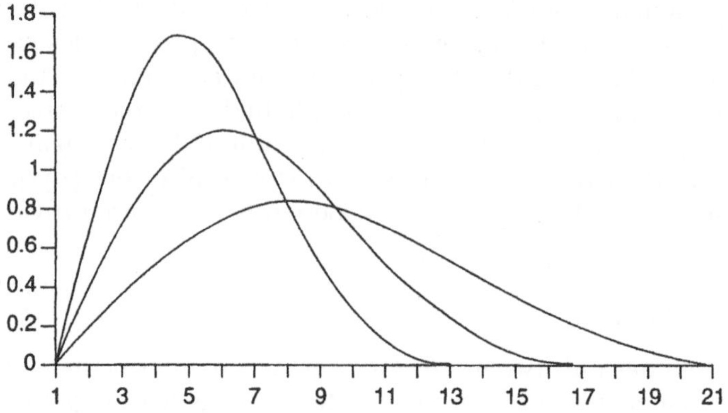

SOURCE: T.G. Lewis, *CASE: Computer-Aided Software Engineering* (New York: Van Nostrand Reinhold, 1991)

Exhibit 17.2. Rayleigh Curves

approach and solve problems, and R&D projects are just a series of problem-solving opportunities. The rising force of the Rayleigh curve models the increasing knowledge (i.e., the learning curve) associated with continued problem solving. The decaying-force models the decreasing amount of work or problems remaining to be solved over time. Therefore, each phase in the development of a new product would conform to the shape of a Rayleigh curve, as shown in Exhibit 17.3, and the sum of all the individual curves would also follow a Rayleigh distribution.

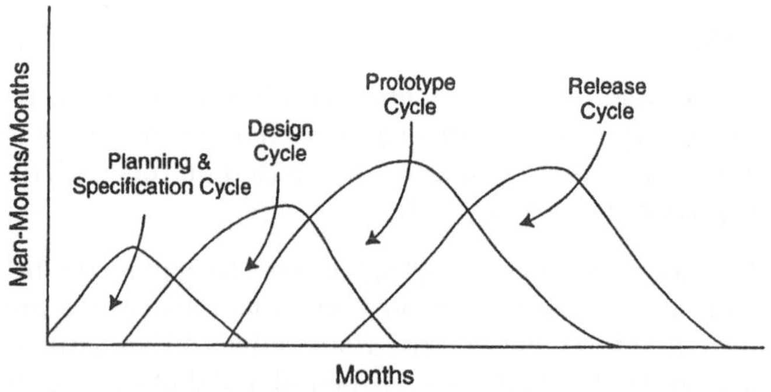

SOURCE: Victor R. Basili, "Resource Models," *Tutorial on Models and Metrics for Software Management and Engineering.* (New York: Computer Society Press, 1980)

Exhibit 17.3. Norden Characterization of an R&D Project Using Rayleigh Curves

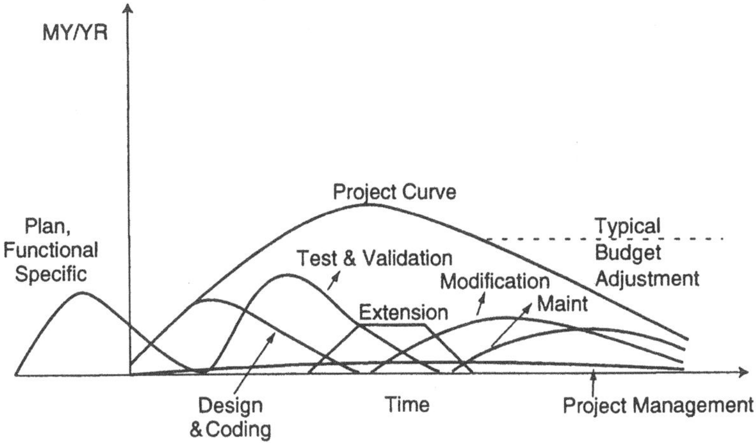

SOURCE: Lawrence H. Putnam, "A General Empirical Solution to the Macro Software Sizing and Estimating Problem," *IEEE Transactions on Software Engineering* SE-4 (1978)

Exhibit 17.4. Putnam Characterization of a Software Development Project Using Norden/Rayleigh Model

Putnam extended Norden's work to the description of the phases in the software development cycle, as shown in Exhibit 17.4, and the cycle itself. He validated this extension using data from approximately 200 large systems developed for the U.S. Army's Computer Systems Command. For most of these systems, the software development process followed the Norden/Rayleigh model well.

The general form of the Putnam curve to describe the software development process is $y = K(1 - e^{-at2})$,

where:

- y = the cumulative effort expended through time t
- K = total effort required for the entire life cycle
- a = shape parameter
- t = number of time periods since the beginning of the project

The shape parameter a is calculated by taking the first derivative of the general form and solving for a when y′ is at a maximum. The first derivative *y′* represents the peak staffing level for the project and is expressed as $y' = 2Kate^{-at2}$.

For large systems, Putnam's empirical analysis determined that y'_{max} occurs when t is approximately equal to the system development time (t_d), which is at the end of the design and coding phase. Based on the shape of the total project curve, Putnam concluded that 39.35% of the total life cycle effort is expended developing the system and 60% expended testing, maintaining, and modifying it.

Putnam used the Norden/Rayleigh model and his empirical data to determine several other mathematical relationships to explain the software development process. Two of the most interesting relationships are the project difficulty and the time-effort conservation law. Putnam observed that project difficulty (D) could be expressed as:

$$D = K/t_d^2$$

where:

K = total effort required for the entire life cycle
t_d = development time

A small value of D indicates a relatively easy system to develop; a large D value corresponds to a hard system.

The time-effort conservation law is based on Putnam's observation that Kt_d^4 is a constant. This indicates that effort (K) and development time (t_d) are inversely related, an intuitively obvious relationship, but as a function of the fourth power of t_d^4. The practical use of this relationship becomes apparent when evaluating the effect of reducing td to compress the project schedule. The total effort required (K) increases as a function of t_d, yielding a very large increase in effort (ΔK) for even relatively small development time reductions (Δt_d).

Putnam's curve and its various mathematical relationships are used to predict costs, development, and total schedules, and work effort required to support the software life cycle. The relationships are also employed to evaluate the effects of various resource constraints and to perform what-if scenario analyses. The few basic assumptions required to use the curve can be made during the requirements analysis phase and later refined and updated as the project progresses.

Analysts have found Putnam curve predictions to consistently overstate the effort and development time required, especially for small- and medium-sized systems. Nevertheless, it provides viable estimates that can be used in worst-case scenarios or with other process metrics.

The Putnam curve is sometimes referred to as Putnam's Software Life Cycle Model (SLIM). However, SLIM is a proprietary CASE tool offered by Quantitative Software Management, Inc. that uses Putnam's concepts.

PRODUCT METRICS

Process metrics concentrate on how the overall software development process performs (i.e., costs, schedule, and resource allocations); product metrics, on the other hand, concentrate on what the process produces. Product metrics focus on the quantitative evaluation of the output of individual phases in the development process. The majority of the product metrics focus on code-related attributes, such as size, complexity, and reliability, but the trend is moving toward the evaluation of the output of the system design and detailed design phases. These product metrics attempt to measure design structure.

SOFTWARE SCIENCE

Software science metrics are size-oriented code metrics, but they are not lines of code counts. Instead, all of Maurice Halstead's metrics are theoretically derived and focus on a count of the operands and the operators in a program or module. Operands are all the variables and constants used in the program (e.g., x, y, Π, 57; whereas operators are all the symbols used to affect or to order an operands (e.g., +, –, *, <, >, GO TO). The operands and operator counts for a program are defined as follows:

n_1 = number of unique or distinct operators

n_2 = number of unique or distinct operands

N_1 = total number of occurrences for all operators

N_2 = total number of occurrences for all operands

From these counts, two basic program attributes are calculated. One is program vocabulary (*n*) where:

$$N = N_1 + N_2$$

The other is observed program length (N), where:

$$N = N_1 + N_2$$

All software science metrics are calculated from these counts and totals and are summarized as follows. For the mathematical details of each metric, interested readers are referred to Halstead's monograph.

- Estimated Program Length (N) is calculated from the number of unique operators (n_1) and operands (n_2).
- Program Volume (V) is the size of the program in bits of information. This value is dependent on the programming language used; the more powerful the language, the lower the V value.
- Program Volume (V*) is the minimum theoretical volume in bits of information. This value is programming-language independent.
- Program Level (L) indicates how well a given algorithm has been implemented in a specific language. It is the ratio of V* and V. Values of L vary between 0 (i.e., poor) and 1 (i.e., perfect).
- Intelligence Content (I) is the language-independent information content of a given algorithm. The value of I should remain constant for

implementations of a given algorithm in different programming languages.

- Programming Effort (E) is the total number of elementary mental discriminations required to generate a program.
- Estimated Programming Time (T) is the estimate of time required to generate a program. Calculated using programming effort (E) and the Stroud Number, typically 18 mental discriminations per second.
- Language Level (γ) is the relative power of a programming language. The higher the γ value, the more powerful the language.

To use software science metrics, source code must be available. Therefore, the application of these metrics is limited to the coding and unit test phase and the operation and maintenance phase. In these phases, the metrics measure the relative size of the program or module. A large-size measurement may indicate high complexity, poor or inefficient programming, and a large number of faults. In this way, software science metrics identify code that is a likely candidate for rework or additional testing. In the operation and maintenance phase, the metrics are also used to estimate the effort, time, and difficulty required to modify a particular program or module.

Experts have criticized Halstead's metrics for the since-discredited psychological theory on which some of them are based and for ambiguities and variations in the determination of operators and operands. In spite of this, however, conclusive evidence of their validity remains elusive. For almost every book and journal article that uses or supports them, there are just as many that do not. Still, Halstead's software science metrics remain the benchmark against which most other metrics are evaluated.

CYCLOMATIC COMPLEXITY

Whereas Halstead's software science metrics employ a size-oriented approach to analyze programs, Thomas McCabe based his metric on program complexity. He reasoned that complexity is directly related to the paths created by control and decision statements. As the number of paths increases, the complexity of the program or module increases. As complexity increases, the testability and maintainability of the program decreases.

McCabe's cyclomatic complexity metric uses graph theory to illustrate the number of linearly independent paths in the program or module. From the source code, a control graph is created. This is a directed graph with a distinct entry node and a distinct exit node. In the graph, nodes represent blocks of sequentially executable code, and the arcs connecting the nodes represent the flow or paths through the program. For McCabe's metric to function correctly, the program control graph must be strongly connected; that is, every node must be reachable from every other node. To meet this requirement, most programs require the addition of a dummy arc from the

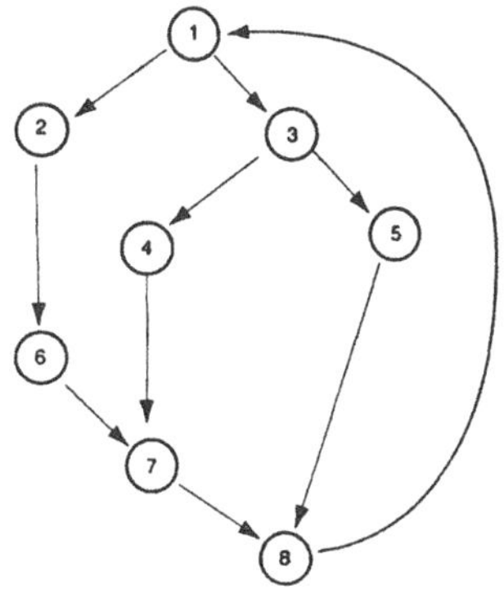

SOURCE: Thomas J. McCabe, "A Complexity Measurement," *IEEE Transactions on Software Engineering* SE-2 (1976)

Exhibit 17.5. Program Control Graph

exit node back to the entry node. A representative program control graph is presented in Exhibit 17.5.

McCabe's cyclomatic complexity metric V(G)is taken directly from the cyclomatic number C(G) in graph theory, and it is expressed as:

$$V(G) = e - n + p$$

where:

e = number of edges (arcs)
n = number of vertices (nodes)
p = number of components (for a single program or module, p = 1)

According to the example in Exhibit 5, the number of arcs (e) equals 10; the number of nodes equals 8, and there is only one component, p equals 1. Substituting into the equation for V(G) yields:

$$V(G) = 10 - 8 + 1$$

$$= 3$$

This value represents the number of linearly independent paths in the graph, and by extension, the program. There are three unique paths in Exhibit 5. These are 1-2-6-7-8,1-3-4-7-8, and 1-3-5-8.

McCabe, based on his working experience with Fortran programs, proposed 10 as the ideal upper limit for a program's cyclomatic complexity number. Below this level, McCabe reasoned that a program was easy to test (i.e., there were a manageable number of paths to validate) and to maintain (i.e., with a reasonable number of paths, the program was easier to understand and modify). If a program had a V(G) value greater than 10, McCabe recommended that it be rewritten or partitioned into less complex modules. The consensus opinion appears to be that there is nothing particularly special about a V(G) of 10 or less, but it is a sensible value. In general, programs or modules with low cyclomatic complexity metric values are easier to test and to maintain than those with high values.

At first, McCabe's cyclomatic complexity metric was used to analyze code after it was written. This approach confined the metric to the coding and unit test phases, and the operation and maintenance phase. In keeping with the current trend of applying metrics as early as possible in the software life cycle, this metric is now routinely employed to analyze the control and data flow charts created in the detailed design phase. The early detection of complex programs or modules significantly lowers the time and effort expended to code, test, and maintain them in subsequent life cycle phases. This reduces the cost of the entire software development process and improves quality.

Integration Complexity

In 1989, McCabe proposed an extension to his cyclomatic complexity metric that enables it to be used in the system design phase. This extension, integration complexity employs similar graph theory concepts, but it applies them to structure charts or hierarchy trees, rather than code or control flow graphs. Integration complexity is a function of design complexity and the number of modules in the software system. From an intuitive standpoint, the metric is sound, but as yet there is little or no empirical evidence to support it. However, this work represents another serious effort to focus software metrics on the early stages of the software development process.

INFORMATION FLOW

In conjunction with a metrics program, a Total Quality Management–oriented IS department should adopt structured design techniques. These techniques reduce the complexity of the design, allowing coding, debugging, and modification to be performed easier, faster, and cheaper. One of the design characteristics that structured design attempts to minimize is coupling, a measure of the interconnectivity between modules. If a module exhibits a large number of interfaces and interconnections with other modules, it is strongly coupled and therefore difficult to understand, test, and modify by itself, because it is highly interrelated with other modules.

One of the most popular metrics to quantitatively measure coupling is Henry and Kafura's Information Flow Metric. The metric is based on the flow of information between a procedure and its environment. A procedure can be a module or a group of modules (i.e., a subsystem). Information flow is defined in terms of fan-in and fan-out. Fan-in is the number of local flows into a procedure plus the global data structures from which a procedure retrieves information. Fan-out is the number of local flows from a procedure plus the global data structures that the procedure updates.[4] The information flow metric is expressed as:

$$C_p = (\text{Fan-In} * \text{Fan-Out})^2$$

The information flow metric is also classified as a structure metric. Structure metrics, like structured design, focus on the system design rather than its physical implementation (i.e., code).

Structure metrics are intended for use early in the software development process. As soon as control and data flows are identified for a module, the information flow metric is also classified as a structure metric. Structure metrics, like structured design, focus on the design of the system, not its physical implementation (i.e., code). Structure metrics are intended for use early in the software development process. As soon as control and data flows are identified for a module, the information flow metric is available to analyze its complexity. This usually occurs in the system design phase and no later than the detailed design phase. The metric may also be used in the integration and system-test phase, and the operation and maintenance phase. It highlights overly complex modules that are likely candidates for additional testing or maintenance modifications. In addition, when a module is identified for maintenance, it can assess the relative complexity of that module and how many other modules are affected.

Hybrid Metrics

There is also a hybrid metric form of the Henry and Kafura Information Flow Metric. Hybrid metrics usually combine a structural complexity metric with a code complexity metric to provide a complete picture of the module's complexity. The structure metric measures the module's external complexity, whereas the code complexity metric measures the internal complexity. The hybrid form of the information flow metric is:

$$C_p = C_{ip} * (\text{Fan-In} * \text{Fan-Out})^2$$

Fan-in and fan-out have the same definition as the structure metric form; and C_{ip} is any code complexity metric, such as McCabe's Cyclomatic Complexity Number [V(G)] or Halstead's Length (N). Hybrid metrics are used primarily in the detailed design phase, but they may also be employed in the integration and system test phase and the operation and maintenance phase.

RELIABILITY METRICS

One of the major objectives of the TQM approach is the early prevention and detection of errors and faults. As an example, the cost per fault to correct problems in the field has been shown to be from 20 to over 300 times greater than correcting problems in the design phase for a particular Siemens software product. Therefore, the importance of early fault elimination cannot be overemphasized, and the key to fault elimination lies in product metrics.

The goal of all the previously discussed product metrics is to reduce a program or module's size or complexity, or both, so the number of errors and faults is reduced correspondingly; but their primary focus is not on faults, per se. Reliability metrics' sole objective is to predict, find, and measure faults. Reliability metrics are applicable to every life cycle phase, but not every reliability metrics is appropriate for every phase. According to Goel, reliability models can be divided into four classifications:

- Times between failures models
- Failure count models
- Fault seeding models
- Input domain based models

These classifications are based on the approach taken by the model to predict remaining faults. The first three models are measurement-oriented techniques that can be categorized as product metrics. The input domain–based model is more of a test strategy, providing a methodology for selection of test data for black- or white-box tests, and therefore this chapter does not discuss it. In addition to his classifications, Goel also suggests the appropriate life cycle phases in which to employ each model.

Time Between Failure Models

These metrics predict the time interval between the ith and the $i^{th}+1$ failure using a statistically derived hazard function. These hazard functions are determined by statistically analyzing the actual time intervals between previous failures and fitting them to a known distribution, such as the exponential or gamma distributions. Examples of time between failure models are the Jelinski and Moranda De-Eutrophication Model, the Schick and Wolverton Model, and the Goel and Okumoto Imperfect Debugging Model. The most appropriate life cycle phase for using these metrics depends on the definition of failure. If failures are defined as module, subsystem, or system crashes, these metrics are appropriate for all phases between coding and unit test and operation and maintenance, inclusive. When a broader view of failure is taken to include human errors in the preparation of design requirements, specifications, or other documentation, then the metrics are also appropriate for the system design and detailed design phases.

Time between failure models are concerned with the time interval between successive failures, whereas fault count models are concerned with the number of faults occurring in a specified time interval. Several simple fault count metrics can be employed in every phase of the software development life cycle. An example is a fault rate metric calculated from the number of faults detected per unit time. When this rate is constant or increasing, the software product requires additional review or testing before release to the next life cycle phase.

Fault count metrics use stochastic methods to analyze and predict the number of faults remaining in a module. Typically, a nonhomogeneous Poisson distribution is used. Examples of the stochastic fault count metrics are the Goel-Okumoto Nonhomogeneous Poisson Process Model, the Musa Execution Time Model, and the Shooman Exponential Model. The statistically derived metrics are appropriate for both test phases and the operation and maintenance phase. During unit or system testing, the metrics provide an indication of the status or relative success of the testing process. In the operations and maintenance phase, they identify modules requiring corrective maintenance.

The premise underlying fault-seeding models appears to be counterintuitive to the elmination of faults and errors. In fault seeding, known faults are intentionally but randomly inserted into the software product. The theory behind this model is that if all or a large portion of the known faults are detected by the testing process, all or a large portion or the indigenous faults are also detected. At the end of each testing phase, the number of seeded faults detected is compared to the total number of seeded faults. If the detected number is significantly below the total number, additional testing is required. Mills and Dyson's Hypergeometric Model is an example of this type of metric. It is appropriate for use in the unit and integration test phases but not for final system acceptance tests. The objective of final acceptance testing is to demonstrate conformance to specifications and performance requirements, not to detect faults. Therefore, fault seeding is inappropriate for this type of test.

CONCLUSION

To become or to remain competitive, IS departments must embrace the Total Quality Management strategy and adopt a process-oriented approach toward the development and maintenance of software. Instituting a metrics program quantitatively measures and controls that process. Emphasizing this need for total software quality management, this article and its companion, "Software Metrics: Developing Software for TQM" (33-30-71), present a concise yet comprehensive review of the software development and maintenance process and recommend a few appropriate software metrics to quantitatively measure and control the overall process and each phase of the software life cycle.

In addition to the improvement of existing metrics and the application of metrics to earlier phases in the life cycle, research must be conducted to develop appropriate metrics for fourth-generation languages and for object-oriented environments. Virtually all the existing process and product metrics were developed and evaluated using third-generation, or earlier, languages. Several authors have said that these metrics are inappropriate for software developed in a fourth-generation language environment, but no one has presented empirical evidence to substantiate that assertion.

The object-oriented environment is emerging as the development process of the near future. This approach is radically different from the approaches used to develop current software metrics. Research must be conducted to establish whether current metrics are able to function in an object-oriented environment, and if not, to develop metrics that are. A first step in this direction has been taken with Chidamber and Kemerer's six object-oriented design metrics. However, much more work remains to be done in this area.

1. Jessica Keyes, "Peeling Back Layers of Quality Equation," *Software Magazine* (May 1991), pp. 42-61.
2. Chris F. Kemerer, Chris F. Kemerer, "Reliability of Function Points Measurement. A Field Experiment," *Communications of the ACM* 36, no. 2 (1993), pp. 85-97.
3. Lawrence H. Putnam, "Trends in Measurement, Estimation, and Control," *IEEE Software* (March 1991),pp. 105-107.
4. Sallie Henry and Roger Goff, "Comparison of a Graphical and a Textual Design Language Using Software Quality Metrics," *Journal of Systems and Software* 14, no. 3 (1991), pp. 133-146.

Section III Checklist

1. What is your definition of a software tool? Is it a tangible entity or methodology?
2. How would you categorize the tools, techniques, and practices used in your organization?
3. Is your definition or understanding of software tools consistent with the manner in which tools are used in your organization?
4. From your experiences, what is more valuable; tools that are powerful but require long learning periods or tools that are limited in scope but can be mastered and implemented quickly?
5. Do your experiences in tool use influence the decision of which tools your organization acquires? If not, why?
6. In your opinion, when are software tools inappropriate? Should this be acknowledged by tool providers?
7. Does your organization favor broad based tool products or are narrowly focused tools more commonplace? What is the affect of this on your development and support efforts?
8. Have you observed differences between tools aimed at the mainframe and those for micro platforms? If so, are these differences related to platform technology or the nature of the application system?
9. Do you think that tools used for development can also be used for support? Does your organization have such tools?
10. How are software tools or new methodologies evaluated in your organization? Does this seem reasonable to you?
11. What techniques have you learned and then passed on to other members in your organization? Do these techniques still hold value in current technology environments?
12. Does your organization document or provide guidelines on the tools and techniques used in your organization. If not, how does a new staff member gain knowledge?
13. Does your organization have a procedure to measure the success or failure of development and support projects?
14. Have you ever tried to measure programming productivity? If so, have the results been accurate?
15. Can productivity measurement of tools, methods, and practices be accurately performed in your environment? If not, how do you determine return on investment?

Section IV
Programming Techniques

Object Oriented Programming (OOP) has become an established alternative to the aging nature of third generation programming languages. The justification for implementing OOP has been well documented. And based on numerous studies of object-oriented development, there have been significant gains over past programming practices. However, there remains considerable debate over "inherent" OOP languages vs. those that implement OOP-like features and functionality. Furthermore, the software industry has been struggling with both proprietary and standard OOP language implementations. This impacts the choice of programming language as well as influences associated tools, methodologies, and middleware technologies. Development managers should be encouraged by potential gains that object-oriented technology offers in the creation of new application systems. But, as with all software technology, caution should be exercised in selecting the appropriate products and services.

One of the more prevalent OOP languages is C++ and its popularity stems from the widespread use of the C language used over the last twenty years. Although C++ advocates praise the strengths of the language, there is evidence that may suggest performance issues when compared to C. Many OOP languages suffer performance problems because of the embedded logic of object-oriented functionality. And accurate methods for performance measurement of object languages has been difficult. In Chapter 18, "Performance of Object-Oriented Programs :C++," the authors examine several experiments where the speed of C++ is compared to C. These tests were limited in size and scope; nevertheless, the results provide important information about the performance characteristics of C++. This can be very beneficial in environments that have an invested base of C programs and desire migration to C++.

Java has entered the object-oriented programming arena as the next evolution of application development languages. The tremendous interest in this programming tool is based on the cross platform strengths and portability. Despite the competition between vendors regarding the standardization of Java, the language continues to gain popularity against C++ implementations. Chapter 19, "Java and C++: Similarities, Differences, and Performance," offers valuable insight to the internal operations between the two language environments. This information is extremely useful in determining the appropriate deployment strategy for Java-based applications.

Technical advancements in software used for Internet/Intranet applications have generated interest over earlier implementations of client/server technology. In particular, Java is recognized as a significant step for enabling more practical improvements. In Chapter 20, "Web and Java Risk Issues," an interesting discussion is given on the benefits of Java technology to the overall Internet development process. Some critics argue that Java may not employ an exhaustive command set when compared to other languages. But the simplistic, yet powerful functions of Java are proving extremely productive to both older legacy systems and newer client/server systems.

As Java's popularity grows it has become recognized as an important tool within the framework of distributed computing. Chapter 21, "Java's Role in Distributed Computing," outlines the various concepts that enable Java to operate beyond the boundaries of stand alone applications. This provides development managers the opportunity to use Java applications across diverse platforms which can help simplify development and support of enterprise software applications. In conjunction, Chapter 22, "Component Architectures with JavaBeans," describes the component features of Java that have capitalized on the reusability of Java code. The use of reusable components is not new, but the combination of JavaBeans with the other strong features of the Java programming language provides a strong and solid foundation for building applications that can be highly independent of operating system characteristics and network attributes.

Application portability is being promoted as one of the major benefits of the two leading (and competing) object middleware standards, CORBA and COM. Chapter 23, "Programming Components: COM and CORBA," examines how to develop components that enable applications portability. Like the preceding chapter, it focuses on application development for a client/server environment. As Internet-based and object technology continue to converge, the distinction between client/server systems and Internet-based systems will blur as these two systems architectures begin to meld into one.

Many organizations are reviewing existing legacy systems as part of an overall initiative to upgrade application systems. In conjunction with program upgrades, organizations face considerable challenges addressing the vast amount of information stored in proprietary data files. In Chapter 24, "Automatically Migrating COBOL Indexed Files," a case study reviews how to leverage the power of new technology by exporting data into newer file structures. This represents an important issue for many organizations who must eventually migrate legacy systems. Development managers should weigh the advantages of new application implementation through careful assessment of program logic and repository architecture.

Chapter 25, "Building Database-Enabled Web Applications with IDC," examines another aspect of SQL.IDC (Internet Database Connector) is a technology developed by Microsoft that enables an SQL statement to execute against a database and return results in HTML page format. This technology works only with another Microsoft offering, Internet Information Server (IIS), but any browser that interprets HTML pages can be used to access database information with IDC. As the Internet and World-wide web are used as a standard platform, Web-based programming technologies will become more commonplace.

Structured Query Language (SQL) has been one of most widely used languages for accessing database information. Originally designed as a simple reporting tool, SQL is often used to facilitate complex queries against large scale relational databases. More often, SQL is invoked through on-line interfaces that have been useful to end user departments. But SQL also has powerful batch capabilities. Chapter 26, "Creating Effective Batch SQL Jobs," explores the vast power of the SQL language in the batch execute ion environment. For organizations that process and manipulate large quantities of database data, understanding the strengths of batch SQL can be an effective agent in maximizing computing resources.

Chapter 27, "Improving Performance in New Programming Environments: Java," shows that while the techniques for improving performance are somewhat different for Java than for compiled languages, the potential for reducing a Java application's execution time is vast.

Chapter 18

Performance of Object-Oriented Programs: C++

Paul J. Jalics
Ben A. Blake

BJARNE STROUSTROP, the creator of C++, said he wanted "something that ran like greased lightning and allowed easy interfacing with the rest of the world." The authors examine this performance aspect of C++ and compare it with C, which has a fine reputation in the performance area.

There are many aspects to program performance; for the purposes of this chapter, the authors limit the meaning to the execution performance of C++ programs (i.e., the amount of time required to execute specific C++ statements and programs).

THE SPECIFICATIONS OF THE EXPERIMENTS

Jalics and Heines developed a set of performance tests to measure the performance of C programs and the C statement level, including CPU, I/O statements, some routine-level modules, and some C library routines. These tests were augmented by a number of statement-level C++ tests and a few whole program C and C++ benchmarks. Execution times throughout are shown in microseconds, unless otherwise specified. These experiments were run on various C and C++ compilers: Borland C and C++ (3.1) on a 386-20 machine, Gnu C and C++ on a Digital Equipment Corp. (DEC) 5000 workstation, and Gnu, AT&T C and C++, and Gnu C++ on a SUN SLC Sparc workstation. Thus, the observations encompass not just a single C++ implementation but a broader picture of C++ performance.

0-8493-9822 3/00/$0 00+$.50

Sun4SLC AT&T		Sun4SLC Gnu		DEC5000 Gnu		Intel 386-20 Borland		
C	C++	C	C++	C	C++	C	C++	Description
0.74	0.74	0.74	0.74	0.32	0.32	1.63	1.63	if(a==b) true
0.70	0.72	0.70	0.70	0.32	0.32	1.40	1.76	if(...&&...)first true
1.04	1.21	1.21	1.21	0.57	0.55	1.76	1.76	if(...LL...)false both
1.15	1.15	1.10	1.15	0.53	0.49	2.28	2.18	nested if false,true
0.75	0.80	0.80	0.80	0.35	0.40	0.78	0.77	for(a=1;a<32;a+=1){;}
0.60	0.85	0.75	0.85	0.45	0.45	0.78	0.79	do{a+=1;while(a<32);
0.75	0.80	0.75	0.70	0.45	0.45	0.95	0.92	x:a+=1;if(a<32)goto x
2.77	2.79	2.68	2.66	1.23	1.30	3.83	3.80	switch(a)0,1,...:d=1
3.34	2.58	2.60	2.58	1.08	1.10	15.48	15.56	switch(a)0,1000,...:d=1
0.42	0.42	0.42	0.40	0.19	0.14	0.67	0.65	a=a + b;
0.38	0.42	0.40	0.40	0.19	0.17	0.71	0.72	a=a - b;
3.60	3.45	3.47	3.49	0.61	0.61	1.07	1.05	a=a * b;
1.34	1.21	1.21	1.23	1.47	1.51	1.73	1.73	a=a/b;
1.36	1.23	1.21	1.23	1.42	1.45	1.75	1.74	a=a & b;
0.46	0.40	0.42	0.44	0.17	0.14	0.88	0.87	a=b + c;
1.70	1.53	1.53	1.51	0.66	0.66	4.62	4.62	a=addm(b,c);
0.27	0.23	0.25	0.25	0.06	0.06	0.17	0.18	d=1
49.72	48.83	48.30	48.46	23.11	23.01	83.72	84.18	total

Exhibit 18.1. C Versus C++ CPU Tests (in Microseconds)

C LANGUAGE SUBSET PERFORMANCE

C++ is approximately a superset of C, so one area of interest is the subset of features contained in the C language. Exhibit 1 shows a small subset of results from the earlier C experiments. These and other results of the experiments show that there is little difference between the C and the equivalent C++ program performance when only the C features of the language are used. This was an expected result and worth the effort to observe on the various systems, especially because performance measurements often deliver surprising results. The sum of times on two of the four systems are actually faster for C++ than for C, although the difference is probably not significant statistically.

C+ + Procedure Call Overhead: The Ctax Benchmark

An object is a collection of data, like a C struct mechanism, that also has a collection of procedures to manipulate that data. These procedures are called member functions. The key word class defines objects in C++. One observation from looking at object-oriented programming (OOP) programs in general and C++ in particular is that the OOP discipline tends to create many objects, each with several relatively small member functions (i.e., 30 to 100 lines). If most procedures are smaller in comparison to non-OOP programs, it seems logical that OOP programs cross substantially more procedures boundaries than non-OOP programs in accomplishing the same task. This factor increases the importance of procedure call overhead in OOP programs.

The following list contains features of C++ that are likely to influence the function call overhead:

1. An inline attribute can be specified for any member function of a C++ class in the class declaration. When code is generated to call such a member function, the executable code in the member function is actually inserted instead of code to put the parameters on the stack followed by a subroutine call instruction. This means that if there are 10 calls to this member function in a program, the machine instructions that implement the procedure are actually generated 10 times instead of 10 procedure call instructions to a single procedure implementation. Thus, when inline is used, the procedure call and return overhead are eliminated altogether, and the implementation code is simply inserted into the calling procedure in each instance that member function is called.
2. A simple procedure call, as in C, that is unrelated to a C++ class needs to be distinguished from a member function of some class. One would expect some performance difference between these two because when calling a member function, a hidden parameter (i.e., the address of the C++ object instance the function is to work on) must also be passed by the compiled code.
3. In a program with inheritance, the inherited class may override some member functions of the base class. For example, the base class has a member function SumIt(), and the inherited class also implements SumIt(). Thus, the second SumIt() will be called for the inherited class, and the question becomes, Does this overridden member function execute as quickly as the base class function?
4. Finally, virtual versus nonvirtual functions must be considered. Virtual functions, or polymorphism, create the ability to decide at execution time which exact member function is to be called. (Usually the function to be called is decided on at program compilation time.)

   Whereas the inline feature of C++ is intended to reduce this procedure call overhead, experience shows that C++ compilers often give up or abort inlining because of procedure length or complexity. An effective optimizing compiler should, as a standard feature, do the same inlining as the Unisys 2200 C compiler or the IBM VS/COBOL II, which does inlining for up to two levels of nested PERFORMs.

Test	Sun4SLC AT&T	Sun4SLC Gnu	DEC500 Gnu	Intel 386-20 Borland	Test Description
1	0.61	0.7	0.46	3.5	call normal function
2	0.38	0.39	0.13	0.85	call inline member function
3	0.69	0.73	0.49	4.74	call non-inline member function
4	0.39	0.39	0.12	0.9	call virtual inline function
5	0.7	0.73	0.5	4.65	call virtual non-inline function
6	0.4	0.39	0.12	0.91	call overridden inline member function
7	0.69	0.72	0.5	4.74	call overridden non-inline member function
8	0.38	0.39	0.12	0.86	call overridden virtual inline function
9	0.7	0.74	0.5	4.63	call overridden virtual non-inline function
10	0.68	0.78	0.5	4.84	polymorphism base (ptr to member function)
11	1.2	1.42	0.7	5.63	polymorphism of non-inline virtual classes
12	1.2	1.4	0.7	5.75	polymorphism of in-line virtual classes
13	0.69	0.82	0.46	3.85	call normal function with 1 param
14	0.33	0.39	0.22	4.04	call normal function with 2 param
15	0.42	0.44	0.26	3.97	call normal function with 3 param
16	0.43	0.48	0.3	4.28	call normal function with 4 param
17	1.17	1.12	0.61	6.03	call normal function with 8 param

Exhibit 18.2. Measuring C++ Procedure Call Overhead (in Microseconds)

The authors developed a procedure call overhead measurement program and named it Ctax.cc. The rest of this section looks at the results of running Ctax on the three platforms using four compilers. Exhibit 2 shows the results to be as follows.

A comparison of tests 1, 3, and 13 shows that in most cases the additional overhead of calling a member function is the same as adding an extra parameter to a normal function. One would expect this, because in calling member functions, C++ adds one hidden extra parameter, namely the pointer to the object being referenced. The actual increase in overhead for the four systems ranges from 4 percent to 35 percent.

Making a member function inline, as shown in a comparison of tests 2 and 3, often reduces the calling overhead by 45 percent to 82 percent. The best reduction, of 82%, is on Borland C++; this reduction may also be indicative of a relatively high procedure call overhead on the Intel 386 when compared to DEC and Sun workstations, which are especially fast in procedure calls. The smallest reductions are on the two Sun systems, on which the role of the procedure call overhead may be even lower.

Also noteworthy is the extra overhead of adding parameters one at a time, as in tests 1 and 13 through 17. Whereas the additional overhead is fairly constant on the Borland C++, at about 10% for adding one parameter, the workstations do much worse in this regard. The overall increase going from two to nine parameters on workstations is 214 percent to 361 percent, as compared to 59 percent for the PC. Virtual member functions and overridden member functions do not have any performance penalties over other member functions when the compiler can figure out at compile time which function is to be called. This is shown in tests 2 through 9.

When member function access is through a pointer, as in tests 10 through 12, the performance slows down to a normal member function that is not inline. Specifying inline has no effect in these cases.

When polymorphism is involved, as in tests 11 through 12, the member function is accessed by pointers, when the appropriate possibly inherited function needs to be decided on at execution time by a virtual array. The execution time for polymorphism goes up further from that mentioned previously by 20 percent, in Borland C++, to 82 percent, on the two Sun Sparc systems.

There is a substantial difference between the two compilers on the same SUN SLC Sparc system. For example, the increase for the Gnu C++ for polymorphism is 40 percent, whereas for the AT&T, it is around 80 percent. So as usual, performance is a function of the compiler, the language, and the hardware.

C++ I/O Streams Performance: the X18S Series Benchmarks

C++ does include the standard C I/O facilities, such as printf, fprintf, getc, and putc. There is, however, a new Stream I/O library that can replace most of the C I/O library. A set of benchmark programs was constructed that attempts to look at the relative performance of the C versus C++ I/O mechanisms. The tests are based on benchmarks and are augmented by testing equivalent I/O mechanisms from the C++ Stream libraries. For example, one test measures the speed of execution of

```
printf("the answer is % d ",dx).
```

The corresponding test for C++ is

```
cout << "the answer is" << dx << ' '.
```

Even though Exhibit 3 compares the C I/O facilities with the new C++ I/O stream facilities just for one C++ implementation (i.e., Borland C++), it can still give some insights into the performance implications of using the new C++ mechanisms. The Borland C++ tests measure elapsed time on a standalone MS-DOS system, which does not have a concept of CPU execution time.

Exhibit 3 summarizes the results of running these benchmarks on the Borland C++ on a 20 megahertz 386 PC system without a floating-point processor. The following observations can be made from the benchmarks.

The C++I/O stream output to the screen is about 21 percent slower

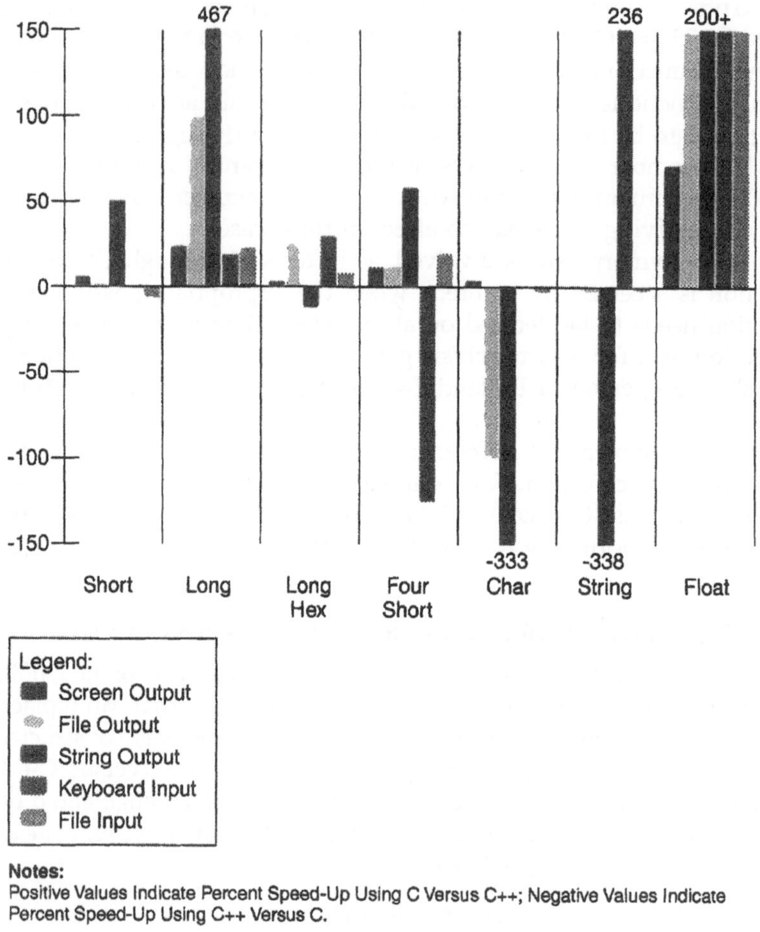

Exhibit 18.3. Comparing C and C++ I/O

than the printf overall; the handling of longs is about 30 percent slower; and float is over 80 percent slower.

The C++ stream output to a disk file is, overall, twice as slow as fprintf to a disk file, with great variations on individual data types. It is the same as fprintf for a third of the tests; it is almost twice as slow for longs; and it is three to five times as slow for gloat (off the chart). Surprisingly, char and string are faster in C++ streams.

For in-memory output conversions, the C++ streams are four times slower than sprintf overall, with longs and floats being five times as slow, but chars and strings are again about four times as fast as the C sprintf.

For in-memory input conversions, using C++ mechanisms are overall three times slower than sscanf. C++ is about the same for the majority of tests, except for floats, which are again five times slower.

For input conversions of data read from a disk file, the C++ mechanisms are overall twice as slow but seem to be only slightly slower—by about 10 percent — in most cases except longs, which are 70 percent slower, and float and double, which are about three times slower. Char and string are again 20 percent faster than for fscanf.

Overall, the C++ I/O streams on Borland C++ seem to be somewhat slower than the corresponding C mechanisms on the same compiler, but they certainly are of the same order of magnitude. Some of the slowness may simply be a lack of tuning on a relatively new class library. Surely the floating-point results show a lack of tuning and would be dramatically different with hardware floating point support on the test system.

The same experiments were rerun on the Sun SLC AT&T C++ system, with quite different results. The overall figures show I/O streams to be faster by about 33 percent in CPU execution time and 4 percent slower in elapsed time, indicating that C++ I/O stream performance need not be worse than C I/O and very much a function of software implementation and tuning. The experiments could not be run on the Gnu C++ compilers because they do not yet implement the C++ Release 2 I/O streams.

It is not really clear that the I/O streams provide a significant new dimension to programming. Well-practiced C programmers may find them harder and more inconvenient to use, especially when using manipulators instead of clear and concise format strings in C. Also, the I/O stream libraries are not described well enough in C++ books and compiler manuals, and there is a scarcity of detailed examples of the many ways that they can be used. One thing certainly favors C++ I/O streams: the whole methodology of I/O streams is in better harmony with C++'s philosophy of complete type-checking each data item being input or output.

SCREEN EMULATOR PERFORMANCE

A problem is posed: how to model a screen object for a terminal emulation system. Normally, the screen was modeled as a two-dimensional array in which each entry contained a data byte and an attribute byte specifying color. Thus, several solutions were implemented using C++ objects and normal C one- and two-dimensional arrays. The function measured by the benchmarks was to add together all the byte values on the screen. The results for the three systems are shown in Exhibit 4.

The simplest implementation is as a one-dimensional array of char [4000], as shown in test 1. This was the fastest on the Borland C++, but surprisingly

Test	Sun4SLC AT&T	Sun4SLC G++	DEC5000 Gnu	Intel 386-20 Borland	Test Description
1	1110	1240	820	11680	sum char[4000] array
2	750	1030	560	16720	sum char[25][160] array
3	940	1180	720	17370	sum [25][80] array of classes
4	3060			21800	sum [][] oper overload array inline
5	3310			21880	sum [][] oper overload dynamic array inline
6	4930			56970	sum [][] oper overload dynamic array not inline
7	1940	1310	780	16070	sum (r,c) with rowindex inline

Exhibit 18.4. Screen Emulator Object Performance (in Microseconds)

the two-dimensional array char, as in test 2, was the fastest on the three workstation systems.

The next attempt, test 3, was to use an array of structures with two char items in each class but no member functions. This was slower than the two-dimensional array on all systems but was still faster than the one-dimensional array on the three workstation systems.

The next three attempts, tests 4 through 6, used real classes with member functions that implemented double subscripting by using inheritance with one object to specify the row subscript and the other to specify the column. There is no [][] operator. These three tests use operator overloading, which is a C++ feature that allows programmers to ascribe new meanings to the standard operators, such as +, -, *, =,>, and []. Unfortunately, the Gnu C++ compiler was not able to compile these tests, so the results are only for the Sun AT&T system and Borland C++.

The results show the huge impact of inline member functions for solving real problems. On Borland C++, the inline solution (see tests 4 and 5) are about three times faster than the on-inline test 6. On AT&T Sun, the inline solutions are one-third faster than the on-inline one. The final version is a simple class with a member function ref(row, column), which selects the appropriate screen position and returns a reference to it. This inline solution proved to be the most efficient of all the real class solutions (see tests 4 through 7) on both Borland C++ and the AT&T Sun, showing above all that simple object solutions such as test 7 may perform better when compared to complex schemes such as double subscripting using two classes and inheritance. In any case, the obvious solution yields a more readable and easier-to-understand implementation.

The best object solutions (see test 7) were still much slower than the best original nonobjects solutions (see tests 1 through 3). On the AT&T Sun the object solution is 158 percent slower than char[25][160]. On the SUN Gnu

Test	Sun4SLC AT&T	Sun4SL C G++	DEC5000 G++	Intel 386-20 Borland	Test Description
dr1	6437	7481	16574	5000	using **Int** and **char**
dr2	3717	4160	2695	1388	Using **Int** and **Char** inline
dr3	1243	1832	2633	373	Using **Int** and **Char** (not inline)
dr4	1006	1541	2013	306	Using **Int** and **Char** (not inline) return by value
dr5		1221	1794	301	Using **Int** and **Char** (no inline)
dr6	5780	6493	7194	1612	Using **Int** only inline
dr7	4016	4958	3405	3333	Using **char** only inline

Exhibit 18.5. Int and Char Classes Used in Dhrystone Benchmark (in Microseconds)

the object solution is 27 percent slower than char[25][160]. On DEC Gnu C++ the object solution is 39 percent slower than char[25][160]. On Borland C++ the object solution is 39 percent slower than the char[4000] solution. These increases in execution time are large, and the question is, Where is the additional time spent? Procedure call overhead is eliminated, because the member function ref is inline. In the generated code for Borland C++ (with all optimizations turned on), there are about one-third more machine instructions in the inner loop, having to do with generating a reference to an object and then dereferencing it to get at the table entries.

THE DHRYSTONE C++ BENCHMARKS

There is a C++ version of the Dhrystone Benchmark that was used to look at C++ performance. The two classes Int and Char were implemented to replace the standard built-in data-types int and char. This test accurately measures the worst-case performance cost of introducing new data types that are used throughout an application. Exhibit 5 shows the results of executing several versions of the C++ Dhrystone on various systems.

The results show the performance of the tested system in Dhrystones (i.e., a bigger number is faster). The following observations can be made:

- Replacing int and char by inline (dr2 versus dr1) implementations of Int and Char in the entire benchmark degrades performance by 43 percent on the two Sun C++ compilers, by 84 percent on the DEC5000, and by 72 percent on the 386. Perhaps the DEC5000 and the 386 do less inline work than the Suns.

	SUN_SLC_AT&T_C++ (CPU Sec)	(Elapsed Sec)	386_20_Borland_C++ (Elapsed Sec)
Cperf (C)	1.8	2.3	1.21
Gperf (C++)	2.1	2.4	0.88

Exhibit 18.6. The Gperf Benchmark

- If the implementations are changed to use procedure calls for member functions (i.e., noninline, dr3 versus dr1), the degradation factors go up to 81 percent for the Sun AT&T, to 76 percent for the Sun g++, to 85 percent for the DEC, and to 93 percent for the 386.
- Using by-value return of results instead of by-reference (dr4 versus dr3) reduces performance further by about 25 percent.
- Making the member functions virtual (dr5 versus dr4) further reduces performance by 1 percent to 26 percent.
- Tests dr6 and dr7 separate out the performance differences due to Int and Char and indicate that performance degradation due to the introduction of just inline Char is only about 12 percent for the two Sun systems, 57 percent for DEC, and 68 percent for the 386.
- Performance degradation due to the introduction of just inline Int (see test dr6) is 34 percent for the two Sun systems and the 386, and 80 percent for the DEC.

THE GPERF BENCHMARK

Gperf is a program that generates a perfect hashing function for a known set of keys; it was designed in C++, and a separate version exists in C (Cperf). This Gperf benchmark consists of 3,906 lines of code and is a reasonable object-oriented design whose performance might be compared to the C version. Whether this is a fair comparison might be debated, but any performance samples are of interest. The results of running this benchmark are illustrated in Exhibit 6.

The results show a 16 percent increase in CPU time for the C++ version on the Sun; the same program, however, shows only a 4 percent increase in elapsed time on the Sun and a 28 percent decrease in elapsed time on the PC. Again, there is not a clear trend that is identifiable in C versus C++.

THE XREF BENCHMARK

This benchmark inputs a list of files, lists them (including file name and line number), and then provides a cross-reference listing of all symbols. The

	SUN_SLC_AT&T_C++ (CPU sec)	(elapsed sec)	386_20_Borland_C++ (elapsed sec)
Cperf (C)	8.8	9.2	37
Gperf (C++)	6.9	7.4	34

The Xref Benchmark

Exhibit 18.7. The Xref Benchmark

original xref0.c program (375 lines) is of poor design, as it was transported originally from COBOL and has seen many modifications. It has, however, been in widespread use by one of the authors for over a decade. Cxref.cc (303 lines), on the other hand, is a completely new object-oriented design that was undertaken as part of learning about object-oriented programming and C++.

Results of running the xref benchmark are illustrated in Exhibit 18.7. Even though the algorithms are not identical in these two programs, the inputs, outputs, and the work done are meant to be the same. The results show a 20 percent improvement for the C++ version on the Sun and an 8 percent improvement on the PC. The results may be explained as follows. The potential loss of performance in a C++ program (when compared to a C program) can be more than overcome in some cases by improving the design and paying attention to performance.

OBJECT LIBRARIES: THE CLASS TEST BENCHMARK

One of the most compelling reasons for choosing OOP and C++ is the availability of object libraries and application frameworks that have hopes of fulfilling the dream of producing reusable software objects, much in the way integrated circuit chips are used in hardware. The I/O stream library is an example of such a library that exists in every C++ implementation. Others include the Borland Container Class Library and the Turbovision Application Framework, which supports the use of multiple windows. The authors have performed a number of experiments on the use of the Container Class Library in Borland C++ and want to look at the performance of those library objects versus building proprietary code to do the same.

Exhibit 8 shows the result of running comparison benchmarks on the Borland C++ Container Class Library. For each of the containers (e.g., String, Stack, List, Sorted Array, ListIterator, DoubleLList, Dictionary, Hash Table, Stack with Date and Time, and a Dictionary with alphabetically sorted associations), a timed measurement was made using the class object, and then compared to a manually written piece of code that attempts to perform the same function. Observations are as follows:

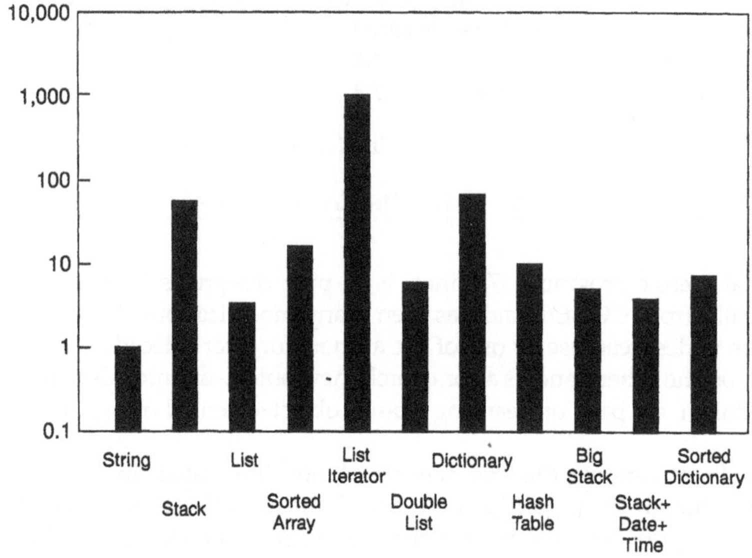

Exhibit 18.8. Timing Ratio of Straight C Code to C++ Code Using Container Classes

- The container class objects are slower in 10 of the 11 measurements by a factor that ranges from 3 to 930.
- The performance of the class implementation is typically three to five times as slow as the C code.

The performance of the object library functions was expected to be less than the specifically targeted code that an organization might write. Because of the simplicity of the object library functions, however, the size of the performance degradation was surprising.

USE OF APPLICATION FRAMEWORKS: THE TVEDITX BENCHMARK

The authors started with an interactive file editor TVEdit, which is written using the Turbovision Application Framework and is provided by Borland as a demonstration program. It is a full-function file editor with mouse support, using multiple windows, scroll bars, cut-and-paste, window movement, and management. TVEdit consists of 562 lines of C++.

The authors extended this program to list all occurrences of a specified symbol in a collection of source files in a new window; the program then allows the user to move quickly between multiple windows, showing the context of each of the symbol references using mouse points and clicks. The code to do the above required a total 260 new lines of C++ code.

The performance of the new functions may be slower, but it would have taken thousands of lines of code and many hours to implement. Actually, performance does not play a role in this case, because the code performs much faster than the human eye and hand can interact with the application. The real performance issue here is development time and debugging time. This benchmark is perhaps the best of all the ones above because it delivers the promise of OOP and class libraries, which serve as reusable modules. Looking at the 260 lines of modifications and additions, the idea of reusability and adaptation is everywhere: a number of existing menu-related classes are instantiated, and new member functions are added to two different classes, which inherit most of their functionality from classes defined and implemented by Turbovision.

SUMMARY

C++ performance can be made as good as C performance because C++ is close to a superset of C, and most C++ compilers give an identical performance when using only features available in C. Thus, C++ is as good as C from a performance standpoint, given the same C code.

C++ I/O Stream library performance can be as fast as C I/O, but much depends on the details of the implementation. Developers are able to affect this performance by a few compiler options but cannot easily otherwise change this performance. Developers are able to have a big impact on I/O performance by their choice of a C++ Compiler system, when that is possible. For example, Intel 80x86 systems have several very fine compiler systems from which to choose.

Procedure call overhead on a given hardware plays a substantial role in performance. This is especially important in C++, in which member functions tend to be small. Compiler optimizations can play a big role in reducing this overhead. The inline attribute for a member function can also greatly enhance performance, but often compilers may ignore this attribute. In some cases, developers may choose a particular computer platform just because it has a low procedure call overhead.

The use of new data types via C++ objects is one of the outstanding features of C++ but should be used with some care when performance is a critical issue. Developers should prototype the new data type and compare its performance to that of comparable built-in types, as the authors did for the screen emulator benchmark.

The performance of C++ implementations varies widely, and users should run experiments on their target system to help make design decisions that ensure that performance goals can be met.

Use of object libraries is still in the early stages, and certainly performance is just one of the issues to be considered. The Borland C++ Container Class Library is not very impressive in execution performance. Because the objects supplies are so simple and do not give functionality that cannot be written simply in a few lines of code, it is hard to understand why the performance should be so low, so for now users might be best advised to stay away from such objects in favor of using their own techniques when execution performance is essential. Also, these class libraries will become more attractive once they are standardized across compilers and platforms. Again, the best approach for performance critical code is to compare use of the object libraries provided with code written by the developer.

Application Frameworks, such as Turbovision, has impressive functionality to which users gain access using only a few lines of code. This is coming close to the software chips idea, which is analogous to hardware microchips that have revolutionized computer hardware design. Performance measurements here are not practical, but development time and debugging time might be considered. The major negative impression is that it takes a lot of time for a novice to use the classes in Turbovision. The programs are very hard to compile, but debugging time was quite short. Perhaps better documentation with many complete examples for Turbovision objects would help to shorten the learning curve. Subsequent experiments with Windows-oriented graphical user interface application frameworks, such as the Microsoft Foundation Classes, gave even more impressive results to the difficult task of windows programming.

The developer interested in performance must measure that performance, run experiments with different options, and compare the performance to best select the one with the best performance.

Developers interested in C++ program performance must become very familiar with their compiler's performance-related options.

Chapter 19
Java and C++: Similarities, Differences, and Performance

Adam Fadlalla, Paul J. Jalics, and Victor Matos

OBJECT-ORIENTED PROGRAMMING (OOP) IS AN IMPROVEMENT IN PROGRAMMING TECHNOLOGY and C++ is the most visible and commonly used OOP dissemination vehicle. However, C++ drags with it a lot of the "history" of C, which includes assumptions from the 1960s that a system implementation language needs to be completely "open" and (consequently) "sloppy" so that programmers can implement, inside the confines of an operating system, all the artifices and "magic" that might be desired. [1]

While this position for "total openness" could be arguably justified, it clearly brings an undesirable amount of language inconsistencies, ambiguities, exceptions, and clumsiness. On the opposite side, an experience [2] from Xerox's Mesa language indicates that a strongly type-checked language can go a long way in avoiding or eliminating execution-time errors. C++ was intended to go in this direction, but backward compatibility to the very important C language had the side effect of leaving a great deal of the "slop" that was in C to remain in C++.

To make matters worse, the architecture of the initial C++ implementations was geared to converting the C++ source programs to C code, so that existing C compilers could be used for compilation. As a result a number of unwanted side-effect anomalies can occur. For example, it is possible in C++ to cast any variable or pointer to anything else; functions without a return type may still return an integer; pointers are most often used without any checking as to whether they were initialized; subscripts for arrays are not checked; # preprocessor commands and variables can generate a multitude of erroneous code.

Adding to all these problems, there is one more disturbing factor: C++ is a compiled language that interacts with "real" computers. For each real computer there is an OS interface to C++, and unfortunately it is different

0-8493-9822-3/00/$0.00+$.50

for each operating environment! Try to convert a Borland C++ GUI application to Microsoft C++. It is akin to starting over, in one sense, especially if the original author did not design his application to be portable [3]. Bear in mind that all this portability conflicts we refer to are, at the moment, confined to the same Intel machine architecture and the same Windows 95 operating system.

This is much more so than in newer programming environments like the two mentioned above because the integrated debugging environments (IDE) and their "wizards" often generate a good deal of C++ source code. The programmer than inserts his application code in the midst of all the automatically generated code.

In summary, C++ is an extraordinary programming language that is unfortunately too complex, too error-prone, difficult to teach or learn because of its wealth of features. We believe the intent of the Java developers [4] was to retain the important features of C++ while eliminating unnecessary complexity and error-prone language features. At the same time, Java introduces some new techniques that are superior to their C++ counterparts. For instance, all pointers are eliminated, all objects are always passed by reference, and address arithmetic is forbidden.

DIFFERENCES BETWEEN C++ AND JAVA

Java is different from its predecessor programming languages (C, C++, Modula, Ada) in several ways, for instance [8]:

- Java is a small language; however it provides support for object-oriented programming.
- Arrays are the only predefined data structure type offered by Java, yet it provides access to classes that could be used to support any user-defined data structure.
- Java includes a rich Graphical User Interface (GUI) and multimedia facilities (sound, images, animation). Java is intrinsically GUI oriented. Its applications — called applets — are displayed by a web browser rather than directly delivered to the computer's monitor.
- Java provides a self-contained environment for concurrency control, as well as a set of primitive programming facilities to support networking operations.

Exhibit 19.1 takes a piecemeal approach in our comparison of the two languages. Concepts from a C++ standpoint are mapped into their equivalent versions in Java. Even though the list is not exhaustive, it contains many of the building blocks needed for a good perspective of the differences between C/C++ and Java. Exhibit 19.2 summarizes the table in Exhibit 19.1.

Exhibit 19.1. A Comparison of C/C++ and Java

C and C++	Java
Program Organization C and C++ programs normally consist of two parts, a header file (.h) containing the class definition and a (.cpp) file containing the implementation of the class. However, one can write very unobvious C++ programs using the preprocessor commands: *#define*, *#ifdef*, and *typedef* constructions.	Each complete logical unit of Java code is placed alone into one single piece of code (.Java file). This creates a single source for a class, which sometimes has the disadvantage that one is not able to get a good overview of the class declaration as it often spans many pages. Projects are made by combining several independent Java files together. There is no preprocessor activity. There are no header files. #ifdef, #include, #define, macros, and other preprocessor commands are not available.

Constants
C/C++ constants have no explicit type, they could be defined in a global mode.
 	
#define MILETOKMS 1602
#define PI 3.141592
class circle {
  double radius;
  circle(double r) {radius = r; };
  double area() { return (2*PI*radius); }
};
Note: 1- Semicolon at the end of the class is needed.
        2- #define variables are global.
	The data type of Java constants must be explicitly defined. Constants must be made *public* and placed inside a class.
	class circle {
	  //constants
	  static final double MILESTOKMS = 1602;
	  public static final PI = 3.141592;
	  //variable
	  double radius;
	  //method
	  circle(double r) {radius = r; };
	  double area () {return (2*PI*radius);};
	}
	Note: 1- Semicolon at the end of class is not needed.
	        2- Public constant *circle.PI* is global.

Global Variables Variables, constants, and data types could be made *global* by positioning them outside of a class definition or the implementation of a class's methods.	Java has no global variables and so all variables must be defined in some class. This implements more fully the object-oriented nature of the language. There are **static** variables just like in C++ and if they have a **public** access they can be used like global variables with a class prefix. For example,: myCompany.phoneNumber; myCompany is the class, and phoneNumber a public static variable).

Structures
C++ structures offer a rude method of providing *Data Encapsulation*.
struct EnglishDistance {
        int feet;
        double inches;
 	
};
 	
an instance is defined as
struct EnglishDistance myboat;
	In Java there are no structures. Therefore C++ structures must be converted into Java classes:
	class englishDistance {
	        int feet;
	        double inches;
	}
	an instance is defined:
	englishDistance myBoat = new myBoat();

Exhibit 19.1 (Continued). A Comparison of C/C++ and Java

C and C++	Java

Functions and Methods
C/C++ programs are collections of functions. There is a distinguished function called *main* that is the first to be executed. C++ supports a heterogeneous mix of both methods inside classes and C-like functions.
 	
double calculateCircleArea (double radius)
{
return (2 * PI * radius);
}
 	
Used in the context:
Double r1 = 5.4;
Area1 = calculateCircleArea (r1);
e
	Java has no functions. All the activity provided by functions must be written as methods inside a class.
	Methods in a function need to receive a fixed number of parameters. Java functions that return no value must be declared as returning void.
	Class circle {
	double radius;
	circle(double r) {radius = r; };
	double calculateArea()
	{return (2*myConst.PI * radius);};
	}
	Used in the context
	circle circle1 = new circle(r1);
	Area1 = circle1.calculateArea();
	here circle1 is defined as an instance of the circle class, with an original radius r1.
	All Java methods are *virtual* so that the actual function called is determined at execution time. Also, the final modifier declares that a method may not be overridden by subclasses.

Access Modifiers Visibility (*Hiding*) of data and member functions inside a class is controlled using access specifiers: **Private:** Can be accessed only *within* the class. **Public:** Visible outside of the class as class.part. **Protected:** Similar to private but accessible to the methods of any derived class.	Java uses the concept of *packages*. A package is a container for classes and other packages. A class is a container of data and code. Java uses combinations of the access modifiers: public, private, and protected, but it adds more control in visibility by ruling how classes and packages interact with one another. Table 1 summarizes the scoping of variables and functions. [9]

Automatic Typecasting
C++ allows coercion in which loss of precision could occur. For instance, assigning a double to an integer (loosing decimals) is a valid C operation
int age = 20;
double dogAge = age/7.0;
//next is a valid assignment in C++
//however it may produce a warning msg
age = dogAge;
	Java forces the programmer to *explicitly* typecast assignments operations in which a loss of representation may occur
	int age = 20;
	double dogAge = age/7.0;
	//explicit coercion is needed below
	age = (int) dogAge;

Operator Overloading C++ offers operator overloading, which in many cases offers a great degree of elegance in dealing with data objects. Consider the C++ example.	Java does not support operator overloading. Overloading is implemented with normal methods, which are functionally equivalent to the action of the operator.

Exhibit 19.1 (Continued). A Comparison of C/C++ and Java

C and C++	Java

class eDistance {//English Distance
private: int feet;
double inches;
public:
eDistance (int f, double i)
{feet= f; inches= i;};
eDistance operator + (eDistance d2) {
inches+=d2.inches;
feet+=d2.feet;
if (inches >12) {
feet++;
inches-=12.0;
};
return eDistance(feet, inches);
};
};
which could be used in the context
d3 = d1 + d2;
where d1, d2, d3 are instances of eDistance.
	Class eDistance {//English Distance
	int feet;
	double inches;
	eDistance add (eDistance d2)
	{
	double sumInches = inches + d2.inches;
	double sumFeet = feet + d2.feet;
	if (sumInches >12) {
	sumFeet++;
	sumInches-=12.0;
	}
	return new eDistance(sumFeet, sumInches);
	};
	}
	
	Used in the context
	d3 = d1.add (d2);
	where d1, d2, d3 are instances of englishDistance.

Strings
C/C++ does not include support for strings. Those must be either treated as a user-defined object or a zero-terminated array of characters. For example.:
#include <string.h>
char Name[20];
strcpy(Name, "Don Quixote");
size = strlen(Name);
	Java offers strings as *primitive* objects. Strings are part of the Java language specification; therefore their behavior is rigorously well defined across programs.
	String Name = new String( );
	Name = "Don Quixote";
	size = Name.length( );

Input-Output Streams C++ offers three standard streams: in, out, error, as well as the overloaded operators << and >> int age; cout << "Enter your age: "; cin >> age; cout << "you said " << age << " years";	Java applications also support the concept of *streams*. However there is no << or >> operators int age; System.out.println ("Enter your age: "); System.out.flush( ); age = System.in.read( ); System.out.println("You said " +age+" years");

Command-Line Arguments
C/C++ passes an integer argc indicating the total number of arguments present in the command line, and argv[ ] which is an array of pointers to chars
int main (int argc, char* argv[ ]) {
for (int i = 0; i<argc; i++)
cout << argv[i];
};
	Java applications use a *String* collection to pass parameters. Path/Prog name are not displayed.
	public class test2 {
	public static void main (String[ ] arg) {
	for (int j = 0; j<arg.length;j++)
	System.out.println (arg[j]); }; }

Exhibit 19.1 (Continued). A Comparison of C/C++ and Java

C and C++	Java
Friends and Packages C++ classes use *friend* functions to act as a bridge between two unrelated classes, or to improve readability by providing a more obvious syntax. When another class declares your class as a friend, you have access to all data and methods in that class.	Java has no *friend* functions. This issue has been controversial in the design of C++. The Java designers decided to drop it. However, Java variables, which are (1) in a class that is part of a package, and (2) introduced without an access modifier, acquire the *friendly* access type of the package. Those variables could be called without *get* and *set* functions from other classes in the same package

Inheritance
C++ provides multiple inheritance. An object has access to all the data and methods of its ancestors.
class student: public person,
public athlete,
public intellectual
{
//derived class definition
...
};
the student class is derived from the three ancestor classes: person, athlete, and intellectual. Any data and methods defined in the upper classes are reachable from the subclass.
	Java implements single inheritance. Each object has only one ancestor, however *interfaces* could be used to support dynamic method resolution at runtime. Java *interfaces* are like classes, but lack instance variables and their methods contain only a signature but no body. An interface is similar to a C++ abstract class which specifies the behavior of an object without specifying an implementation. A class may include any number of interfaces. The body of referenced methods must be provided in the subclass.
	class student **implements** person, athlete,
	intellectual
	{
	//subclass definition
	...
	}
	keyword *implements* is used to introduce the names of *interfaces* other than the primary ancestor

Basic Data Types C++ offers the following primitive data types (given with their field widths in bits): char:8, int: 16, long:32, float:4, double:64, long double:80, unsigned char:8, unsigned int:16, unsigned long:32 C++ also has bitfields, enumerated types, unions, structs, and typedef to enrich the possibilities.	The following built-in data types with field widths in bits are available: boolean:1, byte:8, char:16, short:16, int:32, long:64, float:32, double:64. Please note that char is 16 bits wide and supports the international Unicode standard for all foreign alphabets including Japanese and Chinese. Java has no *enumerated type*, no *bitfields*, no variable number of arguments for functions, no *struct*, no *unions*, no *typedef*.
Strings C++ has no direct support for strings. Programmers must use zero-terminated arrays of characters or include add-in libraries (MFC, OWL, STL) to provide additional facilities to handle strings	Java uses the built-in class *String* to replace most uses of null terminated character strings as used in C++. class Greetings { public static void main(String args[ ])

Exhibit 19.1 (Continued). A Comparison of C/C++ and Java

C and C++	Java

#include <string.h>
...
char myStr [80];
strcpy(myStr, "Hello");
strcat(myStr, " World");
This example uses an array of null-terminated chars, and the <string.h> library to support strings.
	{
	String myStr;//a reference to the string
	myStr = new String("Hello World");
	myStr = "Hello" + " World";//assign concat
	}
	}

Arrays
An array definition defines a starting address and reserves storage for allocation
int deptNumber[4];
int dNumb[ ] = {10, 20, 30, 40 };
	Arrays are defined in two steps. First a reference to the repeating group is made, then new is used to allocate storage and define the array's size.
	int deptNumber[ ];
	deptNumber = new int[4];
	int deptNumb[ ] = new int[4];
	int dNum[ ] = {10, 20,30,40};
	Arrays that have no claimed space using the new command are set to *null*. Since array subscripts are always checked, the most common form of program failure in Java is trying to use a null reference type which is caught by the Java virtual machine.

Pointers
C and C++ make extensive use of pointers. The addressing and dereferencing operators are used to signal a pointer to data and the value of such address
int Number = 10;
int *ptrNumber = &Number;
This example has no equivalent translation in Java.
	Java has no pointers and thus no pointer arithmetic. Referencing and dereferencing operators (*,&) do not exist. There are, however, *references*, which is a safe kind of pointer.
	BTreeType mytree;//reference
	mytree = new BTreeType();//initialization
	Both arrays and objects are passed by *reference*. When one creates an instance variable of a class (BTreeType mytree;), it is just a reference variable to an instance of that class. The instance variable *must be initialized* with a **new** operator (mytree = **new** BTreeType();) to create an actual instance of that class. The default value of all objects and arrays (i.e., reference types) is *null* (which means an absence of a reference).

Operators There is a large number of arithmetical and logical, operators such as: ++, --, +, -, *,/, %, &&, !, ||, etc.	Java supports almost all of the C++ operators, including bit-wise logical operators, and has minimal extensions .
Flow Control Typical flow control structures are: if [else], for, while, switch, break, continue, goto.	Same as C/C++ with the exception of the **goto** statement which is not implemented. Java also includes a **synchronized** statement to protect critical sections of multi-threaded applications.

Exhibit 19.1 (Continued). A Comparison of C/C++ and Java

C and C++	Java
OS Utilities Input-output operations are not intrinsically defined in the language, but they are rather acquired by using the standard C libraries (stdio.h, stdlib.h, etc.). Another alternative is to use the more powerful set of classes or class libraries provided by the Microsoft MFC, and the Borland OWL. However, those libraries are different and incompatable [3] for every compiler.	Java has designed into it a set of predefined and standardized classes for *I/O, Graphical User Interface (GUI)* access at a high-level, *networking, multiprogramming* with threads, and other operating system services.
Linking In C++ one typically links the application into an executable (myBtreeApp.exe), which is all loaded into memory when the program is started.	Uses a built-in *dynamic linker* and it is common to load new .class files in the middle of execution. Java has no .exe form but is instead a *collection* of .class object files. Thus Java .class 'es are often downloaded from the Internet and executed with subsequent parts (.class modules) downloaded as needed.
Executing C++ is compiled into highly efficient machine language.	Java is typically *interpreted*, thus Java has (for the present) compromised performance to get portability. We will discuss performance in a later section.
Security C++ has an infinite number of ways in which its integrity and security can be defeated.	Java has a *Code Verifier* that checks each .class module before it is loaded to verify that it is well-behaved and obeys the basic rules of the Java language. The *Class Loader* maintains a list of classes it has loaded, as well as the locations from which they came. When a class references another class, the request is served by its original class loader. This means that classes loaded from a specific source can be restricted to interact only with other classes retrieved from the same location. Finally, the *Security Manager* can restrict access to computer resources like the file system, network ports, external processes, memory regions outside of the virtual machine, etc.
Internet C++ was not designed with the Internet in mind; therefore, there is nothing directly connecting them.	Java provides a GUI "interpretable" code-type called an Applet. Applets are applications that can be *run in a standardized environment*, which happens to be provided by a browser such as Netscape or MS-Internet Explorer. Therefore, one can develop a GUI application which can run on the Internet browser of any computer.

Exhibit 19.1 (Continued). A Comparison of C/C++ and Java

Miscellaneous

- Debugging code can be included in your source directly and conditioned on constant variables: thus the Java compiler will remove the code if these variables are not set.
- We do not need a *destructor* member function very often in Java because returning new and other heap storage is done automatically by Java when it is no longer pointed to by any reference types.
- Java exception handling is similar to C++ but not exactly the same. The try block is followed by potentially several catch functions, and a clean-up function finally which is executed in any case. The throw statement generates an exception, and a throws clause in a function declaration indicates that a specific exception might occur in that function. This policy promotes error information to the same level of importance as argument and return typing.
- C++ classes sometimes have a "fragile base class" problem which makes it difficult to modify a class which has many derived classes: changing the base class may require recompilation of the derived classes. Java avoids this problem by dynamically locating fields within classes.

Exhibit 19.2. Summary of Differences between C/C++ and Java

Data Hiding Object	Access Modifiers applied on a variable or member function				
	Private	No Modifier	Private Protected	Protected	Public
Same class	Yes	Yes	Yes	Yes	Yes
Same package subclass	No	Yes	Yes	Yes	Yes
Same package nonsubclass	No	Yes	No	Yes	Yes
Different package subclass	No	No	Yes	Yes	Yes
Different package nonsubclass	No	No	No	No	Yes

IMPACT OF THE MISSING C++ FEATURES IN JAVA

With about 10,000 lines of Java programming behind us and 7+ years of C++ programming, we wish to hazard a guess as to the impact on Java's potential of some of the features of C++ that are missing in Java:

- *Multiple Inheritance*: While one can give many examples of cases where multiple inheritance might be the "best" solution, the concept is not totally clear, and it is at least bothersome. In our experience we find that we have not used it in C++ much at all, so the impact of losing it should be minimal. Nonetheless, there is the possibility of implementing multiple inheritance in Java using *interfaces*.
- *The C++ preprocessor* is certainly the source of many possible errors, but it is also a powerful tool for managing different versions such as the performance tests described below. For example, the timing code in the benchmarks was inserted into each benchmark using #include. In Java these were simply manually copied into each benchmark (when a bug was discovered in the timing code, it was time to hand-edit

19 different versions of the same code). Also in the C++ timing code we used an array of structures where the test procedure address was stored along with the repetition count, etc. In Java this could not be accomplished and so another procedure layer needed to be inserted that used a switch statement to call any of the tests in the current group with appropriate parameters.

- *Pointers.* While it is true that traditionally C/C++ have relied heavily on "pointer logic" to access data, and manipulate parameters, it is also clear that a significant portion of the program development effort is related to cleaning-up that type of logic. Dangling pointers and long chains of indirect addressing are by far the most perturbing and error-prone elements of C/C++ programming. Certain retraining might be needed by the C programmer to adjust to a pointer-free environment. Notice, however, that the concept of *reference* to an object is somehow similar to the pointer notion, just simpler. [10]

We do not feel too many other limitations will imperil the C programmer from making a smooth transition to Java.

JAVA PERFORMANCE CHARACTERISTICS

Among the greatest concerns in Java is execution performance: Java is designed to be *interpreted*— rather than executed. Java .class "executable" programs are pieces of machine code for a non-physically-existent computer. This hypothetical computer is totally implemented in software, and is called the *Java Virtual Machine*. In order to execute .class programs we use a computer program (a Java enabled browser such as Netscape, or an emulator such as Jview.exe), which interpretatively executes the machine instructions in the .class files.

The industry rule of thumb for the execution speed of interpreted code is that it is slower by an *order of magnitude*. While it is true that computer hardware speeds are getting ever faster, our appetite for solving larger and more complex problems means the execution speed is still very much crucial.

We started looking at the issue of execution evaluation with the Sun Microsystems White Paper. [5] Later on, we found a number of Java benchmarks, most of those studies are meant to compare the following:

- The speed of one Java implementation vs. another
- The relative merits of different Internet browsers when executing Applets
- The rating of different hardware platforms when executing the same code. However just a few of those benchmarks made some comparison between C++ vs. Java. [6a–6f]

We decided to do an exhaustive analysis of the two languages on a feature-by-feature basis. The focus was to obtain a gross evaluation of how far

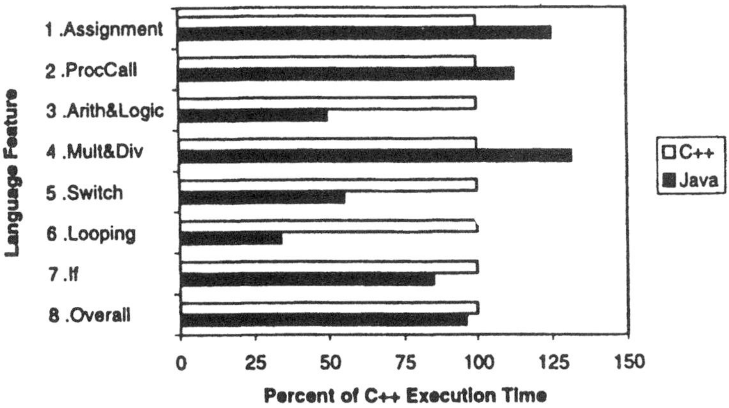

Exhibit 19.3. CPU Language Features: Java vs. C++

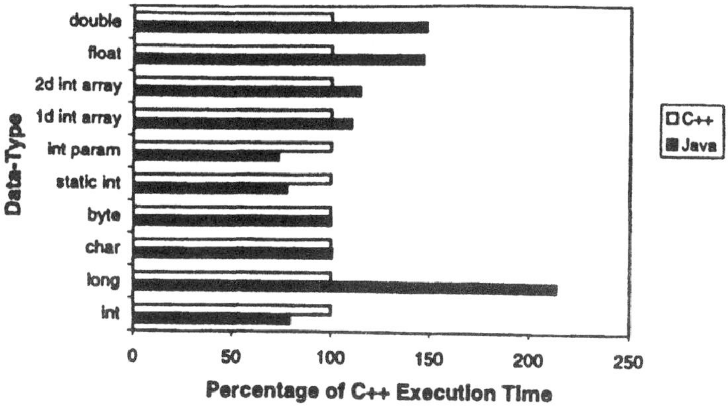

Exhibit 19.4. Java Data-Type Performance vs. C++

apart is one tool (C++) from the other (J++). We converted to Java a number of C++ benchmarks programs that were written earlier to study C++ performance. [7] We then ran all of them first in C++ and then again in Java to study the relative performance of C++ vs. Java.

The performance tests were executed on the same computer, a Pentium 133 megahertz laptop with 32 megabytes of memory, running Windows-95. The software systems were: Visual C++ 4.0 compiler from Microsoft and Microsoft Visual J++ version 1.1.

A battery of tests called the *X tests* measures CPU execution speeds of different language features (see Exhibits 19.3 and 19.4). Both the Java and the C++ test programs were executed using a non-GUI interface. C++ code in the form of .exe files targeted a plain DOS platform, while the Java programs were produced as "applications" to be executed by the JVIEW emulator.

As summarized in Exhibit 3, we found that in a test of CPU language features, Java vs. C++,

- A simple assignment is 25 percent slower in Java as compared to C++.
- Procedure call overhead in actual time is 13 percent slower in Java when compared to C++. However, in C++ a procedure to add two integers executes 8.1 times as long as the "in-line" assignment c = a+b; in Java this factor is 2.1. Thus the additional overhead for the procedure call in this case in Java is one fourth as much when compared to C++.
- Arithmetic, logical, and shift statements overall appear to be about 50 percent faster in Java.
- Multiply and Division statements (*,/,%) appear to be about 32% slower in Java as compared to C++.
- The switch statement performance in Java is 45 percent faster than in C++.
- Looping statements (for,do while,while) appears to be 3 times as fast in Java as in C++.
- If statement execution times in Java are faster by 15 percent.
- The overall execution time of Java is about 4 percent less than the corresponding C++ measurement.

The only surprise here is the low procedure-call overhead in Java, and just the insight that the performance of the main language facilities in Java is comparable to the known-to-be-efficient C++.

As summarized in Exhibit 19.4, Java data-type performance testing found:

- Double precision floating point in Java is 52 percent slower than in C++.
- Java single precision floating point is 53 percent slower than in C++.
- Two-dimensional array access in Java takes 14 percent longer than in C.
- Accessing elements of a one-dimensional array in Java takes 10 percent longer than in C++.
- Int parameters in Java take 27 percent less execution time than in C++.
- Statements involving Java static variables perform 22 percent faster than in C++.
- The Java byte data-type (8-bits) takes about the same execution time as the 8-bit char types do in C++.
- The Java char data-type (16-bits) takes about the same time as the C++ char (but the C++ 16-bit short takes 6.5 percent more execution time than the Java char).
- Java statements involving longs take 113 percent more execution time than C++ longs. Note that Java ints are 32-bit and Java longs are 64 bits, whereas C++ ints and longs are each 32-bits on the Pentium chip.
- Java ints perform 21 percent faster than ints in C++.

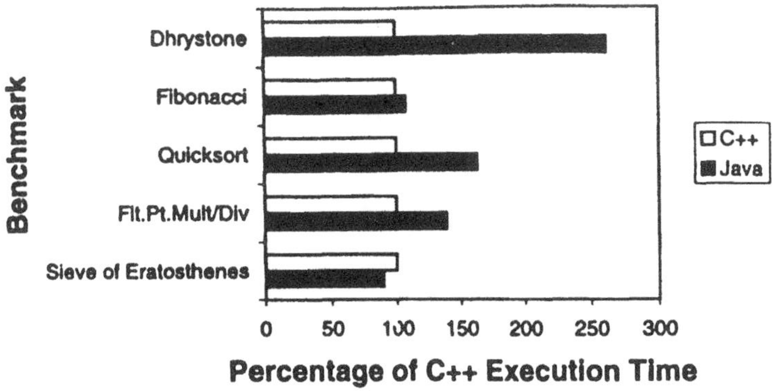

Exhibit 19.5. Routine-Level CPU Benchmarks

All-in-all, paying attention to the choice of data-types can have a significant impact on performance. The single most striking example is the use of longs, which has no performance penalty in C++ on the Pentium, but is over twice as slow in Java, where it is a 64-bit "super long."

As summarized in Exhibit 19.5, routine-level CPU Benchmarks found:

- The Dhrystone benchmark, which is designed to be typical of the CPU part of what programs do (no I/O), takes 2.61 times as much time as in C++.
- The highly recursive Fibonacci number calculation performs 8 percent slower in Java when compared to C++.
- The QuickSort sorting algorithm performs takes 63 percent more time in Java when compared to C++.
- A floating point multiply and divide sequence takes 39 percent more time in Java when compared to C++.
- The Sieve of Eratosthenes code takes 10 percent less time in Java when compared to C++.

These measurements simply confirm that the measurements in the first two sections above can be reaped in a routine that does some specific useful task.

What is clear from the above tests is that unless one pays extraordinary attention to I/O performance, there is little hope of getting a reasonable whole program execution time when compared with what is possible in C++.

As summarized in Exhibit 19.6, routine level I/O test discovered the following:

- Writing 23-character records to a disk file takes 12.2 times as long in Java as in C++.
- Copying a file using readByte/writeByte of a Random AccessFile takes 505 times as long in Java as the corresponding getc/putc commands in C++.

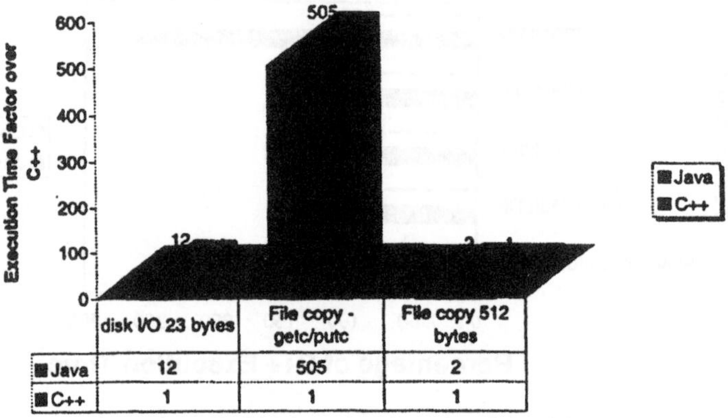

Exhibit 19.6. Routine-Level I/O Test

- Copying the same file by using 512-byte write statements in Java takes only 56 percent more time than in C++.

What is clear from the above tests is that unless a programmer pays extraordinary attention to I/O performance, there is little hope of getting a reasonable whole-program execution time when compared with what is possible in C++.

As summarized in Exhibit 19.7, a simple whole-program benchmark found that

- An electric bill processing benchmark takes 56 times as much time in Java as in C++.
- A string search of a file benchmark takes 63 times as long in Java as the C++ version.
- A bowling scores calculation program takes 224 times as long in Java as the C++ version.
- A TreeSort benchmark takes 15 times as long in Java as in C++.

The actual performance factors here probably have a great deal to do with the I/O usage in the above benchmarks, which we will try to improve below.

The Ctax benchmark found the following:

- A Java procedure call of a static function takes only 60 percent of the time of a global function in C++.
- A normal Java member function takes 8 percent less than in C++. Also, the normal member function in Java takes 45 percent more time than a static function.
- Since all Java member functions are virtual (i.e., exact function is decided at execution time), performance is identical to the above even if using polymorphism, overridden or final.

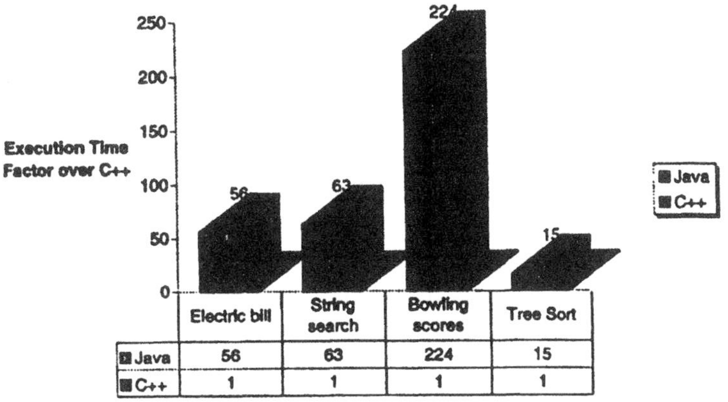

Exhibit 19.7. Simple Whole-Program Benchmarks

- The performance of passing parameters to a procedure is about 4 percent extra for each parameter used. (In C++ the factor is about 3.5 percent extra.)
- The performance of a new of a 4-byte class without member functions is identical to the corresponding C++ new.

The Screen Emulator Benchmark discovered the following:

- Summing up the contents of a CGA 4000 char screen buffer in Java takes 16 percent more time than in C++.
- Summing up a char[25][160] in Java takes 56 percent more time than above in Java (the increase in C++ is 27 percent).
- Summing up a Java class aspot {char a,b;} in an array of classes [25][80] takes113 percent more than item 1 (in C++ this takes 24 percent extra time).
- Summing up a Java class cga that has a member function caref(row,col), which returns a reference to an aspot class instance, takes 263 percent more than the item 1 above (in C++ this takes 216 percent extra).
- Accessing class variables of another class instance in Java is 33 percent slower than a local variable (in C++ it is 3 percent slower).

IMPROVING THE PERFORMANCE OF JAVA PROGRAMS

The purpose of the section above is to give an idea of the overall performance of the Java language using C++ as a framework of reference. The results were mixed; however, they seem to indicate that Java can be as fast as C++ thanks to the intervention of Just-In-Time (JIT) compilation, which does a "mini-compile" into native code as the program is being executed. Looking at the results we questioned our methods a great deal since *so many of the tests showed Java to be as fast or even faster than C++*. However, we were relieved to find that other experimenters have found similar results. [6.f]

To compound this evaluation we must add the obvious issue that not all Java compilers/Viewers are the same. We speculate that most of the relative gains in performance appear to depend primarily on the combination of the Java compiler used to generate the bytecode, and the Java Virtual Machine interpreter utilized for execution. To prove this point we tried a combination of compilers and viewers. Let us consider the following findings:

- One of the measurements yields an execution time of .155 seconds when compiled with the Symantec Java 1.0d compiler and executed with the Microsoft Visual J++ 1.1 Jview interpreter.
- If we use the Symantec Java interpreter, the performance doubles to .327 seconds.
- If we use the Microsoft Visual J++ compiler instead to compile and execute, the execution time doubles again to .675 seconds.
- If, on the other hand, we compile with the Microsoft Visual J++ compiler but run on the Symantec Java interpreter, the execution time is highest at .793 seconds.

A dramatic factor of the above measurements is that while Java "looks good" in most of the measurements, it also provides a disconcerting wide range of variability. We found the execution factor of Java/C++ to be 2, 5, 10, 100, or even 500 in our small number of measurements. To shed some light on this issue we attempted a few performance improvements on some of the benchmarks programs. For instance:

- The electric bill calculation benchmark started with an execution time of 23.79 seconds. Suspecting that the I/O time was causing the problem, we replaced the input file of 8000 integers with a table in memory. This had little effect. The only thing left was to put a *buffering into the print output file: this reduced the execution time by 53.5 percent* down to 11 seconds.
- The string search benchmark originally took 52 seconds (*a factor of 63 times* the C++ version), and was basically searching for a word in an input file and writing the matching line with some trivial formatting. We were already using Java's substring match facility, so there was not much obvious to improve. We again put the maximum file buffering into both the input data file and the output report. This had the dramatic effect of reducing execution time to 4.5 seconds (*a factor of 11.9 times* the C++ version).
- The bowling scores program took 47 seconds to execute (*a factor 191 times* the C++ version). For this program there is no input file and the output report is only a dozen lines. Yet when we put in maximum buffering for the report file the execution time went down to 43.5 seconds

(*a factor of 177 times* the C++ version). The rest of the program does some calculations on two-dimensional arrays.

- The Java program profiler was used to assess where the time is spent in individual applications. In a large medical application with many screens, the time to bring up a given screen for the first time was excessive and the profiler indicated that most of the time was spent in class initialization for the various classes involved. The reason for this was a great mystery and a workaround was attempted: create the classes involved right as the program starts when we do not even know the identity of the patient. Sure enough this reduced the excessive screen switching times substantially. We speculate that the Just-In-Time compiler might be generating native code for member functions for the class as it is being constructed (under VisualCafé).

I/O PERFORMANCE SUMMARY

So just from these few experiences one can see that I/O performance can be improved in a big way by simply using Buffered streams for both file input, file output, and report output. Also, Java has a readFully method that reads in an entire file in one I/O call. Now that virtual and actual memories are so large, this can be a dramatic way of achieving performance improvement, of course at some cost! In one medical data application, bringing up a patient screen *took 20 seconds*, an "eternity" if you're staring at the screen. When the reading of the patient file was changed to readFully, the time *was reduced to 0.4 seconds* (an improvement factor of 50). Obviously, those applications deemed to be real-time critical will benefit tremendously from this "read-ahead" protocol; on the other hand, not all applications need such a solution.

CPU PERFORMANCE SUMMARY

The CPU-bound portions of a program can also be improved with the knowledge derived from the measurements of the different data types described above. But one should always be aware of the relative performance of different compilers, and Java interpreters, which are changing fast as the Java development platforms come of age. It is important to point out that *Java applications are nearly 100% portable between any platform, operating system, and development system.* We took turns using the Sun development kit, Symantec VisualCafé, and Microsoft Visual J++ with no compatibility problems so far.

CONCLUSION

Java is probably a very important software development language for the present and the future. The combination of practical choices made in terms of language features for an Object-Oriented Programming Language, a standardized set of system interfaces for input/output, Graphical User Interfaces, networking, Operating System facilities, and a platform independent executable code will likely make it an important tool for some time to come.

While performance is a serious issue, our measurements show that Java bytecode behavior can approach executable C++ code in a very impressive way. However, we also witness cases in which much work is needed to make the gap between both languages shrink to a reasonable value. The authors have seen some production-level software developed that generally meets the performance requirements of an interactive Windows application. Also, the technology is still emerging so there will likely be more optimization of the JVM code generated, compilers that generate native code, a steady improvement in the performance of Java Virtual Machine emulators and Just-In-Time optimization, and even the possibility of auxiliary hardware CPU's that implement the Java Virtual Machine.

Recommended Reading

[1] Brian Kernigham, Dennis Ritchie, *The C Programming Language*, Prentice-Hall, 1978.

[2] P. Jalics was a researcher at the Xerox-Parc Palo Alto Research Center in Palo Alto California where the super strongly typed Mesa language was developed and used to implement an Operating System and applications.

[3] A. Fadlalla, P. Jalics, Victor Matos, "Portability of GUI based Object-Oriented Applications," *Systems Development Management*, Auerbach Publishers, accepted January 1997.

[4] James Gosling, "The Java Language: A White Paper," Sun Microsystems, 1993.

[5] "The Java Language Environment: A White Paper," Sun Microsystems, October 1995.

[6a] "The CaffeineMark Java Benchmark" from Pendragon Software.

[6b] "Jmark 1.0 Java Benchmark", *PC Magazine*, January 7, 1997, vol. 16, No. 1, p.182.

[6c] Doug Bell, "Make Java Fast: Optimize!," *JavaWorld*, http://www.javaworld.com/javaworld.

[6d] Jonathan Hardwick, Java Optimization site: http://www.cs.cmu.edu/~jcl/java/optimization.html.

[6e] The Fhourstones 2.0 Benchmark (ANSI C,Java), tromp@cwi.nl.

[6f] f. "Jstones" by Sky Coyote, (Java, C++), sky@inergalact.com.

[7] P. Jalics, B. Blake, "Performance of Object-Oriented Programs: C++," *Systems Development Management*, Auerbach Publishers, 1992.

[8] Judith Bishop, *Java Gently*, Ed. Addison-Wesley, 1997.

[9] Patrick Naughton, *The Java Handbook*, Osborne – McGraw-Hill, 1997.

[10] Deitel and Deitel, *Java — How to Program*, Prentice Hall, 1997.

Chapter 20
Web and Java Risk Issues

Louise Soe and Frederick Gallegos

The Internet has been around for years, but private industry only became interested in its commercial possibilities after the graphical World Wide Web emerged during the early 1990s. The Web version of the Internet offered a potentially inexpensive and platform-independent network over which to conduct business and disseminate information. In addition, companies grew excited about the possibility of developing intranets (internal Internets) that would give them access to all of their legacy data via one simple Internet browser interface.

All of this was to be enabled by a programming language, Java, that would work on any operating system or computing platform. In addition, this language could be used to deliver to client machines the program and data elements (in the form of a Java applet) that the client needed to use at any given time. Companies envisioned desktops equipped with Internet appliances that would not need to contain expensive copies of application programs such as word processors and spreadsheets. It is little wonder that corporations were ready to embrace both the Internet and Java, and to build such high expectations about these technologies. These expectations have not died. Many corporate executives and managers expect these technologies to drive economic growth well into the next century.

THE PERCEIVED RISKS

However, the Internet and its most promising language, Java, present an interesting mix of opportunities and risks to organizations. On the one hand, organizations want to stay competitive and embrace technologies that provide so much promise. Yet, both corporations and individuals still perceive the Internet as insecure and the use of Java applets as unsafe. Corporations are wary of the very serious security threats from outside hackers to which a connection to the Internet might expose them. Individual users of the Internet are wary of the possible destructive use of Java applets that they download to their computers over the Internet. Thus, while the promise of the Internet and Java pushes companies toward expectations of free and open communication over the Internet, fear pushes companies toward isolation because they want to protect their information assets from theft, corruption, or destruction.

0-8493-9822-3/00/$0.00+$.50

The remainder of this chapter discusses ways in which corporations can use the Internet in a secure fashion by implementing security measures that are currently available. It also discusses the Java programming language, which is still somewhat immature, and the measures that are being taken to strengthen its security so that it will become the powerhouse language of the Internet.

INTERNET SECURITY

Security tools and procedures exist right now to reduce risk when a company gives its customers access to business resources over the Internet. Security measures are available to provide access security to protect the company's own computers, disks, memory, and other computing equipment from outside interference, and transaction security to ensure that two individuals or organizations on the Internet can privately and safely execute a transaction.

Properly implemented, these security mechanisms will:

- Protect the company from intruders who attempt to enter the internal network from the Internet;
- Provide authorized users with access to Internet services such as HTTP, FTP, Telnet, and Gopher;
- Deliver required Internet applications from the internal network to the Internet;
- Deliver SMTP and Netnews services to the internal network from the Internet;
- Prevent unauthorized use of resources on the internal network;
- Give users an easy way to understand network security status without being Internet security experts;
- Assure expert round-the-clock, seven-day-a-week monitoring and response to security events; and
- Maximize protection from the Internet and minimize the cost of operating and monitoring protective devices, such as the application proxy firewall.

SECURITY TOOLS AND TECHNOLOGIES

Effective security solutions rely on several tools and technologies designed to protect information and computers from intrusion, compromise, or misuse: encryption technologies, security policies and procedures, and various types of firewalls.

Encryption Technologies

Encryption technologies electronically store information in an encoded form that can only be decoded by an authorized individual who has the appropriate decryption technology and authorization to decrypt. Encryption provides a number of important security components to protect electronic information:

- Identity............................ Who are you?
- Authentication................ Can you prove who you are?
- Authorization.................. What can you do?
- Auditing........................... What did you do?
- Integrity........................... Is it tamper proof?
- Privacy............................. Who can see it?
- Nonrepudiation............... Can I prove that you said what you said?

When information is encoded, it is first translated into a numerical form, and then encrypted using a mathematical algorithm. The algorithm requires a number or message, called a key, in order to encode or decode the information. The algorithm cannot decode the encrypted information without a decode key.

Security Policies and Procedures

In the rush to establish an Internet presence, many companies have overlooked perhaps the most important foundation piece in an effective security solution: a sound security policy that identifies who has access to a company's electronic resources, and under what circumstances they have access. Many companies have overlooked this strategy in their rush to establish an Internet presence. Thus, security policies in some companies are almost nonexistent and clearly defined in others. For example, the use of stateless filters means that the organization is relying on defaults set by the vendor of the security package, whereas the use of state-maintained filters means the organization is actively ensuring certain types of activity or patterns are reviewed to prevent possible intrusion or loss.

Security policies fall along a continuum that ranges from promiscuous at one end to paranoid at the other. The promiscuous policy allows unchecked access between the Internet and the organization's internal network to everyone. The paranoid policy refuses access between these two networks to everyone. In between are two more palatable alternatives, the permissive policy and the prudent policy.

The permissive policy allows all traffic to flow between the internal network and the Internet except that which is explicitly disallowed. Permissive policies are implemented through packet-filtering gateways, where stateless filters prevent individual packets of data from crossing the network boundary if the packet is coming from or going to a specific computer, network, or network port. There are two major drawbacks to a permissive policy, however. First, it requires an exhaustive set of filters to cover all possible addresses and ports that should be denied access. Second, it is virtually impossible to block certain undesirable packets without also blocking other desirable and necessary packets, because network protocols are dynamic and often change network port numbers, depending on the protocol state.

A prudent policy, on the other hand, selectively allows traffic that is explicitly allowed by the protocol and excludes any other. Prudent policies are implemented by a set of application proxies that understand the underlying application protocol and can implement a set of state-maintaining filters that allow specific application data to pass from one network to the next. Because the filters can follow the state of the protocol, they can change dynamically when the protocol changes state. This way, rules allow only properly authorized data to flow across the network boundary. Prudent policies are implemented through application proxy firewalls.

Because prudent and permissive policies act as the network boundaries, they are referred to as perimeter security solutions.

Once a company selects the appropriate security policy, the policy can be implemented according to a strict set of procedures with the support of software systems. These security procedures, which include a documented set of rules governing the management and administration of the security system and its generated events, record a trail of all modifications to the security system (auditing) and set off signal alarms when someone attempts to violate the policies. Properly followed, they protect an organization from all types of security violations, including accidental administrative mistakes, human factor attacks (i.e., people characteristics) and unauthorized modifications to the security policy.

To reduce the risk of "inside" break-ins, many companies also require a background check of security systems personnel, and separate security management and auditing to prevent an administrator from altering the audit of management actions.

Internet Firewalls

Internet application proxy firewalls are a prudent perimeter security solution. These systems sit between the Internet and the organization's internal network, and control the traffic flow between the Internet and a company's internal resources. A firewall provides application proxies for most popular Internet applications, as well as support for a more restrictive prudent policy. This policy might restrict the establishment of network connections from within the company outward to the Internet. In addition, rather than forwarding packets between networks, the firewall can require the application client to establish an application service connection to the firewall. The firewall then maintains the connection with the outside server. The firewall will only pass data for applications that it currently supports, which eliminates most security holes.

Security holes created by incorrectly configured computers on the internal network are not visible to the Internet and therefore cannot be exploited by external Internet users. The organization's own Internet application servers then sit outside the firewall in what is called the demilitarized zone. This eliminates the need for outside traffic to travel through the firewall into the organization's internal network when it is using Web, FTP, or Telnet services.

To maintain the integrity of the perimeter, the firewall must be constantly monitored for potential security breaches. Should a breach occur, an Internet security expert must be available to survey the damage and recommend a solution.

Internet Firewall Configurations

Bastion Host. This is the only host on the customer's internal network that is visible to the Internet. It has no customer-accessible accounts for logging into the bastion host.

Customer communications travel through the bastion host via proxy applications. This is the most secure method of performing perimeter security today.

In the popular dual-homed bastion host configuration, the toolkit software is installed on a host with two network interfaces. The toolkit software provides proxy services for common applications like FTP and TELNET, and security for SMTP mail. Since the bastion host is a security-critical network strong point, it is important that the configuration of the software on that system be as secure as possible.

Dual-homed gateways provide an appealing firewall, since they are simple to implement, require a minimum of hardware, and can be verified easily. Most Berkeley-based UNIX implementations have a kernel variable _ipforwardign, which can be set to indicate to the operating system that it should not route traffic between networks, even if it is connected to them (which would normally cause the system to act as a gateway router). By completely disabling routing, the administrator can have a high degree of confidence that any traffic between the protected network and any untrusted network has to occur through an application that is running on the firewall. Since there is no traffic transferred directly between the internal network and the untrusted network, it is not necessary to show any routes to the protected network over the untrusted network. This effectively renders the protected network invisible to any systems except the bastion host. The only disadvantage of this type of firewall is that it implicitly provides a firewall of the type in which that which is not expressly permitted is prohibited. This means that it is impossible to weaken the firewall's security to let a service through should one later decides to do so. Instead, all services must be supported via proxies on the firewall.

Choke Router/Screened Host. The choke router reinforces the bastion host, enforces security policy, and isolates the internal network from the Internet.

A screened host gateway relies on a router with some form of packet screening capacity to block off access between the protected network and the untrusted network. A single host is identified as a bastion host, and traffic is permitted only to that host. The software suite that is run on the bastion host is similar to a dual-homed gateway; the system must be as secure as possible, as it is the focal point for attack on the network. Screened host gateways are a very flexible solution, since they offer the opportunity to selectively permit traffic through the screening router for applications that are considered trustworthy, or between mutually trusted networks.

The disadvantage of this configuration is that there are now two critical security systems in effect: the bastion host and the router. If the router has access control lists that permit certain services through, the firewall administrator has to manage an additional point of complexity. Verifying the correctness of a screened host firewall is a bit more difficult. It quickly becomes increasingly difficult as the number of services permitted through the router grows. Screened host firewalls also introduce management risks; because it is possible to open holes in the firewall for special applications or influential users, the firewall administrator must be careful to resist pressure to modify the screening rules in the router.

In a screened subnet firewall, a small isolated network is placed between the trusted network and the untrusted network. Screening rules in routers protect access to this network by restricting traffic so that both networks can only reach hosts on the screened subnet. Conceptually, this is the dual-homed gateway approach applied to an entire network. The main utility of this approach is that it permits multiple hosts to exist on the outside network (again referred to as the demilitarized zone). An additional advantage to the screened host subnet is that the firewall administrator can configure network routing in a way that does not advertise routes to the private network from the Internet, or internal routes to the Internet. This is a powerful means to protect a large private network, since it becomes very difficult for an outsider to direct traffic toward the hidden private network. If the routing is blocked, then all traffic must pass through an application on the bastion host, just as it must in the dual-homed gateway.

Firewalls in a Partitioned Network. Not every network is a single, isolated network attached to an untrusted network. As the use of large-scale networks continues to increase, businesses increasingly form business partnerships and transmit sensitive corporate information over public networks. In addition, single corporations seek to establish a common security perimeter among multiple facilities connected over a public backbone. In this type of situation, a business can effectively combine a firewall with network-level encryption hardware (or software) to produce a virtual network, with a common security perimeter.

A company can establish a common security perimeter between two facilities, over a public Wide Area Network (WAN). The encryption is separate from the router, but need not be if integrated encrypting routers are available. Currently, there are several products that act as encrypting bridges at a frame level. These products work by examining the source and destination address of all packets arriving via one interface and retransmitting the packet out via another interface. If the encrypting bridge/router is configured to encrypt traffic to a specific network, the packet data is encrypted, and a new checksum is inserted into the packet header. Once the packet is received at the other computer, the peer encrypting bridge/router determines that it is from a network with which the router is encrypting traffic, and decrypts the packet, patches the checksum, and retransmits it.

Anyone intercepting traffic between the two encrypting networks would see only useless cipher text. An additional benefit of this approach is that it protects against attempts to inject traffic by spoofing the source network address. Unless attackers know the cipher key that is in use, their packets will be encrypted into junk when they go through the encrypting bridge/router. If the encrypting bridge/router gets traffic for a network with which it does not have an encryption arrangement, traffic is transmitted normally. In this manner, a firewall can be configured, with encrypted tunnels to other networks. For example, a company could safely share files via NFS or safely use weakly authenticated network login programs, such as rlogin over their encrypted link, and still have a strong firewall protecting access between the corporate perimeter and the rest of the world. Two companies that wanted to establish a business connection for proprietary information could apply a similar approach, in which traffic between the firewall bastion host on one corporate network and the firewall bastion host on the other corporate network was automatically encrypted.

PRACTICAL WEB SECURITY SOLUTIONS

Thus, it is easy to see that businesses need not be intimidated into bypassing the opportunities available to them on the Internet. Several security solutions exist immediately to reduce or remove the risk involved in connecting to the Internet. We list and summarize a few of them:

A Back Door Connection

This method connects the Internet server (Web server, List server, etc.) to other company computer systems through a dial-up link, which is not made available anywhere on the Internet.

A back door data transfer method might include setting up a program like ProComm Plus (by Datastorm) on a computer connected to the Web Server. The company's other computer systems then periodically dial into that back door computer via ProComm to upload files that are then imported to the Web server's database via a custom import program. This same method works well for sending order or questionnaire data in batches from a Web server to other computers within the company.

In using this approach, the communications lines between the company's computers and its Internet presence are severed most of the time. Even when the link is established between computers, it does not use an insecure network protocol like TCP/IP, which is easy for hackers to penetrate. This prevents Internet hackers from drilling through to vital company systems and information.

A Network Firewall

A network firewall connects the Internet server into the company's existing computer network system via a permanent firewall router.

Firewall routers are sold by a growing number of network hardware and software companies. They serve as a security barrier between network systems. By placing such a barrier between the company's Web server and the rest of the company's network, a network administrator can restrict the flow of network data packets between these segments. The firewall could restrict all inbound packets to those generated by the Web server itself; thus only the Web server can access internal information.

A good hacker can get through a firewall, although attempting to gain access beyond the firewall would require the use of sophisticated IP source-address spoofing techniques. These techniques fool the firewall into believing that the hacker's connection has the same network address as the Web server or some other privileged user. At this point, the hacker would need sufficient motivation to expend the effort and time to get through.

Any time a company plans to connect their in-house computer network directly to an Internet server, a firewall should be used to deter casual hacking and other less malicious security risks.

A Pseudo-Firewall

A pseudo-firewall connects the Internet server into the company's existing computer network system via standard router equipment, but segregates network traffic with different network protocols (i.e., TCP/IP and IPX/SPX).

The main security problem on the Internet exists due to certain flaws in the Internet network protocol (TCP/IP). Thus, using a different protocol to connect the company's internal computers to its Internet server solves this problem.

For example, if a company's Internet server used a Pentium PC running Microsoft Windows NT as its Web server over a leased line connected to an Internet Service Provider, this method would entail running two network protocols on the Web server. The Web server must use TCP/IP to connect to the Internet. Yet, to access information on internal computer networks, that same Web server could be configured to use something else, such as IPX/SPX, which is native to Novell's Netware. The hacker could spoof the TCP/IP address, but would find no other network connections beyond the Web server.

This method is not proven to work more effectively than a firewall. However, its appeal is that it can provide a similar level of security to a firewall router, at lower cost.

Our discussion now moves to the application language, Java, and the risks and opportunities it provides to organizational computing.

JAVA RISK ISSUES

Another area for management review in corporate use of the World Wide Web is the use of Java. Java is an object-oriented programming language in which small programs (called applets) can be compiled and run on any computing platform. Within an internal intranet, applets could deliver software and data to client workstations only as needed. The applet would only need to include the functions of a software application and the data that the client needed to accomplish a specific task. Thus, corporations could save on software licenses and workstation computing power across the enterprise. On the Internet, Java applets are downloaded by the client from a server on the Internet. However, many individuals fear the destructive potential of Java applets from unknown sources. Current browsers allow users to refuse Java applets or accept them only from trusted sources.

Although Java provides benefits and cost effective measures to a corporation, the current versions of Java are not mature enough to satisfy the needs of corporate security. Java may be fine for building Windows applets, but it is not yet a real tool for mission critical programs that draw on legacy data. The earlier Java tools provided weak data validation and relied too heavily on object linking and embedding (OLE). These older Java tools were geared too much towards Windows and often lacked some of the key features such as debuggers and compilers that are essential in a workbench.

Recent studies by universities and private industry groups have identified three areas which pose the most significant risks to Java applications: (1) the lack of audit trails, (2) the variances between Java language and bytecode semantics, and the (3) deficiencies in the design of the language and byte code format and the input/output object classes.

Presently, the Java environment does not provide a standard or default mechanism to produce audit trails. The developer must customize all verification into the application. Java needs built-in accountability functions to maintain protected and selective auditing information much like an audit log, which identifies the parties responsible for various actions performed on the computer.

Users also need to understand that they do not control a Java applet once it is downloaded into the local environment. For example, users may not necessarily know that an applet has been downloaded or may not have information on how many applets are in operation, unless they set up adequate security on their Internet browsers. A common form of malicious applet can continue running on the client and force the user to restart the system.

There are other security problems as well. Today, compiler languages such as C or Ada can produce bytecode that looks like Java bytecode to the verifier. If the verifier erroneously accepts the non-Java bytecode, it is unlikely to follow Java's language restrictions and it may allow performance of illegal procedures. For example, a hostile applet could be used to create a classloader containing unacceptable statements. The classloader, which is responsible for defining namespace seen by other classes, could then allow the attacking applet to customize the user's computer environment.

Finally, from an IS audit standpoint, Java input/output object classes are public. Even though this feature improves the usefulness of Java, it provides hackers with a way to deliver damage. This major weakness of Java makes the use of audit tools critical to safe use of Java programs.

For the average corporate IS developer, accustomed to Visual Basic and similar drag-and-drop development tools, the early Java environments seemed to take two steps backwards. Therefore, Java's competitors took advantage of this weakness and prepared a second generation of Java toolsets to resolve some of the weaknesses of the Java programming language. These tools were intended to give corporate IS developers the same warm, fuzzy feeling of confidence they get from other visual development environments.

Corporate IS developers want to build Web applications for the long term. Many corporate and government IS departments are caught up in testing new Web-based development technologies, primarily centered on Java-based development. These include tools such as Visix's-eleven, and emerging technologies such as remote method invocation (RMI) and object serialization. One of the documented weaknesses that most toolsets do not redress is Sun's implementation of the abstract Windowing Toolkit for building user interface features. Developers are still working to resolve this problem.

JAVA SECURITY IMPROVEMENTS

Java has additional shortcomings in the area of security. Most companies that use Java will not yet use it for security-sensitive data because it lacks the necessary security functions. Development experts describe the programming language as "a few cups short of a full pot." Unresolved issues revolve around database access, security, bi-directional communication, and the way in which Java handles compound documents. Sun Microsystems has several initiatives to make Java more suitable for utilizing security-sensitive data. These include creation of several API programs for encryption, digital signatures, authentication, and support for a key management system.

The latest version of the Java tools addresses many concerns by offering:

- Strong memory protection. Java applications and applets cannot gain unauthorized memory access to read or change accounts because Java removes the possibility of either maliciously or inadvertently reading and/or corrupting memory locations outside boundaries of the programs.
- Encryption and signatures. Java uses powerful encryption technology to verify that an applet came from an authorized source and has not been modified.
- Rules enforcement. Java objects and classes make it simple to represent corporate information entities, and the rules governing their use are embedded within the objects themselves. The result is that the introduction of ad hoc access and manipulation methods can be controlled.
- Runtime Code verification. The Java run-time verification system inspects all code for viruses and tampering before running it, ensuring that all applications and applets downloaded to the client do not violate the integrity of the environment.

Even with these improvements, there is no singular approach to solve the major concerns with Java.

Recently, Microsoft Corporation and Netscape announced a security plan, which includes a series of security techniques for forthcoming products. These include ways to verify authorship, improvements to proxy-server and firewalls, and an information database on the security status of Java applets. However, the continued competition between Microsoft and other companies over definition of Java language standards may not be doing much to contribute to the development of a mature, stable Java programming language.

CONCLUSIONS

For CIOs and CEOs, the new millennium promises many exciting opportunities and risks in information technology. As unsettling and unnerving as many of these changes are, managers must employ common sense and informed business judgement to understand both risks and benefits. We have attempted to provide an overview of Web and Java security issues facing business today. We understand the technical complexities and encourage decision-makers to carefully weigh the investment in security against the potential risks. We also reiterate that there are answers and solutions for many of the security issues we discuss. Effective measures exist to protect both access security and transaction security over the Internet. As improvements are made to Java and as the programming language matures, we can also expect that it will incorporate more and better security measures, because Java language developers realize that security is critical to the acceptance and success of the language.

Java provides an entirely new kind of cross-platform computing environment that can be used to integrate and work with an organization's existing systems and networks. As Java matures, it may well replace costlier, less efficient elements in existing computing systems and make feasible the continued use of existing legacy systems. This is especially important today, when multiple incompatible platforms and legacy systems are typical in global corporate and private information systems infrastructures. The Web and Java hold great promise for organizations that want to integrate their existing, incompatible applications and make them available through one common user interface, an Internet browser.

Web platforms and application platforms are incredibly complex and resource-intensive, expensive to buy and maintain, and costly to update or expand. But, as troublesome as these existing systems may be, the CEO and CIO have to consider whether they can afford to scrap huge corporate investments in existing information systems. It is very costly to replace systems, convert databases that contain invaluable information, and retrain workers in new computing environments and techniques.

Throughout the business and personal computing world, industry leaders, software vendors, and software developers are showing utmost support for Java, the programming language that they believe will transcend all barriers. Most business organizations will benefit by using adaptable application architecture. This new technology can save a company millions of corporate dollars per fiscal year on hardware, software, and systems development by converting a "custom fat client" into a "thin client."

While Web technology and Java are still somewhat immature, there is no doubt that they are here to stay. Major software developers continue to give credence to Java's future, and have addressed user concerns by announcing plans to embed Java in future versions of their operating systems. As other higher-order tools are built up around it, Java should become one of the best enablers on the market. Those higher order tools are on their way to the marketplace now, so sit tight, and be prepared to embrace the Web and the Java revolution.

Chapter 21

Java's Role in Distributed Computing

J.P. Morgenthal

Although Java is rapidly becoming the premier tool for building Internet applications, the fact that seemingly simple Internet applications, such as Web browsers, are actually distributed applications is often overlooked. Internet applications carry with them all the complexities associated with any distributed environment, although the severity of problems is admittedly lighter.

The term distributed applications encompasses many technologies and development techniques, and a clear definition of it remains elusive. For clarity, a distributed application is one in which two or more components are cooperatively operating over a process boundary. The process boundary introduces the need for concurrency and shared memory. Concurrency represents the capability to share resources in a mutually exclusive manner with all the guarantees that it implies.

A growing trend in the industry today is transitioning existing enterprise applications to Web applications. Web applications are best defined as those that present a Hypertext Transfer Protocol (HTTP) interface for operation from within a Web browser. Employing this new motif for interacting with the user has given new life to many of these applications by creating a more intuitive user interface and expanding the platforms that can access it.

Inside of the Web pages that represent this new interface are Java applets — code modules that can execute within a Java virtual machine — that enhance the Web browser's ability to interact with the user. For many, this defines the extent of Java's utility in developing distributed applications. This article presents a greater role for Java in the world of distributed computing. Java distributed computing represents a body of Java programming interfaces that enables Java applications to communicate with each other across a process boundary. The simplest form of this type of computing is two Java applications passing data over a Transmission Control Protocol/Internet Procotol (TCP/IP) network connection. The more complex form is two Java applications sending and receiving Java objects.

0-8493-9822-3/00/$0.00+$.50

JAVA'S BENEFITS

Is Java hype or reality? Java is not a panacea for computing, but a very well thought out tool for building applications that need to operate in a networked environment. Like any tool, Java assists with certain jobs and is completely wrong for others. At this stage in Java's technology adoption, users are trying to see what this new tool can do.

Java has provided some immediate benefits through its use:

1. Owing to the nature of its programming language design, Java suits complex object-oriented development without some of the pitfalls associated with other languages in this category. For example, C++ requires detailed control of memory allocation and de-allocation. Java handles this automatically through garbage collection. This one small change in philosophy adds a tremendous amount of quality to software and reduces the number of problems caused with memory leaks and overruns.
2. The Java virtual machine is a widely accepted standard that is supported on all major commercial operating systems. Java's design theoretically supports the concept of write-once run-anywhere, but the mass deployment of virtual machines makes the theoretical concept a reality.
3. Java simplifies the deployment of applications in the organization. Some Java applications can be deployed as applets running on Hypertext Markup Language (HTML) pages in Web browsers. Still others can be full-blown stand-alone Java applications that automatically download their new components as a standard practice of the virtual machine. Here again, the promise of write-once run-anywhere is an important one because these types of deployments are unencumbered by hardware and operating system differences.
4. Java offers the promise of consolidated development resources. Today, many IT departments are strangled by the different hardware and system software platforms requiring support. With Java on all these platforms, many of the specialized resources can be combined to work jointly on multiplatform efforts. These combinations also help to spread understanding of the business' core applications across the development staff.
5. With companies clamoring to get at and manipulate their legacy data locked away on mainframe computers, a Java virtual machine can be a saving grace. IBM is currently porting the virtual machine for OS/390 and AS/400. Both of these machines store roughly 85 percent of corporate data today. Java will provide access to this data as well as offering new ways to process and distribute data throughout the organization.

In general, it could be said that Java simplifies the development, deployment, and maintenance of applications in the enterprise. Since most applications in this environment are for data entry or data retrieval, Java offers enough capabilities and performance today. For some specific applications such as computer-aided design or real-time monitoring, Java cannot provide the performance or features required. Java's strong suit is thus development of distributed applications — applications that are partitioned into multiple tasks running on different machines.

DISTRIBUTED JAVA APPLICATIONS

Network application programming is never a trivial task, but sending and receiving a simple set of data over the network using Java is greatly simplified. However, there is far more utility when the communicating components maintain context along with the data. To accomplish this, not only data needs to be transmitted, but its functional and structural components as well. Existing distributed computing middleware currently supports maintaining context by using references to running executables. Generally, these references are literal strings that identify the machine where the executable is running. Distributed Java also maintains context as references, but the references are fully functional Java objects.

To define Java distributed computing, one must understand the differences between applications running in the same address space and those running in different address spaces. Two Java applications running in the same address space can simply call functions on each other as long as the functions are programmed to be exposed publicly. In this case, there are no barriers stopping this behavior; however, when the applications are running in separate address spaces, there is a virtual barricade that surrounds each application. This barricade stops one application from seeing and being able to call functions into the other address space. The only way to subvert the virtual barricade is to make the function calls by passing the data over defined pathways into and out of it. In Java, the facility that performs this subversion is called Remote Method Invocation, or RMI.

To provide some familiar vocabulary that will help provide context for Java applications; applications that expose their functions publicly are sometimes referred to as servers, and the applications that call them are referred to as clients. Hence, the client/server paradigm that has become so popular applies again with the rise of Web applications. When discussing these terms relative to a pure-Java application, applications that expose their functions publicly are referred to as remote Java objects and the applications using them are referred to as Java clients.

Remote Method Invocation

The Remote Method Invocation facility is core to distributed Java and defines a framework for Java-to-Java application communications that extends Java over process boundaries in a natural manner. Designed using techniques learned from the experiences of the Distributed Computing Environment's (DCE) Remote Procedure Calls (RPC) and Common Object Request Broker Architecture (CORBA), Java RMI is an advanced inter-object communications system. The primary difference between inter-application and inter-object communications is the requirement for inter-object communications to support pass-by-value for objects. Pass-by-value will be explained in detail later.

As previously stated, RMI extends Java naturally over process boundaries. This means that Java communicates with remote objects — those in another address space — in a manner that is transparent to the user. That is, remote Java objects will behave in the prescribed manner of all Java objects. By upholding this contract, remote Java objects will support the same behavior of a local Java object providing the desired local/remote transparency that is one of the core focuses of distributed computing. To accomplish this level of local/remote transparency, three important requirements must be met:

1. The two communicating components must agree on a common messaging protocol.
2. The two communicating components must use the same transport mechanism, for example, TCP/IP networking protocol.
3. Code and data must be marshaled — packaged in a byte-oriented stream — in a consistent manner.

The work on behalf of JavaSoft to develop and implement these requirements represents an outstanding body of computing research and technology. Actually, points 1 and 2 are fairly simple if experienced in network programming. However, the third point requires the cooperation of multiple Java subsystems, including Introspection, Object Serialization, Garbage Collection, and Remote Method Invocation itself.

Introspection

Java's Introspection facilities allow the virtual machine to identify all of a Java object's methods and fields from the Java class description. With this knowledge, the virtual machine can "flatten" Java objects from their in-memory state to a sequential stream of bytes. Once in the latter format, the object can be stored on persistent media or transferred over a network. This facility is not exposed directly to the programmer, for this would pose an opportunity to subvert the built-in security mechanisms. Instead, this facility is exposed through the Reflection programming interface and object serialization.

Reflection is a programmatic interface for allowing Java objects to identify public, and sometimes private, methods and fields on Java objects. However, the method calls to the Reflection interface are checked by the virtual machines security manager, thus allowing the security manager to restrict access. Of note, Introspection and Reflection can only be used on local Java objects. While a useful tool for building a remote procedure call mechanism, it cannot be used to examine remote Java objects. Therefore, the contract between the client and the server must be designed before the application is programmed.

Object Serialization

Object serialization uses Java's powers of introspection to store and retrieve objects from a persistent form without requiring additional programming. To accomplish this task, the serialization layer must be able to identify and read all fields on a Java object. Furthermore, the serialization layer must define a format for flattened objects that allows for identification of class type and simplified retrieval.

The data format chosen for object serialization is publicly distributed from JavaSoft with the Java Development Kit (JDK). This format implements certain required functionality for this facility. For example, if two fields within an object reference the same object, only one copy of the object is serialized along with the two individual references. This provides a level of integrity by ensuring that any changes to the object are reflected via both fields. This format also includes the class name for each object that is serialized so that the corresponding code can be associated when retrieved. Additionally, each serialized object is stored with a unique identifier that represents that object within the stream. This allows the object to be updated within the stream without having to serialize the entire graph again.

A common problem associated with persistent objects is reconciling hine. The Naming class is used by Java objects that wish to use remote Java objects and exposes an interface for finding and retrieving a reference to a remote object.

These classes allow Java applications to implement RMI in a modular manner. That is, it does not make applications that use them reliant on any particular implementation of RMI, thus allowing RMI to operate over a host of networking protocols and vendor independent implementations. The following is a sample RMI transaction.

Sample RMI Transaction

The transaction presented in the steps that follow is based on Sun Microsystems' implementation of RMI that ships with the JDK release 1.1. Again, the only parts of this transaction that are vendor independent are the parts that use the Registry and Naming classes.

Step 1. A Java client object wishing to obtain a reference to a remote Java object running on a particular machine uses the Naming class to perform a lookup on that object.

Step 2. If the remote object is running and properly registered in a RMI Registry on that machine, the Registry will return a reference. A reference in RMI is a Java object called a stub, which implements all publicly exposed methods on the remote Java object and maps the calls over the network.

Step 3. The Java client object makes a method call on the remote Java object that requires an integer parameter. The stub object uses the object serialization facility to serialize the integer object into a stream, along with the method call signature, and delivers it to a dedicated listening network service called the skeleton.

Step 4. The skeleton parses the serialized data from the client and builds a properly formatted method call on the remote Java object, which is local to itself. Any return values are serialized and passed back to the Java client. Exhibit 21.1 clarifies how the transaction operates. On machine 1, a client application uses the Java Naming class to access the Registry located on machine 2. This is done over a lookup operation. Upon successfully locating the requested object in the Registry, a Stub object is dynamically downloaded onto the client. The Stub and the Skeleton work in tandem to marshal data and method calls from the client application to the server application. The line from the Server to the Registry represents a registration process that must occur before the object can be located.

To simplify the transaction description, only an integer was passed from client to server. However, RMI implements the functionality to pass entire objects in this manner. To do this requires pass-by-value functionality for objects. This is a Herculean feat, requiring a system that can encapsulate

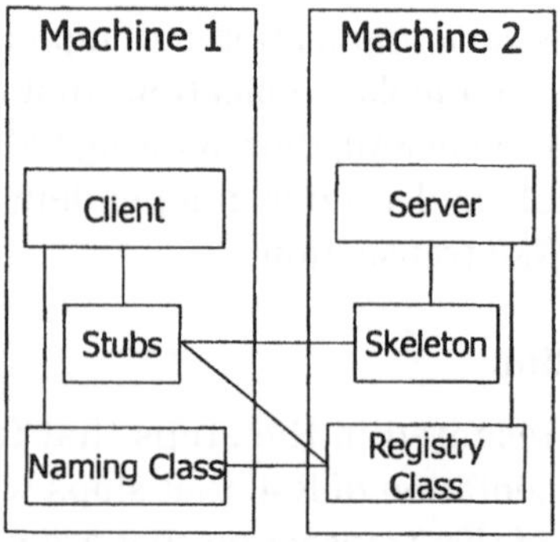

Exhibit 21.1. RMI Transaction Flow

code and data together; without both there is no assurance that an object's data will have the proper coherence. That is, pass-by-value transmits entire objects between process boundaries, including the explicit object being passed and all of its implicit objects defined as fields. When designing distributed systems, coherence will be maintained for explicitly passed objects, but implicitly passed objects may require code definition inside the remote address space.

To accomplish this feat, Java builds on the object serialization facility that stores inside the object's stream the name of the Java classes. These names are then used to request for the Java class files to be transferred if they do not exist locally. The capability to pass classes in this manner is not unusual for Java as this is exactly how Web browsers retrieve Java applets from Web servers. Indeed, the logic inside of RMI to accomplish this uses the class loader functionality associated with automatically downloading Java applets.

Ongoing debates in the industry illustrate the lack of appreciation by programmers for this capability: a severe problem for the industry's overall growth. This is most noticeable in technical discussions at industry events and over the Internet in which developers argue that Java-to-Java communications could have been handled by existing inter-object messaging protocols. However, these existing protocols do not inherently support pass-by-value for objects or distributed garbage collection — both requirements of distributed Java.

AGENT TECHNOLOGY

The new capability to pass entire objects, and the objects they contain, has bred a new type of application called the agent. Agent technology is a rapidly growing field within the Java community. The primary reason for this rise is the solution that agents provide to the problem of possible disconnected network states. Java RMI, as well as all remote procedure call mechanisms, are highly synchronous. That is, the client issues a method call and waits for a response. If the network connection is broken at any time during this waiting period, the client application will never receive its response. This could cause the applications to "hang" or to enter into exception handling logic.

Agents allow clients to send processing code to the server when the connection is up that will execute on the server. If the network connection breaks after the agent is delivered, the entire process can still continue normally. This is because agents work in an asynchronous manner; when the client wants the response to the processing, it will make a separate request to the server to return the agent and all of its collected data. Until the client receives this response, the agent will continue to exist, allowing the client to retry multiple times until it receives it successfully.

Java enables agents such as the Web browser to download an applet and call a method on it to start it running. It requires a contract between client and server to send and receive agents, but this is required of all distributed applications. The combination of synchronous and asynchronous programming allows one to design and build robust distributed applications that operate seamlessly across heterogeneous networked environments.

CONCLUSION

Many different solutions exist for distributing a task over multiple address paces and over a network. This article has presented a method for inter-object communications within a pure Java environment. For some, the simplicity provided by the distributed Java platform may be reason enough to use it over other distributed computing technologies, such as the Common Object Request Broker Architecture (CORBA), OSF Distributed Computing Environment (DEC), and Distributed Component Object Model (COM). However, even if companies choose not to use this platform, the perceptions of how to build distributed applications have been forever altered.

As this article was being written, Oracle, Netscape, IBM, and SunSoft submitted a proposal to the Object Management Group (OMG), requesting that the introspection and pass-by-value be incorporated into CORBA. Interestingly, these are the same features that provide the distributed Java platform with its power.

Chapter 22
Component Architectures with JavaBeans

Doug Nickerson

With each new development in software engineering, developers hope to have the solution — the silver bullet that will kill (or at least tame) the werewolf of software productivity. And indeed, methodologies and advances such as high-level languages, information engineering, rapid application development, application reengineering, and object-oriented programming have made software developers more productive. Still, advances in software productivity do not match the gains in hardware.

Component software, the idea of creating applications from plug-in parts, is a recent weapon in the continuing battle against recalcitrant software projects. There are component architectures now available from a number of different vendors, with minor and major differences among them.

Architectures such as JavaBeans, OLE, and ActiveX support technologies addressed to client-side applications. Enterprise JavaBeans, DCOM, and CORBA provide services for the server side. All of these promise to make development of applications easier, faster, and cheaper by using reusable and interchangeable component parts.

This article focuses on component architectures — the backbone of what makes component software work. Just as a well-planned software project starts with an analysis of the problem to be solved, this article analyzes the need for components before describing them in detail. Discussion includes:

1. what component architectures try to accomplish — why they are needed
2. the minimum requirements a component architecture needs to be viable
3. the features of the JavaBeans from Sun Microsystems, a component architecture built on Java, as an example of one implementation of a component-based system

0-8493-9822-3/00/$0.00+$.50

THE NEED FOR COMPONENTS

Object-oriented programming, which dates back as far as the language Simula in the 1960s, is currently a widely popular development technique. Proponents of object-oriented programming cite its ability to create large applications from self-contained parts, applications that are easily maintainable, extensible, and benefit from extensive code reuse.

Traditional object-oriented methods go far toward meeting the goals above. However, many experts would agree that objects have not become as easy to use as integrated circuits are for the hardware designer.

The tight binding between an operating system and the binary code that runs in it hinders the reusability of objects. Objects are not always interchangeable between different operating systems or compilers. Object interchangeability is mostly achievable only when a project stays within one programming language and one computer type.

For example, when writing a C++ program using an object class library, one might want to use objects provided by a vendor other than the library provider. There are two ways to go: the objects were written in C++ and have been compiled for use with a specific compiler and linker, or one has the source code for a C++ class that one can recompile and link them with one's program. But one cannot select an object off the shelf, plug it in, and be sure that it will work.

Component architectures are proposed as a solution to these problems. They make it possible to create interchangeable, self-contained units of functionality (components) that can work across different hardware and operating systems. To do this, they go beyond the basics of the object-oriented model and add other features. First, a brief review about the object-oriented model for analysis and programming.

OBJECT-ORIENTED SOFTWARE

Although the term "object" means different things to different people, the characteristics of encapsulation, polymorphism, and reusability (often through inheritance) are widely accepted features in the definition of object oriented.

Encapsulation requires that both data and implementation (methods) of an object be encapsulated. Usually, data fields are made private and the object provides an interface to them. (Languages like C++ and Java do not prevent one from making public all the data in an object; one follows this approach as a stricture of good design.)

Data and function encapsulation reduces the coupling of objects in a program: objects cannot change the data of another object without going through an interface or, when no interface is provided to internal data, perhaps have no data access. Encapsulation also eases maintenance by localizing changes to data fields or implementation of an object to one section of a program.

Polymorphism is the ability to send the same message to different objects, and have the object behave differently — call a different method. The concept of reuse is often mentioned in the definition of objects. Although it is not the only method of reuse, object-oriented languages such as C++ and Java provide code reuse through inheritance. One inherits data fields and implementation of a base class (or superclass), creating subclasses that are specializations of the base class.

COMPONENT ARCHITECTURES

Component architectures have much in common with objects, especially the practice of data and functionality encapsulation. Unlike objects, they are required to be usable in many different computing environments, possibly bridging different operating systems or over networks.

A component architecture solves the tight binding problem by providing a layer between the component and the operating system in which it is running.

To a developer of components for a specific architecture, this layer is similar to a protocol like HTTP. If one creates a component in accordance with a specific component architecture (whether JavaBeans, OLE/COM, CORBA, or others), it works in any target environment that implements the particular protocol.

Considering these concepts, one can generate a list of requirements for a component architecture, including:

- a way to contain state information (data)
- a way to provide functionality (callable functions)
- a way to enable communication among components whose types and behaviors are not yet known
- an ability to function across different computing systems/operating systems
- customization features
- persistence: a way for the component to be saved.

The data and functionality requirements are required for component encapsulation. The communication or connections between components are very important because components are to interact with other components in arbitrary software environments.

Cross-environment functioning is the one of the hallmarks of components. For example, Microsoft's Component Object Model (COM) defines a binary standard for the implementation of its COM objects. COM objects can be coded in different languages as long as they are compiled to this standard.

JavaBeans relies on the Java Virtual Machine to be present in the environment in which beans are running. Since beans are Java classes, they will run wherever Java will run. Of course, this solution is a Java-specific one (JavaBeans are created in Java, whereas COM/ActiveX objects can be created in C/C++, Visual Basic, and other languages).

Most architectures also provide the ability to customize components because it may be necessary during development. In a typical scenario, a component is loaded into a graphical application builder tool, and the developer uses it with other components to create a complete application. The developer can make changes to components, their appearance, location, etc. After the developer is satisfied with the application, it may be possible to save the components, retaining the changes made (this is called persistence).

JAVABEANS: JAVA'S COMPONENT ARCHITECTURE

JavaBeans, a component architecture that was introduced by Sun Microsystems in Java 1.1, is implemented in Java. How does JavaBeans meet the requirements in the previous section?

From the language viewpoint, a component (a bean or JavaBean) is simply a Java class. Create a Java class, provide it with some simple facilities, and one has now created a component in Java. JavaBeans encourages one to follow some additional conventions (mostly naming schemes for methods), but a bean is still just a Java class.

The first three requirements in the previous section can be summarized as data, functionality, and component connections. JavaBeans provides the features of properties, methods, and events to implement these features.

The JavaBeans support for properties, methods, and events is based on built-in Java features. Once a developer knows Java, he or she does not have to discard knowledge of the language when learning JavaBeans. The trio of properties, methods, and events is discussed in more detail below.

Properties

Define a bean in JavaBeans by creating a Java class. Any properties required by the bean become normal variable definitions. The convention encourages one to make these variables private to the Java class and to provide an interface to them. The names of the methods accessing the data field use a standard naming convention to assist the reflection mechanism in discovering a property at runtime. The convention of providing interface methods encourages a design that uses data hiding.

An example bean follows:

```
public class SimpleBean extends java.awt.Canvas
{
private int intData;
int getClassData()
{
return intData;
}
void setClassData (int inputVal)
{
        intData = inputVal;
}
} // end class
```

In the above class, access methods have been provided for the local data of the bean SimpleBean. Were this bean running in a container application supporting JavaBeans, JavaBeans would analyze the names of these methods and discover a property named ClassData. In Java terminology, the method by which the properties, methods, and events of a bean are analyzed is called introspection. The integer data field intData can have a different internal name than the external name, classData.

Methods

Once one has decided what functionality is required as an interface to a bean, one can define public methods in the usual way. A bean can contain other methods besides its public interface; methods not called by client code outside the bean can always be declared private.

As mentioned before, there are naming schemes (in JavaBeans terminology, called design patterns) that one can follow — although not strictly required — to aid the introspection mechanism in finding methods at runtime in a container application. The getClassData/setClassData pair shown in the last example is an example of such a design pattern.

The introspection of methods by a container application uses the reflection support in the java.lang.reflect and java.lang packages, which contain classes to represent constructors, methods, fields, and classes. This analysis code is the responsibility of the implementers of a bean container; the average bean user or developer does not have to worry about it.

Events: Component Communication

Events are the methodology for linking beans in a container application. The Java 1.1 event model implements events by way of event sources and event listeners. A particular bean is designated as the source of an event; other beans listen for the event. The listener for an event usually responds by calling other methods on receiving the event.

To listen for an event, a bean goes through a process called registration. The source of an event provides the means for registration. Effectively, the source bean keeps a list of other components that have registered. When it sends an event, it iterates through its list, sending an event to each listener in turn. The source also maintains list management code — code to add and remove beans from its list.

This approach has certain efficiencies over the way events were handled in the first versions of Java (1.0, 1.02). It is more efficient just to deliver events to those objects that are interested in the events. The previous event model broadcast an event across the entire system. The programmer wrote a switch or case construction to distinguish one event from another and called a method for whatever response was required.

JavaBeans provides support for customization and persistence through special classes. A user of a bean builder tool can customize the properties of bean in a design-time environment and save it. The bean can later be reloaded, and still has the same state it was saved with.

Java provides additional JavaBeans support by way of its libraries. In particular, a special package java.beans contains support code for beans. These facilities are mostly used by a container environment.

SOFTWARE CONTAINERS

The ultimate goal of creating a component architecture is to be able to create plug-in components to use in a software project. An environment supporting a particular component architecture is broadly known as a component container.

The container's main responsibility is to provide the services necessary to support the component architecture. A container can be a complete application in its own right. Microsoft Excel and Microsoft Word can be programmed using Visual Basic by way of their support for an OLE technology called Automation. In this mode, they act as container applications supporting the OLE architecture. The first JavaBeans release included a bean container called the BeanBox.

A container for JavaBeans uses the JavaBeans support to provide an environment to run and build with beans. A builder container would make heavy use of Java's built-in reflection mechanism (reflection is similar to runtime type information in C++) to discover and analyze beans.

A typical application builder would be able to scan the current environment for available beans, and present their properties, methods, and events to the developer. The user can use an application builder to develop an application with the beans, possibly modifying properties of various beans and connecting them to create a complete application. The persistence feature implies that the user can save the beans and reload them later without losing their context.

OTHER INDUSTRY MODELS

Although it is beyond the scope of this article to discuss other component architectures in detail, for comparison purposes some information on OLE is provided herein. Microsoft's OLE was developed originally to link and embed objects among different Microsoft applications; for example, linking a spreadsheet with a word processing document. Today, the scope of OLE is much wider.

The Common Object Model (COM), Microsoft's component architecture, is the basis of OLE and ActiveX. OLE Automation and ActiveX controls, as well as many other OLE technologies, are based on COM.

A developer uses COM by accessing the COM library to start up a COM server. A COM server can then load one or more COM objects. A COM object groups functions together by way of its interfaces. A COM object may have multiple interfaces, but always has at least one.

Interfaces group related functionality together. A single interface would implement a certain service that the object provides. Functions of a certain interface might manage a telephone list: looking up a number, adding a number, etc. Another interface in the same object might support a different feature, an address database, for example.

A comparison between JavaBeans and the COM is educational in studying the different approaches to meeting the requirements mentioned earlier. COM interfaces implement a type of function and data encapsulation; the user of a COM object must fetch an interface pointer from the before accessing any object services. Data from a COM object is usually not accessed directly. COM objects also have a type of two-way communication using connectable objects and events (also called notifications).

In terms of ease of use, Sun Microsystems has made much of the fact that JavaBeans is implemented on top of Java in a natural way, introducing very few new concepts or support libraries to the developer interested in creating beans. And, in fact, Microsoft's OLE/ActiveX does require a larger

Exhibit 22.1. Checklist for Evaluating or Learning a New Component Technology

1. How is data and functionality addressed in the technology (properties and methods)?
2. How do components interact in the technology (the event model)?
3. What is important to you and your organization? Assess the technology in those terms.
4. Is cross-platform development important?
5. Is it important to develop components in multiple languages?
6. Is extensibility important?
7. How is customization and persistence of components accomplished? Are they easy to use?
8. Does the component technology require learning a whole new way of thinking? Or, like JavaBeans, does creating components merely involve using some features of the existing environment in a different way?

investment in learning new concepts, familiarity with COM and with the COM library.

If evaluating or learning a new component technology, ask the questions listed in Exhibit 22.1.

References

1. Brockschmidt, Kraig. *Inside OLE*, 2nd ed., Microsoft Press, 1995.
2. Chappell, David. *Understanding ActiveX and OLE*, Microsoft Press, 1996.
3. Cox, Brad, Object Oriented Programming: An Evolutionary Approach, Addison-Wesley Publishing, 1987.
4. Flanagan, David. *Java in a Nutshell*, 2nd ed., O'Reilly, 1997.
5. Nickerson, Doug. *Official Netscape JavaBeans Developer's Guide*, Ventana, 1997.
6. Yourdon, Edward. *Decline and Fall of the American Programmer*, Prentice-Hall, 1993.

Chapter 23

Programming Components: COM and CORBA

T.M. Rajkumar and David K. Holthaus

DATABASE TECHNOLOGIES HAVE EVOLVED from the 1970s' hierarchical databases to relational database management systems in the 1980s and to object databases and client/server systems in the 1990s. While the shift from central processing to client/server did not fully leverage object technology, Internet-based technologies promise to provide the infrastructure for objects. Web-based browsers are poised to become the universal clients for all types of applications. These applications increasingly depend on components, automation, and object layers linking systems.

During the same period, it became less and less possible for software developers to quickly, efficiently, and inexpensively develop all of the functions and modules demanded by customers. Therefore, software development methodologies for Internet and Web applications are increasingly focused on component technologies. Component technology breaks the application into intrinsic components and then glues them to create an application. Using components, an application is easier to build, make robust, and deliver quicker.

WHAT IS A COMPONENT?

A component is an independently delivered package of software services. A component is language independent and allows reuse in different language settings. Software components can be either bought from outside or developed in-house. Implementation requires that it must be possible to integrate them with other applications using standardized interfaces. They must implement the functionality specified in the interface efficiently. Components may be upgraded with new interfaces.

A component encapsulates methods (i.e., behavior) and data (i.e., attributes). Component must provide encapsulation, but inheritance is not as rigid a requirement. Components may include other components. Components do not necessarily have to be object-oriented, though a large

0-8493-9822-3/00/$0.00+$.50

majority of them are because it provides mechanisms to hide the data structure (i.e., encapsulation). Using objects makes components easier to understand and easier to create.

Components may be classified in many different ways. One such classification is based on their function within applications: business or technical components.

Business components usually include the logic that supports a business function or area. These must be developed in-house because it forms part of the core knowledge of an organization. In addition, business knowledge required to create them generally does not exist outside. They are also difficult to develop because organizations must standardize in some manner. There must be a common vision for the organization, and a common architecture must be present to develop business components.

Technical components are represented by elements that are generic and that can be used in a wide variety of business areas. These typically come in the form of GUI components, charting, or interapplication communication components.

A second classification is based on granularity of components. Fine-grained components such as class libraries and encapsulated components are typically small in size and are applicable in a wide range of applications. Although they have large reuse across multiple applications, they are close to code and provide limited productivity to a developer in large-scale applications.

Large-grained components provide broader functionality, but they have to be customized for use. A framework is an example of a large-grained component. Frameworks provide two benefits: flow of control and object-orientation. A framework can be thought of as groupings of components packages or components that belong to a logically related set and together provide a service. They provide a substrate or lattice for other functional components, and a framework can be composed of other frameworks. They also provide the flow of control within components. This helps in the scale of the solution developed.

Object orientation of frameworks helps with the granularity of the components. Ideally, during the assembly stage one wants a small number of large components. However, to increase generality of the solution created, one wants a large number of small components. Large components must be customized prior to delivering needed functionality. Frameworks allow developers to modify and reuse components at various levels of granularity. Frameworks are examples of "white-box" components (i.e., you can look inside the components to reuse it). With inheritance, the internals of parent classes are visible to subclasses in a framework. This provides a developer with flexibility to modify the behavior of a component. Thus,

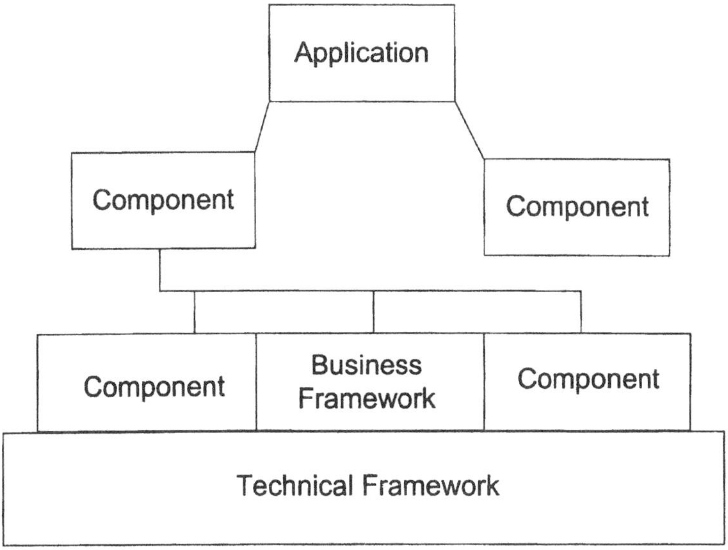

Exhibit 23.1. Application Integration with Components

frameworks enable customization, allowing developers to build systems quickly using specialized routines.

Frameworks come in two categories: technical and business. Technical frameworks encapsulate software infrastructure such as operating system, graphical user interface (GUI), object request broker (ORB), and transaction processing (TP) monitor. Microsoft Foundation Class (MFC) is an example of such a framework. Business frameworks contain the knowledge of the objects in a business model and the relationships between objects. Typically, they are used to build many different components or applications for a single industry. Technically, while not based on components, Enterprise Resource Planning (ERP) such software as SAP are examples of business frameworks. An application is generally built with both technical and business frameworks (see Exhibit 23.1).

CLIENT/SERVER COMPONENTS

Client/server systems typically use three tiers — presentation layer, business layer, and data or server layer (see Exhibit 23.2). The objective behind the three tiers is to separate the business layer from the presentation and data layers. Changes in one layer are isolated within that layer and do not affect others. Within component technologies, the business layer communicates to the presentation layer and the data layer through an object bus, which is typically an object request broker (ORB). This layering makes the system very scalable.

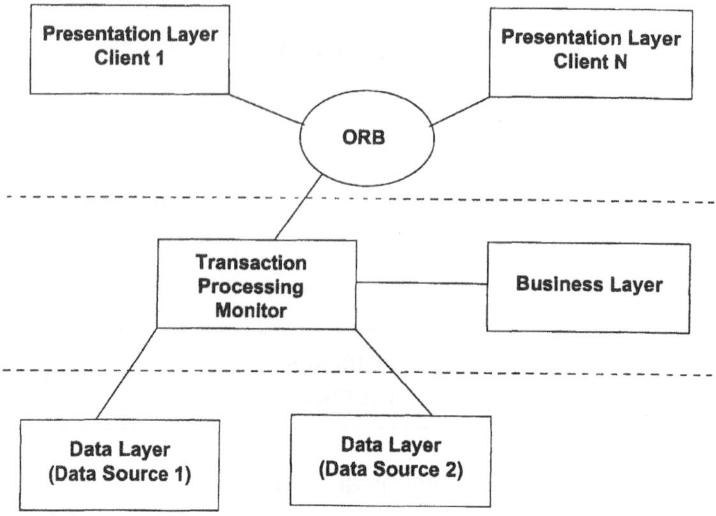

Exhibit 23.2. Three-Layer Client/Server Architecture

An ORB is a standard mechanism through which distributed software objects and their clients may interact. Using an ORB, an object and its clients can reside on the same process or in a different process, which they can execute on different hosts connected by a network. The ORB provides the software necessary to convey the requests from clients to objects and responses from object to client. Since the ORB mechanism hides the details of specific locations, hosts, and conversion of data representation, and hides the underlying communication mechanism, objects and clients can interact freely without having to worry about many details. Thus, distributed applications can incorporate components written in different languages and are executable on different host and operating system platforms. This flexibility allows the data layer to be composed of both legacy software, and relational, object databases.

Business logic may reside on multiple server computers and data may reside on multiple servers. A TP monitor must be used to manage the business logic to provide centralized control. A TP monitor also manages the logic on the serves by providing an array of mission critical services such as concurrency, transactions and security, load balancing, transactional queues, and nested transactions. A TP monitor can prestart components, manage their persistent state, and coordinate their interactions across networks. TP monitors thus become the tool to manage smart components in a client/server system with components.

The real benefit of components in client/server applications is the ability to use the divide-and-conquer approach, which enables clients to scale through distribution. In this approach, an application is built as a series of ORBs. Since an ORB is accessible by any application running on a network, logic is centrally located. Developers can change the ORB to change the functionality of the application. If an ORB runs remotely, it can truly reflect a thin client. ORBs are portable and can be moved from platform to platform without adverse side effects to interoperability and provide for load balancing.

COMPONENT STANDARDS

Object models such as ActiveX, which is based on COM, CORBA, and Java Beans define binary standards so that each individual component can be assembled independently. All component standards share the following common characteristics:

- A component interface publishing and directory system
- Methods or actions invocable at run time by a program
- Events or notifications to a program in response to a change of state in an object
- Support for object persistence (to store such information as the state of a component)
- Support for linking components into an application

The following paragraphs describe each standard.

ActiveX, COM, and DCOM

ActiveX is based on COM technology, which formally separates interfaces and implementation. COM clients and objects speak through predefined interfaces. COM interfaces define a contract between a COM and its client. It defines the behavior or capabilities of a software component as a set of methods or properties. Each COM object may offer several different interfaces but must support at least one Iunknown. COM classes contain the bodies of code that implement interfaces. Each interface and COM class have unique IDs, IID, and CLSID, which are used by a client to instantiate an object in a COM server. There two types of object invocations:

- In process memory (DLLs), where a client and object share the same process space
- Out-of-process model, where a client and object live in different processes

Clients can call either easily. A remoting layer makes the actual call invisible to a client. An ActiveX component is typically an in-process server. An actual object is downloaded to a client's machine. DCOM is COM extended for supporting objects across a network. DCOM allows objects to be freely distributed over several machines and allows a client to instantiate objects on remote machines.

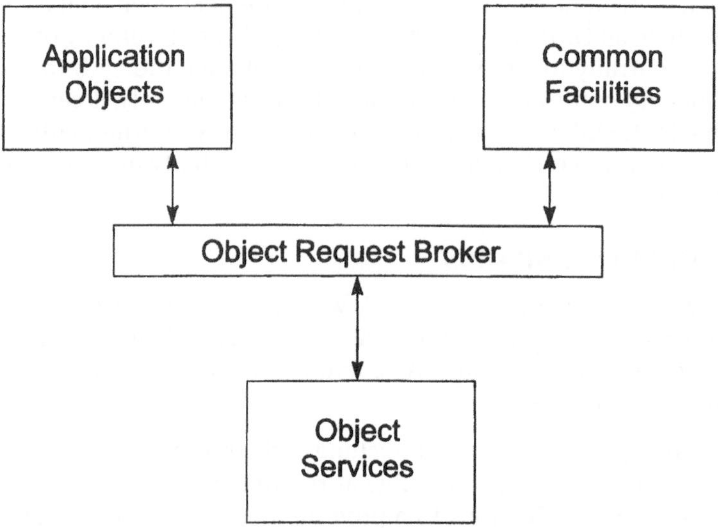

Exhibit 23.3. CORBA Architecture

CORBA

The Common Object Request Broker Architecture (CORBA) is a set of distributed system standards promoted by an industry standards organization, the Object Management Group. It defines the ORB, a standard mechanism through which distributed software and their clients may interact. It specifies an extensive set of bus-related services for creating and deleting objects, accessing them by name, storing them in a persistent store, externalizing their states, and defining ad hoc relationships between them.

As illustrated in Exhibit 23.3, the four main elements of CORBA are the following:

- *ORBs.* This defines the object bus.
- *Services.* These define the system-level object frameworks that extend the bus. Some services are security, transaction management, and data exchange.
- *Facilities.* These define horizontal and vertical application frameworks that are used directly by business objects.
- *Application objects.* Also known as business objects or applications, these objects are created by software developers to solve business problems.

A Comparison of CORBA and DCOM

Both CORBA and DCOM use an interface mechanism to expose object functionalities. Interfaces contain methods and attributes as a common means of placing request to an object. CORBA uses standard models of inheritance from object-oriented languages. DCOM/ActiveX uses the concept of multiple interfaces supported by a single object. DCOM requires that multiple inheritance be emulated through aggregation and containment of interfaces.

Another difference is the notion of object identity. CORBA defines the identity of an object in an object reference, which is unique and persistent. If the object is not in memory, it can be reconstructed based on the reference. DCOM in contrast defines the identity in the interface, the reference to the object itself is transient. This can lead to problems when reconnecting because the previously used object cannot be directly accessed.

Reference counting is also different in both. A DCOM object maintains a reference count of all connected clients. It uses pinging of clients to ensure that all clients are alive. CORBA does not need to do remote reference because its object reference model allows the re-creation of an object if it had been prematurely deleted.

CORBA uses two application program interfaces (APIs) and one protocol for object requests. It provides the generated stubs for both static and dynamic invocation. In addition, dynamic skeleton interface allows changes during runtime.

DCOM provides two APIs and two protocols. The standard interface is based on a binary interface that uses method pointer tables called *vtables*. The second API, object linking and embedding (OLE) automation, is used to support dynamic requests through scripting languages. OLE automation uses the IDispatch method to call the server.

CORBA is typically viewed as the middleware of choice for encapsulating legacy systems with new object-oriented interfaces, since it provides support for languages such as COBOL and mainframe systems. DCOM has its roots in desktop computing and is well supported there.

JavaBeans

JavaBeans enables the creation of portable Java objects that can interoperate with non-Java object systems. Unlike ActiveX, which predominately operates in Windows environments, JavaBeans is intended to run in diverse environments as long as there exists a Java Virtual Machine that supports the JavaBean API. JavaBeans provides the standard mechanisms present in all the component technologies. This standard is still continuing to evolve.

Comparison of Java and ActiveX

A trusted JavaBean has all the capabilities of a Java application. However, if you run a JavaBean that has not been signed by a digital source, its capabilities are limited like any other applet. Java also has limited multimedia support. In contrast, ActiveX objects cannot run from the Web unless they are trusted and have access to all of Windows's capabilities. Hence, ActiveX supports multimedia.

ActiveX and Java both use digitally signed certificates to protect against malicious attacks. In addition, JavaBeans is available for a large number of machines and has cross-platform capability. ActiveX is most widely available on the Windows desktop.

Irrespective of the technology standard, bridges, available from different vendors, can translate between standards. Hence, organizations should choose a standard in which they have the greatest expertise for analysis, design, and development.

HOW TO DESIGN AND USE COMPONENTS

As shown in Exhibit 1, applications are built from the composition and aggregation of other, simpler components, which may build on frameworks. Application design is broken into component and application development. Component development is divided into component design and implementation. A good knowledge of an application's domain is necessary to develop frameworks and components. In general, the steps of domain definition, specification, design, verification, implementation, and validation must be done prior to application. The following sections explain these steps.

Domain Definition. This defines the scope, extent, feasibility, and cost justification for a domain. An organization must define the product it plans to build as well as define the different business and technical areas that must be satisfied through the use of software.

Domain Specification. This defines the product family (i.e., framework) used for application engineering. It includes a decision model, framework requirements, and a hierarchy of component requirements. The decision model specifies how components will be selected, adapted, and reused to create complete application systems. Product requirements are arrived at by analyzing similarities in functions, capabilities, and characteristics as well as variances among them. The component part of the product family is represented hierarchically. When an organization considers components, it must consider not only what the component will do for the domain now but also in the future.

Domain Design. A domain expert must work with component designer to use a modeling methodology and extract the design patterns that occur in that domain. Design patterns are repeatable designs used in the construction of an application. The architecture, component design, and generation design are specified here. Architecture depicts a set of relationships among the components such as hierarchical, communication, and database. Component design describes the internal logic flow, data flows, and dependencies. Generation design is a procedure that describes how to select, adapt, and compose application systems using the decision model and architecture.

Domain Verification. This process evaluates the consistency of a domain's requirements, specification, and design.

Domain Implementation. During this procedure, components are either developed or acquired off the shelf to fit the architecture. Each component must be tested within the common architecture it supports as well as any potential architecture. Certification of components must be acquired when necessary. It must also decide how to store it in repositories, the implementation of application generation procedures, and how to transition to an assembly mode.

Domain Validation. This evaluates the quality and effectiveness of the application engineering support. Application engineering consists of the following:

- *Defining requirements.* In this process, an application model that defines a customer's requirements is defined. This model uses the notation specified in the domain engineering steps. Typically, a use case model can be used to identify requirements. Use cases are behaviorally related sequences of transactions, that a user of a system will perform in a dialogue
- *Selecting components and design.* Using rules in the decision model, reusable components are selected based on the component specification (capabilities and interfaces) and design (component logic and parameters).
- *Generating software.* The application is then generated by aggregating components and writing any custom software.
- *Testing.* Testing involves the testing of use cases, components, integration testing, and load testing.
- *Generating documentation.* The application documentation is created.

MANAGING THE COMPONENT LIFE CYCLE PROCESS

Developing with components means an organization must move from doing one-of-a-kind development to a reuse-driven approach. The aim is to reorganize the resources to meet users' needs with greater efficiency. The steps in this process are discussed in the following sections.

Establishing a Sponsor. This involves identifying component reuse opportunities and shows how their exploitation can contribute to an organization's IS goals. Sponsors must be identified and sold on the various ideas.

Exhibit 23.4. Assessment of Component Potential for Reuse

Concern	What to Ask
Domain potential	In the given domain, are there applications that could benefit from reuse?
Existing domain components	Are expertise and components available?
Commonalities and variables	Is there a sufficient fit between need and available components? Can they be customized?
Domain stability	Is the technology stable? Do the components meet stable standards? Are the components portable across environments?

Exhibit 23.5. Assessment of an Organization's Capability to Reuse Components Columns

Application Development	Component Development	Management	Process and Technology
Component identification for use in application	Needs identification, interface, and architecture definition	Organizational commitment, planning	Process definition and integration
Component evaluation and verification	Components needs and solutions	Managing security of components	Measurement and continuous process improvement
Application integrity	Component quality, value, security, and reusability determination	Intergroup (component and application) coordination	Repository tool support and training

Developing a Plan. This plan should guide the management of the component development process. The plan includes the following:

1. *Reuse assessment.* This assessment should evaluate the potential opportunity for reuse, identify where the organization stands with respect to reuse, and evaluate the organization's reuse capability Exhibits 23.4, 23.5, and 23.6 can be used to conduct the assessment.
2. *Development of alternative strategies.* On the basis of the assessment, an organization can develop a strategy to implement and align the process as well as choose the appropriate methodologies and tools.
3. *Development of metrics.* In the planning stage for implementation, metrics must be used to measure success.

Implementation. The organization finally implements the plan. Incentives can be used to promote reuse by individuals and the organization.

Exhibit 23.6. Organizational Reuse Capability Model

Stage	Key Characteristics
Opportunistic	• Projects individually develop reuse plan – Existing components are reused – Throughout project life cycle reuse of components is identified – Components under configuration and repository control
Integrated	• Reuse activities integrated into standard development process – Components are designed for current and anticipated needs – Common architectures and frameworks used for applications – Tools tailored for components and reuse
Leveraged	• An application-line reuse strategy is developed to maximize component reuse over a set of related applications – Components are developed to allow reuse early in the life cycle – Process performance is measured and analyzed – Tools supporting reuse are integrated with the organization's software development efforts
Anticipating	• New opportunities for reuse of components build on the organization's reuse capability – Effectiveness of reuse is measured – Organizations reuse method is flexible and can adapt to new process and product environment

CONCLUSION

Component technology is changing the way client/server applications are being developed. Supporting tools for this software environment are rapidly emerging to make the transition from regular application development to a component-based development. With proper training of staff, planning, and implementation, organizations can smoothly transfer to this new mode of development and rapidly develop and efficiently deliver client/server applications.

Chapter 24

Automatically Migrating COBOL Indexed Files: A Case Study

Andrew J. Swadener and Lee Janke

Many organizations are faced with addressing the modernization of what has come to be known as their "legacy systems." Unfortunately, the definition of a legacy application has become obscured in the industry. A negative connotation has sometimes been assigned to the term for purposes of selling an agenda of reengineering applications that have been developed in presumably mature (a.k.a. old) software environments — COBOL programming environments are a case in point. Scrutiny toward the goal of identifying such tactics should be undertaken, as an organization may be swayed into buying technology for the sake of the technology, with the primary benefactors being the technology's providers.

It is important to always remember the layperson's fundamental rule of software development, as we all learned it: "Let the requirements drive the technology ... not the other way around." An organization's software environment may be mature, but it may also have been appropriately developed, for the most part, in that environment. A major reengineering effort is not always automatically warranted.

In choosing how to evolve an organization's application into its capitalizing on modern technologies, automation services providers must orient themselves toward identifying where the changes need to take place — in the short, intermediate, and longer terms. It is important to provide a strategy that is cost-effective and dynamic by design, and maximizes the organization's previous software investment. For many application stewards, the definition of the correct direction along these lines may appear daunting or illusive.

As is the case in most projects, dissecting this problem into component parts provides for more manageable, tangible solutions. When attempting to strategize the efforts described above, business rules can be analyzed separately from data stores. The solutions for each may be surprisingly more diverse and, in some cases, easier than originally imagined. The par-

0-8493-9822-3/00/$0.00+$.50

adigm shift is in mentally separating how an application and its users generate data (the programs/processes) and what the data is (data stores). Both programs and data can be considered product lines, and are, at a minimum for all organizations, valuable assets. The important fact is that the programs and the data can be managed differently.

For the most part, the following discussion focuses on the data assets of an organization. The business rules, or software programs, of the original application are assumed to be already functionally rich — at least enough so that existing short-term, mission-critical business requirements are met with them. Even if there are areas where the existing functionality of the application is lacking, there are strategies that can be employed which have proven to work in conjunction with the solutions outlined here for the evolution of the application's data stores. In the discussion provided here, the application's programs are assumed to have been written in ANSI-85 Standard COBOL. From the data store perspective, COBOL programs are intimately tied to proprietary file-handling systems, due to the equally proprietary nature of COBOL compilers and "runtime" components.

When focusing on the data component assets within an application, the above-mentioned paradigm shift opens exciting possibilities for access to and re-use of data stores inside and outside of the original application (see Exhibit 24.1).

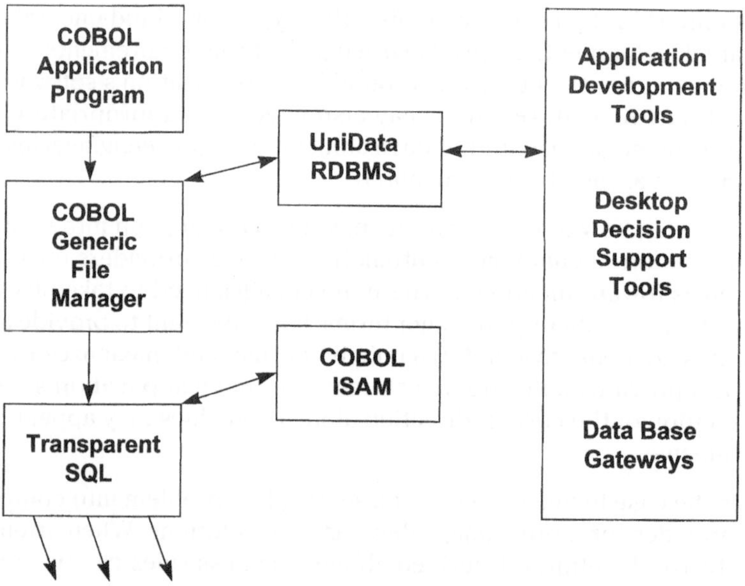

Exhibit 24.1. COBOL Reuse through Open Systems

CHOOSING AN OPEN ARCHITECTURE

There is no doubt that organizations are in the midst of rapidly changing technologies, and are all faced with needing environments that can no longer be thought of as exclusively proprietary, or that are held-up behind our organizations' closed doors. With the burgeoning intra/Internet and World Wide Web marketplaces, advances in personal computer "desktop" technologies, and widespread easier standard accessibility options for automated applications (especially for the data associated with them), there are very few organizations that are not faced with needing to open their applications' doors — while, at the same time, controlling the process with intelligent future-sighted decisions.

After serious evaluation, a decision on the "open architecture" question needs to be formulated. This is especially the case for legacy applications, since they were usually designed without the advantages or requirements of today's open features. Not all applications, or not all the components of an application, *need* to be changed. Candidates for open architecture deployment must be evaluated on the basis of:

- Data access requirements (from the desktop or from tools not necessarily developed by one's organization)
- Ease of use and end-user exposure to newer technologies (for consistently providing nearly the same methods for application usage or access)
- Functionality
- Future development requirements

Potential rehosting and/or component-based modifications may be the identified route to be taken. It is important to evaluate the best approach for accomplishing an open architecture goal from the onset of the feasibility analysis phase of the project. Targeting the right mix of required changes, based on an organization's needs is critical to control the scope (and expense) of the transitions ahead.

This discussion is based on an identified need for an application to be in an open environment — for reasons coming out of the above-mentioned analysis activities.

Case Study

A case study examined in this and subsequent sections outlines the previously discussed activities for BancTec, Inc., a Dallas-based provider of electronic and document-based transaction-processing systems, applications software, and support services. The company is responsible for maintaining and managing systems software for more than 4000 document-processing systems that BancTec has manufactured and for maintaining network software.

BancTec was interested in open architecture for the following reasons:

- Data querying capabilities
- Desktop data access capabilities in a client/server mode
- Post-implementation follow-on development

BancTec's application was initially implemented in a DG-INFOS COBOL DG-MV/AOS environment. After evaluating various options for deploying their application into a new open environment for the reasons above, it was determined that a multidimensional data base was needed, in order to avoid a major reengineering effort. BancTec needed a way to map indexed data structures in COBOL to a relational data base, which posed important questions for BancTec regarding a relational data base that could maintain and accept OCCURing data and data REDEFINEs. (See following sections for detailed discussions on these topics.)

BancTec chose Unidata, Inc.'s Nested RDBMS and COBOL Direct Connect for these reasons. The ability to migrate the data and to accommodate data access requirements in an open environment with no significant data structure changes was critical to a feasible application transition.

Beyond initial migration, BancTec needed options available in order to be able to also get to the data. They wanted to be able to access the data in a "native" fashion, directly taking into account the multiple dimensions of their data base — Unidata's UniQuery and Integrate QueryBuilder satisfied these needs. These mechanisms allow the ability to retrieve the COBOL-oriented data in a predictable fashion, automatically formatted for the original OCCURs and REDEFINEs.

In addition to native access, though, BancTec realized the need to access their application's data in an industry-standard open fashion (e.g., ODBC), which presently does not directly accommodate multidimensional data bases. Unidata's product set allowed for this type of access as well. These technologies allow them to access their application's data from popular desktop applications offered by Microsoft or Lotus Development Corporation.

Lastly, with the above access capabilities, BancTec was presented with a large number of options for future development, and possibly reengineering with other state-of-the-art open environment tools.

The major effort for BancTec's transition to this ideal environment for them was focused on the transition from the original COBOL environment to a COBOL environment that Unidata supports (DG-INFOS was not one of the environments supported). BancTec chose to migrate their application to Acucobol-85 (Acucobol, Inc., San Diego, CA) on a Data General AViiON-9500 computer, under the DG-UX operating system.

The remaining discussion provides some insight into BancTec's experiences in the overall migration process. It is important to note that BancTec chose to migrate their application in two phases:

- Phase 1 migrated the COBOL environment to Acucobol-85 and implemented that environment into production first.
- Phase 2 migrated the Aucocobl-85 Vision indexed files into a UniData RDBMS using COBOL Direct Connect

SELECTING TARGET FILES FOR MIGRATION

Depending upon the goals of the organization in moving their data to an open environment's RDBMS, the purposes for choosing targeted application files may differ. It is important to ensure that the strategy for migration focuses on providing options. A migration strategy that, by default, places all of an application's data into relational format will usually not serve most organizations' needs. If it is important to provide customers with open access to their application's data for ad hoc querying; for example, internally used transient data files can be excluded from the data base. The option should be available to *not* migrate selected data files (i.e., to retain their native/proprietary structure).

In addition to selecting files for migration based on eventual usage requirements, some data may not lend itself easily to migrating to a RDBMS structure, by their intrinsic characteristics. COBOL Indexed Files usually fall into three categories:

- Indexed (primary and alternate keys)
- Relative (dynamic keys)
- Sequential (no keys)

Indexed files are those that should be analyzed for RDBMS deployment. Each indexed file should be reviewed for deployment applicability for the reasons just mentioned.

Case Study

The BancTec application is a corporate mission-critical solution that requires high reliability and availability. Named BancTec Automated Service Executive (BASE), the application helps BancTec's cusotmer service representatives manage nearly 10,000 calls about customer contracts per month.

When project management initially reviewed the migration requirements, it was obvious that these requirements must be met for the migration to be a success. Only then could the added benefits of the relational data base be employed. To achieve that goal, the decision was made to migrate all indexed data to an RDBMS, which supported full system backup and recovery. Although some of the new tables may never be used in a manner to maximize their existence in the relational model, by moving all data the customer can take advantage of any of the standard recovery products, which were offered by Unidata. Also, this will allow them to move to a desired future solution involving data replication on a second server that can be deployed in the event of a significant system hardware failure.

Another issue that was considered here — and should be for all migrations — was the idea of ongoing access to the application data by IS and user staff members. By migrating all indexed tables, the customer is assured that any desired ad hoc reporting or desktop access can be supported either through query to the migrated indexed structures or by constructing views that can span multiple tables. This decision at BancTec has ultimately allowed the customer to open up the data to the end-users without concern over data availability in multiple data base structures.

REDIFINED AND MULTIPLY DEFINED COBOL DATA

Data that occurs, is redefined, or is in multiple COBOL file definitions can be very complex in its design. At first glance, it may appear that logical modeling of the data into a relational data base requires an entirely new file/table design. Capturing these file definitions and constructing a relational table that complies with program I/O logic can greatly reduce the data migration and program testing windows. Creation of this model must allow for a variable data store that can relate to the COBOL-specific variable data fields allowed under redefines, occurs, and multiple record type logic. A normalized relational representation will not easily lend itself to the flexibility inherent in these features and can require significant "background" table manipulation activity when driven out of COBOL with standard relational SQL logic. Techniques used to leverage these COBOL characteristics become the driving force in the estimation of migration timeframes and, ultimately, project success or failure.

Case Study

Using the UniData RDBMS data model, accessed through the COBOL Direct Connection Interface, BancTec was able to redirect its file I/O into the relational environment without affecting the existing business logic of the COBOL application. COBOL data structures involving multiple record definitions in the same file were translated into a relational table containing attributes for all possible data fields. Using a mapping constructed during the COBOL Direct Connect migration phase, attributes are populated only when the logic of the application dictate and the data is reflected in the manner in which it is populated by the COBOL program rules. This allows for multiple record types in a single relational table and allows for a one-to-

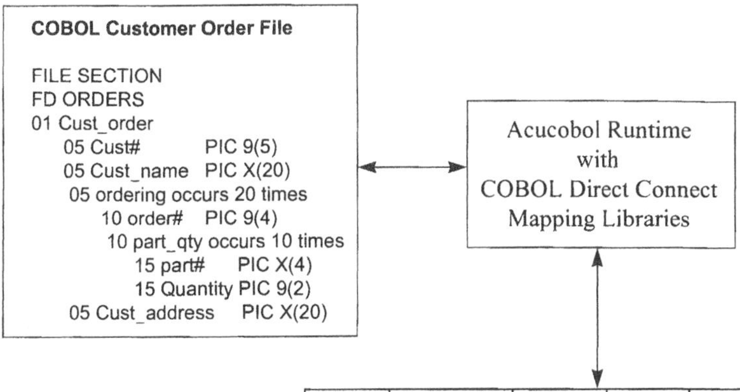
COBOL Customer Order File
FILE SECTION
FD ORDERS
01 Cust_order
05 Cust# PIC 9(5)
05 Cust_name PIC X(20)
05 ordering occurs 20 times
10 order# PIC 9(4)
10 part_qty occurs 10 times
15 part# PIC X(4)
15 Quantity PIC 9(2)
05 Cust_address PIC X(20)
Acucobol Runtime
with
COBOL Direct Connect
Mapping Libraries

Cust#	Cust_name	Order#	Part#	Qty
A123	Action Inc	97-0125	K123	60
			L456	50
		97-0216	M789	100
B456	Bluebird Inc	97-084	P001	20
			K123	200

Exhibit 24.2. File I/O Reduction

one correlation between existing file/record structure and the new table/row storage implementation (see Exhibit 24.2).

This same logic supported the integrity of the existing group redefine logic and allowed for data base access under naming conventions familiar to the BancTec programming staff. Table data implemented under the COBOL occurs clause logic was easily mapped to the UniData RDBMS multivalued and multisubvalued storage repository. This allowed the existing application to continue to retrieve records with a single I/O request, while supporting the query requirements of multiple tuples native to the non-first-normal-fort (i.e., nested or NF2) data base.

DATA INTEGRITY

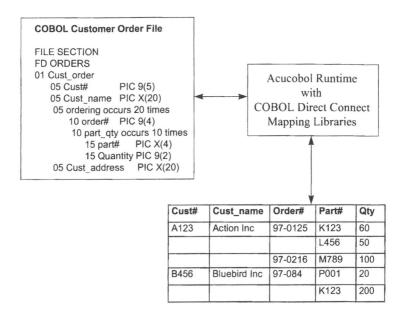

In any migration, regardless of the platform and the data structures, the issue of data integrity must be addressed. To migrate COBOL indexed data structures into a relational model, one must first understand the inherent systems allowance for data fields to be populated in a manner that is contradictory to its definition. COBOL indexed structures by nature allow for this by putting the emphasis for data validation in the hands of the programmer. Block movement of data and the use of working storage redefine structures allow for fields to contain values and structures that will not necessarily match the record definitions described in the file definition layouts. Field and record initialization techniques are also optional procedure in many

COBOL environments and have been left to the individual programmer to develop when systems standards are not apparent or actively enforced.

Along with these issues, there is certainly the need to evaluate and resolve issues relating to date field integrity in both structure and ability to support larger Year 2000 compliance issues. Any migration not examining these issues will fall short in scope and will require a follow-up project covering data functionality. For these reasons, care must be taken in a migration to examine data as it is migrated and not to rely on the file definitions as the final word on data file integrity.

Case Study

The nature of the BancTec migration involved a two-phase migration of application data (see Exhibit 24.3). Initially, it was "flattened" and unloaded from the INFOS data base into sequential files for importing into the UNIX Acucobol VISION indexed structure. From there it was moved into the UniData RDBMS using the COBOL Direct Connect product. Because of the two-phase approach, care was taken at each phase to validate data integrity. "Unload" programs included field validation and initialization as application testing revealed issues with data consistency. Some clean-up was accomplished with C language programs to perform specific field manipulation when issues dictated modifications to the extracted data. During the UniData load phase, the COBOL Direct Connect product provided record-by-record verification of the data as it was loaded into the relational data base. Data inconsistencies appearing at this phase were addressed through modifications to load programs.

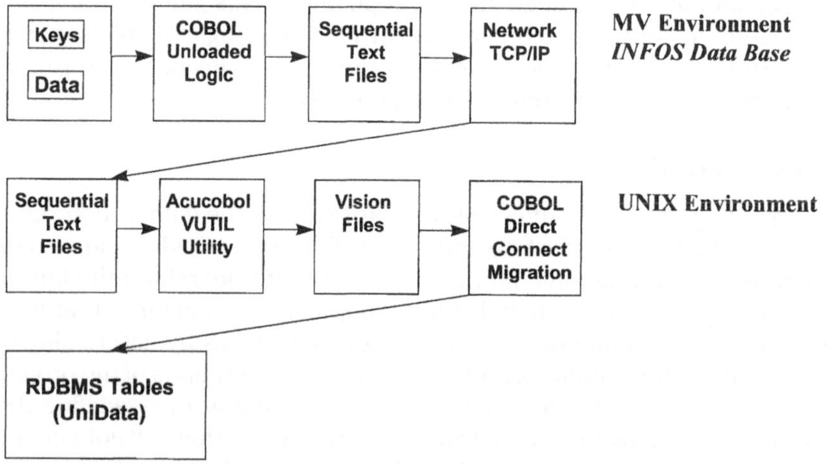

Exhibit 24.3. A Two-Phase Migration of Application Data

A known issue was the problem of dates that were not correctly validated and in some cases incorrectly defined in structure (e.g., a field defined as YYMMDD contained MMDDYY data). BancTec chose to move data fields over as pure numeric data and to address the correction of this data in conjunction with a later project to open for desktop access. With the scope of the problem fully defined during the migration, a project was begun to implement the UniData elapsed day/date formats to allow for proper date sequence query capabilities and to export back into COBOL programs a value that will support date logic into the next century.

PROVIDING OPEN ACCESS MECHANISMS

Opening data to ad hoc query and desktop access is where the relational data base shows its most outstanding values within the goals of the migration. Having a repository of data defined by structure data dictionaries and accessible to any attribute, can rapidly change an organization's ability to understand and manipulate its legacy data. User reliance on IS as the only means of solution delivery can be redirected into self-sufficiency in many of the ongoing day-to-day requirements. These features are often delivered as standard products in a relational environment and can be integrated into the enterprise solution either during the migration or as post-migration enhancements.

Case Study

Upon the completion of migration, BancTec chose to go forward with a number of UniData query and reporting tools. The IS staff is using native UniData UniQuery command line capabilities to support ad hoc reporting, application data review issues, and data base maintenance activity. This product has allowed for the viewing of data structures in a COBOL look and feel that has supported the staff's understanding of the relational model. From this, development of more sophisticated interface logic in SQL and ODBC access tools has progressed.

The BancTec user community is in the process of expanding its access to the BASE application through the implementation of solutions based in the wIntegrate GUI modernization product. This product, along with supporting terminal emulation needs, provide a desktop access interface to relational data allowing for point-and-click query building and downloading into desktop spreadsheets and data stores. BancTec IS staff is building data access views that are concatenations of the COBOL data to support the more involved access requests. The data base administrator is in charge of refining the existing data dictionaries to support greater access and understudying of all application data, driving the organization to greater user independence from IS staff requests to information.

PRODUCTION ENVIRONMENTS

During the migration of a COBOL application to an RDBMS, it is necessary to understand the underlying rules under which each data model has been constructed. Indexed files are designed to provide both rapid random access on keyed inquiries and sequential access through a data file on a record-oriented basis. Access is typically driven through a COBOL application program, and all data grouping and reporting is done within the record-level access of the program I/O.

As applications are moved to an RDBMS, it is important to note that the capabilities now exist to go beyond the record processing paradigm. It is these features that will supplement the standard process and allow for the introduction of replacement or new logic to processing requirements. For example, it certainly will be more efficient in the relational model to use table-oriented processes for requirements such as data purging, as opposed to writing a COBOL application that will sequentially read through an entire table examining each record for compliance to purging criteria.

While sequential record access through an entire table may be efficient within the constraints of the COBOL language, a strong argument can be made for the flexibility and speed of new development under the relation native tool solution. This idea can also be expanded in the area of data sorting and reporting, which, while effective once completed in COBOL, are often overshadowed by the need for application modification and "one-time" usage. By employing these and other relational processing techniques, any performance or functionality issues that arise during the migration process can be addressed in a manner that will provide comparable results.

Case Study

To fulfill existing processing window requirements, certain tasks have been modified to include native Unidata relational table processing activity. Using functionality based upon "select list" processing, these applications now take better advantage of the power of the relational environment. Data extractions that previously read entire data files are now driven by smaller subsets of data that contain only table data pertinent to the task at hand. Whenever possible, ad hoc reporting has been moved to the requesting department level, and through the use of the Unidata tools, these requests are being formalized for access by all personnel involved in similar activity.

Data clean-up and purging activity is now accomplished outside the application when requirements allow. This activity is coordinated with global data base administration tasks done under command line activity, which was previously confined to solution development in COBOL programs. Training and pilot projects have followed for moving existing solutions from the COBOL file extract mentality to an ODBC-compliant data access solution, which will serve as a model for all future access processes.

FOLLOW-ON DEVELOPMENT

Open system functionality either at the RDBMS vendor tool level or through standards ODBC interface levels, is one of the strongest value propositions of migration to the relational data structure. This feature brings to the forefront the many options for future development outside the COBOL environment that, if properly structured, can lead to higher programmer productivity and increased application functionality. The merging of the COBOL-based legacy business rules with the newer visual and rapid application development tools on the market is an effective deployment solution in most open systems environments. It is at this point in the migration life cycle that the decision to migrate the application, as opposed to rewriting, becomes fully validated in both cost and time categories.

Case Study

Although BancTec has continued to develop in Acucobol as requests for maintenance and new development surface, the emphasis has moved to review and selection of supplemental development environment for future requests. Because of previous staff experience with Visual Foxpro, some pilot project activity is proceeding with that product. Unidata's Unibasic language has been used for utility application development, as it allows for rapid data base manipulation at the base attribute level, fully understanding the Unidata data structure and the native storage formats.

CONCLUSION

BancTec's conversion took approximately 1 year and cost approximately $300,000. BancTec's BASE application is now running on series AViiON server hardware running the DG/UX operating system, both from Data General.

The three most measureable benefits to BancTec from its COBOL migration solution are:

- Time savings due to stronger system performance
- More open data access by the systems users themselves
- Increased efficiency of staff serving customers

Chapter 25
Building Database-Enabled Web Applications with IDC

Ido Gileadi

THE WORLD WIDE WEB (THE WEB) HAS BEEN PRIMARILY CONSTRUCTED from static HTML pages. These pages generally contain text, graphics, and hyperlinks that give net users the ability to search and view information easily with the click of a mouse. The static page always displays the same information regardless of individual user selections or personal preferences. Furthermore, the static page displays the whole range of information available to it without consideration of the specific requirements of unique, busy individual users accessing the web site.

In recent years, there has been a strong movement toward a more dynamic approach for web page design. Web pages can now be created on the fly, customized to an individual viewer's requirements, and linked with database servers to provide accurate, up-to-the-minute data. There are many techniques for creating dynamic web pages. Some of the technologies available involve creation of a web page on the fly based on selections a viewer makes in previous pages. Active pages and CGI scripting can easily achieve these tasks.

In many cases we would like to create dynamic web pages that contain subsets of data based on the viewer's selection of a query. A simple example of this type of application is a telephone directory publication on the web. Such an application requires the ability to select and display one or more entries from the database, based on a selection (query) the user makes on the screen. Most likely the selection will involve a last name and/or first name combination.

The traditional way of creating a database-enabled web application, such as the telephone directory, is to use CGI scripting. The CGI script is a program that is referenced by the selection screen. It is invoked by the submission of the selection criteria (last name and first name) and receives the selections as input parameters. Once invoked, the CGI script works like any other program on the server and can access a database server to retrieve the information that is required. It then builds the dynamic web page based on the retrieved data and presents it back to the user on the web page.

0-8493-9822-3/00/$0.00+$.50

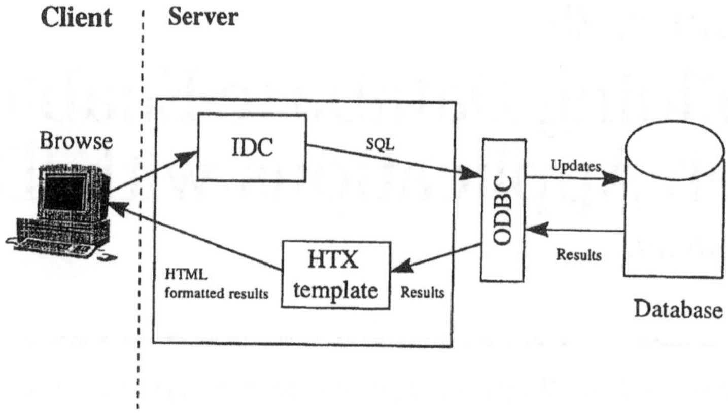

Exhibit 25.1. IDC Operation

This approach is lacking in execution speed and requires programming knowledge in Perl or some other computer language that is used to construct the CGI script. In this chapter, we will write a database-enabled application using the Internet Database Connector (IDC) technology. Building this application will require no traditional programming skills and relies only on minimal coding statements.

INTERNET DATABASE CONNECTOR (IDC)

IDC is a technology developed by Microsoft to allow the execution of an SQL statement against a database and represent the results in an HTML page format. This technology works only with an Internet Information Server (IIS) that is a Microsoft web server offering. Any browser can be used to access database information using IDC because the only requirement is that the browser be able to interpret HTML pages. Exhibit 25.1 depicts the way in which IDC operates.

In this example, a client machine (e.g., your PC) is running a web browser. The browser requests an IDC page, which happens to be a text-based page. The server intercepts the request and sends the SQL statement included in the IDC file to the ODBC data source defined in the IDC file. The database returns a result set or performs the insert/update operation. The data returned is formatted using the format specified in the HTX template into a valid HTML stream that is in turn sent back to the requesting client to be displayed by the browser.

In the following sections of this chapter, this functionality will be demonstrated by building a simple telephone directory application.

Exhibit 25.2. Example Database Structure

Field Name	Description	Type	Comments
id	The directory entry unique id	Counter	This is an automated counter that will be incremented every time a new record is inserted into the database
LastName	Last name	Text	
FirstName	First name	Text	
tel	Telephone number	Text	

DEVELOPING THE TELEPHONE DIRECTORY APPLICATION

Requirements

This is a small sample application designed for the sole purpose of demonstrating some principles of database access over the web. The requirements are identified in terms of the required functionality and access. The functionality required is as follows:

- Store first name, last name, and telephone number of multiple individuals.
- Allow the user to search for a specific directory entry using a part or the whole of the last name and first name.
- Display a list of all matching entries as the results of a search.
- Allow the users to add a new entry to the directory.
- Allow users to access the telephone directory through a web browser and their Internet connection.

The preceding requirements are sufficient to begin developing the application. The following sections provide a guide that can be used on a step-by-step basis to develop the application.

The Database

An Access database will be used to support this sample application. Any database with an ODBC-compliant driver can be used. A new database that contains only one table will be created to contain the directory entries. The structure of the table is shown in Exhibit 25.2.

IDC requires an ODBC datasource to communicate with the database. We will create an ODBC datasource for the access database we have just created using the 32bit ODBC manager in the control panel.

Programming Tip. The datasource must be defined as a system datasource for the web server to be able to access it.

The datasource will be named Tel_Directory and pointed to the newly created access database. Security will not be added to the database for the purpose of this example. In a real-life application you will most likely want to create a user id and a password for the users accessing the database over the network and have them key it in at run time. Another alternative is to create a user id and a password with very limited permissions and include the login parameters in the IDC file to avoid the extra step of logging in.

Warning. The IDC file is a plain text file and can be viewed easily by anyone with access to the web. When storing the login parameters in this file, you must execute great caution to restrict the user access to the very minimum required.

The Application Directory

Any directory that will be accessed by the web server (IIS) has to be defined in the administration section of the web server. This allows the web server to know about the directory and allows the developer to set some parameters for each directory. The parameters of interest in this discussion include the access rights. There are two access parameters:

- **Read** access allows the server to read the files in the directory and send their contents to the requesting browser. This is sufficient for regular HTML files.
- **Execute** access allows the server to execute the program stored in the files in the directory. This is required for CGI scripts as well as IDC files.

For our application we will create one directory that will contain all the files we need to run the application with the exception of the database file. We will grant both read and execute permissions to this directory.

Programming Tip. Create the directory under the web server's home directory (typically .../wwwroot) and make sure you grant read and execute permissions to the home directory. The home directory is marked in the directory property window of the web administration section.

The Search Screen

As defined in the requirements we must allow a search by a combination of first and last name. We will define the search screen as an HTML form, which will allow us to pass the user's selection as parameters to the IDC script. Exhibit 3 shows the search screen as it will display on the browser.

The HTML code for the preceding screen was created using Microsoft Front Page and it consists of the following:

```
<!DOCTYPE HTML PUBLIC "-//IETF//DTD HTML//EN">

<html>

<head>
```

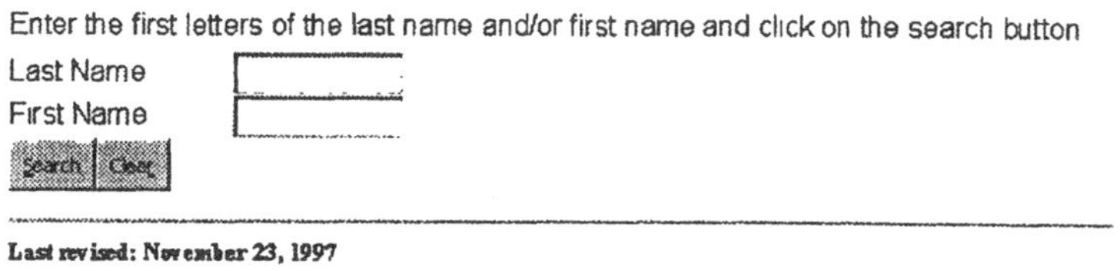

Exhibit 25.3. Search Screen

```
<meta http-equiv = "Content-Type"
content = "text/html; charset = iso-8859-1">
<meta name = "GENERATOR" content = "Microsoft FrontPage 2.0">
<title>Search Directory</title>
</head>
<body>
<h1>Search Directory</h1>
<hr>
<p>Enter the first letters of the last name and/or first name and click on the
search button</p>
<form action = "Search.idc" method = "POST">
    <table border = "0">
        <tr>
            <td>Last Name</td>
            <td><input type = "text" size = "20" maxlength = "20"
            name = "lname"></td>
        </tr>
        <tr>
            <td>First Name</td>
            <td><input type = "text" size = "20" maxlength = "20"
            name = "fname"></td>
        </tr>
    </table>
    <p><input type = "submit" value = "Search"> <input type = "reset"
    value = "Clear"> </p>
```

```
</form>
<hr>
<h5>Last revised: November 23, 1997</h5>
</body>
</html>
```

The HTML code is a standard form with fields that are arranged into a table for cosmetic reasons. Highlighted are the names of the input fields that will be passed as parameters to the IDC script.

The Search IDC Script

The general format of an IDC script is as follows:

```
Datasource: <Name of a system ODBC datasource>
Username: <User id for accessing the database>
Password: <Password for the user>
Template: <A URL of the HTML template file *.HTX>
SQLStatement:
+<Lines of the SQL statement>
+<Lines of the SQL statement>
```

There may be more than one SQL statement in the file. This feature will be revisited in the following sections.

The IDC script used with the search screen is as follows:

```
Datasource:Tel_Directory
Username:
Password:
Template:Directory.htx
SQLStatement:
+SELECT id,FirstName,LastName,Tel from Directory
+WHERE LastName like '%lname%%' and FirstName like '%fname%%'
```

A username or password has not been included for this sample. In a production environment you would definitely include a user id and password or prompt the user for one using a login screen.

The SQL statement containing the SELECT statement will typically return a result set. The result set may be empty or contain one or more rows. The HTML template file will have to handle the display of multiple rows. We also observe that the field names in the SELECT section reflect the names of the columns in the database, and the parameter names in the WHERE clause reflect the field names on the search HTML form. The parameters coming from the HTML form are enclosed in a percent sign (%). In our case, we also enclose the percent signs (%) in single quotes so that the WHERE clause will contain the correct syntax for a text field. In addition we want to allow the user the flexibility of keying only the first few letters of the name. We include an additional percent sign (%) that acts as a wild card character indicating that any string of characters can replace it. The final SQL statement may look like:

```
SELECT id,FirstName,LastName,Tel from Directory
WHERE LastName like 'Smi%' and FirstName like '%'
```

This will return all the entries where the last name starts with 'Smi' regardless of the first name.

The Search Result Screen

The search results are displayed using the HTX template. The HTX file is a regular HTML file and can contain any codes included in an HTML file. In addition to the standard HTML codes it contains the following construct:

```
<%BeginDetail%>
    Any valid HTML code <%FieldName1%><%FieldName2%>
    Any valid HTML code <%FieldName3%><%FieldName4%>
<%EndDetail%>
```

Anything contained between the <%BeginDetail%> and the <%EndDetail%> will be repeated in the constructed HTML file for each row of results coming from the database. The <%FieldName%> parameters are the field-names as they appear in the database and will be substituted with the values returned from the database.

Following is the listing for the Search results HTX file. The name of this file is stated in the IDC script, it is 'Directory.htx'. This template was created using Microsoft Front Page. Highlighted in the following example are the important construct elements, including begindetail, id, LastName, FirstName, Tel, enddetail, if CurrentRecord EQ 0, action = "AddEntry.idc", and endif:

```
<!DOCTYPE HTML PUBLIC "-//IETF//DTD HTML//EN">
<html>
<head>
<meta http-equiv = "Content-Type"
```

```
content = "text/html; charset = iso-8859-1">
<meta name = "GENERATOR" content = "Microsoft FrontPage 2.0">
<title>Directory Listing</title>
</head>
<body bgcolor = "#FFFFFF">
<p><font color = "#0000FF" size = "5"><em><strong>Telephone Directory
Listing</strong></em></font></p>
<table border = "2" cellpadding = "2" cellspacing = "3">
    <tr>
        <td><font color = "#0000FF"><em><strong>Entry
        ID</strong></em></font></td>
        <td><font color = "#0000FF"><em><strong>Last
        Name</strong></em></font></td>
        <td><font color = "#0000FF"><em><strong>First
        Name</strong></em></font></td>
        <td><font color = "#0000FF"><em><strong>Tel
        Mumber</strong></em></font></td>
    </tr>
<%begindetail%>
    <tr>
        <td><%id%></td>
        <td><%LastName%></td>
        <td><%FirstName%></td>
        <td><%Tel%></td>
    </tr>
<%enddetail%></table>
<p> </p>
<%if CurrentRecord EQ 0%>
<table border = "0" cellpadding = "0" cellspacing = "4">
    <tr>
        <td><form action = "AddEntry.idc" method = "POST">
            <p><input type = "submit" name = "B1" value = "Add
Entry"></p>
        </form>
        </td>
```

```
    </tr>
</table>
<%endif%></body>
</html>
```

In the preceding listing we notice that there is an additional conditional construct that looks like

<%if CurrentRecord EQ 0%> any HTML code <%endif%>

This conditional construct allows for better control over the creation of the HTML code. In our example, we use the construct to add an AddEntry button that will activate the add entry screen.

Tip. The conditional construct can also contain the element <%else%> that will allow the creation of a completely different HTML code based on the result set.

Warning. The conditional construct will not work if used before the <%BeginDetail%>

The CurrentRecord is one of the built-in variables that can be used in the template. It indicates the current record being processed. If used after the <%BeginDetail%> <%EndDetail%> construct will hold the last record number. The record number relates to the sequential number within the result set.

The Add Entry Screen

The Add Entry button will appear on the search results screen only when there are no records in the result set. Having no records in the result set will indicate that the entry was not found and therefore may be entered into the database. The Add Entry button is a submit button within an HTML form that points to the AddEntry.idc script.

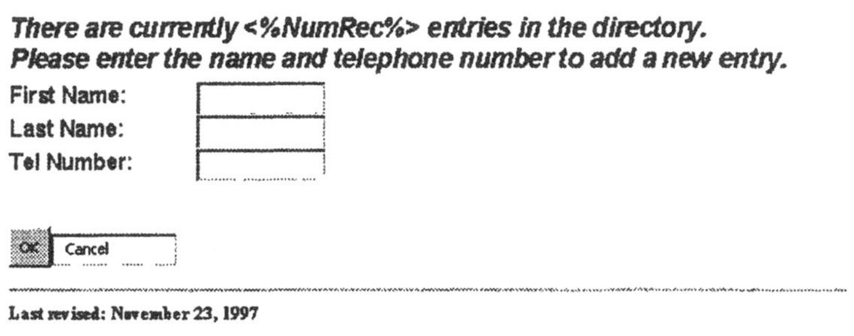
There are currently <%NumRec%> entries in the directory.
Please enter the name and telephone number to add a new entry.
First Name:
Last Name:
Tel Number:
OK
Cancel
Last revised: November 23, 1997

Exhibit 25.4. Add Entry Screen

The AddEntry.idc script will fetch the total number of entries in the database and invoke the HTML template named AddEntry.htx. Following is the listing for the AddEntry.idc script:

```
Datasource:Tel_Directory
Username:
Password:
Template:AddEntry.htx
SQLStatement:
+SELECT count(id) as NumRec from Directory
```

The AddEntry.htx template is different from the search result template we have seen previously. We only expect one record to be returned to this screen. That record will contain the total number of records in the database. The rest of the template is an HTML form that will allow the user to enter the details of the new directory entry and submit them to the database. Exhibit 25.4 shows the Add Entry screen.

The following example is the AddEntry.htx HTML listing supporting Exhibit 25.4: Add Directory Entry Screen:

```
<!DOCTYPE HTML PUBLIC "-//IETF//DTD HTML//EN">
<html>
<head>
<meta http-equiv = "Content-Type"
content = "text/html; charset = iso-8859-1">
<meta name = "GENERATOR" content = "Microsoft FrontPage 2.0">
<title>Add Entry</title>
</head>
<body>
<h1>Add Directory Entry</h1>
<hr>
<%BeginDetail%>
<p><font size = "4"><em><strong>There are currently
&lt;%NumRec%&gt; entries in the directory.</strong></em></font></p>
<%EndDetail%>
<p><font size = "4"><em><strong>Please enter the name and telephone
number to add a new entry.</strong></em></font></p>
```

```
<form action = "Add2DB.idc" method = "POST">
    <table border = "0">
        <tr>
            <td><strong>First Name:</strong></td>
            <td><input type = "text" size = "20" maxlength = "20"
            name = "fname"></td>
        </tr>
        <tr>
            <td><strong>Last Name:</strong></td>
            <td><input type = "text" size = "20" maxlength = "20"
            name = "lname"></td>
        </tr>
        <tr>
            <td><strong>Tel Number:</strong></td>
            <td><input type = "text" size = "15" maxlength = "15"
            name = "tel"></td>
        </tr>
    </table>
    <blockquote>
        <p> </p>
    </blockquote>
    <p><input type = "submit" value = "OK"> <input type = "button"
    value = "Cancel"> </p>
</form>
<hr>
<h5>Last revised: November 23, 1997</h5>
</body>
</html>
```

In the above listing, note the <%BeginDetail%> and <%EndDetail%> around the <%NumRec%> variable without which the %NumeRec% variable will not be assigned a value. Also note the form action is referencing yet another IDC script named Add2DB.idc. The Add2DB.idc script contains the SQL INSERT statement that will insert the new record into the database. The listing for the Add2DB.idc script is as follows:

```
Datasource:Tel_Directory
Username:
Password:
Template:Directory.htx
SQLStatement:
+INSERT INTO Directory (FirstName, LastName, Tel)
+VALUES ('%fname%', '%lname%', '%tel%')
SQLStatement:
+SELECT id, FirstName, LastName, Tel FROM Directory
```

Let us examine this script carefully. It has an SQL INSERT statement that takes as parameters the values that had been entered in the HTML form. The INSERT statement is not the only statement in the script. There is a second SQL statement that selects all the records in the telephone directory. The second select statement will populate the Directory.htx template that we have seen before. This script performs the insert action and then displays all records in the directory including the newly inserted record.

Tip. Results returned from the database must match the template.

Each result set returned from the database will correspond with a single <%BeginDetail%> <%EndDetail%> in the template. There may be more then one <%BeginDetail%> <%EndDetail%> in the template. If one SQL statement does not return a result set, it will be skipped and the next result set will be matched to the <%BeginDetail%> <%EndDetail%> in the template. In our example, the INSERT statement does not return a result set. The second SQL statement does return a result set and will therefore be used by the <%BeginDetail%> <%EndDetail%> in the template.

Organizing the Application

The application directory was created previously. All the HTML, IDC and HTX files should now reside in the same directory. They are all built to reference each other in a cyclic fashion. Exhibit 25.5 depicts the relationships between the various screens and scripts.

CONCLUSION

The sample application created in this chapter demonstrates the principles of accessing a database through a web server. The task is accomplished without the need for traditional programming. All the developer

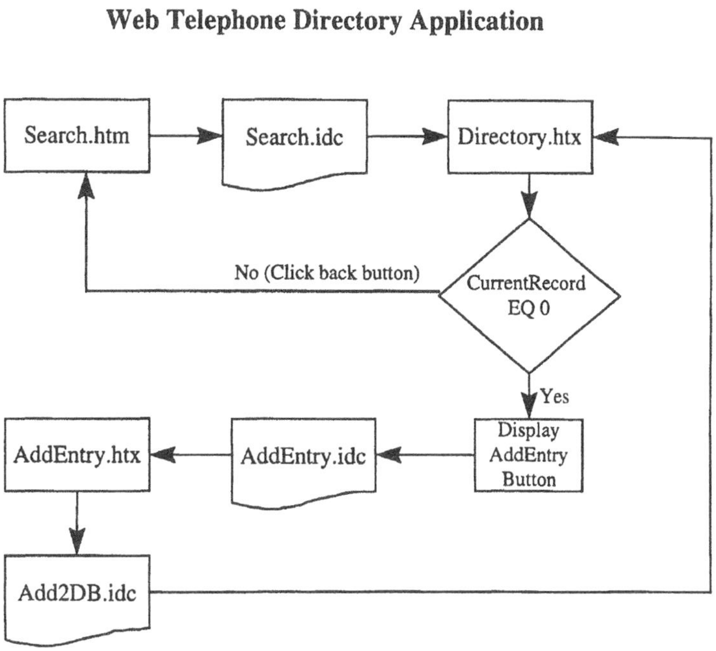

Exhibit 25.5. Web Telephone Directory Application

needs to know are basic SQL statements and some HTML coding. With this basic knowledge we have managed to create an application that can be useful and provide value.

The IDC technology is compatible with a Microsoft Internet Information Server. The personal web server version was used to test this application. Users accessing the telephone directory can do so with any browser that can read and interpret HTML code (e.g., Netscape or Microsoft).

There are many ways to access data through the web, IDC is the simplest and quickest way of doing so. If the requirements for your applications can be met with this method, it will be a convenient and low maintenance solution.

Chapter 26
Creating Effective Batch SQL Jobs

Len Dvorkin

IN RECENT YEARS, THE ARRIVAL OF MATURE RELATIONAL DATABASES powerful enough to handle mission-critical functions has provided systems developers with the ability to perform complex processing much more simply than was possible using traditional data repositories and languages.

This power, however, has represented a double-edged sword when combined with traditional programming approaches and styles. When complex business requirements are combined with the power of SQL, the result can be code that is syntactically correct, but that runs poorly or not at all at production-level data volumes.

This problem commonly occurs during the creation of online transaction processing (OLTP) systems, when a frequently encountered scenario has developers coding and testing an application in a test environment, certifying it as ready for production, and watching it fail with a higher number of users, more data, and so on. Fortunately (or unfortunately), this type of failure generally manifests itself directly and clearly in the form of an online function that stops working or only performs slowly.

A more subtle trap relates to batch processing in SQL. Most significant DBMS-based systems have batch components to support them. These components include:

- *Internal processing:* Using data from tables in the system to update other tables within the system
- *Data loading:* Updating the system's database with data from other systems
- *Data extraction:* Creation of tables or flat files for use by an outside system
- *Reporting:* Collection of data from within the system in order to present it for user review

These components are not as "flashy" as their online cousins; however, they have the potential to seriously impact a system if they are not created and managed correctly. And batch routines are here to stay — the power

0-8493-9822-3/00/$0.00+$.50

represented by relational databases does not exempt mature systems from requiring tasks to run automatically and unattended, separately from any online components.

Most of the recurring problems in batch SQL are also frequently encountered when creating SQL for online purposes — after all, the language is the same. However, given the usual purposes of batch SQL, certain traps tend to manifest themselves with annoying frequency, even when coded by experienced developers. This chapter describes principles and techniques that represent good practice when designing any SQL job, but seem to be forgotten or left out more often when the batch environment is concerned (see Exhibit 26.1).

SQL CODING PRINCIPLES

Joins

A common operation in batch SQL involves combining data from multiple tables that have a relationship to each other. These may be a series of transaction tables coming from different sources or a single transaction table with several foreign keys that need to be referenced.

In these cases, it can be hard to resist the power of SQL's ability to join database lookups across multiple tables. While careful design of queries can result in a tightly tuned, fast-performing join, most databases use rules coded in an internal optimizer to examine a query and develop the plan that will guide the database engine in processing the query. In complicated joins, it is not uncommon for the database optimizer to make an unexpected decision on the join order and turn what should be a simple query into a large, slow-running database killer.

For example, assume that a report extract is needed for a table with four foreign keys to code tables. As a join, this could be coded as follows:

```
INSERT INTO report_table
SELECT t.column1,
        t.column2,
        a.description,
        b.description,
        c.description,
        d.description,
        <other columns>
FROM transaction_table t,
        code_table1 a,
```

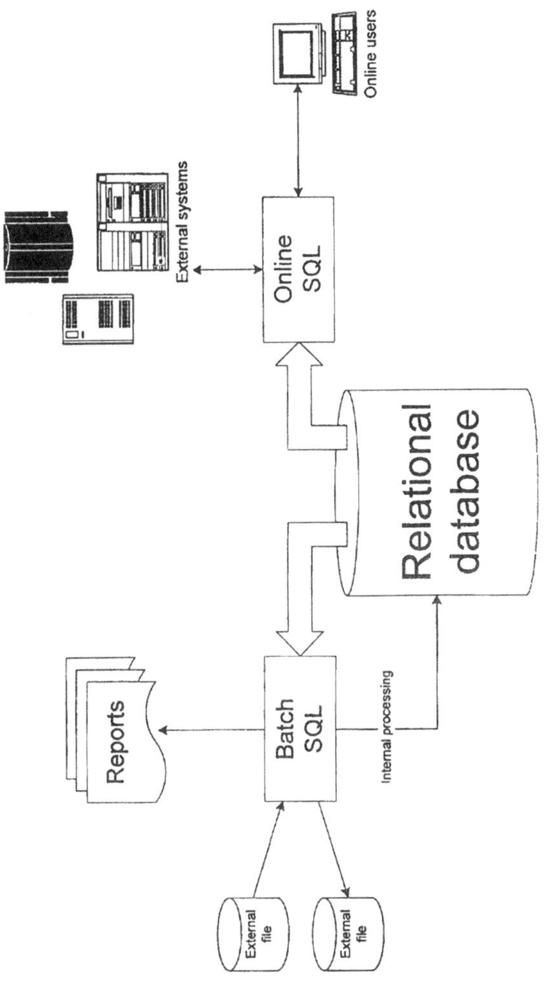

Exhibit 26.1. Common Functions of Online and Batch SQL

```
        code_table2 b,
        code_table3 c,
        code_table4 d
  WHERE t.code_a = a.code
  AND t.code_b = b.code
  AND t.code_c = c.code
  AND t.code_d = d.code
  AND <other conditions>
```

Under low-volume conditions, or under high-volume conditions when the database statistics are current and the database's query optimizer is working effectively, this query will run well. The first table to be examined will be *transaction_table*, and code values found there will be used to reference the required code tables.

Sometimes, though, a large number of *where* clauses or a significant change in database volumes can confuse the optimizer, resulting in disastrous query plans (building the result set in the above example from one of the code tables, for instance).

In a batch SQL job, we are generally not worried about shaving seconds off of transactions. What we are much more interested in is predictable, arithmetic increases in performance time directly related to database table volumes. (There are exceptions to this statement — some systems have a very restricted batch processing time window within which their processing must be completed. However, the techniques in this chapter can be used to reduce the server load of a given batch job, or to permit multiple jobs to run concurrently, potentially fixing these "batch window squeeze" situations.) To that end, splitting the single multitable join into separate queries involves a relatively small performance penalty in exchange for a predictable overall run time. For instance:

```
loop for each qualified record in transaction_table:
    SELECT:col1 = t.column1,
        :col2 = t.column2,
        :code_a = t.code_a,
        :code_b = t.code_b,
        :code_c = t.code_c,
        :code_d = t.code_d,
        <other columns>
```

```
        FROM transaction_table t
        WHERE <other conditions>

        SELECT:description_a
        FROM code_table1
        WHERE code = :code_a

        SELECT:description_b
        FROM code_table1
        WHERE code = :code_b

        SELECT:description_c
        FROM code_table1
        WHERE code = :code_c

        SELECT:description_d
        FROM code_table1
        WHERE code = :code_d

        INSERT INTO report_table
        VALUES (:col1,
                :col2,
                :description_a,
                :description_b,
                :description_c,
                :description_d,
                <other columns>)
    end loop
```

At the cost of a few extra lines of code, the 5-table join in the first example becomes a bullet-proof routine with predictable performance under virtually all conditions of data volume or database statistics.

Note that the number of required database lookups in the code above has not changed from the more complicated example, leaving only a small net extra cost in separate processing of the SQL statements. If these statements are running inside the database engine (in a stored procedure, for instance), the overhead becomes even smaller.

DECLARATIONS AND INITIALIZATIONS

The top section of any routine should contain declarations of any variables that will be used in the job. If a data value is likely to be changed during testing or after the job is running in production, consider changing it to a "constant" variable. This makes it easier to read and maintain the code. Similarly, table columns containing code values are easier to deal with if their code values are stored in constants. Consider the example below:

```
declare:MIN_DOLLAR_VALUE float = 10.0

declare:SALE char(1) = "S"

declare:RETURN char(1) = "R"

<other processing>

SELECT sum (trans_value)

FROM trans_table

WHERE trans_value >:MIN_DOLLAR_VALUE

AND trans_type = :SALE
```

Read Once, Write Once

Depending on the specific driver program type and database implementation being used, the cost of an SQL table hit is easily 10 times or more expensive than processing a simple logic statement. However, many batch programs are profligate in their use of table access statements. In the example below, a single row in a source table is read once for its index value, a second time for a lookup value, and a third time for other information needed to write to an output table:

```
loop for each qualified record in transaction_table:

        SELECT:index_field = t.index_field

        FROM transaction_table t

        WHERE t.transaction_date = <today>

        < processing of the record >

        SELECT:transaction_type = a.type_description

        FROM transaction_table t,

                code_table1 a

        WHERE t.index_field = :index_field

        AND t.type_code_a = a.type_code_a
```

```
        < other processing of the record >

        INSERT INTO report_table
        SELECT t.column1,
               t.column2,
               :transaction_type,
               <other columns>
        FROM transaction_table t
        WHERE t.index_field = :index_field
    end loop
```

When examining this program structure, developers often explain that this is a straightforward approach to satisfying the program's requirements — what's wrong with it? They may be influenced by the method in which one reads a traditional/hierarchical data store, where the first access to a record brings all of its data directly into a program cache, and subsequent access to fields on the record are virtually "free" reads of local memory.

However, this is certainly not the case when we are discussing database access. Each time that the (same) row in a table is referenced in a select statement, a nontrivial amount of database work must take place. Most database implementations will cache the affected data row in its local memory pages after the first read, preventing hard disk access in subsequent reads. However, the overhead cost of parsing the statement, determining a query path, supporting a join, identifying the desired row, determining that it is resident in memory, etc. is still significantly higher than that of a simple reference to a local variable in the program's memory space.

The routine above can be rewritten with a minimum of effort to access each table only once, retrieving all columns that will be required in this select statement and saving them locally for use later in the process:

```
    loop for each qualified record in transaction_table:
        SELECT:index_field = t.index_field,
               :type_code_a = type_code_a,
               :column1 = column1,
               :column2 = column2,
               <other columns>
        FROM transaction_table t
```

```
        WHERE <conditions>

        < other processing of the record >

        SELECT:transaction_type = a.type_description
        FROM code_table1 a
        WHERE a.type_code_a = :type_code_a

        < other processing of the record >

        INSERT INTO report_table
        VALUES (:column1,
                :column2,
                :transaction_type,
                <other columns>
    end loop
```

An analogous situation can occur when writing an output record. Rather than adopting a simple structure that first inserts a skeleton of a new output row, and then updating elements of the same row during processing, the column data to be inserted can be saved in local variables and inserted in a single SQL statement.

Indexes

The optimizers in today's database engines have matured tremendously compared to those of several years ago. For ad hoc, complex queries, it is now often possible to rely on the optimizer to determine the optimum query path that should be taken to minimize a query's run time.

However, even the best optimizers cannot be used as a safety net for all queries. If a database's internal table statistics are not up to date, for instance, many optimizers will choose poor query plans or even switch to table scans with sometimes disastrous results. This problem can be avoided, to some extent, by regularly running an "update statistics" routine that re-creates internal table data volume and distribution statistics. However, in cases where the volume or type of data is changing frequently in a table, even daily or weekly updates of table statistics may be not be adequate to guarantee the use of a desired index.

For that reason, good defensive coding practices take the approach that "It is nice to have a database optimizer, but let's not leave anything to chance." Every query on a table of nontrivial size should be examined, with particular attention to ensuring that its where clauses correspond to an existing index. If an appropriate index does not already exist in the database, it should either be added to the table or, if this is not practical, consideration should be given to redesigning the query.

An extremely common development scenario has normally careful developers designing batch jobs without consideration of indexes ("After all, we won't have any users sitting at their desks waiting for this job to finish tonight"), testing the jobs under low-data-volume conditions and verifying their correctness, and then watching in horror as the batch job run time grows steadily under regular data volume conditions.

There can be some exceptions to this principle — for instance, when an entire table is being read and processed using a cursor, direct sequential access can be faster than involving any indices. But, in general, every database access in the routine should be explicitly designed to use a predefined index. If this is done, then overall job performance may grow geometrically in proportion to the volume of data being processed, but the time should be manageable and predictable from the start.

Transaction Commitments

One of the common design tradeoffs in batch routines involves decisions around committing transactions. As in other aspects of the batch routines, developer approaches adopted in the construction of online routines do not always correspond well to the design requirements of a batch routine.

Within a transaction block, either all updates are applied to the database, or none of the updates are applied. This makes the approach to determining whether a transaction is required for an online SQL routine (and, if so, what its scope should be) a relatively simple exercise. The programmer simply identifies the logical unit of work, in terms of database changes, which may not be left partially complete in case of data or database problems.

The logical extension of this concept to batch routines would be to place a transaction block around every set of inserts and updates that comprised a single block of work. The problem with this straightforward approach is that the impact of processing individual transactions blocks in a routine reading an input table of, say, 20,000 rows can seriously affect the database's performance and logging.

A compromise approach to transaction design in batch routines involves grouping together a larger number of individual input records into a single transaction, and repeatedly beginning and committing transactions when that number of input records has been processed. The example below groups input records into batches of 500 for the purpose of transaction processing:

```
declare:counter int = 0
declare:MAX_RECORDS_IN_COMMIT int = 500
BEGIN TRANSACTION
loop for each qualified record in transaction_table:
        SET:counter = :counter+1
        if:counter = :MAX_RECORDS_IN_COMMIT
                COMMIT TRANSACTION
                BEGIN TRANSACTION
        end if
        <process record>
end loop
COMMIT TRANSACTION
```

Some experience is necessary to determine the best number of rows to include in a single commit block, as this decision depends on the specific database implementation and environment. Establishing this number as a local constant or parameter to the routine (as in the example above) is an effective way to make it easily tunable based on actual experience.

Note that if the batch routine will be running while online users are working on the system, the MAX_RECORDS_IN_COMMIT value should be kept relatively low to avoid locking an excessive number of rows or pages needed by other processes.

If the input records are not being deleted or flagged in a specific way when they are processed, transaction parameters can be used in conjunction with transaction diagnostic messages to facilitate restartability of the routine. They allow a person responding to a problem encountered when running the routine to determine quickly and accurately how much data had been processed successfully before a problem occurred. In this way, steps can be taken to reset the input source and restart the job without incurring the risk of missing or double-processing input data.

Data All in a Row

Most batch routines, either as part of a recurring loop or as a one-time operation, must read data and conduct processing based on that data. The "read-once, write-once" approach discussed elsewhere in this paper applies here. Data All in a Row, the aim is to select data from tables as few times as possible. This may mean storing data in local variables, or organizing the routine in order to defer executing the select statement until all required selection criteria have been established.

If the source data is read in a loop, there are several useful techniques available to "walk through" the qualifying rows.

Cursors. Cursors support a single selection of input data, and one-by-one processing of the results. Depending on the database implementation, it may not be practical to use cursors when the number of input rows is large.

Ascending Key Read. This method stores a starting key position and repeatedly reads additional records with larger key values. This method is simplest when the routine can count on the existence of a sequential key in the source table. If that key is indexed properly, this can also be a very efficient way to read the table rows:

```
declare:current_key int

SET:current_key = <appropriate starting value>

loop:
        SELECT <columns>
        FROM trans_table
        WHERE trans_key = :current_key

        if <no rows found>
                exit loop
        else
                SET:current_key = :current_key + 1

        <process the selected row>
end loop
```

Read and Delete. This is appropriate for cases when the data in the input table does not need to be saved after the routine is complete. This is implemented simply by deleting the rows from the source table as they are processed.

This approach is most suitable for cases where a flat file needs to be processed in a database. The batch jobstream can first transfer the flat file data into a temporary table, and then invoke the batch routine to process the records one by one. If a problem halts the batch routine in midstream, it should be automatically restartable with the (presumably) smaller input table, which would contain all unprocessed rows.

Reading a table in this approach can be highly efficient, especially in database implementations that allow the programmer to specify a row retrieval limit in its syntax (for instance, the "*set rowcount 1*" statement in SQL Server). With this restriction in place, the read can be a simple, nonindexed select statement that permits the database to retrieve the first physical record encountered with no need to refer to indices or complicated query plans.

The program structure for this approach is somewhat similar to the example above:

```
loop:
        <restrict selection to 1 row>
        SELECT:key_field = key_field,
                <other columns>
        FROM trans_table
        <remove the single-row restriction>

        if <no rows found>
                exit loop

        <process the selected row>

        DELETE trans_table
        WHERE key_field = :key_field
end loop
```

Read and Flag. This is very similar to read and delete, but it is used when the input table must be kept intact after being processed. Rather than deleting each input row as it is processed, a status flag is set in one of its columns, indicating that it has been used and should therefore not be picked up on the next loop iteration:

```
declare:PROCESSED char(1) = "P"
loop:
        <restrict selection to 1 row>
        SELECT:key_field = key_field,
                <other columns>
        FROM trans_table
```

```
        WHERE processing_status ! = :PROCESSED
        <remove the single-row restriction>

        if <no rows found>
                exit loop

        <process the selected row>

        UPDATE trans_table
        SET processing_status = :PROCESSED
        WHERE key_field = :key_field
    end loop
```

GENERAL PRINCIPLES

Consistency

In many development environments, database routines seem to suffer often from a lack of structure, design, and clean formatting. This is perhaps due to the ease with which they can be coded and the relatively relaxed formatting restrictions of most SQL implementations. When compared to regular 3GL or 4GL processing code, many database routines are characterized by few (or nonstandard) comments, inconsistent indentation, and capitalization of keywords, resulting in an erratic look and feel. Batch routines, because they tend to be longer and more complex, are particularly impacted by this lack of consistency.

While there are many standards that could be described as clear, and this chapter does not attempt to define a single "best" one, the important thing is to choose a standard and stick with it for all SQL routines in a system. This coding discipline generally pays for itself many times in reduced overall maintenance time in the long term.

In addition to these cosmetic issues, an objective of clarity can lead a structured development shop to convert complex batch routine syntax into simpler statements, even if this involves a small cost in terms of performance. For instance, even if a complex table join has been tested and verified to be correct in all circumstances (including tests under high-volume conditions), it can be worthwhile to review the performance and coding cost involved in splitting it into separate but more simple queries. If this cost is not excessive, it will almost certainly be recovered with interest when the routine needs to be modified due to system problems or new business requirements.

Diagnostics

If a batch routine is running without a user sitting at a screen waiting for its completion, it is very tempting to build it with a minimum of inline diagnostics. Sometimes a small set of control totals may be generated and saved as part of the job run, but batch routines are commonly built without even that level of output.

While it is true that there is little need for detailed diagnostics when a job is working correctly, their lack is felt most deeply in the most stressful situations — when problems manifest themselves. In a typical real-life scenario, the complex batch job runs for several months without problems and then, due to some unforeseen data input scenario, starts producing incorrect results. The support staff designated to investigate the problem are faced with a sometimes daunting task of diagnosis and repair, often complicated by less-sophisticated debugging tools for the database environment.

To speed up diagnosis and resolution of these problems, a relatively small amount of developer time and batch job run time can be applied to producing diagnostic messages directly from the batch routine. A simple, but comprehensive approach involves issuing two types of diagnostic messages:

Control Diagnostic Messages. These act as milestones along the road of a batch routine. If one section becomes slow or fails to work, then the offending section should be immediately obvious by referencing the control diagnostics. These could read, for instance, as follows:

ddMMMyyyy hh:mm:ss Routine "process_transactions" started

ddMMMyyyy hh:mm:ss Beginning to process input rows from trans_table

ddMMMyyyy hh:mm:ss Processed 1000 input rows

ddMMMyyyy hh:mm:ss Processed 2000 input rows

ddMMMyyyy hh:mm:ss Processed 3000 input rows

ddMMMyyyy hh:mm:ss Processed 4000 input rows

ddMMMyyyy hh:mm:ss 4692 input rows processed

ddMMMyyyy hh:mm:ss Beginning generation of report_table

ddMMMyyyy hh:mm:ss Generation of report_table complete, with 2456 adds and 1205 changes

The level of detail and wording can depend entirely on development shop standards, as long as they satisfy their primary purpose — to facilitate quick identification of the likely location of problems.

Transaction Diagnostic Messages. These support a more detailed look at the data being processed by the batch routine. Their existence acts as a record of the data processed and can be used to quickly answer questions like "Why didn't product #5682 get reset last night?" or "Why do the sales to customer #7531 appear twice on this morning's reports?"

Transaction diagnostics can represent quite a large quantity of data and, for that reason, they are generally overwritten on a daily or, at least, weekly basis. Using the same example as above, they could look like this:

ddMMMyyyy hh:mm:ss Routine "process_transactions" started

ddMMMyyyy hh:mm:ss Beginning to process input rows from trans_table

ddMMMyyyy hh:mm:ss Processing product #14, status "A"

ddMMMyyyy hh:mm:ss ... Sales record: Sold 50 units to customer #5532 at $45

ddMMMyyyy hh:mm:ss ... Sales record: Sold 14 units to customer #5532 at $48

ddMMMyyyy hh:mm:ss ... Returns record: Returned 12 units from customer #5532 at $43

ddMMMyyyy hh:mm:ss Processing product #18, status "A"

ddMMMyyyy hh:mm:ss ... No sales records found

ddMMMyyyy hh:mm:ss ... No returns records found

ddMMMyyyy hh:mm:ss Processing product #22, status "D"

ddMMMyyyy hh:mm:ss ... Skipping discontinued product

ddMMMyyyy hh:mm:ss Processing product #23, status "A"

ddMMMyyyy hh:mm:ss ... Sales record: Sold 10 units to customer #5532 at $2.50

ddMMMyyyy hh:mm:ss ... Sales record: Sold 12 units to customer #18006 at $2.75

ddMMMyyyy hh:mm:ss ... Sales record: Sold 985 units to customer #34925 at $2.60

... and so on

If applicable (or necessary), control diagnostics and transaction diagnostics can be combined into a single output file. The emphasis here is not on a cosmetically fancy report layout — rather, the point should be to produce useful diagnostic information that can be referenced when results of the batch process are in question and details of its processing are needed.

If disk space is not adequate to generate transaction diagnostics on a regular basis, the routine can be coded to issue them only when an input "debug" parameter is set. In normal situations, the debug parameter would be turned off. When specific problems arise and there is a need to trace the routine's running more carefully, the parameter would be turned on. By coding the parameter into the routine from the start, production diagnostics can be turned on and off months or years later without changing a single line of code.

Affecting Other Batch Jobs

In many cases, batch processes will be scheduled for times when there are no online users accessing the database. In these cases, using the power of SQL to access many rows in a single statement can have the dual advantages of simplicity and speed. For instance, to copy details from today's transactions to a reporting table, the statement

```
INSERT INTO report_table
SELECT t.column1,
       t.column2,
       <other columns>
FROM transaction_table t,
WHERE t.transaction_date = <today>
```

can certainly be very effective (assuming an appropriate index on the transaction date field).

However, it is very important to realize that, in most database implementations, even a single statement like this one places an implicit transaction on all data accessed in its select statement. This lock ensures that either the entire selection is made and inserted into the destination table, or none of it is.

This means that all rows selected by the query are locked for its duration. If the table and/or number of rows being affected is large, this has the potential to freeze any online users or other batch jobs attempting to access the locked records (or pages, depending on the database implementation of locking).

Running this type of query during the day — to create an ad hoc report, for instance — is often responsible for frustrating calls to the help desk where online users report intermittent freezing of their systems in no discernible or reproducible pattern.

The same phenomenon can occur if multiple batch jobs are scheduled concurrently by system administrators. In the worst case, two batch jobs can fall into a deadlock situation where each is holding resources needed by the other.

To avoid this trap, the most important point is to remember that "you're not alone." If query speed and simplicity is paramount, then designers and database/system administrators must be very conscious of the database access contained in these routines and consciously schedule them in such a way to preclude conflicts.

If robustness of the system is important enough to accept a small speed penalty in running the routine, then a walkthrough approach can produce the same ultimate results as the single query, but without locking tables or inflicting performance penalties on other users or processes sharing the database:

```
loop for each qualified record in transaction_table:
        SELECT:col1 = t.column1,
              :col2 = t.column2,
              <other columns>
        FROM transaction_table t
        WHERE t.transaction_date = <today>

        INSERT INTO report_table
        VALUES (:col1,
              :col2,
              <other columns>)
end loop
```

CONCLUSION

Many problems in batch SQL jobs can be avoided by developing and applying a good set of SQL programming instincts. These instincts comprise rules of thumb that sometimes represent simple common sense, but in other cases are not in the natural toolkit of a developer coming from other technology platforms.

However, applying an ounce of prevention in the design and construction phases of a project's batch SQL components can easily pay back several "pounds" of savings in future maintenance effort.

Chapter 27
Improving Performance in New Programming Environments: Java

Paul J. Jalics and Donald Golden

Java is different from other commonly used programming languages because object code is not compiled into machine instructions for a given machine, but instead is designed to be interpreted by the Java Virtual Machine. This would imply a very substantial performance degradation from compiled languages like C++. The process of performance improvement in this environment is discussed and demonstrated step by step using a specific Java case study application. It will be shown that while the techniques for improving performance are somewhat different for Java than for compiled languages, the potential for reducing a Java application's execution time is huge.

INTRODUCTION TO JAVA

Java is an effort by Sun Microsystems to bring the thirty-some year-old C language into the next century by thoroughly cleaning it up of all its sloppiness, including most of the object-oriented (OOP) features of C++, and providing it with the built-in functionality needed today, and which is so sorely missing in most older languages.

The most striking feature of Java programs is that they are executed with the help of a software component called the Java Virtual Machine (JVM) which executes "Java machine instructions" that are defined as part of the Java language. Thus when a Java source program prog1.java is compiled, the compiler generates a prog1.class file which contains only JVM machine instructions. To execute the Java program, the JVM interpreter is called upon. Sun's compiler is named javac, and its JVM interpreter is named java. Thus to compile and execute prog1, one might type javac prog1.java, which generates prog1.class, which is then executed by typing java prog1.

Java executables (.class files) are totally portable from any architecture computer to any other and from any operating system to any other. This is

0-8493-9822-3/00/$0.00+$.50

one reason that most Internet browsers have the JVM implemented so that sophisticated actions can be implemented by downloaded Java .class files. The JVM checks each .class file before loading it for execution to make sure that it is well behaved and obeys the basic rules of the Java language. Hopefully the security features of Java will be found sufficient to prevent downloaded .class files from doing damage to the machines running the Java-enabled Internet browsers.

There is another twist in Java code management: some JVM's include a "Just in Time" compilation feature. Instead of the JVM interpreting the instructions of a method directly, it translates or compiles the Java code into the native Pentium machine instructions (on PCs at least) the first time a given method is executed. The resulting Pentium code is put into a cache, so that subsequent executions of that method during the current program's execution will be found in the cache and executed at maximum speed.

INTRODUCTION TO PERFORMANCE IMPROVEMENTS

Program performance is often considered to be synonymous with the speed with which a program solves a specific problem. The speed, in turn, is influenced by a number of factors, some of which are programmer controlled, while others are dependent on the hardware and software environment of the program's execution. While it may not be necessary to tune all programs for performance efficiency, there frequently exist one or more "critical programs" where such tuning is essential.

Performance has received too little attention in the programming workplace. Reasons for this lack of emphasis include the still immature nature of the discipline and the rapid performance gains realized through faster hardware. However, program performance is and will continue to be a software issue since, given the increasingly complex nature of software products, the desired throughput of a program is not always realizable through hardware advances alone. As in engineering, where performance standards are usually a part of a product's specifications, a program's performance may become an integral part of a matured software engineering process.

Speed of execution is only one of the dimensions of a program's performance. Other performance factors include memory usage, code portability, and readability. Unfortunately, tuning a program for improvement in speed of execution can lead to compromises in other dimensions of performance. However, speed of execution (referred to as performance hereafter) is not a critical consideration for all programs. For example, performance is irrelevant if a program generates results faster than they can be used. Also, for many other programs, it may be more cost effective to use a faster hardware platform, if one is available or can be acquired, than to spend the effort required in tuning; this becomes increasingly common as labor costs continue to increase and hardware costs continue to decrease. However, there still exists a small percentage of programs, say 10 percent, for which performance is important. We shall call these programs "critical programs."

A program may be considered critical for any of several reasons. For example:

- The user may need the output shortly after the input is available, and a short delay may be life-threatening or lead to serious economic loss. Many real time operations fall into this category when sensor generated data (as in process control, and command and control systems) needs to be analyzed and results fed back to an appropriate decision maker. Computer control of a car engine is an example of this type of system.
- A variation on the first type of critical program occurs when the program is part of an interactive system in which the user's productivity would be adversely affected if there is a wait for the system to respond to input.
- In some systems, hardware upgrades are not feasible for economic or technical reasons, yet the performance goals still must be achieved within the existing configuration.
- The system may need to process very large volumes of data. No matter how fast a program runs, a sufficient volume of data can make it run too long.

Fortunately, in most cases a program's execution time is not uniformly distributed across its statements. Experience has shown that a small part of a program, typically 10 percent or less, largely determines its performance. Therefore, most of the performance improvements are achievable by concentrating on the 10 percent and ignoring the remaining 90 percent of the code. This 10 percent will be called the *critical part* of a program.

There is certainly no implication that noncritical parts of a program cannot yield performance improvements. Such improvements are possible, but would lead to diminishing returns on the labor invested. In other words, a disproportionate amount of labor may be needed for small improvements in execution time.

A PROCEDURE FOR IMPROVING PERFORMANCE

Four steps to improving program performance:

1. Measure the performance of the initial program
2. Identify the critical parts of the program
3. Improve the performance of the critical parts
4. Test the modified program, re-measure the performance, and compare it to the initial performance. If not satisfied, go back to step 2.

Exhibit 27.1. Measuring the Execution Time of a Java Program

```
                          --> CULLER PROGRAM LISTING <--          Thu Feb 04 10:24:51 1999
 1. fig1.java   1.1  public class NHScheckByteArray {
 2. fig1.java   2.2  public static void main(String args[ ]) { long counter=0;
 3. fig1.java   3.   System.gc(); // run garbage collector synchronously
 4. fig1.java   4.   time1 = System.currentTimeMillis( ): //get start time
 5. fig1.java   5.   for(int I=0; I++; I< 100000)/loop being measured
 6. fig1.java   6.   counter +=5000:// body of loop
 7. fig1.java   7.   long time2 = System.currentTimeMillis( ): //get ending time
 8. fig1.java   8.   System.out.println((time2 - time1)
 9. fig1.java   9.   + " milliseconds to add 5000 to counter 100,000 times. ");
10. fig1.java  10.1  }
11. fig1.java  10.0  }

### CULLER CROSS REFERENCE LISTING
  add        9
  args       2
  being      5
  body       6
  class      1
  collecto   3
  counter    2 6 9
  currentT   4 7
```

Step 1: Measuring a Program's Initial Performance

Measuring the execution time of a program can be as simple as using a stopwatch to note the start and finish time of a program. Although this is a very crude method, it may be adequate in cases where the program executes long enough (say 60 s or more) so that manual time keeping does not lead to too much error in the calculated elapsed time. For example, a human being typically can respond to an event in a tenth of a second or less. This means that human inaccuracy should introduce error of less than 0.2 percent in timing a 60 s program.

A more precise technique is to let the program compute its own execution time by recording the start and finish time through calls to the host operating system. Current system time is available from all operating systems. Exhibit 27.1 shows a Java program which reports on its own execution performance measured in elapsed milliseconds.

Step 2: Identifying Critical Program Components

One can identify critical components of a program through manual inspection. For example, inner loops of a program may contribute more significantly to the execution time. However, proper identification of such code is difficult even for experienced programmers who know the program well. Correct identification would require the programmer to be aware of details such as the amount of work done by various statements and the relative frequency of data access from the input files.

A better approach is to use special tools called *profilers* to profile the performance characteristics of the program. A profiler evaluates an executable program (a collection of .class files). The user describes what areas of the program are to be profiled, i.e., which methods from the application and which Java system methods. The test program is then run under control of the profiler which collects information about the execution, including the number of times a procedure is executed and the execution time spent in each method included in the profiling. The resulting data can then be used to identify the program's critical parts. Note that profiling has the disadvantage of increasing execution time dramatically, sometimes by a factor of 5 to 1,000 or more.

In our experiments, Sun's Java Workshop 2 Profiler tool was used to identify the critical parts of the program at the method level, although some other profilers can also give information at the statement level. Typically, the results of the profiling are stored in a data file for later analysis. These results can then be viewed in the Java Workshop profiler in three basic ways:

- Display the time spent in each of the methods profiled
- Display the *cumulative time spent* in each method profiled, which also includes the time spent in methods called from that method
- Display the *number of times* the various methods were called

First Profiling Results

Exhibit 27.2 shows the initial performance profile of the program jxreff.java which will be discussed below. In this exhibit, only the last entry refers to a user-written method; all remaining methods are system methods and cannot be modified by the user.

Note that the time spent in a method is not directly related to the number of times the method is called. As can be seen from Exhibit 27.2, just two methods (String.toLower and StringBuffer.append) account for 50 percent of the execution time excluding input/output, in spite of the fact that the program used hundreds of system methods.

Step 3: Improving the performance of a program

Once the critical program components have been identified, code changes can be implemented to improve performance. The discussion of these code changes will follow in the next section.

Testing the Modified Program. A modified program needs to be tested to verify that it continues to execute correctly and that its performance has improved. If the execution time is not reduced, it would be necessary to return to the premodification state of the program. Therefore, it is essential to retain older versions of the program until changes are successfully

Exhibit 27.2. Partial Profile Results

Method	# of Times Executed	Amount of time spent in the method
String.toLowerCase	447,126	192,999 milliseconds
StringBuffer.append	2,666,970	192,549 milliseconds
Character.toLowerCase	2,652,386	75,516 milliseconds
StringBuffer.ensureCapacity	2,676,565	61,871 milliseconds
StringBuffer.copyWhenShared	2,681,003	54,220 milliseconds
String.<init>	454,642	51,308 milliseconds
String.toLowerCase	447,126	28,902 milliseconds
StringBuffer.toString	454,642	21,009 milliseconds
StringBuffer.<init>(I)	454,958	19,098 milliseconds
StringBuffer.<init>	449,289	18,955 milliseconds
sym_table.find_sym	2,179	17,555 milliseconds
Object.<init>	915,011	15,518 milliseconds
String.equals	450198	15,103 milliseconds
String.compareTo	223,562	12,392 milliseconds
	...	
identifier.tell_identifier	18,560	2,946 milliseconds
	...	

tested. If the performance of the revised program improves without meeting the overall goals, one needs to go back to step 2 to identify anew the critical parts of the modified program. Note that the critical parts of the modified program may be substantially different from those of the previous version. Thus a new profiling run is needed after each improvement to see where the most fruitful area of scrutiny for future performance improvements is located.

IMPROVING JAVA PERFORMANCE USING AN EXAMPLE APPLICATION: CXREFF/JXREFF

Cxreff.cpp is a sample application consisting of 330 source lines of C++. The program reads the file(s) named on the command line parameters, produces a line-numbered listing of the lines of each file preceded by the file name, with indication as to the level of curly bracket nesting ({,}) whenever that changes. Finally, a cross-reference listing of all symbols encountered is produced, including line numbers in the program in which they were encountered. The output shown in Exhibit 27.1 is taken from a report produced by cxreff.cpp.

The same program was also implemented in Java and stored in the file jxreff.java. By comparing the results of executing cxreff.cpp and jxreff.java we can see how closely C/C++ execution performance is to Java, as well as study the process of improving Java execution performance.

The programs were executed using an input file of 326 kilobytes of source text. The Java program was compiled with Microsoft Visual J++ 6.0 into .class files, and executed with the Visual J++ JVM, the SUN JDK 2.0 JVM,

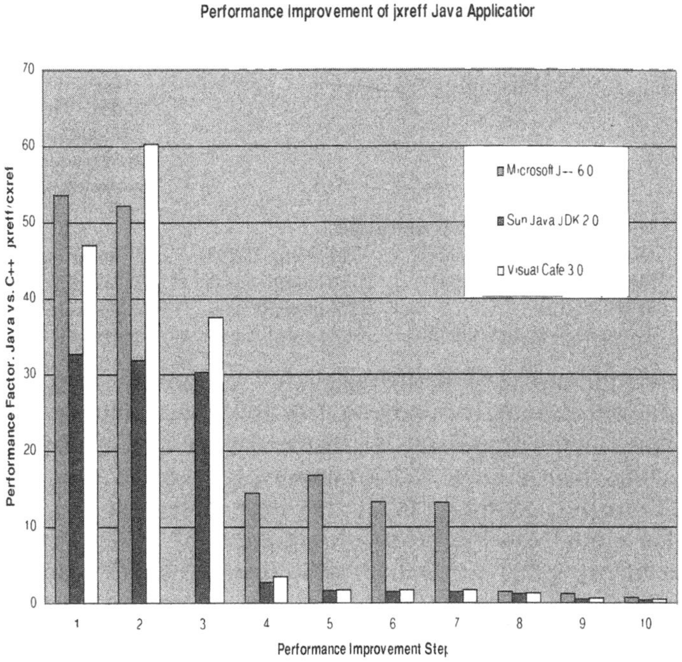

Exhibit 27.3. A Summary of Performance Improvement Results

and the Visual Café 3.0 JVM. The J++ compiler can also create an executable file (jxreff.exe). However, experiments indicate that this executable file does not execute any faster than executing the .class files under the J++ JVM.

Other experiments indicated that programs compiled by the Sun JDK compiler and the Visual Café compiler generate the same execution performance as those compiled by J++. Thus the main focus of performance is on the JVM, and the experiments demonstrate that choosing the JVM to execute the .class files is more important than the choice of the Java compiler. The main interest in all cases is the execution speed of the program with the specific JVM.

Rather than simply showing execution times, we computed a performance factor using the execution time of cxreff.cpp (the C++ version of the program) as a base. We measured the execution time of cxreff.cpp and divided that into the execution times of the various Java programs to produce the performance factor. Thus, the execution time for cxreff.cpp was 12 seconds, while the initial execution time for jxreff.java using the executable (.exe) program produced by Microsoft Visual C++ 5.0 was 642 seconds. Therefore, the performance factor was 53.5. Obviously, the lower the ratio the better the performance. The step-by-step performance improvements are discussed below; for a summary of the results, see Exhibit 27.3.

1. Base Version: The original performance results

cxreff.cpp	using Microsoft Visual C++ 5.0:	12 seconds	—the original program
cxreffMap.cpp	using Microsoft Visual C++ 5.0:	7 seconds	—same as the program above but uses the C++ STL **map** hash table mechanism to improve performance

Performance Factor: jxreff/cxreff:

Microsoft Visual J++ 6.0	JVM using .EXE:	53.5 Java/C++
Microsoft Visual J++ 6.0	JVM using .class:	53.5 Java/C++
SUN JDK 2.0	JVM using .class:	32.6 Java/C++
Symantec Visual Café 3.0	JVM using .class:	46.9 Java/C++

These results are very disturbing! C/C++ programs are compiled into native code and executed directly, so they are expected to be as fast as one can get. Java, on the other hand, is executed by the JVM by interpreting the "Java machine instructions." A degradation of a factor of 10 is expected for interpretation, but a factor of 53.5 is very high. Note, however, that the Sun JDK 2.0 has a much lower performance factor at 32.6. Nevertheless, a performance factor of 32.6 is still too high in many cases. What can be done? Knowledgeable programmers have been able to improve the performance of any program by using some well-known techniques (see references 1 through 8), and we applied these techniques to the Java programs.

Steps in Improving the performance of jxreff.java

2. Try collapsing the most frequently executed method in the application

Looking at the jxreff program and the results from the profiler, the most frequently executed method in jxreff.java is tell_identifier which is called for every character input. Since this tell_identifier method is called from only one place in find_sym, it was collapsed into the find_sym method, thereby saving the call overhead and the return. The results are puzzling since they show some improvement for J++ and the Sun JDK 2.0, and show a substantial *increase* in execution time for Visual Café 3.0.

New Performance Factor: jxreff/cxreff:

Microsoft Visual J++ 6.0	JVM using .EXE:	52.1 Java/C++
SUN JDK 2.0	JVM using .class:	31.8 Java/C++
Symantec Visual Café 3.0	JVM using .class:	60.2 Java/C++

Note that the profiler output in Exhibit 27.2 indicates that by far the largest amount of time is spent in the Java system classes for **String**, **StringBuffer**, and **Character**, which are called from the jxreff application. How these system library classes are used needs to examined and improved.

3. Symbol table comparisons too slow: call C++ strcmpi function from Java using Java Native Interface

Looking at the jxreff program and the results from the profiler in Exhibit 27.2, a great deal of time seemed to be spent on comparing symbols in a case-insensitive manner using the toLowerCase methods for both operands. Since C++ has a good case-insensitive string compare, the Java code was interfaced to call the C++ strcmpi subroutine. The results were disastrous for the J++ program which aborted! The Sun JDK 2.0 had a slight improvement while Visual Café 3.0 had a substantial one.

New Performance Factor: jxreff/cxreff:

Microsoft Visual J++ 6.0	JVM using .EXE:	aborted
SUN JDK 2.0	JVM using .class:	30.2 Java/C++
Symantec Visual Café 3.0	JVM using .class:	37.5 Java/C++

4. Symbol table comparisons still too slow: try to use Collator class instead

The above was not satisfactory for two of the three platforms, so another alternative was sought. The problem was still the same: a great deal of time seemed to be spent comparing symbols in a case-insensitive manner using the toLowerCase methods for both operands. This was modified to use the **Collator** class provided by Java using PRIMARY strength for case-insensitive and NO_DECOMPOSITION for efficiency. Also the collation keys were used to order the symbols in the symbol table. Compare the results to the original ones in the base version, and then to step 2 above. These changes improved the performance dramatically:

New Performance Factor: jxreff/cxreff:

Microsoft Visual J++ 6.0	JVM using .EXE:	14.4 Java/C++
SUN JDK 2.0	JVM using .class:	2.7 Java/C++
Symantec Visual Café 3.0	JVM using .class:	3.5 Java/C++

5. Symbol table comparisons still too slow: minimize conversions to lower case

The profiler still indicated that, as in the original program profile in Exhibit 27.2, String.toLowerCase used the largest amount of computer time. To reduce converting symbols to lowercase for the comparison (using String.toLowerCase method), the symbols in the symbol table were all stored in lower case, and new symbols just scanned were immediately converted to lower case using a quick method that subtracted 32 from uppercase symbols. The performance results show J++ a little slower, but Sun and Visual Café improved further and significantly:

New Performance Factor: jxreff/cxreff:

Microsoft Visual J++ 6.0	JVM using .EXE:	16.7 Java/C++
SUN JDK 2.0	JVM using .class:	1.6 Java/C++
Symantec Visual Café 3.0	JVM using .class:	1.7 Java/C++

6. Symbol table comparisons still too slow: eliminate toLowerCase by using a mapping table

This version of jxreff tried to improve efficiency by creating a mapping table to convert upper case characters to lower case characters. The table provides a lower case value simply by indexing into it with the original value of the character. This is used to make comparison strings case neutral prior to using the String class compareTo method, and eliminates the need to use toLowerCase method of the String class. This change brought a modest improvement for J++ and little change for the other two.

New Performance Factor: jxreff/cxreff:

Microsoft Visual J++ 6.0	JVM using .EXE:	13.2 Java/C++
SUN JDK 2.0	JVM using .class:	1.5 Java/C++
Symantec Visual Café 3.0	JVM using .class:	1.7 Java/C++

7. Reading input file too slow: use ReadFully method to read the whole file in one read.

The profiler now indicated that much time was spent in reading the input file in cross_referencer.get_line. The code was modified to read the input file in one I/O call using Java's ReadFully I/O method. This caused practically no change for any of the systems, probably because input buffering was adequate already in each JVM.

New Performance Factor: jxreff/cxreff:

Microsoft Visual J++ 6.0	JVM using .EXE:	13.1 Java/C++
SUN JDK 2.0	JVM using .class:	1.5 Java/C++
Symantec Visual Café 3.0	JVM using .class:	1.7 Java/C++

8. String comparison too slow: write own case-insensitive String compare using character arrays

Much time was still spent in the string compare routine, so the use of the String class in the application was eliminated in favor of char arrays. A Java case-insensitive string compare function was written using char arrays rather than Strings. This caused a very substantial reduction in execution time in every platform, and huge one in J++.

New Performance Factor: jxreff/cxreff:

Microsoft Visual J++ 6.0	JVM using .EXE:	1.5 Java/C++
SUN JDK 2.0	JVM using .class:	1.2 Java/C++
Symantec Visual Café 3.0	JVM using .class:	1.3 Java/C++

9. Linked-list processing too slow: use Java HashTable class

This application is still about symbol table management, so the Java HashTable collection class was used rather than the previous linked list of symbols. The results are dramatic. Java is faster than the base C++ program by a significant **40 to 50 percent** for all but J++, which is still 20 percent slower than C++!

New Performance Factor: jxreff/cxreff:

Microsoft Visual J++ 6.0	JVM using .EXE:	1.2 Java/C++
SUN JDK 2.0	JVM using .class:	0.5 Java/C++
Symantec Visual Café 3.0	JVM using .class:	0.6 Java/C++

This Java version should also be compared to the cxreffMap.cpp which, similar to the Java HashTable, speeds up symbol table access using hashing. Even with this tougher comparison, the performance of Java is faster than cxreffMap.cpp for both the Sun JVM and Visual Café; however, it is still twice as slow using the J++ JVM.

New Performance Factor: jxreff/cxreffMap:		
Microsoft Visual J++ 6.0	JVM using .EXE:	2.0 Java/C++
SUN JDK 2.0	JVM using .class:	0.9 Java/C++
Symantec Visual Café 3.0	JVM using .class:	1.0 Java/C++

10. Symbol table processing still slow: use Java TreeSort class

The Java TreeSort class was used to replace the previous linked list of symbols (instead of the Java HashTable class used in step 8 above). The results are even more dramatic than in step 8 and show Java is faster than C++ by a significant **25 to 60 percent**!!

New Performance Factor: jxreff/cxreff:		
Microsoft Visual J++ 6.0	JVM using .EXE:	0.7 Java/C++
SUN JDK 2.0	JVM using .class:	0.4 Java/C++
Symantec Visual Café 3.0	JVM using .class:	0.5 Java/C++

This Java version should also be compared to the cxreffMap.cpp which, like the Java TreeSort, speeds up symbol table access using hashing. Even with this tougher comparison, the performance of Java is faster than cxreffMap.cpp using the Sun JVM and the Visual Café, but 30 percent slower using the J++ JVM.

New Performance Factor: jxreff/cxreffMap:		
Microsoft Visual J++ 6.0	JVM using .EXE:	1.3 Java/C++
SUN JDK 2.0	JVM using .class:	0.7 Java/C++
Symantec Visual Café	JVM using .class:	0.9 Java/C++

11. More Improvements if needed

The goal of obtaining a performance better than the base C++ program has now been reached. One could, however, continue with the process and improve the Java program still further. Any program that runs so much faster than the original C++ would be very acceptable to most developers and their managers. A summary of the results from the above experiments are shown in Exhibit 27.3.

12. Potential for Java performance improvements is much greater than C++

The results demonstrate the great potential for execution-time performance improvements of Java programs. The reader may well ask, "Could one have done the same with the C++ cxreff.cpp program?" The answer is certainly, "Yes."

However, the C++ program was written to be as efficient as possible, and C++ code generation is already very good. Thus cxreff.cpp is a good comparison vehicle. Note also that making Java improvements often has more dramatic results because the underlying interpretation by the JVM (or execution time Just in Time compilation results) is inherently less optimized than C++ code is. So, in some sense, Java code is ripe for the performance pickings.

CONCLUSIONS

Java is a programming language with a great deal of promise. Computer science is still in its infancy, so we all have to get used to learning new tools on a continuous basis. Java is certainly not the ultimate tool, but it is one that is much superior to many previous tools. Java programs may be slower than C/C++ but speed of execution is not of major concern in a majority of applications. Furthermore, Jalics[1] has shown through a series of measurements that Java performance can be on the same order of magnitude as C/C++.

In this paper, the results are extended to show that in many cases Java programs can be as fast or faster than corresponding C++ programs if the programmer spends some effort in improving that performance. Thus, in this case study, the Java application originally took 5,250 percent more time to execute than C++, but after the improvements the same program took 30 percent less time than the corresponding C++. Also, note that for a better optimizing JVM (Sun JDK 2.0), Java initially took only 3,160 percent more time than C++, but the improved program took 60 percent less time than the C++.

The choice of the Java Virtual Machine is very critical to Java program performance. The Microsoft JVM took from 1.25 to 10.44 times as long as the Sun JVM to execute the same program.

Programmer choices of Java language features have a tremendous impact on program performance.

Calling C/C++ procedures from Java (using the Java Native Interface (JNI)) is relatively slow and should only be attempted for procedures that do a lot of work in a single call.

Some Java systems have program profilers available. These can pinpoint the most critical sections of Java code in a program, and the user can choose from a variety of techniques to improve these critical sections of code.

There might also be the possibility of an improved implementation in the future of some Java system classes like String, StringBuffer, and Character, which could improve the performance of many programs. This would likely have to be left to the Java developers since these classes are at the core of Java and are used in the Java system software, and, therefore, are not easily changed.

While most of the performance improvement techniques are similar to ones that can be used with C++, Java also has some advanced language features like the Collator class, HashTable class, etc. that can bring better performance.

The case study program has demonstrated that Java applications may be incredibly slower than corresponding C++ ones when the programmer does not pay attention to performance factors when the program is written. However, through the use of Java profilers and by insights into Java performance characteristics, one can easily identify the critical sections of a given program and improve their performance substantially. One can experiment with alternate data structures, advanced language features and library routines, alternate algorithms and data-types, etc. All of these techniques take expertise, time, and patience, however.

ACKNOWLEDGEMENTS

This project started as a research course (CIS 695) for graduate student William Zhukovsky at the Computer & Information Science Department of Cleveland State University. Mr. Zhukovsky was tireless in his efforts to learn about performance improvement techniques and specifically to squeeze more and more performance out of the case study programs.

REFERENCES

1. Jalics, P. and Misra, S., "Java and C++: Similarities, Differences, and Performance," *Systems Development Management*, 21, 6, February 1998.
2. Jalics, P. and Misra, S., "Performance Improvement Techniques," *Systems Development Management*, 21, 6, December 1996.
3. Jalics, P. and Misra, S., "Measuring Program Performance," *Systems Development Management*, 21, 6, December 1996.
4. Jalics, P. and Blake, B., "Benchmarking C++ Performance," *Systems Development Management*, 21, 3, June 1996.
5. Jalics, P. and Blake, B., "Performance of Object-Oriented Programs: C++," *Systems Development Management*, 21, 3, June 1996.
6. Jalics, P. and Blake, B., "An Assessment of Object-Oriented Methods in C++," *J. Object-Oriented Programming,* May 1996.
7. Jalics, P.,and Misra, S., "Improving C Program Performance: Techniques and Examples," *Handbook of Systems Management and Support*, Auerbach, June 1993.
8. "Performance Evaluation of Computer Systems," *Macmillan Encyclopedia of Computers*, Macmillan, 2, 764-769, 1991.

Section IV Checklist

1. Have you concluded that object-based technology is superior to traditional programming techniques? If not, what concepts of object technology would you improve upon?
2. Assuming your support of object technology, would you endorse a rapid conversion of your organization's development efforts to object-oriented programming? If not, how would you implement this technology?
3. How would you prepare your programming staff for migration to object-based system development? Is this a skill that traditional programmers can adapt to easily?
4. Which object-oriented programming languages has your organization researched or used? Are these languages fundamentally the same?
5. Would you choose a development language based on strict inherent compliance to object principles or are object supported languages acceptable? What pros or cons are there in your reasoning?
6. How should development managers determine the selection of an object-based language? Does your organization have guidelines?
7. Is language performance more important than language functionality when selecting an object-oriented language? Would this change based on the application?
8. Does the struggle between vendors for proprietary control over newer languages such as Java cause your organization to take a wait and see approach before committing to an object programming adoption?
9. Do you think that your organization should adopt several OOP languages standards in order to "right-size" development projects?
10. When was the last time your organization evaluated the success of object technology, including the value of reusable code?
11. Is reusable code practical in your environment? If not, is this due to security and administrative issues with object libraries?
12. Do you envision a vast change in using Internet technology to develop application systems? In particular, is Java better suited for this?
13. What is your perception of SQL as a reporting/query tool for online and batch execution. Does SQL have any merits for application programming, or do you view it as an extension to the database utility environment?

14. Has there been a serious endeavor to migrate legacy applications in your environment to new technology? If so, is there a fixed time frame for this conversion?
15. How should your organization evaluate the existing worth of information stored in legacy data files? Would your organization support migration or new deployment of such data?

Section V
Database Functionality and Design

Enterprise Data Management has become a crucial concept in the overall strategy of leveraging information as a corporate asset. Isolated, autonomous, and proprietary data structures used in the past are no longer acceptable repositories for most organizations. Instead, there is a mandatory requirement for accessing all corporate data via simple, expedient and comprehensive techniques. The ongoing pursuit of "distributed databases" and "data warehousing" can be attributed to the increased need for accessing such organizational information. This need has also triggered a growth in communicating and linking data structures worldwide. While database development was important in past computing environments, it is now perceived as critical to those who understand the power of information.

Even though the goals of uniform data access are easily justifiable, they can be complicated, if not difficult, to achieve. Disparate file structures and inconsistent database designs are some of the impediments associated with an enterprise wide data architecture. Multi-tier Client/Server and Distributed Computing add further complexities by raising questions about the overall data access philosophy that is needed. The spectacular growth of information databases, in terms of size and scope, has occurred very rapidly in many organizations. Maintaining an accurate index of accumulated data items is often laborious and ineffective. As a result, there is a tendency to lose meaningfulness in stored data. Chapter 28, "Knowledge Discovery, Data Mining, and Database Management," explains the process used to extract value from large data repositories. The trend toward data mining has received considerable attention in recent years. Much of the interest is focused on the potential for discovering vital business information to be used for competitive advantage. To date, no single method for data discovery has yielded the greatest result. However, it is expected that further research into this form of database technology will continue with much anticipation.

Numerous Data Warehousing systems have become virtual extensions to existing database structures rather than a redundant collection of data. On the other hand, some argue that very nature of Data Warehousing requires a unique structure to enable better utilization of information when compared to traditional databases. Chapter 29, "Critical Factors in Developing a Data Warehouse," outlines a five-step technique for successful implementation of warehouse repositories. While the concept of warehousing may appear simple, the underlying structure can be complex. And if not implemented correctly, performance and data access problems are likely to occur. Chapter 30, "Web-Enabled Data Warehousing," offers yet another viewpoint on the benefits of warehousing beyond the traditional corporate boundaries via remote access. This can yield opportunity for decentralized access, and also provide the basis for e-commerce information distribution. Collectively, these two chapters provide development managers with a comprehensive review of how data warehousing can be incorporated effectively in the development of mission critical business applications.

Alternative methods for retrieving information across multiple database platforms have posed serious challenges to the development of client/server applications. Various approaches to solving this dilemma would enable interoperability with different database management systems and allow application programs universal data access. Chapter 31, "Software Architectures for Distributed DBMSs in a Client/Server Environment," describes the various options available in designing databases for client/server applications. The nature of client/server systems provides the advantage of having broad access to disparate data sources. But it also poses some challenges when designing the most efficient path for data access across the server network. This chapter includes information about design considerations as well as discussion on replication, transparency, and multi-site update capabilities.

Object-oriented and component-based technologies are enhancing the speed and strength of newer development applications. Correspondingly, there is a great interest in extending the same object and component technology into the database arena. However, most organizations are highly dependent on existing relational database systems. It is unlikely that such databases will be immediately replaced with object technology. Therefore, development managers must learn how to couple newer development techniques within the relational database environment. Chapter 32, "Component Design for Relational Databases," explores the new approaches for matching relational and object-based technologies and is described as the "data-component approach." New application programming techniques are usually ahead of most database paradigms. As such, there is the continuous need to couple the newer application with its legacy data counterpart.

Chapter 28

Knowledge Discovery, Data Mining, and Database Management

Patricia L. Carbone

BOTH THE NUMBER AND SIZE OF DATABASES in many organizations are growing at a staggering rate. Terabyte and even petabyte databases, once unthinkable, are now becoming a reality in a variety of domains, including marketing, sales, finance, healthcare, earth science, and various government applications. As their databases grow, organizations have realized that there is valuable knowledge buried in the data that, if discovered, could provide competitive advantage.

Data mining and knowledge discovery are the processes that organizations are using to extract knowledge from their databases. Knowledge discovery is the overall process, in which data mining is used to extract or identify knowledge in large data sets. Examples of data mining applications include:

- *Customer segmentation.* Retailers, credit card companies, banks, and other such organizations are very interested in determining if there are groups or clusters of people who exhibit certain similar characteristics. For example, banks and credit card companies use classification for credit scoring to create segments of those customers that are better credit risks than others. Factors that are analyzed include income, current debt, past payment history, and potentially even geographic area and other demographics.
- *Relationship management.* Retailers and advertisers are interested in the buying patterns of customers. Such attributes that are analyzed include items purchased, dates of purchase, and the type of payment. These attributes can perhaps be used in combination with the customer segments described above. Based on certain buying patterns, such as seasonal purchases of camping equipment by upper-middle-class people in the northeast U.S., retailers and advertisers can better target their advertising dollars toward specific media, items, or geographic areas to capture the customers they want to

0-8493-9822-3/00/$0.00+$.50

attract. Relationship management is becoming of particular interest in electronic commerce.

Knowledge discovery and data mining rely on many underlying technologies, which include:

- Data warehousing and online analytical processing (OLAP)
- Human computer interaction and data visualization
- Machine learning (especially inductive learning techniques)
- Knowledge representation
- Pattern recognition
- Intelligent agents

This chapter looks at how these supporting technologies enable data mining and how knowledge discovery can be applied in several different domains.

THE PROCESS OF KNOWLEDGE DISCOVERY IN DATABASES (KDD)

Data mining is actually a step in a larger *KDD process*. The KDD process uses data mining methods or algorithms to extract or identify knowledge according to some criteria or measure of interest, but it also includes steps that prepare the data, such as preprocessing, subsampling, and transformations of the database. To follow one particular example, consider the application of credit card fraud, or determining when credit card users are purchasing items with a stolen credit card.

Targeting Data

To begin the KDD process, the application or analysis must first have an overall purpose or set of goals. For the credit card fraud example, the purpose of the analysis would be to identify those customers with credit card usage patterns that differ from previously established usage patterns. Databases must be identified that contain the desired data to be analyzed. In this example, incoming credit card transactions must be analyzed to halt fraud immediately. In addition, to identify the fraud trends, historical data should be examined.

The first step in the KDD process is to select data to be analyzed from the set of all available data. In many cases, the data is stored in transaction databases, such as those databases that process all incoming credit card transactions. These databases are quite large and extremely dynamic. In addition, there may be several different transaction databases running simultaneously at various sites. Again, with the credit card example, large credit card companies typically have several processing sites to handle specific geographic areas. Therefore, a subset of data must be selected from those databases, since it is unnecessary in early stages to attempt to analyze all data.

Preprocessing Data

Target data is then moved to a cache or another database for further preprocessing. Preprocessing is an extremely important step in the KDD process. Often, data has errors introduced during the input process, either from a data entry clerk entering data incorrectly or from a faulty data collection device. If target data are being extracted from several source databases, the databases can often be inconsistent with each other in terms of their data models, the semantics of the attributes, or in the way the data is represented in the database.

As an example of the data models being inconsistent, a credit card company may have two different sites handling transactions. If the two databases were built at different times and following different guidelines, it is entirely possible that they may be two different data models (relational and object-oriented) and two different representations of the entities or objects and their relationships to each other (e.g., a customer-centric view versus an account-centric view).

As an example of the differences in the way the data may be entered into the database, it is possible for the same customer to be represented in the two databases in different ways. In one database, the name field may contain the last name of the customer only. In another database, the name field may contain the first name followed by the last name. The preprocessing step should identify these differences and make the data consistent and clean.

Transforming Data

The data can often be transformed for use with different analysis techniques. A number of separate tables can be joined into one table, or vice versa. An attribute that may be represented in two different forms (i.e., date written as 3/15/97 versus 15-3-1997) should be transformed into a common format. If the data is represented as text, but it is intended to use a data mining technique that requires the data to be in numerical form, the data must be transformed accordingly.

Mining the Data

At this point, data mining algorithms can be used to discover knowledge (e.g., trends, patterns, characteristics, or anomalies). The appropriate discovery or data mining algorithms should be identified, as they should be pertinent to the purpose of the analysis and to the type of data to be analyzed. In the example, an algorithm could be chosen that would automatically look for clusters of behavior in the data.

This type of algorithm might find, for example, a set of customers that make relatively low numbers of purchases over time, a set of customers that make large numbers of purchases over time, and a set of customers that make large numbers of purchases in very short periods of time. These behaviors could be examined further to determine whether any of the patterns is representative of credit card fraud behavior. If subsets of data have been established that represent fraud behavior versus normal usage, algorithms can be used that would automatically identify differences between the sets for discrimination purposes. Again, in the example, in looking at two sets of data, the algorithm might characterize fraud behavior as numerous purchases over a short period of time and often in a different geographic area than the user typically shops, as opposed to credit card usage that is relatively consistent for that user over time.

Role of Domain Information. Often, the data mining algorithms work more effectively if they have some amount of domain information available containing information on attributes that have higher priority than others, attributes that are not important at all, or established relationships that are already known. In the credit card fraud example, domain information might include a known relationship between the number of purchases and a period of time. Domain information is often collected in a *knowledge base*, a storage mechanism similar to a database but used to store domain information and other knowledge.

Patterns and Knowledge. When a pattern is identified, it should be examined to determine whether it is new, relevant, and "correct" by some standard of measure. The interpretation and evaluation step may involve more interaction with a user or with some agent of the user who can make relevancy determinations. When the pattern is deemed relevant and useful, it can be deemed *knowledge*. The knowledge should be placed in the knowledge base for use in subsequent iterations. Note that the entire KDD process is iterative; at many of the steps, there may be a need to go back to a previous step, since no patterns may be discovered, new data should be selected for additional analyses, or the patterns that are discovered may not be relevant.

Visualization. In many steps of the KDD process, it is essential to provide good visualization support to the user. This is important for two reasons. First, without such visualizations, it may be difficult for users to determine the usefulness of discovered knowledge — often a picture *is* worth a thousand words. Second, given good visualization tools, the user can discover things that automated data mining tools may be unable to discover. Working as a team, the user and automated discovery tools provide far more powerful data mining capabilities than either can provide alone.

TECHNOLOGIES ENABLING DATA MINING AND KDD

Data mining and KDD are supported by an array of technologies. This section examines how database management, data warehousing, statistics, and artificial intelligence enable data mining and KDD.

Database Management

One of the basic differences between machine learning and data mining or knowledge discovery in databases is the fact that analysis or learning (i.e., the induction of patterns) is being done on database systems, rather than on specifically formatted file structures of the data for use with one algorithm. Database management systems (DBMSs) provide a number of essential capabilities to data mining, including persistent storage; a data model (e.g., relational or object-oriented), that permits data to be managed using a *logical* rather than physical view; and a high-level query language (e.g., SQL), that allows users to request *what* data they want without having to write complex programs specifying *how* to access it. In addition, database management systems provide transaction management and constraint enforcement to help preserve the integrity of the data. Database technology also provides efficient access to large quantities of data.

As discussed in the previous section, the KDD process implies that one is performing knowledge discovery against data that resides in one or more large databases. Typical properties of databases that complicate knowledge discovery include:

- *Large volume.* Databases are capable of storing terabytes, and now petabytes, of data, therefore requiring a need to focus or preprocess the data.
- *Noise and uncertainty.* As discussed in the previous section, noise can be introduced by faulty data collection devices. This causes uncertainty as to the consistency of the data.
- *Redundant information.* For a variety of reasons, data can be stored multiple times, causing redundant information. This is especially a problem if there are multiple source databases.
- *Dynamic data.* Transaction databases are specifically set up to process millions of transactions per hour, thus causing difficulty for data mining tools which are oriented to look at static sets of data.
- *Sparse data.* The information in the database is often sparse in terms of the density of actual records over the potential instance space.
- *Multimedia data.* DBMSs are increasingly capable of storing more than just structured data. For example, text documents, images, spatial data, video, and audio can now be stored as objects in databases, and these databases are used to handle World Wide Web sites. It is becoming extremely desirable to mine this data in addition to the traditional structured data.

Recent advances in data warehousing, parallel databases, and online analytical processing tools have greatly increased the efficiency with which databases can support the large numbers of extremely complex queries that are typical of data mining applications. Databases provide a metadata description that can be used to help understand the data that is to be mined and can also aid in determining how the database should potentially change (e.g., its schema, indices, the location of data, etc.), based on what has been learned.

Data Warehouses

Data warehousing is a technology that is currently being employed at a growing number of large firms. Data warehouses are extremely large DBMSs that are designed to hold historical data. The data model for the data warehouse is oriented to support the processing of analyses and potentially complex queries (known as online analytical processing, or OLAP), as opposed to handling large numbers of updates (which is the purpose of traditional online transaction processing, or OLTP, databases). Because the data is stored over time, the data warehouse must support temporal queries.

An example of a data warehouse is one created for a company with transaction processing dispersed to numerous sites. The process for creating and maintaining the warehouse involves selecting the data from the source databases that will be stored in the warehouse. The selection process involves replicating the new data in the transaction databases at some regular interval for further processing. Once selected, the data is passed through applications that scrub the data to ensure the warehouse is clean (i.e., error-free) and consistent. The fusion applications draw the data from the separate databases together into one model for storage in the warehouse. The extraction, scrubbing, and fusion parts of the data warehousing process match the selection, preprocessing, and transformation parts of the KDD process.

Once a data warehouse has been created, an organization can create smaller views of the warehouse that are oriented toward a particular function. These more focused views are called data marts.

It is important to note that data warehouses are increasingly being used to store not only structured data that is collected from transaction databases, but also textual data. Several vendors have constructed large DBMSs that can be used for data warehousing and also to perform data management for an Internet web site. In addition, online analysis processing tools are being extended to handle not only temporal and spatial queries as part of the complex query and analysis process, but also to perform textual queries.

Metadata Repositories. An important technology associated with data warehousing that could potentially be better utilized in data mining is the metadata repository. The metadata repository is essentially a database that contains information about the data models of the transaction databases, the data warehouse, and any data marts. The information can include the meanings of the attributes, agreed-upon conventions for attribute representation, and relationships among attributes, tables, and databases. Metadata can also contain information regarding the rankings of attributes (e.g., attribute "X" from the western U.S. database is often more current than the same attribute "X" from the north/central American database), or even the validity of the sources of the data.

The goal of the metadata repository is to aid in maintaining consistency among the data warehouse, data marts, source databases, and any analysis applications. Applications performing the selection and scrubbing, and fusion functions rely on input from the metadata repository for criteria on the extent to which the data must be cleaned and transformed.

As discussed earlier, many data mining algorithms can employ domain information when it is available to aid in the analysis of the data. The information in the metadata repository is similar to the domain information and should be used by the data mining algorithms. Some research on data mining techniques includes the use of metadata.

Contributions of Statistics

The area of statistics is an important one to data mining. For many years, statistical methods have been the primary means for analyzing data. Statistical analysis methods are still the standard means of analysis for determining credit scores for loan or credit card companies, for analyzing clinical trials data when determining whether a drug should or should not be approved by the Food and Drug Administration, and for performing other types of market basket analysis and customer segmentation.

Statistical methods differ from machine learning techniques (discussed in the next section) in that the user must typically have a hypothesis of the attributes that are in relationship to each other, then search the data for the mathematical expression the describes the relationship. In some data mining systems, this is called "top-down" learning.

There are three basic classes of statistical techniques with implementations used in data mining today: linear, nonlinear, and decision trees. Linear models describe samples of data, or the relationship among the attributes or predictors, in terms of a plane so that the model becomes a global consensus of the pattern of the data. Linear modeling techniques include linear regression (for prediction) and linear discriminant analysis (for classification). Recent advances in this area allow a model to adapt to data that involve multiple attributes (multivariable linear regression) or that are not described easily by only one linear function and may need several functions (e.g., a different function for each time period).

Nonlinear or nonparametric methods characterize data by referring to existing data when a new point is received in order to estimate the response of that point. An example of this is a higher-order regression curve; another example is the nearest neighbor. In the nearest neighbor technique, a new point is matched against existing data. Based on proximity to already characterized data, the new point is classified as being fraudulent usage or normal usage.

A variation on nonlinear techniques is the creation of decision trees. Decision trees describe a set of data in terms of a set of decision points. Based on the response to the decision point, the data are subdivided into regions. In the statistical community, Classification and Regression Tree (CART) algorithms are used to build decision trees.

Very popular commercial tools used for statistical analysis include

- SAS
- SPSS
- S/S-Plus
- MATlab
- DataDesk

Artificial Intelligence

Artificial intelligence (AI) technology provides many capabilities that support the KDD process. Principally, these contributions are in the more specific fields of machine learning and visualization.

Machine Learning. As opposed to statistical techniques that perform a "top-down" analysis approach, machine learning techniques do not need a priori knowledge of possible attribute relationships, thus providing a "bottom-up" analysis approach. Machine learning techniques are automated systems that use artificial intelligence search techniques to look for patterns and relationships in the data. These search techniques should be flexible and employ adaptive or heuristic control strategies to determine what subset of the data to focus on or what hypothesis to test next.

Machine learning techniques are able to perform several types of discoveries. They can generalize, or produce a more generalized set of rules or patterns to describe a specific set of data. A more specialized case of generalization would be to be able to predict. Generalization is typically an inductive process. Deduction occurs when there is a pattern such that if A implies B, and B implies C, then one can deduce that the existence of A will imply the existence of C. However, if C exists, one can only induce that A exists also. For example, given a set of data that describes a series of events in time, the system induces that an event at a later time may be correlated to the original pattern. As an example of generalization, a set of data may describe valid credit card usage, and an algorithm could learn that purchases are generally spread over a longer period of time in a regional area near where the customer resides.

The algorithms can also cluster data. Given data that describe specific instances, the system can identify groups of instances that are more similar to each other than to instances in other groups.

Models that are discovered are represented in a knowledge representation language that is sufficient to allow description of the model. These representations include symbolic ones (e.g., rules, decision trees, semantic networks), neural networks, and mathematical models. If the representation language is too limited, then the model will not be accurate enough to describe the data. Finally, the machine learning technique must evaluate how well a discovered pattern actually describes the data. The evaluation can include how accurately the model is able to perform prediction, utility of the model, and understandability.

Systems that employ symbolic representation of the data such as rules or decision trees are quite easy to understand by a user, particularly if the variables being tested have threshold splits (i.e., a threshold split applied to the number of purchases variable). Of course, the larger the number of attributes represented in the rules or trees, or the more complex the split descriptions, then the more complicated the rule or decision tree representation will actually be.

Commercial tools that provide a rule-based output include:

- WizSoft's WizWhy
- REDUCT
- Lobbe Technologies' Datalogic
- Information Discovery's IDIS

Commercial tools that employ the use of decision trees include

- Isoft S.A.'s AC2
- Angoss Software's KnowledgeSeeker
- NASA COSMIC's IND

Commercial tools that cluster data include:

- NASA Ames Research Center's Autoclass III
- COSMIC's COBWEB/3

Neural Networks. Neural networks are quite popular in the field of credit card fraud detection, as they are easily trainable and quite fast at processing incoming data. Neural networks can be trained to perform classification and other such tasks. The problem in the past, however, has been that one cannot see inside a neural network in the same way as with rules or trees to understand how the algorithm is classifying and where it may fail. However, recently neural networks have been expanded to output a rule representation of the learned model.

Some popular commercial neural network packages include:

- Right Information System's 4Thought
- NeuralWare Inc.'s NeuralWorks Professional II/Plus
- California Scientific Software's BrainMaker

There are also neural network components for SPSS and MATLAB.

Multistrategy Learning. Because each type of machine learning technique has positive and negative aspects, depending on the type of data being analyzed and the goal for the learning, it is increasingly desirable to employ more than one technique during a data mining session. *Multistrategy learning* allows a high-level controller to choose two or more machine learning algorithms to be applied to the data, based on characteristics of the data, the available algorithms, and the goals for the learning. Although there is no fully automated tool that will perform multistrategy learning without user intervention, more commercial tools are including multiple techniques in the overall package.

Some of these tools include:

- Thinking Machine Corporation's Darwin
- Integral Solutions' Clementine
- IBM's Intelligent Miner
- Information Discovery Inc.'s Data Mining Suite

Limitations of Machine Learning. Having pointed out the benefits of machine learning to data mining, it is important to note that these techniques have limitations also. Machine learning can only learn or discover general categories of things for which they are programmed to look. The representation language, as pointed out earlier, can limit the effectiveness or expressiveness of the model of learned behavior. Also, learning algorithms have a learning bias, so they are not always effective on all problems.

Visualization

A picture is worth a thousand words, as the old saying goes. This is particularly true in the area of data mining. Many tools are currently being developed that allow a user to interact with the data and the way that data is portrayed on the screen. One such method that has been employed for a number of years is link analysis. Link analysis portrays relationships among data in terms of links connecting nodes. For example, if an analyst wanted to look at telephone call records using link analysis, the number from which the calls were made would be displayed in the center of the screen with links to all numbers that were called. Depending on the number of times a number was called, the link between the two numbers might be heavier or lighter or color-coded in some manner. This method of portraying the data would allow an analyst to make connections that are not readily visible by simply looking at tables of numbers.

Increasing research is being done to find more effective ways to portray data. Interactive visualization allows a user to change the attributes shown on a screen, or the scale of the attributes. Users can change the scales on the axes of a chart or zoom in on particular portions of the data in order to get a better understanding.

Virtual Reality. Virtual reality is increasingly being touted as the future way to perform visual analysis of the data. The idea is to allow users to "fly through," touch, and manipulate the data to see relationships that were not previously visible from a two- or three-dimensional representation. Virtual reality may be a method that is used in the future to perform data mining against large amounts of textual documents such as those available on the Internet. The visualization technique would group documents according to some criteria, then allow the data to move through those groupings in order to better choose the desired publication, similar to looking through a library in order to select a book.

Commercial tools are becoming more mature in their capability to provide more effective mechanisms for data display. Some of the tools include:

- ALTA Analytics' NetMap
- IBM's DX: Visualization Data Explorer
- Artificial Intelligence Software's VisualMine
- Data Desk
- Belmont Research's CrossGraphs
- Information Technology Institute's WinViz

PRACTICAL APPLICATIONS OF DATA MINING AND KDD

Many successful systems have been constructed and are now in daily use in a variety of domains. For example, A. C. Nielson has a system called OpportunityExplorer that analyzes retail point-of-sale information to help formulate marketing strategies. Customers for such systems include retailers, advertisers, and product producers, to name a few. IBM's Intelligent Miner is being used by retail stores to better analyze customer buying trends and product popularity. NCR has also been doing research in this area and has developed tools to aid their retail customers.

Another interesting application is the use of data mining by the Traveler's Insurance Company to determine the cost of hurricane insurance to various coastal locations, based on analyses of historical hurricane tracks and the amount of damage caused to coastal areas.

There has been a great deal of activity in the area of analyzing dynamic financial markets, but little of it has been publicized (because of the huge financial gains that can result from even a slight competitive advantage). The Lockheed Artificial Intelligence Center has a system called Recon that has recently been moved from the research lab to become a commercial product. Recon has been used in a number of applications, including one to select a stock portfolio. Currently, that application analyzes both historical and current dynamic data on thousands of stocks and makes recommendations for stocks to purchase by predicting stocks that may do well based on certain predictors. Typically, this area has been dominated by the use of statistical analysis, although neural networks and are also being explored for this domain.

In the area of credit cards and loans, there is the application involving credit scoring and credit card fraud detection. In these areas, statistical analysis and neural networks are quite popular. Neural networks have proven quite efficient at being able to distinguish between good and bad credit risks, and between valid and illegal credit card purchases. The neural network is trained based on collected data that characterizes the types of credit risks or the types of credit card purchases. HNC has a popular neural network application being used by credit card companies for both credit scoring and fraud detection that has proven quite accurate and very able to handle the immense numbers of transactions that are being processed.

Many organizations have become extremely interested in the reduction, analysis, and classification of data in large scientific databases. For example, the SKICAT at NASA's Jet Propulsion Laboratory was developed to catalog sky objects from the second Palomar Sky Survey. The input to the system is a digitized photographic plate, and the output is a set of catalog entries for all objects in the image (e.g., stars, galaxies, or other artifacts). SKICAT has been used successfully with a 3 terabyte astronomical data set and has generated catalogs on billions of objects, including 2×10^7 galaxies, 2×10^8 stars, and 10^5 quasars.

In addition to these and other specific applications, there are general-purpose toolkits for building KDD applications. Many of the tools discussed in the previous section are applicable for use in a variety of domains, including financial and banking applications, the petroleum industry, and in marketing analyses, among others. The limiting factor on any use of a data mining tool is to ensure that the appropriate tool is being used with the given data and goals for the analysis.

Information Retrieval and Text Processing

Information retrieval has typically been concerned with finding better techniques to query for and retrieve textual documents based on their content. Data mining is being applied to this area so that the vast amounts of electronic publications currently available may be brought to users' attention in a more efficient manner.

Data mining and information retrieval are being merged to provide a more intelligent "push" of information to a user. Information retrieval techniques have included the use of a user profile to help focus a search for pertinent documents. The addition of data mining techniques to the creation of a profile is currently being researched to improve the documents that are retrieved or brought to the user's attention. For example, if a user's profile shows that a user is interested in reading articles with the topics of "football," "baseball," and "soccer," a data mining algorithm could generalize these specific topics to "organized outdoor team sports." This type of generalization is increasingly necessary when one considers that topics of interest can change over time (i.e., the three above-mentioned sports are typically run during specific seasons), so the data mining can allow the profile to be more proactive.

CONCLUSION

Knowledge discovery has been defined as the extraction of explicit, previously unknown, and potentially useful information from data. Data mining combines artificial intelligence, statistical analysis, and database management systems to attempt to pull knowledge from stored data. A number of terms have been used in place of data mining, including *information harvesting*, *data archaeology*, *knowledge mining*, and *knowledge extraction*. In fact, all the terms imply the process of sifting through potentially vast quantities of raw material (i.e., the data) and extracting the "gems" or useful knowledge that can drive an executive's decision making.

Data mining continues to receive enormous attention by both commercial and scientific communities for three reasons. First, both the number and size of databases in many organizations are growing at a staggering rate. Terabyte and even petabyte databases, once unthinkable, are now becoming a reality in a variety of domains, including marketing, sales, finance, healthcare, earth science, molecular biology (e.g., the human genome project), and various government applications. Second, organizations have realized that there is valuable knowledge buried in the data that, if discovered, could provide those organizations with a competitive advantage. Third, some of the enabling technologies have only recently become mature enough to make data mining possible on large data sets.

Data mining is actually a step in a larger *KDD process*. The KDD process uses data mining methods or algorithms to extract or identify knowledge according to some criteria or measure of interest, but it also includes steps that prepare data, such as preprocessing, subsampling, and transformations of the database.

Data mining and KDD are hot technologies. They will continue to be so because they give organizations such great advantages that most companies find they need data mining and KDD. As the supporting technologies and applications examined in this article are refined, the need for these technologies will continue to grow.

Acknowledgments

The author thanks David Duff and Eric Bloedorn for their helpful comments. The author also thanks Len Seligman for his work on the previous version of this paper.

Recommended Resources

There are a number of resources available to readers who would like to remain current on the latest developments in this fast-evolving area. Those with access to the Internet can explore the Knowledge Discovery Mine, a World Wide Web home page maintained by Gregory Piatetsky-Shapiro of GTE Labs. This page has a great deal of information on both research projects and commercial products, and it has links to many other Internet resources related to data mining: http://info.gte.com/~kdd.

Chapter 29
Critical Factors in Developing a Data Warehouse

Duane E. Sharp

Data warehousing has become one of the most significant technologies of the past decade, and has permeated virtually every business sector, from retailing to finance, in one form or another.

The International Data Corporation (IDC) estimates that revenue from the total worldwide data warehouse software market, including data access, warehouse management/storage, and data transformation/warehouse generation, will grow at a compound annual growth rate (CAGR) of 30.8 percent, during the period from 1995 to the year 2000. Worldwide market revenue was $1.4 billion in 1995; based on this forecast, it will grow to $5.4 billion by the year 2000. This growth pattern is a certain indication that data warehousing is well beyond the stage of early adoption and has been accepted by pragmatic businesses as a proven technology for enhancing their business operations.

As an example of the proliferation of this major corporate application of information technology, it is worth noting that NCR Corporation, a world leader in data warehousing technology, had over 500 data warehousing installations worldwide in 1997, in a broad range of business sectors.

ARE COMPANIES REALIZING A RETURN ON THEIR INVESTMENT?

A recent IDC ROI study, published as "The Foundations of Wisdom: A Study of the Financial Impact of Data Warehousing" by Stephen Graham, interviewed 62 sites that have successfully implemented a corporate data warehouse. The study covers a wide range of industries, including financial services, health care, telecommunications, retail, government, and manufacturing. The average initial investment by the surveyed sites was $2.2 million. The major finding of the study is that organizations recouped their initial investment within an average of 2.3 years. The average return on the initial investment over 3 years was more than 400 percent, dramatic confirmation that data warehousing can be a good investment.

0-8493-9822-3/00/$0.00+$.50

INTERNAL ACCESS TO THE CORPORATE DATA WAREHOUSE

A data warehouse takes time-oriented data from multiple applications and organizes it according to subjects meaningful to the corporation or business. Corporations, concerned with informing their decision makers, are pursuing this strategy for two major reasons:

1. Reduced complexity. The data in the decision-support database or warehouse is made available in a form that is relatively easy to understand.
2. Improved performance. The warehouse can be tuned to provide better performance and faster response to complex queries and analysis.

BUILDING THE DATA WAREHOUSE

From a qualitative perspective, according to the IDC survey, the key benefits of a corporate data warehouse are:

- More streamlined systems administration; and
- More productivity for internal analysts.

Building a data warehouse is one of the most complex processes a corporation can undertake. It will change the corporate decision-making process without necessarily reengineering the corporation. Traditionally, corporate decisions have been based on the analysis of data, without detailed information to support the data. Corporations analyzed data from reports and made decisions based on limited information. Data warehousing changes this process dramatically, by quickly transforming all available detailed data (irrespective of volume) into meaningful business information. The end results are timelier and better informed business decisions.

Experience based on successful data warehouse implementations points to five critical factors, which are essential for a successful implementation. The following analysis of these factors decribes why they are important to any data warehousing project.

Focus on a Real Problem

It is a fundamental axiom that a successful data warehouse implementation needs to be based on solving a real business problem, and the corporation will have to solve this problem. A data warehouse which does not address a critical business problem is destined for failure.

The business problem selected must have senior management backing which correlates with the desire to solve the problem. Most successful data warehouses are cross-functional, because the ROI increases with both the breadth of data they hold and the impact they have on the business.

Business problems that have been solved by a data warehouse solution include:

- Credit card risk management;
- Sales and inventory management;
- Supply chain management;
- Exposure management; and
- Target marketing.

Solving these business problems requires large volumes of data from many business functions and, in some cases, even from outside sources. It also involves structuring the data based on input from end users who will use the system, as to what data is important and how it should be presented.

History has shown that if a data warehouse is built without end-user input, end users will not use it and the development exercise will be a spectacular, expensive failure. Information technology professionals alone cannot build a data warehouse: user organizations must be involved from the beginning.

There are several approaches to implementing a data warehousing system. One solution which is often applied to solving a business problem is the so-called packaged data warehouse. A packaged solution is usually a single-vendor solution, with a pre-defined front-end application, a standard database management system, and an industry-generic database design. It often fails because it does not solve the critical business problems of a corporation; however, it is implemented to prove the concept. Since it is designed to meet a variety of requirements, it usually fails to address the specific needs which are always a part of any organization's data warehousing business.

The data warehousing solution which is most likely to be successful is one that provides a solution to critical business problems, specific to the organization for which it is designed, with significant end-user involvement and senior management support.

Select the Right Data Warehouse Champion

The second critical success factor is acquiring a strong champion for the data warehouse implementation. The complexities of the implementation are enormous, ranging from maneuvering the project through the corporate political environment to gaining consensus among cross-functional business users with different objectives. Usually, a data warehouse champion has to spearhead the project to ultimately make the data warehouse successful.

The data warehouse champion is typically a fairly senior business user with a strong understanding of the information technology environment. He must understand the political landscape, have the capability to bring tough issues to a consensus, and should report to a senior corporate sponsor during the data warehouse implementation. Meeting these criteria is the best way to ensure that the champion will prove to be a real champion when the chips are down.

The champion must be firmly convinced that a data warehousing solution will meet the requirement and solve the defined business problem, to the extent of betting his or her reputation on the implementation. He will also ensure that the right team of professionals is involved in defining the business problem to be solved, and ultimately in developing the data warehousing solution that will meet the requirements.

A key element in the champion's involvement is the requirement to challenge information system specialists, to work with them for the benefit of the corporation, and to represent the business users in defining methods of access and presentation of the wide range of information to be derived from the data warehousing system.

Use Detailed Historical Data

The foundation of every successful data warehouse is the detailed historical data on which it is based, and this is the third critical success factor. One approach, which has been used by information systems departments to manage the volume and complexity of the issues associated with navigating through weeks, months, or even years of detailed transaction data, is summary data structures. Although these elements have often become a preferred strategy for implementing decision support systems, they frequently become a detriment to the data warehousing system and its original intent. Summary data structures inevitably fall short of meeting requirements, for several reasons:

- Obscuring data variations: Because they are only summaries of information, they tend to obscure important data variations, masking important variations in corporate data which may point to problems, indicating areas where successful techniques have been applied in the past and may be applied in the future.
- Complex maintenance: Another deficiency of summary structures is that their maintenance can be fairly complex and quite resource intensive, requiring a significant amount of updating to reflect adjustments to transaction data.
- Single static scheme: A final deficiency of summary structures is that they are usually created using a single static scheme for organizing transaction level details into a coherent and manageable information format. This limitation ultimately causes the summary structure to fall

short because it prevents the business user from viewing the data in a manner conducive to a discovery process. In short, most of today's business problems or opportunities cannot be identified using a few, limited static views of the business activity.

Summary data tables do have a place in data warehouse design. However, they should not be considered as an alternative to storing detailed data, but rather as a technique for solving some very well-defined performance problems.

Apply Technology

The fourth critical success factor is that a successful data warehouse implementation will apply technology to the business problem. One technology which has been applied to the data warehousing solution is symmetric multi-processor (SMP) computer hardware supporting a relational, multi-dimensional, or hybrid database environment.

More advanced solutions use massive parallel processor hardware (MPP). In a decentralized data warehouse architecture, this solution will probably employ middleware to coordinate wide area access. Furthermore, it will entail the use of graphic user interface (GUI) application tools (either developed in-house or purchased off-the-shelf) and online analytical processing (OLAP) tools to present the volumes of data in meaningful formats.

There are a broad range of architectures which can meet the requirements of a data warehousing system, and the selection of the right technology is a critical factor. However, architectural issues should only be approached when the business problems to be addressed are clearly understood. The technology should always be applied as part of the solution.

Evaluations of different technology can consume significant amounts of time and energy. It is better to work with vendors that can provide references which relate to an organization's requirement. Other sources of information are technical publications, seminars and conferences, and research organizations that have conducted studies and evaluated a variety of different issues around data warehousing. Knowledgeable individuals in organizations that have implemented a data warehousing solution are also a major and extremely useful information resource.

Trust The Data — History Does Not Lie

The fifth and final critical success factor in a data warehousing implementation is realizing that historical data is a strategic asset, since it is a source of corporate truths that do not forget or deceive. Human perception and memory can be faulty, and the data warehousing system should not be entrusted to a process which relies on the human memory.

Precise point-in-time readings of key business indicators can help recreate a thumbnail sketch of past business events. They can also forecast the success of a future event, potentially reducing the probability of recreating previous business disasters.

However, data alone will not solve a business problem. Specialists with specific information system skills will be needed to scrub, load, access, and present the gigabytes and terabytes of transaction data generated each year by the business. Statisticians and business analysts can interpret the business information distilled from all the detailed data, and provide the business analysis and predictive models that project future business trends.

While history does not lie, it can sometimes mislead. Inconsistencies, incomplete or absent metadata definitions, data loss from media corruption, or unnecessarily restrictive retention cycles, are potential serious threats to the quality of data residing in a data warehouse.

CONCLUSION

There are no guarantees with data warehousing implementation; however, the probability of success will be increased significantly if these five critical success factors are addressed. Therefore, it is important to consider these critical factors long before the first query is run or the first gigabyte of data is loaded.

A data warehouse system is one of the most complex applications which an organization can implement, since it involves the core business of the organization and a large part of its transaction and business history. It will have a dramatic impact on each information user. While it is not in itself a solution to a business problem, it provides a means to a solution, one which will involve the entire organization in a major cultural change. This change will enable employees to use detailed information as a key to knowledgeable corporate decision-making.

Chapter 30
Web-Enabled Data Warehousing

Nathan J. Muller

A data warehouse is an extension of the database management system (DBMS), which consolidates information from various sources into a high-level, integrated form used to identify trends and make business decisions. For a large company, the amount of information in a data warehouse could be up to several trillion bytes, or terabytes (TB). The technologies that are used to build data warehouses include relational databases; powerful, scalable processors; and sophisticated tools to manipulate and analyze large volumes of data and identify previously undetectable patterns and relationships.

The benefits of data warehousing include increased revenue and decreased costs due to the more effective handling and use of massive amounts of data. Data warehousing applications are driven by such economic needs as cost reduction or containment, revenue enhancement, and response to market conditions. In being able to manage data more effectively, companies can improve customer satisfaction and cement customer loyalty. This can be done by sifting through the data to identify patterns of repeat purchases, determine the frequency and manner with which customers use various products, and assess their propensity to switch vendors when they are offered better prices or more targeted features. This kind of information is important because a change of only a few percentage points of customer retention can equate to hundreds of millions of dollars to a large company.

The benefits of data warehousing now can be extended beyond the corporate headquarters to remote branch offices, telecommuters and mobile professionals. Virtually anyone with a Web browser and an Internet connection can access corporate data stores using the same query, reporting and analysis tools previously reserved for technically elite number crunchers using expensive, feature-rich client/server tools. The Web-enabled data warehouse makes it possible for companies to leverage their investments in information by making it available to everyone who needs it to make critical business decisions.

0-8493-9822-3/00/$0.00+$.50

SYSTEM COMPONENTS

The data warehousing framework typically encompasses several components:

- An information store of historical events (the data warehouse).
- Warehouse administration tools.
- Data manipulation tools.
- A decision support system (DSS) that enables strategic analysis of the information.

A key capability of the DSS is data mining, which uses sophisticated tools to detect trends, patterns, and correlations hidden in vast amounts of data. Information discoveries are presented to the user and provide the basis for strategic decisions and action plans that can improve corporate operational and financial performance.

Among the many useful features of a DSS are an automatic monitoring capability to control runaway queries; transparent access to requested data on central, local, or desktop databases; data-staging capabilities for temporary data stores for simplification, performance, or conversational access; a drill-down capability to access exception data at lower levels; import capabilities to translators, filters, and other desktop tools; a scrubber to merge redundant data, resolve conflicting data, and integrate data from incompatible systems; and usage statistics, including response times.

The latest trend in data warehouses is to integrate them with the corporate intranet for access by remote users with browser-enabled client software. The primary purpose of Web-enabling a data warehouse is to give remote offices and mobile professionals the information they need to make tactical business decisions.

A variety of toolkits are available that allow developers to create canned reports that can be hosted on the corporate Web site. In some cases, users can drill down into these reports to uncover new information or trends. With more sophisticated Web-based online analytical processing (OLAP) tools, users can access directly the corporate data warehouse to do simple queries and run reports. With the resulting information, reports can be culled to provide information that remote users need for their everyday decisions.

At a retail operation, for example, a store manager might tap into a canned sales report to figure out when a specific item will run out of stock, whereas a business analyst at the corporate headquarters might use client/server OLAP tools to analyze sales trends at all the stores so strategic purchasing decisions can be made.

For users who need more than static HTML documents, but like the convenience of Web browsers, there are plug-ins that dynamically query the back-end database. With such tools, employees can do things like drill down into the reports to find specific information. At an insurance company, for example, users might have the ability to drill down to a particular estimate line within a claim. This granularity might let a user determine how many claims relate to airbags and how long and at what cost it takes to repair them. Such information can be used to determine the discount drivers qualify for if their vehicle is equipped with airbags.

Making a data warehouse accessible to Web users solves a dilemma faced by many companies. On one hand, they do not want to limit users by only providing predefined HTML reports that cannot be manipulated. On the other, they do not want to overwhelm users with an OLAP tool they are not trained to understand. A Web-based OLAP tool that allows some interactivity with the data warehouse offers a viable alternative for users who are capable of handling simple queries. In turn, this makes corporate information more accessible to a broader range of users, including business analysts, product planners, and salespeople.

Because not everybody has the same information requirements, some companies have implemented multiple reporting options:

- Canned reports: these are predefined, executive-level reports that can only be viewed through the Web browser. Users need little to no technical expertise, knowledge of the data, or training because they can only view the reports, not interact with them.
- Ready-to-run reports: for those with some technical expertise and knowledge of the data, report templates are provided that users fill in with their query requirements. Although dynamic, these reports are limited to IS-specified field values, fill-in boxes, and queries.
- Ad-hoc reports: for the technically astute who are familiar with the data to run freeform queries, unlimited access to the data warehouse is provided. They can fill in all field values, choose among multiple fill-in boxes, and run complex queries.

WEB WAREHOUSE ARCHITECTURE

Many vendors offer Web tools that support a tiered intranet architecture comprising Web browsers, Web servers, application servers, and databases (Exhibit 30.1). The Web servers submit user requests to an application server via a gateway such as the common gateway interface (CGI) or server API. The application server translates HTML requests into calls or SQL statements it can submit to the database. The application packages the result and returns it to the Web server in the proper format. The Web server forwards the result to the client.

This model can be enhanced with Java applets or other client-side programs. For example, the query form can be presented as a Java applet,

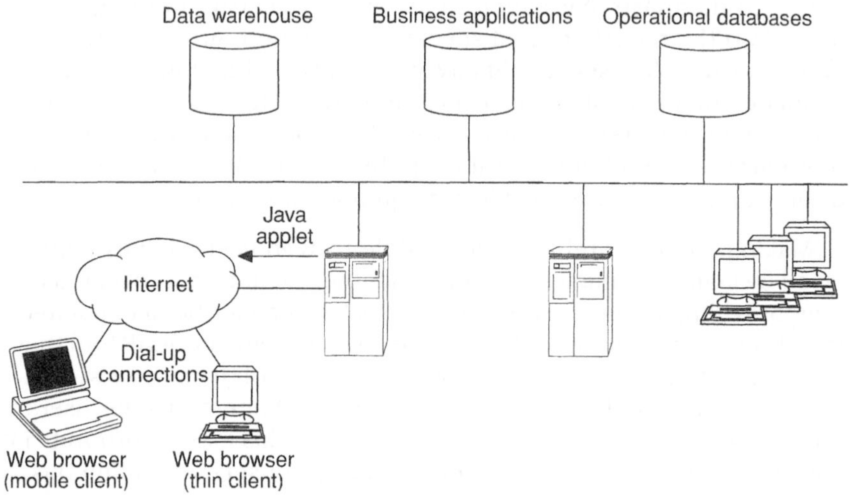

Exhibit 30.1. Tiered Architecture for Web-Enabled Warehouses

rather than the usual CGI. Among the advantages of a Java-based query form is that error-checking can be performed locally rather than at the server. If certain fields are not filled in properly, for example, an appropriate error message can be displayed before the query is allowed to reach the server. This helps control the load on the server.

An all-Java approach provides even more advantages because connecting clients and servers at the network and transport layers is much more efficient than doing so at the application level using CGI scripts. This means users can design and execute queries and reports much more quickly than they can with other types of tools.

SECURITY

Obviously, a data warehouse contains highly sensitive information, so security is a key concern for any company contemplating a Web-enabled data warehouse. Not only must the data warehouse be protected against external sources, many times it must be protected against unauthorized access from internal sources as well. For example, branch offices might be prevented from accessing each other's information, or the engineering department might be prevented from accessing the marketing department's information, and all departments might be prevented from accessing the personnel department's records. Security can be enforced through a variety of mechanisms from user names and passwords to firewalls and encrypted data transmissions.

The use of Java offers additional levels of security. Applets that adhere to the Java cryptography extensions (JCE) can be signed, encrypted and transmitted digitally via secure streams to prevent hackers from attacking applets during transmission. Specifically, JCE-based applets make use of Diffie-Hellmann authentication, a technology that enables two parties to share keys, and data encryption standard (DES) for scrambling the data for transmission.

Some Web-enabled OLAP and DSS tools are designed to take advantage of the secure sockets layer (SSL) protocol, which protects data transferred over the network through the use of advanced security techniques. The SSL protocol provides security that has three basic properties:

- Connection privacy: encryption is used after an initial handshake to define a secret key.
- Data protection: cryptography algorithms such as DES or RC4 are used for data encryption. The peer's identity can be authenticated using a public key.
- Connection reliability: message transport includes an integrity check based on a keyed message authentication code (MAC).

SSL is being considered by the Internet Engineering Task Force (IETF) as the official Internet standard for transport layer security (TLS).

OPTIMIZATION TECHNIQUES

Some Web-based development tools optimize database interactivity by giving users the ability to access back-end databases in real time. Users can submit queries against the entire database or refresh existing reports to obtain the most up-to-date data. In addition to providing for more flexible report generation, this dynamic report creation environment minimizes the need to manage and store physical reports online, which streamlines storage requirements. However, some servers also can deliver copies of pre-executed reports to users who do not need to filter existing reports and want to optimize data delivery.

Other Web tools optimize functionality by giving users the ability to manipulate returned data in real time. Users can drill up, down or across data, apply calculations, toggle between charts and tables, and reorganize the local data. Through the use of Java and ActiveX, a high degree of interactivity between the user and data is now possible over the Web.

VENDOR OFFERINGS

Many vendors of DSS and OLAP tools now offer Web versions of their products, each differing in terms of features and ease of use. Exhibit 30.2 summarizes the offering of the five vendors discussed here. All of them strive to extend data warehouse query and reporting capabilities to a greater number of users who otherwise may not be able to access corporate information stores and database systems, because conventional tools

Exhibit 30.2. Select Vendors of Web-Enabled DSS and OLAP Tools

Company	Product	Platform	Databases
Brio Technology, Inc. 3950 Fabian Way Suite 200 Palo Alto, CA 94303 USA Tel. +1 650 856 8000 Fax. +1 650 856 8020	brio.web.warehouse	Windows NT, Macintosh, Unix	Oracle Express
Business Objects, SA 2870 Zanker Road San Jose, CA 95134 USA Tel. +1 408 953-6000 Fax. +1 408 953 6001	WebIntelligence	Windows NT	Arbor Essbase, Oracle Express
Information Advantage, Inc. 7905 Golden Triangle Drive Eden Prairie, MN 55344 USA Tel. +1 612 833 3700 Fax. +1 612 833 3701	DecisionSuite Server, WebOLAP	Unix	IBM DB2, Informix, Oracle, Red Brick, Sybase, Tandem, Teradata
Infospace, Inc. 181 2nd Avenue Suite 218 San Mateo, CA 94401 Tel. +1 650 685 3000 Fax. +1 650 685 3001	SpaceOLAP, SpaceSQL	Unix, Windows NT or IBM mainframe	Arbor Essbase, IBM DB2, Oracle Express
MicroStrategy, Inc. 8000 Towers Crescent Drive Vienna, VA 22182 Tel. +1 703 848 8600 Fax. +1 703 848 8610	DSS Web	Windows NT	IBM DB2, Informix, Oracle, Red Brick, Sybase, SQL Server, Tandem, Teradata

are either too complex for the average person to use, or too expensive for general distribution and maintenance by IS staff.

Brio Technology

Brio Technology, Inc. (Palo Alto, CA) offers a scalable server suite called brio.web.warehouse that provides a full-featured Web-based query, reporting and analysis solution for the extended enterprise. Through the use of push and pull technologies, organizations efficiently and economically can distribute business-critical information to a broad range of users, across mixed computing environments.

Brio offers a choice of servers. One provides information on-demand through the use of client pull technology and the other distributes information on a scheduled basis through the use of server push technology. The choice depends on how the organization wants to make information available to users. Both servers are available in Windows NT and UNIX versions.

The company's Broadcast Server runs scheduled queries and pushes precomputed reports and documents to Internet, client/server and mobile users via FTP, E-mail, Web, and file servers. Reports also can be sent directly to any network printer from the Broadcast Server. With push technology, the user subscribes to predefined reports and documents, which are delivered automatically when ready — without having specifically to request them. The canned reports are viewed with Web client software called Brio.Quickview.

The company's OnDemand Server is a Web application server that delivers full-featured ad-hoc query, reporting, and analysis functionality over the Web using client pull technology. Pull technology simply means that the user specifically must request information from the server using a query form.

The OnDemand Server provides users with the capability to conduct queries across the Web. Query execution is performed on the server, which then builds reports and transmits them in compressed form back to Brio.Insight Web clients. Recipients then can engage in personal reporting and analysis using the exact same functionality and user interface offered in the company's client/server based BrioQuery Navigator product.

However, analysis often leads to new questions, which require ad-hoc querying. Brio.Insight can adapt its functionality based on the contents of the report and the user's security profile. This means that users can do a certain amount of ad-hoc querying, but without having free-form control over information they only should be allowed to view.

The reporting backlog of busy IS departments can be reduced by granting analysis and ad-hoc querying capabilities to specific users or groups of users on a report-by-report basis. Five different functional modes dynamically can be enabled from view-only to full query-and-analysis. A built-in Wizard creates a Web page where decision makers can find a list of available reports — each with its own set of analysis and formatting functionality privileges. This frees IS staff to focus on publishing or giving access to data anywhere in the extended enterprise.

The OnDemand Server also supports zero-administration of clients. The server automatically installs and updates Brio.Quickview and Brio.Insight on client machines. Upon opening a report on the Web, users are notified to download the appropriate Web extension, new patch, or latest upgrade. This capability lowers the total cost of ownership for IS organizations because the need to install and maintain complex middleware and client/server software across diverse platforms is eliminated.

Business Objects

Business Objects, SA (San Jose, CA) offers IS organizations the means to deploy broadly DSS capabilities and extend DSS beyond the enterprise to reach suppliers, partners, and customers over the Web. The company's multitier, thin-client WebIntelligence solution provides nontechnical end users with ad-hoc query, reporting, and analysis of information stored in corporate data warehouses, data marts, and packaged business applications.

Via a Java query applet, users autonomously can request data using familiar business terms, analyze the data by viewing it from different perspectives and in different levels of detail, and share the information with other users in the form of formatted reports.

The WebIntelligence report catalog and search engine enable users to find and access specific documents quickly. Like Brio Technology's product, WebIntelligence takes advantage of both the push and pull models of document distribution. With a few drag-and-drop actions, users can pull fresh data in new or existing documents and, after applying simple formatting options, push the reports to wide populations.

Users also can reach beyond the corporate data mart or data warehouse and tap into the resources of the Web to enrich their reports with other useful information. WebIntelligence includes a feature called hyperdrill, which allows the report cells themselves to be hyperlinks that can drill out of a report and into any Internet-based data source. Using hyperdrill, for example, an accounts receivable report can include a hyperlink for each customer that, when pressed, activates a credit service to produce a current credit report for that customer.

WebIntelligence can run on a single machine or be distributed across multiple servers. With multiple servers, WebIntelligence automatically performs load balancing to make the best use of system resources and ensure optimal response times. A multiserver configuration allows a backup server to be designated for automatic cutover in case another server becomes unavailable. It also allows components to be added easily to the system to meet increased user demand.

Together, the distributed architecture and Java query applet eliminate the need for client-side installation and maintenance of both application software and database middleware. As a Java-based solution, users require only a standard Web browser on their desktop to access to the information they need. Because the Java query applet does not take up permanent residence on the client machine, the most current copy of the applet is called by the Web browser when the user wants to perform a database query. This zero-administration client eliminates one of the key obstacles to wide-scale deployment of decision support technology — deployment cost.

User administration can be streamlined by assigning new users to groups. For each user or group, the resources they are allowed to access can be specified by the system administrator. In addition, WebIntelligence is designed to work with Web security standards such as the secure socket layer (SSL), which protects data transferred over the network through the use of advanced encryption algorithms.

With the WebIntelligence administration utility, distributed components can be started, stopped, configured and tuned over the Internet. At any time, the administrator can check which users are connected to the WebIntelligence system and monitor their activity. This information can be stored in a system log file for auditing purposes.

WebIntelligence can share the same metadata (e.g., the same business representation of the database) and the same security information as BusinessObjects, the company's client/server tool for decision support systems. The business representation of the database (also called a semantic layer), which is created to insulate users from the complexity of the data source, is available to both WebIntelligence and BusinessObjects users. Similarly, the security privileges defined to control each user's access to database information apply to both tools. Thus, only one DSS environment needs to be set up and maintained to support both Web and client/server users.

Information Advantage

Information Advantage, Inc. (Eden Prairie, MN) offers WebOLAP, a browser-based reporting and interactive analysis tool that extends the delivery of warehoused data over a corporate intranet, to business partners over an extranet, or to remote users over the Internet.

WebOLAP is supported by the company's DecisionSuite Server, a system that maximizes throughput in high-volume reporting environments by dynamically adding, managing and deleting concurrent processes initiated by requests from multiple users. This multi-user, network-centric design eliminates bottlenecks by maintaining persistence and state between the server and database, providing the means to create as many concurrent server processes as required to fulfill incoming requests.

Unlike Brio Technology and Business Objects, Information Advantage's WebOLAP does not provide a Java-based query applet. Instead, a CGI script is used to provide a link between the Web and its application server, which is still the most prevalent integration method. The DecisionSuite Server outputs OLAP report files in XLS, WK5, ASCII, or HTML formats.

WebOLAP indexes the data warehouse to corporate intranet or extranet metadata. Live, interactive OLAP views can be accessed directly from search engines, bookmarks, directories, hyperlinks and E-mail attachments for seamless integration of data warehouse analysis into corporate intranet sites.

Users can create, pivot, drill, and save reports and convert and download data to popular desktop productivity tools, such as spreadsheets and word processors. The WebOLAP system retains each new report so users have a clear audit trail of their journey through the data warehouse. WebOLAP saves and shares reports as live objects that contain the data and instructions used to create the reports. More than one user can interact and explore a single report. Each user receives a temporary instance of the object, so that he or she is free to take the analysis in any direction without affecting other users or the original report.

Users also can benefit from the monitoring and filtering capabilities of intelligent agents that work on their behalf to find information stored in the data warehouse. Agents filter out low-priority information and proactively deliver personalized OLAP information back to the user. Agents can deliver results to directory listings and/or notify the user directly through alerts or E-mail with interactive report attachments. A number of agents can be launched by the user and be active at the same time within the data store. Agent requests run in the background, keeping desktops free for other tasks. Agents save the user from having to personally surf and filter through gigabytes and terabytes of warehoused and derived data.

WebOLAP develops reports using a personalized library of private and published filter, calculation, and report template objects. Information objects can be recombined to create new and different analyses of the data warehouse. Reports can be delivered in multiple file formats, allowing users to integrate information within their current business workflow and personal productivity tools.

WebOLAP gives users the ability to cross-analyze data simultaneously from multiple data marts or data warehouses, regardless of data location or vendor RDBMS. A report subscription feature provides access to previously built report templates that can be personalized quickly with a user's parameters to save time and prevent the reinvention of popular reports. A groupware application provides seamless sharing of interactive reports and their assumptions to eliminate duplication of effort, ensure consistent analysis, and encourage collaboration.

Infospace

Infospace, Inc. (San Mateo, CA) offers two scalable, server-based data access and analysis solutions that work over the Web: SpaceOLAP and SpaceSQL. Both applications are written in Java. With the familiar Web browser, users are provided with data access to any relational or multidimensional database, data mart, or data warehouse, and even to other legacy data sources and objects via an open API.

Persistence and state are maintained between client and server and server and database, allowing data to pass freely and efficiently. To improve efficiency and performance, the server caches data and only delivers small packets of information to the user as needed. As the number of users increases, a load-balancing option also allows additional machines to start up automatically to meet demand.

Operating in UNIX, Windows NT, or mainframe environments, SpaceOLAP delivers most of the same functions as traditional client/server-based data analysis tools. It provides native access to Oracle Express Server 6.0, Arbor Essbase, and IBM DB2 OLAP Server.

SpaceOLAP consists of three client modules and one server module. Each client module is a different application that is accessed through a browser. The server module, called the Infospace Java Server, resides on the Web server. This module pulls data from data sources as requested by modules running on the client. SpaceOLAP Administrator is where administrators set up the users, user groups, and data sources of the system. SpaceOLAP Designer lets users and administrators create reports and graphs for the system. OLAP queries can be built from scratch, or the user can simply use predefined queries. SpaceOLAP Runtime lets users view the reports and graphs that have been created for them in their browsers.

SpaceOLAP enables the user to interact fully with the data in real time. In addition to drill-down, drill-up, pivoting, and selection capabilities, interactive presentations can include Java-based charts (SpaceCharts) and Java-based pivot tables (SpaceTable). With SpaceCharts, users can sort and select data dynamically, and resize and rotate charts. With SpaceTable, users can present the information with a Java-based pivot-table, which allows the user to slice and dice via pivoting and drill-down in a spreadsheet-like environment.

The company's other product, SpaceSQL, is a Java-based query, reporting, and charting tool that provides Web access to relational databases. It integrates graphical reporting with the Web-based point-and-click interface for direct access to Oracle, Informix, Sybase, and other relational databases over a corporate intranet.

The architecture comprises a client that runs within a Web browser and a server that resides alongside the Web server. SpaceSQL includes a Java-based design version for query, report, and chart definition and a runtime version for end-user viewing. It installs itself automatically on the client system when called.

The SpaceSQL designer allows users to define queries through a point-and-click interface. Advanced users can also use the SQL editor to directly import or enter SQL queries. Query results can be presented and analyzed by designing customized reports and interactive three-dimensional charts using the browser's intuitive interface. A Java-enabled Web client, like Netscape Navigator, is the only requirement on the client system; no additional hardware or software is required.

SpaceSQL produces output in a variety of formats including HTML, Java charts, .GIF, VRML, CSV (for Microsoft Excel compatibility), and Java tables. This allows users to gain insights into data, then communicate their ideas through standard E-mail by attaching one of the chart formats suited for the recipient's system.

Existing chart technologies provide static images only and offer less flexibility in presenting and viewing the chart according to each user's preferences. However, SpaceSQL enables users to interact with data and manipulate the displayed data. The interaction takes two forms — drill-down reports and three-dimensional charts.

Native RDBMS drivers and the multithreaded server provide database interaction. The persistent database connection is an improvement over typical HTML-based solutions, which constantly need to reconnect to the database. The charting is done completely on the client side, freeing up the server and facilitating scaling to a large number of users.

Reports can be scheduled to run when the system load is low. SpaceSQL also allows for periodic scheduling of reports — daily, weekly, or monthly. This is especially useful for running large reports without tying up network and processor resources. Depending on the sophistication of the user, he or she can design, run, and view reports and charts and immediately communicate the insights gained from this analysis over the corporate intranet.

MicroStrategy

MicroStrategy, Inc. (Vienna, VA) offers DSS Web, an OLAP tool that provides all types of end users with dynamic, interactive access to decision-support information. Starting with version 5.0, users can take advantage of webcasting for decision support. DSS Web 5.0 incorporates Internet push technology to automate the delivery of information to end users. Users can decide which reports they wish to subscribe to and have those reports automatically pushed to their desktops. DSS Web's Alerts & Exception Reporting feature enhances the automation of report delivery by allowing users to run reports that provide text alerts to exception conditions, such as record weekly sales or low item in stock. This feature allows users to focus on immediate business action instead of report creation.

Via a Web browser, remote users can share a central, corporate information repository to access data and conduct sophisticated analysis. For example, the DSS Web Report Wizard provides step-by-step instructions that allow users to define and save new reports. DSS Web AutoPrompts provide runtime customization of reports. And with features such as On-the-fly-Sorting and Outline Mode, users can view and modify their data in a variety of different ways. Reports in grid and graph modes can be sliced and diced with drill everywhere functionality. Interactive reporting features are achieved with Java and ActiveX technologies.

System administrators have the ability to manage the system from remote locations. Administrative changes can be made once through DSS Web and distributed to all Web browsers, eliminating complicated and expensive upgrades. In addition, decision support systems deployed with DSS Web can have up to four tiers of security at the browser, firewall, DSS Web and RDBMS levels.

Among other enhancements scheduled for later this year by MicroStrategy, DSS Web will support newspaper-like overviews of canned reports and other enhancements aimed at less technology-savvy users.

SELECTING A TOOL

In selecting a Web-enabled DSS or OLAP tool, attention must be given to the critical areas of security, data management, ease of use, and scalability.

Security

A data warehouse solution must include authentication so that the organization can be certain that each party requesting access to its information is indeed who they say they are. Authentication will prove the identity of a remote user, whether on the public Internet, an intranet, or an extranet that is shared by several business partners.

End-to-end encryption is vital to the protection of data during transmission, preventing eavesdropping. Public key technology is an effective solution. It uses a secret and a public key — the public key is sent with the query. The system encrypts the return data using that key. The user's secret key is then used to decrypt the coded information. If the DSS or OLAP vendor does not provide encryption, it can be added with a third-party solution.

The data warehouse solution should also provide the administrator with tools that control the access level each user should have. These tools can be used not only to stop departments from stepping on each other's toes, but to minimize the chances that databases will be corrupted by user error or mischief. Being able to set access levels is an important enforcement mechanism that imposes order on the otherwise chaotic flow of data to and from the company.

Data Management

Virtually everyone within an organization has the ability to create the documents that go into databases. What organizations lack most are the skills to manage all this data. Therefore, the warehouse product must include tools that facilitate the management and ongoing maintenance of vast stores of information.

At a minimum, the product should provide authors with the means to prioritize, label, and set expiration dates on the documents they create and, ideally, allow them to set access levels based on a corporate policy. If the documents are to have embedded hypertext links, there has to be some automated way of checking periodically the integrity of the links, which can become broken over time as new data is added and expired data is deleted.

Regardless of the warehouse product under consideration, it must be remembered that none is going to substitute for experienced staff who have a thorough understanding of the business and who can establish appropriate data definition parameters.

Ease of Use

Ease of use is perhaps the most difficult criterion to apply to the selection of a Web-enabled data warehouse solution, especially within an environment of diversely skilled users. The reason is that the same product must appeal to both low- and high-skilled users if the organization expects to leverage its investment in information systems.

Ideally, the product should not overwhelm less-experienced users by requiring technical mastery before a basic query can be launched. A warehouse product that supports push technology to serve predefined reports and documents automatically may be adequate for most users and does not require any training. Power users, however, must be provided with the features they need to dig deep into the information store and perform sophisticated trend analysis.

Picking the right tool requires an understanding of how various users intend to use the information. Do they just need to look at and refresh reports, for example, or do they need the capability of inputting new values and building queries from scratch? Can a range of user needs be accommodated in the same product, without imposing feature and performance tradeoffs on everyone?

Scalability

Scalability refers to the ability of the data warehouse solution to grow and adapt incrementally as organizational needs change. The data warehouse application must be scalable in several ways: the amount of data to be managed, the amount of users to be accommodated, and types of functions to be supported.

Because data tends to accumulate rather than diminish over time, the data warehouse solution must be able to maintain an acceptable level of performance to ensure optimal response, regardless of how much data there is to plow through. There are a number of ways to enhance server performance, such as implementing caching and balancing the load across several connected machines. In addition, the database server should be designed to accommodate easily such components as processors, memory, disk drives, and I/O ports to meet increased user demand.

In terms of functionality, the data warehouse solution should not only support the broadest range of users, but allow new functionality to be added with minimal disruption to business operations. Furthermore, it should be easy for users to migrate to higher level functions as they become more experienced or as their information needs change over time.

CONCLUSION

The Web enables organizations of all types and sizes to provide applications that deliver content to the end user without the traditional, costly barriers of installation, training and maintenance. Web-based decision support tools and data warehouses provide scalable solutions that can handle diverse requirements in dimensional analysis, support a large variety of financial calculations and enable secure collaborative analysis across all levels of the company.

In the mainframe-centric environment of the past, employees had to submit their information requirements in writing to IS staff and then wait two or three weeks for a report. Today, with a Web-enabled data warehouse, users can have immediate access to the information they need. The Web offers unparalleled opportunity to deliver business reports to huge numbers of users without the information bottlenecks of the past and without the headaches typically associated with rolling out and configuring new software.

In addition, the Web is easy to access on a global basis, supports a high degree of interactivity, and provides platform interoperability — capabilities that are difficult and expensive to achieve over non-TCP/IP networks. All the end user needs is a Web browser. The two most popular Java-enabled Web browsers — Microsoft's Internet Explorer and Netscape Navigator — are free. End users get the most updated versions of Java applets automatically whenever they log onto the data warehouse, which virtually eliminates the need for IS staff to extend software support to every client machine.

Although the rich functionality and high performance of client/server tools cannot be duplicated yet on Web-based data warehouse offerings, this is not necessarily a handicap because the overwhelming majority of users only need to access predefined reports or execute limited queries. For this class of users, basic Web OLAP and DSS tools are appropriate. The relatively small number of technically elite users, who require the ability to interact with large data sets or create decision-support applications for others in the corporation, will continue to use the more powerful client/server tools to which they have become accustomed.

Chapter 31
Software Architectures for Distributed DBMSs in a Client/Server Environment

James A. Larson and Carol L. Larson

A client/server architecture consists of several computers connected by a communications system. Some computers act as servers, and some act as clients. A user interacts with a client to formulate requests for information. The requests are transmitted to one or more servers through a communications system for processing. Each server accesses its local database or file system to respond to the requests and transmits the results back to the client through the communications system. The client/server architecture also allows multiple users to share data by accessing data on a data server through multiple clients.

Businesses are motivated to use a distributed client/server architecture because it enables them to:

- Save money by replacing expensive mainframe hardware with less expensive server hardware. A large savings in cost may be realized if mainframe computers are phased out and replaced with servers and desktop computers.
- Leverage the existing investment in personal computers. Users want to access, analyze, and modify data using their PCs.
- Upgrade existing clients and servers or to add additional clients and servers. This gives upgrade flexibility to the system.

A distributed database management system (DBMS) enables users to access multiple servers. The remainder of this article discusses how to choose a distributed DBMS whose software architecture supports the features users need to perform their jobs.

0-8493-9822-3/00/$0.00+$.50

DISTRIBUTED DBMS TECHNOLOGY

Database administrators are responsible for organizing the database so it can be accessed efficiently. The collection of interrelated records in the database is maintained by a data manager, such as a DBMS or a file system. If data managers exist on several computers, they are interconnected with a communications system. If several data managers share a computer, data is transmitted among them by facilities provided by the local operation system. Both cases are examples of distributed databases because different data managers maintain the data.

Access to Multiple Servers. With more and more essential data being collected and stored in desktop computers, users in many organizations are finding they need to access several computers as well as their organization's mainframe system. Distributed DBMSs enable this accessibility.

A data server provides all of the advantages of centralized databases, which allow users to share up-to-date information managed by the server. However, accessing data becomes more difficult for the user when there are multiple data servers. Users must perform the following tasks to access information stored in multiple servers:

- Determine which computers contain the data to be accessed.
- Formulate several queries, which will be executed on a different computer.
- Copy or transfer the results to a single computer for merging.
- Combine and merge the results.
- Extract the answer to the original request from the combined results.

A distributed DBMS helps users to perform these tasks.

DISTRIBUTED DBMS FEATURES

Three important features available in some distributed DBMSs are location and replication transparency, DBMS transparency, and multisite update capability. The availability of these features depends on the software architecture supported by the distributed DBMS. Database administrators choose software to support the desired features.

Location and Replication Transparency. This feature supports a type of data independence, which enables the database administrator to change the physical location and replication of data without modifying existing application programs.

A distributed DBMS supports location transparency if the user is not aware of the location or site of the data being accessed. Replication transparency is supported if the user is not aware that more than one copy of the data exists. Although these features provide increased data independence, they may require the use of sophisticated and expensive software optimizers.

DBMS Transparency. DBMS transparency is the second important feature. A distributed DBMS needs DBMS transparency when it contains multiple types of local database managers. For example, a distributed DBMS that interconnects a file system located at one site, a relational DBMS at a second site, and an IMS DBMS at a third site contains three types of local data managers. When a distributed DBMS supports DBMS transparency, the user formulates requests using structured query language (SQL). A translator, or gateway, transforms each SQL request to the language understood by a participating data manager.

Multisite Update Capability. The third important feature is the ability to update multiple local databases with a single request. Distributed DBMSs require sophisticated distributed concurrency control protocols which guarantee that two or more users do not attempt to update the same data simultaneously. They also require distributed commit protocols that allow distributed DBMSs to determine if and when updates to the database are completed. These protocols add to the complexity of the distributed DBMS, which in turn adds to the communications cost and response time of distributed requests.

DISTRIBUTED DBMS COMPONENTS

Exhibit 31.1 depicts the major software components of a distributed DBMS in a client/server environment. Distributed DBMS products differ in their components, so the availability of key features also differs.

Distributed DBMSs containing a request optimizer support location and replication transparency, whereas distributed DBMSs containing gateways provide DBMS transparency. Distributed DBMSs containing a sophisticated distributed execution manager enable updates across multiple data managers. The keyword here is sophistication; that is, all distributed DBMSs contain a distributed execution manager to retrieve data from multiple data managers, but not all distributed execution managers are sufficiently powerful to support distributed updates.

Distributed Request Optimizer

The distributed request optimizer hides the existence of multiple databases from the user. The three relational database tables shown in Exhibit 31.2 illustrate this point. Assuming the three tables are visible to a user who wants to retrieve employee Davis' salary, the user needs to retrieve the Davis information from the Employee1 Table at Site1 and Davis information from the Employee2 Table at either Site1 or Site2. The SQL request (query 1) would be written as:

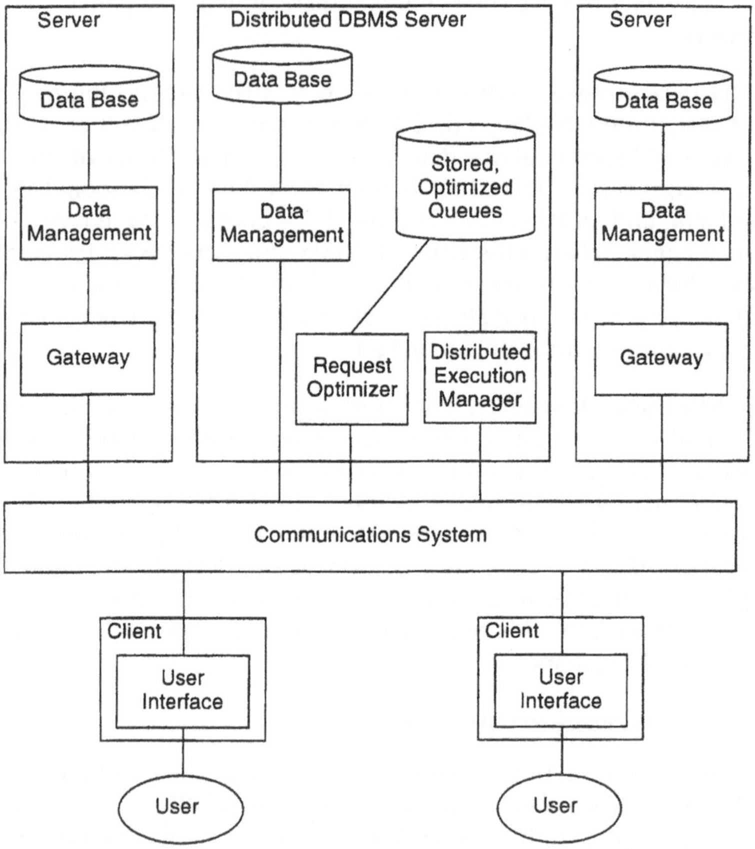

Exhibit 31.1. Major Components of a Distributed DBMS

Employee 1 — Site 1

Name	Salary	Department
Ackman	5000	Car
Baker	4500	Car

Employee 2 — Site 2

Name	Salary	Department
Carson	4800	Toy
Davis	5100	Toy

Employee 2 — Site 3

Name	Salary	Department
Carson	4800	Toy
Davis	5100	Toy

Exhibit 31.2. Employee Database Information Replicated and Distributed to Three Sites

Employee

EmpId	Name	Salary	Tax	ManagerNumber	Department
100	Smith	10000	1000	20	3
200	Jones	1333	122	40	14

Exhibit 31.3. Centralized Employee Information

```
select Salary
from Employee1 at Site1
where Name = "Davis"
UNION
select Salary
from Employee2 at Site2
where Name = "Davis";
```

Alternatively, the user could formulate the request as if all of the data were in a centralized database. The simplified request (query 2) would be:

```
select Salary
from Employee
where Name = "Davis";
```

The distributed request optimizer accesses data location and distribution information maintained by the distributed DBMS and converts query 2 to query 1.

Exhibit 31.3 illustrates a more compelling example. To change the department number of Smith from 3 to 15, the user or programmer would write query 3:

```
update Employee
set Department = 15
where EmpId = 100;
```

However, if the information in the table in Exhibit 31.3 is stored in four tables at four different sites (as shown in Exhibit 31.4), the distributed request optimizer modifies query 3 to the following complex program (query 4):

```
select Name, Sal, Tax, into $Name, $Sal, $Tax
from Employee1
where EmpId = 100;
select ManagerNumber into $ManagerNumber
from Employee2
where EmpId = 100;
```

Employee 1 (Department <10)

EmpId	Name	Salary	Tax
100	Smith	10000	1000

Employee 2 (Department <10)

EmpId	ManagerNumber	Department
100	20	3

Employee 3 (Department ≥10)

Name	Name	Department
200	Jones	14

Employee 4 (Department ≥10)

EmpId	Salary	Tax	ManagerNumber
200	1333	122	40

Exhibit 31.4. Employee Information Distributed to Four Sites

```
insert into Employee3
(EmpId, Name, Department)
(100, $Name, 15);
insert into Employee4
(EmpId, Sal, Tax, ManagerNumber)
(10, $Sal, $Tax, $ManagerNumber);
delete Employee1
where EmpId = 100;
delete Employee2
where EmpId = 100;
```

As this example illustrates, a distributed request optimizer greatly simplifies the task of the user or programmer because the request optimizer hides the four tables in Exhibit 31.4 from the user. The user or programmer can express the relatively simple request in query 3 terms rather than using the more complicated query 4.

When the database administrator moves a table from one site to another, the users or programmers do not need to modify their requests. Instead, the distributed request optimizer translates the user request with updated information about the table location.

Distributed request optimizers have some disadvantages, but each disadvantage has a counter argument. For example:

- Distributed request optimizers are expensive to build or purchase. However, the expense should be offset by savings in time necessary for users and programmers to formulate requests.
- Like any general optimizer, it may be possible to program a request that executes faster than the same request generated by the optimizer. However, optimizers take only seconds while programmers may require hours to implement the optimizations.

Gateways

Some distributed DBMSs support multiple types of local data managers. When this occurs, each request or part of a request to be executed by the local data manager must be translated to a format that the local data manager can execute. Gateways perform this type of translation.

If the global request is expressed in SQL and a data manager supports SQL, the transformation may be trivial and only needs to consider different SQL dialects. However, if the global request is expressed in SQL and a database manager does not support SQL, then a much more sophisticated gateway is necessary. The translation problem can be illustrated with some examples.

Example 1. Suppose that a local data manager consists of two files: a Department file containing DepartmentName and Budget and an Employee file containing EmployeeName, Salary, and DepartmentName. The following SQL request must be translated to a program containing file I/O commands:

```
select *
from Employee
where DepartmentName = "Car";
```

Depending on the file structures used by the file system data manager, the resulting program may perform one of the following:

- Search linearly for all records in the Employee file containing the value "Car" in the DepartmentName field.
- Perform a binary search for records in the Employee file ordered by the DepartmentName field.
- Do an index lookup for records in the Employee file indexed by the DepartmentName field.

Example 2. The following SQL request requires that the generated program access and join together records from both the Department and Employee files that have the same value for the DepartmentName field:

```
select *
from Department, Employee
where Department.DepartmentName = Employee.DepartmentName;
```

Depending on the file structures used by the file system data manager, the resulting program may perform one of the following:

- Nested (inner-outer) loop. For each record in Employee, every record in Department is retrieved and tested to determine whether they match.
- Index. For each record in Employee, the index to DepartmentName is used to retrieve matching records in Department.
- Sort-merge join. If both Employee and Department are sorted physically by DepartmentName, then both files should be scanned at the same time to locate matching records.
- Hash join. Records from both Employee and Department files are mapped into the same file using a hashing function applied to DepartmentName. Records with the same value for DepartmentName are placed in the same location within the file.

Gateways have the same disadvantages and advantages as request optimizers:

- Gateways are expensive to build or purchase. However, the expense should be offset with savings in user and programmer time.
- Like any general optimizer, it may be possible to manually translate a request that executes faster than the corresponding request generated by the gateway. However, gateways take only seconds to execute, whereas manual optimization may require hours of programmer time.

Distributed Execution Manager

A distributed execution manager controls and coordinates the execution of requests or pieces of requests by one or more data managers. It also provides distributed concurrency control and commit protocols.

A transaction is a set of reads and writes and ends with a commit (if all operations are successful) or with a rollback (if one or more of the operations is not successful). A distributed DBMS may execute several transactions concurrently as long as one transaction does not try to update data being accessed by another transaction. The execution of several concurrent transactions is said to be serializable if the results are the same as a serial execution of the transactions.

Several approaches are used to guarantee the serializability of concurrently executing transactions, including locking, timestamp ordering, and optimistic approaches. These approaches also are used in centralized databases, but their implementation is much more complicated in distributed systems.

TWO-PHASE COMMIT PROTOCOL

Distributed transactions that update data in several databases need a mechanism to determine whether to commit or rollback changes made in each database. Protocols have been developed to solve these problems; the most popular is the two-phase commit protocol. In the two-phase commit protocol, each local data manager reports its results to the distributed execution manager. When the distributed execution manager determines that all subrequests are completed, it performs the following two-phase commit protocol:

1. It sends a message asking each local data manager if it still can make local changes permanent.
2. After receiving an OK to commit message from each local data manager, it sends a final commit message to each local data manager. If anything goes wrong either before or during the two-phase commit protocol, the distributed execution manager sends rollback messages, which cause all local data managers to undo any changes made to their local databases.

The distributed concurrency control and commit protocol messages add expense and delay to the execution of requests that update data at multiple sites. To avoid these expenses and delays, some distributed database management systems do not permit updates at all, while other only permit updates to a single database. If updates to a single database are permitted, the local data manager performs the concurrency control and may not support the two-phase commit protocol. It is very difficult to modify the local managers to accommodate the distributed concurrency control and commit protocols. This is why most distributed DBMSs that support multisite updates usually support only one type of data manager.

DISTRIBUTED DBMS PRODUCT CLASSES

There are many products that provide various combinations of facilities for managing distributed DBMSs. Exhibit 31.5 identifies four product classes and three of their features.

Message-oriented middleware (MOM) transfers database requests from the user's site to one or more data servers. While these requests may

Tool and Replication	Multisite Updates	DBMS Transparency	Location Transparency
MOMS	Somewhat	No	No
TP Monitors	Yes	No	No
DB Middleware	Yes	Yes	No
Distributed DBMSs	Yes	Yes	Yes

Exhibit 31.5. Distributed DBMS Product Classes

involve updates, there may be no distributed concurrency control and distributed commitment. Examples of MOM products include MessageQ from Digital Equipment Corp. (DEC), MQSeries from IBM, Pipes from PeerLogic Inc., and MSMQ from Microsoft.

TP monitors process transactions involving data within multiple databases. However, the application must be aware of the command formats in the underlying DBMSs, be aware of the location of each database, and update all copies of any replicated database. Popular TP monitors include BEA Systems' Tuxedo, Transarc's Encina, and Microsoft's Transaction Server.

DB middleware includes Java Database Connectivity (JDBC), Open Database Connectivity (ODBC) and its enhancement, OLE-DB, and IBI's EDA/SQL. All of these middleware toolkits contain facilities that convert user requests into the formats required by the underlying DBMS or file system (DBMS transparency), as well as processing transactions involving multiple databases (multisite updates). However, the application must know the location of each database and update all copies of any replicated database.

Distributed database management systems are marketed by Microsoft, Oracle, IBM, Sybase, and Informix. These systems support transactions involving multiple databases, as well as DBMS transparency and location and replication transparency. For more vendor information, see the recommended Web sites at the end of this paper.

RECOMMENDED COURSE OF ACTION

Database administrators should assess the needs of users and decide if the client/server system is to support one or several data servers. If several data servers are needed, then the database administrator determines which of the following features are needed:

- Location and replication transparency. If this feature is needed, the database administrator should purchase a distributed DBMS that supports a request optimizer.
- DBMS transparency. A requirement for this feature means that the database administrator should build or buy gateways to hide the languages required by heterogeneous data managers.
- Multisite updates. If this feature is needed, it is best to build a sophisticated distributed execution manager that supports concurrency control and commit protocols among the data managers.

After the database administrator has determined which features are necessary, a product should be chosen to meet the user's needs.

Recommended Web Sites

For more information about the products mentioned in this article, see the following Web pages:

- BEA Systems, Inc. (Tuxedo)
  385 Moffett Park Drive
  Sunnyvale, CA 94089-1208
  Telephone: (408) 743-4000
  Fax: (408) 734-9234
  http://www.beasys.com
  http://www.beasys.com/products/tuxedo/index.htm
- Digital Equipment Corp. (DECMessageQ)
  111 Powdermill Road
  Maynard, MA 01754-1418
  Telephone: (978) 493-5111
  http://www.digital.com/decmessageq/
- IBM Home Page
  http://www.ibm.com
- IBM (MQSeries)
  http://www.software.hosting.ibm.com/ts/mqseries/
- Information Builders Inc. (EDA/SQL)
  Two Penn Plaza
  New York, NY 10121-2898
  Telephone: (212) 736-4433
  Fax: (212) 967-6406
  http://www.IBI.com
- Informix Home Page
  http://www.informix.com/
- Java Database Connectivity (JDBC) Home Page
  http://java.sun.com/products/jdbc/index.html
- Microsoft Corporation Home Page
  http://www.microsoft.com/
- Microsoft Message Queue Server (MSMQ)
  http://www.microsoft.com/ntserver/guide/msmq.asp
- Microsoft Open Database Connectivity (ODBC)
  http://www.microsoft.com/data/odbc/
- Microsoft OLE DB
  http://www.microsoft.com/data/oledb/

- Microsoft Transaction Server
  http://www.microsoft.com/ntserver/guide/trans_intro.asp
- Oracle Home Page
  http://www.oracle.com
- PeerLogic, Inc. (Pipes)
  555 De Haro Street
  San Francisco, CA 94107-2348
  Telephone/Fax: (800) 733-7601 or (415) 626-4545
  Fax: (415) 626-4710
  E-mail: info@peerlogic.com
  http://www.peerlogic.com
- Sybase Home Page
  http://www.sybase.com
- Transarc (Encina)
  The Gulf Tower
  707 Grant Street
  Pittsburgh, PA 15219
  Telephone: (412) 338-4400
  Fax: (412) 338-6977
  E-mail: sales@transarc.com
  http://www.transarc.com/afs/transarc.com/public/www/Public/ProdServ/Product/Encina/index.html

Chapter 32

Component Design for Relational Databases

Ashvin Iyengar

Component-based object-oriented architectures are becoming increasingly popular in building industrial strength applications. However, relational databases are not going to be replaced by object databases in the foreseeable future. This paper explores the ramifications of component-based designs on data management and offers strategies which could be deployed in the use of relational centralized databases with object-oriented component-based application architectures.

WHY RELATIONAL DATABASES ARE HERE TO STAY

From a pure application design perspective, object-oriented databases would be much more suitable for use with object-oriented component-based application architectures. However, the business realities are more complex and include the following considerations:

- Object-oriented databases are not mature enough to be entrusted with the job of managing large corporate data;
- It is more difficult to find professionals with experience in administration as well as the design of object-oriented databases;
- The vast majority of corporations are currently using relational databases to manage business information; and
- Most current live applications have been designed and developed to work with relational databases.

MOVING TOWARDS A COMPONENT-BASED ARCHITECTURE STANDARD

The subject of object-oriented design and programming involving relational databases has been well explored. More often than not, the data model is constructed using pure relational database modeling techniques with little if any consideration for object-oriented design techniques. This necessitates the use of impedance matching techniques to allow object-oriented applications to interact with relational data models.

0-8493-9822-3/00/$0.00+$.50

Application architectures are becoming increasingly component based to satisfy the need for flexible as well as manageable systems. The effort to move away from large monolithic applications has been underway for a number of years. This has resulted in the adoption of client-server based architecture as the de facto standard in the industry. However, with lack of proper design, client-server architectures became just as monolithic as mainframe applications and thus inherited all the maintenance problems associated with large monolithic applications. Object-oriented design techniques and multi-tiered architectures were adopted in order to solve this problem. Component design is a natural next step in the evolution of application architectures since it combines the principles of object-oriented design with multi-tiered application architecture. In addition, industrywide acceptance of the incremental and iterative software development methodology over the old waterfall development methodology has provided an additional thrust towards component-based design.

Some of the other factors contributing towards making component-based application design the de facto standard are:

- The maturing of technologies like DCOM (distributed component object model) and CORBA;
- The plethora of new technologies encouraging the design and deployment of components over the Web (e.g., JavaBeans);
- The ability to design, develop, and deploy components using high level, widely used applications like Visual Basic;
- The potential for using third-party components along with in-house applications in order to fulfill specific needs (e.g., a professional third-party charting component); and
- The resulting relative ease of component replacement.

BACKGROUND OF MULTI-TIERED ARCHITECTURES

The current thrust is towards the use of distributed, component-based application architectures. The ever-increasing need to deploy applications over the Web and the resulting security considerations have led to a n-tiered architecture, using, at the very least, three distinct tiers, as follows:

- Web server;
- Application server; and
- Database server.

Whereas, a number of studies have shown that pure object-oriented applications are difficult to design and develop and that the payoffs information technology (IT) executives had hoped for in terms of reuse are seldom realized, multi-tiered architecture is here to stay. Three-tiered architecture is, in fact, the industry standard and a wide variety of application development environments from Smalltalk to Visual Basic support and encourage the use of this standard architecture.

In general, a three-tiered architecture has the following layers:

- Interface layer;
- Business layer; and
- Data layer.

The driving force behind three-tiered architecture is the need to support both flexibility and robustness in applications. De-coupling the interface layer from the database offers the advantage of changes in the database that need not affect the interface layer directly, thereby isolating the effects of a change in either layer. The interface layer describes how the application interacts with the outside world. If the outside world is comprised of end users, then the interface layer refers to a user interface. Alternatively, if it is comprised of client applications, it refers to an application interface.

Arguably, the main payoff involved in object-oriented architectures is not reuse but rather change management. Effective change management is also the goal of three-tiered architectures. Since three-tiered architectures are easier to implement with object-based (if not object-oriented) systems, new life has been extended to object-based systems. In this article, a distinction is being made between object-oriented and object-based systems. Object-based systems implement classes and objects, but do not permit other aspects of object-oriented programming like inheritance and polymorphism. So whereas the three pillars of object-oriented programming can be said to be encapsulation, inheritance, and polymorphism, object-based programming concerns itself with mainly encapsulation.

A leading example of an object-based application development is Visual Basic. Visual Basic is to the client-server world what Cobol is to the mainframe world. Since classes in Visual Basic are implemented using DCOM (distributed component object model), it is extremely easy to develop and deploy components using Visual Basic.

An object-based component can be described as a set of objects collaborating to provide a common functionality and implementing a common interface. Thus, an object-based component improves the encapsulation aspect of object-based applications. By virtue of this it also increases the flexibility as well as robustness of an object-based application, since changes to the component are isolated.

It has already been argued that the main thrust towards three-tiered architecture is coming from a need for effective change management. Change management, as used in this paper, encompasses the concepts of flexibility and robustness. It has also been argued that object-based applications by virtue of their support for encapsulation are a natural choice for the implementation of business solutions with underlying multi-tiered architectures. Since a component-based architecture enhances the ability of multi-tiered architectures to deliver on its promise, it would be logical to conclude that component-based multi-tiered architectures are here to stay.

So the prevalent application development environment can be said to have the following features:

- Multi-tiered architecture;
- Relational databases;
- Object-based applications; and
- Component-based application architecture.

APPLICATION ARCHITECTURE EXAMPLE

Now this article will take an example where a set of three tables provides a certain functionality (e.g., hold information pertaining to interest rates in a portfolio management system) and three discrete applications that interact with these three tables. It will start with a simple two-tiered application architecture example and note the problems in the chosen context.

Then it will move to a more object-oriented version of the same problem and again note the problems with the approach. Finally, it will illustrate a solution to the same problem using a data-component approach.

In Exhibit 32.1, Application A1 is responsible for displaying and maintaining information in M1 (the set of tables T1, T2, and T3 constituting a sub data model). Applications A2, A3 use the information in M1 to do their processing. Note that Application A1 interacts with all the tables in M1, whereas Applications A2, A3 interact with only T3.

The shortcomings of two-tiered applications have already been noted. In this case, the tight coupling between the applications and the data is obvious, and consequently, flexibility is severely compromised. Also, there are three different applications interacting with the same data and consequently, complexity is increased since a change in data storage/design would necessitate change to all the client applications.

To make this design more object-oriented, now move to Exhibit 32.2 which illustrates a three-tiered object-oriented architecture. Applications A1, A2, and A3 contain their own relational to object mapping layer (also known as impedance matching layer). Now consider that new business rules necessitate a change to M1. M1 is a sub data model corresponding to functionality F1 (e.g., performance history of various investment options in a portfolio management system). If the new data model involves changing the way information is represented in T3, then all applications involving T3 (in this case Applications A1, A2, and A3) have to be updated. In addition to requiring duplication of effort this design increases the risk of applica-

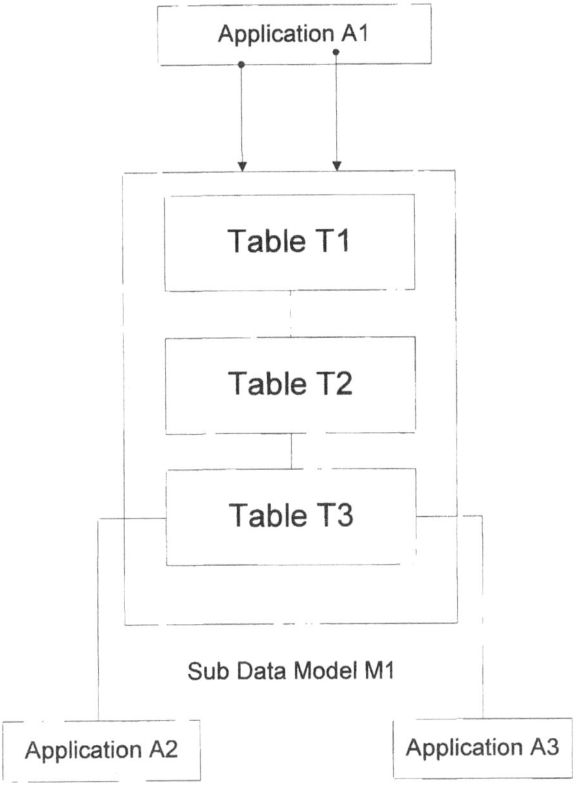

Exhibit 32.1. Two-Tier Application Architecture

tion malfunction, since it is possible to miss updating an application which needs updating. Also note that even aside from complicating change management, this design involves duplication of effort in terms of data access as well as relational to object mapping.

In order to solve the above-mentioned problems, modify the design to produce a more object-oriented approach by introducing components. Exhibit 32.3 introduces a component C1 that encapsulates sub data model M1. This makes C1 a data-component. Consequently, to the methodology illustrated in Exhibit 32.3 is referred to as the data-component approach.

ADVANTAGES/FEATURES OF THE DATA-COMPONENT APPROACH

The data-component approach, as illustrated in Exhibit 32.3, offers the following features and advantages:

- Applications do not access the tables directly but use the interface functions provided by the interface layer in C1;

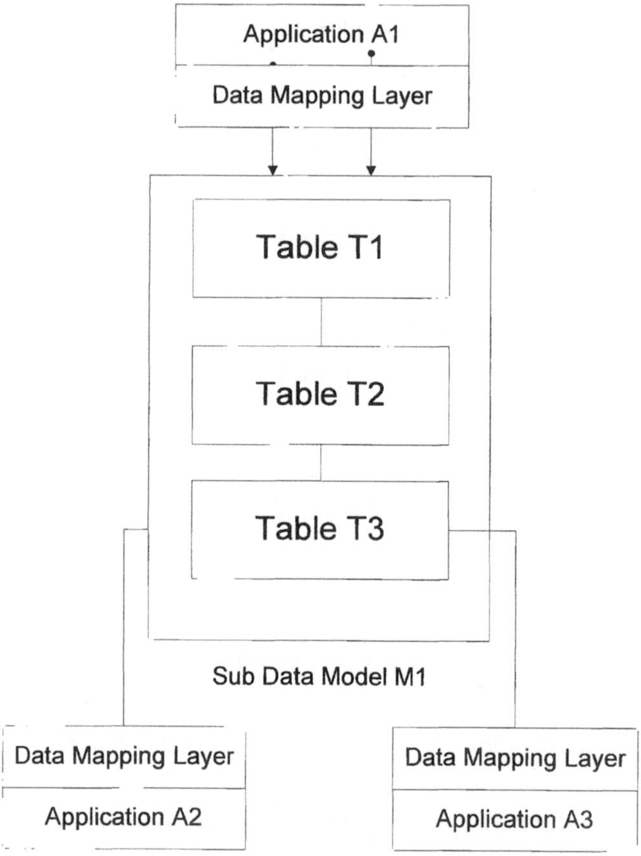

Exhibit 32.2. Three-Tier Application Architecture with Data-Mapping Layer

- Satisfies an important OOD (object-oriented design) requirement: keep function and data together;
- Eliminates redundant data access as well as data mapping;
- Separates the GUI from the business logic — an important requirement of three-tier client server computing;
- Allows implementation of n-tiered architecture since C1 can be deployed on an application server;
- Provides much better change management (which as elaborated before, is an even greater benefit of object-oriented development than reuse), since changes in the data model no longer affect client applications directly. The only time the client applications are affected is when changes to the data model/functionality affect the interface between C1 and the client applications;

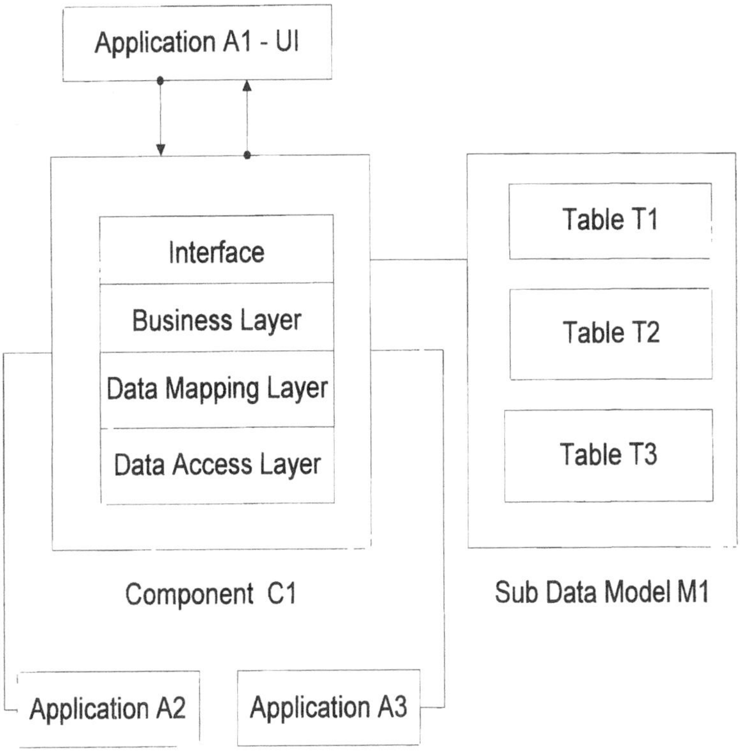

Exhibit 32.3. Application Architecture Example Using Data-Component Approach

- Allows implementation of multiple interface or different views of data thus adding a new twist to the classic MVC (Model View Controller) object-oriented architecture;
- Provides data source independence, since changing the source of the data will affect only the data access and data mapping layers of the component and the client applications will be insulated from any such change; and
- Reduces the effort involved in allowing new applications to access the data.

DISADVANTAGES/LIMITATIONS OF THE DATA-COMPONENT APPROACH

The data-component approach as illustrated in Exhibit 32.3 has the following possible disadvantages or limitations:

- If used indiscriminately, this approach could lead to a proliferation of components thereby increasing the number of applications;

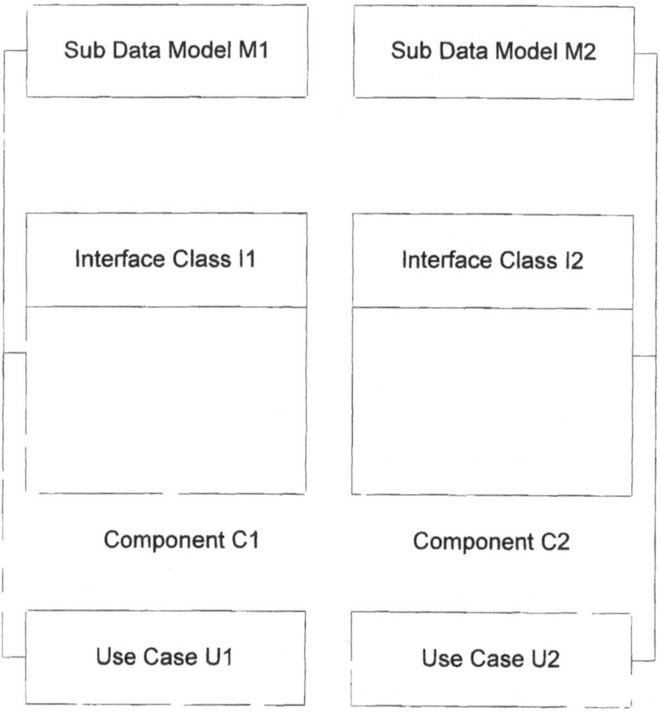

Exhibit 32.4. One-to-One Component to Sub Data Model Example

- Large applications using a large number of components could experience performance degradation, especially while loading the application;
- Each component will possibly have registration requirements, so the task of installing and distributing applications will be more complex; and
- This approach deals primarily with discrete, non-overlapping use cases. Overlapping use cases will create additional complexities that have not been addressed in this approach.

DATA-COMPONENT GRANULARITY CONSIDERATIONS

To prevent proliferation of components, the granularity of the components can be increased. For example as shown in Exhibit 32.4, use cases U1 and U2 use sub data models M1 and M2 correspondingly.

Instead of having components C1 and C2 that correspond to use cases U1 and U2, if U1 and U2 are closely related, a single component C (with interfaces I1 and I2) can serve U1 and U2, as illustrated in Exhibit 32.5.

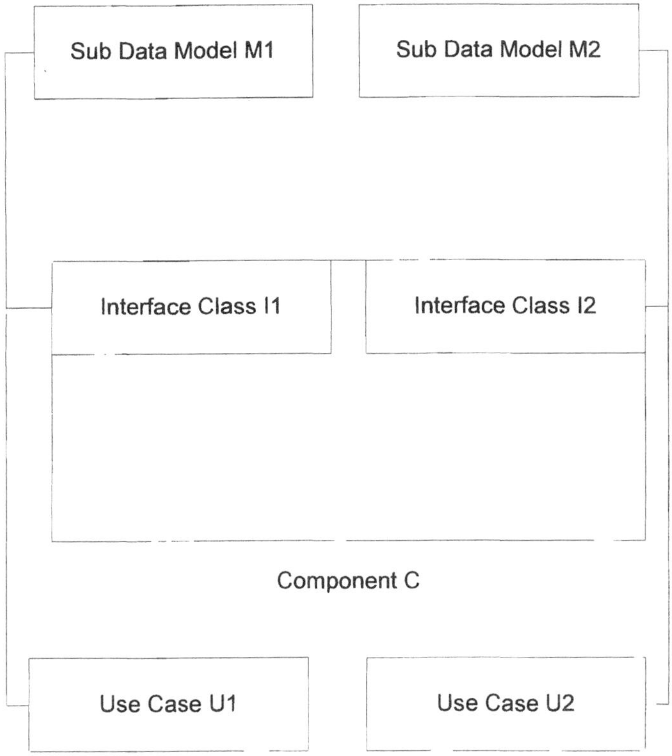

Exhibit 32.5. One-to-Many Component to Sub-Data-Model Example

The same exercise of combining related use cases into components could be carried out through the application design space thereby bringing component proliferation under control.

IMPLEMENTATION OF THE COMPONENT-BASED DESIGN USING MICROSOFT'S ARCHITECTURE

Even though the component technology war between CORBA and DCOM is far from over, the fact remains that DCOM (in some form) has been around longer and is used widely in the industry. It also has, arguably, more opportunities to mature into a stable industrial strength technology. Consequently, Microsoft's DCOM platform is discussed in the implementation of the data-component approach illustrated in Exhibit 32.3.

In Microsoft's DCOM technology there are two main types of components:

1. ActiveX Exe; and
2. ActiveX DLL.

The difference between the two types of components is that the ActiveX Exe is an out-of-process component while the ActiveX DLL is an in-process component. In-process components usually offer significantly better performance than out-of-process components. However, in-process components and their client applications must reside on the same physical machines. With out-of-process components there is no such restriction, therefore out-of-process components offer greater flexibility in terms of deployment at the cost of application performance.

The choice between in-process and out-of-process components would therefore depend on the physical architecture. Note that three-tier software architectures can be deployed using two-tier physical architectures. In a two-tier implementation, the database runs on a database server and the user interface layer as well as the business layer runs on the client desktops. This kind of implementation is also called fat-client, since most of the applications are deployed on individual workstations. Whereas this might be sufficient for a small shop, for larger shops, distribution as well as maintenance of all the various components on individual workstations can prove to be a daunting as well as error-prone task. For this reason, larger shops may prefer to implement a physical three-tier architecture which would involve client workstations interacting with an application server which in turn would interact with a database server. While this approach alleviates some of the distribution problems inherent in the two-tier architecture, a new problem is created with multiple workstations accessing the same application on the application server concurrently. Clearly, it would be counter-productive to start up a new copy of the application for every workstation that needs it. Therefore, some sort of a queuing solution is inevitable. It is in this respect that the DCOM architecture is yet to mature. Microsoft's solution to the problem involves use of MTS (Microsoft's transaction server), but that may not be a universally viable solution for every situation.

It is also worth noting that even though it is technically easy to convert an ActiveX DLL to an ActiveX Exe, there are other considerations involved which might necessitate knowledge of the physical architecture in advance. The main consideration is network traffic. With out-of-process components, performance requirements usually dictate the use of fewer but longer messages, whereas with in-process components, frequencies of messages do not result in performance penalties.

If the generic architecture example illustrated in Exhibit 32.3 were to be implemented on a Microsoft platform, the following notes may apply:

- The interface layer of component C1 interfaces with Applications A1, A2, and A3. Since A2 and A3 are inquiry-only applications, they can share a common interface. So, we would have two interface classes, I1 and I2. I1 will implement the interface needed for A1 and I2 would implement the interface needed for applications A2 and A3. In some cases, classes I1 and I2 could be implemented in a separate ActiveX DLL. This has the advantage of providing de-coupling between the client and server applications. In practice, this has to be weighed against the cost of distributing this additional component. There will also be a minor performance penalty involved in separating the interface classes in a separate component, since an additional program will have to be loaded;

- Another factor to be considered while designing the interface layer is the number of parameters needed for the component to query and present the information. Assume for starters a method M1 in component C1, where the number of input parameters is n and the method returns only one value. A change in the input parameters would entail changing method M1 and therefore changing the interface. Therefore, except for trivial methods, it would make sense to encapsulate the data flowing between the component and its client applications, in classes. In this example a class C1M1 would contain all the input parameters as well as result values for method M1 in Component C1. M1 now would be passed a reference to object OC1MI (corresponding to class C1M1). With this approach, if method M1 were to need a new input parameter or need to return an extra result value, the interface would remain unchanged and changes would be restricted to class C1M1 and its usage;
- The business layer of the component should contain most of editing rules and the business logic. Including the editing logic in the business layer of the component goes a long way towards ensuring data integrity since applications that update the data maintained by the component have to use the interface layer of the component. Note that the business layer is not exposed directly to the outside world. External applications can only use the methods exposed by the interface layer, which in turn will interact with the business layer. Also, since the interface layer does not directly interact with the data layer of the component, the business layer has a chance to enforce its business rules and ensure logical integrity; and
- The data layer of the component typically consists of two internal layers namely a relational to object mapping layer and a data access layer. The data access layer is responsible for the actual interaction with the database. The data mapping layer is responsible for mapping relational data into objects. Each record in a relational database is essentially an array of values. If a query returns more than one record (a RecordSet in Microsoft-speak), then we are dealing with a two-dimensional array. The data-mapping layer typically converts a single record to an object and a RecordSet to a collection of objects. Also, for persistent data, the object in the data mapping layer must know how to access the objects in the data access layer in order to store updated

data. It is also worthwhile noting that the data access layer could be implemented as a separate component in itself. That way multiple applications can use the data access layer to manage their interactions with the physical database.

Following are examples of the architectures discussed in this paper:

1. The business layer has classes B1 and B2 that correspond to the interface layer classes I1 and I2. B1 and B2 interact with classes R1,R2,...., RN which implement various business rules. B1 and B2 also interact with corresponding classes DM1 and DM2, which belong to the data mapping layer of the data layer. DM1 and DM2 in turn interact with classes DA1, DA2, and DA3, which access/update data in Tables T1, T2, and T3.
2. Instead of having separate classes B1 and B2, depending on the application, a single class B may suffice.
3. Again, depending on the application, a single class DA may provide the functionality provided by DA1, DA2, and DA3.
4. Note that DM1 and DM2 provide the business view of the data model and this case is basically driven by the choice of B1 and B2 as the business classes. Depending on the requirements, classes DM1, DM2, and DM3 could correspond to DA1, DA2, and DA3 or any other combination that makes sense.
5. Note that classes DM1 and DM2 could create and return a variety of objects. For example, object O11 might correspond to a specific record in the table T1. Object O12 might correspond to a collection of records. Alternatively, O12 may be implemented as an object containing a collection of O11 objects. Similarly, objects O21 through O2N might correspond to Table T2. Alternatively, O21 through O2N might correspond to data linked between Tables T2 and T3 if appropriate.

The possibilities are endless. The examples listed previously illustrate some of the considerations that might come into play during the design of the component. To reiterate one of the main points in this article, effective change management, assume that a change is to be made to this design. Instead of accessing data in Tables T2 and T3 directly, applications must use a View instead. In this case, only relevant classes in the data access layer and maybe the data mapping layer will need to be changed. All other classes in the business and the interface layer of the component can remain unchanged. Also, the client applications using the component remain unaffected. Thus use of a multi-tiered component-based architecture has provided for flexibility (providing ease of change by restricting the area of change) as well as robustness (limiting the scope of the effect of change).

DATA-COMPONENT MINING

Data-component mining is the process by which an existing data model can be analyzed and broken up into sub data models with associated data-components. One approach to component mining is to study the data model to identify loosely coupled sets of entities. Each such set of entities can be called a sub-data model. Each such sub-data model is a good candidate for a component and more so if the sub-data model is used by more than one application. Use cases have become a standard way of defining requirements/functionality in object-oriented design. A list of existing as well as future use cases can also provide a valuable perspective during data-component mining design. Related use cases can be combined to help identify sub-data models and consequently corresponding data components.

For example, in a portfolio management system, analysis of the ERD (entity relationship diagram) of the data model might suggest that the set of entities containing historical performance data could constitute a sub-data model M1. Similarly, the set of entities pertaining to investment choices in a client's portfolio could constitute another sub-data model M2. There is now a potential use for two data components: C1 corresponding to model M1 (historical performance data) and C2 corresponding to model M2 (client's investment choices). Alternatively, it could start with use cases. For example, consider the following use cases:

- U1 — Provide inquiry of client's investment elections;
- U2 — Provide investment election change update/change;
- U3 — Provide inquiry of investment performance data;
- U4 — Provide update of investment performance data; and
- U5 — Calculate portfolio values for a given client.

U1 and U2 deal with the same information (a client's investment choices). Similarly, U3 and U4 deal with the same information (investment performance data). U5 deals with the client's investment choices as well as investment performance data. Since investment performance data is independent of a client's investment choices, the entities in the data model corresponding to investment performance data, can be said to be loosely coupled with the entities pertaining to client investment elections. Therefore, investment performance data as well as client investment choices are both candidates for sub-data models with corresponding data components. The implementation of U5 would then involve use of both data components.

CONCLUSION

The data component approach to data management can be valuable in an environment involving object-oriented applications and relational databases. The primary advantage provided by this approach is ensuring that the application responsible for updating information is responsible for providing inquiry of the same information, thereby providing for superior change management. This approach can be used in any environment that allows development of component-based applications.

Section V Checklist

1. Does your organization have a dedicated staff for data administration? If not, does this present difficulties for data integration?
2. Is your organization considering either implementation of distributed database or data warehousing? If so, would this work?
3. What factors would need to change in your organization in order to implement a new database concept such as data warehousing?
4. In your opinion, are most database configurations fundamentally the same? Has this been demonstrated in your environment?
5. How is database information managed in your environment? Is there a dedicated group for data administration? If not, should one be created?
6. Does your organization suffer from multiple database repositories that do not communicate or share data dictionary information? How will this be resolved?
7. Is the lack of Enterprise Data Management contributing to the difficulties of system development and support in your IS environment? If so, can this be measured in a quantifiable manner?
8. Has the use of client/server techniques presented challenges in managing database over traditional application systems?
9. Does your organization treat each client/server application differently when designing the database access technique or have guidelines been established that standardize the link?
10. How complicated is the production data flow in your environment? What tools or techniques are used to document or identify data processes?
11. Has data analysis become more important to your application development efforts? If so, how much emphasis is placed on accurately assessing data processes?
12. Based on your perception of data maturity, how would you assess the state of your organization's database stability and organization? What steps would you take to improve this?
13. Has your organization attempted a portfolio analysis of the various data repositories in your organization? If not, would this be worthwhile to improve consolidation of enterprise data?
14. Does your organization struggle from proprietary data structures that cannot communicate with each other? If so, how is data shared between environments? Has this caused more redundant data to exist?

15. What are the processing demands of most data transactions in your environment? Does this force frequent upgrades of hardware, or is its increased demand handled through performance tuning?

Section VI
Operating Platforms

Ongoing advancements in hardware platforms and corresponding operating systems have brought about new opportunities for building new systems. Development managers now have numerous technical options in which to create and deploy enterprise level business applications. However, selecting the most appropriate combination of platform and system environment has become critical to the overall success of application development efforts. In addition, many operating platforms have been proprietary in nature which potentially limits true portability of some applications. Although some vendors are striving toward common operating system standards, industry competition will continue to challenge those who seek uniformity in building operating-neutral software applications. This is especially difficult when so much press has be given to breaking up monopoly driven vendors. It becomes questionable as to whether single vendor operating systems bring more standardization to an organization than multiple level operating systems. The rise in popularity of new systems, such as Linux, indicates an interest but not necessarily a commitment at the corporate level.

One of the most significant differences between vendor operating environments exists in the object middleware arena. The two strongest standards have been the Common Object Request Broker Architecture (CORBA) and the Component Object Model. However, each proposes different mechanisms that affect the development of object-based systems. Chapter 33, "Evaluating Object Middleware: DCOM and CORBA," furnishes an important discussion about these two technologies and the impact on application development efforts. Microsoft's COM vs. Object Management Group's CORBA has been the topic of much debate. Neither technology has emerged as the single standard, and it is expected that application managers will need to understand both technologies before choosing one over the other.

Windows NT has steadily gained popularity as a Network Operating Environment as well as a Desktop Operating System. The benefits of Windows NT have been lauded by those who seek stronger functionality in operating platforms. But migration to Windows NT may be complicated, even for existing users of Windows 9x software. Chapter 34, "Transitioning to Windows NT," describes some of the issues required for users of Unix and NetWare operating systems. But it also includes other important aspects of migration that could be applicable to other operating environments. In conjunction, Chapter 35, "Windows NT Architecture," offers meaningful insight into the subtle but important components of the operating system as applied to servers and workstations. Current versions of Windows NT, and the newer version Windows 2000, are sophisticated packages that can offer solutions not found in other operating software. However, implementation and support, as it relates to the development of application software, requires a willingness to accept the overhead that comes with Windows NT platform.

In contrast to Windows NT, NetWare has been used longer in many organizations. Despite perceived weaknesses with the NetWare platform, many environments still rely on the established connectivity built on the NetWare protocols. Recent and long awaited improvements to NetWare include functionality to enable NetWare to become more compatible with other communication protocols. Chapter 36, "NetWare/IP," describes the TCP/IP implementation within the product. The proprietary IPX/SPX protocol traditionally used by NetWare requires additional overhead when used in conjunction with TCP/IP. However, as with any communication interface, there are arguments for and against the use of native NetWare drivers as opposed to the more generic TCP/IP. This chapter offers a balanced view of NetWare's capabilities within the Internet-based environment.

Supporting changes to applications over networks has become more complicated due to the size and scope of many files used by a system. Determining how a file was corrupted or the impact of an update across the network environment can be difficult to assess without better synchronization. Chapter 37, "Software Configuration Management in a Client/Server Environment," discusses the fundamental principles associated with the synchronization process needed for reliable system functionality. Many organizations have poor methods for assessing file access and often waste time and effort tracking down problems during development and post-implementation periods. Although some vendors offer tools to ease this problem, it requires a basic understanding of the issues in order to choose the right strategy and/or packaged solution. As applications and networks grow with more complexity, it will become more difficult to support client/server applications without a configuration management technique in place.

Chapter 33

Evaluating Object Middleware: DCOM and CORBA

T.M. Rajkumar and Richard J. Lewis, Jr.

OBJECTS IN THE FORM OF SOFTWARE COMPONENTS ARE CHANGING the way applications are developed and delivered. Component technology breaks the application into intrinsic components and then glues them to create the application. Using components, the application is easier to build, robust, and delivered quicker. A middleware is used as the object communication bus to enable distribution of these components across heterogeneous networks and operating systems.

The need for reliable distributed computing middleware environments is becoming pressing as three-tier client-server networks become commonplace. While much of the industry backs the Common Object Request Broker Architecture (CORBA) as the standard object bus, Microsoft is pushing its own Distributed Component Object Model (DCOM). Managers and system architects have to determine what object bus to use in their companies. This chapter reviews the two primary forces in distributed object technology, CORBA and DCOM. It discusses their individual strengths and weaknesses across a wide spectrum of categories, and gives some sensible advice on what technologies might be best applicable to current projects. Finally, it takes a look into what the future has in store for these architectures.

WHAT IS CORBA?

CORBA is a set of distributed system standards promoted by an industry standards group called the Object Management Group (OMG). The idea behind CORBA is to allow applications to communicate with one another no matter where they are located or who has designed them. The CORBA standard defines the ORB, a mechanism through which distributed software and their clients may interact. It specifies an extensive set of bus-related services for creating and deleting objects, accessing them by name,

0-8493-9822-3/00/$0.00+$.50

storing them in persistent store, externalizing their states, and defining ad hoc relationships between them.

History

OMG has more than 700 member companies who have been working on the CORBA standard for eight years. CORBA 1.1 was introduced in 1991 by OMG and defined the Interface Definition Language (IDL) and the Application Programming Interfaces (API) that enable client/server object interaction within a specific implementation of an Object Request Broker (ORB). CORBA 2.0, adopted in December 1994, defines true interoperability by specifying how ORBs from different vendors can interoperate.

Since 1989, the Object Management Group has been working to create standards for object-based component software within the framework of its Object Management Architecture. The key component is the Common Object Request Broker Architecture (CORBA), whose specification was adopted in 1991. In 1994 CORBA 2.0 defined interoperability between objects in heterogeneous systems. Since then the world has seen a growing list of CORBA implementations come to market. Dozens of vendors have recently announced support for the CORBA Internet Inter ORB Protocol (IIOP), which guarantees CORBA interoperability over the Internet. Specifications of several generally useful support services now populate the Object Services segment of the architecture, and work is proceeding rapidly in specifying domain specific technologies in many areas, including finance, healthcare, and telecommunications.

CORBA Architecture

The four main elements of the object management architecture are shown in Exhibit 33.1 and are the following:

- **ORBs:** The ORB defines the object bus and is the middleware that establishes the client/server relationships between objects. The ORB provides interoperability between applications on different machines in heterogeneous distributed environments and seamlessly interconnects multiple-object systems.
- **Object Services:** These define the system-level object frameworks that extend the bus. They include services such as security, transaction management, and data exchange.
- **Common facilities:** These define horizontal and vertical application frameworks that are used directly by business objects. They deal more with the client than a server.

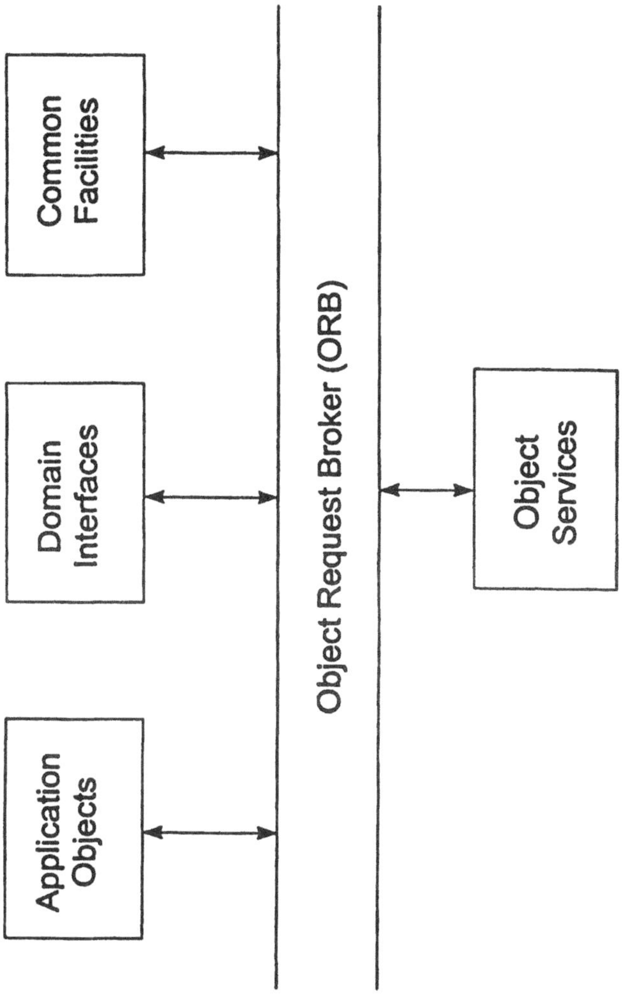

Exhibit 33.1. The Main Elements of the Object Management Architecture

- **Domain interfaces:** These are interfaces like common facilities but are specific to a certain domain, such as manufacturing, medical, telecommunications, etc.
- **Application interfaces:** These objects are defined by the developer to solve the business problem. These interfaces are not standardized.

ORB Component and CORBA Structure

Interface definition language (IDL) stubs provide static interfaces to object services. These define how clients invoke corresponding services on the servers. The ORB intercepts the call and is responsible for finding an object that can implement the request, pass it to the parameters, invoke its method, and return the results. The client does not have to be aware of where the object is located, its programming language, its operating system, the communication protocol that is used, or any other system aspects that are not part of an object's interface. The CORBA structure as shown in Exhibit 33.2 specifies the workings of the ORB component of the OMG specification.

While IDL stubs are static, dynamic invocations enable the client to find (discover) at run time a service that it wants to invoke, obtain a definition, issue a call, and return a result.

On the server side, the object implementation does not differentiate between a static or dynamic invocation. The ORB locates an object adapter, transmits the parameter, and transfers control to the object implementation via an IDL skeleton or a dynamic skeleton interface (DSI). The IDL skeleton provides support for the IDL-defined methods of a particular object class. The DSI provides a run-time binding mechanism for servers by inspecting the parameters passed by the message to determine the target object and method.

The object adapter accepts the requests for service on behalf of the server objects. If necessary, it starts up server processes, instantiates or activates the server objects, assigns an object id (object reference), and passes the requests to them. The object adapter also registers the classes it supports and their run-time object instances with the implementation repository. Object adapters are specific to each programming language, and there can be multiple object adapter for every object.

Inter-ORB protocols allow CORBA products to interoperate. CORBA 2.0 specifies direct ORB-to-ORB interoperability mechanisms when the ORBs are resident in the same domain (i.e., they understand the object references, IDL type system, etc.). Bridge-based interoperability is used otherwise. The bridge then maps the ORB-specific information across domains. General Inter-ORB protocol specifies the transfer syntax and a set of standard message formats for ORB interoperation. Internet Inter-ORB Protocol is the implementation of this specification over a TCP/IP network. These

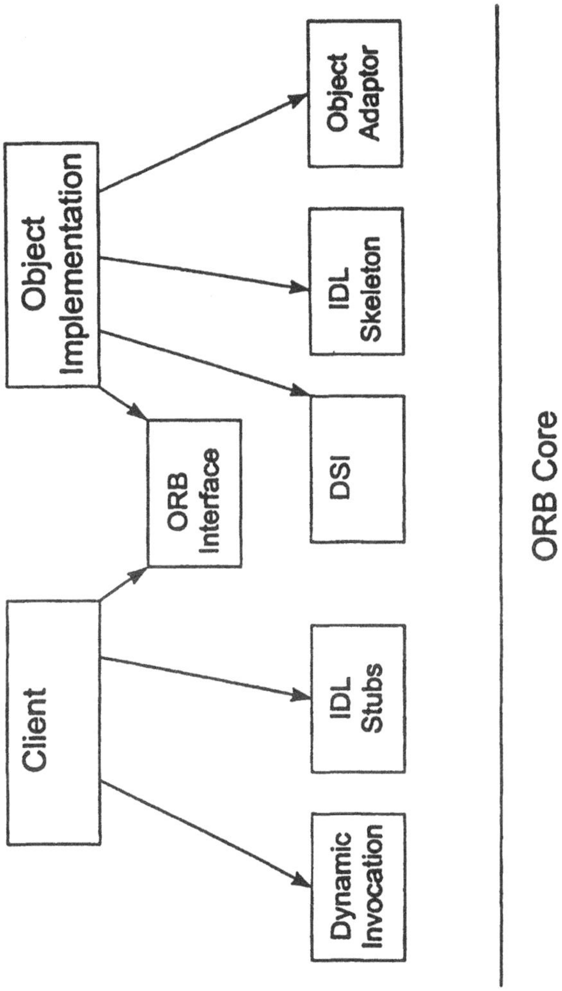

Exhibit 33.2. CORBA Structure Specifying Operation of the ORB Component

systems also support interobject references to locate and identify an object over the TCP/IP network.

CORBA IN THE REAL WORLD

CORBA has been around for a long time, but differences in early CORBA implementations made application portability and interoperability between implementations difficult. Different CORBA implementations fragmented an already small market, thereby rendering CORBA ineffective. Only recently have issues such as interoperability been addressed.

Other recent events have given rise to the hope that the industry can overcome these early missteps. First, the World Wide Web has created an incentive for a mainstream component architecture. Second, Netscape, Novell, and Oracle have licensed the Visigenic Software ORB, targeting one CORBA implementation. And Netscape has the potential to propagate large numbers of that implementation in its browser, which could create critical mass. Third, IBM, Netscape, Oracle, and Sun have agreed to ensure interoperability between their CORBA and IIOP implementations. Still, these vendors are fighting an uphill battle, and significant interoperability problems remain.

WHAT IS DCOM?

Microsoft's Distributed Component Object Model (DCOM) is object-oriented middleware technology that allows clients and servers in a distributed system to communicate with one another. It extends Microsoft's Component Object Model (COM) technology to work on the network. As is the case with Windows, Microsoft owns DCOM and controls its development. There will be no differing DCOM implementations to fragment the market, and Microsoft has begun shipping DCOM on both Windows NT and Windows 95. In other words, critical mass is quickly building.

COM Architecture

COM is an object-based framework for developing and deploying software components. COM lets developers capture abstractions as component interfaces and then provide binary classes that implement those interfaces. Encapsulation is enforced by COM such that client applications can only invoke functions that are defined on an object's interface.

COM interfaces define a contract between a COM object and client. It defines the behavior or capabilities of the software component as a set of methods and properties. COM interfaces are implemented by COM classes. COM classes are bodies of code that implement at least one COM interface. All COM classes implement two functionalities: lifetime management and interface management. COM classes may implement several interfaces. COM clients must explicitly request the interface they need. It also lets clients widen their interface requirement at run-time or query whether a component supports an interface. Lifetime management is accomplished by reference counting.

COM classes reside in a server either as DLLs or EXEs. COM classes implemented as DLLs share the same address space (in-process) as their clients. COM classes implemented within EXEs live in different processes (out-of-process) than their client. Such out-of-process clients are supported via remote procedure calls.

COM classes are like meta classes. They create instances of COM classes, and also store static data for a class interface. For example, if a COM server has four different COM classes inside, that COM server will also have four class objects — one for each kind of COM class within the server.

OLE is a set of system services built on top of COM for constructing compound documents that is also used for supporting components. OLE Automation allows a component object to expose its methods through the Idispatch interface, allowing late binding of method calls. OLE Controls (OCXs) provide exposure to the interface of an object using method pointer tables called vtables.

COM's binary interoperability standard facilitates independent development of software components and supports deployment of those components in binary form. The result is that software vendors can develop and package reusable building blocks without shipping source code. Corporate application developers can use COM to create new solutions that combine in-house business objects, off-the-shelf objects, and their own custom components.

DCOM Architecture

DCOM, or Distributed Component Object Model, extends COM to the network with remote method calls, security, scalability, and location transparency. With COM objects may be loaded into the client's process or launched in a separate process on the the same machine. DCOM extends this transparency to include location transparency, allowing objects to exist anywhere on the network. When the client and the object server are on different machines (see Exhibit 33.3), the remoting layer adds a proxy object in the client's process space and a stub process on the server's process space. The proxy object is then responsible for marshalling the parameters and makes the function call. The stub unmarshals the parameters and makes the actual function call on the component object. The results are then marshalled and sent back to the proxy object where it is unmarshalled and given to the client. The entire process of creating the

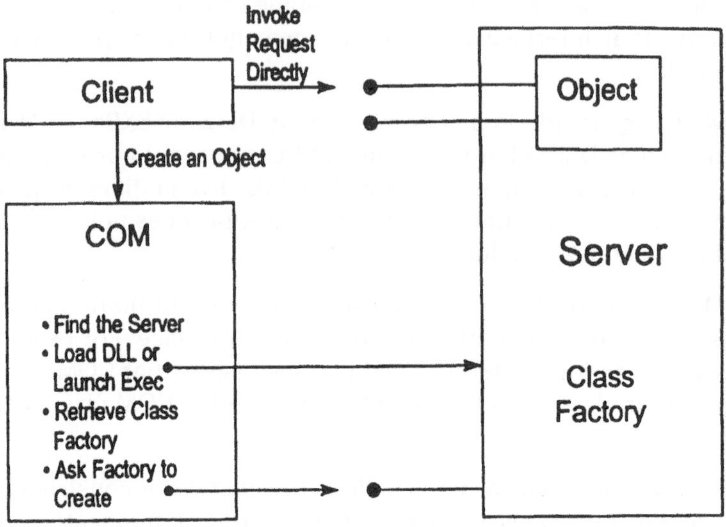

Exhibit 33.3. A COM Object and an Invocation by a Client

proxy and stub is invisible to either the client or the server, and they use remote procedure call as the interprocess communication mechanism.

ARCHITECTURE: CORBA VS. DCOM

The member companies of the Object Management Group have shared one consistent vision of an architecture for distributed, component-based object computing since OMG's inception in 1989. The architecture is described in the Object Management Architecture Guide, first published in 1990, and has been incrementally populated with the specifications of the core interobject communication component (CORBA), and with common services for handling transactions, security, concurrency control, and other vital support functions for object-based applications. Both the architecture and the individual specifications are vendor-neutral, and control of their technical direction and definition is via a public process that ensures broad cross-industry consensus. The specifications are available to all (OMG members or not), and free rights to implement software using the specifications are guaranteed by the terms of the OMG's constitution.

DCOM, being a version of Microsoft's COM, has deep roots in the client desktop GUI side as well as the server side. However, CORBA's main focus has always been on the server side. ORB vendors were in the past expecting the now defunct OpenDoc to compete with Microsoft's COM on the client side. Today CORBA has no model specification to compete with desktop COM components for heterogeneous client GUIs. However, JavaBeans, a component technology from SUN, is being integrated to support client components with CORBA. This technology is still evolving. Until COM is ported to other platforms, however, Microsoft's client side advantage exists only on 32-bit Windows platforms.

The CORBA Object Reference differs from DCOM's Interface Reference in several ways. CORBA supports multiple inheritance of object interfaces, whereas DCOM has a mechanism allowing multiple independent interfaces per object.

Interfaces. Both use the interface mechanism to expose object functionalities. Interfaces contain methods and attributes as a common means of placing requests on an object. CORBA uses standard models of inheritance from object-oriented languages. DCOM/ActiveX uses the concept of multiple interfaces supported by a single object. DCOM requires that multiple inheritance be emulated through aggregation and containment of interfaces.

Identity. Another difference is the notion of object identity. CORBA defines the identity of an object in an object reference that is unique and consistent. If the object is not in memory, the reference is used to reconstruct the object. DCOM in contrast defines the identity in the interface, but the reference to the object itself is transient. This may lead to problems when reconnecting because the previously used object may not be directly accessible.

Reference Counting. Reference counting is also different in both. A DCOM object maintains a reference count of all connected clients. It uses pinging of the clients to ensure that the clients are alive. CORBA does not need to do remote reference, because its object-reference model allows the re-creation of the object if it had been prematurely deleted. CORBA does not attempt to track the number of clients communicating with a particular object. If a client releases the object on the server while another is using it, the object will be destroyed and an error will return to the other client on the next method call. Thus, it is up to the object implementation to provide life-cycle management if such behavior is unacceptable. Without a transaction manager integrated into the distributed system, it is very difficult to implement a reliable life-cycle management system.

APIs. CORBA uses two application protocol interfaces (APIs) and one protocol for object requests. It provides the generated stubs for both static and dynamic invocation. In addition, dynamic skeleton interface allows changes during runtime. DCOM provides two APIs and two protocols. The standard interface is based on a binary interface that uses method pointer tables called vtables. The second API OLE Automation is used to support dynamic requests through scripting languages.

PROGRAMMING DCOM AND CORBA

CORBA defines a finite set of primitive data types used for argument passing and structure definitions. CORBA interface definition language (IDL) files are similar in syntax to the C language, but deals only with interface-related details.

Two of the primary differences between COM and CORBA are structure and naming. A COM object consists of one or more categories of interfaces, where each one is named and has its own derivation hierarchy. A CORBA object follows a standard object model in that its interface is defined by its class and all the ancestors of that class. In the COM interface definition, the developer provides a universal identifier (UUID) that uniquely identifies the interface and class definitions. The UUID identifies classes instead of a class name so that you can have multiple classes with the same name but different vendors and functionality. CORBA, on the other hand, uses a naming system that includes the class name and an optional module name. Module names are equivalent to the C++ namespace concept, where class names can be scoped (assigned) to a particular module. The COM approach ensures that a collision will not occur. The CORBA version would allow a program to use two or more classes of the same name if their module scopes are different.

Error conditions and the amount of information they return is another difference. CORBA implementations provide an exception mechanism that returns errors as a structure embedded within another object called the Environment. A standard System Exception structure is defined for system-level and communications errors that can occur during a remote method call. Since CORBA is generally implemented with an object-oriented language, the exception systems of CORBA and the language can be tied together. Thus in C++, an error that occurs on the server will result in an exception being thrown on the client. In contrast, all methods in COM return an HRESULT integer value that indicates the success or failure of the call. This integer value is split up into a number of bit fields that allow the programmer to specify context, facility, severity, and error codes, making error handling more laborious.

The error-handling example is an area that CORBA is better at supporting than DCOM. Though both promote the aspect of location transparency, the reality that object implementations exist in other processes and the complications that can result from this are exposed in the way errors are handled. Developers like to know where an object exists when an error occurs. CORBA seems better, with its support for reporting system errors separate from application-level errors, which makes it easier for the developer to build appropriate exception-handling code.

Existing Services. To quickly implement distributed object technologies, it is important to have a built-in core set of components that applications can use. While DCOM comes bundled with a few more than CORBA, both suffer from a lack of existing components.

SECURITY

DCOM has a more flexible security implementation than does CORBA. DCOM provides multiple levels of security that can be selected by the administrator. DCOM uses access control lists (ACLs) on COM components. Administrators can use ACLs to determine who has access to the objects. DCOM methods can also programmatically control authorization of individual method invocations. By combining NT APIs and registry keys, a method can implement custom security. DCOM's security managers are platform-dependent. However, they employ readily available authenticators from third parties.

CORBA object services specify three levels of security. Level 0 specifies the authentication and session encryption using technology similar to that of the secure sockets layer (SSL) on web servers. This requires that the IIOP be secure, and object servers have to register themselves with the ORB as secure. Levels 1 and 2 are differentiated based on whether the CORBA clients and server objects are aware of the security layer. In Level 1, they are not aware, and in Level 2 they are aware of the security layer. Because CORBA's security specification has only recently been completed, ORB vendors have in the past had to come up with their own security implementations, which were incompatible with each other. Most vendors are currently only supporting SSL and Level 0 security.

SCALABILITY

Transaction Processing (TP) monitors help with scalability of any application by providing two critical services:

- Process management — starting server processes, filtering work to them, monitoring their execution, and balancing their workloads.
- Transaction management — ensures atomicity, consistency, isolation, and durability (ACID) properties for all processes and resources under its control.

Both DCOM and CORBA leverage TP monitors to provide for scalability and robustness.

DCOM is designed to work with the Microsoft Transaction Server, which began shipping in early 1997. Transaction Server is a transaction processing system that enables development, deployment, and management of multitier applications composed of COM and DCOM objects. DCOM is used for all object communication among machines. Transaction Server transparently provides transaction support to objects; manages threads, processes, ODBC database connections, and sharing data among concurrently executing objects. Transaction Server has a tight integration with SQL Server, and it can be used with a wide range of databases. Transaction Server currently does not support failover and load balancing, though it is expected to in future releases. In addition, DCOM is scheduled to work with a next-generation Directory Services, scheduled to ship with Windows NT 5.0. These services will provide a highly scalable store for object references and security information for DCOM.

CORBA has a specification called Object Transaction Services (OTS) that is designed to interoperate with X/Open-compliant transaction monitors. Hence, CORBA OTS is designed to work both with ORB-based and traditional TP transaction processing services. OTS offers the capability of supporting recoverable nested transactions that supports ACID and two-phase commit protocols. IDL interfaces can be used to provide a way to access the TP monitor application remotely. Integrating TP monitors within an ORB allows the CORBA components to be wrappers of existing business functionality, and to support legacy data.

PLATFORM SUPPORT

DCOM will currently only run on 32-bit Windows platforms. It is currently integrated into Windows NT 4.0, both Server and Workstation, and is available free for Windows 95.

However, cross-platform support for DCOM is coming, with third-party ports coming for UNIX, including one for Linux, Digital UNIX, HP/UX, and Sun's Solaris, as well as IBM's MVS and DEC's OpenVMS. Microsoft is actively seeking partners to port DCOM to other platforms, although some are concerned that Microsoft will favor its Windows-based implementations over the published DCOM standards. Applications using DCOM running on non-Windows platforms are only able to invoke the services on the Windows platforms, as opposed to allowing applications to be built anywhere.

Among UNIX users, there is a driving need to have an easy means to connect application on the desktop and the server. Software AG, a developer of three DCOM-on-UNIX ports, estimates that of the 600,000 UNIX servers in production systems worldwide, about 80% need an easier way to bridge the worlds of UNIX and Windows.

Critics of DCOM point out that the DCOM component model isn't inherently distributed. It has to be ported to every platform where it is to be used in order to get portability, which is clumsier than CORBA, which was built from the ground up to be distributed.

In order for DCOM to be widely used for creating enterprise applications, cross-platform services such as Transactions Server and Message Queue Server must be in place. Although Microsoft is expected to provide versions of its COM-based messaging and transaction services on other platforms, directly or through a third party, no formal commitment has been made.

LANGUAGE SUPPORT

CORBA is well suited for use by object-oriented languages. The code is much cleaner, because the bindings fully exploit the features of the host language. DCOM, on the other hand, has done nothing to provide management classes for the method arguments or a way to link error conditions to the C++ exception mechanism. CORBA also has a superior mechanism for handling arrays and sequences and provides an "any" data type for marshaling arguments whose type you do not know in advance. For object-oriented languages such as C++, the DCOM interface is cumbersome and requires more low-level code.

On the other hand, since DCOM supports OLE automation, applications can be developed with popular, nonobject-oriented languages such as Visual Basic or Delphi. If you are developing a PC-based application within these environments DCOM is definitely easier. For those dealing with object-oriented languages and significant object models, the CORBA model is more of a natural fit, because of COM's inability to support polymorphism and framework development.

INDUSTRY SUPPORT

Although many key companies such as Netscape, Oracle, and Sun Microsystems have agreed to support the emerging CORBA standards, there is some doubt whether they are fully committed to the standard, or if they will shift to DCOM if it gains considerable market share. DEC has announced it will use more than one technology, and HP has indicated interest in supporting COM on their versions of UNIX, but remains uncommitted to DCOM.

Others, such as IBM, seem to be firmly backing CORBA. IBM has introduced a CORBA-based development suite of middleware products, including Component Broker Connector and Component Broker Toolkit, which it plans to offer free with many of its products.

Tools vendors such as Oracle are hoping to find a middle ground in the battle for market share between DCOM and CORBA. Oracle has released a development environment that supports both native COM and CORBA components.

MATURITY

CORBA and DCOM have great potential for creating seamless distributed computing environments, despite the fact that today CORBA is struggling to establish its standards and DCOM has yet to prove it can operate as a cross-platform solution.

A Complete Tool?

While both architectures can create the structure for enterprise-level applications, neither is capable of generating an actual enterprise-ready application, which requires other services such as transactions, event notification, concurrency control and naming. While neither CORBA nor DCOM is a complete solution for network programming, CORBA offers good code for object-oriented languages. DCOM is easy to use with non-object-oriented languages such as Visual Basic.

PERFORMANCE

The network performance of DCOM is comparable to that of CORBA's IIOP, with each accomplishing reasonable request-reply response times. However, a standard method of communicating over an asynchronous transport is needed for both DCOM and CORBA. Currently, because of their highly synchronous operation, these technologies are limited to operating over LANs and server backbones. Internet use, or use over a company WAN, is not practical with the current technologies because of the high rate of synchronous request-reply activity required.

The OMG is in the midst of finalizing the Asynchronous Messaging service. This service extends CORBA's synchronous processes and provides a notion of "store-and-forward" processing with a variety of quality of service guarantees for messaging, reporting, and similar functions.

SUPPORT FOR THE WORLD WIDE WEB

Netscape has declared the Internet Inter-ORB Protocol (IIOP) as its standard for communicating between distributed objects and has included object broker technology in Communicator and SuiteSpot. Microsoft continues to position its Windows, DCOM, and ActiveX as its distributed object solution, and Explorer is the only browser to support ActiveX.

Notification services are being provided in conjunction with the asynchronous messaging services in CORBA to enable an object to subscribe and receive notification of changes. This is essential to support the various push technologies emerging on the Web. Along with Event services, this provides support for publish and subscribe to be effectively supported. Many CORBA vendors have provided support for this technology. However, they are not very scalable, since by their very nature the Event-services uses a point-to-point connection oriented approach.

PROTOCOLS SUPPORTED

DCOM supports several protocols, such as TCP/IP, IPX/SPX, and Named Pipes. Though not limited to IIOP, CORBA ORBs only support the TCP/IP-based Internet Inter-Orb Protocol (IIOP) or proprietary inter-ORB protocols. DCOM's core network protocol is called Object Remote Procedure Call (ORPC). It is based upon DCE RPCs (Distributed Computing Environment Remote Procedure Calls), with extensions such as the addition of a primitive data type to support object references.

EASE OF USE

DCOM has just a few key management tools and has based the transport and security mechanisms on familiar Distributed Computing Environment (DCE) standards. This has made managing distributed components much less of a challenge.

INTEROPERABILITY BETWEEN CORBA AND DCOM

Currently, the Internet Inter-ORB Protocol (IIOP) is the OMG-approved method of linking distributed CORBA objects. Microsoft says it has no plans to support IIOP in DCOM, and there is currently no built-in COM support in CORBA. This battle of standards is making the implementation of both CORBA and COM services difficult.

As most enterprises will have both COM and CORBA environments, it is necessary that the objects in each be able to communicate with each other. OMG published a specification two years ago called "COM/CORBA Interworking" (now part of the CORBA 2.0 specification), which defines standardized mappings between COM and CORBA objects. There are several companies shipping implementations of this specification, including IONA, HP, Digital, and Expersoft. Basically, one of two approaches are used: encapsulation or converter. In the encapsulation approach, a call to the server object system is wrapped in an implementation of the object from the client system. ORB vendors provide generators to create such a bridge from the interface description of the object. In the converter approach, conversation proxies are generated during runtime based on the interface description of the object it represents. Both support bidirectional calls to and from either object systems.

THE FUTURE

Microsoft is about to release a new version of COM called COM+, which is designed to simplify the creation and use of software components. COM+ will provide a runtime and services that are readily usable from any programming language or tool. It is intended to enable extensive interoperability between components regardless of how they were implemented.

Where COM+ really shines, and where it most affects DCOM, is how COM+ will address the difficulties inherent in writing component-based distributed applications. COM+ will introduce an extensibility mechanism called interception, which will receive and process events related to instance creation, calls, returns, errors, and instance deletion. Services that the Microsoft Transaction Server provides today will become a part of COM+, and thus will be a core part of future Microsoft operating systems.

Similarly, OMG is defining and filling in the services required for most of the service layers, such as directory service, transactions, and security. Vendor implementations of these are starting to appear. Others such as persistence, concurrency, time, query, trader, collection, and versioning will slowly trickle in over the next couple of years. In addition, JavaBeans technology is being pushed as the client component technology, and Java support for CORBA is emerging. This may help provide additional support for CORBA on the desktop.

CONCLUSION

DCOM is more accessible than CORBA at this stage of the technologies, because of Microsoft's experience and focus on the included DCOM management tools. For Microsoft-centric companies, DCOM is a solution that is tightly integrated with the Windows operating system. Customers have the most to lose in the object wars, and interoperability between CORBA and DCOM will likely be an important issue for many years. Where cross-platform capability or access to legacy objects is required, CORBA is currently the clear winner. CORBA provides companies with the highest degree of middleware flexibility through its extensive third-party support. More likely, all enterprises will use a mix of the two technologies, with DCOM at the desktop, and CORBA at the enterprise level.

In essence, DCOM and CORBA provide similar enough services that debates on minor technical issues ought to be dismissed in favor of more practical concerns, such as scalability, openness, availability, and maturity. Other important issues to be considered are the operating systems and programming languages used in the current project. Availability of CORBA and DCOM bridges may render the choice moot, and users will not be aware nor care whether it is DCOM or CORBA under the covers, because what they will use will be higher services (such as business facilities) built on top of either architecture.

Notes

[1] Object Management Group, 1997, "CORBA vs. ActiveX," http://www.omg.org/activex.htm..
[2] Object Management Group, 1997, "What is CORBA?," http://www.omg.org/omg00/wicorba.htm.
[3] T.M. Rajkumar, 1997, Client Server Development with Components.
[4] *InfoWorld*, August 4, 1997, v19 n31 p6(1), HP to push DCOM as part of CORBA, McKay, Niall.
[5] *Network Computing*, July 15, 1997, v8 n13 p98(5), Is DCOM truly the object of middleware's desire?, Frey, Anthony.
[6] *Network Computing*, July 1, 1997, v8 n12 p101(1), Three's a crowd with object lessons, Gall, Nick.
[7] *InformationWeek*, May 26, 1997, n632 p122(1), Component software war, Harzog, Bernd.
[8] *InfoWorld*, May 19, 1997, v19 n20 p51(2), Microsoft's cross-platform DCOM plans raise questions, Bowen, Ted Smalley.
[9] *PC Week*, May 12, 1997, v14 n19 p8(1), DCOM-to-Unix ports on the way, Leach, Norvin.
[10] *PC Week*, May 12, 1997, v14 n19 p93(1), Single victor unlikely in object protocol war, Lewis, Jamie.
[11] *Byte*, April 1997, v22 n4 p103(3), Programming with CORBA and DCOM, Pompeii, John.
[12] DBMS, April 1997, v10 n4 p26(6), Inside DCOM, Roy, Mark and Ewald, Alan.
[13] Object Management Group, 1997, IIOP, http://www.omg.org/corba/corbiiop.htm.
[14] Microsoft Corporation, 1997, "COM and DCOM," http://www.microsoft.com/cominfo/.
[15] *Byte*, April 1997, v22 n4 p93, Distributing Components, Montgomery, John.
[16] *Microsoft Systems Journal*, 1997, v12 n11, Object-Oriented Software Development Made Simple with COM+ Runtime Services, Kirtland, Mary.
[17] *Object Magazine*, July 1997, p. 68-77. CORBA/DCOM interoperability, Kotopoulis, Alexander and Miller, Julia.
[18] BMS, March 1997. p. 43-50 CORBA Masterminds Object Management, Kueffel, Warren.
[19] *Application Development Trends*, October 97, p. 41-46. Deeper Inside CORBA, Dolgicer, Max.

Chapter 34 Transitioning to Windows NT

Nathan J. Muller

Windows NT provides a secure, easy-to-manage, powerful foundation for a new generation of business applications using low-cost PC hardware. Microsoft's Windows NT 3.5 builds on the reliability and stability of Windows NT 3.1 (the first version of Windows NT) to greatly enhance speed and provide better connectivity to other systems, particularly Novell NetWare and UNIX environments.

NT 3.5 offers a high degree of protection for critical business applications and their data, and provides complete security for desktop systems. By supporting industry standards, Windows NT works with existing systems and networks. Windows NT delivers a networking architecture that fully optimizes the power of desktop and server operating systems and interoperates with other vendor's systems in the corporate computing environment.

As a 32-byte operating system with preemptive multitasking, strong networking support, no memory limits, and no dependency on DOS, Windows NT 3.5 surpasses Windows NT 3.1 and Windows 95 and matches the power of UNIX. Users can run both technical and business applications on a single desktop platform, which in most cases is far less expensive than a UNIX workstation.

UNIX INTEROPERABILITY

Because UNIX works well for large, networked organizations, most IS managers are hesitant to change hardware and software for anything less than very compelling reasons. Windows NT is interoperable with UNIX, allowing Windows-based products to be added as the need to add more users arises. Interoperability is achieved through:

- Common, standard networking protocols.
- Character and graphical terminal support.
- Standards-based distributed processing support.
- Standards-based file systems and data sharing.
- Application portability.

0-8493-9822-3/00/$0.00+$.50

UNIX VARIANTS

At the most basic level, Windows NT Server includes communications protocol support, network utilities, and APIs that allow it to communicate with most UNIX variants, including TCP/IP, TCP/IP utilities, and SNMP support.

TCP/IP

Windows NT Server has TCP/IP support built in, which means the Windows NT server can communicate right out of the box. The core TCP/IP protocols included with Windows NT include the UDP, address resolution protocol (ARP), and the Internet control message protocol (ICMP).

TCP/IP Utilities

More than a dozen basic network utilities are included with Windows NT that provide terminal access to, or file transfer capabilities to and from, most UNIX-based systems. The basic TCP/IP connectivity applications include finger, File Transfer Protocol, RCP, Telnet, Rexec, Rsh, and TFTP. TCP/IP diagnostic utilities include ARP, hostname, ipconfig, nbstate, netstap, ping, and route.

SNMP Support

Windows NT Server provides several facilities for integrating Windows NT-based systems into networks that use SNMP, a common TCP/IP-based network management facility. This component allows a Windows NT Server to be administered remotely using such enterprise-level management platforms as Hewlett-Packard's OpenView, IBM's NetView, and Sun's Solstice SunNet Manager.

Assigning IP Addresses

With regard to TCP/IP, Windows NT Server is the only server operating system that provides Dynamic Host Control Protocol (DHCP) management. DHCP is the facility that assigns TCP/IP addresses, eliminating the process of manual address allocation every time users request a connection.

The proliferation of TCP/IP-based networks, coupled with the growing demand for Internet addresses, makes it necessary to conserve IP addresses. Issuing IP addresses on a dynamic basis is a way to recycle this increasingly scarce resource. Even companies with private intranets are using dynamic IP addresses instead of issuing unique IP addresses to every machine.

With DHCP, which was developed by the Internet Engineering Task Force (IETF), IP addresses can be doled out from a pool of IP addresses as users need them to establish network connections. When they log off the net, the

IP addresses are released and become available to other users. Assigning addresses can consume a majority of a network manager's time if done manually. With DHCP support, Windows NT automates this task.

A related feature provided by Windows NT is the Windows Internet Name Service(WINS), which maps computer names to IP addresses, allowing users to refer to their machines with an easy-to-remember plain-text name rather than by an IP address such as 123.456.789.22, for example.

Windows NT includes native support for NetBEUI and IPX/SPX as well as TCP/IP. Regardless of the protocol used, each system hides the details of the underlying network from the applications and the end user. The network administrator can choose the protocol that best addresses the company's network requirements.

Character and Graphical Terminal Support

Although designed to support business-strength client/server computing, Windows NT can also host a variety of terminal emulation capabilities for easy integration with UNIX-based hosts, including the ones described in the following sections.

Telnet and Third-Party Terminal Emulators. Basic character-oriented terminal access using Telnet is included with Windows NT and integrated with the Windows Terminal applet. A variety of terminal emulators with more advanced features are also available from third-party vendors.

X Servers. X servers are available from a variety of third-party vendors to allow users of Windows NT to access and run existing X-based application on their UNIX-variant hosts.

Standards-based Distributed Processing Support

Windows NT Server includes API to support computing in a distributed environment. The APIs provided are discussed in the following sections.

DCE-compatible RPC. Remote procedure calls (RPCs) are a critical component needed to build distributed applications. The RPC built into Windows NT Server is compatible with the Open Software Foundation's DCE RPC. Using this RPC, developers can build distributed applications that include other Windows NT-based systems, as well as any system that supports Data Circuit-terminating Equipment-compatible RPC–including those from Digital Equipment Corp., Hewlett-Packard, and other vendors.

Windows Sockets. Windows Sockets is an APIs that is compatible with Berkeley-style sockets, a popular distributed computing mechanism among UNIX variants. Windows Sockets enables developers to build applications that interoperate with any other system that supports this industry-standard APIs.

Windows Open Services Architecture (WOSA). WOSA is a set of Microsoft-developed open APIs for integrating Windows platforms with a broad range of back-end services from multiple vendors.

Standards-based File Systems and Data Sharing

Windows NT supports the following standards for file systems and data sharing.

LAN Manager for UNIX (LMU). LMU is an implementation of Microsoft Windows networking for servers that run UNIX variants. LMU allows Microsoft network clients to access data stored on UNIX hosts, including data on remotely mountable UNIX file systems. LMU uses Server Message Blocks (SMBs), a set of protocols developed by Microsoft that are now an X/Open standard.

Network File System (NFS). Sun's Network File System is a popular tool for sharing files among different UNIX operating systems and is available for Windows NT Server from several third-party vendors, including SunSelect.

File Transfer Protocol (FTP). Microsoft has also developed client and server versions of FTP for Windows NT Server. FTP is a popular TCP/IP-based utility that allows users to copy files among diverse systems, including UNIX and non-UNIX systems.

Application Portability

Native Application Ports. There are thousands of 32-byte applications for Windows NT, including many applications originally developed for UNIX variants, virtual memory system (VMS), or multiple virtual storage (MVS). In fact, approximately 25 percent of the applications being developed for Windows NT are ports from these other platforms. Many of these are high-end technical and business applications.

POSIX. The IEEE 1003.1-1990 standard–usually referred to as POSIX.1–specifies a set of APIs that describe an interface between applications and an operating system. Windows NT Server includes a protected subsystem that provides full support for POSIX.1.

Windows Libraries for UNIX. Microsoft has licensed Windows source code and test suites to several companies that will develop products that allow Windows-based applications to run on all major implementations of the UNIX operating system, including Solaris SunOS, UNIXWare, SCO UNIX, Advanced Interactive Executive, and HP-UX. These agreements make the

Windows APIs a universal standard for both the Intel and RISC-based UNIX platforms and help ensure that users can take advantage of evolving 32-byte Windows technology in both their operating systems and applications development.

SERVICES FOR NETWARE

Microsoft's networking strategy is to ensure that any desktop computer can access any server. Therefore, Microsoft has equipped Windows NT Server (and NT Workstation) with several utilities that make it easier for NetWare users to make the transition to Windows NT.

File and Print Services for NetWare

File and Print Services for NetWare is a utility that makes Windows NT Server look like a NetWare 3.x-compatible file and print server. Without changing their NetWare client software, users can access file and print services, as well as their server applications, on the same multipurpose Windows NT Server-based machine from their desktops. The Windows NT directory service provides single network logon, replication, and centralized management.

Client Service for NetWare

Client Service for NetWare provides NetWare client capabilities for the Windows NT Workstation. It allows the Windows NT Workstation to connect to file and print services provided by NetWare servers. Windows NT Workstations can store and print information on NetWare servers, and they can have access to many of the most commonly used NetWare-aware applications, such as NetWare SAA and Lotus Notes. Users who have supervisor rights are also able to run administrative utilities, such as Syscom and Pconsole, commonly used in managing NetWare servers.

Client Service for NetWare integrates into both the Windows NT and NetWare environments. It can be configured so that a single logon provides access to the Windows NT Workstation, NetWare file and print servers, and Windows NT-based application servers.

Gateway Service for NetWare

Gateway Service for NetWare provides networked and remote users connected to a Windows NT Server access to the file storage and printer resources on NetWare servers. This gateway is a useful integration tool for companies that run both NetWare and Microsoft clients in a heterogeneous server environment. The network administrator controls access to the gateway so only those with permission can use file and print resources on designated NetWare servers.

Gateway Service for NetWare can be used to isolate IPX/SPX traffic and ease the transition to TCP/IP, as well as to run the remote access capability available with Windows NT Server. With remote access, clients can securely dial into the network from a remote location and access all services as if they were directly connected to the LAN.

NWLink

NetWare users can access server applications such as Microsoft SQL Server, SNA Server, and others running on Windows NT Server without changing their client software. This capability is accomplished by using NWLink, the IPX/SPX-compatible transport that comes standard with Windows NT Workstation and Windows NT Server. These applications appear to a NetWare user in the same way as a NetWare Loadable Module (NLM) does. During installation, Windows NT Server automatically checks the network to see which transport is running. If it finds IPX/SPX, the server automatically defaults to the NWLink (i.e., IPX/SPX) transport.

Migration Tool for NetWare

Migration Tool for NetWare in Windows NT Server aids network administrators by copying user accounts and files from NetWare servers to a Windows NT Server while maintaining security. It has the capabilities of both a migration and an integration tool.

For migration, the Windows NT Server Migration Tool for NetWare lets administrators transfer users and data to the Windows NT Server platform. They can migrate a single NetWare server to a single Windows NT Server, multiple NetWare servers to a single Windows NT Server, or many other configurations, allowing for the redistribution of information across the servers on a network.

Because there are some security differences between NetWare and Windows NT Server, the Migration Tool includes a trial migration process that generates detailed log files. These files assist the administrator in keeping track of any changes that may occur during the migration process.

When integrating new servers into the network, administrators are always looking for ways to avoid duplicating user accounts across a variety of servers. The Migration Tool for NetWare simply copies the users, groups, files, and directories to the Windows NT Server, leaving the NetWare server fully intact. For example, if an administrator is setting up an application server in a NetWare environment, user accounts can automatically be populated on the Windows NT Server running SQL Server, for example, by copying the NetWare binary information. These accounts would mirror the user accounts that already exist on the NetWare server, saving the administrator valuable time in the initial server setup.

To test the interoperability of Windows NT Server with NetWare, Microsoft recommends the following procedure:

- Set up Windows NT Server as an application server with Microsoft SQL Server using the NWLink protocol.
- Install the Client Services for NetWare on a Windows NT-based machine and test its functionality as a NetWare client.
- Install the IPX/SPX transport protocol on both a workstation and the server and test its functionality in a routed environment.
- Set up the Gateway Services for NetWare on Windows NT Server and test its effectiveness.

REMOTE ACCESS

Portable systems represent a large and growing share of personal computers. They are used by telecommuters, systems administrators, and mobile workers. Through Windows NT Server's Remote Access Server (RAS), network administrators can extend the local area network across a telephone line, allowing remote computers to appear as if they are directly attached to the network. Up to 256 sessions are supported. Remote users can participate fully in the network, sharing files and printers, accessing databases, connecting to hosts, and communicating with colleagues over E-mail. Windows NT Server also supports Point-to-Point Protocol (PPP) and serial-line IP (SLIP), making Internet access a routine task.

PPP is a set of industry-standard framing, authentication, and network configuration protocols that allows remote access solutions to interoperate in a multivendor network. PPP support allows Windows NT Server to receive calls from and provide network access to other vendors' remote access workstation software.

SLIP is similar to PPP, except that it is an older standard that only addresses TCP/IP connections over serial lines. It does not provide automatic negotiation of network configuration without user intervention. It also does not support encrypted authentication. Although SLIP is not recommended, it is supported by Windows NT to accommodate users who already have SLIP servers installed.

RAS supports any combination of NetBEUI, TCP/IP, and Internetwork Packet eXchange protocols to access remote networks. Internetwork Packet eXchange turns Windows NT Server into a remote access server for NetWare networks. TCP/IP support makes Windows NT an Internet-ready operating system, allowing users to access the vast resources of the World Wide Web with any browsing tool.

Windows NT Server enhances the RAS architecture by adding an IP/IPX router capability. This allows clients to run TCP/IP and IPX locally and run Windows Sockets applications or NetBIOS applications over their local

TCP/IP and IPX protocols. This feature enhances RAS's multiprotocol support and makes it a good solution for NetWare and UNIX networks.

DIRECTORY SERVICES

Windows NT implements a distributed directory model that tracks user accounts and resources across a network. Users, groups, and resources such as volumes, directories, files, and printers are divided into domains for distributed access. Each domain is an administrator-defined collection of workstations and servers where one sender is designated the primary domain controller (PDC). The PDC contains a directory of users' accounts and resources within its domain. The directory itself is replicated to Backup Domain Controllers for fault tolerance.

When a user logs on to the network, the directory authenticates the user's identity using the password stored in the directory. The directory also keeps track of the groups to which users have been assigned by administrators based on their workgroups or activities. Based on the user's ID and assigned group rights, the directory grants access to all appropriate resources across all the workstations and servers in the domain. Administrators as well as users can set access control privileges for resources as specific as individual files.

For very large networks where access to the domain controller cannot be guaranteed for the administrator or user, the NT Directory Server employs a "trusted" domain model. Administrators in one domain can certify other domains as "trusted," thereby granting full access to all users from the foreign domain. Using this domain model for directory services, users have the benefit of a single logon to the entire network while preserving administrative control through trust certifications and access control lists.

In addition to primary and backup directory controllers, a member server can be set up. The member server can participate in directory security, although it does not have to. A server that participates in a directory gets the benefits of the directory's single logon, but without having to spend resources authorizing logon attempts or receiving replicated copies of the directory's user database. Instead, it can perform time-critical tasks or devote all of its resources to running applications.

PERFORMANCE

One of the goals of Microsoft has been to reduce memory use and improve system performance. Accordingly, the size of the working set needed by Windows NT Server has been reduced by 4M bytes to 6M bytes. This means that the operating system functions more efficiently with the same amount of system memory.

According to Microsoft's internal testing, Windows NT Server 3.5 performs better on typical server tasks, including file and print. Using the BAPCo network load benchmark, the performance of Windows NT Server 3.5 is more than double that of Windows NT. For example, running a 48-client BAPCo network load, the performance was 6,296 seconds with Windows NT 3.1 versus 2,641 seconds for Windows NT 3.5–an improvement of 2.38 times that of Windows NT 3.1.

These improvements are most evident when using the preferred client, Windows for Workgroups 3.11, which supports the use of 32-byte protect mode networking components to communicate with Windows NT Server. These networking components include 32-byte protocols such as NetBEUI and an IPX/SPX compatible transport, as well as a 32-byte protect mode network redirector. The use of a 32-byte network card driver provides a 32-byte code path from the network card to the network redirector, resulting in improved performance over DOS-based solutions while consuming only 4K bytes of conventional memory.

Windows for Workgroups 3.11 supports the use of client-side cache with a feature called 32-byte File Access. This is a 32-byte protected mode replacement for the DOS-based SmartDrive disk cache program. The caching routines provided as part of 32-byte File Access differ from that offered by SmartDrive in the following ways:

- 32-byte File Access caching routines are implemented as 32-byte protected mode code, thus reducing the need to transition to real mode to cache disk information.
- 32-byte File Access read-ahead routines work on a per-file basis rather than on a per-sector basis, resulting in a higher probability that information read into the disk cache will be used.
- 32-byte File Access caching routines share cache memory with the protected mode network redirector, thus reducing the memory overhead for maintaining multiple cache buffers.

Windows NT Server provides thread scheduling that allows dynamic load balancing across multiple Central Processing Unit. Microsoft has concentrated on providing smooth scalability for up to four processors, the maximum supported by Windows NT Server. Although OEMs can optimize Windows NT Server to support more processors, no operating system provides application performance that increases linearly by a factor of the number of CPUs installed. There are several reasons for this, including hardware designs, the application itself, performance limits caused by physical input and output, and the overhead associated with the operating system's management of multiple Central Processing Unit.

With regard to Windows NT Workstation, performance tests using WinBench, a benchmark testing a range of graphics and disk access capabilities, revealed that performance tripled on the graphics portion–from 4.1 WinMarks on Windows NT 3.1 to 12.6 WinMarks on Windows NT Workstation 3.5. The tests used Microsoft's minimum memory configuration of 12M bytes. In other similar tests, the graphics performance of Windows NT 3.5 Workstation running on dual Pentium machines was as much as four times as high, demonstrating the scalability of performance.

SECURITY

One of the biggest advantages of Windows NT over UNIX is in the critical area of security. Hackers are attracted to UNIX because it offers many weak spots and back doors. Although NT does have some weak spots (for example, NT's built-in File Transfer Protocol server by default gives root access to the disk volume selected for sharing), it was built with a much tighter security model than UNIX, which makes it more difficult to hack. For example, pressing Ctrl+Alt+Del is a hacker's easy way into a DOS or Windows system, making it simple to cut through the password on a screen saver. If this is tried on NT, the computer's security module is invoked, which requests a user name and password.

Another important security feature is Account Lockout, which provides the ability to lock a user's account after a specified number of unsuccessful logon attempts. This feature makes Windows NT Server more secure from intruders who try logon by guessing the passwords of valid user accounts. The administrator can lock the account for a specified period of time or until the account is reset.

EASE OF USE

Another advantage Windows NT has over UNIX is ease of use. Configuring a UNIX server is so complicated that it can take days to get things running properly. On the other hand, it takes relatively few mouse clicks to get an off-the-shelf Pentium up and running with Windows NT Server. After installation, the NT system is far easier to administer and maintain than a UNIX system.

To complicate matters for UNIX, there is no single UNIX platform. This means users cannot run a UNIX program designed for one type of system on a UNIX platform from a different vendor — it is as if Compaq, Dell, IBM, and Gateway 2000 all sold slightly different versions of Windows and users had to buy special software for each of these variants. When Novell bought the main UNIX standard from AT&T a few years ago, it looked as if the competitors might finally unite around a common UNIX standard. But that did not happen, leaving Microsoft to successfully exploit the market with an easier to use platform than that of UNIX.

APPLICATIONS DEVELOPMENT

Windows NT attracts mainstream software developers because it has inherited many applications that run with Windows 95 and Windows 3.x. It has also netted a supply of native applications, especially those related to the Internet. One of the leading applications on the Internet is the Netscape server software, which was originally sold only for UNIX. Now a Windows NT version is available that offers all the functionality of the UNIX version. Making it even more of a lure is its price: the NT version costs about 75 percent less than the UNIX program.

Megabyte for megabyte, an NT Server system costs less to construct than a UNIX system. NT is also cheaper to configure with the critical software needed to run a World Wide Web server. Although UNIX servers currently maintain a slight performance edge, that will dissolve quickly because of parallel processing, the Pentium Pro, the Alpha, and the PowerPC.

RELIABILITY

Reliability is another benefit of Windows NT. Although a Windows NT machine crashes at roughly the same frequency as UNIX machine, when a crash does occur under Windows NT, the system does not have to be rebooted — only the affected window is closed out and it is immediately restarted. When a UNIX workstation crashes, on the other hand, the user has to power down and reboot.

An administrator can specify how Windows NT Server behaves when a fatal system error occurs. This feature — Dump Facility with Automatic Reboot — writes an event to the system log, alerts the administrator, dumps system memory to a file that can be used for debugging, and then automatically reboots the server. The clients can take advantage of the Remoteboot Service, whereby their operating systems are rebooted using software on the server's hard disk instead of their own hard disk.

CONCLUSION

Much of the success of Windows NT Server is attributable to the substantial improvements in version 3.5 over version 3.1. Although a good application server, version 3.1 suffered in comparison to NetWare as a file and print server. In addition, version 3.1 required too much memory to compete against workstations with similar performance. The current version of Windows NT Server combines excellent file service with a wide variety of performance and management features needed for mission-critical applications. This enables Windows NT Server to play an important role in enabling members of the organization to make optimal use of information and processing power throughout the enterprise. Today,

Windows NT Server 3.5 is a viable alternative to Novell's NetWare as an application server and file and print server, while Windows NT Workstation 3.5 is rapidly gaining against UNIX variants running on workstations.

Chapter 35
Windows NT Architecture

Gilbert Held

Windows NT is a 32-bit, preemptive multitasking operating system that includes comprehensive networking capabilities and several levels of security. Microsoft markets two version of Windows NT: one for workstations — appropriately named Windows NT Workstation — and a second for servers — Windows NT Server. This chapter, which describes the workings of the NT architecture, collectively references both versions as Windows NT when information is applicable to both versions of the operating system. Similarly, it references a specific version of the operating system when the information presented is specific to either Windows NT Workstation or Windows NT Server.

ARCHITECTURE

Windows NT consists of nine basic modules. The relationship of those modules to one another, as well as to the hardware platform on which the operating system runs, is illustrated in Exhibit 35.1.

Hardware Abstraction Layer

The hardware abstraction layer (HAL) is located directly above the hardware on which Windows NT operates. HAL actually represents a software module developed by hardware manufacturers that is bundled into Windows NT to allow it to operate on a specific hardware platform, such as Intel X86, DEC Alpha, or IBM PowerPC.

HAL hides the specifics of the hardware platform from the rest of the operating system and represents the lowest level of Windows NT. Thus, HAL provides true hardware platform independence for the operating system.

Using HAL, software developers can create new software without a lot of knowledge about the hardware platform. This allows software developers to provide enhanced performance capabilities, such as additional device drives. Hardware vendors can provide the interface between the operating system and the specific hardware.

Kernel

The kernel represents the core of the Windows NT operating system. All operating systems have a kernel. The key difference between the

0-8493-9822-3/00/$0.00+$.50

Windows NT kernel and those found in other operating systems is the tasks managed.

The Windows NT kernel manages thread dispatching. (A "thread" is a basic item that can be scheduled by the kernel.) The kernel is also responsible for scheduling and processor synchronization when the hardware platform has multiple processors.

To perform scheduling, the Windows NT kernel attempts to dispatch threads for execution in a way that promotes the most efficient use of the processors in the hardware platform. The actual dispatching of threads is based on their priority, with Windows NT supporting 32 priority levels to maximize processor use.

The kernel always resides in real memory within the hardware platform's RAM and is nonpayable to disk. When NT controls a multiprocessor platform, the kernel will run on all processors at the same time and communicate with each other to govern the distribution of threads.

The NT Executive

The NT Executive can be considered a common service provider because it is responsible for providing a set of services to all other operating system components. The Windows NT Executive is the highest level within the kernel mode of the operating system.

As indicated in Exhibit 35.1, the Executive consists of six core modules that provide an interface between users and computers (represented by Virtual DOS Machines and Environment Subsystems) and the kernel. Virtual DOS Machines support DOS or 16-bit Windows 3.X applications. Windows NT provides support by creating virtual machines and then implementing the required environment within such a machine, resulting in the term "virtual DOS machines."

In comparison, "environment subsystems" are environments that may be required to operate on top of Windows NT. Examples of currently supported environment subsystems include OS/2, POSIX, and Win32 (the Windows NT subsystem).

Object Manager

The object manager names, retains, and provides security for objects used by the operating system. In a Windows NT environment, an object represents physical items as well as the occurrence of defined situations. Thus, an object can represent directories, files, physical hardware ports, semaphores, events, and threads. An object-oriented approach is used to manage objects. If network managers are using Windows NT, they can view the status of event objects through the NT Event Viewer, which is provided in the operating system as an administrative tool.

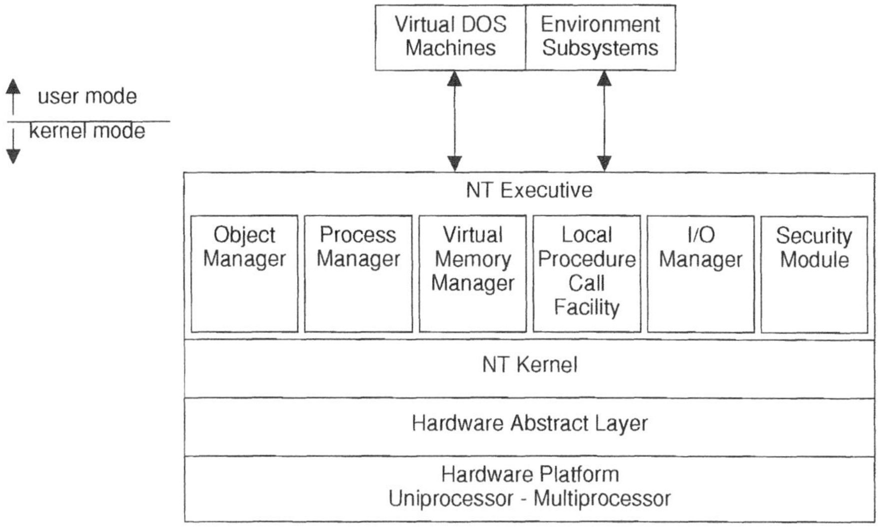

Exhibit 35.1. Windows NT Core Modules

Process Manager

In a Windows NT environment, a process represents an address space, a group of objects defined as a resource, or a set of threads. Thus, each of these entities is managed by the process manager. In doing so, the process manager combines those entities into a "virtual machine," on which a program executes. Here the term "virtual machine" represents a set of resources required to provide support for the execution of a program. Windows NT permits multiple virtual machines to be established, allowing multiprocessing capability.

Virtual Memory Manager

Windows NT uses a special file on the hardware platform's hard disk for additional memory beyond available RAM. That file is referred to as a virtual memory paging or swap file and is automatically created when the operating system is installed.

The Virtual Memory Manager manages the use of virtual memory as a supplement to physical RAM. For example, when one program cannot completely fit into RAM because of its size or the current occupancy by other executing programs, the Virtual Memory Manager might swap one program currently in memory to disk to enable another program to execute, or it could swap portions of the program requesting execution between RAM and the hard disk to execute portions of the program in a predefined sequence.

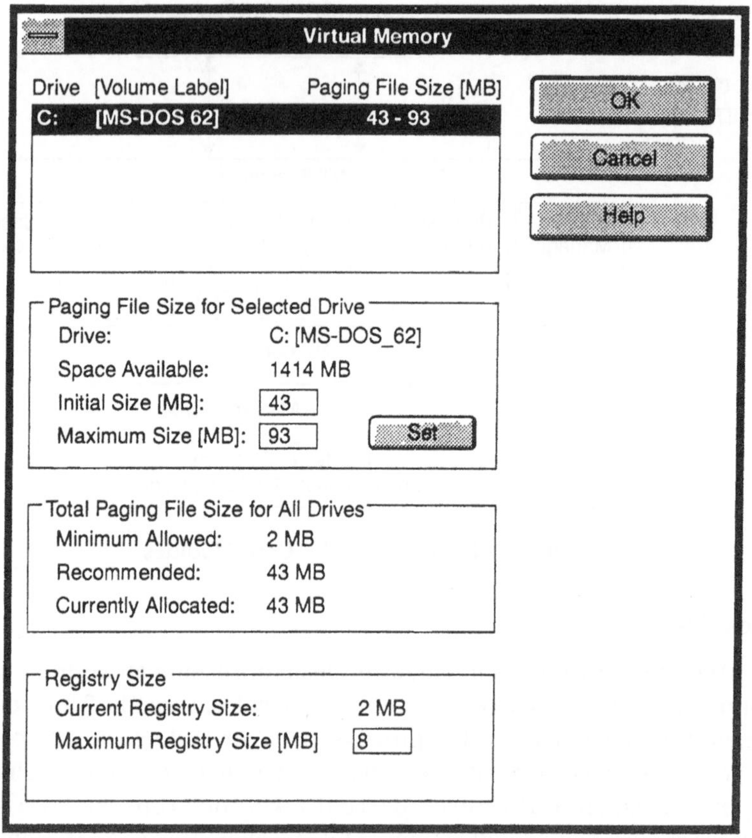

Exhibit 35.2. Virtual Memory Dialog Box

Although the operation of the Virtual Memory Manager is transparent to programs using it, network managers can change the paging file size. To do so, they would first select the System icon in the Control Panel and then select the Virtual Memory entry from the resulting display. This action results in the display of a dialog box labeled Virtual Memory. Exhibit 35.2 illustrates the Virtual Memory dialog box with its default settings shown for a Pentium processor.

Although Windows NT automatically creates a virtual memory paging file and assigns an initial file size based on the capacity of the system's hard disk, the operating system does not know what applications the network manager intends to run or the size of those applications. Thus, if network managers frequently work with applications that require a large amount of memory, they should consider raising the default setting.

In Exhibit 35.2, Windows NT provides a pseudo constraint on the sizes of the paging file. That constraint is in the form of a range of values defined for the size of the paging file; however, that range is a recommendation and is not actually enforced by the operating system. For example, to set the initial size of the paging file to two megabytes, the user would type "20" into the box labeled Initial Size and then click on the Set button. Similarly, if users want to raise the maximum size of the paging file to 100 megabytes, they would enter that value in the appropriate location in the dialog box and click on the Set button.

Local Procedure Call Facility

Programs that execute under Windows NT have a client/server relationship with the operating system. The Local Procedure Call Facility is responsible for the passing of messages between programs.

I/O Manager

The Input/Output (I/O) Manager is responsible for managing all input and output to and from storage and the network. To perform its required functions, the I/O Manager uses four other lower-level subsystems — the Cache Manager, file system drivers, hardware device drivers, and network drivers.

The Cache Manager provides a dynamic cache space in RAM that increases and decreases based on available memory. File system drivers provide support for two file systems, the file allocation table (FAT) and the high performance file system (HPFS). The FAT file system provides backward support for DOS and 16-bit Windows 3.X-based programs, whereas the HPFS enables support of the new file system for Windows NT 32-bit applications.

The hardware device drivers used in Windows NT are written in C++ to provide portability between hardware platforms. This allows a driver developed for a CD-ROM, a plotter, or another hardware device to work with all Windows NT hardware platforms.

Network drivers represent the fourth lower-level I/O Manager subsystem. These drivers provide access from Windows NT to network interface cards, enabling transmission to and from the network and the operating system.

The Security Module

Windows NT includes a comprehensive security facility built into the operating system. Once the user turns on power to the hardware platform, this facility is immediately recognizable. Unlike Windows 3.X, Windows 95, or DOS, Windows NT prompts the operator for a password before allowing access to the computer's resources.

<table>
<tr><th>OSI Reference Model Layers</th><th colspan="4">Windows NT Layers</th></tr>
<tr><td>Application</td><td colspan="4">Environment Subsystems</td></tr>
<tr><td>Presentation</td><td colspan="4">Network Provider</td></tr>
<tr><td rowspan="2">Session</td><td colspan="4">Executive Services</td></tr>
<tr><td colspan="2">Server</td><td colspan="2">Redirector</td></tr>
<tr><td>Transport</td><td colspan="4">Transport Driver Interface</td></tr>
<tr><td>Network</td><td>NetBEUI</td><td>DLC</td><td>TCP/IP</td><td>NWLink (SPX/IPX)</td></tr>
<tr><td rowspan="2">Data Link</td><td colspan="4">NDIS</td></tr>
<tr><td colspan="4">NIC Drivers</td></tr>
<tr><td>Physical</td><td colspan="4">NIC</td></tr>
</table>

Exhibit 35.3. Correspondence Between Windows NT and OSI Reference Model Layers

Windows NT security works by the log-on process and a local security subsystem that monitors access to all objects and verifies that a user has appropriate permission before allowing access to an object. The log-on process is linked to the Security Reference Monitor, which is responsible for access validation and audit generation for the local security subsystem. Another component of the Security Module is the Security Account Manager. The Security Account Manager maintains user and group information on a secure database.

WINDOWS NT NETWORKING

One of the biggest advantages associated with the use of Windows NT is its built-in support of many transport protocols. The Windows NT networking architecture was established in a layered design that follows the seven-layer ISO OSI Reference Model. Exhibit 35.3 illustrates the general correspondence between Windows NT layers and OSI Reference Model layers.

The environment subsystems represent virtual DOS machines as well as 32-bit applications operating on top of NT. At the presentation layer, the Network Provider module is required for each network supported through a redirector. At the session layer, the Windows NT Executive uses a server and redirector to provide capability for a server and workstation, respectively. Both components are implemented as file system drivers and multiple redirectors can be loaded at the same time, so that a Windows NT computer can be connected to several networks. For example, NT includes redirectors for NetWare and VINES, enabling an NT workstation or server to be connected to Novell and Banyan networks.

At the transport layer, the transport driver interface (TDI) provides a higher-layer interface to multiple transport protocols. Those protocols, which represent operations at the network layer, include built-in NT protocol stacks for NetBEUI, used by the LAN Manager and LAN Server operating systems; Data Link Control (DLC), which provides access to IBM mainframes; TCP/IP for Internet and intranet applications; and NWLink, which represents a version of Novell's SPX/IPX protocols. Through the use of TCP/IP, a Windows NT computer can function as a TCP/IP client, whereas the use of NWLink enables a Windows NT computer to operate as NetWare client.

At the data link layer, Windows NT includes a built-in Network Device Interface Specification (NDIS). NDIS enables support for multiple protocol stacks through network interface card drivers. Thus, NDIS allows a network interface card to simultaneously communicate with multiple supported protocol stacks. This means that a Windows NT computer could, for example, simultaneously operate as both a TCP/IP and a NetWare SPX/IPX client.

UPGRADE ISSUES

The key differences between NT 3.5 and 4.0 are speed and user interface. Windows 4.0 added the Windows 95 user interface to NT. In addition, a recoding of the operating system makes it slightly faster than 3.51. However, because the difference in cost between a Pentium and Pentium Pro microprocessor is a few hundred dollars, it may be more economical to purchase the more powerful processor and retain the familiar Windows 3.51 interface. This could eliminate the costs associated with retraining employees.

Conversely, if an organization has already migrated to Windows 95 or is planning to migrate to that operating system, the network manager may want to consider Windows NT Version 4.0. Its use of the Windows 95 interface may be well known to some or most of the organization's employees who will be using NT, which should minimize training costs while providing a slightly improved level of performance.

CONCLUSION

The modular design of the Windows NT architecture makes it both portable and scalable. Windows NT's hardware abstraction layer allows the operating system to run on different hardware platforms. Currently, Windows NT runs on Intel X86, Digital Equipment Corp. (DEC) Alpha, MIPS RISC (reduced instruction set computing), and the PowerPC series of microprocessors jointly manufactured by IBM Corp. and Motorola.

Besides being highly portable, Windows NT supports scalability, which allows the operating system to effectively use multiple processors. Thus, when network managers evaluate Windows NT Server as a platform for different applications, it is important for them to note that they have several options for retaining their investment as applications grow.

For example, because of its scalability, network managers could replace a uniprocessor Intel Pentium motherboard with a dual- or quad-processor motherboard. If this replacement does not provide the necessary level of processing power, network managers might consider migrating hardware to a high-level PowerPC or a DEC Alpha-based computer. If that migration is required and the applications continue to grow, network managers could use multiple processors to ensure scalability.

Chapter 36
NetWare/IP

James E. Gaskin

NetWare/IP allows all NetWare client to NetWare server communications to run over the TCP/IP (Transmission Control Protocol/Internet Protocol) suite, rather than Novell's own IPX/SPX (Internetwork Protocol eXchange/Sequenced Packet eXchange) protocol. The explosion of Internet and related services has made the world lean toward TCP/IP for every computer connection possible. However, the move from IPX to TCP/IP is not necessary for most NetWare customers, and it usually means more trouble, more configuration, higher RAM usage, and lower performance.

There are problems with TCP/IP. Complex routers with complicated software tables are required to maintain a TCP/IP network. Time-dependent protocols, such as SNA and multimedia, poorly fit TCP/IP's "best-effort" delivery methods. Audio stretches TCP/IP to near-breaking points; video transmissions require major TCP/IP surgery to work reliably. TCP/IP network addresses are both mind-numbing to configure and running short because of poor allocation techniques. Between now and the year 2000, the TCP/IP suite will be mutating into the next version of TCP/IP called IPv6 (Internet Protocol version 6).

NetWare/IP is more trouble than it is worth in most cases. If a company is looking for easy Internet or intranet connections, and management can be convinced to use some version of NetWare to TCP/IP gateway, either from Novell or a third party, the company will be better off than fighting its way to NetWare/IP. The company will suffer during the move away from IPX to TCP/IP, although it will ultimately prevail.

NOVELL'S PROTOCOL FOUNDATION

Basically, a protocol is a method that two systems use to communicate. Networks use many protocols, often gathered together under one umbrella and called a protocol suite. Technically, what the systems talk about is separate from the methods they use to talk, but life is not always so convenient.

Modular programming makes the computer world go around today. In late 1979, when Novell engineers were modifying XNS (Xerox Network Systems) into IPX, modular programming did not exist. The result was that many NetWare functions, particularly those of the workhorse NCP (NetWare Core

0-8493-9822-3/00/$0.00+$.50

Protocol) handling most of the file and print requests to the NetWare server, were mixed in with the IPX parts of the client and server control software.

NetWare 3.0 marks the start of structured programming practices that start separating the message from the protocol. By rewriting much of the NetWare operating system in C rather than Assembler, Novell engineers could finally address using TCP/IP in any form with NetWare. Although promised with version 3.0, the NetWare server could not support TCP/IP until version 3.11.

Functions were separated successfully from the underlying protocols. Today, the only restrictions clients will see when using NetWare/IP is the inability to support some NetBIOS broadcasting applications, such as some network monitoring programs. All the 3000+ applications written to address IPX at the client (without NetBIOS involved) will run over NetWare/IP without a problem. Few programs today use NetBIOS; NetWare/IP will support most applications without problems.

Large networks can migrate user groups gradually to NetWare/IP, rather than trying to upgrade everyone at once. Novell provides gateway functions between standard IPX networks and NetWare/IP networks. The administrator will have to do some extra work, but the users will not miss a single server connection.

Naming Functions and Broadcast Packets

TCP/IP clients use DNS (Domain Name Service) to supply names and network addresses to network clients. NetWare/IP supports DNS by creating a NetWare/IP domain servicing the new NetWare/IP clients. The NetWare DNS domain must be a subdomain of an existing DNS domain, but may not have any subdomains itself.

This should not cause a problem. If a company is trying to move to NetWare/IP without already having a large TCP/IP network all over the company, it is making a mistake. Unless a huge installed base of TCP/IP clients, servers, and routers is available, do not consider NetWare/IP.

A company should run the DNS server software on at least one of its NetWare servers to provide local name servers for NetWare/IP clients. NetWare DNS will also support "standard" TCP/IP clients.

How will Novell client software use DNS when the client application requires IPX? Novell uses a DSS (Domain SAP Server) to hold the information normally supplied by IPX broadcasts to NetWare clients. When a TCP/IP client wants to know which machine is the server, that client queries the DNS name server, the address of which is configured in the client's software. NetWare clients broadcast a message to the network and read the responses from all servers. Applications running over NetWare/IP send "broadcast" messages to the network as they do when running on regular NetWare, but NetWare/IP converts those requests into queries to the predefined DSS. The specialized DSS server provides the requested network information, and the application is satisfied, never knowing it is not running on IPX.

This battle between broadcast and configured name server is the crux of the dislike shown by TCP/IP fans toward Novell's IPX protocol suite. TCP/IP was developed with the idea that the remote networks were slow and unreliable, so broadcasts were avoided so as not to chew up precious bandwidth with network housekeeping duties. IPX, on the other hand, was developed for local area networks, where bandwidth and network reliability were plentiful. Therefore, the concept of DNS is new to NetWare networks, and requires some effort to understand on the part of the NetWare administrator. The DSS, the hybrid system that makes NetWare/IP possible, is new to everyone.

When the NetWare/IP product is installed from the CD-ROM (LOAD INSTALL then highlight "Choose an item or product listed above" and press Enter), there is an opportunity to go right into NetWare/IP installation. Do not do this, particularly if TCP/IP support on that server is yet to be installed.

SERVER INSTALLATION AND CONFIGURATION

It is important to have NetWare TCP/IP installed and running on the NetWare server before adding NetWare/IP. If the standard NetWare/IP installation is followed, one is offered a chance to add TCP/IP support during the NetWare/IP installation process. This is tempting and seems efficient, but it will not work.

All installation and configuration is done through Novell's C-Worthy interface, which provides only ASCII graphics in primary colors. At the server console, stifle the urge to type LOAD INSTALL. TCP/IP support is built into NetWare 4.11 and IntranetWare, so it is only necessary to provide some configuration details and bind the protocol to the appropriate network interface card. The INSTALL program will not be used until later. Instead, type LOAD INETCFG.

The user will be asked permission to move all the protocol information from the AUTOEXEC.NCF file to new programs called INITSYS.NCF and NETINFO.CFG. The latter is new to NetWare 4.11.

Asking "permission" is not really a choice, since NetWare TCP/IP demands that these new files be created. One important difference between AUTOEXEC.NCF and these new files is editing: one cannot edit these files directly without bypassing multiple screens promising disaster if one continues. Changes can only be made through the INETCFG program.

The menus in INETCFG change, depending on which products are loaded on the server. What is needed for TCP/IP are Boards, Protocols, and Bindings.

Inside the Configured Boards screen, a list of multiple boards may be seen, even though there is only a single physical board in the server. Add a board by pressing the Insert key, and give the board a name of less than 10 characters. If one board is named "IPX-LAN" already, take the easy road and use "TCP-LAN" for the next board.

NetWare now assumes that the server is Plug and Play ISA, rather than the old-fashioned ISA. If the server does not support Plug and Play, the field to answer "Is the card a legacy ISA Card" to YES from NO, the default, must be changed manually. One must provide either the Plug and Play default slot number of 10001, or the IO port and ID Port values for the board. This is not any different from installing NetWare 4.11 in the first place. Escape to save and move down the INETCFG menu to Protocols. Exhibit 36.1 shows the Board Configuration for TCP/IP setup.

Press "t" for TCP/IP, and press Enter. The "Status" field will say "Unconfigured" until the board is configured, naturally enough. The default choices for the new virtual board will likely work. If the company has no intelligent routers, the user may need to specify a stated routing table, but this is not often necessary.

The IP address of the server board supporting TCP/IP will be missing from this screen. Press the Escape key to save what has been done thus far and choose "Bindings" from the main menu.

The "Configured Protocol to Network Interface Bindings" screen shows each virtual board, along with the protocol supported by that virtual board. If multiple IPX frame types are supported, such as Ethernet 802.3 for older systems and Ethernet 802.2, the new default, each will show up in the "Protocol" field.

The "Binding TCP/IP to a LAN Interface" window finally allows one to give the IP address for the NetWare server. In this example, the address used is 204.251.122.3. If this is new, ask the TCP/IP administrator what address to use for the server, and type that number in exactly. Exhibit 36.2 illustrates how to set the IP address.

The other critical field is the "Subnetwork Mask of Connected Network." The TCP/IP administrator will most likely give a number of 255.255.255.0. One can put that number in, but Novell engineers use the hexadecimal equivalent number of FF.FF.FF.0 instead. Both will work, but the latter is the default.

Press Escape enough times to return to the main menu and choose "View Configuration." The first option on the submenu is to view all

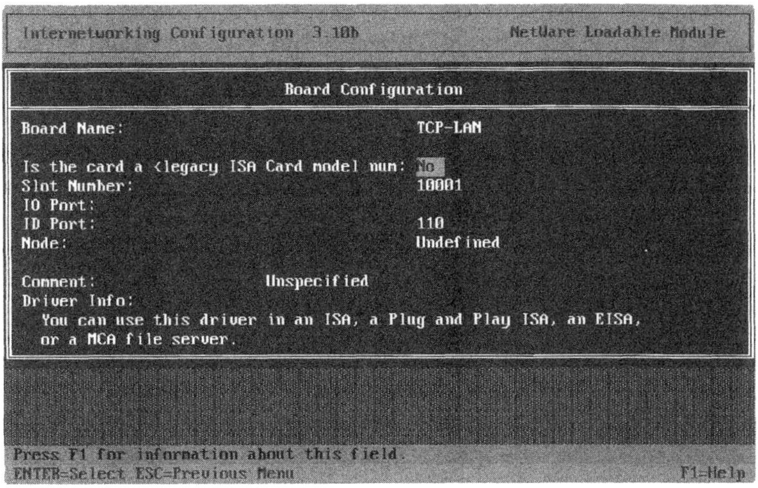

Exhibit 36.1. Board Configuration for TCP/IP Setup

INETCFG commands, meaning view the resulting file created by the configuration choices. This mode is read-only, but it is a good place to check one's IP address and other settings.

Configuring DNS

NetWare/IP will function perfectly well using an external DNS server, such as the Sun SPARCstation supporting a company E-mail server. Many

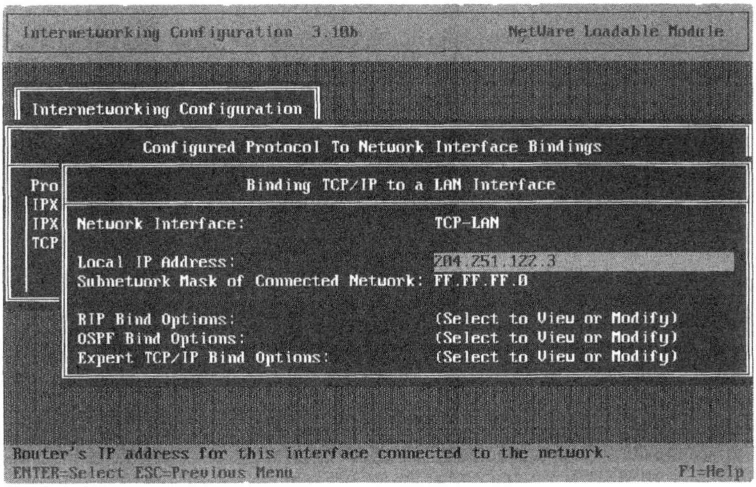

Exhibit 36.2. How to Set the IP Address

customers prefer to designate a NetWare server to support the NetWare/IP clients, to keep NetWare traffic limited to NetWare servers if for no other reason. If NetWare/IP clients want Internet access, they must list an Internet connected name server in the client RESOLV.CFG file.

Once again, the action happens at the NetWare server console. Start the UNICON program on the server console. Only supervisors can control UNICON, so have the ADMIN user password close at hand. Nonsupervisors may later make changes after being granted permission, but only the ADMIN password gains access to UNICON configuration screens. One is asked for the server name, username, and ADMIN password immediately when starting UNICON.

Multiple servers can be configured from a single console, as evidenced by the menu choice "Change Current Server" and the need for the ADMIN password. Remote servers can be handled using RCONSOLE or after starting UNICON at the local server console, whichever is preferable.

The read-only "View Server Profile" screen shows the server's IP name (make it the same as the NDS name for simplicity), IP address, and subnet mask. A pop-up screen shows NetWare information such as the operating system version, current NDS context, and the NDS Tree. More details, such as installed products, server time zone, and some NFS and NetWare user coordination are available from another subscreen of this screen. Exhibit 36.3 shows the information that must be provided.

The meat comes in the "Manage Global Objects" menu screens. Here, the user enables DNS Client Access, sets the domain name, and lists the name server addresses. The \ETC\HOSTS file, used by DNS to find and interact with other hosts, can also be modified.

Configured hosts in the local domain appear after pressing the Enter key twice on the Hosts options. The Insert key allows for the addition of more hosts, and the Delete key dispatches the highlighted host. The only mandatory fields are for host name and primary IP address. Physical address, aliases, other IP addresses (each IP network connection must have a separate address, even on the same host), NDS object, machine type, and operating system may be added.

The "Start/Stop Services" menu option is the next choice, and this opens a window labeled "Running Services." The Insert key opens the "Available Services" window, and one needs only to highlight and press Enter to start a service. The choices? DNS Server, DSS Server, NetWare/IP Server, NetWare-to-Unix Print Gateway, and the XConsole Server, a vt100 terminal support service should the user wish to run RCONSOLE over telnet. Avoid XConsole if possible. However, the NetWare/IP server depends on the active services and support of the DSS Server and a DNS name server, whether NetWare or other.

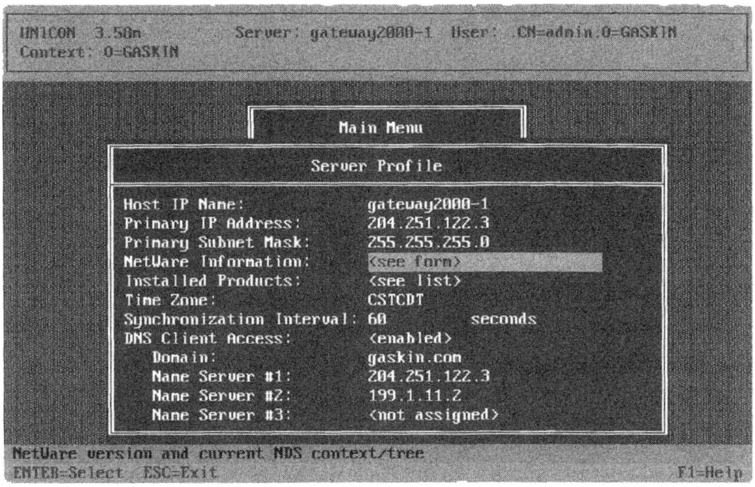

Exhibit 36.3. The "View Server Profile" Screen

Back on the main menu, "Configure Error Reporting" sets the details for NetWare console logging and various SNMP (Simple Network Management Protocol) settings. Do not worry about these until everything else is running. If the company is big on SNMP, it still may elect to cover the NetWare server via NDS.

The menu option "Perform File Operations" makes life easy in large, DNS-aware companies. The NetWare server is now a full-fledged UNIX host, since it runs TCP/IP and has a network address. Use the FTP utility to grab that file, automatically putting it into the correct server directory. File access permissions can also be set, but do not worry about those until all else is running.

Here, the user goes to the main menu important screen: the "Manage Services" menu option that has been ignored thus far. In this menu, there is a list of "Running Services" in the submenu option of the same name, but DSS will not be on that screen. One must go back to the NetWare/IP configuration screen for that.

DNS settings abound, however. One can "Administer DNS," "Initialize DNS Master Database," and "Save DNS Master to Text Files." Under "Administer DNS," one sees "Manage Master Database," "Manage Replica Databases," "Link to Existing DNS Hierarchy," "Query Remote Name Server," and "Disable DNS Service."

"Manage Master Database" leads to "Manage Data," "Delegate Subzone Authority," and "Delegate Subzone by IP Authority." The "DNS Resource Record Information" screen under "Manage Data," where one actually describes the record names and types, is the seventh level from the top of UNICON.

Subzones may be assigned to others to manage, but do not worry about this unless geographically diverse networks exist. In local networks, allow one or two supervisors to manage all the NetWare/IP details.

Back up to the DNS menu under the "Manage Services" menu, and find the "Initialize DNS Master Database" option. Activate this well-hidden, but important option before continuing. DNS entries can be confirmed on this screen as well.

Starting the DSS Software

Back up once again to the "Manage Services" submenu, and choose "NetWare/IP" to configure both the NetWare/IP and DSS servers. Do not jump ahead and type LOAD NWIPCFG at the server console to start NetWare/IP, because it will not work. Go from UNICON to "Manage Services" to "Manage NetWare/IP" to configure DSS details before starting the NetWare/IP server software.

From "NetWare/IP Administration," bypass "Configure NetWare/IP Server" and "Delete NetWare/IP Server Configuration" and choose "Configure Primary DSS." One is first asked to name the NetWare/IP domain, and the default name of the DNS domain will be listed in the field. Be sure to add "nwip" to the beginning of the current DNS domain name so it will work. If the DNS domain name is gaskin.com, make the DSS domain name nwip.gaskin.com and this will work (see Exhibit 36.4).

The other fields that must be filled are the primary DSS host name and a unique IPX network number for the new NetWare/IP virtual network segment. The instructions say the DSS name must be "fully qualified," leading most to think that means an NDS fully qualified name. Actually, Novell wants the DNS qualified name, listing the server and domain (gateway2000-1.gaskin.com) instead.

Other options on the menu are "Tunable Parameters" and "DSS SAP Filters." The first option allows one to set the synchronization details between the primary and secondary DSS server, the DSS server, and NetWare/IP servers. One can increase the ticks between synchronizations to accommodate router lag and transmission delays. At least one secondary DSS server on another NetWare server in the domain is definitely needed. SAP filters allow for control of the amount of information exchanged between servers, if network traffic levels are a consideration. Plenty of SAP (Service Advertising Protocol) and RIP (Routing Information Protocol) details are available in the "Browse DSS Database" menu option. This is not casual information, however, so do not look for help there unless directed by Novell support.

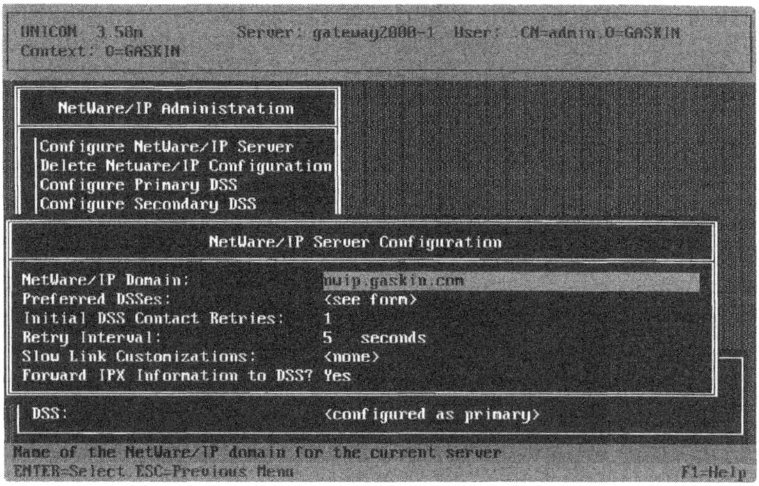

Exhibit 36.4. NetWare/IP Administration

Back to "Configure NetWare/IP Server" so that one can set the name of the NetWare/IP domain and the preferred DSSes (by IP address or host name of up to five DSS servers). The number of contact retries and intervals between connections can be set if desired. "Slow Link Customizations" again allows one to pad the communications times to accommodate slow remote links.

The setting to make this particular DSS server a gateway between the NetWare/IP clients and NetWare IPX clients is here as well. The default is "no." Since few companies can completely convert all users from IPX to NetWare/IP in one fell swoop, at least one of the systems should act as a gateway. Multiple gateways automatically load balance between the two groups, which is a good reason to have at least three gateway systems configured.

Go back to the UNICON main menu, and start NetWare/IP. If it works, there will be a message saying "NetWare/IP Server is initialized and functional." If that message does not appear, delete and start over. It is quicker than trying to retrace steps and correct details.

THE NETWARE/IP CLIENT

NetWare/IP, at least the version that ships with NetWare 4.11 and IntranetWare, expects to see Client32 software on the client. Client software may be installed from the NetWare CD-ROM, a set of diskettes, or the \PUBLIC\CLIENT\WIN31 or \PUBLIC\CLIENT\WIN95 directories on the newly NetWare/IP equipped server. Run the INSTALL program for DOS, and SETUP for Windows of both types. As of this writing, there is not yet a NetWare/IP client for Windows NT, but that may be changed by the time this article appears in print. When NT is supported by NetWare/IP, the client installation will be the same as for Windows 95, judging by how Novell has handled NT systems thus far.

One can install Client32 for DOS or Windows, TCP/IP and NetWare/IP (which does require the TCP/IP box just above on the screen to be checked, as well), desktop SNMP, and the TSA (Target Service Agent) for backup systems.

When installing TCP/IP and NetWare/IP, one must provide IP addresses for the client and the router, the subnetwork mask, domain name, NetWare/IP domain name, and the address of the name server or servers. If using DHCP (Dynamic Host Configuration Protocol), the client needs information about the DHCP server instead. Windows 3.1 systems put details in the NET.CFG file, while Windows 95 hides them in the Networking Property sheets.

The Client32 software change will mask any NetWare/IP problems, such as slightly slower performance and more RAM used at the client. Detractors will say that Client32 causes these problems, but Windows of every flavor can share that blame. Novell rated versions of NetWare/IP before Client32 software as losing 11% of their performance versus native IPX clients. With Client32, there is no discernible difference in casual testing.

NetWare/IP and the Internet

NetWare/IP can act as a springboard for NetWare clients to reach the Internet, but it is a long, hard road to that springboard. One will get there, but it will take longer.

Internet access, or even accessing TCP/IP-based intranet resources within the company, relies on two important configuration details. First, the name server used by the NetWare/IP server must have an Internet connection itself. Using the name server at the Internet Service Provider as the backup DNS server would accomplish that goal. Using a name server within the company that is connected to the Internet will work as well. If the name server is not Internet-enabled, NetWare/IP cannot reach the Internet either.

Second, the Client32 software will not automatically replace the WINSOCK.DLL provided by Windows in the \WINDOWS directory. NetWare/IP's client installation adds a WINSOCK.DLL, but places the file in the \NOVELL\CLIENT32 directory. This is logical, but always behind the \WINDOWS directory in the client PATH statements. When Netscape or any other TCP/IP application starts, it will find the Microsoft WINSOCK.DLL program first, become confused, and crash.

Rename the WINSOCK.DLL program in the \WINDOWS directory rather than deleting it, because one can never tell when Windows will demand some supposedly obsolete DLL file. Copy the Novell WINSOCK.DLL file into the \WINDOWS directory since some applications will not accept the file anywhere else on the PATH statement. Then try everything again.

If Internet or intranet access is the goal, one needs to check out the IPX-IP Gateway included with IntranetWare rather than NetWare/IP. A dozen other companies make NetWare to Internet gateways besides Novell, and all of them are less trouble to configure, use, and maintain than NetWare/IP.

Upgrade Security

TCP/IP has a terrible reputation for security because it has so little. TCP/IP was developed and enhanced with people interested in sharing. Unfortunately, some of the things hackers want to share are the same things that a company and its employees would prefer to keep private.

If any type of Internet connection already exists, do not initiate NetWare/IP until a functioning firewall is in place. Even other departments may cause security problems. If everyone in the company is all together on the TCP/IP network, any security breach is a problem for every department.

CONCLUSION

NetWare/IP is a specialized tool for special situations. IPX works better, faster, and takes less RAM than TCP/IP, so upgrading without a good reason will only cause a company to regret that choice later.

Few activities show the old-fashioned side of NetWare better than an extended console session. The C-Worthy interface looks extremely dated. Windows NT may be winning the marketing war strictly on the appearance of Windows NT administration tools versus the C-Worthy interface applications present on NetWare.

NetWare/IP will completely replace IPX for all client communications to the NetWare server. If a company feels that the installation pain of NetWare/IP is worth the advantages to be gained by supporting a single corporate network protocol (TCP/IP) rather than two (adding IPX), then NetWare/IP will do the job as advertised. Once NetWare/IP is configured, it works and continues to work without problem.

Chapter 37
Software Configuration Management in a Client/Server Environment: A Case Study

John McMullen

When trying to track down a problem — either during development or while maintaining an already-released version — time and money are lost trying to locate the problem files. The reasons are many, including:

- Files change over time. In many distributed environment (such as local area networks, or LAN), file ownership is not enough to determine who last changed a file, and it is never enough to identify who made the second-to-last change. Without a history of those changes, time is wasted reconstructing what probably went into a past release.
- Developers keep copies of source files that inevitably begin to differ. When the time comes for a new release or for post-release maintenance, no one can identify which copy of the file was actually used in the product.
- Developers overwrite each other's changes. Time must be spent repeating bug fixes or other modifications, once the problem is discovered.
- To identify a bug, a tester or programmer needs to work with a stable baseline. A piece of software under development may change hourly, which makes tracking down the root of a particular problem a lengthy, if not impossible, task.
- In post-release maintenance, support people must retrieve the files used to build a customer's release, test against them, find the problem and fix it. The challenge is so great that often support passes on to customers the newest version in hopes that that version will solve the problem. This is a quick solution, and not necessarily the correct one.

0-8493-9822-3/00/$0.00+$.50

All of these problems are magnified when the development environment is multiplatform or when development takes place in a distributed environment, such as a LAN. This article looks at a software development group that is addressing its configuration management situation through a combination of CM software and development discipline.

COMPANY BACKGROUND

This case study focuses on a single product group within a publicly held company that generates annual revenues of more than $128 million (1994 figures). The company produces application development tools that support a wide range of open and proprietary platforms, including UNIX and the Microsoft Windows desktop. The product group discussed in this article produces a visual development environment for building and deploying client/server applications.

The product group involves almost 120 developers and quality control workers networked with Windows NT, Windows for Workgroups, and Window 95 machines. This team deals with over 100,000 source and construction files stored on Windows NT servers.

A related project stores single source for VMS, UNIX, and NT cross-platform modules and on a UNIX machine. Although the cross-platform modules are only peripherally related to the product, those files had been under RCS control; RCS is the Revision Control System, a version control system developed on UNIX.

The company's client base includes both those customers inside the company — the other developers and the beta testers who are waiting for the next release — and the commercial clients.

The company has used configuration management tools for more than a decade. It was one of the very first to use CMS/MMS (i.e., Code Management System/Module Management System) on DEC when it was introduced in 1985. The accepted philosophy within the company is that source code management systems and object code management systems are essential, according to the director of the product group. Source and object code management systems are insurance against problems.

For its configuration management product, the group chose MKS Source Integrity, an integrated network package providing a robust set of features, including network and file security, file histories and audit trails, report generation, and the Sandbox™ development environment, which greatly eases both team-based development and post-release maintenance.

CONFIGURATION MANAGEMENT OVERVIEW

Configuration management is a relatively new term for an old problem: Coordinating the changes made to software by development teams. By careful control of software modification, development problems can be identified quickly or avoided entirely. When time is not spent on problems, it is spent on solutions, and productivity improves.

The need for configuration management appears as soon as two developers are working on a single project, or as soon as a single developer is working on two versions of a project. Yet each organization has had to come up with independent solutions to its configuration management problems. Only in the last few years has it become recognized that these are common problems requiring common solutions. Configuration management software provides the common approach to problems that any team-based development environments require.

Briefly put, configuration management is about knowing what is in the product and controlling how it gets there. CM provides control over which files go into the product, because files change over time, and to control which versions of files go into the product, ensuring that the files work together. Last, it controls how the product is made. Those three legs, content, compatibility, and construction, support configuration management and the construction of any software project. On two- or three-person projects, the delays caused by a lack of configuration management are annoying and expensive; on large projects, they are lethal and expensive.

RULES OF THE GAME

The basic tenets of configuration management are as follows. The development group should:

Maintain a single reference copy of the source

Maintaining two identical copies of a file takes twice the work and twice the opportunity for error, and it is an unnecessary use of resources. Maintaining only a single copy of the source provides access control as well. Developers retrieve a temporary working copy of the source, if authorized, but that copy is not part of the reference source until it is approved and put into the reference copy of the source tree.

The authorization process is normally automatic and is handled by the software, because developers are trusted employees. At any point, however, a manager can remove faulty changes from the source.

Make access for modifying source files exclusive

When one developer has declared an intention to change a source file, no other developer may change the file. This is typically handled by a file-locking mechanism. The same mechanism a developer uses to get a copy of a file also locks the file.

Record all changes to the files

This audit trail is the heart of configuration management. With an accurate record, a developer can re-create any version of the file. Without an accurate record, the project's history is reconstructed by guesswork alone. Files are an asset to the company, an intellectual property that is valuable but fragile. The audit trail protects that asset.

With the system chosen by the company, the audit trail is part of the retrieval and authorization process. It records who changed the file, what changes were made to the file, and when they were put back into the reference source.

Record the files that went into a release

This is essential for post-release maintenance. Once the contents of a release are recorded, the release can be regenerated at any time in the future. Because files change, a list of the files in the release must also contain the version of each file, as recorded in the audit trail. It s a snapshot of the product — a record of its appearance at a point in history.

The software selected has a project feature to record the files involved. It also supports the idea of "checkpointing" a project, in which the current versions of all files are recorded and labeled as a grouped set.

Isolate developers from unnecessary change

If a developer spends a day checking an apparently unsuccessful fix only to discover that the real problem was introduced to another module at the same time by another developer, a person-day has been lost. A solid configuration management system provides a stable baseline for developers to test their own changes against. MKS Source Integrity has a unique solution in its Sandbox development environments.

Because configuration management problems are, in part, social ones having to do with the culture of a particular organization, no single tool provides the complete solution. The full answer to a specific configuration management problem is always a combination of appropriate tools and a willingness to communicate on the part of the development team.

No development manager in the company under study in this article would risk his or her reputation by not using a source code management system. Configuration management is so important to the product group that they have a Build Team, which is in charge of the quality and consistency of the product's construction and file management.

Configuration management pays for itself in reduced quality assurance and support costs. Fixing a bug before the product ships is less expensive than fixing it after.

SOURCE ORGANIZATION

The first issue of configuration management, as mentioned earlier, is that multiple copies of source files exist. Whenever possible, only one official copy of a source file should exist, and only the official source should be used for builds. (The official source is sometimes called the baseline source or the production source.) One of the functions of configuration management tools is to provide a way for developers to modify that official source so that their changes can be verified and tracked. Organizing source is a large part of this.

The product produced by the group has more than 100,000 files stored on a Windows NT server and provided to developers and testers as needed through the LAN. To maintain the files, the product group divides the file groupings into projects of 50 to 100 files. Those projects are then gathered into larger projects, and those projects are gathered again into projects. Three levels of projects handle all of the product's files. When building the product, developers do not have to build each individual project, only the top-level project. Recursion facilities the configuration management software automatically build the included projects.

The construction facility determines which files are actually rebuilt. Although the build facility in their software solution contains a number of advanced features, including automated generation of dependency lists, the group chose to stay with its existing construction tool, because the construction scripts represented a sizable time investment. The configuration management software was able to integrate with other tools rather than relying on its own construction facility.

ISOLATING CHANGES

When testing new code or finding a problem in old code, a developer requires a stable product. In a development environment, this is rare. The source is changing every day, and it may take several days to track a particularly insidious bug. With post-release maintenance, the problem is even more difficult: The files that went into a buggy release may not exist any more.

In the product group, developers use MKS Source Integrity's unique Sandbox feature to provide themselves with a "carbon copy" of the source as it existed at any point in its history. This copy could be of the current source or of the source that went into a former release. This working directory becomes the developer's playground for testing hypotheses and trying fixes.

For new development, developers assume that a project continues while the developer tracks a bug. While stability is essential for bug hunting, currency is also essential to see if the bug fix actually works with the existing source. A developer uses a single command to replace all the unchanged working files with their current equivalents. From that point on, the developer is checking to ensure that a bug fix is consistent with the rest of the product.

FILE ACCESS AND QUALITY CONTROL

Controlling file access is critical to maintaining security. It also has an impact on quality control. The company required these two key features for maintaining security and an audit trail

- Permission to modify source files is controlled, both through the file locking mechanism and through access lists.
- A record is maintained of all changes, including who changed the file, when the file was changed, and how the files were changed, providing the information to recreate the version of that file that existed at any point in its history.

This audit trail — the record of changes and the file's content — is stored in a file archive. Different configuration management systems use different archiving schemes. For the company, compatibility between the configuration management system's file archiving scheme and the UNIX RCS scheme used on the cross-platform legacy code on UNIX was useful. When team members need to examine the cross-platform modules, they can use the commands of the new software, which function identically to the corresponding RCS commands.

By putting the 100,000 files in the product source under the control of the configuration management software, the organization has a record of every change made to each file, who made the change, and when the change was made, back to the start of file archiving. (The project converted to the new software earlier this year, but file compatibility with UNIX RCS means that the histories of some files go back to the beginning of the project.) This audit trail can be summarized using the CM software's report-generation facility, which can print reports summarizing the activities on the file from any arbitrary baseline(e.g., a time, a version number, or a release).

An important feature for this company was the ability to export reports to a database. The company exports the audit trail of files changed into database. Further reports are generated using their proprietary database engine.

When a problem is found, it can often be isolated to one of a set of modules just because of the nature of the problem. Even if it cannot, the problem can often be narrowed very quickly by looking at the list of changed files since the last known version in which the problem did not exist. Rather than comparing individual files, developers can compare product snapshots and see which files have changed. These snapshots, or checkpoints, provide overviews of the changes.

The more often checkpoints are made, the smaller the differences between the contents. With fewer differences to examine, a problem can be found faster. The product group described in this article has about 32,000 checkpoints on their file sets; this is one reason why they checkpoint their files daily. They adhere to the discipline of frequent checkpoints for an important reason: In the long run, it saves time.

CROSS-PLATFORM COMPATIBILITY

Other products at the company are multiplatform (Windows NT, UNIX, and VMS) and are built from a single set of sources on a UNIX server. The product group shares some modules with these products, so the configuration management system must work with the UNIX system as well. The revision control system used on the UNIX system is RCS; obviously, a system that is compatible with RCS is preferable.

Compatibility with configuration management systems on other platforms was useful, but not essential. Most of the PC-based configuration management systems available today provide conversion utilities to convert archive files. These utilities are limited because they are often one-way conversions. If the new configuration management system does not run on all of the platforms, control of files is lost.

Because the multiplatform files are single-sourced on a UNIX machine, the product group takes advantage of the fact that their CM software is history-compatible with UNIX RCS archives.

EASE OF USE

When selecting new technologies, ease of use is often overlooked in favor of other features. When the product group was testing candidates for their configuration management tool, they selected on the base of performance and ease of use. In the final decision, ease of use was the deciding factor.

There are several reasons for choosing the easier-to-use product. An easy-to-use tool requires less support internally, which translates into lowered costs. The lower support costs can begin as soon as the product is installed. Installation was quick and painless, a factor worth considering for a site with 150 licenses. After filling out only three dialog boxes, the configuration is done. A more complex installation and configuration process puts a greater load on the support staff and costs more money.

Understandably, the development process used by the product group requires a certain amount of discipline from the developers. The configuration management tools must be used diligently, or the benefits are greatly reduced. The fact is, a tool that is awkward to use simply will not be used. It must be easier to use the tool than to circumvent the tool. Otherwise, developers conveniently forget to check a file in or out, or to create a new sandbox environment.

THE DEVELOPMENT MODEL

The only way to ensure that all components of a piece of software work together is to build them and test the software. The more often the software is built, the sooner a problem is caught. However, many organizations build infrequently or only at significant points in the development cycle. In the development group, the product under development is built every day. The priority is to get a buildable product, every day.

The entire project is checkpointed every morning. This places a marker, or a "bookmark" that indicates the state of the product that morning. After the day's work is finished, the product development manager builds the product. In later stages of development, the newly constructed product may also be run through an automated suite of tests.

The next morning, the product manager examines the record of the build, and checks for failures, either in the build or in the tests. When there is a failure, it is diagnosed. If the cause is not immediately obvious, the product manager can use the audit trail to see which files have changed in the last day. The problem is somehow related to those files.

As mentioned earlier, the list of changed files is stored in a database. With this guidance, it is usually a quick matter to find the source of the problem. Strictly speaking, the problem may not be in one of the files that changed; for example, if an API changed, the problem could be in a module where the call was not changed.

Once the problem is isolated, the product development manager requests an immediate fix. The first priority is to restore the product to a state in which it can be built, providing a baseline for testing.

The decision to build daily was made partly because building daily enforces a certain discipline on the programmers. It also requires a level of support from the corporate culture. For example, it is a matter of pride among the developers to ensure that their changes do not interfere with the construction. There is informal discussion of instituting a "Hall of Shame" outside the cafeteria; developers responsible for breaking the build will have their pictures displayed there.

CONCLUSION

The stated goal of configuration management is to maximize productivity by minimizing problems. This productivity gain comes through time savings for developers of new software and maintainers of a released product. Managers also gain through improved control, auditing, and tracking.

- Configuration management is a combination of the appropriate policy and the right tools. A configuration management policy must:
- Be orchestrated from above.
- Be easy to use. Some of the ease-of-use can come from the product, but some must lie in the policies.
- Encourage the stability of the product: a clean build is the minimum starting point.
- Encourage frequent checkpoints. The more frequent the checkpoints, the fewer changes each one encompasses, and the easier it is to use differences between checkpoints to find problems.
- Work with other critical development tools.

A configuration management product must:

- Maintain a single reference copy of the source and make it available.
- Control access to the source files. The company needed file locking and access to Novell network security.
- Maintain a history of changes to the source.
- Record the identities of those who changed the files.
- Support the organization and construction of source into logical groups, such as projects.
- Isolate the developer from spurious changes to the project but allow the developer to be current when necessary.
- Run on the platforms to be handled.

Section VI Checklist

1. Would you characterize the operating environment of your computing environment as complex? What factors contribute to this?
2. How many different operating platforms does your organization use for application development? Does this create difficulty in developing enterprise-based applications?
3. Is it important for your organization to develop applications across platforms or between operating systems? Will this continue in the future?
4. What challenges does cross platform application development pose in your environment? Have you found solutions to the problems or have you abandoned the effort?
5. Is the struggle between CORBA and COM standards affect your plans when developing application systems?
6. Assuming both CORBA and COM remain industry co-standards, would you favor one over the other to help simplify development practices, or does it make more sense to use each for their own strengths?
7. How does your organization define and implement client/server and cooperative processing applications? Is there confusion on the implementation strategy?
8. Who governs the connectivity between host-based systems and micro-based systems? What controls or auditing procedures are used to ensure the reliability and integrity of the connection?
9. Could you identify the hardware connectivity options available in your environment? If not, what criteria is used for cross platform development?
10. What changes would you recommend as a means of improving the execution of application systems in a client/server environment?
11. Can you identify the differences between n-tiered applications in your organization? Should these differences be a function of operating platform or application requirements?
12. What is your organization's assessment of Windows NT vs. NetWare as a network operating system. Are you more interested in functionality or stability?
13. Does Windows NT pose any significant challenges to your network environment? If not, is there consideration for using Windows NT as a desktop platform along with the server platform?
14. How is configuration management handled in your environment? Should this be the responsibility of the application development team or the network support group?

15. What techniques could be incorporated in your environment that would improve the methods for tracking down file problems used by applications? Are you concerned about potential failures that could shut down an entire application for an extended period?

Section VII
Networking and Connectivity

Networking and connectivity remain as salient issues in the future role of corporate computing. Continued growth of communication technologies, has prompted many organizations to capitalize on the distributed power of multi-platform processors. This has been especially true for Internet and intranet environments. While the benefits of connectivity are encouraging, there is significant effort in deciphering the various networking options and directions. Since communication is at the heart of computing architecture, it has a profound impact on an organization's technical prowess. Pursuing bleeding edge networking products too rapidly, or delaying implementation of stable technology, can have adverse affects on application development and support. Furthermore, the IS industry is debating the merits of Network Computers (NC) over the prevailing establishment of Desktop Computers. Arguments about the "computer being the network" and visa versa have only added more challenges to the effort for implementing network-centric applications.

One of the more interesting and lively debated topics of network computing has been the future of large-scale mainframe processors. Long regarded as dead, mainframes have surprised many in the IS community. In fact, just the opposite may be occurring through a resurgence in the role of these work-horse machines. Chapter 38, "The Mainframe as Enterprise Server," looks at the trends for incorporating the mainframe as an integral part of the networking environment. As technology advancements increase in the network server arena, the line between mainframe and server computers has become less distinguishable. Given the deployed base of mainframes, organizations would be wise to exploit the vast power of large scale processors for the sake of network servers.

Advancements in technology for e-commerce business applications have generated tremendous interest in the last year. And predication for continued growth in cyber commerce have been meeting or exceeding many expectations. However, there is equal concern that security for e-commerce systems is still lacking and requires careful monitoring. Chapter 39, "Developing a Trusted Infrastructure for Electronic Commerce Services," discusses the diverse issues involved with securing commerce networks. This chapter also proposes ways of confirming sender and recipient identities, protecting confidentiality, and date stamping to ensure trustworthy applications.

Electronic Messaging Systems, in the form of e-mail, are some of the earliest examples of a network centric applications. Most organizations have some form of message systems, and in numerous instances, there can be several that are concurrently implemented in a given environment. Furthermore, it is not uncommon for organizations to migrate from one type of message system to another in order to improve overall communication efficiency. Chapter 40, "Integrating Electronic Messaging Systems and Infrastructures," gives an overview of the issues surrounding consolidation of disparate messaging systems. This information can be useful when developing applications that encompass e-mail as part of the system functionality.

The explosive use of the Internet has also fueled considerate concern about the general security and safety of network environments. Incidents of security breaches seem to occur daily, and there is an expanding need to tighten control on network communications. At the center of Internet security lies the mechanism to encrypt and decrypt information. Chapter 41, "Understanding Public Key Cryptology," reviews the basic structure of cryptological systems. Although many crypotological systems are currently in use, there have been known weaknesses that allow for security violations. Development managers should maintain a close watch on the ongoing changes and advancements in Internet security as it pertains to the application development process.

Chapter 38
The Mainframe as Enterprise Server

Brian Jeffrey

Among companies that have used information systems (IS) to sustain competitiveness, a new kind of IS strategy is emerging. IS technology is being used not only to automate business tasks and processes, but also to turn the information itself into a powerful competitive weapon. Simple, effective techniques enable the IS infrastructure to deliver continuous, accurate, and useful information to executives, line managers, sales professionals, and front-line workers throughout the organization.

At the same time, new integrated software systems increase the efficiency of all business operations. Products and services are delivered more rapidly. Sales and service become more responsive to customers. And organization structures as well as business processes are streamlined to reduce operating costs and eliminate unnecessary administrative overheads.

ENTERPRISE SERVER ROLE

The basis of a new IS strategy is a modernized, upgraded mainframe system equipped with new data base and application tools that enable it to function as an enterprise server. Mainframe-based computing retains its embedded strengths of economy of scale, robustness, and business-critical computing. The mainframe continues to run the core systems without which the business could not function, providing high levels of availability, data integrity, and security.

However, these systems also acquire powerful new client/server capabilities. Central databases play a new role in concentrating, protecting, and providing access to all corporate data resources. Users employ PCs, workstations, and mobile computers to access this data, and to communicate via organizationwide network infrastructures.

New development tools deliver high-quality, flexible applications in a fraction of the time previously required. In most cases, legacy data, applications, and skills carry over to the new IS environment. More importantly, there is no significant business disruption.

0-8493-9822-3/00/$0.00+$.50

The transition from conventional mainframe computing to an enterprise server-based IS strategy uses simple techniques and proven solutions. In most growth companies, it can be realized within 12 to 18 months. Key applications can be brought online even more rapidly. In an organization that already uses mainframe systems efficiently, and employs modern hardware and software technologies, much of the infrastructure will already be in place.

BUSINESS BENEFITS

Costs will vary from company to company. But such an IS strategy, if properly applied, will yield business gains and improvements in efficiency that more than justify the investments. Within the IS infrastructure, data center operating costs are normally reduced by two to eight times. Application development productivity can be increased up to eight times. PC/LAN costs can be reduced 50 to 80 percent. Telecommunications costs can be reduced up to 50 percent. Savings can also be realized in other areas.

TECHNICAL IMPLEMENTATION

The technical infrastructure for a leadership IS strategy is based on upgrading a mainframe system with new capabilities that enable it to function as an enterprise server. The enterprise server is the cornerstone of this strategy. It concentrates key IS resources to better support distributed and remote users. It also increases the volume, quality, and accessibility of information for all users, improves availability of application, data, and network resources, and maximizes the cost effectiveness with which all IS resources are used.

ENTERPRISE SERVER BASICS

An enterprise server combines the following distinct and, until recently, separate computing technology streams.

Mainframe Computing

In most growth companies, this focuses on business control systems, such as accounting, finance, asset management, personnel administration, and payroll, and the core business-critical systems without which the company could not function. The mainframe's key strengths are its robustness, its ability to handle large-scale, organizationwide workloads, its ability to provide high levels of availability and data integrity, and its capability to manage all system, data, and network resources effectively in performing these tasks. Mainframes also leverage economies of scale, benefits of concentrated resources, and consistencies of architecture that are inherent to the central IS environment. Few seriously question the superiority of mainframe systems in these areas.

Client/Server Computing

This refers to the use of PCs and workstations. Although industry debate often treats client/server computing as a single phenomenon, in practice, it involves several different types of applications. A basic category includes text processing, electronic mail, and personal productivity tools. These are useful and fairly easy to implement in an end-user environment. The largest and, from a business standpoint, most valuable category involves "informational" client/server applications that access, manipulate, and process data. Applications include decision support, market research, financial analysis, human resources, and planning applications.

In most organizations, mainframe databases are the primary source of data used by such applications — over 95 percent, according to some estimates. The data is generated by the production business control and business-critical applications that run on mainframes. There is therefore an obvious synergy between mainframe and client/server computing. To realize business benefits from new types of applications, this synergy needs to be exploited to its full potential. By consolidating key databases and implementing reliable, organizationwide network infrastructures, all data can be made accessible at the workstation level.

In combining these technology streams, most growing companies are faced with the choice of upgrading a mainframe to act as a server or trying to equip a UNIX server to act as a mainframe. Upgrading the mainframe is normally both less expensive and less disruptive. Moreover, it is substantially less difficult to provide client/server capability to a mainframe than it is to provide mainframe-class robustness to a UNIX server. The strengths of the mainframe environment have developed over more than 30 years of handling high-volume, business-critical workloads with high levels of availability and data integrity. Few users have been prepared to entrust genuinely business-critical applications to UNIX servers. The experiences of those who have tried are not encouraging.

IMPLEMENTATION PLAN

Establishing an enterprise server involves several steps. A core data base management system (DBMS) must be put in place. This should be capable of handling online transaction processing (OLTP) and batch workloads required for business control and business-critical applications, as well as the new, query-intensive workloads that will be generated by organizationwide client/server computing. Multiple data bases, such as the common customer data base and common operational data base, are created within the core DBMS, which also ensures the accessibility, currency, integrity, security, and recoverability of all corporate data.

In some organizations, it may be necessary to replace older hierarchical data base and file structures. This is, however, a relatively fast and easy process, particularly if automated tools are used. Legacy data and applications can be converted to run on the new core DBMS. Existing applications written in COBOL and leading fourth-generation languages (4GLs) can be ported in this manner without the necessity for major rewrites.

New applications must be delivered. Leadership applications require special types of tools. Conventional COBOL- and 4GL-based techniques are often too slow and do not provide adequate levels of integration and flexibility. Equally, light-duty client/server development tools for PCs and small servers may not be able to handle the size and functional requirements of new, high-value-added solutions.

Packaged software can be used. However, most independent software vendor offerings address only standardized accounting, human resources, and business-critical requirements. They do not usually provide a direct competitive edge for companies that use them, and they are difficult to customize.

The logical candidates to use to develop these new high-volume applications are latest-generation, computer-aided software engineering (CASE), rapid application development (RAD), and object-oriented development tools for the mainframe environment. These deliver high-quality, large-scale applications that fully support client/server capabilities, including graphical user interfaces (GUIs). Moreover, they do so in a fraction of the time required with conventional techniques.

Where existing applications remain viable, a number of techniques can be used to make them more flexible and user-friendly. For example, PC-based GUIs can typically be added to legacy applications without the necessity for major changes in platforms or software architectures. Similarly, existing applications can be redeveloped and maintained using new PC-based COBOL visual programming tools.

Once the core DBMS is in place, considerable flexibility is possible. New systems can co-exist with legacy applications, and light-duty data base query, decision support, and related tools can also be employed.

Data center operations must be rebuilt around modern, efficient hardware and software technologies, automation tools, and improved management practices. High levels of capacity usage, increased performance, reduced operating costs, and minimal outages or production job failures will be the norm.

PC/LAN clusters must be integrated. To support distributed PC users more effectively, LANs are interconnected and managed from a central point. New tools are also put in place to regularly back up data on LAN servers to data center storage. This ensures that departmental data is properly managed and protected, and is accessible to other users within the organization.

These initiatives significantly improve the quality and availability of LAN infrastructures and reduce support costs.

Network infrastructures should be transparent and functional enough to allow information to flow freely throughout the organization. Increased use of client/server computing normally increases network loading, which may mean that more bandwidth is needed at both the local and wide area network levels. In addition, wireless technologies may be used to support mobile sales, logistics, and other applications. Networking for mobile computing is typically simpler and less expensive to implement than for client/server solutions built around traditional PCs and LANs.

RETURN ON INVESTMENT

If the process is properly managed, investment in the technical infrastructure will pay for itself in a relatively short period of time. First, there will be a direct impact on business performance. Sales, customer loyalty, and corporate profitability will increase. If the introduction of new systems is accompanied by business re-engineering or other forms of organizational streamlining, major reductions in personnel and other costs will typically occur. Employee productivity will also increase in all areas of the business supported by new IS solutions.

Second, there will be significant savings in the IS operations. Costs will be reduced as efficiency improves. In many companies, the use of IS resources is highly inefficient. Old systems have low capacity usage and high environmental costs. Aging application portfolios and low-productivity programming techniques mean that application maintenance overheads are too high. Old, inefficient code and poor tuning generate excessive consumption of processor and storage resources. Networks are poorly optimized. And both mainframe and PC/LAN installations are characterized by low value-added, manpower-intensive practices.

Efficiency improvements yield gains in four main areas: data center costs, application costs, PC/LAN costs, and network costs.

Data Center Costs

If the organization starts with low levels of mainframe efficiency, annual operating costs — including hardware acquisitions, software licenses, maintenance, and most categories of IS personnel — can routinely be reduced by two to five times and may be reduced as much as eight times. If the data center is efficient to begin with, reductions of 10 to 20 percent per annum in operating costs can still be expected.

Application Costs

Latest-generation mainframe development tools deliver radical increases in the speed of application development and in developer productivity, compared with conventional COBOL. Applications can therefore be developed more rapidly, with fewer analysts and programmers. They will also have substantially longer life cycles and require less maintenance.

PC/LAN Costs

Hardware, software, support, and other costs for PC/LAN installations are normally in the range of $6000 to $10,000 per user per year. Consolidation, mainframe-based remote LAN management and backup tools, and other techniques can routinely reduce these costs by 50 to 80 percent.

Network Costs

These can be reduced by improved capacity management, data compression, and new technologies, such as frame relay, which has been shown to reduce telecommunications costs for SNA networks by up to 50%, depending on network size and configuration.

The objective may not always be to lower IS costs per se. In organizations experiencing growth in applications and workloads, the result may be that new requirements are met without increasing IS costs, rather than through net reductions in IS budgets. In either case, initial investment to create a more efficient, functional IS infrastructure built around a mainframe-based enterprise server will yield major payoffs both in positive business benefits and in significantly higher yields from IS expenditures.

CONCLUSION

The leadership IS strategy described in this document is about using IS resources for maximum, organizationwide business impact. That means focusing IS strategy not on any single theme in business performance but on all of the variables that affect the market penetration, competitive success, and profitability of a growing company. And it means moving beyond using IS to automate business tasks and processes more effectively, to turn information itself into a dynamic new tool that can be employed throughout the organization, from the executive suite to the front-line worker.

More fundamentally, a leadership IS strategy is also about integration and coordination. A company does not succeed as a collection of individuals and departments. Similarly, the IS infrastructure must do more than empower individual users. It must provide a further level of value by creating a new cohesiveness in the way in which all of the company's resources — human, material, financial, and technical — are focused and deployed for success. In a leadership company, the whole is always more than the sum of the parts.

Chapter 39
Developing a Trusted Infrastructure for Electronic Commerce Services

David Litwack

THE USE OF INTERNETWORKING APPLICATIONS FOR ELECTRONIC COMMERCE has been limited by issues of security and trust and by the lack of universality of products and services supporting robust and trustworthy electronic commerce services. Specific service attributes must be addressed to overcome the hesitation of users and business owners to exploit open systems — such as the Internet — for commercial exchanges. These service attributes include:

- **Confirmation of identity (nonrepudiation).** This indicates proof that only intended participants (i.e., creators and recipients) are party to communications.
- **Confidentiality and content security.** Documents can be neither read nor modified by an uninvited third party.
- **Time certainty.** Proof of date and time of communication is provided through time stamps and return receipts.
- **Legal protection.** Electronic documents should be legally binding and protected by tort law and fraud statutes.

SERVICE ATTRIBUTE AUTHORITY

To support these service attributes, an organization or entity would need to provide:

- Certificate authority services, including the registration and issuance of certificates for public keys as well as the distribution of certificate revocation and compromised key lists to participating individuals and organizations.
- A repository for public key certificates that can provide such keys and certificates to authorized requesters on demand.

0-8493-9822-3/00/$0.00+$.50

- Electronic postmarking for date and time stamps, and for providing the digital signature of the issuer for added assurance.
- Return receipts that provide service confirmation.
- Storage and retrieval services, including a transaction archive log and an archive of bonded documents.

These service attributes could be offered singly or in various combinations. The service attribute provider would have to be recognized as a certificate and postmark authority. The following sections describe how a service attribute provider should work.

Certificate Authority

Although public key encryption technology provides confidentiality and confirmation of identity, a true trusted infrastructure requires that a trusted authority certify a person or organization as the owner of the key pair. Certificates are special data structures used to register and protectively encapsulate the public key users and prevent their forgery. A certificate contains the name of a user and its public key. An electronic certificate binds the identity of the person or organization to the key pair.

Certificates also contain the name of the issuer — a certificate authority(CA) — that vouches that the public key in a certificate belongs to the named user. This data, along with a time interval specifying the certificate's validity, is cryptography signed by the issuer using the issuer's private key. The subject and issuer names in certificates are distinguished names (DNs), as defined in the International Telecommunications Union-Telecommunications Standards Sector (ITU-TSS) recommendation X.500 directory services. Such certificates are also called X.509 certificates after the ITU-TSS recommendation in which they were defined.

The key certificate acts like a kind of electronic identity card. When a recipient uses a sender's public key to authenticate the sender's signature (or when the originator uses the recipient's PKS to encrypt a message or document), the recipient wants to be sure that the sender is who he or she claims to be. The certificate provides that assurance.

A certificate could be tied to one individual or represent an organizational authority that in turn represents the entire organization. Also, certificates could represent various levels of assurance — from those dispensed by a machine to those registered with a personally signed application. Additional assurance could be provided by the personal presentation of a signed application along with proof of identity or by the verification of a biometric test (e.g., fingerprint or retina scan) for each use of the private key.

Exhibit 39.1 shows a possible scenario for obtaining a certificate. The registration process might work as follows:

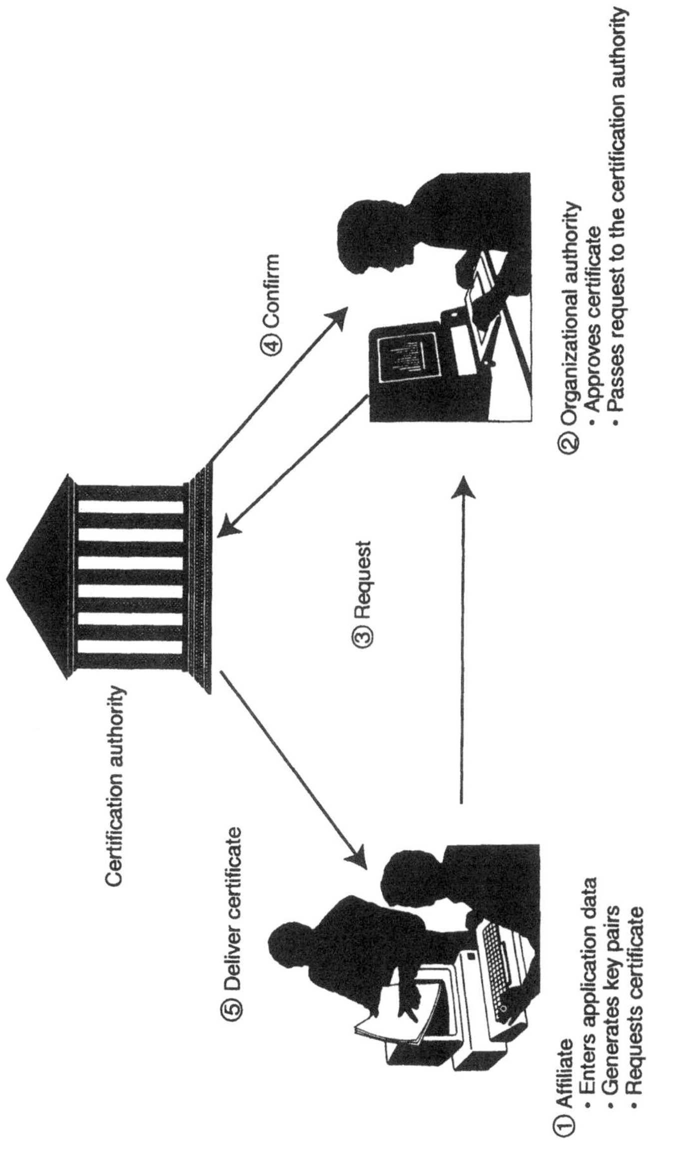

Exhibit 39.1. The Registration Process

- The affiliate (i.e., candidate for certificate) fills out the application, generates private-public key pairs, and sends for the certificate, enclosing his or her public key.
- The organizational authority approves the application.
- The organizational authority passes the certificate application to the certification authority.
- The certification authority sends back a message confirming receipt of the application.
- After proper proofing, the certification authority sends the certificate to the applicant-affiliate.
- The applicant-affiliate then loads the certificate to his or her workstation, verifies the certificate authority's digital signature, and saves a copy of the certificate.

Digital Signatures. Exhibit 39.2 illustrates how a digital signature ensures the identity of the message originator. It shows how a message recipient would use an originator's digital signature to authenticate that originator.

On the Web, authentication could work as follows:

- The originator creates a message and the software performs a hash on the document.
- The originator's software then signs the message by encrypting it with the originator's private key.
- The originator sends the message to the server attaching his or her public key and certificate to the message if necessary.
- The server either requests the originator's public key from a certificate/key repository or extracts the certification from the originator's message.

With this service, the authentication authority could either attach an authentication message verifying the digital signature's authenticity to the originator's message or provide that authentication to the recipient via a publicly accessible database. Upon receipt, the recipient would either acknowledge the originator's authenticity via the attached authentication message or access the public key and certificate from the publicly accessible database to read the signature.

To provide such levels of assurance, the certification authority must establish proofing stations where individuals and organizations can present themselves with appropriate identification and apply for certificates. The authority must also maintain or be part of a legal framework of protection and be in a position to mount an enforcement process to protect customers against fraud.

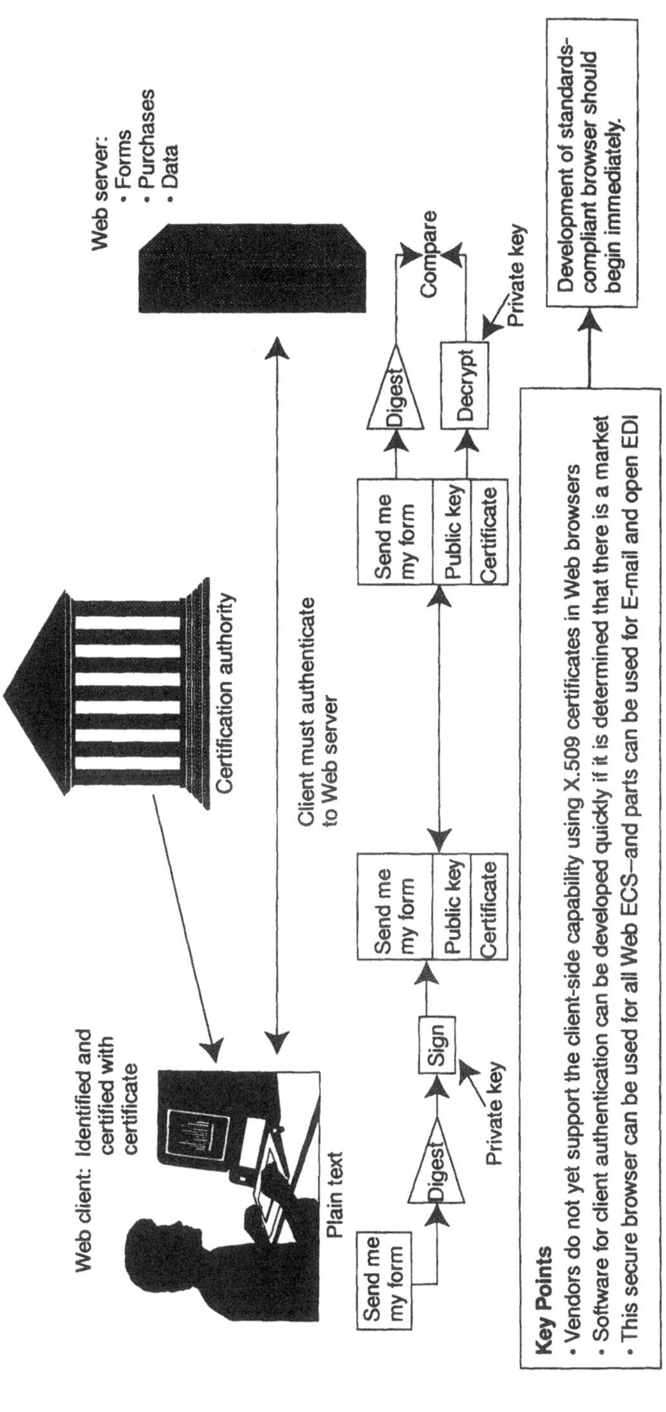

Exhibit 39.2. Client Authentication

Certificate Repository

The certificate authority also provides the vehicle for the distribution of public keys. Thus the certificate authority would have to maintain the public key certificates in a directory server that can be accessed by authorized persons and computers.

Exhibit 39.3 shows how subscribers might use such a repository. Certificates could be retrieved on demand along with their current status. Additional information, such as e-mail addresses or fax numbers, could also be available on demand.

The repository would work as follows:

- The message originator creates a message, generates a digital signature, and sends the message.
- The recipient sends a signed message requesting the originator's public key from the certificate repository.
- The certificate repository verifies the requester's signature and returns the public key to the recipient.

The certificate authority could also use the certificate repository to maintain a certificate revocation list (CRL), which provides notification of certificates that are revoked pursuant to a suspected compromise of the private key. This service could also require that the authority report such compromises via a compromised key list to special customers — possibly those enrolled in a subscribed service — and that such notifications be made available to all customers.

Finally, transactions involving certificates issued by other certificate authorities require that a cross-certification record be maintained and made publicly available in the certificate repository.

Electronic Postmark

A service providing an electronic date and time postmark establishes the existence of a message at a specific point in time. By digitally signing the postmark, the postmarking authority assures the communicating parties that the message was sent, was in transit, or received at the indicated time.

This service is most useful when the recipient requires the originator to send a message by a specified deadline. The originator would request the postmark authority to postmark the message. The authority would receive a digest of the message, add a date and time token to it, digitally sign the package, and send it back to the originator, who would forward the complete package (i.e., signed digest, time stamp, and original message) to the recipient, as shown in Exhibit 39.4.

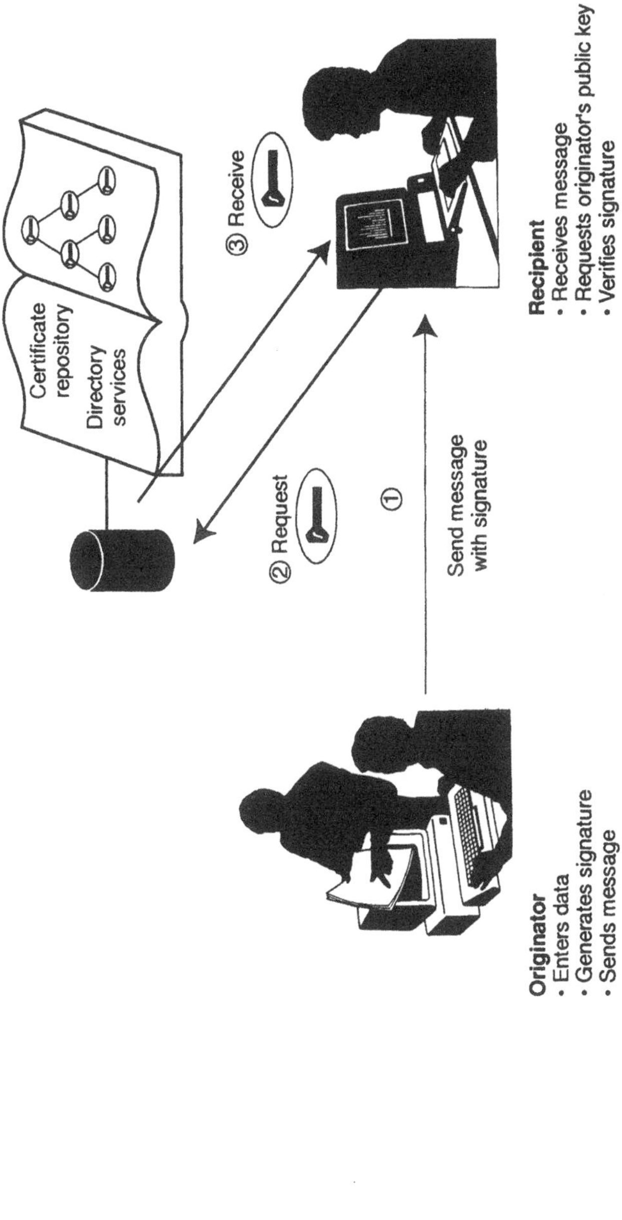

Exhibit 39.3. Certificate Repository

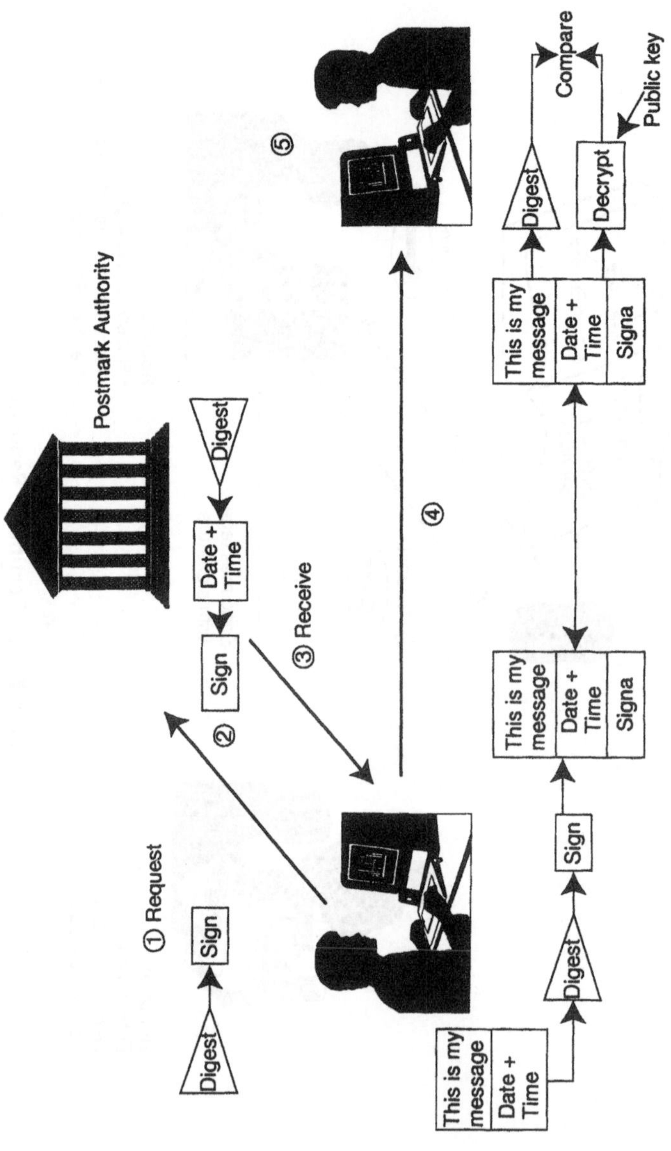

Exhibit 39.4. Electronic Postmark

Electronic postmarking functions as follows:

- The originator sends a request to the postmark authority to postmark a message or document (i.e., a digital digest of the message or document).
- The postmark authority adds date and time to the message received and affixes its digital signature to the entire package.
- The postmark authority sends the package back to the originator.
- The originator sends the original message or document plus the postmarked package to the recipient.
- The recipient verifies the postmark authority signature with the authority's public key and reads the message or document.

Return Receipts

This service reports one of three events: a message has transited the network, it has been received at the recipient's mailbox, or the recipient has actually decoded and opened the message at a specific date and time. In the latter instance, the transaction delivered to the recipient that has been encrypted might be set up only to be decrypted with a special one-time key, as shown in Exhibit 39.5. This one-time key could be provided by the postmark authority upon receipt of an acknowledgment from the recipient accompanied by the recipient's digital signature.

Here is how return receipt might work:

- The originator sends a message digest to the return receipt and postmark authority (the authority) with a request for a postmark and return receipt.
- The authority receives the message digest, adds date and time, encrypts the result, attaches a message to the recipient to request the decryption key from the authority upon receipt of the message, and affixes its digital signature to the package.
- The authority returns the postmarked, receipted package to the originator, who sends it to the recipient.
- The recipient receives the message package and makes a signed request for the decryption key from the authority.
- The authority receives the recipient's request, verifies the recipient's digital signature, and sends the decryption key to the recipient, who then decrypts and reads the message.
- The authority simultaneously forwards the return receipt to the originator.

Storage and Retrieval Services

These services include transaction archiving where copies of transactions are held for specified periods of time, as illustrated in Exhibit 39.6. The service might also include information (i.e., documents, videos, or business transactions) that can be sealed, postmarked, and held in public storage to

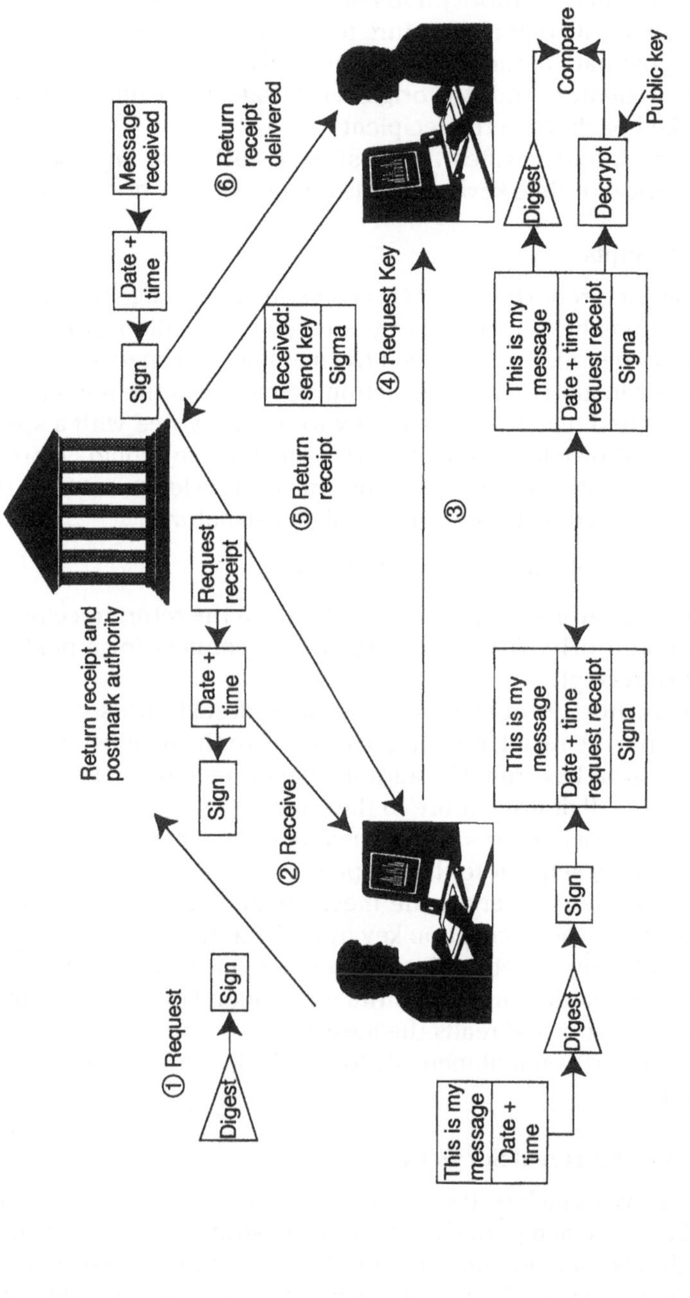

Exhibit 39.5. Return Receipt

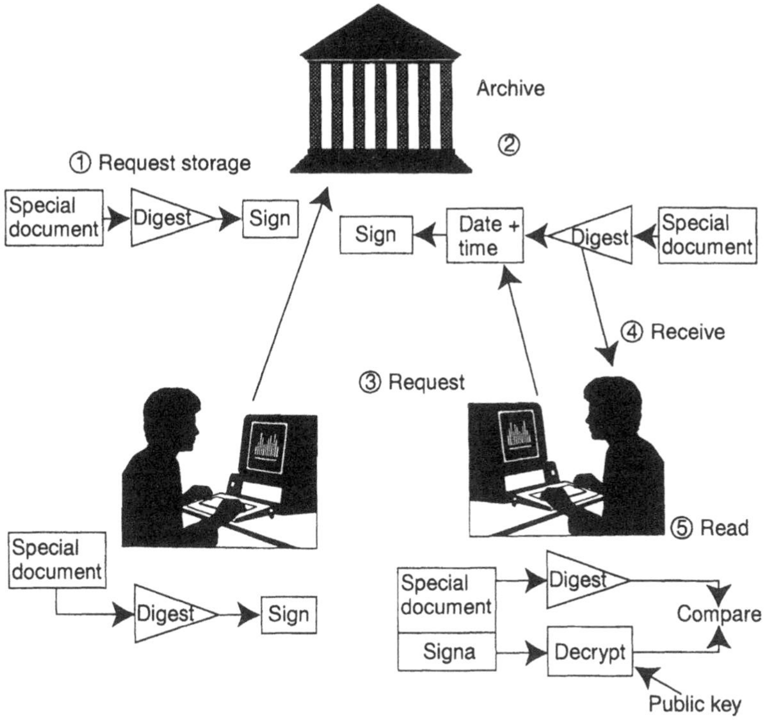

Exhibit 39.6. Storage and Retrieval

be retrieved via any authorized access. Likewise, encrypted information (i.e., documents, videos, or business transactions) can be sealed, postmarked, and further encrypted and held in sealed storage for indefinite periods of time. Each of these storage and retrieval capabilities must carry legal standing and the stamp of authenticity required for electronic correspondents.

Storage and retrieval works as follows:

- The originator sends a request to the archive to archive a document or message for a specified period of time and designates this information as publicly retrievable.
- The archive adds date and time to the message, verifies the identity of the originator, affixes a digital signature to the package, and archives the package.
- A customer requests the document from the archive.
- The archive retrieves the document, adds a date and time stamp to the package, affixes another digital signature to the new package, and sends it to the recipient.
- The recipient verifies the first and second archive signatures and reads the message.

USE OF THESE COMMERCIAL EXCHANGE SERVICES

Electronic Commerce services (ECS) may be used in one of three ways:

- The originator sends a message to the authority with a request for service, the authority provides the service and returns the message to the originator, and the originator then forwards the message to the recipient.
- The originator sends a message to a value added network (VAN), which then forwards the message to the authority with a request for services. The authority provides the service and returns the message to the value added network, which then forwards the message to the recipient.
- The originator sends a message to the authority with a request for service and the address of the recipient. The authority then forwards the message directly to the recipient.

All these services could be provided by a single authority, by a hierarchy of authorities, or by a network of authorities, each specializing in one or more of these services.

AVAILABLE TECHNOLOGIES FOR ELECTRONIC COMMERCE

Currently, three major technologies are capable of providing electronic commerce services — e-mail, the World Wide Web, and open EDI. Typical of advanced technologies, security elements are the last to be developed and yet are essential if these technologies are to be deemed trustworthy for electronic commerce.

The issues of confidentiality, confirmation of identity, time certainty, and legal protection apply to all these technologies. The solutions — certification, key repositories, postmarking, return receipts, and storage and retrieval — are equally applicable to each of these technologies. Although the state of universality and interoperability varies among these technologies, they are all in a relative state of immaturity.

Secure e-mail

Electronic messaging's most classic manifestation is e-mail. Because of its capacity for handling attachments, e-mail can be used to transfer official business, financial, technical, and a variety of multimedia forms.

DMS and PEM. Both the Department of Defense standard for e-mail, which is based on the ITU's X.400 standard for e-mail (called the Defense Message System or DMS), and the Internet e-mail standard, the simple mail transfer protocol (SMTP), have made provisions for security. The DMS uses encapsulation techniques at several security levels to encrypt and sign e-mail messages. The security standard for the Internet is called

Privacy Enhanced Mail (PEM). Both methods rely on a certificate hierarchy and known and trusted infrastructure. Neither method is fully developed.

Secure World Wide Web

The phenomenal growth of the Web makes it a prime candidate for the dissemination of forms and documents. Organizations see the Web as a prime tool for services such as delivery of applications and requests for information. However, Web technology has two competing types of security: one at the application layer that secures hypertext transfer protocol (HTTP) formatted data (known as SHTTP), and one at the socket layer that encrypts data in the format in which it is transported across the network.

In addition, vendors do not yet support either client-side authentication or the use of X.509 certificates. Although software for such activities as client authentication can be developed relatively quickly, vendors have to be convinced that there is a real market for such products. This technology is about to emerge, and although it will emerge first to support Web applications, it will also speed the development of e-mail and EDI security services.

Secure Open EDI

Until now, EDI has been used in closed, value-added networks where security and integrity can be closely controlled. Signing and encryption have been proprietary to the EDI product in use or to the value-added EDI network provider.

By contrast, open EDI, running across open networks, requires adherence to the standards that are still being developed and a yet-to-be developed infrastructure that can ensure trusted keys. To date, the various schemes to accelerate the use of open systems for EDI have not captured the imagination of EDI users and providers.

THE OVERRIDING ISSUE: A PUBLIC KEY CERTIFICATE INFRASTRUCTURE

The suite of services and technologies described in this article depend on trusted public keys and their bindings to users. Users could be completely assured of the integrity of keys and their bindings if they were exchanged manually. Because business is conducted on a national and international scale, users have to be assured of the integrity of the registration authority and the key repository in an inevitably complex, electronic way.

One as-yet-unresolved issue is whether such an authority or authorities should be centralized and hierarchical or distributed. The centralized, hierarchical scheme would mean that certification authorities (and purveyors of the accompanying services) would be certified by a higher authority that, in turn, might be certified by yet a higher authority — and so on to the root authority. This kind certification would create a known chain of trust from the highest to the closest certification authority. This scheme is often referred to as the Public Key Infrastructure (PKI).

The alternative assumes that the market will foster the creation of a variety of specialized certification authorities to serve communities of interest. A complicated method of cross-referencing and maintaining those cross-references in the certificate repository for each community of interest would then develop.

The outcome of this debate is likely to result in a combination of both methods, such as several hierarchies with some kind of managed cross-referencing to enable public key exchanges between disparate communities of interest when required. Following are some of the issues yet to be resolved:

- Agreement on the exact contents of certificates
- Definition of the size of prime numbers used in key generation
- Establishment of the qualifications required for obtaining a certificate
- Definition of the identification and authentication requirements for certificate registration
- Ruling on the frequency with which certificates are renewed
- Agreement on the legal standing and precedence for such technology

CONCLUSION

Groups such as the Internet Engineering Task Force (IETF), the federal government's Public Key Infrastructure (PKI) users group, and even the American Bar Association are tackling these knotty issues.

In fact, with toolkits now available that allow the user to become his or her own certificate authority, everyone can get into the act. Private companies such as VeriSign are establishing themselves as certification authorities so that users will give their public keys and certificates credence. The National Security Agency wants to become the certificate authority for the federal government. The U.S. Postal Service is intent on offering electronic commerce services to businesses and residences by acting as the certificate authority and provider.

An infrastructure will emerge, and it will probably work for users very similar to the way that it has been described in this chapter.

Chapter 40

Integrating Electronic Messaging Systems and Infrastructures

Dale Cohen

IMPLEMENTING A MESSAGING SYSTEM INFRASTRUCTURE requires taking small steps while keeping the big picture in mind. The complexity of the endeavor is directly affected by the scope of the project.

If implementing messaging for a single department or a small single enterprise, a vendor solution can probably be used. All users will have the same desktop application with one message server or post office from that same application vendor.

By contrast, integrating multiple departments may require proprietary software routers for connecting similar systems. When building an infrastructure for a single enterprise, the IT department may incorporate the multiple-department approach for similar systems. Dissimilar systems can be connected using software and hardware gateways.

If the goal is to implement an integrated system for a larger enterprise, multiple departments may need to communicate with their external customers and suppliers. The solution could implement a messaging backbone or central messaging switch. This approach allows the implementers to deploy common points to sort, disperse, and measure the flow of messages.

If an organization already has an infrastructure but needs to distribute it across multiple systems connected by common protocols, the goal may be to make the aggregate system more manageable and gain economies of scale. Implementations can vary widely, from getting something up and running to reducing the effort and expense of running the current system.

HOW TO ACCOMPLISH ROLLOUT AND MANAGE CONSTRAINTS

Messaging is a unique application, because it crosses all the networks, hardware platforms, network operating systems, and application environments in the organization. Plenty of cooperation will be necessary to accomplish a successful rollout. The traditional constraints are time,

0-8493-9822-3/00/$0.00+$.50

functionality, and resources, though implementers must also manage user perceptions.

Resource Constraints: Financial

In an international organization of 5000 or more users, it is not unreasonable to spend $200,000 to $500,000 on the backbone services necessary to achieve a solution. The total cost — including network components, new desktop devices, ongoing administration, maintenance, and end-user support — can easily exceed $2,500 per user, with incremental costs for the e-mail add-on at $300 to $500 per year.

The initial appeal of offerings from Lotus Development Corp., Novell Inc., and Microsoft Corp. is that a component can be added at a low incremental cost. In reality, the aggregate incremental costs are huge, although most of the purchaser's costs are hidden. For a corporate PC to handle e-mail, the corporatewide and local area networks and support organizations must be industrial strength.

Although this investment may at first glance seem prohibitively high, it allows for add-ons such as Web browsers or client/server applications at a much lower startup cost. Vendors argue that they make it possible for the buyer to start small and grow. It is more likely that an organization will start small, grow significantly, and grow its application base incrementally. In the long run, the investment pays for itself repeatedly, not only for the benefits e-mail provides but for the opportunities the foray offers.

Resource Constraints: Expertise

It is easy to underestimate the expertise required to operate an efficient messaging infrastructure. Most IT departments are easily able to handle a single application in a single operating environment. Multiple applications in multiple operating environments are a different story.

Messaging systems must be able to deal with multiple network protocols, various operating systems, and different software applications — all from different vendors. Given these facts, it is difficult to understand why already overburdened LAN administrators would take on the significant systems integration responsibilities of a messaging system rollout.

When confronted with problems during a messaging system integration, the staff must be able to answer the following questions:

- Is it a network problem or an application issue?
- Is it an operating system-configured value or an application bug?
- Can the problem be handled by someone with general expertise, such as a front-line technician or a support desk staff member?

Skill Sets. Individuals performing the rollout must be technically adept, have strong diagnostic skills, and understand how to work in a team environment. They must be adept with multiple operating systems and understand the basics of multiple networks. Ideally they understand the difference between a technical answer and one that solves the business issue at large.

Many organizations make the mistake of assigning first-tier support staff to an e-mail project when systems integrators are called for. The leanest integration team consists of individuals with an understanding of networks and their underlying protocols, operating systems, and two or more e-mail applications. Database knowledge is very useful when dealing with directories and directory synchronization. A knowledge of tool development helps automate manual processes. Application monitoring should occur alongside network monitoring, because nothing signals a network error as well as an e-mail service interruption.

Cross-Functional Integration Teams. The most efficient way to coordinate a rollout is through cross-functional teams. It is important to incorporate e-mail implementation and support into the goals of the individuals and the teams from which they come. Many organizations do this informally, but this method is not always effective. A written goal or service level agreement is extremely helpful when conflicting priorities arise and management support is needed.

When creating the core messaging integration team, it is very helpful to include individuals from WAN and LAN networking, systems, operations, and support desk staff, in addition to the individual application experts from each e-mail environment.

Functionality and Scope

At any point in the project, network administrators may find themselves trying to implement an enterprisewide solution, a new departmental system, a corporatewide directory service, or a solution for mobile e-mail users. When building a house, it is commonly understood that the plumbing and waste systems must be installed before hooking up the bath fixtures. This is not the case with messaging.

A messaging system rollout should start with a basic infrastructure "plumbed" for future expansion, and be followed directly with reliable user functionality. Results should be monitored and measured, and original infrastructure issues should be revisited as appropriate. Project success comes with regular reports on what has been delivered and discussions of incremental improvements in reliability and services.

Supporting Internal and External Customers

No matter how good the features of any product or set of products, if the system is not reliable, people cannot depend on it. If the system is perceived as unreliable, people will use alternative forms of communication.

To satisfy user needs, the IT department should separate internal customers from external customers. Internal customers are those that help provide a service. They may be IT management, support personnel, or networking staff — they could be considered an internal supplier.

Because of the nature of most organizations, internal customers are both customer and supplier. They need to be provided with the means to supply a service. For example, IT management may need to create step-by-step procedures for the operations staff to carry them out. If the information technology group cannot satisfy the requirements of internal customers, it probably will not be able to satisfy the needs of external customers.

External customers are the end users. If they are in sales, for example, external customers may include the enterprise's customers from other companies. It is the job of the IT staff to provide external customers with messaging features, functionality, and reliability so they can do their job.

IMPLEMENTATION MODELS AND ARCHITECTURES

It is helpful for network managers to know how other enterprises have implemented messaging systems. The next few sections describe the various components of the infrastructure, common deployment architectures, and how to plan future deployments.

Infrastructure Versus Interface

Often messaging systems are sold with the emphasis on what the end user sees. Experienced network managers know that this is the least of their problems. The behind-the-scenes components, which make the individual systems in an organization work as a near-seamless whole, include:

- Network services
- Message transfer services
- Directory services
- Management and administration services

Network Services. The network services required for a messaging rollout involve connectivity between:

- Desktop and server
- Server to server
- Server to gateway
- Gateway to foreign environment

It is not unusual to have one network protocol between a desktop device and its server and a second protocol within the backbone server/gateway/router environment. Servers may communicate via WAN protocols such as TCP/IP, OSI, DECnet, or SNA, and the desktops may communicate over a LAN protocol such as IPX or NetBIOS. WAN connections may occur over continuous connections or over asynchronous dialup methods.

The network administrator's greatest concern is loss of network connectivity. It is important to understand how it happens, why it happens, how it is discovered, and what needs to be done on an application level once connectivity is restored.

If the network goes down, e-mail will be faulted. Weekly incident reports should be issued that cite direct incidents (e.g., an e-mail component failure) and indirect incidents (e.g., a network failure) as well as remote site issues (e.g., a remote site lost power). Such information can help to clarify the real problem.

Message Transfer Services. The message transfer service (also termed the message transport system) is the most visible part of the messaging infrastructure. The message transfer service is responsible for moving a message from point A to point B. This service consists of one or more message transport agents and may be extended to include gateways and routers. The most popular services are X.400 and SMTP international standards, and IBM's SNA Distributed Services (SNADS) and Novell's Message Handling Service (MHS) proprietary industry standards.

X.400. More widely used in Europe than in North America, X.400 is popular because it:

- Provides universal connectivity.
- Has a standard way of mapping features.
- Is usually run over commercial WANs so it does not have the security problems associated with the Internet.

SMTP. Simple Mail Transfer Protocol's allure is its simplicity. Addressing is easier and access to the Internet is relatively simple compared with establishing an X.400 connection. Because it is simple, there is not much that can go wrong. However, when something does go wrong, it is usually monumental.

Directory Services. The directory service is critical to a company's e-mail systems, but it is also problematic. The problems are a result of the difficulty in keeping directories up-to-date, resolving redundant or obsolete auto-registered entries, and failures of directory synchronization.

The directory serves both users and applications. End users choose potential recipients from a directory. The directory should list enough information for a user to distinguish between the George Smith in accounting and the George Smith in engineering. Some companies include in their directory individuals who are customers and suppliers. The ability to distinguish between internal users and external users is even more important in these cases.

Management and Administration Services. Management refers to scheduled maintenance and automated housekeeping procedures that involve system-related tasks such as reconfiguration and file maintenance. The constant I/O on messaging components leads to disk and sometimes memory fragmentation. Regular defragmentation procedures, including repro/reorg, tidy procedures, and checkstat and reclaim, are required. Whatever the environment, such procedures should be done more often than is recommended to prevent problems from occurring.

Alerts and Alarms. Alerts and alarms are extremely helpful, because the system can tell the user if there is a potential problem. Alerts generally refer to warnings such as "too many messages in queue awaiting delivery." Alarms are a sign of a more serious problem, such as a disk full condition.

Mail Monitoring. Mail monitoring is typically an administrative function. One way of monitoring a system is to send a probe addressed to an invalid user on a target system. On many systems, the target system will reject the message with a "no such addressee" nondelivery message. When the initiating system receives this message, it indicates that mail flow is active.

Timing the round-trip provides a window to overall system performance. A message that does not return in a preestablished timeframe is considered overdue and is cause for further investigation.

Reporting. Reporting is used for capacity planning, measuring throughput and performance, chargeback, and statistical gathering. At initial implementation, network administrators will generally want to report breadth of coverage to demonstrate the reach of the infrastructure. Breadth can be measured by counting users and the number of messaging systems within each messaging environment.

Performance can be measured by reporting the volume — the average number of messages delivered per hour, or messages in each hour over a 24-hour period. This measure can be divided further by indicating the type of message (i.e., text only, single/double attachments, read receipts). This information gives network managers a measurable indication of the kind of features the user community requires.

For network planning purposes, it may be useful to measure volume or "system pressure," ignoring the number of messages sent and focusing on the number of total gigabytes sent per day.

Exhibit 40.1. Implementation Scenarios

	Enterprise	
	Single	**Multiple**
Single Department	One-Tier Single System	Two-Tier Similar Systems
Multiple Departments	Two-Tier Dissimilar Systems	Three-Tier Cross-Enterprise Systems

IMPLEMENTATION SCENARIOS: A TIERED APPROACH

Manufacturing environments have long used a tiered approach to messaging for distributing the workload of factory floor applications. As environments become more complex, the tiered approach offers additional flexibility.

An entire enterprise can be considered a single department, indicating the need for a one-tier system where clients are tied into a single server or post office. Multiple departments in a single enterprise or a single department communicating with multiple enterprises require routers and gateways to communicate with the world outside. When multiple departments need to communicate with each other and with multiple enterprises, a messaging backbone or messaging switch is called for.

Exhibit 40.1 summarizes the implementation scenarios discussed in this chapter.

One-Tier Messaging Model

A single department in a single enterprise will most likely deploy a one-tier messaging model. This model consists of a single messaging server or post office that provides all services. It may be as large as an OfficeVision system on a mainframe or a Higgins PostOffice on a Compaq file server running NetWare. The department need only concern itself with following corporate guidelines for networking and any naming standards.

Caution should be observed when using corporate guidelines. It is often simple to apply mainframe conventions when standardizing PC LAN-based applications. Many large organizations tend to forget that the whole reason for deploying desktop computers is to move away from mainframe conventions (e.g., 8-character user IDs) that are nonintuitive for users. Exhibit 40.2 shows a typical one-tier model within a single department of an enterprise.

Two-Tier Model: Multiple Servers

As the number of e-mail users grow, or multiple departments need to be connected, an organization will probably deploy multiple servers. This two-tier model can consist of integrating similar messaging systems from the same vendor or from different vendors. Exhibit 40.3 illustrates a connec-

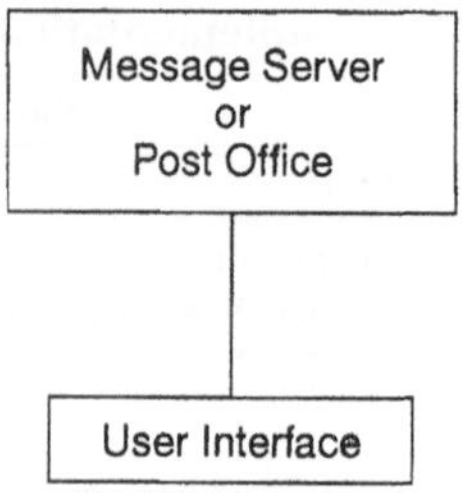

Exhibit 40.2. One-Tier Model

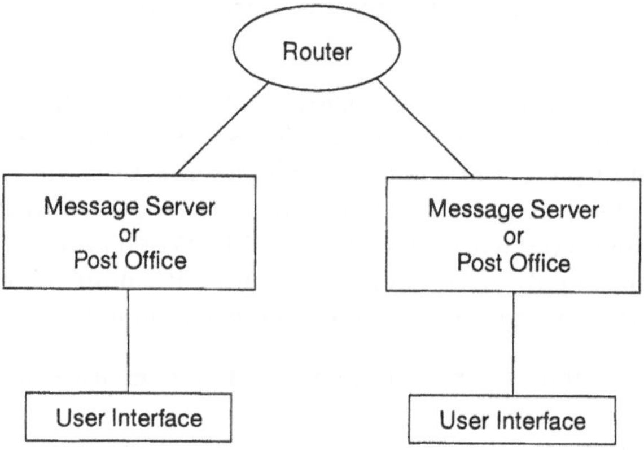

Exhibit 40.3. Two-Tier Model

tion between two departments using the same vendor software connected via application routers.

In a typical PC LAN environment using a shared-file system such as cc:Mail or Microsoft Mail, the router acts the same way as the PC. The post office is completely passive. When users send messages, their workstations simply copy the message to the file server as an individual file or as an insertion into a file server database. In either case the PC workstation actually does the work — the post office simply serves as a shared disk drive. The router is also an active component, but has no user moving messages. It periodically moves messages from one post office to another without user interaction.

Application Gateways for Integrating Dissimilar Systems

Many enterprises have different departments that have chosen their own e-mail systems without a common corporate standard. To integrate dissimilar systems, application gateways can bridge the technical incompatibilities between the various messaging servers (see Exhibit 40.4).

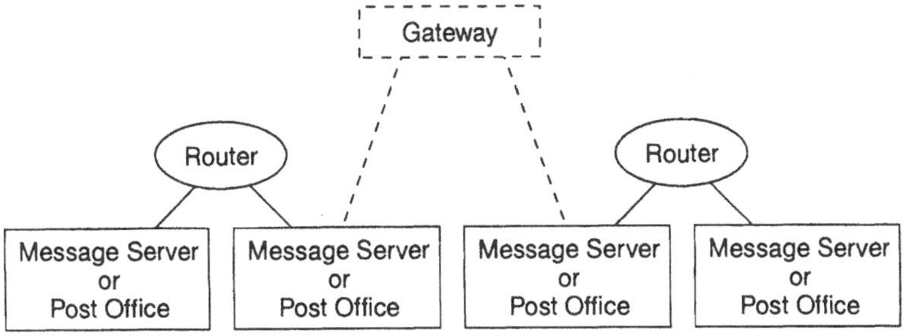

Exhibit 40.4. Using Application Gateways

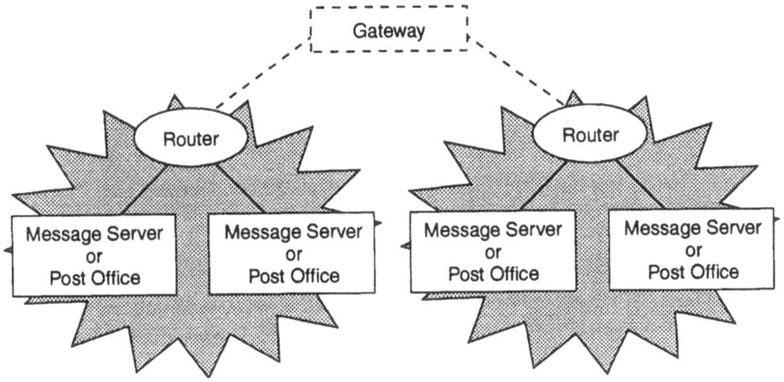

Exhibit 40.5. Placing a Gateway Between Routers

A simple gateway can translate cc:Mail messages to GroupWise. A more complex gateway can bridge networks (e.g., Ethernet to Token Ring), network protocols (i.e., NetWare to TCP/IP), and the e-mail applications.

Converting one e-mail message to the format of another requires a lot of translation. Document formats (i.e., DCA RFT to ASCII), addressing formats (i.e., user@workgroup@domain to system::user), and message options (i.e., acknowledgments to read or deliver receipts) must all be translated.

Gateways can emulate routers native to each environment. They perform message translations internally. The alternative to this approach is to place the gateway between the routers as opposed to between the post office — this is not an end-user design, it is merely a function of the vendor software (see Exhibit 40.5).

If an enterprise is large, network administrators may want to make use of economies of scale to handle common administration, common gateways to X.400, and Internet networks. The network administration staff may simply need points in its network where it can measure progress.

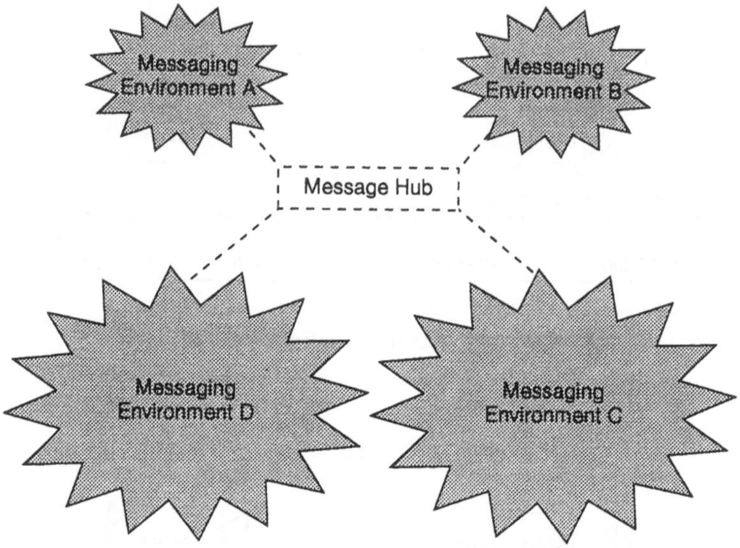

Exhibit 40.6. A Central Switching Hub

Gateways from each environment to every other environment can be provided, but this solution becomes costly and difficult to maintain. A better approach would be to use a central switching hub or a distributed backbone, as shown in Exhibit 40.6.

Distributed Hubs. The central switch or hub allows for a single path for each messaging environment to communicate with all other messaging environments. The central hub, if it is relatively inexpensive, can be expanded into the distributed model. This is often done as the aggregate system grows and requires additional performance and capacity.

However, this implementation can be taken to an extreme, as seen by the number of companies that have grown PC LAN/shared file systems beyond their original design. It is inexpensive to grow these systems incrementally, but difficult to provide end-to-end reliability. Most organizations plug the technical gaps in these products with the additional permanent and contract personnel to keep the multitude of routers and shared-file system post offices up and running.

Some organizations have taken this distributed hub approach to the point where they have multiple connections to the Internet and the X.400 world (see Exhibit 40.7). Some organizations offer the single message switch for their global environment, and their messages are more well traveled than their administrators. A message sent from Brussels to Paris may stop in Los Angeles on the way because of the central switching mechanism. In addition to local switching, the distributed hub allows for redundancy.

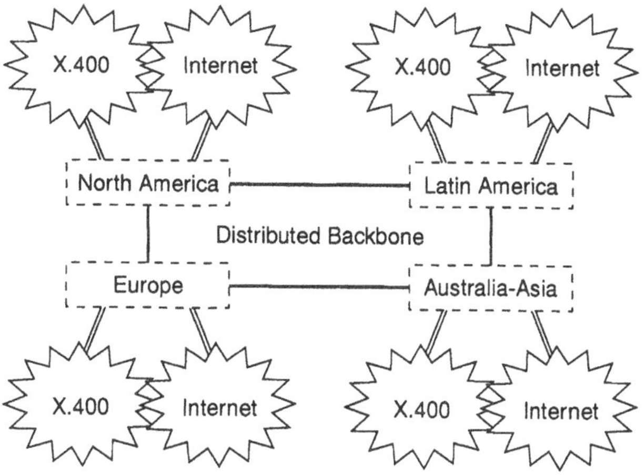

Exhibit 40.7. Worldwide Distributed Hubs

THREE DEPLOYMENT ARCHITECTURES AND OPTIONS

Most companies deploy e-mail systems using variations of three architectures: a common platform, where all e-mail systems are identical; a multiple backbone, where each e-mail environment has its own gateway; or a common backbone, where all systems share common resources. The following sections describe these architectures along with the advantages and disadvantages of each.

Common Platform Architecture

For years, a major automotive manufacturer delayed PC LAN e-mail deployment in deference to the purported needs of the traveling executive. Senior managers wanted to be able to walk up to any company computer terminal, workstation, or personal computer anywhere in the world and know that they would be able to access their e-mail in the same manner. This implies a common look and feel to the application across platforms as well as common network access to the e-mail server. In this company's case, PROFS (OfficeVision/VM) was accessible through 3270 terminal emulators on various platforms. As long as SNA network access remained available, e-mail appeared the same worldwide. This IBM mainframe shop had few problems implementing this model.

The common platform model is not unique to IBM mainframe environments. Another manufacturer used the same technique with its DEC ALL-IN-1 environment distributed across multiple VAX hosts. As long as a DECnet network or dialup access was available, users could reach their home systems. The upside of this approach is that an individual's e-mail files are stored centrally, allowing for a single retrieval point. The downside was that the user had to be connected to process e-mail and was unable to work offline.

This strategy is not limited to mainframe and minicomputer models. A number of companies have standardized on Lotus Notes, Microsoft Mail, or Novell's GroupWise. None of these products are truly ready for large-scale deployment without IT and network staffs having to plug the technical gaps.

Multiple Backbone Model

The multiple backbone model assumes that an organization integrates its e-mail systems as though it were multiple smaller companies. The OfficeVision/VM system may connect via Advantis to reach the Internet and X.400 world. The cc:Mail WAN may have an SMTP gateway for access to the Internet and an ISOCOR MTA for access to the Message Router/X.400 gateway. All the various e-mail environments may have a proprietary Soft*Switch gateway for access to the IBM/MVS host so that everyone who needs to can access their OfficeVision/400systems (see Exhibit 40.8).

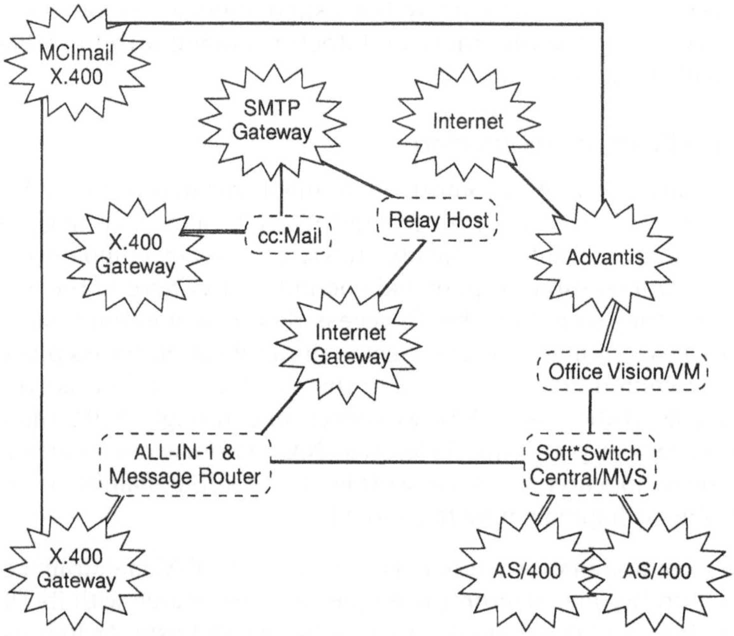

Exhibit 40.8. The Multiple Backbone Model

On the surface, this hodgepodge of point-to-point connections may seem a bit unwieldy, but it does have advantages. Users of cc:Mail can address Internet e-mail users by filling out an SMTP template rather than waiting until the cc:Mail administrator adds recipients to the cc:Mail directory. OfficeVision/VM users can fill out a simple address block within the text of their message to reach an Internet user. AS/400 users can send mail to an application that forwards the message on their behalf. The trouble occurs when the recipients of the AS/400 users try to reply — they end up replying to the application that forwarded the message rather than the original sender, or originator, of the message.

This architecture may still work. If each e-mail environment had its own gateway, network administration could offer multiple connections to the Internet.

Common Backbone

The common backbone takes two forms:

- A central e-mail hub or message switch on a single system that serves as the common denominator among all e-mail environments.
- A distributed model where all backbone components run a common software protocol.

The common hub involves a single switch that serves the users' applications, thus serving their needs indirectly. Each e-mail environment has an application gateway that converts its environmental format to that of the common hub. Other systems are attached to this hub in a similar manner. Messages destined for dissimilar environments all pass through this central point to be sorted and delivered to their final destinations.

The distributed backbone takes the central hub and replaces it with two or more systems sharing a common application protocol. This solution offers the ability to deploy two or more less expensive systems rather than a single, more expensive system. Any system connected to any point in the backbone can use any other service (e.g., gateway) connected to that same backbone.

Network managers may decide to purchase a single hub and gradually add systems to form a distributed backbone. Should you decide to use a common backbone protocol like X.400 or SMTP, there is an advantage. Because these protocols are available from a number of vendors, the cc:Mail/X.400 gateway could connect to an X.400 system running in an HP9000, DEC/Alpha, or Intel/Pentium system — all running the same protocols. It is possible to change distributed servers without having to change the gateways to these servers. Exhibit 40.9 illustrates three-tier flexibility.

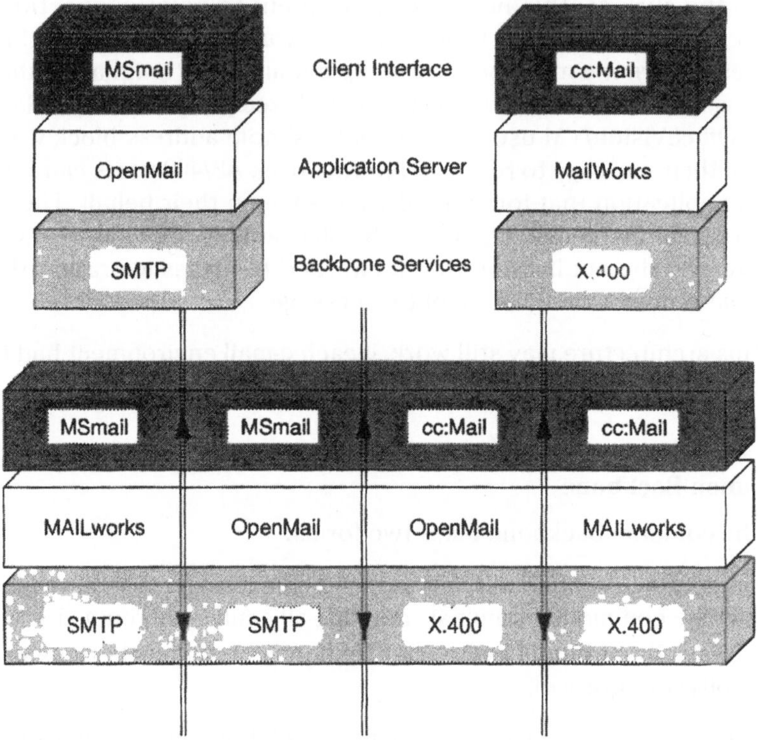

Exhibit 40.9. Three-Tier Flexibility

A third approach is to use one central server or a distributed backbone of similar systems. In the central server/central hub approach, all e-mail environments use application gateways to connect to the central switch. There they are routed to their target environment.

Two-tier models may seem most convenient, because they can use the offerings of a single vendor. One problem is that the system must use that vendor's protocols for a long time. Three tiers allow the layers in the model to be changed, which allows for ease of transition.

Under most application scenarios, changing one component of the messaging environment entails changing all the pieces and parts with which it is associated. It may be necessary to provide adequate support staff and end-user training or hire consultants to handle the need for temporary staff during the transition — a significant business disruption.

For example, in one environment, users have Microsoft Mail on their desktops and a traditional MSmail post office is used, as well as message transfer agents (MTAs), to route mail between post offices. The engineering department uses OpenMail. The IT group would like to begin consolidating systems. With minor changes to the desktop, IT can retain the Microsoft Mail user interface, remove the back-end infrastructure, and use the same OpenMail system as the OpenMail desktop users by consolidating the second tier and simplifying the support environment. The client changes somewhat because it is using a different directory server and message store, but it appears as a minor upgrade to the users — no significant training is necessary.

Likewise, IT can change the back end and still allow the OpenMail systems to communicate with the MAILworks and ALL-IN-1 systems without locking into a single vendor solution. This is a feasible option. Today, users can plug an MSmail client into a MAILworks or OpenMail server. Novell recently announced the ability to plug a cc:Mail or MSmail client into its GroupWise XTD server. A Microsoft Exchange client plugs into various servers, and Lotus's cc:Mail can plug into anything.

ESTABLISHING MESSAGING POLICIES AND PROCEDURES

An organization can prevent misunderstandings, conflicts, and even litigation if it publishes its policies and procedures for messaging applications at the outset. Most important are privacy and confidentiality.

Privacy

A privacy policy serves two purposes: to properly inform employees that their messages may not be private and to protect the organization from legal liability. Most organizations create a policy that cautions users as follows: All electronic data is company property and may be viewed by designated personnel to diagnose problems, monitor performance, or for other purposes as the company deems necessary. While you normally type a password to access your e-mail and you may feel that your messages are private, this is not the case. The e-mail you create, read, or send is not your property nor is it protected from being seen by those other than you and your recipients.

Organizations can contact the Electronic Messaging Association (EMA) in Arlington, VA for a kit to aid in developing a privacy policy.

Proprietary and Confidential Information

E-mail appears to ease the process of intentional or inadvertent disclosure of company secrets. If this is a concern, an organization could try the following:

- Let users know that the IT department logs the messages that leave the company.
- Perform periodic audits.
- Apply rules or scripts that capture e-mail to or from fields, making it possible to search on competitor address strings.

Some systems insert a header on incoming e-mail that says: "WARNING: This message arrived from outside the company's e-mail system. Take care when replying so as not to divulge proprietary or confidential information."

A company may also specify that proprietary information should not be sent to Internet addresses if security measures on the Internet are inadequate for the company's needs. Users may be asked to confirm that only X.400 addresses are used. It is helpful to incorporate any such e-mail ground rules — for example, that the tranmission of proprietary information without a proper disclosure agreement is grounds for dismissal — as part of the new employee orientation process.

RECOMMENDED COURSE OF ACTION

One of the most important elements of a successful messaging system rollout is a staff that is well versed in the workings of the network, operating system, backup procedures, and applications.

Network Connections

An implementation needs individuals who can set up network connections efficiently. A messaging system needs procedures in place to notify users when a network link is unavailable. If the network goes down, often one of the first applications blamed is e-mail. It is the job of the network staff to diagnose the problem quickly and have the right people remedying the problem.

Operating Systems

Many e-mail groups have their own systems and servers and operate them as their own. Consequently, many successful organizations pair systems programmers or senior software specialists with systems engineers who can provide installation services and upgrade support.

Backup

Most messaging support organizations are not set up to provide 24-hour support. It is important to borrow methodologies from the mainframe support environment and staff an operations center that can answer phone calls, fix problems, and backup and archive applications regularly.

Applications Support

This function demands staff members with:

- Excellent diagnostic skills.
- Excellent communication skills.
- Database and business graphics experience.

- Cross-platform network experience.
- A basic understanding of the operating environment of each of the platforms.

E-mail integration by its nature involves cross-platform expertise. Most applications are fairly straightforward. In the case of an integrated infrastructure, an organization may need people familiar with NetWare, SNA, TCP/IP, and LAN Manager. They may also need to understand Mac/OS, UNIX, OS/2, and VMS.

When staffing an implementation, the key is to match expertise across the various groups within the company. The team should be application-centric with contributors from across the enterprise. If an implementation is properly staffed, and the implementers keep in mind the big picture as well as the daily objectives, the messaging system rollout is far more likely to be a success.

Chapter 41

Understanding Public Key Cryptology

Gilbert Held

THE GROWTH IN THE USE OF COMMUNICATIONS now provides end-users with the ability to perform a variety of functions that just a few years were unimaginable. Today, users can avail themselves of CompuServe, Prodigy, or the services of numerous Internet access providers, to order books, CDs, and even automobiles electronically. Although security has always been a limiting factor, holding end-users back from transmitting credit card information to on-line sales organizations, the use of public key cryptology represents a mechanism that can overcome that limitation.

The purpose of this chapter is to acquaint systems development managers with the operation and use of public key cryptology to include how this technology is being incorporated into World Wide Web (WWW) browsers, Web servers, and other computer-based software products. The systems development manager can apply knowledge about the operation of this technology to facilitate secure communications — and understanding the advantages over traditional methods used to secure communications. Because an understanding of the advantages of public key cryptology requires a comparison to traditional cryptology methods, this chapter first examines the general method by which traditional cryptological systems operate.

TRADITIONAL CRYPTOLOGICAL SYSTEMS

In a traditional cryptological system, both the person encrypting information and the person that will decrypt the received information use the same encrypting key. The encrypting device uses the key to perform an additive operation, usually a modular 2 (mod 2) operation. In comparison, the decrypting device uses the same key to perform a subtractive operation, which is normally based upon a mod 2 operation.

An example can best illustrate the operation of a traditional cryptological

0-8493-9822-3/00/$0.00+$.50

system. A one-byte portion of the key sequence used to encrypt data is the binary sequence 10110010.

The mod 2 addition of the key and data results in a mod 2 sum is transmitted as encrypted data. At the receiver, the same key is used to perform a mod 2 subtraction from the mod 2 sum received, resulting in the reconstruction of the original data. Thus, decryption is performed by the mod 2 subtraction of the key from the received encrypted data.

Traditional Systems Limitations

Although traditional cryptological systems are in wide use and, depending upon the key length and method of key selection, are difficult to essentially impossible to break, they have a major limitation: The distribution of keys. When communications are limited to between two nodes or users, only one key is required. When three nodes or users require communications, the number of keys increases to three. Communications between four nodes requires the use of six distinct keys.

In general form, the equation to determine how many keys are required is:

$$k = n^*(n-1)/2$$

where:
k = number of keys
n = number of users

This means that the use of a traditional cryptological system to secure communications for a large number of users can result in the expenditure of a considerable effort to distribute keys (e.g., for 15 users, 105 keys are required). In addition, each user requiring the ability to communicate with two or more nodes in a large network must be careful in his or her selection of keys, as the selection of the wrong key to encrypt or decrypt data will not produce the desired effect.

In a modern communications environment, such as the World Wide Web, with which the potential exists for tens of thousands of vendors marketing products to tens of millions of users, it becomes obvious that the use of a traditional cryptological system would not be practical for general purpose utilization. This is due to the massive number of keys that would be required to be distributed as well as the problem users would face in storing, retrieving, and using an appropriate key from an extremely large data base of keys. Clearly, an alternative method of key distribution and usage is required. A public key cryptological system is that alternative.

PUBLIC KEY CRYPTOLOGY OVERVIEW

A public key cryptological system is based on the use of a one-way function. Here the term *one-way function* represents a mathematical function whose inverse is extremely difficult, if not impossible, to compute. For example, for a given X, Y is easy to compute in the function:

$$Y = F(X)$$

However, in that same equation, for a given Y, X can be very difficult, if not impossible, to compute. The following relatively simple function is an example:

$$Y = X^5 - 2X^4 + 3X^3 - 2X^2 + X - 5$$

When X equals 2, for example, Y equals 13. However, given that $Y=13$, solving for X would be a much more difficult task:

$$13 = X^5 - 2X^4 + 3X^3 - 2X^2 + X - 5$$

Computing X, which represents the inverse of a one-way function, is programatically much more difficult. In addition, without special information, the computation of the inverse of a one-way function can require a relatively long period of time. For example, without special information, such as at what point to start and what increment to use, the end user might employ a trial-and-error process, beginning with $X = 0$ and incrementing X by .00001, each time testing the equation to determine if the new value used for X results in balancing the equation.

Modern public key cryptological systems are based on the use of a large prime number in an exponential operation. The first public key system concept resulted from the work of Diffie and Hellman, professors at Stanford University, during the mid-1970s. In their seminal paper, they noted that exponentiation is a one-way function for a relatively large prime number. For example, if p is a prime number, given an X and N, it is easy to compute the equation:

$$Y = X^N \bmod p$$

However, for a given Y and X, it becomes difficult to compute N.

The basic computations published by Diffie and Hellman for their public key system are based on the use of large prime numbers and exponentiation, as follows:

$$\text{Encryption } Y = X^e \bmod p$$

$$\text{Decryption } X \text{ -} y^d \bmod p$$

where:
X and Y = integers whose values are less than p
X = the plain-text

Y = the cipher-text
e = the secret encryption exponent
and d = the secret decryption exponent

One of the most interesting properties of an encryption and decryption function based on exponentiation is its commutative property. This can be demonstrated by the equation:

$$X^{E1} \text{ mod } p^{E2} \text{ mod } p = (X^{E2} \text{ mod } p)^{E1} \text{ mod } p$$

where:
$E1$ = one secret encryption exponent
$E2$ = a second secret encryption exponent

The commutative property permits two communications in a network to share a secret encryption exponent by only exchanging non-secret numbers. For example, assume Ted and Bob wish to communicate with each other and p represents any integer between 0 and p-1. For Ted and Bob to obtain a shared secret number, Ted would first generate a randomly selected secret number, X_T, and a corresponding public number, $Y_T = a^{XT}$ mod p. Bob would also randomly generate a secret number, X_B, and a corresponding public number, $Y_B a^{XB}$ mod p.

When a large prime number is used, it is for all practical purposes impossible to obtain the secret numbers from the public numbers. Thus, Tom and Bob can share a secret number that is unique to them and only need to exchange their non-secret public numbers. For example, Tom would send his public key Y_T to Bob, while Bob would send his public key Y_B to Tom. Based upon the commutative property of exponentiation, Tom can compute the equation:

$$C = Y_B^{XT} \text{ mod } p$$

Bob can compute the same number by using the equation:

$$C = Y_T^{XB} \text{ mod } p$$

Based upon the preceding, once public keys are exchanged, Tom and Bob can use their private keys to decrypt messages transmitted from one to the other. Similarly, either Bob or Tom can use his private key to encrypt a message that can be decrypted by any person that has the individual's public key. If this concept is expanded to include modern communications systems, such as the World Wide Web, the usefulness of a public key cryptological system becomes apparent. For example, a company wants to sell Widgets via the Internet and has installed a Web server to take credit card orders.

Without a public key system, the server operator would have to send a different traditional encryption key to every person who wishes to place credit card orders on the server in a secure environment. Thus, a person might first have to communicate with the server and request the server operator to him or her, via mail, a key to be used as a secure method to transmit the credit card number when ordering a Widget.

To avoid using the postal service, several server operators started using fax machines. A customer electronically places an order without the credit card number. The server then uses a dial-out fax system, which transmits an order form to the requester. The requester must then verify his or her order, enter his or her credit card number, sign the order form, and fax it back to the server operator. Obviously, this method requires the customer to have a fax machine, which can significantly limit the number of potential customers.

Through the use of a public key system, the server operator only has to identify his or her public key. This means that a person using a Web browser could access the server, retrieve the public key, and use that key to encrypt his or her credit card number. Because only the private key can be used to decrypt the message encrypted with the public key, only the server that has the private key can decrypt the secured information.

The method just described represents the technique used by Netscape Communications and other companies — with some slight modifications to provide secure communications for browser users when ordering information from World Wide Web server operators. For example, Netscape Communications markets secure server software which enables a server operator to generate a public key and a private key. If a Web user has a secure Netscape browser, once they access the Netscape secure server, the browser will automatically retrieve the public key from the server. This enables the browser operator to transmit credit card or other information to the server securely and without delay, avoiding the previously described problems associated with traditional cryptological systems.

OTHER APPLICATIONS

The use of public key cryptology can be used in a variety of ways to secure communications both inside and outside the organization. Concerning internal organizational use, different public keys could be provided to different departments that might require secure communications, and companywide public keys could be provided for secure communications between persons working in different departments within a company. For example, the sales department might wish to secure the transmission of sales forecasts as well as obtain the ability to transmit such information to corporate officers. Then, one public-private key set would be used for transmission of sales forecasts within or between members of the sales department, while a second public-private key set could be used to communicate sales forecasts to corporate officers.

ACTION PLAN

As indicated in this chapter, the use of public key cryptological systems considerably simplifies the management and transmission of keys. If an end-user requires secure communications, the systems manager should consider obtaining products that support the use of public key cryptology. For example, if users want to consider ordering information from Web servers, they should select a Web browser that supports public key encryption. Similarly, if users need to encrypt and transmit files in the form of diskettes or magnetic tapes, the systems manager should consider the use of file encryption software that supports public key encryption. Doing so can significantly reduce the time and effort required to manage keys which can provide an organization with an increase in your while maintaining a very high level of security.

Section VII Checklist

1. Is your organization planning to use the mainframe computer as an integral part of network computing?
2. What considerations should be given to connect mainframe and local servers as a multi-tiered server environment?
3. How should mainframe networks be managed in comparison to local area networks? Are there more similarities or differences in your environment?
4. Are considerations given to the design of networks based on application development and support requirements?
5. Is your organization's network strategy evolving too rapidly? What impact has this created on development and support?
6. Would you consider your network environment as open and flexible or is it closed and restrictive? How has this altered development efforts?
7. How would you assess your organization's network security? Do you consider it vulnerable to breaches?
8. What steps are you taking to develop applications that have integrated network security functions within the developed application?
9. Should your organization be better prepared for security before e-commerce applications are implemented?
10. When does your organization plan to perform a security audit of its network and communication systems?
11. What is your interpretation of electronic message processing?
12. How many different e-mail systems does your organization have? Do these systems talk to each other?
13. Is your organization planning on integrating message systems and application systems together as part of a larger business system?
14. What unique challenges does multi-platform connectivity create when developing or supporting applications?

Section VIII
Testing Software Applications

Testing software applications can be burdensome and demanding for many IS professionals. The challenge of software testing has become even more rigorous due to the utilization of newer development technology that includes multi-platform, client/server processing, and event-based systems. Other factors include lack of qualified testing staff and poorly practiced testing techniques. Despite acknowledgment of testing's importance, development managers are routinely faced with the dilemma of choosing between comprehensive testing or timely project delivery. More often than not, the requirement for punctual system implementation prevails and the test process is compromised.

Development managers can improve the value of software testing by re-establishing an understanding of testing principles and integrating the test process early in design and development phases. Chapter 42, "Reinventing Testing in the Age of Convergence," offers an important foundation for comprehending newer testing concepts and methods. Traditional testing techniques can be costly, time consuming, and yield little return on invested cost. However, there have been successful uses of more streamlined approaches that do not sacrifice testing initiatives for the sake of time or expense. This chapter discusses such a framework and recommends guidelines for appropriate implementation in a variety of testing situations.

Newer development paradigms, such as object-oriented programming and client/server applications, require new tools and techniques that differ from traditional development methods. Likewise, the testing process for client/server-based systems requires a different approach, especially given the Year 2000 support issues. Chapter 43, "Year 2000 Testing on Client/Server Database Applications," explains some of the factors to be considered in testing software outside the traditional environment of mainframe languages. The detailed information in this chapter will help development managers establish new and specific test procedures aimed for multi-tiered database applications. Recommendations and guidelines for establishing date compliancy are also presented.

Numerous testing initiatives are regaining more prominence as a critical phase of the application development process. Part of this acknowledgment is due to more complex application systems, such as web-based, object-oriented and client/server applications, which require extensive testing prior to implementation. Chapter 44, "Software Testing to Meet Corporate Quality Goals," offers insights and recommendations for improving the development process via a strong testing strategy. This chapter emphasizes the need for comprehensive application testing as a means to ensure more reliable business competitiveness. System failures, due to poor testing, can be more costly in the dynamic environment of the Internet and client/server architectures. Establishing strong testing practices is mandatory in the competitive world of e-business.

Software testing should not be limited to the boundaries of application functionality and performance. Given the scope of the entire application environment, it would be prudent to consider testing issues that are tangent to application process. Chapter 45, "Testing Disaster Recovery Plans," presents an informative discussion concerning the reliability of the disaster and recovery process. More often these processes are not checked until an actual failure has taken place, and usually it is too late to modify the plan for correctness. Unlike application testing which assumes that a system is functioning correctly, disaster and recovery testing assumes that a serious failure has already occurred. Many development managers fail to recognize that this is an area that can jeopardize even the most comprehensive application project. This chapter provides an excellent review of those areas that should be routinely examined for effective continuation of production systems.

Chapter 42
Reinventing Testing in the Age of Convergence

Shari Dove

The structured approach to testing advocated in this chapter has been successfully applied to save organizations time and money while increasing software quality and delivery reliability. The savings are realized through the implementation of the "V-model" of testing, metrics, and automation to dramatically improve the productivity and effectiveness of the software delivery processes. This chapter discusses a framework for testing that has been successfully applied to custom development, package installation, and maintenance, in traditional development environments as well as in iterative, rapid development, and object-oriented environments.

WHY REINVENT TESTING?

Testing costs organizations significant amounts of money. Currently, too much effort goes into testing, and many testing approaches waste both time and money. The value derived from today's testing processes does not match the effort expended. For typical systems projects in which 50 percent to 80 percent of the budget goes into testing-related activities, including test execution, impact analysis, and error resolution, a mere 10 percent reduction in the overall testing effort can translate into significant annual savings for the average IS department. Typical testing approaches exercise only 40 percent of application code, leaving an average of 3.79 defects per thousand lines of code (KLOC) and as many as 5 defects per KLOC.

There is cause for concern, then, that testing approaches that are ineffective in the current computing environment will only worsen as the computing environment becomes more complex. The risk to the average company today is significant. Customer expectations are escalating; the average business person is now familiar with computer technology and is less tolerant of imperfect solutions. Also, IS departments are losing control of their user community, as users are now customers and cannot be trained to make up for poorly tested solutions.

Testing approaches were left behind in the client/server revolution. Design, development, code, and architecture were all significantly changed

0-8493-9822-3/00/$0.00+$.50

by the client/server revolution, but testing was not, and testing today looks very much like it did 10 years ago, even though the applications are very different. In addition, software testing has not kept pace with the technology revolution; automation in the testing process has been vastly underused. Tools to automate test planning, test preparation, and execution are now available in the marketplace, as are tools for test data management and configuration management. These are all highly integrated, labor-intensive tasks that can benefit from the use of tools not only to increase speed and productivity but also to reduce the occurrence of human error. However, in spite of the availability of more mature tools in the marketplace, the use of automation in the testing processes remains limited, partially because the tools available have only recently matured to the point where it makes sense to invest in them. Many organizations are either unaware that tools exist to automate testing activities, or they looked at testing tools years ago when the tools market was immature and do not realize the advances made since. Another common reason for a lack of testing automation is that IS departments begin considering the automation requirements of the testing process too late in the project, when there is not enough time to evaluate, select, and implement tools.

Today's testing processes do not address the complexities of client/server computing, much less those of convergence. Multilayered architectures, graphical user interfaces (GUIs), user-driven or decision-support systems, and the need to interface heterogeneous systems and architectures all present new risks and challenges for information technologists. A proliferation of users and user types in netcentric applications all provide and demand information from an enterprise system. This situation presents massively complex design challenges, as well as security and error-avoidance requirements. All of these complexities must be recognized, designed for, and built into a set of applications. Then, just as important, they must be tested to ensure that they perform as expected.

As development in the client/server world matures, and as the industry becomes more comfortable with client/server development, IS departments' attention increasingly turns to testing. Recent recognition of testing as an important facet of successful systems delivery can be seen in the significant increase in the number of seminars and conferences dedicated to testing and software quality. Likewise, there has been a trend toward increased emphasis on testing indicated by the identification of dedicated testing or software quality managers or entire departments within large IS organizations.

All of the factors just mentioned, increased complexity, higher level of effort spent on testing, increased risk, and minimal revision in testing approach, are leading to the inevitable: Software developers must reinvent the way they test systems. Reinventing testing is part of the current movement toward quality in systems development, making use of concepts introduced in manufacturing, such as quality management (QM) and just in time (JIT), which are modified to apply to software development. Applying these manufacturing concepts to systems development requires IS development managers to adopt new or modified models of the development process and project organization. The key components of the V Model testing approach presented in this chapter are:

- Well defined development processes, each with suppliers and customers, in which an overall quality product is achieved only when quality is delivered at every point in the chain.
- Structured, repeatable testing.
- Definition of metrics to be used for continuous process improvement.
- Use of automation to improve speed and reduce errors.
- New management approaches to organization and communication.

By applying a V-Model testing approach, many organizations have realized improved quality, reliability, efficiency, and delivery time. They have also achieved better risk management and cost avoidance. For example, an internal software development organization within Andersen Consulting was able to achieve an 80 percent reduction in the software defects delivered to customers while improving testing productivity and delivery speed. Another example is a large drugstore chain in the US which realized a 100 percent improvement in testing productivity while achieving nearly fivefold improvements in software quality.

A MODEL FOR CONVERGENCE TESTING

This section presents a quick review of the V Model approach. The V Model is a framework for structured, repeatable testing, serving as a basis for the V Model testing approach needed to successfully manage net-centric systems development.

The V Model provides a structured testing framework throughout the development process, emphasizing quality from the initial requirements stage through the final testing stage. All solution components, including application programs, conversion programs, and technical architecture programs, are required to proceed through the V Model development process.

The V Model charts a path from verification and validation to testing. After each process in the development life cycle has been defined, each major deliverable in the development process must be verified and validated, and then the implementation of each specification must be tested. Verification is a process of checking that a deliverable is correctly derived from the inputs of the corresponding stage, and that the deliverable is complete and correct. In addition, verification checks that the process to derive the deliverable was followed and that the output conforms to the standards set in the project's quality plan. One form of verification, for example, is desk checking, or inspection of a design specification to ensure the process was followed, the standards were met, and the deliverable is complete.

Validation checks that the deliverables satisfy requirements specified in the previous stage or in an earlier stage, and that the business case continues to be met. In other words, the work product contributes to the intended benefits and does not have undesired side effects. Given the top-down nature of systems specification, validation is critical to ensuring that the decisions made at each successive level of specification continue on track to meet the initial business needs. For example, using validation techniques, developers seek to avoid the experience of one major reservation call center, which implemented the ability to view recent print ads in the reservation systems when the overriding business case for the system was to improve the speed of the reservation agents. There was no real business need for the reservation agents to view print ads, and a great deal of time was spent designing functionality that, if implemented, would have actually slowed the reservation process rather than speed it up.

Testing is designed to ensure that the specification is properly implemented and integrated. Ideally, testing activities are not in place to ensure the solution was properly specified, that activity being done via verification and validation. Rather, testing activities associated with each level of the specification ensure that the specifications were properly translated into the final solution.

The V-model is depicted in Exhibit 42.1. This figure shows the work flow in the development process, with a series of design activities and systems specifications on the left side (i.e., top-down), and a series of corresponding testing activities on the right side (i.e., bottom-up).

In concept, the core process stages of requirements analysis, design, and construction consist of creating a series of increasingly detailed specifications. The exhibit specifies the systems from the top down, making decisions and adding detail at each stage. Work flows between stages in the V model when a work packet or deliverable has met the exit criteria, that is, all the verification and validation requirements for that stage. Testing is designed to ensure that the components of the application are properly constructed, put together correctly, and that they deliver the functional, technical, and quality requirements.

The specification stages are:

- The business case.
- The requirements definition.
- The technical design.
- The detailed design.

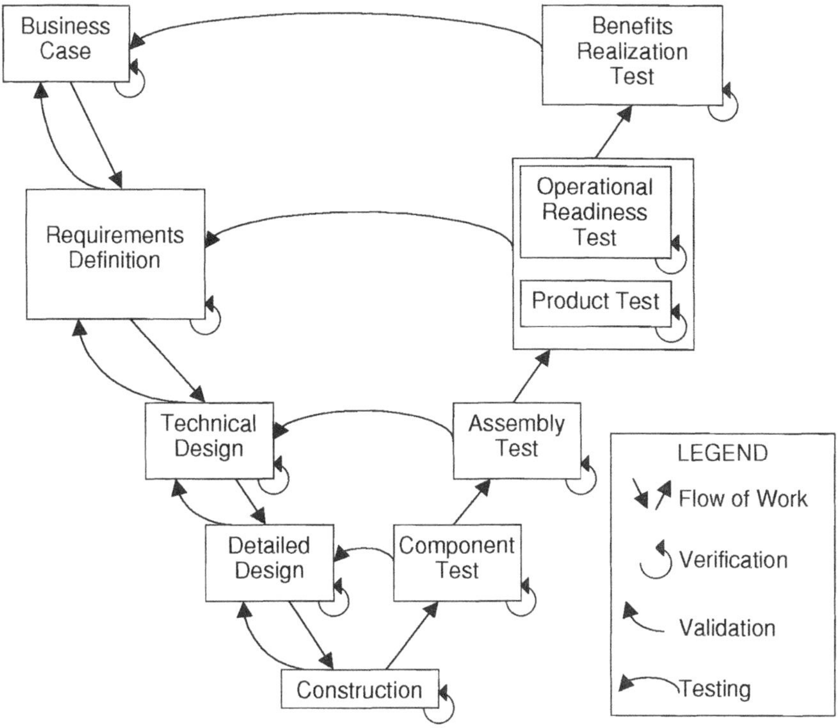

Exhibit 42.1. V-Model of Verification, Validation, and Testing

The test stages are:

- The component test.
- The assembly test.
- The product test.
- The operational readiness test.
- The benefits realization test.

An underlying concept of on the V Model is that the boxes in the exhibit represent distinct development and testing stages. It is essential that the stages of the V-Model, and the processes to complete each stage, are well defined, structured, and standardized. Defined, standard processes are repeatable and measurable. Processes that are not repeatable or measurable therefore do not easily lend themselves to improvement. Testers cannot collect meaningful data about ad-hoc processes because there is no clear understanding of what the steps and outcomes are meant to be. Developers cannot learn from their experiences if they take a completely different approach each time they set out to develop software. Also, there is significant margin for error in undefined processes. Too often, the designers have different expectations of what that process is to produce than do the construction and testing teams. This leads to gaps and overlaps between the processes, which are at best inefficient, at worst, error prone.

ENTRY AND EXIT CRITERIA

Of special importance is the verification and validation performed at hand-off points between work cells or teams or from the project team to the users. Each inspection, performed at hand-off points or other important checkpoints during the development process, must satisfy a set of specific entry and exit criteria. As processes are defined, it must be clearly stated what each process is responsible for, and where it begins and ends. Entry and exit criteria are a mechanism for articulating what is required from previous processes to support a given stage (i.e., entry criteria) and what is required of a given process to determine completeness (i.e., exit criteria). Entry and exit criteria are defined for each stage to ensure quality deliverables from one stage to the next. If a deliverable fails to meet these set criteria, it is demoted to the previous stage or to the stage determined to have caused the nonconformity.

One stage's exit criteria are largely the next stage's entry criteria. Some exit criteria, however, may satisfy the entry criteria of a stage other than the one next in line. Relative to testing, there are three types of entry and exit criteria:

- Those that must be met in one test stage in order to proceed with the next test stage.
- Those that must be met in the specification stage to facilitate test preparation.
- Those that are required for repetition of the current stage, in maintenance or enhancement activities.

All three types of entry and exit criteria should be defined and communicated as part of the standard process definition. Entry criteria may also be inspected throughout the development process, as opposed to right before the test stage requiring the criteria to be met is about to start. Inspection helps to build quality into the process and thus the solution, rather than retrofitting the solution to work correctly, and inspection saves the cost of rework, which only gets more expensive as the life cycle progresses. Although inspections cost time and effort on the front end, experience shows that the cost of formalized inspections is more than gained back in future stages of the life cycle.

Three key success factors with regards to inspection of entry and exit criteria are the developer should:

- Ensure the entry and exit criteria are understood.
- Validate and verify content as well as format.
- Conduct inspections throughout the process.

Developers should not wait until the end of the stage to start inspecting deliverables. People are less willing to go back and rework something from a previous stage if the next stage is well underway. This reduces any rework in the next stage or in the related test stage and ensures that nonconformity to the entry and exit criteria can be communicated to the rest of the work cell or team to prevent replicating nonconformity throughout the remaining deliverables for that stage.

Sample key exit criteria for each stage are:

- Deliverables must conform to standards.
- Requirements specification must be reviewed with user.
- Test cases must be generated.
- Design must be traceable to the requirements specification through cross-references.
- Code must be analyzed for adherence to standards and complexity guidelines, and analysis results must fall within defined thresholds.
- Code must be traceable to the design through cross-references.
- Component test data must be traceable to the design through cross-references.
- There can be no abends in component test results.
- Component test results must be repeatable.
- All paths within the application flow must be executed.
- Assembly test results must be repeatable.
- The product test model must be traceable to the requirements specification (both functional requirements and quality attributes) through cross-references.
- Product test results must conform to predicted results.
- Product test results must be repeatable.

VERIFICATION AND VALIDATION

Verification and validation are a means to test specifications and other deliverables. Approaches to verification and validation include walkthrough or peer reviews, formal inspections, and prototypes. Other approaches are paper system testing, desk checks, and stakeholder reviews.

Verification

Verification is most commonly accomplished through an inspection. Inspections involve a number of reviewers, each with specific responsibilities for verifying aspects of the specification package, such as functional completeness, adherence to standards and correct use of the technical architecture. According to Tom Gilb, software quality expert and author of Software Inspection, inspection, done before an application is finished, can remove 95% of all defects before the first tests.

Validation

Validation is most commonly accomplished through management checkpoints or stakeholder reviews. Two effective techniques of validation are repository validation and the completion and review of traceability matrices. Repository validation can be used when a design repository such as development workbenches, CASE tools, or even very strict naming conventions, are used and cross-checks can be executed against the repository to ensure integrity of dependencies between deliverables. Such a cross-check is designed to confirm that each deliverable is derived from a higher order deliverable, and that each higher order deliverable breaks down into one or more implementation level deliverable. A traceability matrix is a technique used in defense contracting when a matrix is developed of all requirements cross referenced to the designs, code, tests and deployment deliverables that implement the requirement. In either case, what is accomplished is a cross-check that all business-case criteria are directly linked to one or more specification, and at each level of specification, there is a direct link back up to a business case criteria. The objective of validation in this way is the direct relation of the specifications to the requirements and business case items that they implement, facilitating the identification of missing requirements and specifications not contributing to the business case.

How validation is performed depends on the nature of the requirement in the specification document. Certain requirements can be traced directly from the specification to the implementation; they bear the same name, and there is a one-to-one correspondence between the requirement and some component in the implementation. For example, a business objective to support a new operational process may be directly tied to portions of the application under development.

In other cases, the specification concerns a quality factor or an emerging property of the implementation. Therefore, a direct comparison is not possible. In this case, validation can be done by analyzing a model of the implementation, for example, analyzing the workflow to ensure that headcount does not increase and that cost is reduced. It can also be done by creating and testing a prototype or by a peer or expert review, as in validating the design for maintainability criteria.

CONCLUSION

Viewed as opportunity, the V-Model approach to testing positions an organization to move into advanced technology and business challenges. Having processes at a high level of quality and predictability provides a controlled software delivery environment, so that variables like new technology, new enterprises, or new business offerings can more easily be introduced. This minimizes risk and produces the desired results for the IT organization.

Chapter 43
Year 2000 Testing on Client/Server Database Applications

Martin D. Solomon and Scott C. Blanchette

Whenever information systems professionals think of Year 2000 projects and initiatives, they almost exclusively envision examining, maintaining, and performing testing on applications that are over 10 years old and based on third-generation languages such as COBOL, FORTRAN, and PLI. The potential vulnerability of recently designed and constructed client/server database systems is usually never considered. Based on observations taken over the past few years and on work performed in the past 18 months, the assumption that these systems are millennium compliant could prove unwise and be a precursor to a flood of problems when that time arrives.

The following article will provide insight into which client/server systems are likely to be the most vulnerable, what are some of the most common problems and issues found during testing, and recommendations for how to address these issues. All of the scenarios and recommendations recounted and presented here are the sum of the authors' experiences over several projects that tested for millennium-compliance issues on distributed client/server systems. Although most of these items were found through targeted regression testing, some were found serendipitously.

WHAT TO TARGET

Since it would clearly not be cost-effective to inspect closely all client/server applications for potential millennium issues, it was necessary to develop criteria for determining which applications and systems would be the most vulnerable. Drawing from the authors' experiences and those of colleagues with broad-based distributed systems knowledge, it became apparent that the more data sources a system had, the more at risk it would be. While this conclusion seems obvious, what was often not so easy to see is which systems had many data sources. Systems that at first glance appeared to have only a few data sources suddenly mushroomed in

0-8493-9822-3/00/$0.00+$.50

complexity when it was found that those "few" data sources were each partly or wholly composed of other data sources! In one particularly nasty case, the database system that was being examined had what was thought to be two principal data sources, one from a legacy database and the other from an online transaction-processing (OLTP) client/server database. Upon closer inspection, it was found that the legacy system files were composed from nightly batch feeds from other legacy systems and that the OLTP system received a portion of its data from several other completely different legacy systems!

The applications described above commonly fall under the data warehouse category and in general are those that should be targeted first. Specifically, applications that are constructed in-house, are large and complex, and whose database is built from many data feeds from a myriad of sources should be considered primary testing targets. Other key applications to target include seemingly "small" or niche client/server systems that monitor and record data from computer integrated machinery and hardware. It may be possible that these applications have trip mechanisms in them that will shut down or quiesce the items from which they are recording information if date discrepancies are indicated. In addition, it is appropriate that applications that mix vendor-based solutions with customized internal applications should at least be placed under consideration for a formal testing process.

THE TESTING PROCESS

In all cases the ability to replicate completely the client/server application and database on a separate piece of hardware was requested. This allowed the dates on the operating system of the receiving platform to be changed freely. It also helped to limit what would prove to be extensive coordination efforts among all of the platforms, environments, pieces of hardware, and corporate organizations. This way at least the server(s) containing the database(s) and executable code could remain in a "stable" Year 2000 state for the duration of the testing. In all of the cases, the request was fulfilled since there always seemed to be an adequate server that could at least be borrowed for the duration. This was always impractical in the host environment, which could not be cloned because of financial constraints.

The periodic updates and/or feeds to the client/server systems were often manipulated manually. Frequently, there were several levels of data, which in turn required additional manipulation all the way back to the original source data. Repeated trials of host downloads and feeds were run with corresponding application testing on the client/server side. Where it proved worthwhile, separate "one-time-use" programs or queries were written to aid in the data verification process.

After each download was completed, the client/server relational database tables were periodically scanned for data inconsistencies. Once again, several "throwaway" programs were constructed for comparing data from the different host platforms and environments. The dates on the client/server platform and the data feed files were varied from January 2000 to December 2001. In applications deemed particularly vulnerable or critical, these feeds, processes, and testing scenarios were performed for situations that would arise even if the source files or databases were *not* made millennium compliant by the deadline. (This is not at all an unreasonable scenario. In fact, some of the client/server warehouse-type applications and their respective databases which were investigated had, over the years, become more important to everyday business functions than those systems from which they drew their data.)

For all applications, IDs and passwords were changed and/or manipulated to prevent any accidental "production" runs during the course of the testing. Since the client/server platform was nearly always 100 percent replicated with the exception of the network address of the computers, it was felt this was a worthwhile precaution.

WHAT WAS FOUND

The first obstacles or hurdles that had to be overcome occurred even before the formal millennium testing took place. Replicating the batch or bulk feeds and file transfers that these systems received took extensive effort. In nearly every case, the batch feeds used in the distributed systems were managed by several different groups or departments. Coordinating and cajoling the different areas to meet the testing requirements and to provide assistance when and where required proved quite difficult. Decisions regarding what to do if the systems providing the data had not already planned for their eventual millennium compliance also came only with great effort and coaxing. Some of the answers required prior to the testing plan and process included whether the files would be changed to reflect the four-digit year, or if other markers or switches would be added or modified to accommodate the change that would make the source applications millennium compliant.

Once the responsible groups were all on board and it was decided what to do with current noncompliant data feeds, another logistical headache was encountered when authorizations and access were requested for the different platforms and software that were to be part of the testing scenario. Unlike the mainframe testing scenario, the client/server world brought together many different products, machines, and platforms that required user or programmer IDs and the corresponding authorizations. In addition, while these items were being put in place it became apparent that the learning curve for the testing or millennium teams was going to be extraordinarily steep. Here again, the difference between host-based millennium testing and client/server testing paradigm was brought to light by the number of products and components in the systems. Most host-based testing involved prior general knowledge of IBM-based systems, the popular third-generation languages and the common relational database or file systems. In the distributed client/server environment, however, the millennium teams were often up against several software products on differing platforms. In addition, these products were quite frequently of the niche or seminiche variety, so obtaining quick or "just-in-time" training and/or extensive technical support added a few more logistical hurdles to be overcome. (Fortunately, since many of the millennium teams consisted mostly of mainframe professionals and entry-level programmers, the carrot of learning new client/server software made these hurdles that much easier to vault.)

Once testing began and system dates were changed, the client/server application code encountered several bugs because it was converting and manipulating fields in the database that were downloaded as two-byte years. The main culprits were combined indexing fields or fields used to reference and/or look up data in the client/server back-end database tables. The composite nature of these columns lent themselves to overflow problems when the source feed files were changed to accommodate the millennium. If it was assumed that only the source system code would be changed to accommodate the millennium and the programs that manipulated the downloading of the data remained unchanged, the client/server application code would break down and warrant modification. On the other hand, if it was assumed that the source data structures would be changed, the interface programs would fail or deliver incorrect data to the application tables. This situation occurred in several different systems tested. As a consequence it is believed that this fact is at the very core of millennium vulnerability in the relatively new client/server paradigm. Many of these distributed systems get their information from legacy sources that are not yet millennium compliant. Although these distributed applications were designed to withstand four-digit years, it is impossible for them to predict how to handle modified date feeds from existing systems. Of course, this is true for any type of similar data modification in a data warehouse–type system, but it is never of this magnitude. In many cases, there probably was not even an afterthought to the problem, since the front-end client/server application being built, with modern relational database back ends, was unquestionably millennium compliant.

A specific example of this occurred during the very first week of the first millennium client/server testing project. The application being examined used an integer field to contain index "look-up" data for various information searches. This field was composed of a two-digit year, a two-digit month, plus other numbers initially generated in the legacy source systems. This problem was discovered early on in testing when the application logic failed. At this point the first instinct was to update the data in this field to the four-digit year format and then modify the interface programs to deliver the data as such. Unfortunately, when adding the extra two places, the values of the index field exceeded the defined capacity for the integer datatype! To fully fix the problem, the index look-up field datatype had to be changed to decimal in all tables where it was used. Within an hour the first millennium client/server problem became a somewhat costly effort to modify a half dozen very large tables, change some fairly complex interface program code, and thoroughly retest the application.

Another problem that was not quite anticipated was that there were several record structures or fields on the mainframe side that were never going to be made compliant because the application owners assumed that this information was no longer of any consequence. Whether due to employee turnover or lack of communication, there were several pieces of information left out in the source system as "dead space." In the course of the past few years, however, that information was now starting to be used as data sources to systems on other physical platforms and often in other corporate political worlds.

Some of the other problems encountered included noncompliant vendor software experiences. This was despite the fact that the particular version of the software was assured to be Year 2000 compliant. What the vendor did not know, or neglected to mention, was that its product was not compliant when coupled with other back-end databases or linked with other software on some hardware configurations. One such issue occurred early on in the testing. The system, which used Microsoft Access version 2.0 for its back-end database, kept track of expiration dates for various types of equipment. What the application did not account for is the fact that although the software accepted and managed four-digit years, the algorithm it used when two-digit years were placed in the database automatically preceded it with "19." So when users entered expiration dates beyond 1999 the system accepted and displayed the data with the year as "01" or "02." The users had no reason to assume that the information was incorrect, yet the database was storing it all along as "1901" or "1902"!

Perhaps with the complexity of today's distributed systems it is unreasonable to ask vendors, especially the smaller ones, to have accounted for every permutation that could occur, but it is something to keep in the back of the mind from the compliance-testing standpoint.

Another minor problem occurred when a monthly production run failed because the "real" IDs had been turned off during testing and were not turned back for the actual business processing. More of an inconvenience than a major problem, it was still felt to be worth it when compared with the alternative of accidentally running a millennium test against a production server database.

Perhaps most surprising, but what in retrospect should have been anticipated, were the compliance problems found in the application code constructed specifically for the client/server software and written only three years ago! Whether due to careless programming or insufficient testing during the original construction, it was a reminder of how even with the best software nothing should be taken for granted. These problems consisted of the classic millennium errors, such as neglecting to take into account that the year 2000 is a leap year or continuing to use the old function of assigning expiration dates to various media types as "99/99/99."

CORRECTIVE ACTIONS AND RECOMMENDATIONS

First, the logic to handle and synthesize the data delivered from other systems was corrected. Second, the noncompliant application software code was fixed. Next, vendors were called where necessary. In each of the cases, the vendor indicated that it would note the problem for customer inquiries in the future. Finally, where required, the applications providing the source data to this system were modified to ensure a smooth flow of data after the turn of the century. Legacy data left for "dead" was put on the path for compliance, and its supporting application areas were notified to document its usage in other system(s).

These experiences have left the authors with some very specific items that are felt must be addressed when looking at the Year 2000 situation for distributed client/server applications. Once systems have been triaged based on business needs, it is recommended that the plan of attack for testing should be as follows.

Target applications and systems that receive the many feeds from disparate platforms and environments. Most often these will be data warehouse-type systems. The likelihood that these processes will involve an extensive combination of hardware and software components makes these systems extremely vulnerable to millennium problems. Keep in the forefront the assumption that the "owners" or maintainers of the source data systems may not be aware of who or what other business units are using their data.

In all testing scenarios, resist the urge to run individual piece replications of bulk- or batch-feed process into the client/server system. Problems that may emerge from the entire process may not be seen when run piecemeal, so it is essential that the complete load process be replicated with the client/server system at the year 2000 and 2001. All loads, batch copies, and cycles must be therefore be diligently and painstakingly tested and reviewed. "Disposable" data verification programs may have to be written to support this philosophy.

Do not take for granted that, just because a database has attributes defined with the standard datatypes in the client/server world, it is indeed receiving and using these attributes as under normal circumstances. Date and time information might be hidden under the guise of otherwise-defined integer, character, and decimal datatypes in the database. These fields, which are frequently used for indexing purposes, may also be a composite of several data sources from different business units, which makes the detection problem especially complex.

Ensure that all front-end application presentations require four-digit years to be entered and displayed back the user. Otherwise, inaccurate data may be entered and retrieved from the application in question and may not show up as such until reports are generated or calculations are performed on the data in the future.

Be wary of millennium problems even in "new" application software code built only a few years ago, especially that which was built in-house. This may be stating the obvious, but as of this writing, few have expressed concern about it and the experiences here prove that most organizations should be putting more effort into evaluating whether or not these latest and greatest applications are indeed millennium compliant.

Verify that front-end vendor software is compliant with the particular back-end database(s) the site is utilizing. On several occasions, the authors saw front-end software functioning perfectly with one back-end database, but when another was used, millennium compliance broke down. In addition, it may be wise to ensure that the vendor is millennium compliant as well. If the software it is using to run its business is not compliant, it may end up costing the user's business as well. Perhaps this last point seems small, but if this turned out to be the case, users' software investment will be riding with what may become a very unstable supporting company.

In summary, several of the issues regarding client/server application systems that were discussed here are somewhat similar to those that are experienced with mainframe or host-based millennium testing and compliance. As was seen, however, many are not, and those issues proved to be very insidious in nature because of the distributed world in which they live. It is urged that all at least be cognizant of this fact.

Chapter 44
Software Testing to Meet Corporate Quality Goals

Polly Perryman

THE EFFECTS OF SATELLITE COMMUNICATIONS and worldwide Internet use in the business world are among the driving forces in today's software community. The pressure is on to beat the leading technological standards currently available. These pressures come into the world of software development from three distinct areas: business and industry demands, product quality, and world market competition. Each of these areas raises its own issues relative to testing. The result is that software developers and system integrators must alter their view of the work effort to ensure a more thorough and complete testing.

The perspective for a new view includes defining testing processes for the organization that not only overlap the development effort but also fully support the schedule and budgets of the project. These processes must address areas of testing that have traditionally been lumped into the part of the cycle where "a miracle occurs." Processes for planning, requirement mapping, change control, development tools, and testing tools are a few of the areas that are necessary to develop software and to integrate systems that satisfy the dimensions of twenty-first century technology. The development cycle may remain constant, but methods applied within the phases of the development cycle have become more sophisticated, and as a result, testing of these systems needs to be more thorough than when current systems were created.

Traditionally a problem area for containing costs and meeting schedules, testing processes are scrutinized in assessing the quality of a product and in selecting companies to develop software. More important, testing processes must meet the demands of business and industry for demonstrating that the software will meet the interoperability and reliability needed. Defining an approach to software testing that can be used on one or more software development projects can minimize problems previously prevalent throughout the software development community, but to accomplish this, it is necessary to start with a basic testing approach and to understand that there is a test cycle consistent with and complementary to

0-8493-9822-3/00/$0.00+$.50

the software development cycle. Once a basic approach for testing is developed, it can in turn be customized to meet the organization's quality goals.

As competition increases on the international front, business and industry continuously identify greater areas of need. To meet these needs, they are raising an outcry for technological solutions, which in turn translates into systems that are more complex and more secure. As a result, innovative systems of the late twentieth century, such as bank ATMs, home shopping telephones, and nonrestricted scanners, are becoming substructures for twenty-first century technology. Routine, day-to-day tasks common to modern man are becoming automated, and the manual functions performed in corporations today are being reassessed for automation tomorrow. Even relatively simple systems for general business and financial applications must be integrated and perform at high speeds. To meet these technology-driven demands, software systems are becoming more complicated to design, construct, and test.

At every phase of the development effort, methods are needed for ensuring that new product specifications comply with the interface, interconnection, and interoperability requirements set for the software community, not only in the U.S. but the international marketplace. To test these systems adequately, testing processes must be well planned. Test objectives must be carefully defined. This is accomplished by accepting the changes that are already in process within the software community and in becoming knowledgeable about existing industry standards and those under development.

Whether the system to be developed is for corporate or home use, today's consumer expects the best. Corporate end users have, at a minimum, a fundamental knowledge of computer technology on which to base their purchasing decisions. They do their homework to find out which products, software developers, and system integrators offer the best value. What they are looking for is the highest level of usefulness and quality relative to cost.

An important starting place is an assessment of the philosophy and the testing processes already in existence within the corporation. This chapter proposes and discusses the following testing philosophy.

ESTABLISHING A TESTING STRATEGY

For the purposes of this article, a philosophy for testing is proposed to be the process for finding and fixing the inconsistencies and problems present in software and the process of identifying and developing procedural work around for those that are not easily fixed. The testing process is intended to help attain perfection rather than proving perfection.

In building a testing strategy to support that philosophy, it is important to establish a familiarity with testing terminology among developers and managers responsible for testing, because as software is developed and tests are designed to ensure quality, decisions need to be made whether white box testing or black box testing, or both, will be performed.

The term white box test is generally used to describe a controlled test or a series of controlled internal system tests that demonstrate what happens within the system under certain circumstances. Individual modules and strings or threads of code are generally tested using white box techniques. The unit or thread is executed and stopped at various points in the processing to determine what happens when it is stopped and to determine whether the processing that was intended to occur in fact did occur.

The term black box test refers to a test that validates the use and operations of a system with the internal processes of the system transparent to the testers. Black box tests generally consider the input and the output without regard to what is going on within the system. Black box testing of a GUI, for example, would be concerned with the human factors of the GUI, such as ease of use, correctness of the transportation through the system, and the response time of the displays.

Whereas these terms describe specific types of testing techniques, they do not represent or provide an overall strategy or approach for testing. A testing strategy is significant in being able to do one or more of the following:

- Show value (i.e., this product is better than the competition's product).
- Meet customer expectations (i.e., this product performs the functions needed with no failures).
- Contain costs (i.e., the problems are found as early as possible in the development cycle and fixed without exploding development budgets).
- Meet schedules (i.e., the defined processes used for development support better planning and execution).

In establishing a test strategy for single or multiple software development projects, five issues must be addressed: testing goals, pretest procedures, test methods and techniques, test cycle, and test activities.

TESTING GOALS

All organizations that are interested in finding ways to ensure the quality of their products through testing have a common goal, but the methods for achieving that goal employ many different testing methods and techniques. One way to determine if the methods and techniques meet the growing and changing technological advancements is to review what is being required in specific industries and for particular types of software. In the recently published book, *Software Engineering Standards and Specifications*,[1] 146 national and international standards development organizations are identified. These organizations are making headway in projecting the needs of software within particular industries and in general. The standards they are developing are affecting the future of software development in the areas of requirements definition, design, code, integration, project management, verification and validation, configuration management, quality assurance, and others. Forty-five of these organizations deal specifically with standards for software testing in some form.

A review of these standards points to specific testing requirements at various levels and for particular types of software. The standards provide valuable guidelines in industries in which safety is foremost, as it is in nuclear and air transport. They are also useful to organizations whose software products require accuracy and integrity but that may not be mission critical. The usefulness is in reviewing the standards, editing them to meet explicit needs in the organization, and then using them to customize a testing approach for independent corporate use and to meet the expressed quality goals of the organization.

PRETEST PROCEDURES

Creating testing procedures is an intricate part of having a defined testing approach. It does not have to be a painful experience, but it does require decision makers to document the steps that will be taken as each new development effort is begun.

Acceptance Criteria

At a minimum, a procedure should exist to ensure that the software acceptance criteria are put into place while system requirements are being defined. Defining the acceptance criteria for the software to be developed before the design work begins is one of the first steps in containing costs. The acceptance criteria sets the baseline standard on which testing will be conducted, by giving the high-level measurements against which compliance with requirements will be evaluated. This measurement is used to judge the completeness and usability of the software by the end user in deciding the acceptability of it for its intended purpose. For example, if a requirement states that the system must be available 99 percent of the time, the acceptance criteria must include those statements that explain precisely what constitutes 99 percent of the time. For example, does that mean 99 percent of a 40-hour work week or 99 percent of a 24-by-7 operation? If the requirement states that the system is to process 4 million documents annually, the acceptance criteria must clarify what constitutes a

[1]S. Magee and L.L. Tripp, *Software Engineering Standards and Specifications: An Annotated Index and Directory* (Global Professional Public Publications, 1994).

single document. For example, is a document a single sheet of paper, or is a document some number of related papers between 1 and 100?

Test Methods and Techniques

Defining the minimum types of tests to be run before the development cycle begins is also critical. This procedure ensures that the testing approach put into place will consistently review individual software projects. It will make certain that scheduled testing activities meet the minimum level of testing needed for specific types of software, including, for example, the mission-critical software included in weaponry, information-processing software, such as tax returns and bank statements, and automation-processing software for automated teller machines and robots. The types of tests to be considered include reliability, usability, interoperability, accuracy, safety, performance, and stress testing.

Compiling a written list of the minimum types of test acceptable for the software to be developed provides a point of reference in analyzing software requirements during the requirements-definition phase of the development effort. A checklist may be included with the procedure. This procedure helps project managers understand the scope of testing needed for individual software projects, a key factor in ensuring that planned schedules and budgets are realistic from the beginning of the effort.

The Level of Testing Detail. Once the procedure specifying the types of tests is complete, guidelines are generated designating the level of detail that is needed for each type of test. The level of detail addresses both the technique and timing. The technique refers to the method to be applied, and timing states when in the development cycle the test will be conducted. Determining the level of detail needed to perform thorough testing for each type of testing means that planned testing techniques for a given project are identified and recorded before the development work commences.

Defining both the testing techniques and the type of testing establishes a clear testing picture, and the intended approach to testing becomes more definitive. For example, the technique for usability testing might be a peer review of flowcharts and decision tables during the design phase or path testing by the programmer or team leader during the coding phase.

Establishing the correct level of detail for testing in relationship to the complexity of the system enforces a definitive level of testing and precludes subjective testing decisions from being based solely on schedule issues. In other words, the approach not only reduces the risk that the software will be more grandiose than necessary or not usable at all, it also ensures that realistic schedules and budgets can be established and met. Just as important, in defining the level of testing, the level of understanding needed to meet quality goals is demonstrated.

By identifying criteria, defining which tests to use, and establishing a level of testing detail, an organization shows a commitment to quality. It also establishes the foundation for a repeatable testing approach and can reasonably establish a testing tool kit that can be reused from one project to another, effectively improving productivity during the testing phase of the development cycle.

TEST MANAGEMENT AND TEST AUTHORITY

An organization should also define how it will control all testing efforts and should identify, by position, the authority structure for every testing effort. The value of having these procedures in place as part of the organization's overall testing approach is threefold. First, they provide consistency, and consistency is, in today's market, translated into quality. This is highlighted by the growing requirement to demonstrate quality both internationally, through the ISO 9000 series of standards for quality management, and nationally, at least for government projects, through the Capability Maturity Model, created by the SEI at Carnegie Mellon University. (See Exhibit 44.1 for a more detailed discussion of ISO 9000 and SEI CMM.)

CONCLUSION

Because the test management procedures call out the way in which testing will be accomplished, it is essential that test authorities be established. This means that the positions or roles of a project are designated for test personnel, and assignments stating the responsibilities for each position, including who has signature authority to show successful test completion, are defined. When a project is staffed, a single individual could possibly fulfill the responsibilities of all the defined positions; however, having a clear understanding of what those responsibilities are could prevent untimely surprises — a skills shortage — from interfering with either the cost or schedule, or both.

Exhibit 44.1. The Software Engineering Institute's Capability Maturity Model (CMM)and ISO 9000 Guidelines

The SEI CMM, initially developed and implemented in the United States for use by the Department of Defense, is now a feature of the commercial world, as the technology of today's businesses expand for greater and greater personal access and use in areas of finance and security. The SEI CMM quality guidelines were created specifically to measure and validate software development processes, and compliance results in a level rating somewhere between 1 and 5, with a rating of 5 being the highest. The SEI CMM rating is established though an assessment process defined and structured as part of the model. The SEI CMM is finding its way into the international software community via United States representatives working on international communities.

ISO 9000 is composed of a series standards and guidelines initially prepared to ensure that the processes used in the manufacturing of products met minimum criteria that could then be translated to assured quality of the product. Compliance with ISO 9000 is certified by registered ISO certification auditors. There are continuing efforts by representatives of ISO's subcommittee on software engineering and system documentation and by SEI CMM representatives to broaden the ISO 9000 quality-management guidelines in a manner that addresses software development quality issues.

SEI CMM and ISO 9000 are similar in that they both relate quality to process, both provide methods for validating the processes of an organization, and both result in recognized and accepted ratings or certification. Both the CMM and ISO 9000 seek to ensure consistency in the processes of an organization as part of the rating and certification assessments.

Second, consistency improves productivity by allowing personnel to do the job rather than trying to figure out how to do the job and how to get around personal agendas that can sabotage a project. These test management procedures also provide a baseline method from which process improvement can be attained and measured. Developers who work on one or more projects within an organization will find the snags in the process and be able to bring suggestions and recommendations for implementing day-to-day operations that support improvement of the procedure and ensure its smooth execution.

The third benefit is that an organization can correctly staff an upcoming development effort. Whether individuals are going to wear one hat or support multiple roles on a project, management must make several decisions before the project begins. It must define in advance how the testing effort is to be managed. Management must also determine what type of decision makers are going to be needed. By doing so, it minimizes the risk that the staffing process omits the skills necessary to complete the job on time and within budget. In other words, the planning can be more accurate and cost overruns can be minimized.

When establishing test management procedures, management must remember that the procedure will be the guidelines not only for managing staff, test environments, and schedules, but also for determining the test readiness of software. Consideration must be given to configuration management in terms of version control, problem reporting and tracking, and the overall integrity of the test environment.

Chapter 45
Testing Disaster Recovery Plans

Leo A. Wrobel

Determining the effectiveness of a disaster recovery plan, or whether a plan works at all, is as crucial to the plan's development as the documentation of operating and security standards and recovery procedures. This article presents checklists of issues and errors that often occur during disaster recovery tests. It is based on an exercise conducted by a large fictitious company whose EMT works in coordination with other logistical teams to oversee a highly visible disaster. Reviewing the functioning of these varied teams can help other IS managers develop or refine a test and ensure a more cohesive recovery exercise for their organizations.

THE EXECUTIVE MANAGEMENT TEAM

At a minimum, an Executive Management Team (EMT) should comprise a chief executive, a director of technical services, a building facilities manager, and a small administrative staff. It is called together only under specific circumstances, such as a destructive disaster that necessitates moving the company's primary place of business to a disaster recovery facility; an environmental disaster, such as a hazardous chemical spill, that poses a complicated public affairs problem; or a disaster that is considered a threat to investors, shareholders, or customers who depend on the organization and require a high level of public contact and reassurance. The primary requirement of an EMT is a predefined location — such as a training facility, hotel suite, or one of the executive's homes — to which the executives know to report after a disaster.

Activating the EMT

Successful activation of an EMT depends foremost on the ability to contact team members during the difficult and unusual circumstances a disaster poses. Several basic issues can arise during the notification process: Do key executives have unlisted telephone numbers that are not documented in the plan? Even if they do not, what if telephone service is out to the area? Do they have a backup, such as a pager or a cellular phone?

0-8493-9822-3/00/$0.00+$.50

Contacting employees at their homes regarding disasters at the facility involves other more subtle issues. For example, what if an employee was at the facility when the disaster occurred? People making the calls to employee homes should be prepared to deal with hysterical relatives who may be hearing for the first time that a disaster has occurred at the facility where a loved one works. Providing a preapproved checklist that contains not only names and telephone numbers but also a brief procedure to follow when contacting employees' families can help circumvent these problems.

Once notified, the correct EMT members should assemble at the predetermined location or command center. Under already difficult conditions, EMT members may have trouble following directions to the command center. Planners should choose a location that is central enough for easy reach by team members. These issues can be mitigated in large part by establishing the command center at a landmark that has ready access to telephone service.

Operating the Command Center

The EMT needs to be able to begin work on arriving at the center. Several items must be immediately available to the EMT, such as telephones, fax machines, a small copier perhaps, and, although less apparent, a place to sit. Documenting the command center's setup allows technical personnel to ensure that the center can begin operations promptly.

To prevent EMT members from wasting precious time trying to figure out how to use emergency telephones, a basic touchtone analog telephone set should be used. Workers should be able to plug in a fax, laptop machine, or modem to the telephone as well.

The EMT must receive critical status and damage reports in the time frame prescribed in the recovery plan. A successfully activated EMT works with several logistical teams involved in the technical aspects of the recovery process. Once notified of the disaster, the teams fan out citywide or perhaps nationwide to implement the company's recovery plan. One team is dispatched to the disaster recovery center, if one is in use; another is dispatched to the affected facility to aid in restoration; and still more teams travel to perform such functions as retrieving stored magnetic media and picking up and delivering equipment.

Refining the Test Process

The importance of testing disaster recovery plans must be communicated, as well as the ability of even the most advanced organizations to learn something each time they test their recovery plan. To strengthen their company's plan, team members should make notes during and after the test. For effective updating, the plan and test procedures should be reviewed immediately following any test and activation, when memory is fresh. EMT members can learn lessons from the exercise, including what procedures they would change next time they test the plan. For example, EMT members may feel that recovery could have been facilitated by the representation of other areas in the company on the team, such as the real estate department and human resources.

TECHNICAL SERVICE TEAMS

Many organizations use commercial off-site disaster recovery facilities from a variety of sources. While these sources specialize in recovery, they cannot do the job alone. Several teams of technical service personnel must be mobilized to staff and configure a recovery center. Some of the most basic are suggested here.

Despite the trend toward distributed processing, mainframes are still used by many companies. The team responsible for what is generally the oldest but still core component in many recovery plans must be activated.

Mainframes, however, are only one component of a business and its recovery plan. Today a mainframe supports many functions that it did not support in the past. One of these things, of course, is LANs. Restoring LANs means more than restoring a server and wiring. To effectively restore a LAN business function, the three components of a business recovery solution are needed:

- An attendant position.
- The data that resided on the LAN.
- The communications link that turns the employees using the LAN into revenue generators for the company. These links will play a prominent role in recovering LANs, both for voice and data communications.

Other teams involved in the recovery include field services teams comprising personnel who may normally support personal computers or terminals from a maintenance standpoint and can serve as emergency installation technicians for the new configurations.

Various engineering teams, or teams of senior analysts, may also be involved to provide high-level trouble-shooting and support when complex equipment configurations must be literally built overnight.

Mobilizing Technical Service Teams

Mobilizing technical service personnel involves many of the same issues as mobilizing the EMT. For instance, team members obviously will need easy-to-follow directions to the recovery center. Planners, however, must address additional factors. In cases of widespread disasters, as many as 50 percent of employees will go home to check on their homes and families before reporting to work. It is therefore imperative to test how the recovery plan would work in the absence of key technical personnel. Removing a few personnel in a simulation effectively tests how others will compensate.

Setting Up the Recovery Center

Commercial disaster recovery centers are shared by many organizations. A company must be aware that its site probably was used by others between tests and that configurations most likely were changed.

Personnel unfamiliar with a company's day-to-day environment will rely on diagrams and a documented recovery plan to set up equipment. The company's key technical people will know where equipment goes and how to set it up, but there is no guarantee they will be available during a disaster. Even when company personnel are present, they will be installing overnight what originally took years to create. Equipment service or installation manuals should be readily at hand in the event they are needed. Similarly, commercial recovery sources must provide on-site guides to demonstrate the subtleties of equipment used at the center, such as complex matrix switches.

Restoring Communications

Technical service teams must deliver a report to the EMT within a prescribed time frame. Restoring communications is therefore one of the teams' priorities. If the recovery center does not provide regular touchtone analog telephones, personnel should be trained in advanced on the telephones at the center.

Efficient restoration of communications involves several tasks. When a large amount of technical equipment must be installed in a short time, keeping the same help desk or network control number enables vendors supporting the recovery process to contact a company easily, avoiding unnecessary delays. Dial-in data, switched digital service, and Integrated Services Digital Network links must also be successfully established.

The complement of telecommunications services that support data transmission for users must be checked in advance. One common problem with T1 links, for example, concerns the fact that most T1 local loops to recovery centers are shared among a broad user community. Because each customer using these links may be using a different line code for the T1, the links may have been reoptioned since a company's last disaster test and may not work without modification.

Procedures for reoptioning CSUs and other components that may have changed should be detailed in the recovery plan. The best test in all of these cases is a live test. Even if live production data is not transmitted, running a test pattern across these facilities can ensure that the telecommunications facilities are in tact, work properly, and would support data if necessary.

Data Delivery and Restoration

Data stored off-site must be delivered to the recovery center for such components as the mainframe and LAN ; telecommunications, switches, and multiplexers; the voice mail system; and automated call distribution (ACD) units. Procedures for retrieving mainframe and LAN data, which are typically stored off-site, are already in place. With coordination, telecommunications data may also be picked up during this procedure.

Problems in removing software from one system and reinstalling it on another stem from subtleties in operating systems or even minute differences in components such as tape drives. Although this problem is common, shortcuts that facilitate a more graceful reload on the new systems can be learned.

Evaluating Performance

Like members of the EMT, technical personnel should document what they learned from the exercise and what should be changed for the next test. Some of the issues requiring documentation are basic, such as whether the test equipment installed at the center for general use was surveyed in advance, appropriate for the company's test processes, and functioning properly. Even seemingly insignificant items, such as hand tools, should have been available and adequate. It is also highly recommended to request of principal equipment vendors that a representative be present at the recovery center, and to rate each vendor's response to the request.

No team can accomplish its goals without an overall environment reasonably conducive to the company's work environment. This issue is especially important in cases of distributed processing. While ergonomics may be a problem and people may be working on folding tables, the recovery assembly should help everyone get the job done. If not, team members should specify what is needed to bring the recovery center up to par.

Successful performance of tasks also depends on effective use of personnel at a time when personnel are at a premium. Team members should evaluate whether representatives of other areas of the organization would have facilitated work at the recovery center. Or, stated another way, they should ask whether an area was unnecessarily represented at the center. Someone who may be a fifth wheel at the recovery center could be reassigned to assist in restoring the damaged facility, for example.

Thorough documentation also includes communicating to management that the true test of a plan is whether it can uncover failure points. Consistent flawless results on recovery tests indicate that an organization should tighten its standards.

The Facility Reconstruction Team

The facility reconstruction team comprises a complement of personnel who are dispatched to the damaged site to survey conditions, report to the EMT, and coordinate with local and emergency authorities. The team could include members of the company's building services group and representatives of the production, LAN, mainframe, telecommunications, or other divisions that have a high content of equipment in the building. Other teams, such as administrative or logistical supply teams, should also be considered, as well as a media affairs representative.

Again, testing criteria for the facility reconstruction team are similar to those discussed previously, with notable exceptions. A checklist for the reconstruction team follows.

Restoring the Damaged Facility

The Right People for the Job. Only employees required for the recovery process should assemble at the site after a disaster. Others who report to satisfy their curiosity may interfere with the recovery process, especially by tying up valuable cellular telephone frequencies with personal or unnecessary calls.

The specific complement of personnel who report to the damaged site depends on the type of disaster that has occurred. In the case of a fire, the building facilities manager should be present to interface with local emergency personnel who control the facility until it is deemed safe for entry. A knowledgeable building facilities manager could help these personnel decide issues more quickly. Similarly, in cases of a highly visible or widely broadcast disaster, a media affairs representative is needed to interact with the inevitable high volume of media presence. In almost all disasters, it is a good idea to have at least one security person on the team to assess the situation and determine whether additional security reinforcements are required to secure the building from theft.

A smoothly functioning reconstruction team also depends on clearly delineated responsibilities. Without them, conflicts or turf issues may develop over such issues as which department is responsible for rewiring the building. There are probably five different people in the organization (from facilities, LAN management, telecommunications, and other departments) who will believe themselves responsible for rewiring, so predefined responsibilities will avoid overlap, wasted efforts, and squabbles during the recovery.

Adequate communication among members is also a must. Team members should feel like a cohesive unit during the test. If they frequently feel out of touch with others, communications must be improved to foster cohesiveness.

Appropriate Equipment. Each member of the team that enters what may be a severely damaged facility needs certain standard equipment, such as a flashlight with a spare set of batteries; a hard hat; an identifying badge or, preferably, an identifying vest to quickly differentiate between employees and looters; a copy of the recovery plan; a small notebook to annotate critical events and document important command decisions made during the recovery process; and at least one roll of quarters in the event that a major telecommunication disaster renders other services unavailable or overwhelmed. The team should also have at least two cellular telephones, two two-way radios, two pagers to keep track of people on-site and expedite the recovery process, and at least one cellular fax and a laptop computer with a fax modem card to aid in reporting to the EMT in the prescribed time frame.

A Staging Area for Recovery Operations. When a building is totally inaccessible or lacks the required telecommunications, water, or sanitary facilities, facility reconstruction personnel should promptly report to a prearranged staging area for recovery operations, such as in a nearby hotel. Telephone numbers must be promptly diverted to the staging area. The network control number may be diverted to the recovery center, for example, for technical questions regarding mainframes or LANs. The help desk number, however, may be diverted to the staging area.

Notifying Professional Clean-Up Personnel. Professional clean-up companies have the answers to such questions as what to do with magnetic tapes that have been wet in a disaster (they should be put in the freezer). The companies use a freeze-dry process to save valuable data stored on magnetic media and similar processes for wet paper and smoke-damaged equipment. Immediate notification is crucial, since the processes must be performed within the first 48 hours following a disaster.

Evaluating and Documenting Test Results

Facility reconstruction personnel must evaluate similar issues as their colleagues on the EMT and technical service teams. Most important is whether an initial status report was dispatched to the EMT within the 90 minutes specified in most disaster recovery plans. Other issues include whether equipment was adequate, whether on-site vendor representatives were immediately summoned and current telephone numbers listed for them, whether the complement of team members was effective, and what should be changed for the next exercise.

CONCLUSION

The teams involved in a disaster recovery test have different tasks, goals, and needs, yet the testing procedure holds the same overriding message for all of them: Testing a plan is a learning experience. Organizations should not expect their first test to run perfectly, nor aim for perfect results each time they test. Testing until failure makes for a true test.

Once testing procedures become routine, criteria should be tightened, or key personnel removed from the process to ensure that the plan executes in a variety of circumstances. Successful testing of a plan provides greater peace of mind and assures management that the time and money spent in developing and honing the test was a wise investment.

Section VIII Checklist

1. Does your organization have a dedicated testing group? If not, who performs most of the application testing in your environment?
2. What conflicts do you think occur when programmers test their own software? How does this affect program quality?
3. Is your development environment conducive for testing? Does your organization support a formal testing methodology?
4. Are you more likely to delay a project because of needed testing or forego testing for timely project implementation? Is this true in all situations?
5. What benchmarks do you use when evaluating the benefits of software testing?
6. Should software testing be aimed at finding errors or confirming functionality or both? Are these issues factored into your test plans?
7. Could the testing process be outsourced in your organization?
8. What are the differences between software and data testing in your environment? Are these treated the same in importance?
9. Assuming that you acknowledge the importance of testing, when was the last time you reviewed the basic principles behind the software testing process?
10. What book, seminars, conferences or outside sources have you utilized in your testing efforts? Have these been worthwhile?
11. To what extent have you automated testing functions? Does your organization use automated tools or procedures?
12. How would you describe the ideal test environment? Is this based on time, staff, or technical tools available to you?
13. When does testing become troublesome in your environment? Is testing considered during or after development?
14. Does your IS environment use various testing procedures based on platform or other development paradigms?
15. Do you approach software testing as a necessary evil, or as part of the design and development of the system? What is the opinion of your co-workers?

Section IX
Quality and Productivity Initiatives

Improving the quality and productivity of application development is a tenacious goal for most IS organizations. Few managers would debate the virtues of these objectives as related to overall programming efforts. Despite this fact, many organizations struggle in achieving the caliber of excellence that is often desired by the software industry. Some of the adversity can be attributed to lack of sufficient time and availability of resources. More often, however, there is uncertainty on defining the exact criteria for success. Perhaps the more realistic solution should be acknowledging that quality and productivity are continuous processes throughout the software life cycle. Finding a specific endpoint to these attributes is less important than incorporating diligent procedures in everyday software development. In either case, it is important that development managers understand and pursue the ongoing trends used successfully by the computing industry.

Most IS professionals strive to develop software programs that meet functional goals without sacrificing execution performance. Unfortunately, not every program can meet both on an equal basis. And in some cases, performance becomes a secondary goal to functional specifications. Typically, achieving the necessary performance criteria can occur from upgrades to the processing hardware. In lieu of this, however, programmers are forced to review the options inherent in specific programming languages or run time compiler settings. Chapter 46, "Measuring Program Performance," provides suggestions for assessing the actual run time performance of deployed software applications. Although the examples are based on the C++ language, the concepts can be applied to other language environments. Development managers should encourage programmers to pursue a harmonious balance between program function and program performance in order to satisfy the overall goals of application systems.

Chapter 47, "Creating A Development Environment for Quality," presents a case study for building systems through a "get-it-right-the-first-time" methodology. By leveraging the knowledge and experience of the development staff, it was possible to foster a commitment for quality in all aspects of the project life cycle. This requires managerial leadership and determination, especially when there can be conflicting priorities of implementation timeliness and system quality. Quality can only be obtained when the principles for building systems are fully accepted and practiced by all levels of the development team.

The debate for improving development productivity has included many concepts and ideas that are aimed at satisfying the human side of the development process. One concept that is growing in acceptance is found in Chapter 48, "Telecommuting: Distributed Work Programs." The premise of telecommuting is simply, allow software professionals the opportunity to develop applications in a non-work environment or "virtual office." In principle the idea has much merit, especially given lifestyle demands and the need for skilled workers. But telecommuting may not work in all cases, and there is the potential for less productivity if the employee lacks the needed discipline to stay focused. Nevertheless, telecommuting will become another alternative to solving the work crisis and development managers should understand the issues before engaging in any offsite development strategy.

Chapter 46
Measuring Program Performance

Paul J. Jalics and Santosh K. Misra

PROGRAM PERFORMANCE IS OFTEN CONSIDERED SYNONYMOUS with the speed with which a program solves a specific problem. The speed, in turn, is influenced by a number of factors, some of which are programmer controlled and others that are dependent on the hardware and software environment of the program's execution. Whereas tuning all programs for performance efficiency may not be necessary, some programs do exist that are "critical," and such tuning is essential.

PERFORMANCE

Performance has received too little attention in the programming workplace. Reasons for the lack of emphasis include the not-as-yet-mature nature of the discipline and rapid performance gains realized through faster hardware. However, performance may be more of an issue in the future, because the desired performance of a program may not be completely realizable through hardware advances alone, given the increasingly complex software products. As in engineering, when performance standards are usually a part of a product's specifications, a program's performance may become an integral part of a matured software engineering process.

Speed of execution is only one of the dimensions of a program's performance. Other performance measures include issues such as memory usage, code portability, and readability. As will be shown in this chapter, tuning a program for improvement in the speed of execution can lead to compromises in other dimensions of performance.

Critical Programs

Speed of execution, referred to as performance hereafter, is not an primary consideration for all programs. For example, performance may be irrelevant if a program generates results faster than they can be used. For many other programs, using a faster hardware platform may be more cost effective than spending the effort required in tuning. There is, however, a

0-8493-9979-3/99/$0.00+$.50

small percentage of programs, say 10 percent, for which performance is of some importance. This chapter calls these critical programs.

A program may be considered critical for a number of reasons, including:

- The user may need the output shortly after the input is available, in a situation in which a short delay can lead to economic or more serious loss. Many real-time operations fall into this category when sensor-generated data, as in process control and command and control systems, need to be analyzed and results fed back to an appropriate decision maker. Computer control of a car engine is a good example.
- The user's productivity is adversely affected if there is a wait for the interactive system's response.
- Systems are critical when hardware upgrades are not feasible because of economic or technical reasons and when the performance goals must be achieved within the existing configuration.

Critical Parts of a Program

The execution time is not uniformly distributed among a program's statements. The authors' experience shows that a small part (e.g., 10 percent) of a program largely determines its performance; therefore, most of the performance improvements are achievable by concentrating on that 10 percent and leaving the remaining 90 percent of the code alone. This 10 percent, for the purposes of this chapter, is called the critical parts of a program.

It is not the authors' intention to imply that noncritical parts of a program cannot be used to derive performance improvements. Such improvements are possible but would lead to diminishing returns on the labor invested; that is, disproportionate amounts of labor may be needed for small improvements in execution time.

A PROCEDURE FOR IMPROVING PERFORMANCE

Four steps can lead to improving program performance:

- Measuring the initial performance of the program
- Identifying the critical parts of the program
- Improving the performance of the critical parts
- Testing the modified program, remeasuring the performance, and comparing it to the initial performance. If the results do not meet expectations, Step 2 is repeated

Measuring the Program's Initial Performance

Measuring the execution time of a program can be as simple as using a stopwatch to note the start and finish time of a program. Though this is a very crude method, it may be adequate in some cases when the program executes long enough (e.g., 10 seconds or more) so that manual timekeeping does not lead to too much error in the calculated elapsed time.

A more precise technique is to let the program compute its own execution time by recording the start and finish time through calls to its host operating system. Elapsed times can be reported by all operating systems.

Identifying Critical Program Components

One can identify critical components of a program through manual inspection. For example, inner loops of a program may contribute more significantly to the execution time. However, proper identification of such code is difficult even for experienced programmers who know the program well. Correct identification would require the programmer to be aware of such details as the amount of work done by various statements and the relative frequency of data access from the input files.

What Is a Program Profiler? It is most practical to use special tools to profile the performance characteristics of a program; the profile can then be used to identify the critical parts. The authors used the Borland C++ profiler tool to identify the critical parts of the program. Such a profiler supports an executable program that was compiled with debugging options, so that the user can talk to the profiler, a separate utility program, using source line numbers, procedure names, and source module names. The profiler also supports a source code window, so the user can point to places of interest in the program. The user describes what areas of the program are to be profiled: any procedure, module, or individual source code lines.

The user specifies a profiling mode to be active or passive. Active profiling means that code is modified to intercept the execution of the areas of interest, whereas passive means that the profiler samples the program counter during execution and generates a table of how often the areas measured are sampled. The active mode has the advantage of collecting all the information, but it has the disadvantage of increasing execution time dramatically, sometimes by a factor of 5 to 1000, depending on what level of detail is measured. The test program is then run under control of the profiler, which collects information about the execution. Information includes the number of times a procedure or individual source code line is executed and the execution time spent on that module or code line.

First Profiling Results

Just two procedures, fsscan and symlkins, out of a total of 30 account for 55percent of the execution time, excluding input and output. Exhibit 46.1 shows the initial performance profile (module level) of the program in the case study.

Exhibit 46.1. Initial Performance Profile (Module Level)

Turbo Profiler Version 4.5 Fri Jan 12 14:56:00 1996
Program: C:\T\ASM990.EXE → CPU Execution Profile(by Procedures)
Total CPU Execution Time: 2.5 sec
Total Elapsed Time: 24.7 sec

fsscan	0.296 sec	36p erc ent	|*************************************
symlkins	0.140 sec	19%	|********************
wrasl	0.044 sec	5%	|******
bchecksum	0.044 sec	5%	|******
oplook	0.034 sec	4%	|*****
pass2	0.033 sec	4%	|*****
getval	0.027 sec	3%	|****
bpackout	0.024 sec	2%	|***
plalloc	0.021 sec	2%	|***
expreval	0.019 sec	2%	|**
evopnd	0.018 sec	2%	|**
optabinit	0.015 sec	1%	|**
wrasl1	0.014 sec	1%	|**
boutdata	0.014 sec	1%	|**
pass1	0.013 sec	1%	|**
refsym	0.011 sec	1%	|*

(<1%: wrasl2, poper, outext, bwrline, doarith, regchk, syminit, tss, pcomma, chksflgs, treedump)

A statement level profile of symlkins, illustrated Exhibit 46.2, shows that 3 out of a possible 39 statements account for 85 percent of the execution time of the procedure. Because symlkins accounts for 19 percent of the program's execution time, the three critical statements of symlkins contribute 16 percent toward the overall CPU execution time. Special profilers can not only identify such critical code but also guide the improvement efforts, which, for the following example, should be directed toward the three statements of symlkins.

Setting the Goal: CPU vs. Elapsed Time Measurements

To be useful in performance analysis, a program profiler should have the capacity to report not only overall elapsed time, as measured with a stopwatch from the beginning of program execution to the time the program is finished, but also the CPU execution time (CPU) at various levels of detail. The authors define CPU execution time as that part of a program's elapsed time in which the program is executing CPU instructions; CPU execution time does not include other activities, such as waiting for input/output(I/O) to complete, executing operating system calls, or running other processes.

Before discussing improvement experiments, this chapter must describe a goal for the improvements (i.e., should the goal be to seek to

Exhibit 46.2. Statement Level Profile of Symlkins

Turbo Profiler Version 4.5 Fri Jan 12 15:00:26 1996
Program: C:\T\ASM990.EXE module FS.C → CPU Execution Profile(Line-by-Line Profiling of symlkins Procedure)
Total CPU Execution Time:
2.5 sec
Total Elapsed Time: 24.7 sec

293.	[symptr]))>0)0.056 sec	35%	|**
if((ret = strcmp(id.symname			
295. else	[symptr];switlr = 1;}0.055 sec	34%	|**
if(ret<0){stmptr = slinkl			
296. else found = 1;	0.027 sec	16%	|**********************
319.	0.005 sec	3%	|****
if(debgdict)dbddum(sympt			
r);			
282. int symlkins(char *id.	0.004 sec	2%	|***
int *symp)			
291. csymdepth++;	0.003 sec	1%	|**
320. *symptr = symptr;	0.002 sec	1%	|*
290.	0.002 sec	1%	|*
for(csymdepth = 0.found = 0;			
found == 0 && symptr! = 0;)			
{			

(<1%: lines 294. 299,288. 313. 312)

reduce the elapsed execution time of the test program or to reduce the CPU execution time of the program). The elapsed time can be measured with a stopwatch, as just described, but measuring CPU execution time is a bit trickier.

Most multiprogramming operating systems (e.g., UNIX) provide built-in services that can measure both elapsed and CPU execution time between any two points in the execution of a program. Microcomputer operating systems, such as Windows and MS-DOS, do not provide services to measure CPU time. However, most competent compilers, such as Microsoft Visual C++ and Borland C++, offer profilers as part of the compiler software, and the profiler can estimate CPU execution time.

The most straightforward performance measure is elapsed time. On a multiprogramming computer system with dozens of processes executing concurrently. It is, however, unwise to measure elapsed time, because when the CPU is shared, elapsed time depends on what work is being done for the other processes. In such a case, repeatable experiments can only be run if the system is running standalone, with no other processes active. CPU execution time, on the other hand, is repeatable under any load, because the operating system accumulates CPU time only when the CPU is executing the process's CPU instructions.

CPU execution time is important, because it is easily repeatable and also because it measures the amount of work done by the CPU for the program. CPU time does not include waiting for disk reads and writes, as this does not involve the use of the CPU. Further complicating the question is the fact that the most common machines, personal computers, cannot as yet measure CPU execution time. Unfortunately, elapsed time is what is important to the user. Very little other work is typically done by such a computer concurrently, and few users care about how busy or idle the machine is, since it is inexpensive.

TESTING THE MODIFIED PROGRAM

A modified program needs to be tested to verify that it continues to execute correctly and to verify that its performance has improved. If the execution time is not reduced, it will be necessary to back up to the premodification state of the program. Therefore, it is essential to retain older versions of the program until changes are successfully tested.

If the new performance improves without meeting the overall goals, the programmer should go back to Step 2 (identifying the critical parts of the program) to identify anew the critical parts of the modified program. The critical parts of the modified program may be substantially different from that of the previous version. For example, if the three statements that contribute 85percent of the execution time of symlkins can somehow be eliminated, the procedure may no longer be in the critical part of the program at all.

REDUCING CPU EXECUTION TIME BY 50%

This section describes a test case that the authors used to demonstrate the process of performance improvement.

Asm990, a cross-assembler program for a TI 9900 microprocessor, was used as the case study program. It accepts assembler source code for the TI 9900 as input and produces an assembly listing and an object file as output. Asm990 is written in C with some emphasis on making it as efficient as possible. The source program for Asm990 is about 1660 lines of code and consists of five modules: bnc29c.c is the highest level main module; pass1.c scans the source; p1alloc.c allocates memory; expr.c evaluates the expressions; pass2 generates the object code and produces the listing file. The case-study uses a synthetically generated input file consisting of 2745 source lines.

The authors implemented nine rounds of improvements (Rounds A to I) on Asm990 with a goal of reducing its CPU execution time by 50 percent. They chose the reduction of CPU execution time as their goal because that is where they find most of the techniques in performance improvement that they wish to demonstrate. Furthermore, reducing CPU time also reduces elapsed time. Finally, the authors will focus on elapsed execution time reductions in the final round (Round J).

The experiments were carried out on a Pentium 75 with a Windows development environment, but program execution took place in an MS-DOS window, because the application is not a GUI Windows application. This platform used Borland C++ 4.5. Exhibit 46.3 presents the elapsed and CPU for each of the 10 rounds. The initial elapsed time for Asm990 on the Pentium is 24.7 seconds and the profiler estimated CPU time is 2.5 seconds.

A summary of the improvements is presented in the following sections. The improvements in the test program involve only a few of the many techniques that are possible.

The sequence of experiments described in the following sections, concerning Rounds A to J, reduced the CPU execution time by 60 percent on the Pentium (2.5 to 1.0). Thus, the user might expect a 60 percent reduction in elapsed time from 24.7 to 10 seconds. However, the actual elapsed time decreased from 24.7 seconds to 18 seconds, a savings of only 29 percent.

Exhibit 46.3. Elapsed and CPU for Ten Rounds

IMPROVEMENT	ELAPSED	PENTIUM 75 CPU	NATURE OF CHANGE
Round A	24.7	2.5	original program
Round B	24.0	2.0	hashing randomizing 1
Round C	23.2	1.8	hashing dispersion 2
Round D	22.5	1.6	hashing buckets → 500
Round E	22.7	1.1	macros for sprintf,strcpy
Round F	18.0	1.2	xgetc #def macro: buf = 8,192
Round G	18.4	1.3	xgetc #def macro: buf = 24,576
Round H	18.0	1.1	* → <<,setmem to init struct
Round I	18.0	1.0	-Ox max compiler optimization
Round J	5.8	2.6	setvbuf 32,767 byte buffering

Round A. This is the initial program, the outputs of which are used later to verify that the modified versions still work correctly. A profile of the program, the first table shown in this chapter, indicates that 55 percent of the CPU execution time is being spent in two procedures: fsscan (36 percent), which is the lexical analyzer, and symlkins (19 percent), which is the symbol table search routine. These two procedures then clearly constitute the critical parts of the initial program, and they are targeted for improvement. The profiling report also indicates that the CPU execution time was only 2.5 seconds, so that 90 percent of the time was spent on waiting for I/O, system calls, and library functions.

Round B. The symlkins is a small symbol table insert procedure consisting of only 40 lines, so it was chosen for improvement. The hashing algorithm used in symlkins was changed, resulting in a 61 percent reduction in the CPU execution time used. The old algorithm did not distribute well, and most of the symbols fell into three buckets of the 27 alphabetics possible. Symlkins, which took 19percent of the program's CPU execution time, now takes only 9 percent. The overall CPU execution time is down to 80 percent of the original, and the elapsed program time was also reduced by 3 percent. This change was limited to only five lines of source code.

Round C. The hashing algorithm still did not distribute well enough to the 27 buckets, so it was modified to include a weighted sum by character position of the symbol character values. This resulted in a fine distribution of the symbols into the 27 buckets and reduced symlkins execution time by another 4 percent, so that it ended at 13 percent of the original. This change only involved two source lines. The whole program CPU execution time is down to 72 percent of the original.

Round D. This iteration involved changes in the size of the hash table for the symbol table from 27 buckets to 500 buckets. The change in size resulted in a further 45 percent reduction in CPU time for symlkins, to a level of 9 percent of the original. The whole program CPU execution time is down to 64 percent of the original.

Round E. This iteration involved minor changes to some 95 source lines in a number of functions in the pass2.c source module. The general principle was to replace library routines, such as sprintfand strcpy, by user-written preprocessor macros that perform the required actions inline. The advantage is derived from avoiding the procedure call overhead of the C++/C library routines. Also for sprintf, the preprocessor macro takes advantage of the simple hex formatting required rather than the completely general formatting done by sprintf. The overall program Central Processing Unit time was reduced to 44 percent of the original.

Round F. At this time, the fsscan procedure accounted for 35 percent of CPU execution time, and the line profiling for this procedure indicated that a line with a getc library call took the most time. Thus this round focused on writing a preprocessor macro to substitute the getc routine of the library. A large buffer of 32,767 bytes was created, and fread filled it up with a single read. The xgetcmacro then picked out single characters from this buffer and replenished the buffer when it became empty. Total CPU execution time actually went up slightly (8 percent), but the elapsed time dropped from 22.7 to about 18 seconds, a decrease of 21 percent.

Round G. This was a continuation of the previous round. The data buffer for the user-written preprocessor xgetc macro was increased by a factor of three to 24,576 bytes. The change in CPU execution time was negligible, as was the elapsed time. Apparently a buffer larger than 8192 produced no additional benefit.

Round H. Still trying to reduce the CPU execution time in pass2.c, the authors replaced a loop zeroing out individual fields including an array of structures with a setmem library call that zeros out a range of memory cells. This reduced Central Processing Unit execution time to 1.1 seconds, and elapsed time stayed at 18 seconds.

Round I. This final try involved turning on all possible compiler optimizations. The previous tries were with the compiler defaults. This resulted in an extra 10percent Central Processing Unit reduction to 1 CPU seconds. The total program time is now at 40 percent of the original. The authors have surpassed their goal by 10 percent.

Round J. This application is clearly I/O intensive, so the above CPU execution times are tiny when compared to the elapsed times. The only round that saw a significant reduction in elapsed time significantly was Round F, in which the I/O buffering for the source input file was improved. The authors realized that the program uses several files: source input, intermediate output then input, a list file output, and an object file output. Therefore, the code was changed to add a setvbuf library function after each open, and the I/O buffer was set to 32,767 bytes for each. This change is similar to the xgetc change, but it is better and simpler, and the normal getc, putc, fread, and fwrite functions work faster. This results in the elapsed time being reduced to 5.8 seconds, which is a 77 percent decrease from the original. Unfortunately, more time is spent on buffer management, so the Central Processing Unit execution time jumped to 2.6 seconds, to be slightly higher than the original. Nevertheless, this last change is very much worthwhile, as the user will see the program work four times as fast as in Round A.

REDUCING THE ELAPSED EXECUTION TIME

Another way of looking at the results is as follows: The CPU execution time of 2.5 seconds is only 10percent of the total elapsed time of 24.7, so what the authors have done is reduce the 2.5 seconds to 1.0, and — all things being equal — the elapsed time should have decreased by only 1.5 seconds as well. Instead, it decreased 6.7 seconds! The explanation is that the changes have had a big impact on the time spent executing system calls, especially I/O-related ones. For example, the xgetc #define macro used in round F executed fewer freadlibrary calls by reading huge blocks of a file into a large 24K buffer, so the number of system calls was reduced by a factor of 100, and the I/O wait time was also reduced by doing fewer larger read system calls.

To reduce the elapsed time further, Round J was initiated to reduce the elapsed time further. Taking a lead from the xgetc experience above, the authors looked for a runtime library to improve I/O buffering on all four of the files the program accesses. The setvbuflibrary function allows the user to set the I/O buffer size.

The authors set the I/O buffer to its maximum of 32,767 bytes for all files in the program and reran the experiment, arriving at an elapsed time of 5.8 seconds, which is just 26percent of the original. Unfortunately, the additional buffer management brought the CPU execution time back up to 2.6, which is slightly higher than the original.

CONCLUSION

The results of the experiments show that a program initially written with some attention to performance can still be improved substantially if it is analyzed systematically. The gain in performance would be even more dramatic if the original program were a typical C program (i.e., written without performance considerations in mind).

CPU execution time improvements should also reduce elapsed execution time. But in this case study, the real benefits came by actually increasing CPU time, which was a side effect of using the setvbuf library routine. The user was delighted because his 24.7-second execution time was reduced to 5.8. On a real multiprogramming system, such as UNIX, with 100 such assemblies executing at once, this change can be viewed as negative. Because it increased CPU execution time from 1.0 to 2.6, the throughput of the whole system might be reduced, and this could lead to slower program execution for an individual program.

In addition, the direction and magnitude of the improvements on one system, such as the Pentium 75, cannot be used to predict the improvements on another system, such as a HP9000 UNIX workstation. Some of the techniques yield similar results on all architectures, but others may vary substantially.

Chapter 47

Creating a Development Environment for Quality: A Case Study

John Care

Increasing corporate reliance upon technology as a competitive weapon places extreme stress upon the IT organization to reduce product development cycles further in parallel with product marketing cycles. As a result, the confluence of shrinking project cycles and the lack of sufficient senior development talent lead to more code being written by entry-level staff.

The issue then becomes how to retain and even renew the commitment to quality by an organization's long-term employees, while simultaneously teaching first- and second-year developers the importance of getting it right the first time.

Case Study: Company Background

The case study examined in these sections outlines the activities undertaken by the author as a new director of software development for a commercial software applications provider with $50 million in annual revenues. The company had about 1500 customers throughout the United States, running its packaged applications for financials, inventory control, order processing, and shipping. Although the company had been in business for a number of years, it had grown very slowly (in the single digits) and was starting to stagnate, both in terms of technology and employee development.

The development environment was a combination of an old proprietary file system and BASIC-like language married to a Progress database running host-based character-mode on an IBM RS/6000. A new development effort was underway utilizing the Sybase, Inc. Powerbuilder accessing a Microsoft SQL Server on Windows NT.

The issues were numerous.

- The company had been through three QA managers in 15 months.
- Hiring new developers for the current product set was difficult.

0-8493-9979-3/99/$0.00+$.50

- Product updates were shipped every two weeks.
- There were no automated QA testing tools.
- The vice president of sales set product release dates.
- Customer support was overrun and development schedules slipped when critical bugs in the product had to be fixed.
- The code was never stable because most new customers had custom code added to the base code line.
- Senior programmers had no time or inclination to mentor junior programmers.

Total headcount for the entire development organization was budgeted at 50 staff, including QA, product maintenance, and production support. Actual headcount had historically averaged 85 percent, due to a steady stream of developers with 18 to 24 months of experience departing for greener pastures.

Climbing into the Trenches

When an IT executive needs to justify an investment and seek approval for a project, the tried and trusted approach is to turn to the numbers. A return on investment analysis or a total cost of ownership study yields excellent results when the benefits can be quantified. The key issues when dealing with quality are twofold. First, how does an organization measure the effect of improved software quality on the bottom line and, second, many of the side effects have been historically categorized as soft and intangible.

To measure the impact of any change, it is crucial for executive management to experience life in the trenches. This is analogous to the standard practice of sending IT analysts into business units to spend a day with sales or accounting prior to undertaking the specification of a new project. If this is truly a requirement of analysts within an organization, then the same should hold true for IT management. Otherwise any commitment to excellence will be questioned by those who are affected the most.

Psychologists say that people are the products of their environment. This piece of conventional wisdom is a powerful statement in examining why a program or process is not functioning correctly. The vast number of younger IT professionals are driven primarily by direct and indirect compensation and then by pride of ownership. Before rushing into the management maxim of "you cannot manage what you cannot measure," take a more holistic view of quality as it relates to the environment within IT.

Case Study: Getting Started

Prior to commencing any activities, a town hall meeting was held to introduce the new quality initiatives and to set expectations. After some initial resistance and suspicions of spying, the program caught fire as the staff realized the implications of the ultimate objectives. So as to counter the "you are just another exec promising everything and delivering nothing" attitude, a large board was mounted prominently outside the corner office. This noticeboard detailed meticulously every promise and commitment made by the management team and was updated at least twice weekly.

Over the course of the next two to four weeks, IT management spent time in the cubicles, either working out of a temporary setting or shadowing staff in their own cubicles. Should the daily environment in which staff is placed not reflect a commitment to quality, then the entire process faces an uphill battle. If developers need to reboot their PCs twice a day, restart the browser at least once a day, and live through network, E-mail, and server outages on a weekly basis — what are the realistic expectations for them to "get quality"?

A host of environmental factors, such as ambient temperature, noise level, screen size and glare, desk space, and chair comfort were examined. Notable issues in the workstation setup, such as the speed and capacity of machines, non-uniformity of release levels, lack of Internet access, and check-in/out of code, were discovered. An even more astounding statistic was the copious use of E-mail for discussions between groups less than 15 yards apart.

As a result of these studies, the development organization implemented a customer care system to upgrade every development workstation to a corporate standard Pentium. Uniform versions of Microsoft Office, Editors and Productivity Tools were installed, and all beta software was deleted. A purchasing program, which introduce 17" and 21" monitors to replace older 14" monitors, was also initiated. Simple ergonomics showed that the use of large screen monitors allowed the development staff to have enough windows visible so that simple cut-and-paste errors were actually reduced tenfold and the accidental opening or closing of programs was halved.

It was also noted that compilation time for some of the larger modules within the system was over three minutes. This is a long-enough period for a developer both to move onto another task and to lose the frame of reference for the current task. A simple upgrade of the base development server reduced compilation times to under a minute. Based upon ten compilations per day per programmer, a $1500 investment in the server yielded payback within the week. An unforeseen benefit of this upgrade was an increase in error traps and error messages within new modules — typically the last pieces added to a system.

Internalize "Getting It Right"

The largest challenge managers faced was making the junior programmers understand that customers were the corporation's biggest asset. The method used to finally help them "get quality" was to draw parallels to their own lives. Yet another town meeting was held, and they were asked to relate one or more occurrences of poor quality and service they had encountered outside of work. Examples such as "my dry cleaning wasn't ready when it was supposed to be," "the new toy I bought my daughter broke after a week," "the phone guy never showed up" were cited. Several of the newer members still did not understand — so they were asked how they would feel if the company "forgot" to pay them because of a bug in the financials program used by the company. How would that affect their lives? Because most of them were young and living paycheck-to-paycheck, the message came across loud and clear.

There is another social issue at work here which is somewhat more controversial. The new generation of IT are of the video game generation. It is acceptable in a video game to get killed, for the car to crash, for the skateboard to wipe out; and that attitude of acceptance is carried forward into their work. There is regrettably, however, no Reset or New Game button in programming schedules.

Externalize "Getting It Right"

Another important step is externalizing the importance of quality to customers both inside and outside the corporation. Rarely, in 20 years of IT life, have customers complained that the software was too good. On several occasions the opportunity presented itself to call a time out on new development and simply fix and stabilize existing code. If this is not a viable, political task to undertake, then imposing a 10 percent to 15 percent development tax on new work and allocating that time to repair existing code and improve infrastructure is also an acceptable option.

The quick fix is the bane of the software developer. Because an end-user can quickly fix or add to applications like an Excel spreadsheet, he or she feels that a developer should be able to fix quickly or enhance an existing enterprise application. It is therefore critical to relate to the user community the importance of structure and architecture. Visual aids usually provide a major benefit to get the point across. Depending upon the industry or user community serviced and the geographic location, it is usually fairly simple to provide the appropriate analogies.

Case Study: Let the Customer Tell You

Once a quarter, a customer was invited in for day to explain how it runs its business and the importance of the product. Covering the financial and emotional consequences of what could occur when and if the product broke allowed several of the development groups to visualize this single customer as representing all users. This arrangement worked best by bartering with the customer — offering free days of education, free consulting, or a promise to add that last requested enhancement. Junior programmers and analysts were also regularly sent out to the business units for a day or two to sit with the users to watch how they performed their job — not just how they use technology.

The director of the support center became a major ally due to this initiative and eventually all technical staff were rotated through the customer support phones over the course of their first year. Customer satisfaction became internalized as they took ownership of problems and understood the impact of quality programming. Several of the developers then actively sought out the customers they had dealt with over the phone, met at user group sessions, and even sponsored their issues within the organization.

Although, at first glance, the productivity of entry-level programmers was adversely affected during their first six months due to time spent in other departments, it was more than covered during the second half of the year. Productivity as measured by lines of code, quality of code (percent of rework, errors, and documentation) was up nearly 20 percent over the historical average of prior classes.

The Buck Stops at the QA Manager's Desk

The company had gone through three QA managers for one simple reason: they had all the responsibility for a quality product and no authority. A policy was instituted whereby pre-release software could only be shipped upon the written signature of an executive of the company. This was later expanded to include software that QA had rejected, but it needed to be shipped anyway because of revenue recognition or contractual commitments. The mere act of forcing the CEO or VP of Sales to sign a sheet of paper to release potentially substandard code had a chilling effect on them. An organization must have a set of standards and measurements which dictates when a product is of beta or of production quality. These measurements should also cover documentation, availability of training, a marketing campaign, and press release, if necessary. By making quality stretch outside of the IT organization, a corporate buy-in results and more departments feel like a part of the ownership process.

Case Study: A Little Planning Goes a Long Way

Just a cursory overview of the corporate processes showed that the entire company was so busy reacting to situations that, as an entity, minimal time remained for proactive planning. This is not an uncommon situation in corporate America, although it is difficult to break the habit. It therefore became imperative to create time for the development groups to catch up. As noted earlier, product updates and fixes were shipped on a maniacal two-week cycle and the code line was never stable enough to be fully tested.

Having been warned by sales and marketing that the customers would react negatively to any changes in this cycle, the senior developers challenged this myth. By enlisting the help of the support desk it was discovered that customers waited an average of five months to install update tapes. The major factor behind this lag was summed up by an old-time client who noted that, once her system was running, she did not want to update it and face weeks of tracking down new bugs. Armed with this information, the production cycle was gradually expanded from two-week to two-month intervals. Production support costs were reduced by 11percent, installation questions called into support dropped dramatically, and the percentage of clients installed on the latest release climbed 35 percent.

The Bucks Stop in the Paycheck

Many programming bonus schemes are dependent on achieving a delivery date, a budget, and a quality target. It is a truism within the community that only two of the three variables can fixed. Should an organization decide to make quality part of its compensation scheme (and it is certainly strongly recommended), the bonus plan needs to drive the correct behavior of all employees. Some successful plans have included:

- Quality payments are not made until the end user signs a piece of paper saying the quality objective has been met.
- Defer an additional percentage of the bonus for 6 to 12 months after the system has been burnt in.
- Award bonuses on a weekly or monthly basis so they become more tangible.
- Provide each employee a bonus, on paper, at the start of each period, and then take part of it away if goals are not met. This is far more effective than losing something you never had.
- Pay senior level staff directly based upon the quality of work generated by the associates they manage or mentor.

Force Decisions

Encourage every member of the development organization to force decisions, and then be prepared to stand behind them. A forced decision usually takes the form of "if I make this change or add this feature, which one of these other tasks can slip?" By taking a hard stance on this issue and refusing to accept the Einstein view of programming — if you code faster then time slows down — the amount of scope creep every project experiences can be dramatically reduced.

As part of the recommitment to quality within the development group, a policy of mandatory monthly status meetings with other departments was implemented. Naturally, sales, marketing, and support are key stakeholders in the success of any quality initiative, as are the finance and human resources departments. The CFO or controller will review requests for future funding in a far more favorable light when a return can be shown on previously soft items. Human resources will find hiring easier if there is documented quality training and mentoring program in place for the programmers.

Fixing Bugs

State that a rotation through the bug fixing group is a requirement for promotion. Many departments now use the name "sustaining engineering" for psychological effect instead of the dreaded "maintenance" word. Every time an error is fixed in the code, ensure that it is documented and the reason the error was introduced is also documented. It is extremely important for an organization to focus on fixing the problem and not the blame. Over the course of a six-month period, the programming standards were updated nearly a dozen times as a result of an error correction. Of far greater importance, the group learned several new questions to ask during the analysis and design phase so that errors could not be introduced during coding. After gathering several months' worth of data on fixes, the managers gained a solid understanding of which modules should be rewritten based upon the development tax discussed earlier.

An external display of progress and current status is of great importance. Status on the bug count — broken down by product, release, and development group — should be made available every day on the corporate intranet for all to see. This not only promotes an open environment and attitude towards IT, but may also cut down on status calls with regard to projects and products.

Recommended Course of Action

Prior to launching any major corporate or departmental initiative involving quality or process, first take a step back to examine the environment in which information technology professionals are working. Use the checklist given in Exhibit 47.1 for guidance.

By following these guidelines, a development organization can improve its effectiveness, meet more customers, produce better code, and improve its infrastructure all in the cause of a quality product. The eventual outcome of all the actions undertaken in the case study at a cost of about one programmer's salary resulted in a total three-month payback and a 10 percent ongoing reduction of operating costs. Only once an organization has examined and optimized these factors should it then introduce all of the traditional computer and process-driven quality functions.

Exhibit 47.1. Checklist for Examining the Development Environment

	Checklist Point	Sample Action
1	Evaluate whether or not offices and cubes are environmentally acceptable.	Reduce glare, modify thermostats.
2	Check floor plans for optimal configuration.	Mix managers and mentors with their staff. Dismantle "Managers' Alley."
3	Comingle departments.	Physically locate QA with key development groups.
4	Does infrastructure fail more often than the programming?	Uniformity of desktop software. No beta products.
5	Have IT managers been in the cubicles in the last six months?	Just do it.
6	Measure response time on development machines.	Upgrade to prevent "compile and coffee" syndrome.
7	Ensure monitors are large enough to multi-task multiple applications.	Initiate purchase of 17" to 21" monitors.
8	Is there sufficient customer contact?	All staff meet with customers on a regular basis.
9	Have customers present their business.	Host quarterly educational sessions.
10	Institute a career rotation requirement.	Have mandatory time in support and sustaining engineering.
11	Monitor bug tracking.	Fix the problem, not the blame. Note why the bug was introduced and how to prevent a similar situation.
12	Encourage behavioral reinforcement of quality.	Have a portion of senior IT bonuses tied to the quality of their staff.

Chapter 48

Telecommuting: Distributed Work Programs

Richard A. Bellaver

The time has come to make the art of telecommuting and its synonyms, the virtual office, or telework, into a science. Benefits for the employee and to the company are available. Several million contract, regular, full-time, or part-time people now are active participants in either formal or informal programs. Obviously the technology to make these concepts viable is here; however, more important than the technology needed to make these programs work is the change in management style needed to get the full benefits of these new working arrangements. Several companies have more than three years experience with employees in satellite centers, hoteling, or working at home. This experience shows that corporate policies are affected by these changes and must be considered before attempting to take advantage of the new arrangements.

Recently government and nature have added the required emphasis to prove the practicality of the virtual corporation. The U.S. Clean Air Act attempted to force large companies in the nation's smoggiest cities to cut commuting by 25 percent and to have in effect plans for employee trip reduction. Although federal legislation has eased up on its demands, many companies have already started to comply. Nature intervened in the form of the January 1994 Southern California earthquake.

This natural disaster showed that distributed work can be a lasting environment not just a passing fad. According to Pacific Bell, 1300 workers had their commuting routine changed by the quake, and nine out of ten who took advantage of the company's telecommuting relief package were still working at home a year later even though most of the roads were cleared by then.

Does this mean that every company should start a telecommuting program? Much investment and much management preparation must take place before a company should get involved. Not everyone and not every job is a good candidate for distribution. Questionnaires for employees and

0-8493-9979-3/99/$0.00+$.50

job evaluation techniques can be used to examine the fit. Although business reengineering should consider work distribution in the redesign of basic business processes, a company must first look to its basic policies concerning evaluation of employees and supervision.

A change to a form of absentee production means that supervisors must establish specific objective outputs that can be measured to prove the value of an employee's activities. This management skill, as well as the skill of giving instructions and taking status over the telephone, may have to be learned before going to a virtual office plan. Many companies may not be ready for such a change to their corporate culture.

TYPES OF PROGRAMS

Telecommuting involves the use of technology to replace the need for employees to travel to or work from a conventional office. The concept is to move the work to the employee instead of vice versa. A fact that cannot be forgotten is that organization of the work, its social parameters, and management of employees so involved also must be considered.

Traditionally management people have taken work home through the years. Many more have attempted to overlap travel time by doing something work oriented while on the road. New technology has assisted this effort greatly. The use of networks to send hard copy messages (E-mail) as well as voice has been practical for many years. Some types of work traditionally have been done out of the office.

People who repair large appliances spend a good deal of the day away from the company office (the exception being the Maytag repairman), only coming in for dispatch. Now some companies are having these people remain at home handling scheduling, parts ordering, and distribution from their home computers and making schedule changes using cell phones for voice and facsimile to the truck. The lack of official criteria for measuring the numbers of telecommutters has made the estimates of its number vary from as little as 2 to as high as 45 million Americans.

The Conference Board estimates that only about 15 percent to 20 percent of U.S. companies practicing telework have formal programs. Formal programs are characterized by specific policies encouraging the program and usually a specific agreement between the company and every employee that participates. Formal programs are specific about who owns equipment and how it is maintained, and in some cases, involve management review and approval of the remote work site. Some formal programs are conditions of employment, involve specific training, test grades and are part of official employment documentation.

Informal programs are much more common and are identified by as little as word of mouth encouragement or enhancement to flexible working hour arrangements. Some training for the employee on how to set up an office or deal with vendors of communications equipment is usually provided even in informal programs. There may be hardware and software recommended and possibly even some financial assistance towards its acquisition even in informal programs.

In the downsizing trend of the past few years a good deal of outsourcing and the use of temporary workers have been seen. These methods of providing human productivity are also a part of the telework equation. The opportunity to use people for short-term needs without having to provide space and equipment is very inviting. Usually the arrangement for these contract workers is developed on an individual basis and is a formal arrangement.

BENEFITS OF DISTRIBUTED WORK

Other than compliance with the various laws, there are more positive benefits to encourage businesses to look at distributing work. There is the ability to recruit employees who cannot work normal hours or commute because of disabilities. There is the possibility to provide better customer service by working the off hours. There is the capability to cut down on moves associated with organization changes or promotions. Growth can be managed faster. Distant resources can be tapped.

There are reduced space requirements at the central site. There is the ability to differentiate through knowledge and innovation growth. There is enhanced reputation of being a human resources leading edge company. Finally there is increased individual productivity. Estimates vary on the increase. Some early studies of small manager groups indicate the number could be as high as 30 percent. More conservative and consistent estimates indicate as high as a 15 percent improvement could be realized.

Employee benefits sometimes center around the family, allowing a more flexible schedule or the elimination of payments and insurance for one car. Many people feel the ecological aspects are beneficial enough, but some look for less expense for clothes or even lunches. Some employees just like to work by themselves or have caregiving responsibilities. Many people would like to telecommute for companies despite where they live or send their children to school. In our present world any way to lessen stress, such as having to fight less traffic, is considered positive.

COMPANY EXPERIENCE

The people of a California advertising agency went virtual on January 3, 1994, when they opened their new building. This company has probably done the fastest job of converting their corporate culture because of the opportunity to design and build a structure specifically tailored to virtual concepts. The interior design of the building, only about a block from the beach, reflects an interesting philosophy, stated by one of the executives as, "Work is something you do, not a place to go."

This company is into the practice of hoteling or assigning shared space to individual people based on a reservation system. Along with the 300 to 900 square feet of project room space comes a large table, several conventional phones, a speaker phone, a desktop computer, and a video tape deck with monitor. The equipment is needed to do intellectual work as well as to put on presentations for customers. Workers are able to engage in company mail, look at data bases, and contact customers by phone from home or their cars using portable devices.

Most employees can be reached by pager. Although the program is quite formal some things have not been demanded. Executives are expected to maintain their calendars online, but this is not part of an agreement. However, missing a meeting due to failure to check the mechanized calendar is not permitted.

Spending more time with the customer is the chief motivation behind a large computer company's telecommuting effort. It has about 20,000 employees in the United States who participate in what is called mobile computing, a concept designed to increase productivity, improve relationships, and save time and expense. Employees are given laptop computers with local area network and long distance dial connectivity software programs.

Other support includes pagers, fax, and cellular tools. Major cost reductions have come in the form of less real estate, heating, cooling, maintenance, phone, computer, and other equipment in the individual offices. The company usually does not break out these savings, but it is assumed that they are in the millions. Most of the people doing mobile computing are in sales and service, but others are in manufacturing, development, research, and staff support.

Many of the company's offices around the country have implemented this formal program of mobile computing based on pilots conducted in Indiana and Florida in the early 1990s. Individual offices remain in most company complexes, but they are few. In most cases, there is an open concept with work spaces, computers, and phones assigned to employees who come to their base locations to work or meet with peers or managers. The ratio of employees to office is generally 4 to 1 and in some locations it is 10 to 1. Employee surveys show 75 percent of the employees have benefited from less commuting expense by being mobile, and studies show that mobile computing allows marketing representatives to spend an average of three more hours each week with customers.

One of the company's East Coast facilities has about two years experience with telecommuting. Some people are away from the office 80 percent of the time. They have home terminals and voice mail transfers to their homes, and some have pagers. They have one group meeting a week in the office. They still need to come in for U.S. mail and some supplies. So far the expense of telecommuting is doing very well versus office space and the work still is providing quality results. At another location, the company has converted a former warehouse complex into a telecommuting center.

The employees of four former office facilities were assigned to the remodeled space. The hoteling concept is used with the exception that the 450 resident spaces are segregated from the space of the 630 hotelers. Only 110 work stations are available for the hotelers. Manager rooms are available and there is shared meeting space. Services are provided to both groups by a third resident organization.

IS LEADS THE WAY

A formal program involving a phased approach to telecommuting was piloted by the information systems (IS) organization of a large insurance company. This company knew that not all jobs are appropriate for telecommuting. The jobs included in the pilot were measurable, contained relatively little face to face communication, did not require access to office equipment or files, and involved thinking tasks. The employees wishing to participate needed to have a minimum of one year of employment. They were allowed to volunteer, but did not participate unless approved by management.

Phase 1

Specific IS positions were identified by management as full-time telecommuting jobs. The positions were allocated to the IS divisions based on population and filled through the job opportunities program. In the first quarter of the year the people selected began telecommuting.

Phase 2

In the second quarter the opportunity to telecommute was offered on a part-time basis to IS officers and managers. Approximately 100 positions were identified as three days at home and two days in the office part-time.

Phase 3

In the following year, telecommuting was designated a corporate program and was adopted by several other business groups, which substantially increased the number of professionals and the types of jobs identified for telecommuting.

Consulting firms would seem to be ideal candidates and several are active participants using virtual office concepts. One such firm has been hoteling in its Chicago office since June 1992. If a consultant or an accountant wants to reserve office space it must be done a least a day in advance. Everything to do the proscribed work, including personal belongings, will be set up beforehand.

In Los Angeles, another global consulting firm started a pilot program in 1993 for 40 of its 200 executives. Based on early feedback and continual input from the participants, both consulting firms were able to overcome psychological space possession problems and poor utilization of the reservation system and they feel they are on the right track. The company is now in the process of standardizing its internal networks and platform specifically in light of telecommuting. Many of the company's customers have gotten into virtual offices on a quick need-to-do basis, like planning to close downtown offices during the Atlanta Olympics.

The firm is now looking at what is really needed for the long run. How many databases are going to be accessed from home? What type of bandwidth will be needed for graphics? How does wireless fit into the equation? The test bed for the newly designed platform and network will be in the firm's new technology park in suburban Chicago.

According to the AT&T publication *Telecommuting Connection* in one of the most measured trials in the United States, AT&T and the state of Arizona conducted a pilot program with 134 telecommuters and 70 supervisors. During the trial, telecommuters worked one day per week at home. After six months they logged 97,078 miles avoiding generating 1.9 tons of vehicle-related pollutants. They saved 3,705 hours of drive time and $10,372 in travel expenses.

Approximately 8 out of 10 participants felt telecommuting better equipped them to work at personal peak times, to become better organized, and to plan more effectively. Ninety-five percent of the supervisors reported adequate communication with their staff. Eighty percent of the supervisors said telecommuting increased employee productivity.

Almost two-thirds of all nonparticipants would telecommute if given the opportunity. In 1992, the state of Arizona and AT&T were selected to receive a national Environmental Achievement award. Since the initial trial, the number of AT&T and state commuters has grown to 648 and in 1993 they drove an estimated one million fewer commuter miles and avoided generating 20 tons of air pollution.

SECOND THOUGHTS

Not all companies are moving as aggressively as those mentioned above. A brewing company in Milwaukee, as a part of a program of its parent organization, conducted a pilot of a telecommuting work option in August and September 1994. The program was very expensive because each employee was equipped with a total home office.

Some preliminary findings indicated that such an extensive set up was not required, women viewed the program more positively than men, and distractions arose in those households where children were home for the summer months. The latter situation improved in September when school started. The company did not include telecommuting as part of their compliance plan for the Clean Air Act; however, it may conduct expanded pilots as part of future work/life initiatives.

CORPORATE INVESTMENT

As brought out above by the brewer's experience, companies react to the potential investment of telecommuting in different ways. For those that want to provide relatively high speed lines, because of database access or videoconferencing requirements, Integrated Services Digital Network (ISDN) is the most common service used. More commonly regular telephone lines are used. In many cases a second line is paid for by the employer. This second line is satisfactory for Internet access, fax, limited file downloads, and certainly voice transmission.

Many times a speaker phone is provided. Once the circuitry is determined, decisions must be made as to the equipment, not just type and capacity, but ownership, maintenance responsibilities and even safety. If the program is formal most of these arrangements are documented in the telecommuting agreement. The agreement can go so far as to the specific times the equipment must be available for access from the office. The kids cannot use the second line to call their friends.

Some companies consider the value of telecommuting to the employee as benefit enough and do not accept any responsibility for the expense. A central Indiana data processing firm has had 45 employees working from their homes for several years. The company does not pay for telephone service, but will help the employee finance the purchase of a computer. This three-shift operation has normal turnover of employees, but never has a problem replacing them. If a worker wants a second line into the house for emergency purposes, it is his or her own responsibility.

In all cases a hardware and software platform must be standardized for telecommuting to work to best advantage. The data entry function above used dial-up service and a modem pool. This approach has been around for years and for relatively slow speed works well. The particular company uses proprietary software with built-in security because the data transmitted is sensitive.

There are many software packages available over the counter that can perform the transmission function well, and some have a form of security built in. More companies are allowing employees access to local area networks. Corporate standards generally have been established before this takes place so that the home work station looks just like any centralized station to the host or router. Security must be considered carefully and a software firewall constructed if there is any potential possibility of abuse of the system or its data.

Some companies have considered use of the Internet as a means of providing a work-at-home environment. E-mail through the Internet, as well as through commercial online services, is used by many employees. The lack of security is a serious problem and in most cases has prevented use of the Internet from serious consideration as a major vehicle to carry telework traffic.

CHANGE IN MANAGEMENT STYLE

For those companies moving ahead, the most difficult part of establishing a virtual environment has been the changes required to their management style. Many managers have talked of management by objective for years, but now the job must be precisely defined to make telecommuting successful. Managers must learn how to give meaningful assignments over the telephone without seeing body language or observing whether the subordinate makes notes. Management by walking around must be modified to calling around.

The ideals of participatory management are imbedded in the new style. Along with more faith in the workers' abilities comes more participation in the decision of how the work is to be done. It will be necessary for a manager to provide access to more background information and information about the problem than in the past. In order for a remote worker to be a self-starter, the data to find one's own way must be available. In the past some managers wanted to keep data to themselves to retain the power the data possessed — this kind of management will not work with remote workers. Managers also will have to learn how to get along with fewer strokes from their subordinates. The old model of the boss getting the credit for everything goes out the window.

For well-defined projects, the supervisor must establish the goals, provide the tools and get out of the way. For more complex projects more status communication must be built in at each milestone and a good definition of the next portion to be completed must be agreed upon. The team concepts of total quality management are compatible with these management characteristics, and even the dreaded reengineering should consider the aspects of virtual office. The idea of testing employees to do the right thing is implicit. The point to be made here is that there must be an investment in management training to shift the corporate culture to accomplish benefits from telecommuting.

If the internal communications model of a company is conversations around the water cooler or coffee pot, a new method, involving possibly an electronic bulletin board, must be developed. If most business gets done at power lunches or breakfasts the locations might have to be shifted or the times juggled. If a manager lives for the hubbub of the typing pool he may need a white noise machine. All these aspects must be considered in formulating a virtual office plan.

In conjunction with the previously mentioned consulting firm's move to the suburbs, a pilot project was established in which lessons learned were shared with all other parts of the organization's worldwide offices. Although it studied many different facets of telecommuting, the research was primarily focused on three areas: planning, teaming, and communications. The firm also used a variety of methods to collect information and assess the program's progress. For example, focus groups were conducted with supervisors of telecommuters as well as the staff that technically supports them. All of the data gathered was analyzed and, if found valid, was used to reinforce the program or make modifications.

THE BEST EMPLOYEES

Not everyone is suited to be a telecommuter. Of course, trust is the key link between company and an absent employee, but most of the other attributes of good employees are found in good telecommuters. Those that require little supervision are usually those that keep up to date on their work load. They are well organized, tend to look for more things to do, and are the best team players.

This latter quality may seem contradictory; however, the good team players are those that keep the communications links open. Naturally people best suited to telecommuting are those that are willing to accept the use of technology and undergo the training necessary. Respect for technology is necessary — love is not required. Company nerds may not be the best telecommuters.

One of the drawbacks documented about telecommuting is isolation. Moving experienced employees from the social contacts of office work has a negative effect on some workers over time. Many plans that called for no office visits or very limited returns to the old office have had to be modified to include extra attention to the social aspects of work. Some aspects of isolation can be eased by additional voice contact with the home-bound employee or more bulletin board activity or even possibly support group meetings outside the office environment.

In some cases the number of days per week for each employee to be in the office has had to be increased. Some people are not suited to telecommuting at all. Questionnaires need to be used to discover employees' desire to telecommute. Supervisory experience should be consulted for present workers and possibly some psychological testing should be done before deciding which specific employees should work at home.

THE BEST JOBS

As with employees, not all jobs are suitable to work at home. Work functions that are easily understood and of a long duration are the best to teleport. Data entry and many clerical jobs are good candidates. Programming works well provided it can be well defined and tested independently. Outward dialing telemarketing is done widely from people's homes. Telemarketing easily fits the criteria of a job that can be well defined and is easily measured.

The number of calls and the number of sales can be matched easily. Provided training is properly administered and maintained, telemarketing is an excellent candidate. Research is another good function to work remotely. Many reporters now do their interviews using laptops and later enter the data to the editor automatically via a home communications device. Of course, travel demands are one of the biggest reasons to equip and train management people in the art of telecommuting.

Cell phones, laptops, and even fax machines move from limo to taxi to airplane to hotel desk with minimal interruption. Many higher level managers are accustomed to working in this environment; however, they usually have been supported by an office full of people. The thought of calling from an airplane to a subordinate's boat in the middle of the day might be somewhat upsetting.

CHANGES IN CORPORATE POLICY

Most companies with formal plans have a specific written telecommuting policy, secure agreements from employees, and data gathered during the telecommuting activity. Most formal programs are not started without a trial or pilot program. Legal advice may be useful to determine ownership of equipment supplied to the home and possible safety requirements.

It even may help to look at zoning laws for potential difficulties. An employee may live in a different municipality with different laws than at the company office. Unions have been concerned about potential effects of telecommuting on their membership. A union, which probably has the most experience with mechanization, has formalized its concerns in a set of demands for employers.

COMMUNICATIONS WORKERS OF AMERICA

Communications Workers of America (CWA) has the following requirements:

- Equal pay and benefits
- Work to be done in the office for a least two days a week
- No more than two visits a month to home by a manager with 24-hour notice
- The company supplies equipment and materials
- The company reimburses for higher utility and insurance costs
- The union has the right to inspect the home for safety and ergonomics
- Telecommuters should see all routine job openings

It can be seen that the union is protecting against the possibility of several abuses with these rules. It is also attempting to assure against isolation of employees and makes sure equal opportunity for advancement is available even though the employee is absent.

Because of the new way of evaluating productivity, new pay programs may be required and management evaluation processes may need to be updated. Workers may be concerned about their career advancement when absent, so human resource employees need to be involved early and continuously. Important HR procedures, such as time reporting, telephone expense, and the use of other home resources, must be spelled out in the telecommuting policy statement or the employee agreement.

One of the consulting firms mentioned previously is developing principles and guidelines for its pilot, which are expected to serve as blueprints for the future telecommuting programs. Although not viewing telecommuting as a substitute for child or elder care, the company would like to develop a framework flexible enough to enable people to use the program as a tool in helping them balance their professional and personal lives. Core hours will be identified, meaning the company can expect the employee to be available during specific hours at a home telephone number. It is also very important for companies to have a thorough understanding of insurance liability and human resource issues that can arise as a result of this initiative.

THINGS TO DO NOW

If a company is interested in becoming a virtual corporation there are some things that can be started today. Just as total quality management methodology advises, a task force of different levels of the organization and different attitudes about telecommuting should be established to examine the situation. This group should look at all aspects, even including the safety, comfort and security of potential home offices. The subject of isolation should be considered when determining how many days per week the program should incorporate and what types of additional communications means need to be considered.

Employees with authority to do something with the results should be included on the team. Those within the company who have some experience with the subject should be included. Consultants can be used, but experienced employees are the best resource. Vendors of telecommuting products and services will provide many services including assistance in network sizing, job requirements and even employee questionnaires.

The company must establish the policies that will be needed as early as possible. Policies can be tested during a pilot phase. The question of ownership of equipment and how maintenance will be handled should be addressed. These items are better thought about up-front before experience dictates a problem. Experience can be used to modify the practices later.

Companies must learn about the technology, its use, and its cost. It is best to sample employees' opinions and attitudes. If the attitude and the culture seem compatible, then it is proper to set up a pilot with specific objectives and specific means of measurement. It is then up to the company to select the proper jobs, the proper people, and the proper managers and give the virtual corporation a try.

Section IX Checklist

1. Does your organization have a formal methodology for software quality? Does it work?
2. How are programmers in your environment educated about the quality process?
3. Is there a dedicated quality control group in your organization? If not, where are quality standards managed?
4. As a development manager, what steps do you take to ensure the quality of the software that is delivered to end users?
5. Do you consider quality management part of the software development process or part of the business development process?
6. Should software quality be reviewed during the testing phase of a project or during the design phase? How is it handled in your environment?
7. Does reduction in maintenance tasks reflect improvement in development quality, or is it a function of application system complexity?
8. Can software quality improvements be measured accurately or is it too difficult to assess?
9. Has your organization ever halted implementation of a development project due to poor quality? If not, does this mean that quality is not important?
10. Are you familiar with software metric measurement techniques? If so, have you applied any metric measurement to development or support tasks?
11. Has your organization utilized software metric tools to establish a baseline complexity for all software programs in your installation? If not, is there a future opportunity for such activity?
12. Does your organization permit telecommuting? If so, how is it monitored and who is eligible for offsite working?
13. Should productivity be measured in the number of written lines of code, the number of written programs, the ability to meet development schedules or the quality of programming syntax?
14. What performance tools would be valuable to your efforts to improve program execution? Do these tools exist?
15. In your opinion, are "productivity" and "quality" textbook attributes that will never be achieved, or do you believe in pursuing these objectives as part of your professional commitment to the computing industry? Do other staff members share your opinions?

Section X
Leveraging Staff Resources

Harmonizing the diverse nuances of human behavior with the technical complexities of application development can be strenuous as well as frustrating. Whether supervising computing professionals, communicating with end users, negotiating vendors' contracts, or maintaining technical expertise, development managers must consider a myriad of personnel situations. This also includes retention, career counseling, turnover, training, disciplinary action, motivation, and hiring. Unfortunately, few managers are fully prepared to embrace such a broad array of nontechnical skills. Nevertheless, within current business environments, the ability to persevere with all types of human resource issues is essential.

Attracting talented software professionals to accomplish development goals remains extremely challenging. Perpetual changes in technology have created fragmented pockets of skilled workers. And many of these workers vary in competency and ability. Additionally, the demands of business competition, including economic globalization, has created a potential shortage of technical expertise. As a result, retaining qualified personnel has become a critical issue. Chapter 49, "Fostering Loyal and Long-Term Employees by Raising Organizational Identification," offers valuable insight on the issues that can affect personnel stability. This is particularly important for those organizations that rely on employees with business and technical expertise. As a follow-up, Chapter 50, "Successfully Hiring and Retaining IT Personnel," examines the techniques that can bring about improvements to staff acquisition. These include the ability for organizations to hire rapidly, remain focused on the position, truthful about the tasks, and decisive in final selection. Development managers have learned that in today's hiring market, it requires more savvy than asking technical questions. Thus, new skills must be used to attract, qualify, and hire the talent needed to implement newer and more challenging technology.

Technical training has been an important, and well-recognized, method for retaining software professionals. Training has also become a critical factor in reducing the shrinking labor pool. Many organizations are re-educating software professionals on newer technologies in an attempt to leverage existing business knowledge. Other organizations view training as an ongoing process that should be incorporated as part of the overall development life cycle. But training is not a panacea, nor is it as easy to implement as may be thought. Chapter 51, "Training Options in a Technical Environment," provides specific viewpoints on retaining skilled software professionals via training. The misconceptions and realities of retraining existing staff are closely examined with suggestions and guidelines that are practical. Development mangers should establish a balanced plan that can attract needed professionals and ensure staff longevity.

Allocating time for self improvement of professional knowledge has been difficult for the vast majority of IS workers. In particular, development managers may be most affected by the substance of their work since they are involved in more business tasks rather than detailed technical chores. This is not necessarily bad, but it does require more acknowledgment about the shifting nature of business and technical skills. Chapter 52, "A Worksheet for Goals and Skills Assessment," provides a method for examining and reviewing professional expertise within the framework of the business environment. This can be useful for realigning career direction with corporate business strategy or reaffirming existing career direction. This technique can also be applied to most IS positions and can be used as part of the annual review process.

Successful application development extends beyond the use of just hardware and software technology. It can be a resource intensive function that demands the cooperation of both technical and business professionals. However, creating the right team environment is critical for successful project implementation. Chapter 53, "Project Teamwork: How to Make It Happen," offers valuable insight to the creation of development teams that can make or break a software project. Teamwork, like other components in development, requires understanding and experience. It is often misunderstood, and many development managers grapple with the task of keeping the key players focused and productive. Clearly, those who often succeed at project management have mastered the skill of creating effective development teams. This chapter is an important part of the development process and should be reviewed carefully for appropriate use in the technical environment.

Chapter 49

Fostering Loyal and Long-Term Employees by Raising Organizational Identification

Carl Stephen Guynes, J. Wayne Spence, and Leon A. Kappelman

THE INCREASED ORGANIZATIONAL RELIANCE on IT has led to the evolution of a group of highly technical IT specialists who display certain distinctive common characteristics. Among these common traits are

- High growth needs
- High professional identification
- Low organizational identification

IS professionals tend to like the change and challenge of their work and generally have high standards of professional conduct and performance.

Unfortunately for most employers, they also exhibit low organizational identification — that is, they do not exhibit a strong sense of identification or commitment to their current employer. Although there is little an organization can do about fostering the growth needs of its employees, and can have only a limited, albeit important, influence upon their sense of professionalism, an organization can take significant actions to foster their sense of identification. All too often, however, these actions are not taken, and organizations experience not only high turnover and all of its associated problems, but, more important and enigmatic, fail to optimally utilize their information assets.

This historical low organizational identification problem is now being manifested by other organizational members as more firms downsize; thus, the prescription for IS personnel may well have a wider context. The IS professional knows that since their skill set is in demand, if they become disenchanted with their current employer, they can find a suitable job with another firm by investing a minimum amount of effort. Perhaps because of

0-8493-9822-3/00/$0.00+$.50

their employment flexibility coupled with the specialized nature of the work, it is not surprising to discover a peculiar cliquishness associated with small, specialized work groups such as that found in IS shops. This exclusiveness of interest and resulting camaraderie fosters a sense of functional identification among some IS staff members at the expense of organizational identification. But these are not mutually exclusive conditions and this does not have to be the case.

IS Employees' Concerns are Not Always the Company's

In many cases, these IS professionals are not really concerned about the organization. They have a job to perform, and it does not matter to whom they report. Organizational problems only secondarily affect them, and they are frequently indifferent regarding the nature of a problem. They do their job in much the same way regardless of whether they are working for a public sector organization or a large private corporation. The problems that they face may be different depending upon the particular organization they work for, but their approach to solving the problem is handled in a similar fashion.

In many instances, the organization's philosophy of management further contributes to the negative attitude held by these specialists. Organizational management often does not identify with its own personnel. Many managers do not understand the technical environment and have no desire to learn about them. These managers are often in a position where they must accept the use of the systems, but they do not try to understand them.

Low Loyalty and High Turnover

Organizational loyalty in IS sections is often minimal and the personnel turnover rate is frequently high. Many information systems managers try to explain this high turnover rate as simply a characteristic of technical personnel. Professional employees tend to stay with organizations and need more justification for making a change. It is generally felt that satisfied workers will not arbitrarily jump from one job to another. However, since some of these highly technical computer personnel do change jobs frequently, they are evidently not satisfied with their work environment. Yet, job-hopping is not a function of technical expertise, since engineers do not seem as prone to rapid employment change.

It is management's task to attempt to determine the source of employee discontent. This task can be extremely difficult when management must deal with technically oriented IS personnel, for it is difficult to make them feel that they are supplying a unique contribution to the organization. These employees must feel that they are part of the organization and not merely a separate group of people unrelated to the organization as a whole. The problem of satisfying the IS employees is, in many ways, similar to providing satisfaction for any type of specialized knowledge worker. It is common to find specialists, especially technical specialists, in any organization being treated similarly to IS personnel. It is, therefore, necessary for human resource management to look into the makeup of IS specialists in order to understand them in their peculiar situation.

WORK PROFILE OF IS PROFESSIONALS

IS professionals quite often feel a great degree of professionalism concerning their duties even though their superiors may not share these feelings, for they have acquired an impressive technical knowledge and talent for efficiency and technique within their own specialized area. Specialists must keep several important IS concepts in mind at all times and must be aware of the concept of change management. They must be prepared to install and maintain multiple systems while maintaining a certain level of efficiency, security, and reliability. IS specialists are rarely satisfied if a system simply works — it must possess the same degree of excellence that other craftsmen would devise. If they are not allowed to act as craftsmen, no personal pride can be attached to the work they completed.

The IS professional also tends to reject historical managerial control, which compounds the problem. Of particular importance is the dislike held for traditional auditing procedures and internal security measures. These procedures and measures are for the most part viewed as nuisances that keep the IS professional from doing the job efficiently and are often inadequate safeguards against error and invasion. It is common for such procedures to be rejected by the highly skilled IS personnel, because they perceive them to reflect upon the character of their immediate work group.

Lack of Organizational Identification

As mentioned previously, the lack of organizational identification can cause many of these problems. Therefore, a look at the IS specialists' profile could help to generate solutions to the problem. Although many IS personnel prefer not to become involved with the employing organization on a personal basis, the organization can emphasize that each individual is an integral part of the whole and does possess special talents worthy of notice. Such recognition of ability will surely help increase the employee's organizational identification.

In many cases, the IS professional feels that his or her contribution to the organization goes unrecognized. This is partly due to the nature of the work. When working on a system, the professional is immersed in the problems and daily activities of other organizational units. However, once the project has been completed, it is common that the IS professional has no idea of what has happened (is happening) to the system. Multiple levels of feedback are necessary to solve this problem.

FEEDBACK FOSTERS ORGANIZATIONAL IDENTIFICATION

Minimally, at least two forms of feedback are important. First, the IS professional needs feedback on how the system is working. This may be in the form of positive and negative information about system consequences. If the system is performing well, the IS professional receives personal satisfaction for a job well done, as well as an element of job closure. If the feedback is negative, the IS professional can use this information for product improvement and later system development. For the IS professional, not knowing how an employer uses and values information systems is a significant element of lack of organizational identification.

The second useful form of feedback is how a system contributes to the organization's bottom line. If IS employees can establish how their efforts are contributing to the overall organizational goals, they will feel more organizational identification.

Promoting Recognition. To amplify the impact of this feedback, recognition of contribution could be easily established. For example, a "best system of the year" award could be established to promote recognition of how individual systems and people are contributing to the organization. These awards would not even have to be monetary, but rather a plaque, certificate, or internal publication citation. The important factor is the recognition, not the form of the award.

COMMITMENT TO THE IS GROUP

However, organizational identification may be the wrong approach. Perhaps it is more important that the IS professional give his or her most significant allegiance to the IS function, even if there are problems. Within the IS function, individuals tend to work in project groups or teams. These groups are charged with the responsibility for completing the activities to which they are assigned. Yet, once the group discharges its responsibilities, the group is disbanded. Thus, any personal relationships with other individuals within the group or personal commitments to the group itself are severed when the group is disbanded. Thus, it is no wonder that the IS professionals feel no organizational commitment — they may not even feel any identification with the IS function within which they serve.

Tactical Teams

The solution to this problem is the creation of tactical work groups or teams rather than the more strategic nature of team development today. Tactical teams would by necessity have to be highly specialized and relatively small. However, the objective to be achieved is to have the individual member develop a sense of belonging and consequently commitment. In today's team environment, individuals often feel like interchangeable cogs in a machine. This feeling is the most significant reason for rapid job movement among IS professionals. There are, at present, few emotional reasons for staying put when another job around the corner has a few more dollars attached to it.

CREATING STRONGER ORGANIZATIONAL IDENTIFICATION BY PROMOTING EMPLOYEES

Many corporations now view IS professionals as potential managers. These employees have worked with many of the functional departments of an organization due to the nature of their work, and if they are knowledgeable concerning the procedures of each end-user department, they could be well equipped to view the organization as a whole. It is sometimes difficult to perceive an information systems analyst as a potential manager because of their seemingly technical role, a problem similarly experienced by engineers and scientists. However, many systems analysts are well suited to assume this type of position and seek the new challenges that a new role would afford.

This is not to say that a low-level IS specialist with a limited educational background is qualified to be a high-level manager. It does mean, however, that a qualified individual with a good educational background in business, who has a strong technical background and organizational experience, could excel at other responsibilities within an organization and have an understanding of an organization's aims and accomplishments. This person would be in a position to move into management and would, no doubt, have few organizational identification problems because of their more holistic perspective on the organization. It is, then, top management's responsibility to analyze the technically oriented computer personnel and consider their potential as management talent.

Managers who possess an information systems background should have the opportunity to follow a career path that is arranged in such a way that individuals that have potential managerial talent are recognized for that talent and can move along this the path. Many organizations have been well served by providing such opportunities (e.g., John Reed, CEO of CitiBank was once the CIO of the IS organization there). IS personnel who are not management-oriented should not be promoted into managerial positions merely because of seniority. The same people that do excellent network maintenance, for example, may not, by their technical nature, be qualified for advancement to top management levels. On the other hand, to stifle a valuable client/server analyst who is quite capable of being a manager is an excellent way to destroy any sense of organizational identification that may have existed.

Cultivating Talent

The lack of personnel planning has caused many bright IS professionals to become disenchanted with and disenfranchised from their organizations; thus they move on to other companies in hopes that they will be recognized as talented and will be, hopefully, more efficiently used. This lack of attention to planning may well extend into the realm of educational opportunities and other forms of job enrichment for the IS specialist. Many IS skills are indeed perishable — necessitating continued skill enhancements, and in some cases, altering the direction of new skill attainment. Thus, both the personnel function and the IS organization need to establish the skill sets that will best serve the overall organization in the future and establishing a training plan to achieve that goal. However, simply establishing the goal is insufficient — this goal must be communicated to the IS specialist, along with his or her place in achieving this goal. On a more personal level, this goal may be established in the sense of "we have a plan for your future" rather than dealing with the IS specialist as an indiscriminate entity within the organization.

MAKING IS PERSONNEL FEEL AS PART OF THE COMPANY

The fact that it often takes a large number of people to run a truly efficient information systems group poses a problem for some organizations. Unless cooperation and understanding are organizational characteristics, the IS group may not be working for the maximum good of the total organization. It is critical that the IS function be integrated into the overall organizational structure. The major way that management can integrate IS personnel activities into the organization is by the maximization of the employees' organizational identification. An employee must be made aware of where systems development fits into the overall organizational structure. IS personnel must also be familiarized with other areas of the organization and be included in meetings between the various department heads, or at least feel that they are represented at such meetings and be in communication.

Last, personnel should be encouraged to participate in informal meetings with personnel from other areas so that they might become acquainted with each other and feel less isolated in the area of the computer world. An accompanying solution would have the executives from throughout the organization visit the IS area to see what is being done relative to integrating departmental activities.

CONCLUSION — ORGANIZATIONAL RECOGNITION OF THE INDIVIDUAL

Any employee will become bored if left to stagnate in a job for a number of years. The high growth needs of IS professionals makes it unlikely that they would remain in an organization that allowed such a situation to exist.

IS personnel are a specialized group who possess characteristics exhibited by other specialists. If this personnel can be treated as professionals and be motivated by a challenge, business may be able to eliminate some of the organizational identification problems that currently exist among technical IS employees. If top management can create an environment that fosters employee well-being and promote loyalty to the organization, the organizational identification problem will eventually be minimized and more IS personnel will stay with the organization.

To retain IS personnel by fostering their sense of commitment and identification with an employer, this chapter recommends the following steps:

- Understand the profile of IS professionals.
- Recognize IS professionals' talents and contributions to the organization.
- Inform IS employees how they contribute to the organization.
- Create tactical teams in which each IS member is an integral part.
- Promote business-minded IS staff members to managerial positions.
- Offer training and education to enhance IS skills.
- Have IS personnel become more familiar and participate in other areas of the organization.

Chapter 50
Successfully Hiring and Retaining IT Personnel

John P. Murray

This article examines the hiring techniques practiced at a Midwest consulting agency. In the middle of 1995, this branch of a large international information technology consulting organization mounted a campaign to aggressively increase its headcount.

Despite a tight IT labor market, the total headcount for the branch had increased from 75 to 230 employees by mid-1998. The branch has enjoyed the benefits of its hiring model, which is applicable to many IT organizations.

The branch's hiring record is impressive. However, it is more impressive when considered within the context of the hiring standards established in the branch. The hiring goal is based upon interviewing only those candidates who appear to be within the top 20 percent of all prospective candidates. The selection of candidates is based upon clearly defined hiring criteria. Those criteria form the basis for deciding whether or not the candidate will be invited to a formal interview. Therefore, the process focuses on increasing the headcount within the branch, but only within the established hiring standards.

It is important to understand that, while the growth of the branch is and will continue to be, to some extent, a numbers game, it is a game with constraints. The goal, of course, is to continue to increase the headcount because of the correlation between headcount and ultimate branch performance. While it is important to continue to increase the total headcount, the priority of the branch is to place quality above increasing headcount numbers. There is no doubt, should the approach simply have been to increase headcount, that today the branch headcount would be above 350.

ACKNOWLEDGING THE COMPETITION FOR INFORMATION TECHNOLOGY PERSONNEL

When considering IT hiring and retention issues, the place to begin is with the recognition that prospective employers face a "seller's market." Because there are many more employment opportunities for IT people than there are people available, prospective employment candidates enjoy

0-8493-9822-3/00/$0.00+$.50

the luxury of being selective with regard to their next employer. That circumstance is particularly valid for the high-quality candidates. The favorable job climate for IT people is a reality that is likely to continue for some time. Given that reality, it is mandatory that organizations interested in finding and retaining high-quality IT people adopt more creative methods to address IT hiring and retention concerns.

It is important to recognize the value of focusing on, and hiring, high-quality IT people. Again, given the strong market for IT employees, there is often not going to be much difference in terms of salary between the highest quality people and people in the second rank. While the difference in salary expense between the best and the next tier of employees may not be great, the difference in quality can be significant. The best and brightest people will often make a considerably higher contribution over time. That being the case, it should be easy to justify extra compensation, where needed, to attract those people.

Quality is an important factor in the decision to hire an individual, but the topic transcends individual hiring concerns. Good IT people are attracted and challenged by association with IT professionals of the same caliber. An organization that has built a strong IT department is going to have an advantage in hiring candidates, because those candidates will be able to see that the organization cares about the IT effort within the organization. When an organization can point to an IT environment that both stresses and delivers high-quality work, the best people are going to be interested in coming on board.

Because people with IT skills are at a premium, the market for people with those skills is very aggressive. One result of that circumstance is that IT people have an understanding of the market value of their skills; they understand the competitive nature of the marketplace. Therefore, the process of attracting, hiring, and retaining skilled IT people has become increasingly aggressive and competitive. Organizations that fail to recognize the realities of the marketplace, and to make a strong commitment to compete, are not going to succeed in the race to find and retain good people.

It may come down to a simple business consideration about whether or not there is a willingness to make the appropriate commitment within the organization. When a commitment to the technology is not in place, attempting to hire and retain good IT people is simply going to be futile.

Many IT people receive a constant stream of calls from recruiters attempting to persuade them to change employers. In most instances, those callers are making very tempting proposals. Items such as signing bonuses, large salary increases, and additional time off become routine offers to encourage job changes. In addition, there will be promises that the candidates will be working in areas that use the newest technology.

Promises will be made about the willingness of the employer to provide technology-related educational opportunities. There will be references to the potential opportunity to manage interesting IT projects.

Hearing those blandishments sets high levels of expectation in the minds of those being recruited. Sometimes the candidate, upon joining the organization, finds that the promises are not honored. When that happens, it is likely the person will move on to something else. The concern here is not with the keeping of promises, but with the expectations those promises raise in the minds of the candidates. Those expectations, valid or not, become a baseline for IT people considering changing jobs. Poorly managed employee expectations ultimately encourage the employee to move on to something else. Obviously, when good employees leave the organization, everyone involved loses.

THE FRAGILE NATURE OF THE TECHNOLOGY-BASED HIRING PROCESS

Success in the hiring of IT personnel must be based upon a clear understanding of the marketplace and the needs and desires of the IT candidates. Like it or not, technical people often do tend to have a different set of goals and interests than other types of employees. The purpose here is not to pass judgment on those differences, but to make it clear that a successful hiring and retention program must acknowledge those differences and use them to the advantage of the potential employer.

The first item to be recognized is the ability of the particular organization to offer competitive salaries. Again, given the realities of the marketplace, a failure to become and remain competitive with salaries is simply going to exacerbate the problems associated with hiring and keeping IT personnel. This is a dual problem, in that competitive salaries will attract good employees, but it will also require competitive salary adjustments to retain those employees. There is another aspect of the salary issue in that salaries for existing IT employees are going to have to be reviewed and, where appropriate, adjusted. If a continuing review of salaries is absent for all IT employees, retention difficulties will increase.

One aspect of the salary issue is to consider moving away from the traditional process of annual salaries to a nine-month review cycle. If that change occurs, it will be important to advise all IT employees as part of an approach to forestall offers from competitors. Making a salary review timing change will create some level of difficulty with other departments within the organization; however, doing so will help the IT retention effort. Whether the improvement is worth the additional difficulty is an issue for each organization, but doing so represents an effective approach to the problem.

While it may be a difficult concept to sell within the organization, because it disrupts the traditional human relations structure, it is worthwhile to give serious thought to adopting a new approach to IT hiring. The approach taken will depend upon the size of the organization and the particular IT installation. In medium and larger organizations, the responsibility for the hiring and retention of IT personnel should be within the IT department. Again, given the size of the IT department, it might have its Human Resources section within the department.

In smaller organizations, several approaches should be considered. One approach would be to work out an agreement between the IT department and the Human Resources department to work very closely in hiring IT people, with someone from the IT department accepting primary responsibility for the effort. Another approach would be to engage the assistance of an outside consultant to assume responsibility for finding, hiring, and retaining IT employees. Of course, any approach can only be successfully developed with the support and cooperation of the Human Resources department, but making such a change is worth considering.

The idea here is not to circumvent the Human Resources department, nor to lessen the importance of that department in any way. Usually the Human Resources department has involvement in all hiring decisions across the organization. As a result, given the magnitude of the hiring effort, the process can be lengthy. When the hiring process takes too long, the candidates will move on to other opportunities. It is imperative, when a good IT candidate is identified, that an offer be made as quickly as possible. One way to deal with this is to shift the primary responsibility and focus for IT hiring to the IT department.

There are several valid reasons for taking a different approach to IT hiring. First, being in a position to talk comfortably about technology-related issues with candidates will send a signal that the organization is interested in them as technicians and will put them at ease. Organizations do sometimes send IT candidates the wrong signal because several of the primary hiring contacts tend to be with people who have little practical understanding of the technology. Being involved early on with someone who can relate to the candidate and the associated technology constitutes a hiring plus. Second, a person with a technical background is going to be more sensitive to the interests and needs of the candidates. An important aspect of a successful IT hiring campaign is that a strong relationship is developed between the candidate and the person doing the hiring. The existence of a mutual understanding of the technology will work to strengthen that relationship.

Many times the decision to join a particular organization occurs as the result of subtle issues that arise during the interview process. In that regard, having someone who can make the candidate comfortable and to whom the candidate can relate is going to be a benefit. In addition, taking such an approach will help to set the organization apart from those where the approach is to simply hire everyone through the Human Resources department. Being able to send a signal that the organization really does care about its IT effort represents a hiring strength.

SUCCESSFUL HIRING CRITERIA

There are four basic components associated with the successful process of hiring IT personnel. The hiring process must be rapid, focused, candid, and decisive. An examination of each of the components, the ways they affect the hiring process, and their relationship to each other will provide guidelines for dealing with the hiring issues.

A salient reason why employers fail in their effort to hire IT people concerns the use of standard hiring approaches for all types of employees. It is not unusual to find organizations where it takes an average of 15 or more working days to respond to a resume after it comes into the office. In responding to the resumé, the first interview may be scheduled for several weeks in the future. To make matters worse, an offer may be contingent upon multiple interviews involving a number of people. When that amount of time constitutes the normal hiring schedule, any hope of finding good IT candidates is unrealistic in today's market; they will have gone somewhere else. It should be obvious that the ability to react quickly to good IT candidates is imperative. That approach can only be used when the organization is well prepared.

Like it or not, a "one size fits all" approach is not going to produce success in hiring IT people. One way to look at the current situation as it applies to hiring IT personnel is to think of it as a commodities business. With high demand and low supply, those prospects who are available are going to be hired quickly. Expecting that a lengthy hiring cycle will not affect hiring IT people is incorrect. The reality is that there are just too many jobs available, and while the organization is grinding through the employment process, someone else, who is more nimble, is going to hire the candidate.

An important component of moving to a successful hiring effort is to reduce the IT hiring cycle from weeks to days. Doing so may, given the current status in many organizations, seem a difficult, if not impossible, cultural change. However, if the organization is serious about the IT hiring effort, this is a change that needs to be accommodated.

The realities of the marketplace must be acknowledged. A candidate, having a number of job opportunities available, is not going to be very patient waiting for an organization to respond. Those other organizations making offers are going to put pressure on the candidate to accept, which works against the slow-moving organization. When an organization moves quickly with the hiring process, there are two positive results. First, the organization sends the candidate a signal that it values the candidate and wants him or her to join the organization. Second, moving rapidly sends a message that this is an organization where decisions are made quickly.

Success in hiring IT people is contingent upon the development of a focused hiring approach. Understanding the requirement for speed with IT hiring is critical, but doing so is only possible within the framework of a clear process. Those doing the hiring must be comfortable with two sets of criteria: the appropriate technical skills to do the work and personal traits that fit the culture of the organization.

The technical skills may vary with the needs of different departments or projects; specific technical skills and experience will vary. However, within the general context of the organization, there should be a baseline of technical skills. As an example, if the organization operates in a UNIX environment, UNIX experience is going to be an important factor. Beyond the basics, there will often be some "nice to have" skills or experience that adds to the candidate's attractiveness. Perhaps there is a need for Access experience in the Marketing department; obviously, someone with that skill and experience would be of interest.

As the technology needs of the organization change, those doing the hiring have to be made aware of those changes. With a clear technology focus, people not meeting the hiring criteria will be bypassed, saving time and effort for everyone. There may be some gray area because those with a strong technology interest and aptitude, yet without the identified specific skills, will be considered. The idea here is to come to a clear understanding regarding technical area needs and to focus the recruiting effort on that area.

Again, the importance of having someone who understands the technology at the beginning of the process needs to be stressed. Sometimes a candidate surfaces without the exact skills required, but with good experience and adaptability. When that happens, a knowledgable interviewer will be in a position to make an offer to a candidate who otherwise would be passed over.

Developing and maintaining a strong understanding of the current and anticipated uses of the technology within the organization is a strong IT hiring factor. Having a person with a strong technology background (and appropriate people skills) directly involved in IT hiring will smooth the process. That involvement will also forestall future disappointments on the part of candidates who feel they did not receive a clear picture of the current technology.

The model used to identify personal traits considered in hiring IT personnel is more general. In determining the personality criteria, the place to begin is with an understanding of the culture of the organization. Just as all organizations differ, the same is true of their cultures. The values of the organization must be clearly understood by those doing the interviewing. The interviewer has to be in a position to explain those values to the candidate so that he has a clear understanding of what is going to be expected if the candidate is hired.

As an example, the culture of the organization may be based upon a high level of structure and control. In that environment, people usually receive specific instructions about their assignments and about the anticipated results. If the candidate has a strong interest in being "creative," i.e., wants to go ahead and do things on his own, with very limited supervision or direction, the environment within the organization is probably not going to provide a good fit.

One of the mandates of the IT department may be to develop and maintain high levels of customer service. In such an environment, the interviewer must make certain the candidate understands the importance of customer service and is going to be comfortable in such a culture. If that is not the case, it will be much better to come to that decision quickly and for both parties to recognize that not going forward is the most appropriate choice for everyone.

In order to move the hiring process along, it is important that someone directly involved with interviewing has the authority to make an offer or to reject a candidate. If the appropriate hiring model is in place and carefully followed, it will ease the hiring decision. Again, any delay through the hiring process represents a risk. Failing to quickly close the hiring loop means that the candidate remains available to the competition. If the proper hiring structure is in place, there is no need to prolong the decision to hire or to reject a particular candidate. In order to speed the process, a reasonable approach would be to make offers contingent upon acceptable reference checks. Again, in a well-managed hiring process, checking references should not consume too much time.

In moving to a more focused and rapid process of interviewing and hiring IT candidates, the risk of making a hiring mistake is going to increase. It may happen that an unsatisfactory candidate is hired who, in a more structured, more traditional environment, would not have been considered. However, if the hiring focus and criteria are clear, and if the proper discipline is in place, such mistakes will be rare. Success in the hiring process is sometimes worth the risk of a mistake.

MANAGING THE EXPECTATIONS OF THE CANDIDATES

A substantial number of people interviewed for IT positions will have a definite set of ideas about what they expect from a job and an employer. The interviewers need to anticipate the candidates' willingness to express their views about those interests. During the interview process, the focus should be on precisely what the candidates consider important with regard to their work.

Although practical, the concerns of the candidate should be separated from the technology-related and other quality-of-life issues. Without that separation, it is too easy to glide over the technology interests and discuss the standard benefits offered by the organization. The importance of the technology-related items to the candidates has to be recognized and covered in sufficient detail.

There are two goals here. The first is to determine if the interests of the candidate can be met by the IT department. The second goal is to correctly set the expectations of the candidate as they relate to the realities of the job and the organization. It is important that an open and candid environment be established so that, should an offer be made and accepted, all parties understand what is expected.

While there can be a number of answers to the question about the candidates' work interests, some basic issues are likely to be raised. Usually, candidates will want to know about the current technology within the organization. They will want information about the role of the IT function and how it is viewed by the rest of the organization. They will also want to know about the future course of the technology.

Candidates will be interested in the career ladders available within the organization. This is an area where candor is important. If the candidate raises the issue of career development, the interviewer should ask questions that will identify the specific interests behind the questions. The goal here is to determine the basis for the question, i.e., is there really an interest in moving into a management role, or is the interest in moving to management based upon the desire to move to a higher salary level? If the answer has to do with salary and the organization rewards strong technical performance with increased salary, that point should be discussed with the candidate.

An important issue is continuing training. Many candidates, particularly good ones, will want to know if the organization supports continuing IT training and at what support level. The rapid changes in IT technology mandate a continual upgrading of skills for people who want to make a strong contribution. If the organization makes an effort to hire the best possible people, there needs to be an understanding that those people will have a strong interest in education.

Educational support should be seen as a critical component of the hiring approach. If the organization is supportive of education, that should be presented as a strong point and stressed in the interview. Conversely, if the organization does not value continuing education, the interviewer should be candid about that fact.

It is important to recognize that IT training, appropriately managed, represents an investment, not an expense. The rapid changes in IT technology require a continuing upgrading of technical skills. Training good people in the current technologies is in the best interest of the individual and the organization. A link exists between a strong IT training program and the retention of high-quality IT people, and it should be seen as a critical success component of the IT effort.

Dealing with high-quality IT people raises the bar for the IT department. Well-motivated employees are going to work hard at their careers. The IT managers must recognize that high-quality people will take an aggressive approach to their continuing education. If there are representations of educational commitments to employees, those commitments must be honored.

In answering questions from the IT candidates, candor is the only policy that will serve the organization well over time. It is a mistake to allow the pressure to fill open IT positions to cause the interviewers to be less than forthcoming about the organization's ability to meet the candidates' desires. Of course it is important to make the hire, but that hire should not be made based upon a set of false assumptions on the part of the candidate. In today's market it is likely, once the candidate faces the realities of the job, and if there has been misrepresentation, he will to move on to something else. When a good employee leaves, everyone loses.

While presenting a less-than-candid scenario is an obvious mistake, in today's competitive hiring environment, it does happen. Taking that approach can be seen as having an upside in that it will improve the hiring success rate. Conversely, the approach carries a downside — the mistake of being less than candid will generate unrest within the IT department and will result in a high rate of resignations.

"SELLING" THE CANDIDATES ON THE ORGANIZATION

Being candid with prospective employees does not preclude opportunities to sell the organization. It will pay to take the time to identify the positive aspects of the organization and to explain them when talking to candidates. Again, it is important that the interviewer takes the time to uncover the interests of the particular candidates. Having that understanding, they will be in a position to emphasize those positive aspects that fit the interests of the particular candidate. It is important to recognize the pressure level to find and hire strong IT candidates. Making an effort to sell the organization is simply one way to counteract that pressure.

Clearly, any area where the candidate's interests can be supported represents an opportunity to encourage the individual to join the organization. Beyond that, there should be focus on what makes the organization unique.

Some ancillary selling points would include: the values of the company, the culture under which the organization operates, and attractive benefits not commonly found in other organizations. Taking the time to understand components that make it a good place to work and emphasizing those strengths are appropriate and effective hiring tools.

As an example, in the case of the success of the branch office used in this piece, one of the strong points of that organization is the commitment to "doing the right thing." Taking time with candidates to discuss that commitment and using examples of how the process works within the branch, have been very effective tools in helping people reach decisions to join the branch.

DEALING WITH THE ISSUE OF RETENTION

IT organizations are generally uncomfortable with the issue of employee turnover. While keeping good IT people is important, indeed critical, to the health of the IT installation, some limited turnover is not a bad circumstance. There are benefits to bringing in people with different perspectives and ideas, those familiar with new technologies, who can infuse a higher level of energy and excitement.

Conversely, people do become stale, or grow restless; they may develop an interest in moving on to something else for a variety of reasons. When that occurs, if the organization cannot meet the changed needs of those employees, it is in the best interest of all concerned for that employee to move on.

The goal should be to keep total turnover low and to concentrate on retaining the good people within the IT installation. Beyond that, an additional emphasis should be placed on retaining the most valuable people — the perceived "stars" of the installation. Just as with hiring, it is going to be important to understand the needs and goals of the current IT professionals and to work to accommodate those needs and goals. Again, those needs and goals will change based upon changes in technology and on the pressures from competitors to lure the employees away.

It is critical in the development of a retention effort that someone remains in close contact with the IT employees and is alert to changing needs and interests. The absence of continuous, open communication within the department is going to create opportunities for people to be lured away.

Again, the issue of IT retention begins with the hiring process. Those items identified within the hiring model will lay the groundwork for a continuing employment relationship. The model works — it should be seen as the basis for not only successful hiring, but also for improved retention.

CONCLUSION

One way to view hiring and retention of IT personnel is to consider the process as a project. As with any project, success is dependent upon the ability to develop processes that work and, once developed, consistently adhere to those processes. Having developed a project approach provides the ability to install a hiring and retention model and to improve the IT success record.

Of course, circumstances are going to change over time and what works today may no longer be effective. Obviously, when that happens, it may be time to review the model and to make the appropriate changes. The technology- and money-related sections of the model will be the most likely to change. The idea is to remember that changes will occur and to be in position to shift the hiring criteria appropriately.

An important aspect of the hiring model is that it formalizes the process. Given that the model is used to address IT hiring issues, modifications can be made as changes occur within the industry. That ability allows the organization to remain current with whatever may be occurring within both the organization or the IT industry.

Following the usual hiring practices will not work in the pursuit of IT personnel. That is not to say that IT people will not be found and hired, but they are not likely to be the best candidates. Even when good hiring practices are in place and work well, finding IT candidates is expensive. In order to obtain the best return on the hiring investment, it is important to hire, and to retain, the best possible candidates.

The first step in the process, as is the case with any project, is to decide whether or not the organization is willing to make the commitment to develop a successful IT hiring and retention program. If the answer to that question is yes, the opportunity exists to make significant progress in a relatively short time.

While hiring IT candidates is expensive, moving to a more effective IT hiring process need not require additional expense. What it does require is the development of a particular culture within the organization, focused on the goal of attracting, hiring, and retaining high-quality IT professionals. Again, the idea of a model is an appropriate way to think about the issues involved. The points considered in this article cover the issues required to move to a strong IT hiring retention environment. This process has been tested and found to be very effective. Attracting and retaining high-quality IT people is a process that can be improved in any organization, whether or not that happens is up to those charged with the task.

Two IT hiring scenarios exist. A certain level of pain will be associated with either approach. Not making any changes to the current process will lessen the stress on the culture that would be associated with developing a new hiring model. The pain will be in the inability of the organization to find and retain high-quality IT people. Conversely, moving to the IT hiring model is going to create disruption. The benefit in moving to the new model will be the improvement of experience with IT hiring and retention.

It is in the best interest of every organization to find and retain high-quality IT people. Doing that may require change and it may cause some stress within the organization. Each organization must determine willingness to make the changes and to act or not as they deem appropriate.

Chapter 51

Training Options in a Technical Environment

Gilbert Held

The advent of client-server processing and the growth in the use of open-system technology resulted in most data centers using a wide mixture of hardware and software products. This, in turn, resulted in a dramatic change in the scope and depth of employee training requirements, as well as in options available to the data center operations manager (DCOM) to satisfy those requirements. By understanding the advantages and disadvantages associated with different training options, the DCOM can construct a training program that is best structured to meet the needs of the organization in a cost-effective manner. The objective of this article is to provide the DCOM with detailed information concerning viable training options that should be considered.

INTRODUCTION

Although there are literally hundreds of different types of training programs offered by thousands of vendors, these programs can be divided into six major categories. Major training method categories are listed in Exhibit 51.1, with the "technical seminar" entry further subdivided into two classifications that are discussed later in this article.

BOOK-BASED TRAINING

Even before vendors established formal training courses, they distributed equipment training manuals. Book-based training represents perhaps the oldest method used for training data center employees.

Since the 1950s, book-based training has significantly evolved, with formal "courseware" programs now being offered on a large number of topics. These programs allow employees to read the material at their own pace and usually include assignments that reinforce key topics. Some courseware programs are used by certification programs, which are described in the next section of this article. Other courseware programs may be developed by hardware and software vendors as instructional aids designed to enhance the ability of a person to use a specific product or to

0-8493-9822-3/00/$0.00+$.50

Exhibit 51.1. Training Method Categories

Book-based training
Certification program
Computer-based training (CBT)
College/university courses
Technical seminars
Public
Vendor developed
Video-based presentations

learn a specific subject (e.g., how to test a cable using the XYZ Corporation cable tester).

The key advantages of book-based training are its relatively low cost in comparison to other training methods and the fact that users can go through the material at their own pace.

The major disadvantages include (1) the fact that it is usually necessary to obtain a set of manuals for each employee, and (2) the lack of assistance when an employee has a question that is not answered by the material. To help with this problem, some courseware developers now provide a limited amount of telephone consultation via an 800 toll-free number, while other courseware developers offer assistance via a 900 number, which results in additional charges that can rapidly mount up as employee questions increase.

CERTIFICATION PROGRAMS

The rapid expansion of local area network (LAN) technology resulted in the recognition that new areas of vendor-specific information were required by hardware and software users. Several vendors attacked this problem by establishing certification programs that require trainees to complete a core curriculum of courses and pass one or more tests to be certified as "proficient."

The earliest certification programs required trainees to attend courses conducted by a specific vendor. Recognizing that the rapid expansion of LAN technology required a more flexible training schedule and location availability than could be offered by hardware and software developers, vendors considerably expanded their certification programs. Today, many resellers and third-party training organizations are licensed by hardware and software vendors to provide a core series of training necessary for persons to obtain a particular type of certification.

Exhibit 51.2 lists popular certification programs currently offered by six hardware and software vendors. Fields of specialization are commonly offered within each program, which results in a varying designation of the

Exhibit 51.2. Popular Vendor Certification Programs

Vendor	Program
Banyan	Certified Banyan Engineer
Compaq	Accredited System Engineer
IBM	Certified LAN Server Engineer
	Professional Systems Engineer
Lotus	Certified Lotus Professional
	Certified Lotus Instructor
Microsoft	Certified Systems Engineer
Novell	Certified Novell Engineer (CNE)
	Master CNE

program. For example, Lotus Education, which is now part of the IBM Corporation, offers five Certified Lotus Professional (CLP) programs. Those programs include:

- *Applications Developer.* Focused on the construction of a Lotus Notes Data base.
- *Principle Applications Developer.* Focused on constructing applications that require meshed data bases and linking to other tasks inside and outside of Notes.
- *System Administrator.* Focused on the installation, monitoring, maintenance, and operation of a Notes server.
- *Principle System.* Focused on the integration of administrator-communication product technology.
- *Certified cc:Mail.* Focused on the installation and specialist-operation of cc:Mail across multiple networks and hardware platforms.

In addition to the five CLP programs, Lotus also offers a Certified Lotus Instructor (CLI) program. This is the program that enables more than 50 Lotus Authorized Education Centers operated by third-party training organizations to offer CLP certification programs. Thus, the Lotus CLI represents a "train the trainer" program.

The key advantage of specialized certification programs is that they focus on a specific area or topic that is normally directly applicable to the training requirements of the organization. Other advantages include their availability and location. Most vendors have hundreds to thousands of authorized education centers located in most major metropolitan areas. This enables organizations to economize on travel costs. In addition, because of the popularity of many courses, they are offered frequently so that organizations can rapidly upgrade employee skills.

The two primary disadvantages associated with certification programs are their cost and the fact that after completing a program, the employee will have new marketable skills and may choose to seek work elsewhere.

Even without factoring in the cost of travel or salaries while employees are working in an authorized education center away from their jobs, costs can run between $10,000 and $30,000 for courses and examinations required to obtain certification in a particular area.

Employee mobility is another significant issue. The completion of many vendor certification programs is considered to represent a passport to new employment opportunities. With more than 100,000 LANs being installed on an annual basis and each network requiring a manager or administrator, Novell and Microsoft, as well as their authorized education centers, are capable of teaching just a small fraction of the administrators that business, academia, and government seek. This fact is easily verified by scanning the Help Wanted columns in the Sunday paper, particularly the advertisements for LAN administrators, and noting the certification credentials required.

Although it is often difficult to retain trained and knowledgeable personnel under the best of circumstances, the completion of a certification program can make it more difficult. One method that data center managers may wish to establish is a career ladder, which works in conjunction with the completion of the various stages of most certification programs. As milestones are reached, the employee can be given added responsibility as well as an increase in compensation. In addition to this "carrot," DCOMs may wish to examine corporate policy concerning the investment of a large expenditure of funds for a certification program. Some organizations now require persons enrolled in a certification program being paid for by the organization to agree to remain employed by the company for a defined period of time. That period is typically 1 year from the completion of the certification program; if the employee should leave earlier, he or she must reimburse the company for the cost of training. Although this policy can be considered to represent a "stick," some organizations now mesh the "carrot" and the "stick" together, adding responsibility and periodically increasing the compensation level of employees as they successfully move through a certification program while requiring the employee to agree to stay with the organization for at least a year after the program is completed.

COMPUTER BASED TRAINING

The personal computer can be considered the guiding force for the development of computer-based training (CBT). Although a few vendors prior to 1981 offered mainframe- and minicomputer-based courses of instruction, when a large number of vendors could afford personal computers, a mass market opened for CBT products. Today, companies can obtain courseware covering mainframe, communications and networking, programming, and a variety of other topics for both mainframe and client-server technology.

The key advantages of CBT include its general ability to be reused by more than one employee and the fact that training can take place on a flexible schedule. Concerning the reusability of CBT courses, many vendors license a course for use either on one computer or as a network version. When licensed for use on one computer, the license allows the software to be removed and used on a different computer. Thus, it becomes possible to amortize the cost of the CBT course over several employees; however, only one employee can legally use it at a time.

When a network version of a CBT course is obtained, multiple persons can use the course at the same time. However, license restrictions for a network-based CBT course usually prohibit its removal onto a laptop for an employee to use at home. In comparison, it is perfectly legal for an employee to use a CBT course at work and then remove the diskettes and take them home to use during the evening or on a weekend. Another advantage associated with CBT courses is the fact that they can be taken on site so that it is unnecessary for employees to travel. This type of training is relatively economical in comparison to training that requires employees to leave the office.

Disadvantages associated with CBT courses include an inability to ask questions about the material, the fact that the structure of some courses makes them awkward to take, and the scope and depth of the material. Fortunately, many CBT development vendors provide demonstration diskettes that will give an indication of the structure of a course as well as the scope and depth of the material. Because of the significant differences in quality between courses on the same topic, time spent previewing demonstration diskettes is highly worthwhile.

COLLEGE/UNIVERSITY COURSES

Both continuing education as well as regular college and university courses represent an excellent source for employee technical training. Unfortunately, a majority of technical courses offered by colleges and universities may not be directly applicable to the operational environment of an organization. However, many educational institutions have recognized the training requirements of business organizations and government agencies by considerably expanding their continuing education programs to cover a variety of PC-related topics, such as word processors, spreadsheets, and data base management programs.

Although there are many courses in programming, data base design, and similar topics that can be very beneficial for employees to apply to their work environment, many training topics necessary for operating a data center cannot usually be obtained from educational institutions. A few examples of such topics in specialized or recently evolving technologies include Web server design, programming in HyperText Markup Language

(HTML), mainframe operations, and a variety of LAN topics ranging in scope from NetWare administration and Windows NT server setup to router and bridge configuration. Employees requiring this kind of specialized training may have to consider one or more of the other training methods listed in Exhibit 51.1.

Some additional advantages associated with courses offered by educational institutions include evening sessions that facilitate after-hours employee attendance, regular scheduling of courses, and a professional instructional staff. As far as course scheduling is concerned, many educational institutions now recognize the business potential obtained by developing specialized courses that better reflect the technical training requirements of industry. Recently, several universities established degree programs for such topics as data communications and data base management.

Some of the disadvantages associated with training provided by educational institutions include scheduling and cost. For employees who travel frequently, it may be difficult to attend courses that meet on a defined schedule. As for cost, a three-credit course at some colleges now represents an expense of approximately $2000 for tuition. For these reasons, many organizations have shown a greater willingness to send employees to public and vendor-developed technical seminars.

TECHNICAL SEMINARS

Technical seminars represent one of the best methods of obtaining information on narrowly defined or rapidly evolving topics. In the U.S., there are more than 20 organizations that specialize in the development and presentation of technical seminars covering topics related to mainframes, PCs, and data communications. Such organizations range in scope from Amdahl and IBM Education Centers to Verhof, DataTech, Business Communications Review, The Learning Tree, and the American Research Group.

The major advantage associated with technical seminars is the fact that they often represent the only mechanism of obtaining training on rapidly evolving technology. Other advantages include their intensive presentation—typically over 2, 3, or 4 days — and the frequency with which they are offered plus the convenience of the training sites. It is often easier to send employees to a seminar and reschedule a portion of their work for part of a week than to attempt to modify their schedule so they can take a 3- or 4-hour class one day a week over the course of a semester. In addition, many seminar organizations schedule presentations in 10 or 20 major metropolitan areas, which can considerably reduce or eliminate travel expenses. This advantage can also represent the major disadvantage associated with technical seminars since they are usually presented over a period of 2 or

3 months on a rotating schedule that results in the presentation in different cities on different dates. This means that to minimize travel expenses, an employee may have to wait several months until the seminar is presented in the city where he or she works. Other disadvantages associated with technical seminars include the fact that if an insufficient number of persons register for the seminar, it will be canceled. The cost of specialized seminars can also be prohibitive. Costs typically range between $1000 for a 2-day course and $2000 for a 4-day seminar. Travel expenses for attending several seminars in distant cities can rapidly deplete an organization's training budget.

RECOMMENDED COURSE OF ACTION

There is no one best method for obtaining technical training for employees. Instead, a mixture of the six major training methods should be considered by the data center operations manager. By carefully considering the advantages and disadvantages associated with each training method and comparing them to the training requirements of employees, the manager can select the best methods for each situation. Considerations include the size of the training budget, employee availability for training, subject matter, and the time period during which the knowledge should be acquired.

Although training is costly, when organizations consider the alternative, which can be the inability to correct problems in a timely manner, install new hardware or software, or support the organization's evolving data processing and data communications requirements, properly selected training can be a bargain.

Chapter 52

A Worksheet for Goals and Skills Assessment

Kenneth P. Prager

IT departments are aligning with their companies much differently than they once did. Companies now change more frequently and view IT as a strategic resource — looking to IT not only for strategic advantage but also to contribute directly to the bottom line.

This changing strategic alignment is an external driver of internal IT change, creating the need for different mind-sets and behaviors from IT professionals. Today, managing an IT career requires more than mere technical excellence — which most corporate executives take as a given. IT professionals must align thinking and behaviors with corporate strategy, understand and manage a different set of expectations about what IT can and should deliver, and learn to build different kinds of working relationships throughout the company.

This article first explores how today's changing business environment affects IT professionals and then presents strategies for career management.

EFFECTS OF THE CHANGING BUSINESS CLIMATE

Today's IT professionals face a very different world than just a few years ago, when technology was a back-room operation supporting back-room business functions. Today, technology is a strategic resource helping organizations achieve goals and gain competitive advantage, and leading strategic change. Along with this new view of technology comes a new view of IT professionals evidenced by five interrelated factors that now influence their jobs:

- There are no guarantees.
- Technical excellence is not enough.
- Rapid and frequent change is a constant.
- Organizations are flatter.
- Companies are outsourcing the technical jobs.

0-8493-9822-3/00/$0.00+$.50

There Are No Guarantees

Many people remember when jobs were secure and companies were proud of never laying off their employees, but these conditions no longer exist. Today, most employees feel much less secure in their jobs. They watch companies merge, acquire, divest, downsize, reengineer, and generally try to survive more volatile marketplaces and regulatory environments. And they see how those survival tactics affect the people and jobs in their companies.

When jobs were secure, technology jobs were particularly secure because only the technologists understood the mysteries. However, many of today's executives understand more about technology, more about how technology can help them achieve corporate objectives, and more about how their competitors are using technology. Because these executives understand more, they expect more from IT people. Even those executives who are still mystified are no longer afraid to challenge IT professionals and demand more strategic use of technology. IT managers and professionals who fail to live up to these new expectations and challenges will find their careers in jeopardy.

Beyond Technical Expertise

As executives challenge IT, they are asking IT professionals to participate in creating business strategies and to fully understand existing and potential markets, regulatory environments, and competitive pressures. These executives no longer merely say, "We'll tell you what we need and you do it for us." They now ask IT professionals to "Help us figure out how we can use technology."

Clearly, these demands are driving the need for broad-based business knowledge, forcing technocrats out of their glass-walled inner sanctum into the heart of the business areas.

Living with Rapid and Frequent Change

Beyond understanding existing business and competitive drivers, today's IT professionals are surrounded by rapid and frequent changes in organizational direction. These directional changes force similar rapid and frequent changes in organizational strategy that subsequently force changes in organizational design and functioning. Even chief executive officers of major companies cannot always tell what businesses those companies might be in several years down the road.

However, those same executives still expect IT to "be there in time," no matter how quickly or how often they change strategies. So, IT people are often forced to rapidly change both IT infrastructure and applications.

Flattened Organizations

Another by-product of the recent years of downsizing and reengineering is the so-called flatter organization. In this model, employees throughout the organization work differently: They make decisions they did not make before, they connect across the organizational boundaries that once kept people isolated in functional areas, and they work cross-functionally on formal and informal teams. In flatter organizations, everyone learns everyone else's business, strategies, and goals.

These new work models demand new skills and competencies and make it impossible for IT managers and professionals to hide behind the technology mystique.

Outsourcing of Technical Jobs

As the IT professional's role becomes more strategic, and as flattened organizations have fewer technocrats to do the back-room functions, more of these functions are being outsourced. Increased outsourcing shifts the demand for the more technical jobs toward the outsourcing service providers.

This demand is not new. For years, systems consultants, systems integrators, and systems and programming contractors housed mostly technical positions. These firms served two different kinds of clients: smaller firms that did not need the skills full time, and larger firms that needed an extra pair of hands.

However, the changing strategic alignment of IT changes the way companies are using these outside resources. Today, many organizations expect their in-house technologists to learn the business of the business and help users determine the best use of technology. Organizations do not want in-house talent dedicated to long-term applications development, maintenance of existing systems, or version upgrades to system and application software packages. Therefore, companies are beginning to selectively outsource these functions.

MANAGING AN IT CAREER

This new era of strategic technology and rapidly changing, flatter organizations with no guarantees demands a new mind-set and new behaviors from IT professionals that fall into four broad categories:

- Align with strategy.
- Understand expectations.
- Build bridges.
- Measure up to new criteria.

Clearly, these new behaviors raise the bar for successful IT professionals because they are still primarily responsible for understanding technology and making it work. The new behaviors do not replace certain job requirements; they add to them. The following sections explore these four categories in more detail and describe the new behaviors in each.

Aligning with Strategy

"Alignment" is an often used, and often misunderstood, term that can mean either matching current goals or matching future direction. Current goals exist within the envelope of future direction, and, in a rapidly changing environment, IT should align with future direction rather than current goals. Aligning with current goals is short term and reactive and generally follows this formula: "Tell me your current goals and I'll match my IT strategy." Aligning with future direction is long term and proactive: "Together let's figure out how to use technology in whatever business we're going to be in."

For example, a company's current strategic goal might be to expand market share by acquiring companies in related businesses. Aligning with this fairly specific goal would drive fairly specific IT infrastructures and applications. However, this goal exists in an envelope of future direction driven by changes in external customers' directions, competitors' directions, regulatory direction, and corporate governance direction. A change in any of these future-direction drivers might lead a company to dramatically change its strategic goal. For instance, reacting to deregulation, a change in the regulatory future-direction driver, the company might change the goal to increase sales by looking for new products and services outside the business.

Aligning with these future-direction drivers and predicting changes in them would lead the IS manager to a more flexible IT strategy — resulting in more flexible infrastructures and applications that allow changes to current goals along the way. And thinking in terms of these future-direction drivers changes conversations. The IS manager or executive will talk with corporate executives about new revenue opportunities, cost pressures, marketplace intelligence, liability, regulatory issues, and strategies for long-term growth of the company and impact on shareholder value. Strategic conversations will not be about hardware or software upgrades, or a defense of IT's past contributions as a means for selling new IT ideas. One IT executive summarized this new behavior as follows: "In the past we had a technical focus with a business application. Today we need a business focus with a technical foundation."

The new behavior demands IT leaders with intimate business knowledge. And if technocrats are not able to live up to the demand, companies will find the knowledge elsewhere. There are many examples of CIOs of major companies who did not rise through IT. At lower levels, business analysts from the functional areas are often served by IT rather than promoted programmers.

The new mind-set and behavior also has major implications for the IT professional's skills and competencies. They demand more than technical competence — they demand the ability to discuss future direction with top corporate executives, business knowledge, an understanding of strategic thinking, and a philosophy of flexibility. Strategic thinking means that IT managers and professionals will continually ask "What businesses are we going to be in?" driving new and ever-changing conversations with their peers and executives throughout the company.

Understanding Expectations

Corporate executives have always expected IT professionals, particularly IT leaders, to have a technology vision. That is, executives have always expected IT professionals to keep abreast of major technological trends, watch competitive technology uses, and understand business processes to create the hardware and software infrastructures and applications that the business needs.

Today, however, executives expect more. They want the technology to be flexible enough to support constant and rapid business change. These expectations are driving a wider separation between infrastructure and application because the applications will come and go while infrastructure survives. Consequently, many technologists are focusing on flexible infrastructures while pushing applications out to the users and business units. Witness the move to client/server and desktop decision support based on the underlying data warehouses. And notice organizations with IT professionals reporting directly to business units instead of to centralized IT.

As this infrastructure/application split widens, IT professionals will need to help users understand the application development tools — at whatever level possible — and focus more on the hardware and software infrastructure issues. Indeed, many CIOs are already hiring infrastructure experts as new employees and are concerned about long-term employees still mired in traditional but diminishing applications development. The question these CIOs ask is, "What do I do with my veteran Cobol programmer who doesn't want to change?"

This shift in IT's work processes is consistent with another executive expectation that IT leaders facilitate technology throughout the organization — that they go out into the business units and functional areas and help non-IT leaders integrate technology. This expectation creates the need for even more new skills: communicating effectively, influencing peers, persuading others, and building consensus.

Facilitating technology integration is a 180-degree behavioral shift from the old world of controlling technology integration. Controlling means standardization; facilitating means flexibility and, at times, accepting nonstandard platforms. Controlling means that IT professionals design the application and then show users what they are being given. Facilitating means that IT professionals help the business units and functional areas create their own solutions and then integrate those solutions back to the central systems.

Building Bridges

Aligning with strategy and understanding expectations require IT professionals at all levels to build and maintain strong interpersonal relationships, particularly outside the IT department. IT professionals cannot think strategically or facilitate technology throughout the organization without relying on those relationships. Success will come as much or more from influence and persuasion as from technological savvy, and influence and persuasion are based on strong interpersonal relationships.

Although IT professionals need to build strong interpersonal relationships across the organization, it does not mean that they have any particular skill or experience at doing so. False starts at IT realignment and failed reorganization occur because no one built successful working relationships. As a result, IT professionals must learn new skills and reach out to proactively build these bridges.

Moving Out to Functional Areas. One way to begin is to change the traditional meeting between IT and business areas in which IT professionals ask about current needs, prioritize those current needs, and establish projects to meet those needs.

Instead, IT professionals should find a way to live in the functional areas — formally or informally. This means that they must spend a great deal of time following people around, asking them questions, engaging them in conversations, attending their staff meetings, and inviting them to lunch. These conversations should be about understanding the business process and where it is headed in order to strategically align with that business area. By understanding and exhibiting that understanding, IT professionals will gain the confidence of the business area leaders. The focus here is understanding where the functional area is headed by participating in predicting future direction.

After gaining that confidence, and after conversations about the direction of the business areas are commonplace, the IT manager or professional and the business area manager can jointly invent a future technology direction and both can actively participate in creating the business case. That is, IT professionals must first understand the business issues, the revenue possibilities, and the cost issues — both technical and nontechnical — so that together, the IT professional and the user can hammer out an appropriate ROI calculation. The traditional meetings between IT and business areas deal reactively with current needs and current goals. The approach described here proactively seeks future flexibility and strong working relationships with business areas.

Ensuring Rapid Deployment. Bridging one gap has been particularly troublesome. That gap is the time lag between when users need technology projects delivered and when IT can actually deliver them. Today, the tension is even greater because the need for strategic technology changes as quickly as the organizations' strategies change. In the past, IT professionals may have had one or two years to install and modify significant applications. Today, that time shrinks to as little as three to six months, forcing IT to work together with end users to install applications much more quickly. And both IT people and users are seeing that those applications have shorter useful lives than in the past.

One way to accomplish this rapid deployment is to find a department to test market an application early in the development process. Together, IT professionals and that department should develop a mini-application showing whether there are actual strategic benefits, and how much those benefits are. This test marketing is not new: It resembles prototyping or phased implementation. However, the practice may be crucial in today's fast-changing organizational world and is applied differently. Prototyping and phased implementation both imply that all affected business areas will eventually implement the application. Test marketing is just that. The organization can cut its losses after the initial installation if it finds no strategic benefits.

Another way to build bridges is to stop trying to sell technology ideas to management — a word the author of this article frequently hears from many IT executives. Today's expectations run counter to a selling relationship and instead dictate educating, leading, and coaching relationships. Selling implies an arm's-length, self-protective relationship. Educating, leading, and coaching imply working closely together toward common goals.

Consequently, bridge-building behaviors are those that help the IT professional align with strategy and understand expectations: living in functional areas, jointly discovering technology direction, working together for rapid deployment, allying early for strategic benefit, and educating rather than selling.

Measuring Up to New Criteria

All the behavioral changes described so far, of course, affect performance criteria. Job evaluations deal more openly with soft skill items as companies expect their IT people to work differently. The clear theme in these new feedback and performance review processes is that today's business executives expect IT professionals to develop the same soft skills as non-IT professionals. That is, organizations that once accepted IT behaviors different from organizational norms no longer will.

For instance, in one company, technology managers are assigned to cross-functional coaching teams. These teams meet several times each year to review how well the technology manager is meeting expectations and working cross-functionally. Although not yet part of the formal evaluation and review process, cross-functional coaching is one way that this organization is trying to change how technologists are measured.

Similar to cross-functional coaching is business unit review. Here, business unit managers regularly feed back to IT and review performance — a practice intended to measure how well IT is meeting the needs of the user community.

The 360 review process is also gaining popularity. Here, employees receive feedback from their managers, peers, subordinates, and sometimes external customers. The feedback is often used as part of larger coaching and management development programs intended to help people manage more effectively.

Highlighting these new measurement criteria are new formal evaluation and review forms at several different organizations. In these new-behavior IT departments, staff is measured against words such as communication, customer focus, initiative, judgment, learning orientation, self-confidence, vision and direction, tenacity, drive for change, building ownership, making tough decisions, global awareness, critical thinking, forward thinking. out-of-the-box thinking, profit focus, interpersonal astuteness, getting organizational support, managing external relationships, developing others, attention to detail, collaboration, professionalism, results, attitude, coaching, responsiveness, cross-functional drive, and energy.

Here again are the double pressures of today's IT job: companies expecting superb technical skill while measuring against criteria well beyond it. The double pressures are necessary, however, because it is not just technical skill that spells success. It is also the new set of behavioral skills that will better help the organization achieve its strategies, goals, and future direction.

ASSESSING PERSONAL PROGRESS

Managing an IT career in today's business world means looking beyond just being a really good technician. To succeed, IT professionals must achieve the following competencies:

- Learn how to think and act strategically using technology for bottom-line results and to support future direction.
- Understand new expectations from the other managers and executives to whom IT professionals will reach out to educate, lead, and coach.
- Learn to build bridges and proactively manage successful interpersonal relationships.
- Recognize the new performance criteria growing out of the new demands — performance criteria that go well beyond just being technically good.

Managing an IT career means mastering these skills. They are what companies now need and actively seek. In the absence of guaranteed employment, IT professionals must make themselves eminently employable either inside or outside their current organization.

IT professionals who wish to see where they stand should fill in the self-administered alignment measurement presented in Exhibit 52.1. It is derived from the *Organizational Flexibility Profile®*, an organizational behavioral assessment developed by Riverton Management Consulting Group, Inc. Exhibit 52.2 contains a scoring matrix.

Score Interpretation

Low scores in the subcategories indicate concentration is needed on the following activities.

Match Belief Sets. The IT professional should discuss the company's vision, mission, values, and philosophy with superiors, peers, and subordinates, whether they are written down or not. It is important to observe and decide whether behavior matches philosophy — whether employees, particularly the IT professional, walk the talk.

Align with Strategy. The IT professional should find more and more frequent opportunities to talk with those responsible for corporate strategy and direction. Strategic initiatives should be discussed with superiors, peers, and subordinates. The IT professional's own job responsibilities and authorities should be linked with company strategy and with the company's external customers. If it is not linked, more serious conversations with superiors as to why they are not linked are warranted.

Understand Expectations. For many employees, only a supervisor evaluates job performance. The IT professional should seek feedback from peers, subordinates, and internal customers — and even try to make this part of the formal evaluation process. IT people should go beyond getting job instructions and information just from a boss; they should seek and

Exhibit 52.1. Personal Alignment Questionnaire

1.The basic theme or message of the company's philosophy matches your personal philosophy. ***(Mark one with "X")*** ***(16)***

9) ______ very strongly agree
8) ______ strongly agree
7) ______ somewhat agree
6) ______ sometimes agree, sometimes disagree
5) ______ somewhat disagree
4) ______ strongly disagree
3) ______ very strongly disagree
2) ______ does not apply
1) ______ do not know

2.You know what you need to know about your company's strategy in order to do your job effectively. ***(Mark one with "X")*** ***(20)***

9) ______ very strongly agree
8) ______ strongly agree
7) ______ somewhat agree
6) ______ sometimes agree, sometimes disagree
5) ______ somewhat disagree
4) ______ strongly disagree
3) ______ very strongly disagree
2) ______ does not apply
1) ______ do not know

3.Which one of the following phrases best describes the authority and responsibility you typically have in your job? ***(Mark one with "X")*** ***(0)***

8) ______ develop directions and decisions based on strategic guidelines
7) ______ develop directions and decisions based on your superiors' input
6) ______ help develop and shape directions and decisions
5) ______ modify your superiors' directions and decisions as needed
4) ______ provide input to your superiors for their decisions
3) ______ provide feedback to your superiors about your results
2) ______ follow the directions of your superiors
1) ______ do not know

4.Who typically evaluates you for your appraisal/performance review? ***(Mark <u>all that apply</u> with "X")*** ***(0)***

1) ______ immediate supervisor
1) ______ other functional supervisors
1) ______ superior(s) in other functions
1) ______ functional subordinates
1) ______ other function's subordinates
1) ______ functional peers
1) ______ other function's peers
1) ______ external customers
0) ______ does not apply
0) ______ do not know

5.Which of the following phrases describes what your salary increases are based on? ***(Mark one with "X")*** ***(0)***

9) ______ your ideas and suggestions for improvement
8) ______ developing and shaping directions and decisions based on your superiors' input
7) ______ helping develop and shape directions and decisions
6) ______ modifying your superiors' directions and decisions as needed
5) ______ providing input to your superiors for their decisions
4) ______ providing feedback to your superiors about your results
3) ______ following the directions of your superiors
2) ______ does not apply
1) ______ do not know

Exhibit 52.1 (Continued). Personal Alignment Questionnaire

6. My performance-based salary increases strongly reflect the results of my performance appraisal. ***(Mark one with "X")*** *(31)*

8) ______ very strongly agree
7) ______ strongly agree
6) ______ somewhat agree
5) ______ sometimes agree, sometimes disagree
4) ______ somewhat disagree
3) ______ strongly disagree
2) ______ very strongly disagree
1) ______ do not know

7. My **supervisor has** the information and knowledge I need to do my job. ***(Mark one with "X")*** *(38)*

8) ______ very strongly agree
7) ______ strongly agree
6) ______ somewhat agree
5) ______ sometimes agree, sometimes disagree
4) ______ somewhat disagree
3) ______ strongly disagree
2) ______ very strongly disagree
1) ______ do not know

8. **I get the information** I need to do my job from my supervisor. ***(Mark one with "X")*** *(39)*

8) ______ very strongly agree
7) ______ strongly agree
6) ______ somewhat agree
5) ______ sometimes agree, sometimes disagree
4) ______ somewhat disagree
3) ______ strongly disagree
2) ______ very strongly disagree
1) ______ do not know

9. My **peers and others within my company have** the information and knowledge I need to do my job. ***(Mark one with "X")*** *(40)*

8) ______ very strongly agree
7) ______ strongly agree
6) ______ somewhat agree
5) ______ sometimes agree, sometimes disagree
4) ______ somewhat disagree
3) ______ strongly disagree
2) ______ very strongly disagree
1) ______ do not know

10. **I get the information** I need to do my job from my peers and others within the company. ***(Mark one with "X")*** *(41)*

8) ______ very strongly agree
7) ______ strongly agree
6) ______ somewhat agree
5) ______ sometimes agree, sometimes disagree
4) ______ somewhat disagree
3) ______ strongly disagree
2) ______ very strongly disagree
1) ______ do not know

11. In your company, employees have easy access to any information within the company that they need to improve doing their job. ***(Mark one with "X")*** *(48)*

8) ______ very strongly agree
7) ______ strongly agree
6) ______ somewhat agree
5) ______ sometimes agree, sometimes disagree
4) ______ somewhat disagree
3) ______ strongly disagree
2) ______ very strongly disagree
1) ______ do not know

12. When employees change jobs within the company, they know what they must do to perform well in the new job. ***(Mark one with "X")*** *(50)*

8) ______ very strongly agree
7) ______ strongly agree
6) ______ somewhat agree
5) ______ sometimes agree, sometimes disagree
4) ______ somewhat disagree
3) ______ strongly disagree
2) ______ very strongly disagree
1) ______ do not know

Exhibit 52.1 (Continued). Personal Alignment Questionnaire

13. In your job, functional area, or team, you are always aware of how satisfied your internal customers are. ***(Mark one with "X")*** *(53)*

9) ______ very strongly agree
8) ______ strongly agree
7) ______ somewhat agree
6) ______ sometimes agree, sometimes disagree
5) ______ somewhat disagree
4) ______ strongly disagree
3) ______ very strongly disagree
2) ______ does not apply
1) ______ do not know

14. In your company, you are always aware of how satisfied your external customers are. ***(Mark one with "X")*** *(56)*

9) ______ very strongly agree
8) ______ strongly agree
7) ______ somewhat agree
6) ______ sometimes agree, sometimes disagree
5) ______ somewhat disagree
4) ______ strongly disagree
3) ______ very strongly disagree
2) ______ does not apply
1) ______ do not know

15. When individuals in your company disagree with each other, usually: ***(Mark one with "X")*** *(0)*

8) ______ both try to integrate their ideas
7) ______ both find a way to reach consensus
6) ______ both try to compromise
5) ______ they resort to the formal dispute resolution program
4) ______ one concedes to the other
3) ______ one dominates the other
2) ______ one avoids the other
1) ______ do not know

16. The behavior of your company's executive management team is consistent with the **company's philosophy** as you understand it. ***(Mark one with "X")*** *(67)*

8) ______ very strongly agree
7) ______ strongly agree
6) ______ somewhat agree
5) ______ sometimes agree, sometimes disagree
4) ______ somewhat disagree
3) ______ strongly disagree
2) ______ very strongly disagree
1) ______ do not know

17. The behavior of your company's middle managers is consistent with the company's philosophy. ***(Mark one with "X")*** *(68)*

8) ______ very strongly agree
7) ______ strongly agree
6) ______ somewhat agree
5) ______ sometimes agree, sometimes disagree
4) ______ somewhat disagree
3) ______ strongly disagree
2) ______ very strongly disagree
1) ______ do not know

18. The behavior of your company's employees is consistent with the company's philosophy. ***(Mark one with "X")*** *(69)*

8) ______ very strongly agree
7) ______ strongly agree
6) ______ somewhat agree
5) ______ sometimes agree, sometimes disagree
4) ______ somewhat disagree
3) ______ strongly disagree
2) ______ very strongly disagree
1) ______ do not know

Exhibit 52.1 (Continued). Personal Alignment Questionnaire

19. The behavior of your company's executives is consistent with the behaviors needed to successfully execute the **strategic plan.** ***(Mark one with "X")*** *(70)*

8) ______ very strongly agree	4) ______ somewhat disagree
7) ______ strongly agree	3) ______ strongly disagree
6) ______ somewhat agree	2) ______ very strongly disagree
5) ______ sometimes agree, sometimes disagree	1) ______ do not know

20. The behavior of your company's middle managers is consistent with the behaviors needed to successfully execute the strategic plan. ***(Mark one with "X")*** *(71)*

8) ______ very strongly agree	4) ______ somewhat disagree
7) ______ strongly agree	3) ______ strongly disagree
6) ______ somewhat agree	2) ______ very strongly disagree
5) ______ sometimes agree, sometimes disagree	1) ______ do not know

21. The behavior of your company's employees is consistent with the behaviors needed to successfully execute the strategic plan. ***(Mark one with "X")*** *(72)*

8) ______ very strongly agree	4) ______ somewhat disagree
7) ______ strongly agree	3) ______ strongly disagree
6) ______ somewhat agree	2) ______ very strongly disagree
5) ______ sometimes agree, sometimes disagree	1) ______ do not know

22. Employees receive the training and instruction necessary to do the job properly. ***(Mark one with "X")*** *(121)*

8) ______ very strongly agree	4) ______ somewhat disagree
7) ______ strongly agree	3) ______ strongly disagree
6) ______ somewhat agree	2) ______ very strongly disagree
5) ______ sometimes agree, sometimes disagree	1) ______ do not know

23. Employees are well trained and prepared for job changes as they occur. ***(Mark one with "X")*** *(122)*

8) ______ very strongly agree	4) ______ somewhat disagree
7) ______ strongly agree	3) ______ strongly disagree
6) ______ somewhat agree	2) ______ very strongly disagree
5) ______ sometimes agree, sometimes disagree	1) ______ do not know

24. Most employees like the jobs they do. ***(Mark one with "X")*** *(123)*

8) ______ very strongly agree	4) ______ somewhat disagree
7) ______ strongly agree	3) ______ strongly disagree
6) ______ somewhat agree	2) ______ very strongly disagree
5) ______ sometimes agree, sometimes disagree	1) ______ do not know

25. Most employees feel the company has a good future. ***(Mark one with "X")*** *(124)*

8) ______ very strongly agree	4) ______ somewhat disagree
7) ______ strongly agree	3) ______ strongly disagree
6) ______ somewhat agree	2) ______ very strongly disagree
5) ______ sometimes agree, sometimes disagree	1) ______ do not know

Exhibit 52.1 (Continued). Personal Alignment Questionnaire

26. Most employees feel this is a good place to work. ***(Mark one with "X")*** *(125)*

8) ______ very strongly agree	4) ______ somewhat disagree
7) ______ strongly agree	3) ______ strongly disagree
6) ______ somewhat agree	2) ______ very strongly disagree
5) ______ sometimes agree, sometimes disagree	1) ______ do not know

confirm that information from others throughout the company, and from external customers if possible.

Build Bridges. It is vital to establish strong working relationships with internal customers, to share information readily with them, and to encourage them to do likewise. The IT professional should seek feedback from those internal customers and learn how to resolve operating differences both inside and outside the IT department by striving for consensus, compromise, and integrating ideas for better solutions.

Perform to New Criteria. IT professionals should expand their authority and responsibility by demonstrating that job duties are consistent with corporate strategy and that their job goes beyond technical prowess to organizational effectiveness. They should ensure that their performance evaluation criteria are consistent with corporate strategy and that they are behaving consistently with those criteria and that strategy.

Seek Employability. It is important to try to understand corporate strategies and how they contribute to a company's success or failure in the marketplace. IT professionals should seek more authority and responsibility in the job and make sure that this authority and responsibility will expand the soft-side skills set. Training should be sought for a current job and for potential new jobs inside and outside the department and company — particularly for the nontechnical skills needed to better relate across the organization.

RECOMMENDED COURSE OF ACTION

It is important to remember that IT professionals face a very different world today than they did just a few years ago, when IT was essentially a boiler-room operation. The IT professional and the IT department must be prepared to participate fully in helping the organization achieve strategic change, even, in many cases, leading the way. If the questions in the self-assessment have been answered honestly and resulting scores are low, the time has come to reevaluate the job situation.

Exhibit 52.2. Scoring

Overall Alignment	Match Belief Sets	Align with Strategy	Understand Expectations	Build Bridges	Perform to New Criteria	Seek Employability
1	1					
2		2				2
3		3			3	3
4			4		4	
5					5	
6			6		6	
7			7			
8			8			
9			9	9		
10			10	10		
11			11	11		
12			12			12
13			13	13	13	
14		14	14		14	
15				15	15	15
16	16					
17	17					
18	18					
19		19			19	
20		20			20	
21		21			21	
22			22		22	22
23			23			23
24	24				24	
25	25	25				
26	26				26	
Total	Total	Total	Total	Total	Total	Total
Midpt 119	Midpt 32	Midpt 32.5	Midpt 54.5	Midpt 23	Midpt 59.5	Midpt 27.5
Range 25–213	Range 7–57	Range 7–58	Range 11–98	Range 5–41	Range 12–107	Range 6–49

Chapter 53

Project Teamwork: How To Make It Happen

James R. Coleman

There is a great deal of emphasis on the need for teamwork. It should be on the need for *good* teamwork. If a project requires a variety of skills, has multiple tasks, and shared resources, it usually involves several individuals working together to accomplish it. If the job eventually gets done, then teamwork of some variety has happened. The question is "How well did they work together?"

To determine if teamwork is effective, the following questions should be asked:

- Was the work accomplished in the minimum amount of time, with the resources available?
- Did the individuals performing each task have all information, tools, or material available to them when they needed it?
- Was there any uncertainty on the part of the team members about who was responsible for what?
- Did the individual elements fit together nicely the first time, or was a lot of rework required?
- Were formal team meetings confined to quick status reports, news essential to the entire team, and issues appropriate for group discussion, such as development of high-level specifications?
- Did the project require very little management intervention?
- Did the work meet the goals of the project?

If the answer to any of these questions is no, then the teamwork needs to be improved. Think about last two or three projects done by the team. How do they stack up?

THE THREE ESSENTIAL ELEMENTS

Three activities where astonishing levels of teamwork are common have been studied. They are aircrew coordination on an antisubmarine warfare aircraft, professional motor racing teams, and team sports at the college and professional level.

0-8493-9822-3/00/$0.00+$.50

Crew interaction on an antisubmarine warfare aircraft is one of the most dramatic examples of teamwork ever observed. The aircraft is required to operate at dangerously low altitudes, performing a series of aggressive maneuvers, for long periods of time. Data from multiple sensors must be received, logged, and processed. Decisions have to be made and actions taken. Delays of a few seconds make the difference between a successful mission and lost contact.

What is remarkable is not that this is routinely done well, but that it is was done well by hundreds of crews, with whatever individuals are assigned. Equally remarkable is the fact that individual members can be replaced without seriously degrading the performance of the crew. Somehow, the skills of the group can be maintained in an environment of constantly changing personnel.

In the case of the racing teams and organized sports, one member of the team usually gets all the headlines (drivers, quarterbacks). However, it is inevitably the group that executes the best as a team that enjoys the most success. How many people remember the name of the quarterback for the University of Nebraska during the past NCAA football season, yet Nebraska thoroughly trounced Tennessee and superstar Peyton Manning to win the national championship. It was able to do this because it was better as a team at executing the plays.

These activities represent the achievement of very high levels of teamwork, but they largely depend on repetitive drill for developing it. The luxury of constant drill is not available in the business world. However, there are three elements common to all these teams that define why they work so well; which can use project managers to improve the teamwork in their own projects.

The three essential elements of good teamwork are

- Each member of the team must thoroughly understand the process and the relationships of the individual parts of the process to each other.
- All members of the team must be adequately skilled in their function or part of the process.
- Each member of the team must be committed to the success of the team as a whole rather than to success as individuals.

When these elements exist, uncertainty largely disappears.

UNDERSTANDING THE PROCESS

Understanding the process is not easy. It requires careful analysis. Fortunately, in the case of repetitive processes, if the work is done well, it only has to be done once. Remember, everything else depends on how well the manager and all the team members understand the process.

This is the point where most businesses fail in their effort to improve teamwork. Excuses given for not properly analyzing and specifying development processes are usually some variation of "We don't have time for that." A better statement of why process design is poorly done would be "We don't know how." That situation is at least correctable. A full course on process design is beyond the scope of this article, but, since it is fundamental to achieving teamwork, at least a look at the basics is worthwhile.

Every process consists of three parts, inputs, a transform, and outputs. Each input has to come from somewhere and contain certain items. The transform operates on those items and turns them into something else (outputs). The outputs have to go somewhere and are required to contain certain data, information, or material.

Most processes can be further broken down into subprocesses. The trick is to break them down *properly.* The breakdown should be according to function, not organizational department. Most process designs require at least three levels of breakdown. Very seldom will even the most complex processes require as many as five levels. It is easy to get carried away with breaking down the process. If it is getting out of hand, it would probably be a good idea to rethink the way the process has been partitioned. As a general rule, process breakdown should continue until each subprocess is easily accomplished by one individual or small task group.

The function of each process or subprocess should be clearly stated, but it would be a mistake to be specific about *how* the transformation is done. This allows the individual or group responsible to create and change procedures as necessary to fit their situation. Each individual subprocess should appear as a black box to the rest of the system. This means that, as long as the input or output structures are not affected, the specific procedures for the transform can be changed and revisedwithout affecting any other part of the system.

The form and content of the inputs and outputs should be specified *explicitly.* Identify the direct and ultimate sources and destinations of the material. While it is easy to get carried away with breaking down the process, it is almost impossible to overdo the documentation of inputs and outputs.

Processes can be diagrammed in a number of ways. *Remember,* the objective is to enable those who are is given the responsibility for one part of the process to understand exactly what they are supposed to accomplish, where the needed input is coming from, what form the input will have, where the output is supposed to go, and what form that output needs to have.

The best way to develop a good process design is to involve those who will eventually be assigned to projects. These are the professionals who understand what is necessary for the development project to be successful. It is highly unlikely that one individual could create a good process design without utilizing the knowledge and experience of all the professional resources available.

TRAINING TEAM MEMBERS

Once a good process design document exists, it is relatively easy to train the personnel. They need to be trained to do three things:

- Understand the process as a whole, and how their work fits into it;
- Trust their teammates;
- Do their job first, and then make themselves available to help anywhere else they are needed.

Process Training

Plan your training to ensure *understanding* of the process. This understanding is, after all, the key to making it work. Remember that this is training in the process, not specific disciplines. The manager is trying to give the team members a project organizational structure that will allow them to do their best work.

Training to Trust

Training people to trust their teammates takes a little more thought. Most people are reluctant to believe that the process will truly function as designed. This lack of confidence usually is the result of experience with poorly organized teams. This is not due to any character flaws in the personnel, but is usually a self-defense behavior. In teams where process is poorly defined and teamwork is poorly understood, the natural tendency is either to try to control as much of the activity as possible or to try to shift any blame to another area. Show the team members that the objective of the process design is to define individual responsibility clearly.

The key is to emphasize that *everyone* have a clear understanding of what is required. Point out that as long as everyone performs his or her individual function, the process as a whole will work well. If it does not, it is probably the fault of the process design, not the individual. Most people will be happy to concentrate their efforts on their function once uncertainty is eliminated.

Training in *How* to Assist Others

When people realize they are being evaluated as a team, it is not difficult to get them to help each other. There are two problems that usually happen here. First, there is a tendency to meddle instead of assist, and, second, there is often a reluctance to do menial work. Preventing these can be more difficult than might be imagined.

Point out that the objective is to assist where needed, not to take control of other functions. In most cases, the need for assistance falls in the category of simple administrative help or legwork. These things are not perceived as heroic efforts, but they are just as essential as anything else. Emphasize how they can free up time for a teammate to apply specialized skills to the core problem. Teach them that assistance in specialized skills areas should be given *only* when it is requested and *only* when they are fully qualified to give it.

In the case where a more experienced or knowledgeable person is assisting one who is not at the same level, it is certainly appropriate to share experience and knowledge. However, this must be done in an attitude of teaching or coaching instead of simply taking over the work. The most experienced people should be given a little special training in how to do this. Ensure that they understand the difference between valuable assistance and destructive meddling.

GETTING THE REQUIRED COMMITMENT

The key to obtaining commitment is making the team members understand that they will be evaluated only as a team, not as individuals. In fact, individual performance simply does not matter if the team as a whole does not perform well.

Once this has been said, it is important to be consistent in applying it. It is also essential that management understand this philosophy and is willing to back it up. *Only when people understand that they are being measured as a team will they start performing like one.* This sounds like common sense, but it is the second most common cause of teamwork failures. Under no circumstances, should a manager single out an individual for praise or criticism. All team members must be treated as equally important. If the process is well designed, all functions are part of an essential chain. Even if the most mundane function fails, the effort of the entire team is compromised.

Expect a fair amount of uneasiness about this method of evaluation. No matter how often it is said that this is the way it will be done (and it should be said often), managers will have to prove that they really mean it.

WHAT ABOUT THE "NON-TEAM-PLAYERS"?

Undoubtedly, there will be one or two individuals who simply do not function well in a team environment. Unfortunately, these people tend to be either very experienced, or very skilled in what they do. If this happens, find some other way to use their talents. If you leave these individuals in the team during the formative stages of teamwork attitudes, they will guarantee failure. If their skill set is essential, try to use them as an internal technical consultant, but do not make them responsible for any functions. These people are usually very valuable to an organization. Do not waste them! Just do not let them get in the way of developing effective teamwork.

PUTTING IT ALL TOGETHER

This article is about developing teamwork, not about project management. However, teamwork has no value unless it is applied. With this in mind, how to manage a project will be touched on briefly.

The trick is to *make the project plan match the process design*. This sound obvious, but, more often than not, project plans are organized by department and tend to be very linear. A great deal of effort went into to analyzing and specifing the process; use the work!

Gantt and PERT charts are wonderful tools, but they have serious limits. It will be found that the process design creates a large number of dependencies, and some things will probably have to be blocked. It may be necessary to have a few tasks that include more than one function. Most of the common project management software is going to be difficult to use — not impossible, but difficult. Just make sure that the plan does not conflict with the process design.

Concentrate on ensuring that the requirements of the process inputs and outputs are met. Do not worry too much about discontinuities in the project plan. If the process design is good and the team members are properly trained, the project will be completed in just about the minimum time anyway.

WHERE TO GET HELP

With all of this information, why would help be needed? The answer is because this article touched only lightly on some very important technical areas.

First, if readers are new to some of these ideas and cannot find help within their organization, they should *get some outside help!* A good consultant can save immense amounts of money and time. More importantly, they will prevent mistakes that will cause the initial effort to fail. There probably will not be a second chance. Here are a few things to look for in selecting a consultant:

- Find one with some background in both structured design and leadership development.
- Beware of consultants who are too attached to any particular buzzwords. This usually indicates a lack of flexibility.

- Look for a consultant who approaches this type of situation as a teacher. The manager is going to have to continue this work long after the consultant has collected his or her check and gone.
- Beware of anyone who claims to be able to solve all the problems. Such individuals tend to rely on "canned" solutions that may or may not be appropriate to the organization.
- If a consultant is hired, work together. Managers should make sure that they and their management are committed to the effort.

For internal help in process design, look in the IT or systems engineering departments. There is likely to be someone with knowledge of structured systems design. The techniques of that discipline will provide an excellent framework for doing the process analysis. Some modification of the specifics is necessary, but the principles are the same.

DOES THIS REALLY WORK?

In terms of the original set of questions for evaluating teamwork, how will these techniques help?

- Was the work accomplished in the minimum amount of time, given the resources available?
  If the process design is good, it will eliminate uncertainty and enhance communication. It also defines precisely what work has to be done. If the project plan matches the process, all the work will be done and in just about the minimum amount of time.
- Did the individuals performing each task have all the information, tools, or data available to them when they needed it?
  This is a function of the design and adherence to it.
- Was there any uncertainty on the part of the team members about who was responsible for what?
  The process design explicitly defines what functions are required. All that is necessary to do is assign responsibility by function.
- Did the individual elements fit together nicely the first time, or was a great deal of rework necessary for the project to make sense?
  The process design defines the required interfaces.
- Were formal team meetings confined to quick status reports, news essential to the entire team, or issues appropriate for group discussion, such as development of high-level specifications or functional baselines?
  Once the higher-level issues of the project are decided, the ususal purpose of formal meetings is to maintain communication. With a good process design, communication is a provided for by the input and output specifications. Uncertainty is eliminated, interfaces are defined, and points of coordination are right there for all to see. Formal meetings

may then be used simply for short status updates, or to pass along information useful to the team as a whole.

- Did the project require very little management intervention?
  Beginning to get the idea?
- Did the work meet the goals of the project?
  Adherence to the process design will ensure the project goals are met.

Section X Checklist

1. Which Human Resource issues are the most challenging to your IS environment?
2. Would you support licensing and/or accreditation programs for software professionals? If so, would this improve skills?
3. Do you think that managing today's IS professional is more difficult than ten years ago? If so, why?
4. Does your organization embrace newer methods for work such as telecommuting and flexible work weeks? If so, has this been successful?
5. Should IS professionals be given more latitude in their work based on the technology used in the IS environment?
6. What is your organization's turnover rate? Do you expect programmers to come and go or is that just a myth supported by employment agencies?
7. How much effort should an organization extend to retain qualified professionals? At what cost does this make business sense?
8. In your opinion, should an organization or an individual be responsible for the ongoing training of IS professionals?
9. Should organizations train staff members on future technology in order to build newer systems or train on current technology to extend the benefits of existing software?
10. How would you describe the communication between departments in your organization? Does this communication aid or inhibit software development?
11. Does your organization use methodologies such as Joint Application Development (JAD) to help improve communication between end users and developers?
12. In your opinion, should IS staff learn to speak the business of the company in order to be effective? If so, how is that accomplished?
13. What steps does your organization take to improve overall communication between departments?
14. How do you plan to keep your technical and professional skills updated? Do you have an action plan?
15. Have you ever assessed your own technical skills or completed a skills inventory for yourself? If not, how do decide which technical areas are important for you to continue learning?

Section XI
Supporting Existing Software

Support of existing software remains a rudimentary part of the application system life cycle. Dismissing program maintenance as merely software fixes would be impractical and unwise. Most reported maintenance activity, excluding the Year 2000 date conversion, is not corrective in nature but rather modifications or enhancements which result from changes to business environments.

Enduring the demands of system support has been a hardship for many managers. Although some may argue otherwise, maintaining aging "legacy" systems is often perceived as an unrewarding, and frustrating process. Even maintenance of newer systems, written in the microcomputer environment, poses a motivational challenge for programming staff. Justifying the true cost of support, either in savings or expense, has further added to the burden of maintenance efforts. Various approaches to the maintenance process, including management and technical techniques, continue to improve the success of overall support. However, rigorous challenges still exist and most organizations rely heavily on the maintainability of mission critical applications for business survival.

Extending the useful life of existing software applications is often prudent and economically wise. Unlike the necessary modification for the year 2000 date changes, there can be beneficial reasons to keep mission critical systems in production. Chapter 54, "Refurbishing Legacy Systems: An Effective Approach to Maintenance," discusses the options and opportunities to invigorate the support process through various methodologies. Development managers may want to explore the many ways that these methods can help coalesce disparities between supporting legacy systems and new applications built with different technologies. This chapter offers insight on how to correctly target and identify legacy systems that once refurbished, can still provide a return on investment.

Given the pace of software and hardware advances, it should follow that programmer productivity has grown equally fast. This is not the case, because for many new applications being developed, there is one constraint — it must plug into an established world of corporate data and the processes that manage them. For many companies, the processes that manage their enterprise data were written at least 10 to 15 years ago. Rewriting legacy systems would solve the technology gap experienced today, but the cost and risks are usually too great. Chapter 55, "Interfacing Legacy Applications with RDMSs and Middleware," outlines some options available for interfacing legacy systems with the latest technology, enabling a company to continue to compete in a rapidly changing field.

It is doubtful that software support will ever be eliminated from the list of responsibilities performed by IS departments. However, over time, the level of effort required to maintain any given application should diminish as older code is replaced with higher quality programs. The current popularity of migrating long-standing applications to newer platforms and languages is a serious undertaking. In Chapter 56, "Critical Success Factors in Reengineering Legacy Systems," a comprehensive review of key elements for system redeployment is presented. Consideration should be given for an integrated approach to reengineering that includes methodologies, procedures, and tools.

Another strategy to ease support efforts is presented in Chapter 57, "A Systems Approach to Software Maintenance." Unlike development, formal methods for support and maintenance are less publicized and often ignored. Part of the reason lies in the nature of support activities, which at times, can be unpredictable and unplanned. But in many instances, this does not have to be the case. Using a formal request process, coupled with more formal planning, maintenance, and support tasks can be less stressful and more productive for an organization. Development managers should be aware that the same planning issues for new development can also be applied to support of exiting systems. This can improve staff morale and provide a more consistent approach to planning activities in both development and support projects.

Chapter 54
Refurbishing Legacy Systems: An Effective Approach to Maintenance

William F. Lenihan

In its effort to support the business need for more information to be available in less time, the IS department has implemented a variety of proprietary technologies, developed new systems, and added capabilities to existing ones. The amount of systems integration, development, and maintenance activity required to satisfy these demands has left IS with little time to properly care for the base of old and rapidly aging systems. These legacy systems are often in a state of disrepair, suffering from the use of outmoded technologies and years of changes at the hands of different IS personnel who used different programming styles and formats. For many companies, these systems have been left to age with few (if any) improvements to the program structure, complexity, or hardware and software technologies.

Currently, however, the IS department's new directives are to reduce cost and improve financial performance. Departmental budgets are being cut, business processes and computer systems are being reengineered, application systems are moving away from a centralized data center and distributed to the operating divisions, and IS is being outsourced or downsized. When the cost associated with maintaining legacy systems is evaluated, it is increasingly apparent that, perhaps more than ever, management must seriously consider system refurbishment as an integral component of cost containment and business process reengineering, and as a baseline for outsourcing, systems reengineering, and downsizing activities. This chapter presents an effective approach to maintaining and repositioning legacy systems to align them with the goal of systems that are cost-effective and competitive.

SYSTEM REFURBISHMENT AND BUSINESS PROCESS REENGINEERING

The increasing popularity of business process reengineering has placed greater pressure on IS to keep pace with similar systems reengineering

0-8493-9822-3/00/$0.00+$.50

projects. One study done by G2 Research, Inc., projected that the total market for business process reengineering will have grown from $5.3 billion in 1992 to $12.5 billion in 1997. The systems reengineering market for this same period is expected to grow from $17.6 billion to $39.8 billion. Among the companies that have implemented and realized the benefits of business process or systems reengineering projects are Shearson Lehman Brothers, KLM Engineering and Maintenance, and Nalco Chemical Company. Companies can adopt an approach to maintain and reposition their legacy systems to make them more cost-effective and competitive so that they can support activities associated with business process reengineering.

Legacy systems share similar characteristics regardless of industry, business, or application focus. Usually, these systems are more than seven years old, may or may not be mission critical, use outmoded or different proprietary technologies, have poorly structured program code, have ineffective reporting systems, and use system and human resources inefficiently. To further complicate these systems, the original design and development team may have changed, leaving the current support team without a complete understanding of the detailed operation of the system. In other words, legacy systems are usually the systems that everyone fears and no one wants to support.

How do companies determine the strategic contribution of their legacy systems? How do they know which systems to keep? What if the operations or development staff is outsourced? Is it possible to convert a legacy system into a more competitive tool that allows a company to provide higher-quality products and services in less time? The answers to these questions can be found in a refurbishment approach that has been successfully implemented in a variety of businesses and industries.

THE REFURBISHMENT PROCESS

The refurbishment process encompasses (encapsulates) an entire system, which may be of any size or complexity. The refurbishment process also provides IS with the ability to evaluate its functional and technical attributes and recondition the system to improve cost and maintainability. The process comprises five key phases: preliminary inventory analysis, encapsulation, application analysis, production standardization, and design recovery. Each phase is defined briefly as follows:

- *Preliminary inventory analysis.* This phase determines the scope of the refurbishment effort (i.e., which systems to include) and establishes the priorities of the systems to be refurbished.
- *Encapsulation.* This phase generates an inventory of the components of a system.
- *Application analysis.* This phase evaluates applications according to three aspects:

— Functional fulfillment.
— Technical quality.
— Fit with the IS strategic plan.

Production standardization.

This phase eliminates many past mistakes and provides an understanding of the functional and technical aspects of the system.

Design recovery.

This phase provides detailed system documentation and positions the application software to be reverse and forward engineered.

The results of the refurbishment effort, together with other forces that influence a system's strategic direction, are used to determine the refurbishment strategy for a system. The key phases of refurbishment and the forces that influence the refurbishment strategy are illustrated in Exhibit 54.1. Application refurbishment improves the performance and maintainability of a system while also incorporating internal and external business forces.

PRELIMINARY INVENTORY ANALYSIS

Before jumping into the refurbishment process, a preliminary analysis of the existing systems is performed to determine the overall scope of the refurbishment effort. This analysis is an abbreviated version of the encapsulation and application analysis phases.

During this initial phase, the inventory of applications is quantified and analyzed to determine which systems should be included or excluded from the project. At this point, it is not necessary to develop a detailed inventory of each system's components. However, IS should determine the approximate number of executable jobs, procedures, and programs for each system selected.

While conducting this analysis, IS has the opportunity to determine the relative state of each system (i.e., functional and Technical Quality) as well as to estimate the amount of time required to complete the four remaining project phases. From this analysis, a detailed project work plan can be developed for the remaining phases of the project.

ENCAPSULATION

The encapsulation process is a key aspect of refurbishment because it is this process that ensures that the system components (e.g., job control program source, load modules, copybooks) are identified. An accurate component inventory must be developed before beginning the analysis. Although it is possible to include components in the inventory after the

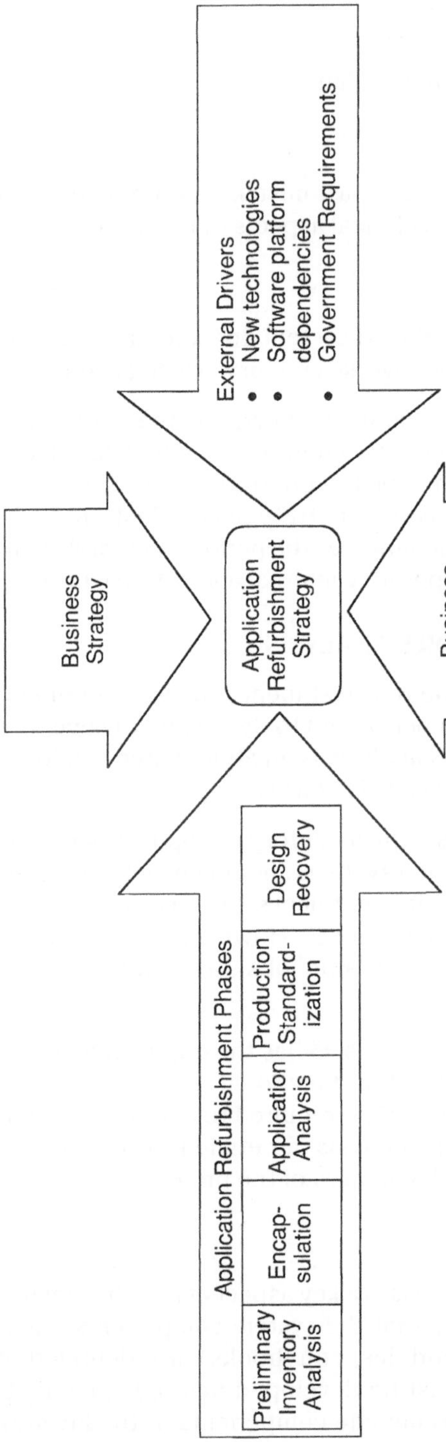

Exhibit 54.1. Forces Influencing the Refurbishment Strategy

analysis has begun, it may be costly to reproduce the analysis a number of times.

After the inventory is completed, it may be necessary to verify that modules that are executed in production are the same as those identified in the inventory. There are several ways to verify the quality and integrity of the inventory, including reviewing source edit statistics, equating source modules to load modules, and systems testing.

The extent of the effort required to develop an accurate inventory is inversely related to the quality of the controls provided within the IS change management procedures. For example, a change management procedure that incorporates excellent controls requires less inventory and verification effort than one with few controls.

Encapsulation identifies all possible system components and shakes out those that are not a part of the system. Although several software tools are available to assist in the process of defining the component inventory, the use of a combination of both manual and automated analyses provides the most accurate inventory in the least amount of time. This is accomplished by digging through the system manually (system utilities may be used) to identify libraries that contain misplaced system components and by using the automated tools to piece together the remaining components.

By completing the encapsulation process, IS establishes a definitive inventory of all system components. The inventory alone may reduce the IS cost associated with analyzing the production and departmental libraries and any other additional activities that may be required to locate the components that satisfy a user's special request. In addition, the accuracy of the systems analysis required by an new development or maintenance activity may be improved because all of the system components have been identified and are easily located.

APPLICATION ANALYSIS

Although refurbishment presents a significant opportunity for IS to effectively improve the performance, maintainability, and cost of legacy systems, it would be shortsighted not to include a more strategic review of these systems. This review should initially evaluate these systems according to three primary attributes:

- Ability to support the functional requirements of the system's users.
- System design and use of technology.
- Conformance with the IS strategy.

The evaluation of these three criteria provides insight about the value that the system provides to the business. A system that adequately supports the business needs of the user but employs outmoded technology is

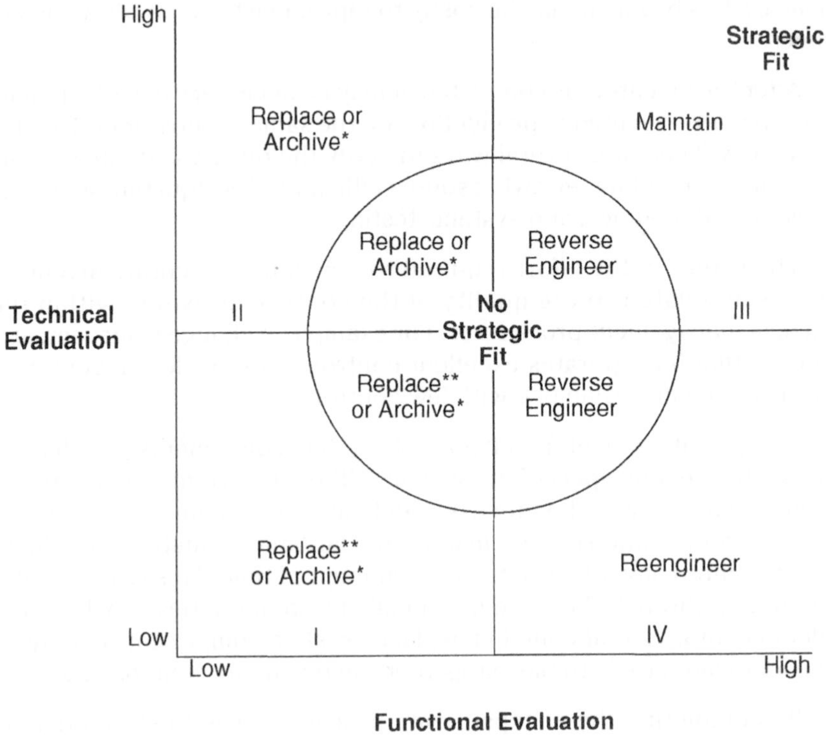

The chart shows four quadrants (I–IV) and eight sectors (two sectors per quadrant). Sector positioning is based on the system's strategic fit. Systems whose core competencies support the IS strategy are placed outside the circle (the bull's eye); those that do not support the IS strategy are placed inside the circle. regardless of the system's functional or technical rating.
*Functional obsolescence
**Technical obsolescence

Exhibit 54.2. System Target Chart

more valuable than one that provides little or no functional support to an organization but uses all the latest technology.

To complete the analysis, the functional and technical attributes of the system are mapped to the IS strategic systems plan to determine the refurbishment strategy for the system, as shown in the System Target Chart in Exhibit 54.2.

The forces that influence the refurbishment strategy must be considered, because they may directly impact the order in which revitalization activities are performed. For example, if the business strategy is to outsource IS operations, management should focus the IS effort on those activities that will maximize resource use. This focus will achieve lower operational costs for production systems. Specific areas of focus would include Central Processing Unit utilization, disk and tape utilization, online performance, database efficiency, system backup and restore procedures, and documentation. The sector in which a system is placed in Exhibit 54.2 provides a basis for formulating a system refurbishment strategy.

Targeting the Refurbishment Strategy

The System Target Chart is a single representation of two separate charts that have been blended to communicate refurbishment alternatives for one or more systems. One chart evaluates the technical and functional attributes of the system and the second chart evaluates the system's core competencies to determine the system's strategic importance. When combined, the charts form four quadrants (I to IV) and eight sectors (i.e., two sectors per quadrant, one which fits IS strategy and one that does not). Positioning a system within a sector provides a basis for formulating a refurbishment strategy.

The placement of a system within a quadrant represents the functional and technical capacity of the system. Within a quadrant, sector positioning is based on the system's strategic importance. Systems whose core competencies support the IS strategy are placed outside the circle (the bull's-eye) and those that do not support the IS strategy are placed inside the circle, regardless of the system's technical or functional rating.

Each system is rated on the basis of the information gathered during the preliminary inventory analysis and encapsulation phases of refurbishment. In general, systems that fall into sectors I or II provide little functional support to an organization and therefore are considered less valuable than systems that fall into sectors III or IV.

Quadrant I

Quadrant I of the Target Chart represents systems that provide little functional support to the business and use outmoded technologies or are poorly designed and constructed. Systems in this sector that provide functional support but are technically obsolete will be replaced, whereas the systems in this sector that are functionally obsolete (i.e., no longer support a business function)can be archived or deleted.

An example best illustrates this point. One organization maintained a system that relied on manual processes to collect revenue data in the form of paper receipts. It took 15 to 20 business days to enter the receipt information into the system using a data entry service bureau. The system was poorly designed and the programs were unstructured and difficult to maintain. The users complained that the system forced them to iteratively print reports, compute adjustments on a microcomputer before entry to the system, and reprint the reports to determine the adjustment's net effect. In addition, analyzing and modifying the system reports took a great deal of time, and in many cases, the users had to resort to building a new spreadsheet or database system to produce their own reports.

Systems in a similar state of disrepair are fairly common. Quadrant I systems usually consume significant IS resources as well as increase user frustration. In the previous example, considerable time was required to create the manual receipts, audit the computerized reports to the manual receipts (what happens if a receipt is lost?), iteratively rerun and analyze reports after adjustments have been made, and develop new or maintain existing unstructured code to create or enhance reports. For this system alone, IS spent a total of one person-year responding to one-time user requests to modify or create reports. This effort was magnified by the fact that the system was supported by only three programmers. A thorough analysis would identify even more areas of cost associated with supporting such systems.

This system is currently being replaced with a new automated data collection system that uses a relational database on the mainframe. A new conversational interface is also to be written to assist the users with the online processes, and all remaining programs are to be reengineered (using an automated program restructuring tool) to improve maintainability.

Quadrant II

Quadrant II of the Target Chart represents systems that provide little functional support to the business but use current technologies or are well designed and constructed. Technology, no matter how advanced, has little value unless it supports a business requirement. Generally speaking, systems that provide functional support to the business should be replaced; those that do not can be archived or deleted. However, for those systems that do not fulfill functional requirements, the best alternative may be to salvage and redeploy technology components to new or other existing systems.

Quadrant III

Systems that fall into Quadrant III or Quadrant IV (which is discussed in more detail in the next section) support the business functions performed by the organizations that use the system. They provide the greatest flexibility with regard to alternative system strategies because they provide more business support than Quadrant I and Quadrant II systems. Although both Quadrant III and Quadrant IV systems support the functional requirements of the business, only Quadrant III systems use current technologies, are well-designed and constructed, and use IS resources efficiently.

Quadrant III represents systems that provide the best functional and technical support to the business. These systems are usually the most cost-effective users of IS resources. Supporting the strategic systems plan, Quadrant III systems are best positioned for the future and should continue to be maintained as usual. Those systems that fall within the bull's-eye are positioned to be reverse engineered to take advantage of other technologies (e.g., hardware platform, database, or communications).

A simplified example of a Quadrant III system is an online purchasing system that satisfies the user's functional requirements, is well designed and coded (i.e., easy to maintain), and uses IS resources efficiently. If the system was based on an Integrated Data Management System database using Canadian Independent Computing Services Association for communications that corresponded to the strategic systems plan, it would be positioned outside of the Quadrant III bull's-eye and therefore would be maintained as is. If, however, the strategic systems plan called for a broad sweeping conversion to dBase 2 using CICS, the system would be placed within the bull's-eye and the system would be reverse engineered to convert the system to the new database architecture.

Quadrant IV

Quadrant IV systems satisfy the business functional requirements but do not score well on their design, code construction, or use of technology. The prognosis for systems in this sector is still positive, however. If a Quadrant IV system fits the strategic systems plan (i.e., its position is outside the bull's-eye), it would indicate that the technological components of the system support the strategy but that the system design or construction are difficult to maintain.

Systems that fall into this category are usually reengineered. In the context of the Target Chart only, computer systems reengineering differs from reverse engineering in that reengineering operates on a system at the source-code level whereas reverse engineering operates on a system at a higher technical level (e.g., hardware platform, database architecture, or communication monitors). Reengineering implies improving the maintainability of a system by eliminating dead code, incorporating structured programming techniques, and adhering to IS standards for program development.

These program-level changes may be made using automated or manual methods. The use of automated tools speeds the modification process significantly. When using these tools, however, IS must review and test the regenerated source code to verify that system functionality is not altered. This method is the preferred approach for large source program because manually converting large programs is extremely time consuming and requires the same level of verification as the automated tools.

Quadrant IV systems that do not fit the strategic systems plan require more than just code-level modifications. These systems usually require a conversion to a new database or other technical architecture. In this case, systems are usually reverse engineered to reposition the system for the new architecture.

PRODUCTION STANDARDIZATION

The goal of production standardization is to revitalize the existing system after years of touch-up work performed by different IS personnel using different programming techniques and styles. The revitalization transforms the legacy system into one that performs better, is easier (i.e., more cost-effective) to maintain and operate, and uses resources more efficiently. Nearly every IS organization has at least one system that can benefit from this revitalization process.

The refurbishment process allows IS to approach the system from two directions simultaneously—from both a functional and technical perspective. A functional knowledge of the system is required to identify and document the business attributes that are supported by the system. The technical aspect of this two-pronged approach provides IS with detailed knowledge of the processing within the system and the information necessary to improve the maintainability and performance of the system. Obviously, the refurbishment of legacy systems and, in particular, production standardization cannot be performed in a vacuum.

To obtain an accurate functional understanding of the system, IS should meet with the system users to determine the functions performed by the organization, the information that is required by the organization, and the information that the organization currently receives from IS. The objectives are to determine the value that the users place on the system and the positive and negative functional and technical attributes of the system.

Simultaneously, IS can initiate the activities that focus on analyzing and improving the technical aspects of the system. A preliminary analysis of the several systems in the inventory can be performed to determined the areas that may benefit most from the use of automated tools. A word of caution before purchasing the newest tools: it is essential to ensure that the tools perform the functions needed to perform the analysis. For example, some tools can restructure program source code to improve system maintainability, document the structure of the system, and document the system's input and output.

For one insurance company, this revitalization approach, and the use of a purchased software package, improved the monthly financial closing time from 25 days to 5 days. For another company, converting tape data sets to disk and improvements in the disaster recovery process (for one batch job) improved the processing time by nearly 3 hours.

When the revitalization effort is completed, IS has a system that is more cost-effective to maintain and operate and is better positioned to react to internal and external business forces, such as outsourcing, downsizing, business process reengineering, or changes in government regulations. Production standardization provides significant benefits to IS and the business regardless of the priorities imposed by internal or external forces.

DESIGN RECOVERY

The final phase of a refurbishment effort is the design recovery phase. Design recovery captures certain elements of the current system design, incorporates these elements into a Computer-Aided Software Engineering tool, and provides IS with the ability to accurately document the functional and technical aspects of the system. This repository of up-to-date system documentation improves systems analysis and maintenance time and cost, improves the learning curve for new IS personnel, and provides a basis for engineering these systems more competitively in a CASE environment.

The process of extracting and loading mainframe system design elements (i.e., program names and their relationships to other programs, data files and records, and data record attributes) to a microcomputer or mainframe-based CASE tool is not always straightforward. Automated analysis and documentation tools designed to pass this information to other products (e.g., CASE or data dictionary) are available; however, this is not necessarily a standard feature of these products. The element extraction process is simplified if this feature is available. Otherwise, an extraction program may be written to perform the extraction function. Currently, the extraction process applies to data elements only. The processing or logic aspect of a system cannot yet be extracted and passed to the CASE tool. Some vendors are trying to develop this logic link between the system and the CASE tool, but such products are not expected to be commercially available in the near future.

The documentation produced from this phase provides insight into the functional purpose of the system, the major components of the system, the technology used to provide system functionality, the organizations that use the system, and the interfaces to other systems. This documentation can be used to support forward engineering, downsizing, and other IS refurbishment strategies.

CONCLUSION

If IS is to play an active role in the effort to better control cost, then system refurbishment should be included as part of an overall cost-reduction plan. Although this chapter has specifically targeted legacy systems, IS can achieve substantial benefits from refurbishing newer systems that have been developed using loose standards or that have experienced several modifications.

Systems refurbishment presents IS management with an effective approach to maintenance because it reduces the operating cost of systems, improves system maintainability, and positions systems to support the IS strategy as well as activities associated with business process reengineering, outsourcing, and downsizing. Refurbishment may also avoid the cost of replacing a system with a purchased package that is in a similar state of disrepair. The approach and tools provided in this chapter were designed through experience, practice, and a few painful lessons, and they provide IS with the road map for accomplishing its performance objectives.

Chapter 55
Interfacing Legacy Applications with RDBMSs and Middleware

Dan Fobes

TODAY PROGRAMMERS HAVE A WIDE RANGE OF OPTIONS when developing applications. There is an endless number of tools and techniques associated with simply writing a program. Hardware advances deliver what used to be the power of a mainframe on a programmer's desktop. Given the pace of software and hardware advances, it should follow that programmer productivity has grown equally as fast. This is not the case, because for many new applications being developed, there is one constraint — it must plug into an established world of corporate data and the processes that manage them. For many companies, the processes that manage their enterprise data were written 10 to 15 years ago. These applications are also referred to as legacy systems. Rewriting legacy systems would solve the technology gap experienced today, but the cost and risks are usually too great. This chapter outlines some options available for interfacing legacy systems with the latest technology, enabling a company to continue to compete in a rapidly changing field.

CLIENT/SERVER AND DECENTRALIZED IS

In the 1970s and early 1980s IBM dominated IS with mainframes, and IS programmers wrote largely in COBOL. All programs were defined by users, then written by IS. As a result all mission-critical applications were coded by one group and executed on one machine. In the mid to late 1980s, the PC started to replace terminals as companies moved to empower the user with word processors and spreadsheet applications. Nontechnical users could move data from the mainframe to their desktop and do some additional client processing within a spreadsheet without the aid of IS. Network operating systems (NOSs) provided a means to connect PCs in a local area network allowing for users to share both the raw mainframe data and PC processed data. Hence the birth of client/server. As a result, companies had distributed their mission critical data processing from a centralized IS throughout the enterprise.

0-8493-9822-3/00/$0.00+$.50

The Failure of Client/Server

All applications can be broken down into three groups of code (or tiers):

1. Presentation Tier — get user information.
2. Business Tier — process user information.
3. Data Tier — write processed information.

When applications were written by one group and run on one machine, these layers were usually intermixed. It was not uncommon for one programmer to write one program that contained all three. With the advent of modular programming, large programs could be broken down into a collection of shared modules, reducing both the time required to finish an application and the risk of writing entire applications from scratch. Unfortunately, the immediate IS benefit of reusing modules would often come at the expense of large modules with large numbers of parameters instructing them how to behave for different types of invocations. However, modular programming presented the opportunity to separate the presentation tier from the business and data tiers.

With client server applications, there is a requirement to distinguish between the presentation, business, and data tiers. There are two computers involved in client/server applications — the client and the server. The client application executes on the client PC, with all presentation input being received locally from the user. However, some data are read from and written to the server for the purpose of information sharing. As a result, unlike a mainframe application, a client/server application is separated from some of its data by a network — the slowest part of any computer.

For applications such as simple spreadsheet calculations the client/server model works fine. However, many corporations, lured by the low cost of client/server technology and a need to standardize, attempted to move all IS applications to a client/server architecture. After investing lots of time and money, many companies found that the tools enabled them to re-create the applications, but the client/server model made it impossible to implement them. No matter how fast the client and server hardware is, the network is a bottleneck. With the business tier executing on the client and saturating the network with file I/O requests, it was not uncommon to see a complex client/server application become unusable when 25 to 50 users begin to use it — something a mainframe could handle easily.

SUCCEEDING WITH DISTRIBUTED DATA PROCESSING

The scalability problem that exists with client/server applications has many proposing a return to mainframes and centralized IS. However, given that data is distributed throughout an enterprise and applications exist on various platforms, others would benefit if the data and the processes that manage them can be tied together. Currently available are several options that provide for both types of solutions:

- Relational Database Management Systems
- Remote Procedure Call
- Messaging

As stated above, most legacy mainframe applications contained all three tiers. Clearly the presentation must be rewritten for the PC. For each of the technical solutions above, consider a simple PC application, PCDEPOS, that collects user information such as an account number and amount of money to deposit. The goal is to have PCDEPOS call an existing COBOL program on a mainframe, MFDEPOS, which performs the transaction (i.e., it represents the business and data tiers only).

RDBMS

One solution to the fragmentation of mission-critical data and their processes is to centralize them to one or more relational databases. Data access through a relational engine can be much faster because data contained within files located across various platforms is moved under the control of a technology built to manage it. Files are moved to tables and selected columns within tables can be indexed. Furthermore, business logic, usually in the form of COBOL programs, can be recoded as SQL-based stored procedures that are compiled then executed within the RDBMS engine for optimal performance. Additionally, most databases support some form of replication whereby tables from one database can be replicated to others, facilitating information sharing. Finally, Transaction Processing (TP) monitors are available for most RDBMS. A separate product, TP monitors interface a client application to a RDBMS and increase performance where large numbers of users require data access. It does this by creating a pool of costly connections to the RDBMS and having the application use a connection from the pool only when necessary.

For the example application, PCDEPOS is created to collect information from the user using middleware, called an open database connectivity (or ODBC) driver, supplied by the RDBMS vendor to facilitate communication between the client and the server. Files that MFDEPOS wrote to and read from, or the data tier, must be moved into RDBMS'$ tables. There are two options for MFDEPOS'$ data processing logic (the business tier) — it can be rewritten as a stored procedure within the RDBMS or modified to perform I/O against SQL tables instead of files.

There are two problems with this solution. For one, it increases the cost and complexity of applications. An RDBMS requires the purchase of a RDBMS, additional server hardware, and one or more dedicated database administrators (DBAs) to install, design, tune, and maintain it. The other problem is risk. Simple applications may be easy to move to a RDBMS; however, no legacy application is simple. Many companies will be required to spend a large amount of resources normalizing or breaking up the data within records, as they move from files to RDBMS tables. This is because an RDBMS table has a limit of 255 columns and no row can exceed 2 kilobytes in size — legacy applications typically exceed this. Also, not all data maps over from a file to a table (e.g., dates), and for each of these, a translation is required. Time and staff must be allocated to not only normalize data and map data types, but also verify that existing data moves cleanly into the RDBMS. Part of the migration to an RDBMS is the modifications to the existing business tier code. In the example application, rewriting the MFDEPOS business tier as a stored procedure introduces significant risk because of the differences between the languages (a form of SQL and COBOL). The alternative of replacing file I/O within the COBOL program with RDBMS I/O is usually not feasible because of the scalability issues (requires the COBOL code to execute on the PC).

An RDBMS solution has many benefits, however the costs and risks associated with moving the data and recoding the business logic must be weighed.

REMOTE PROCEDURE CALLS

For most, there is a significantly smaller risk in tying together existing systems that work. What is needed is a form of interprocess communication (IPC) to have one process send and receive data to another. One form of IPC is Remote Procedure Call (RPC).

Using RPC a program calls a procedure that is executed on a different machine. There is always a one-to-one relationship, and the calling program blocks until the called procedure returns. This sounds simple enough, but since the applications are residing in different address spaces, the only data that each share are the parameters they pass, not global variables within the applications. For an RPC across different machines, data mapping must be addressed, because not all hardware supports the same byte-order (i.e., it stores numbers differently). Finally, either or both machines can crash at any point and recovery must be addressed.

Some vendors of development systems provide proprietary RPC mechanisms that address some of the above issues. There are also standards such as the RPC protocol used by the Open Group's Distributed Computing Environment (DCE). Additionally, third-party vendors provide Object Request Brokers (ORBs) for RPC services. The most common ORB is called CORBA. A standard created by the Object Management Group (OMG), CORBA facilitates RPCs across different machines. Unfortunately, the CORBA standard is just that — a standard. Because CORBA is similar to UNIX, each vendor has a slightly different implementation of that standard, and until very recently different CORBA implementations could communicate with each other. Microsoft has a competing technology called the Distributed Component Object Model (DCOM). Many vendors support both CORBA and DCOM as their RPC mechanism, and although both CORBA and DCOM are complex to program, they are options that should be considered when evaluating distributed processing via RPC.

MESSAGE-ORIENTED MIDDLEWARE

Another form of IPC is messaging. Vendors of message-oriented middleware provide a mechanism to send and receive messages asynchronously from one process to another. A message is simply a string of bytes the user defines. There are two approaches to messaging: message queues and publish/subscribe. In a message queue environment, an application sends messages to and receives messages from queues. In a publish/subscribe model, an application broadcasts and receives messages via a subject. The sender specifies the subject of the message and the receiver specifies the subject(s) it wants to get messages for. There are pros and cons to each; however, both are sufficient for most environments.

As stated above, a message is a user-defined string of bytes — there is no standard that needs to be followed. A typical messaging application sends and receives messages asynchronously across multiple platforms. The messaging subsystem handles the routing with most vendors supporting the concept of guaranteed and assured delivery (i.e., the message will get to the receiver and only once). One of the strengths of messaging, which differentiates it from RPC, is that the sender need not block, or wait until the receiver responds. Another strength is that one message may be delivered to multiple listeners.

For the example application, messages would contain the arguments to the MFDEPOS program. To facilitate messaging, a new server application called MFLISTEN is required, and the client application must be modified to send and receive messages to it. MFLISTEN listens for client messages and calls the server application with the arguments specified in the message. Once completed, MFDEPOS returns control back to MFLISTEN, which sends the arguments back to the client via a message.

Since there is no enforced message type, defining one that is flexible becomes a challenge. Different requests for different server applications will likely require a different message, and over time this may become unmanageable as each request begins to change. There are two ways to solve this problem: message versioning and self-describing messages.

To accomplish the deposit application using message versioning, a message could simply contain the linkage to MFDEPOS with each parameter separated by a delimiter (see Exhibit 55.1).

Exhibit 55.1. Message Containing Parameters with @@ as a Delimiter for MFDEPOS.

```
 -----------------------------------------
 | Parameter 1@@Parameter 2@@Parameter 3@@ ...
 -----------------------------------------
```

Exhibit 55.2. Simple Message with Segments Supporting Message Versions.

```
| 4 bytes | 2 bytes | 2 bytes | 2 bytes | 2 bytes | ...
--------------------------------------------------------------------------
| MessageID | Segment Count | SegmentID | Segment Version | Segment Size | Parameter 1...
--------------------------------------------------------------------------
                          | SegmentID | Segment Version | Segment Size | Parameter 1...
                          -----------------------------------------------
```

Although this works, it requires a dedicated MFLISTEN program for each server program such as MFDEPOS. A more flexible approach would be to break up the message into multiple segments and then build a header to contain segment information (see Exhibit 55.2). Designing messages around segments is not new — a standard called Electronic Data Interchange, or EDI, is also based on segments.

Here MessageID represents the format of the message, Segment Count is the number of segments in the message, SegmentID is the start of the segment and represents the program name (e.g., 1 for MFDEPOS), segment version represents the format of the parameters (number, order, datatypes), and the parameters follow. The parameters can be delimited or fixed length — their layout is defined by SegmentID and Segment Version. The benefit to moving the program name and version down to the segment is that it allows for one MFLISTEN program to serve as an interface to multiple server programs. The only problem with this design is when MFDEPOS'$ linkage changes, the format of the segment changes and the segment version must be incremented. Sending applications such as PCDEPOS would need to be changed to send the new message. Receiving applications such as MFLISTEN would need to be modified to verify the new message version and call the updated version of MFDEPOS.

To accomplish the deposit application using self-describing data, the version number within the message is replaced by field descriptors. Specifically, each parameter value in the message is prepended with a field name that defines it (see Exhibit 55.3).

With self-describing data, the segment remains the same, but each parameter has two components: a descriptor and a value. These two components can be fixed length or delimited (they are fixed length in Exhibit 55.3). The benefit to this structure is that it automates the process of calling legacy

Exhibit 55.3. Segment Supporting Self Describing Data.

2 bytes	2 bytes	2 bytes	8 bytes	?	8 bytes	
SegmentID	Segment Version	Segment Size	P1 Descriptor	P1 Value	P2 Descriptor	...

applications. The best case scenario with versioning saw one listener program created to serve multiple server applications. However, the sending applications (PCDEPOS) and the listener application (MFLISTEN) require an update when there is any change to the server application's linkage (MFDEPOS). With self-describing fields, we can reduce this maintenance to a batch scan on the server. An application on the mainframe can be written to scan a COBOL program and extract the linkage to a table that contains each name and type. The sending applications would then use the names in the COBOL linkage to describe their data, followed by the value of that field. The MFLISTEN program, upon receiving a message, can extract the program name and map the linkage in the message to the linkage in the database automatically, then make the call. New versions of MFDEPOS can be scanned and the database updated. No changes are required to MFLISTEN or PCDEPOS in most cases.

Some message systems allow for field mapping within the message. This allows the MFLISTEN application to query the message for fields instead of parsing it directly. This simplifies MFLISTEN, and combined with self-describing data, which provides the optimal messaging solution.

Not all is golden with a messaging solution. Although guaranteed delivery insures a message gets to its destination, it may be possible that one transaction is composed of several messages. Additionally, one message may require the execution of multiple listener programs. In either case, a program would have to initiate a transaction locally, send the messages, subscribe to the responses, and roll back if any of them failed. Another possible issue with messaging is security. With messages traveling back and forth on a network, a hacker can easily listen in, make a change, and send messages back out. Here, encryption is required.

RECOMMENDED COURSE OF ACTION

The above technologies are not mutually exclusive, and in fact, it may turn out that a combination of all three is the best solution. For example, a client may communicate with a server using RPC, the server may use messaging to perform IPC with another server, and one or both of these servers may interact with an RDBMS.

In general, all programs should be separated into three tiers and corporate data should be managed by an RDBMS. Business logic should be coded in a high-level language such as COBOL, which calls a minimum of stored procedures for I/O intensive requests. Finally, the presentation should be coded in a rapid application tool that supports an RDBMS such as Visual Basic. For companies that require a high volume of transactions, middleware in the form of a transaction server or a TP monitor combined with an ORB should be considered.

Migrating an enterprise to this configuration involves many steps and differs for different companies. Avoid the all-or-nothing approach. Risk can be reduced by using a divide-and-conquer approach that targets subsystems. Below are some high-level steps for accomplishing such a migration:

1. Identify a logical subsystem of the enterprise.
2. Form a team composed of programmers who understand the subsystem and others who understand the target technology.
3. Identify the data of the subsystem.
4. Identify existing applications that manage the data, then tie them together using messaging. This will uncover redundant data and data processing within the subsystem.
5. Design the RDBMS solution (tables, stored procedures, etc.)
6. Create a listener program that listens to the messages created in step 4 and performs the requests on the RDBMS.
7. Once the RDBMS can service all of the messages of step 4, it can be phased in.
8. Go to step 1.

Some applications may span subsystems. Messaging supports this requirement well and should be used. Although most RDBMSs support replication, this usually requires one server to stream over tables of information to another server at scheduled intervals. Not only does this introduce a delay across servers, it does not scale for large databases — messaging the updates as they happen addresses both shortcomings.

When the RDBMS phase-in is complete, new applications should go directly against the RDBMS. Most new technology being introduced provides for access to RDBMSs. The legacy applications can continue using messaging, be modified for direct RDBMS access, or be rewritten.

Chapter 56

Critical Success Factors in Reengineering Legacy Systems

Patricia L. Seymour

ARE ANY SOFTWARE MANAGERS today not concerned about the increasing cost of maintaining and migrating their legacy systems? Many find themselves on the firing line, unable to dodge the bullets, because they have few solutions for their legacy systems. The flush 1980s are gone but not the systems that were inherited.

However, some organizations did begin reengineering early, in the late 1980s. They have shown that reengineering can alleviate the organizational pressures caused by legacy systems. For example, Bruce Skivington of Aetna Insurance informed an audience at a conference on reengineering that Aetna had reengineered one major system and reduced its resource requirements by 60 percent from 1986 to 1988. The Aetna IS organization also standardized and rationalized data and thus reduced errors by 90 percent; such were the data complexities of its legacy systems.

Another reengineering success story comes from DST, in Kansas City MO, a processor of shareholder accounting and recordkeeping services for mutual funds. Estimates for a systems redesign and rewrite exceeded $50 million and three years for completion. The total cost was approximately $12 million, and the project was completed in 14 months

Because reengineering projects deliver often and early, organizations usually receive a return on investment quickly. Thus, scarce resources are made available for other projects.

WHAT IS REENGINEERING?

Over the years, various organizations that promote reengineering have emerged and undergone changes. So have various definitions of the term

0-8493-9822-3/00/$0.00+$.50

reengineering. Some still associate reengineering with code restructuring, and others associate it with a specific set of software tools. Still others include reverse engineering as part of reengineering.

The Systems Redevelopment Methodology (a trademark of James Martin & Co.) defines *software reengineering* as the use of tools and techniques to facilitate the analysis, improvement, redesign, and reuse of existing software systems to support changing business and technical information requirements. The IEEE has defined *reverse engineering* as "the process of analyzing a system to identify components and interrelationships and to create representations in another form or at a higher level of abstraction." The two processes often go hand-in-hand to deliver business solutions. For example, to understand data relationships in legacy systems and to extract business rules, data rationalization — a reengineering activity — must be performed, but the actual recovery and documentation of the business rules are considered reverse engineering activities.

REENGINEERING CRITICAL SUCCESS FACTORS

Why have not more companies followed the examples of Aetna and DST and embraced reengineering principles? Many organizations have approached reengineering with fragmented strategies because they believed that tools alone would solve the problems. What is needed for reengineering to be successful is an integrated approach.

The following sections examine 12 critical factors that must be addressed for reengineering to be successful. Failure to address these factors, which are also listed in Exhibit 56.1, often mean failure for the reengineering effort.

The Silver Bullet Syndrome

Many computer-aided software engineering (CASE) tools, workbenches, methodologies, and processes that organizations bought in the 1980s were bought because they seemed to make the transition from old to new systems as simple as pushing a button. More rigorous and disciplined reengineering concepts and strategies, which required rigor and discipline of IS organizations, struggled to compete with the many panaceas that were available. In fact, the slightest association with the word maintenance could doom a tool's or methodology's debut into the market. Continuing to budget for enhancements of legacy systems was often regarded as a waste of resources. Some organizations hired contract programmers to perform minimal maintenance on existing systems. These organizations spent the bulk of their resources on the latest and greatest state-of-the-art tools for building new systems.

There was one problem with this strategy. The old systems were poorly

- Silver bullet syndrome
- Technology driven
- Internal team
- Sponsorship
- Risk aversion and analysis paralysis
- Infrastructure support
- Ambiguous targets
- Integrated systems options
- Integrated tools
- Resistance to change
- Training and education
- Blueprint framework

Exhibit 56.1. Critical Success Factors in Reengineering

documented, and it seemed that the business rules required to create new systems could be found only in the existing source code. This was compounded by many organizations' downsizing and the forced early retirement of personnel. Those seemingly all-powerful tools, methodologies, and processes were finally seen as what they always were: silver bullets that could not deliver. It has been estimated that $16.5 billion is wasted annually on projects that never are delivered to the user.

Reengineering is not a panacea; it is not performed by pushing a button. It requires the proper set of tools and methods as well as resources and commitment. With these, reengineering can aid organizations in making a cost-effective transition from legacy to new systems that meet current and new business requirements.

Technology Driven

Reengineering began as a bottom-up technology. Programmers were toying with tools, debates about code restructuring began, and the rest is history. Rarely were strategic plans and business issues the motivation for systems reengineering. Attention was on code, and usually business sponsors were not involved. At one time, there was much trade press about whether code restructuring tools could even produce functionally equivalent code.

Such companies as Pacific Bell, Hartford Insurance, Aetna, and General Mills were some of the early pioneers that proved that code restructurers not only produced functionally equivalent code but facilitated reengineering strategies. When integrated into business strategies, these restructuring tools

- Create the team
- Understand the challenge
- Assess organization readiness and culture
- Identify stakeholders and create effective sponsorship
- Review and establish reward and recognition programs
- Market consultatively to the internal client
- Create, implement, and manage partenership agreements
- Communicate the change
- Provide for technology transfer
- Identify critical success factors for pilot projects

Exhibit 56.2. Steps in Human Factors Approach to Reengineering

would guide the migration to new systems. Some of these companies partnered with major reengineering software vendors to define requirements for data equivalency and modularization tools.

The technical debates over restructuring tools soon died, and many organizations rushed blindly to buy these tools. Without an integrated strategy for using the tools, these IS organizations soon found their shelves lined with unused copies of restructuring software.

The Need for an Internal Team

It soon became clear that reengineering required a different support structure than common, standalone maintenance tools did. Tool users lacked the skills to influence strategies of an entire IS organization and capture necessary funding and other resources. If reengineering were to survive, it would need a team approach.

Pacific Bell in San Ramon CA developed a team known as the Systems Renewal Group. Because reengineering was believed to be a technical problem, a technology group was formed. However, the group became greatly bewildered when it failed to influence peers on reengineering strategies. This resistance made the group reevaluate its approach. Exhibit 56.2 summarizes the approach that the group started to develop. It has been further refined by Technology Innovations of Danville CA.

After extensive training and applying the consulting and marketing skills they learned, the group successfully trained several other groups to perform software reengineering throughout the company. They attributed their success to having realized that their lack of understanding of organizational change rather than technology was at fault. Organizational change was found to be key in directing the reengineering methods and approach. Although the Systems Renewal Group was successful, its members have stated that it was a grass-roots effort with minimal sponsorship.

Sponsorship

The lack of IS and business sponsorship is probably the primary reason for failure with reengineering. Because software reengineering is usually started at the technical level, senior management may never become involved nor understand systems reengineering issues. One of the most frequently asked questions at reengineering conferences is, How can I sell reengineering to upper management and internal business clients and sponsors?

Usually, IS projects are approved and funded by business clients. In the last decade, a growing number of enhancements and changes to business applications have caused software to grow significantly more complex. Along with smaller IS staffs, this complexity has resulted in users' charging IS organizations with being unresponsive to their needs. This situation is exacerbated by new development projects that are delivered late or over budget or are never delivered. In many cases, friction has grown to the point that business users are hesitant to fund any project that does not directly support their needs.

When users are involved with every activity from training to reviewing reports and setting priorities, both users and IS staff better understand each other's needs. When business sponsors are able to get their back-log of requests attended to, they are more inclined to pay attention to the needs of IS.

Risk Aversion and Analysis Paralysis

Teams in large organizations frequently become frustrated when they attempt to create a reengineering environment. When considering new technologies, organizations seldom have teams complete necessary research, define their processes, and rank their projects and activities before they evaluate tools.

Often, new technology is considered when an individual or a group becomes interested in a tool and tries to evaluate or buy it. Without further investigation or analysis, the interested party does not have the data needed to influence management of the technology's value. One of two scenarios is usually played out at this point. Either the whole idea is dropped because there is no budgeting for it, or no one has the time to follow it up. Or, the business application has to be determined, standards resolved, and processes defined.

Vendors are continually confused by organizations' evaluation and procurement processes because they find the evaluations to be more expensive than the tools. Perhaps, less emphasis should be placed on the cost of the tool and more on the cost of implementing the tool.

When the United States Automobile Association (USAA), in San Antonio TX, became interested in reengineering technology, a few key reengineering sponsors and technicians visited Pacific Bell's Systems Renewal Group. Based on the data gathered from Pacific Bell, an industry survey was conducted by a small team at the USAA. The product of the survey was a comprehensive internal report, "An Industry Survey of Reengineering Theory and Practice," which discussed all phases of reengineering. The report focused on processes and implementation and not on tools.

Team members collected their information from masses of articles, journals, books, personal interviews, site visits, conferences, and training classes. After having issued the report and won the support of senior management, they formed a corporate team to define their processes and implementation strategies. Team members subsequently evaluated and purchased tools to support their processes.

They successfully avoided analysis paralysis. The project was carefully planned and managed to reduce risk. They completed the prerequisites for successful engineering.

Infrastructure Support

Occasionally, small application teams reengineer an insignificant number of programs without running into organizational policies and procedures. However, reengineering teams must address the following infrastructure support issues:

- Project management.
- Metrics.
- Development and redevelopment methodologies.
- Tools and support.
- Quality integration.
- Process improvement programs.
- Standards.
- Change management.

These issues are listed in Exhibit 56.3 and discussed in the following paragraphs.

Strong project management methods form the basis for improving an organization's processes; these methods turn chaos into repeatable processes. Reengineering projects are not an exception to this rule.

- Project management
- Metrics
- Development and redevelopment methodologies
- Tools and support
- Quality integration
- Process improvement programs
- Standards
- Managing change

Exhibit 56.3. Issues of Infrastructure Support

A written project plan with clear deliverables and defined roles and responsibilities is critical for success. Flaws in program logic are often discovered when code is restructured and data names are rationalized. Analysts and programmers instinctively want to fix incorrect logic. Although errors should be corrected, to do so without the proper project management can cause additional problems and increase the time and tasks required for testing. Instead, logic flaws should be documented and handled subsequently according to stringent project controls. This has caused more than a few reengineering projects to continue longer than they should have and management to believe that there was an insufficient return on their investment.

Data, coding, and testing standards must be in place before a reengineering project begins. Managers often underestimate the difficulty and necessity of this process. Without enforced standards, an organization stands little chance of improving its systems and processes. Strong data administration is also essential.

Most organizations today are involved in major quality and process improvement efforts. Reengineering teams need to unite these efforts and demonstrate that reengineering systems furthers quality and process improvement efforts already under way. For instance, reengineering systems to meet standards creates more flexibility for movement of resources as well as reducing the learning curve for new employees.

Metrics is another key infrastructure support issue. Organizations must develop a pro-metrics climate that fosters change. When performing technical analysis of an application, an organization must not use metrics for process improvement on the current individuals maintaining systems. These individual often maintain what they inherited. An application's metrics can give management an appreciation of its complexities. These metrics can be used to implement a logical plan for making systems improvements.

Ambiguous Targets

Frequently, organizations have a conceptual vision of their target environment but lack adequate models that enable mapping from the existing systems to the target environment. For example, organizations have tried to move their systems to a CASE environment. However, with only high-level models of what is wanted of the new environment and without detailed business area analysis and lower-level requirements completed, an organization cannot map business functions in the existing system to high-level models in the target system. Many organizations realized that they could port their legacy systems into CASE design-level tools. However, without the prerequisite reengineering and business area analysis, this porting most often produced only very large and flat action diagrams. An effective redevelopment methodology addresses this situation and provides the guidelines for functional mapping of the appropriate business area entities.

Integrated Systems Options

Because reengineering is a technology for transforming legacy systems, business scenarios may be altogether different for each project. The business object and legacy systems analysis dictates the reengineering process and methods — not the technology. Exhibit 56.4 shows a high-level framework for thinking about the integration of business needs, processes, tools, and technology. This framework is not intended to be all-inclusive but an example of how reengineering strategies add value to most systems options.

Organizations usually choose a systems option to the exclusion of all other options. An example is the redevelopment of an existing system. New development teams are created and usually start the traditional cycle of planning, requirements, design, coding, and implementation. Frequently, in doing a thorough job, IS project teams become so entrenched in their endeavor to discover and document business rules that the client loses patience or the budget is depleted before the requirements phase is completed or any deliverables are produced.

This often happens because:

- It is extremely difficult to determine when requirements are complete without exceeding the project's scope.
- The complexity of discovering business rules in legacy systems is often underestimated.
- Corporate downsizing has created a scarcity of subject matter experts and a subsequent lack of verbal documentation.

It can be determined what existing systems do not do, but it cannot be specified what they do do. The software assessment management framework

Business Analysis → Technical Analysis → Functional Analysis → Organizational Assessment

SYSTEM OPTIONS					
Maintain	**Replace**	**Enhance**	**Eliminate**	**Technical Migration**	**Develop New**
Document • Process • Tools Implement quality control • Process • Tools Reengineer • Process • Tools Outsource • Process • Tools Port to PC • Process • Tools	Evaluate package • Process • Tools Rewrite application • Process • Tools Package-rewrite combination • Process • Tools Analyze existing systems	Analyze alternative existing systems • Process • Tools Implement quality analysis • Process • Tools Evaluate system function requirements • Process • Tools Populate analysis workstation • Process • Tools	Determine system usage • Process • Tools Phase out strategies • Process • Tools Analyze existing systems • Process • Tools Outsource • Process • Tools	Implement standards • Process • Tools Implement quality control • Process • Tools Create regression tests • Process • Tools Technical analysis to manage portfolio • Analysis • Code restructuring • Rationalize and standardize data • Modularize code • Port personal computer/CASE	Develop plan • Process • Tools New requirements • Process • Tools Reengineer • Process • Tools Reverse engineer • Process • Tools

Exhibit 56.4. Software Asset Management Framework

shown in Exhibit 56.4 is designed to guide the analysis required for determining how to reach a business goal.

It was once commonly held that reengineering was a systems option. The software assessment management framework, however, clarifies that reengineering is a horizontal strategy that should be applied in varying degrees according to business objectives analysis of existing systems. Redevelopment projects often fail because reengineering strategies are not considered and used as an element of the redevelopment life cycle.

Integrated Tools

Reengineering tools evolved from consultants' need to bid for and complete projects. Consultants played a major role in developing the reengineering tool set as they began to be able to perform repeatedly such activities as data name rationalization. Rarely was a project called reengineering. Instead, such terms as *language upgrades, platform migrations,* and *applications replacement* were used. Thus, consultants selected independent, standalone tools that they knew.

Integrated tool sets did not exist in the mid-1980s. Subsequently, a few vendors have built some quality tool benches. One vendor that has been a steady force in maintenance and reengineering is ViaSoft, Inc. ViaSoft has created an integrated set of quality tools, called Existing Systems Workbench, that supports most reengineering activities. This workbench provides metrics to analyze and guide reengineering projects and ongoing maintenance as well as integrated tools for performing mechanized reengineering.

When tools are evaluated, the cost of purchasing the tool should be considered secondary to the cost of implementing the tool. Better-integrated tool sets will require less support and be easier to implement.

Another consideration is choosing a vendor that will remain in the market. Vendors must understand legacy systems and have an overall reengineering vision. Many vendors have lacked this vision, and many tools have subsequently changed vendors several times. This raises support costs in organizations requiring new or revised processes. It is important to find vendors that continually enhance their products as well as their product lines. This information can be easily obtained by asking the vendor for the history of its product line. Vendors should also be asked for industry references. Independent consultants are also a good source of unbiased information about tools and vendors.

Resistance to Change

Organizations often underestimate the resistance to change, even change that is perceived to be good. Such was the case with the reengineering group at Pacific Bell. Projects managed and staffed by external consultants have faced this problem for a long time. External consultants, however, have the opportunity to finish the project and leave the organization. Internal teams do not have that opportunity and must continue to work against the resistance of colleagues. Therefore, it is important to start on the right foot.

Daryl Conner, an organizational development expert based in Atlanta, explains change in an interesting way. According to Conner, capabilities are always balanced against challenge. Status quo is when capability (i.e., ability and willingness) equals challenge (i.e., danger and opportunity). Positive change occurs when capability becomes greater than challenge, and negative change occurs when challenge becomes greater than capability.

Because of the fast pace of technological changes and the demanding nature of business changes, IS organizations, especially large ones, are confronted with employees who experience much change and consequent anxiety. On one hand, these employees want to continue to grow professionally (i.e., willingness); however, they fear that they will no longer be regarded as and rewarded for being experts if they allow their systems to be reengineered. Although these systems may be a complex mess, they are familiar with this mess.

Change requires training and time to assimilate new methods and concepts. The more employees are asked to change, the less time they have for learning and training. Thus, the perception of danger increases and so does resistance, which can lessen productivity.

Change begins at the sponsor level and requires adequate time and training. Unfortunately, few organizations are allowed this training and transition time because management does not really view the reengineered system as a different system. It is usually business as usual with the same or greater productivity expectations. With the proper support of senior management and training, change is not a painful and unpredictable process. The steps listed in Exhibit 56.2 are critical for successfully implementing change.

Education and Training

Although many companies have succeeded with reengineering, many still find that education is a critical issue. Because of constant corporate reorganizations, corporate decision makers are often unaware of the maturity of reengineering technology. They are unaware of the systems options that are possible through reengineering.

Industry experts are brought into the organization to deliver presentations for the purpose of educating and sharing success stories from other companies. In addition to methodology training classes, internal focus groups are another forum for sharing information on methods and processes. Because of the constant change in technology and business, education continues to be important.

Without proper education, internal teams cannot reengineer systems. Because reengineering can be applied to many business areas, specific training is needed to use the proper methods, processes, and tools as well as to understand the related changes.

Blueprint Framework

The method for creating a cost-effective strategy for making the transition from legacy systems is to understand business goals objectively and ask, How can the current system be used to meet these goals? Typically, organizations are reluctant to take the time to do an initial thorough inventory and analysis of their systems.

Metrics are often not kept on programs and systems. Without a set of comprehensive metrics, systems managers cannot measure the effects of new releases of systems and programs. Consequently, systems complexity and maintenance costs soar. With a portfolio of systems and program metrics, standards and software management methods can be enforced. The metrics can help management to see systems option alternatives, which are listed in Exhibit 56.4.

Legacy systems still exist because they do perform a business function. In most cases, the business rules still apply and major portions of the systems are salvageable. By combining the systems option of replacing and developing new (see Exhibit 56.4) systems, reengineers can extract reusable functions and code, thereby reducing project costs.

For organizations that simply want to decrease maintenance costs and improve maintainability, the 80/20 rule still applies; by improving the worst 20 percent of the system, 80 percent of the problems are solved. For example, one or two large, complex, critical path programs can be modularized to reduce complexity, eliminate redundant or dead functions, and improve architecture and processes. Multiple programmers can then work on new modules simultaneously to respond more quickly to user requests. In addition, productivity is increased, because smaller, less-complex modules require less time to analyze, change, and test, and the reliance on a few individual system experts is reduced.

Most companies have life cycle and development methodologies, but most lack a redevelopment methodology that guides the activities discussed in the previous paragraphs. Such organizations are unaware of the value of reengineering activities or how to plan such projects. These organizations can benefit from a redevelopment methodology, however, because at least 80 percent of all IS activity is related to existing systems.

A REDEVELOPMENT METHODOLOGY

A redevelopment methodology should be driven by business needs, provide flexible, robust processes, and integrate enabling technologies. The following sections give an overview of The Systems Redevelopment Methodology (TSRM), which was created by William M. Ulrich. This methodology is examined in depth in Chapter XI-5, "Moving Legacy Systems into the Future."

Business-Driven Scenarios

The scenario concept facilitates rapid analysis of specific IS situations and enables management issues to be matched to areas described in the scenarios. A scenario identifies a unique sequence of methodology activities to accommodate the project requirements. This is especially helpful to organizations that lack reengineering training or experience. The unique sequence ensures that all essential activities are addressed.

A few of the more common scenarios are the following:

- *Application replacement.* This scenario describes design recovery and component reuse processes that leverage application replacement efforts.
- *Infrastructure stabilization.* This is the most commonly applied scenario and is used to reduce maintenance costs and increase reliability and quality of legacy systems. It analyzes basic applications weaknesses, determines user requirements, and produces a detailed implementation plan to upgrade the system.
- *Package assimilation.* This scenario assumes that a package has been purchased and is now ready for implementation and integration into the IS environment. Step-by-step instructions are given for assessing the gaps between the existing system and the ideal target system (i.e., the package), ensuring that critical functions in the existing system are not lost in the implementation.

There are currently 11 such scenarios, with new ones being added with most product releases.

Inventory/ Analysis

As shown in Exhibit 56.5, this phase consists of objective-setting tasks in which the reengineering team establishes the hypothesis and builds the plan that is to be followed for inventory and assessment activities. The technical assessment of environment, processes, and data is carried out with automated metrics that measure the quality and structure as well as assess the systems-level data use. Most of the quality metric tools have been integrated in the

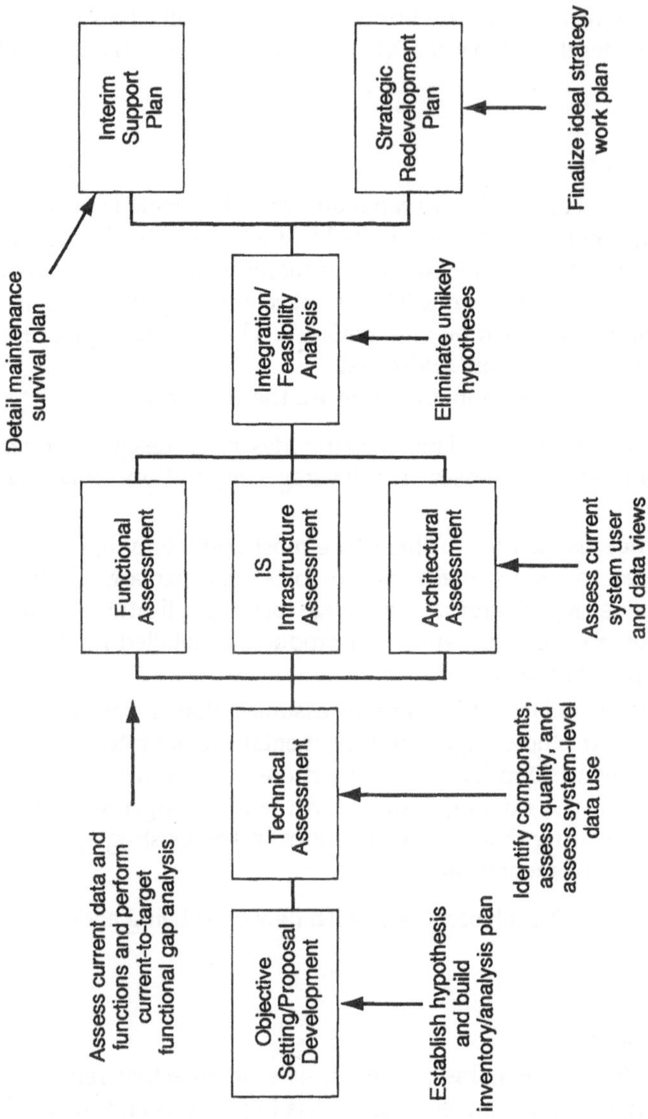

SOURCE: TSG, Inc.

Exhibit 56.5. Process Flow Summary for TSRM Inventory/Analysis Phase

tasks and activities, thus alleviating much of the manual effort. As shown in Exhibit 56.5, once the initial inventory is complete, the technical assessment may be performed simultaneously with the other assessments.

The purpose of the functional assessment is to evaluate current data and functions and perform current-to-date functional gap analysis. In some scenarios, the user backlog is identified, categorized, and ranked during this assessment. The IS infrastructure assessment examines the organization and measures skill and experience levels, tool and methodology proficiency, and testing maturity. The architectural assessment appraises the current systems user and data views. Once all of the assessments have been completed, the metrics and other findings are summarized in the integration and feasibility component. At this time, unlikely hypotheses are usually eliminated, and the team focuses on one objective.

Some scenarios require an interim support plan, which is sometimes referred to as a maintenance survival plan, and others may require a strategic redevelopment plan. This is a long-term plan used to transform the system; transformation is the key component of any redevelopment initiative.

For each component, the methodology provides detailed objectives, entrance criteria, roles and responsibilities, input requirements, tool and technology support, task steps, deliverables, quality checks, metrics, and exit criteria. A team always knows exactly what is required for accurate planning and tracking.

Positioning

Until this phase, only assessments but no changes have been made. Exhibit 56.6 illustrates how the different activities that may occur are designated by the assessments in the prior inventory and analysis phase. Application staging is a support task used in all positioning tasks to ensure that the version control process operates properly. Language changes and upgrades may be as simple as a COBOL II upgrade or as complex as Assembler-to-COBOL conversion.

Code stabilization activities include restructuring accompanied by flaw analysis and removal. The lack of flaw analysis and removal has caused many restructuring projects to fail. Without this step, the quality of restructured code may be very poor.

Data definition and standardization involve multiple tasks that are aimed at improving the quality of existing data definitions across one or more systems and eliminating the redundant record groupings. Remodularization eases maintenance by decreasing complexity, realigning functions, and eliminating redundancies and facilitates transition architecture.

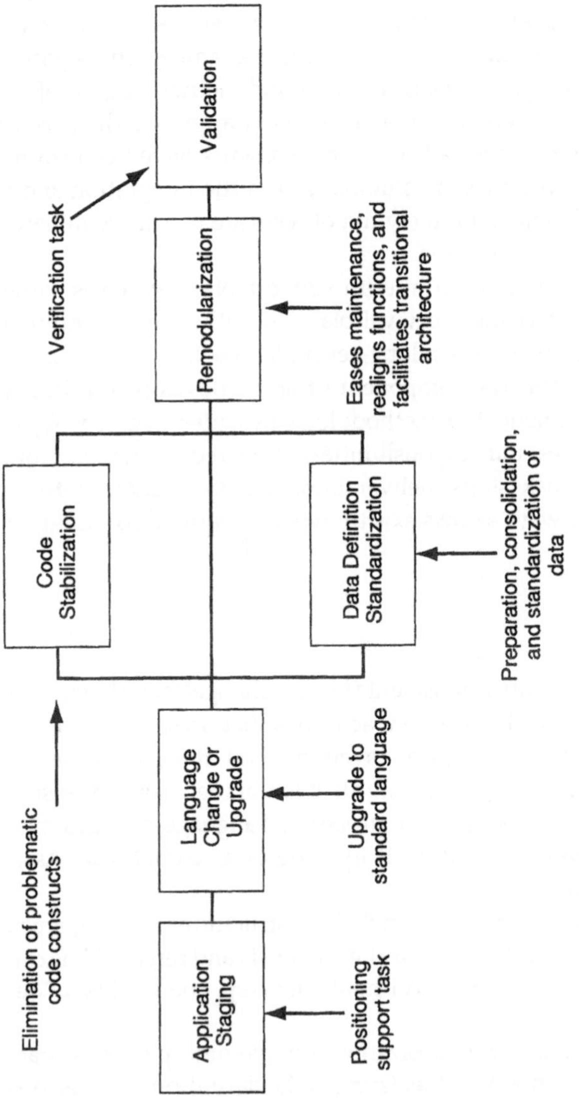

SOURCE: TSG, Inc.

Exhibit 56. 6. Process Flow Summary for TSRM Position Phase

Validation is, of course, the process of verifying that source code improvements, as applied during the positioning tasks, do not introduce any functional changes to the code.

Transformation

The last phase of the methodology is depicted in Exhibit 56.7. In the transformation phase, software redevelopment models are created through the use of top-down and bottom-up analysis of current and target application. The goals of transformation are to specify the tasks required to view existing systems in the form of formal models and, if applicable, to use those models to assist in leveraging the development of a replacement system. Obviously, not all scenarios require this stage of the methodology.

ACTION PLAN

Successes and failures have been discussed throughout this chapter. For the most part, failures can be attributed to not meeting the reengineering critical success factors. Knowing and understanding the pitfalls before beginning a reengineering project can lessen risk factors significantly and increase project successes. Following are additional helpful hints:

- Always ensure that there is a real business need to reengineer. Reengineering can deliver significant value and return on investment if the application or system is of importance to the business.
- IS and business sponsors can form a powerful association. Encourage their continued involvement and support through constant education and project feedback.
- A trained team is essential to success.
- Technical skills are important, but a lack of organizational change skills can kill reengineering. It takes less energy to do the job right.
- The temptation to jump in with both feet is great. Do homework first.
- Assess infrastructure support. Scrutinize methods and standards. Standards should be developed and implemented before reengineering. Metrics education is essential to everyone involved.
- Overly ambitious targets may send reengineering efforts in circles.
- Research vendors as well as tools. The quality of vendor will probably be in business for years to come. Integrated tool sets are easier and less expensive to implement and maintain.
- Never underestimate the power of resistance to change. Remember to expect it, keep things out in the open, and stay constructive and nondefensive. Leveraging resistance can improve processes and products.

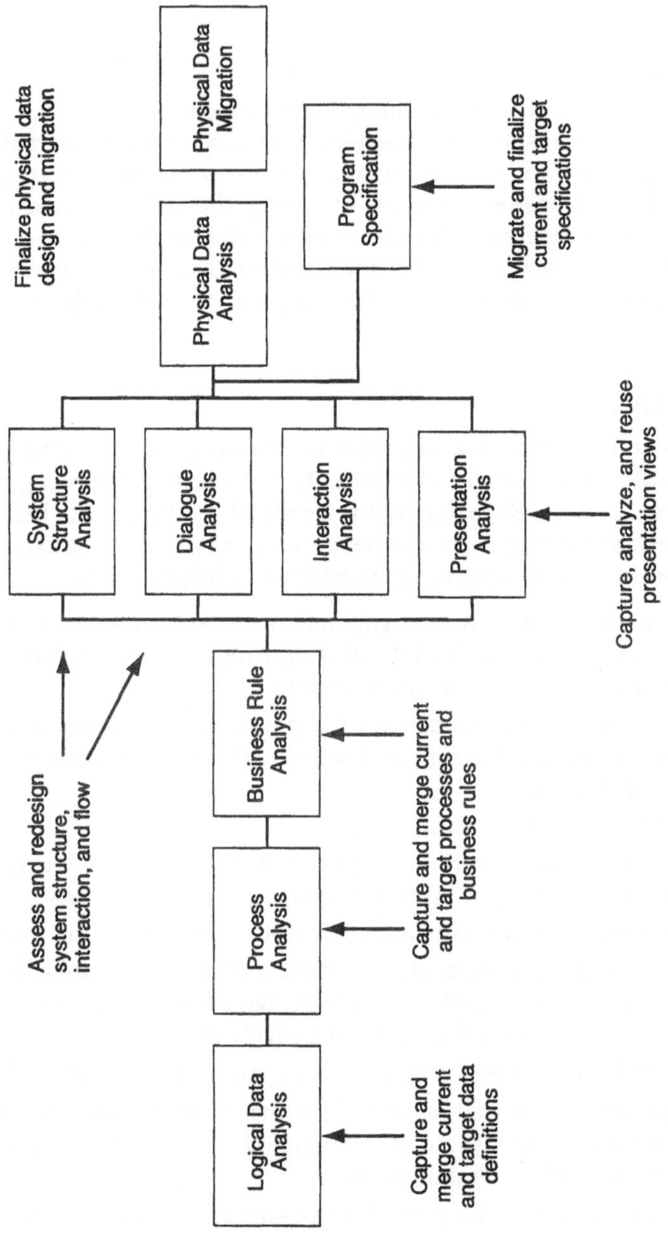

SOURCE: TSG, Inc.

Exhibit 56.7. Process Flow Summary for TSRM Transformation Phase

- Training and education are a constant and never-ending process. Reengineering conferences and user groups are sources for networking with those who have experience. Examine public courses and use industry speakers to influence internal sponsors, managers, and peers.
- Use the software assessment framework (see Exhibit 56.4) to maximize systems options. Remember, reengineering is a technology that has pragmatic strategies, techniques, and procedures, producing cost-effective solutions for many business needs.
- A methodology is essential to success. A flexible, project-oriented framework based on business requirements and integrated with supporting technologies ensures quality deliverables.
- Perhaps the most important point to remember is that there are no silver bullets.

Chapter 57

A Systems Approach to Software Maintenance

John G. Burch and Fritz H. Grupe

Software maintenance is sometimes viewed as a necessary evil — a laborious, uninspiring, and costly task. Nonetheless, maintenance must be performed over the life of a system, which may run for years. Maintenance can be beneficial and well managed, or it can be burdensome and expensive. This chapter suggests methods for making software maintainability a paramount goal of systems development.

TYPES OF SOFTWARE MAINTENANCE

Software (and hardware) maintenance can be categorized into four types:

- Corrective maintenance.
- Adaptive maintenance.
- Perfective maintenance.
- Preventive maintenance.

Corrective Maintenance

Corrective maintenance is the most burdensome part of software maintenance because it corrects design, coding, and implementation errors that should never have occurred. Commonly, corrective maintenance is the result of an urgent or emergency condition that needs immediate attention. The ability to diagnose rapidly and remedy the error or malfunction is of considerable value to the organization.

The need for a significant level of corrective maintenance usually implies that the systems development life cycle (SDLC), various systems development modeling tools and technologies, and testing procedures were not used properly or at all while the software was being built.

Adaptive Maintenance

Adaptive maintenance is performed to satisfy changes in the processing or data environment and to meet new user requirements. The environment in which the software operates is dynamic; therefore, the software must be

0-8493-9822-3/00/$0.00+$.50

responsive to changing user requirements. For example, a new tax law may require a change in the calculation of net pay, or the adoption of a new accounting depreciation method must be installed, or a report's content and format need to be updated. Generally, adaptive maintenance is inevitable. Too much of it indicates, however, that user requirements were not defined adequately during systems development.

Perfective Maintenance

Perfective maintenance enhances performance or maintainability and meets user requirements that had gone unrecognized. When making substantial changes to any software module, the maintenance staff also exploits the opportunity to upgrade the code, remove outdated branches, correct sloppiness, and improve documentation. For example, this maintenance activity may involve reengineering or restructuring software, rewriting documentation, altering report formats and content, and designing more efficient processing logic. The need for perfective maintenance, as for adaptive maintenance, may also indicate that analysts did not discover all user needs or that programmers were unable to fulfill all requirements before the software was released.

Preventive Maintenance

Preventive maintenance — also called proactive maintenance — consists of a periodic inspection and review of the system to uncover and anticipate problems. As maintenance personnel work with a system, they often find defects that signal potential problems. These defects may not require immediate attention; if left uncorrected in the minor stage, however, they could significantly affect either the functioning of the system or the ability to maintain it in the near future.

IMPROVING SOFTWARE MAINTAINABILITY

Maintainability refers to the capacity of maintenance personnel to perform corrective, adaptive, perfective, or preventive maintenance without wrestling with unnecessary obstructions, such as poor design and the lack of documentation. Clearly, these people will have difficulty performing maintenance if the software cannot be understood.

Maintainability should be a paramount goal of software development. The following section discusses ways to reduce obstructions and build applications software that is highly maintainable.

Designing for Software Maintenance

Software maintainability is increased if the system is designed to make changes easier. A maintainable system is more flexible because it allows new features to be incorporated easily, enables programmers to locate and resolve problems, and prevents a change from producing unforeseen side effects. Maintainability encompasses a variety of procedures, some of which are explained in the following paragraphs.

SDLC and SWDLC

The professional application of the systems life cycle and its subcomponent, the software development life cycle (SWDLC), establishes an engineered, structured approach to the development of the total system and its supporting customized applications software. Various modeling tools (e.g., data flow diagrams, entity-relationship diagrams, and structure charts) are used to facilitate the SDLC and SWDLC. The application of these modeling tools can be automated using CASE technologies.

Standard Data Definitions

The trend toward database management systems underpins the need for standard data definitions and data normalization. Redundant and inconsistent data definitions that exist throughout an organization's procedure manuals, source program documentation, and data files add further to the problem of maintenance. A glossary or data dictionary of terms for data elements and other items in the system should be provided. For example, all data elements should have a standard name, description, size, source, location, security, and maintenance responsibility designation. It is also important to use the name precisely in each application. CUST-NAME is not the same as CUSTOMER-NAME, for example.

Standard Programming Languages

The use of a standard programming language, such as C or COBOL, makes the maintenance task easier. If COBOL- or C-based software contains complete and clear internal documentation, even a novice maintenance programmer can understand what the software does. Moreover, C and COBOL are universal languages generally known to many people. Therefore, maintenance programmers turnover has less impact on the company's ability to maintain old C and COBOL programs.

Modular Design

With home appliances, a repair person can determine which part is causing trouble and quickly replace it. Similarly, maintenance programmers can change modules of a program much more easily than they can deal with the total, monolithic program. Many object-oriented and nonprocedural language make true modularization difficult. The flexibility of these languages can be constrained, however, by developing standards to group logically related blocks of code to facilitate debugging and maintenance.

Reusable Code

Modularity fosters reusability. One common module of reusable code can be accessed by all the applications requiring it. Should it need to be changed, modifying this one common module is all that is needed. CASE products provide a central repository in which previously defined data and program modules can be stored and accessed for reuse — a key productivity aid for systems developers. In fact, storing data and program modules in a central repository or library for ready access is a key feature of systems development and software maintenance.

Documentation Standards

Complete documentation is needed (for the system, the users, the programs, management, and operations) so that all the information required to run and maintain an application is available. Documentation must be up-to-date with the code in use. This supportive material should include reference to the changes that have been made to the code. Ideally, changes to code should automatically generate supportive documentation and data that can be assembled in management reports. Effective documentation can include CASE tool products, flowcharts, operator's manuals, and program source code. Although maintenance activities are initiated by many sources, much of the documentation effort focuses on the maintenance programmers.

Central Control

All programs, documentation, and test data should be installed in a central file under the control of a directory and program librarian package. (A change management system that accomplishes this job and more is discussed later in the chapter.)

Test Case Libraries

Test cases that were created during the testing phase of the SWDLC should be retained in a library for maintenance work. Some test cases can be turned over to maintenance programmer; others will be used by the quality assurance group.

Standard Fourth-Generation Design Aids

A software package built years ago may no longer be the best means of processing some applications. A more easily maintained solution may be to scrap the old software and to developing a new system using fourth-generation languages (4GLs), database query language (e.g., SQL and QBE), or function-specific software (e.g., a spreadsheet or a report generator) that is available off the shelf.

CASE and 4GL tools serve as aids to automating the project development life cycle. Indeed, systems analysis, design, construction, and testing are supported by assorted available CASE and 4GL toolsets.

ORGANIZING FOR SOFTWARE MAINTENANCE

There is no clear-cut, best way to organize for systems maintenance; however, three methods are worth exploring. The choices are to:

- Separate systems development and software maintenance.
- Combine systems development and software maintenance.
- Position systems professionals who have responsibility for both systems development and software maintenance within the organization's functional areas.

Separating Development and Maintenance

Traditionally, IS programmers and analysts have been organized into two distinct groups: development and maintenance. This separation of duties provides a natural way for one group to force the other group to perform its work properly. For example, a maintenance programmer would not accept a new program for operations unless it had been thoroughly tested during development.

Maintenance that is performed separately from development has its advantages; it requires better-prepared documentation and formalizes change procedures as well as the system's conversion to an operational system. In addition, senior maintenance programmers may be promoted to development project leaders, because they have acquired in-depth knowledge of documentation requirements, standards, and operations. Maintenance positions are also an effective training ground for junior programmers.

A Combined Approach

The combined approach brings together both development and maintenance personnel into one major group within the IS department. This form of organization creates a closed loop in which systems developers are forced to deal with all maintenance problems as well — a situation that encourages the use of development techniques that ensure the software's maintainability.

If both development and maintenance are performed in the same group, then users have one point of contact with IS personnel who can effect change. User departments often do not know whether a request for work will be classified as development or maintenance, because large revisions or system improvements are often treated as development. Furthermore, the analysts, designers, and coders who originally developed the systems can assess the full impact of changes. Some software is so critical and complex that maintenance must be handled by only the most capable people, and in many cases, the most capable people are those who developed the software in the first place.

The Functional Approach

The functional approach is a variation of the combined approach. The difference is that the functional approach removes systems professionals from the IS department and assigns them to business departments, where they are responsible for both development and maintenance. Specialization is by the organization's functional areas, and is no longer a choice between development and maintenance. The functional approach to organization puts systems professionals much closer to users, in terms of both physical proximity and knowledge of users' jobs and requirements.

By virtue of employing the functional approach, systems professionals are actually members of the user departments and, consequently, have a vested interest in the success and feasibility of systems applications. Moreover, systems professionals become more business-literate and users become more systems-literate. The payoff is understanding, communication, and mutual interest. The downside of the functional approach includes a possible loss of IS control over development standards and procedures and blurring of priorities.

SOFTWARE MAINTENANCE METHODOLOGY

If the development of software requires a structured methodology, then it seems logical that after the software has been converted to operations, its maintenance should also follow a structured methodology. A number of authorities recommend that software maintenance be performed according to a software maintenance life cycle (SMLC). Essentially, the SMLC includes the following phases.

THE MAINTENANCE REQUEST

The user submits a maintenance request that is used to prepare a maintenance Work Order (see Exhibit 57.1). The work order includes information that management is interested in: the work requested, work performed, estimated time versus actual time, maintenance code, and maintenance cost. The maintenance code is structured as illustrated in Exhibit 57.2. Accordingly, maintenance code 116, for example, describes corrective maintenance with emergency priority and a modify activity.

TRANSFORMING THE REQUEST TO A CHANGE

The maintenance staff has a description of both the existing software and the desired software. Transforming the request to a change involves identifying and eliminating the differences between the two.

Maintenance Work Order

Work performed: Add vendor performance code to inventory record.

Name: Tom Barkley Title: Purchasing Agent

Work performed: Added vendor performance code. Tested and documented change.

Name: Maria Gomez Title: Maintenance Programmer

Change Approved: Harry Feldman Date: MM/DD/YY

Number

Request Date

MM | DD | YY

Priority
Emergency
Urgent
Routine

Estimated Time

HH:MM

Actual Time

HH:MM

Maintenance

X | X | X

Labor Cost (actual time x labor rate) $.

Material or Parts Cost .

Total Maintenance Cost $.

Exhibit 57.1. Maintenance Work Order Form

SPECIFYING THE CHANGE

The change may involve all or parts of the existing code, data, and procedures. The new code, data, and procedures are sometimes termed a patch.

DEVELOPING THE CHANGE

The change of patch is designed and coded.

TESTING THE CHANGE

Test procedures are applied to the software after it has been changed. Testing helps to validate and verify that the right change has been made

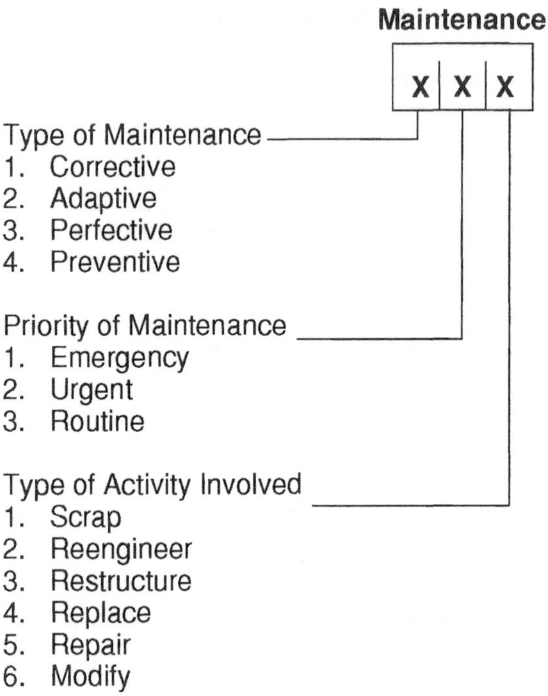

Exhibit 57.2. Deciphering the Maintenance Code

and made correctly. Code walkthroughs, similar to testing in the software development life cycle, focus on the modified code itself (i.e., does the changed code work?).

Regression testing (sometimes referred to as revalidation testing)is done to confirm that modules of the software that were to have been left unchanged still perform as they were intended to perform before the required change. regression testing focuses on the functional integrity of the total software package after the change.

TRAINING USERS AND RUNNING AN ACCEPTANCE TEST

If the change is relatively simple, this step may be skipped. If the change introduces new ways in which users perform their tasks, the users must receive training. After users have been trained, acceptance tests should be conducted using alpha testing — that is, usability or user testing in which users perform their own tests while the maintainer is present.

User involvement in the testing phase may elicit calls for still more changes. These changes should be processed as new work order.

CONVERTING AND RELEASING TO OPERATIONS

When the newly changed software has successfully passed all tests, it is ready to become operational. Simultaneously, the old version of the software should be withdrawn according to a conversion plan.

UPDATING THE DOCUMENTATION

All the documentation pertaining to the maintenance activities should be updated to reflect the newly changed software. Equally important, the out-of-date documentation should be withdrawn from service to avoid confusion.

CONDUCTING A POSTMAINTENANCE REVIEW

The software should operate for a few days or weeks after maintenance has been performed. At that time, the maintenance staff should conduct a postmaintenance review to determine whether the change continues to meet user expectations.

A Source of Management Information

Not only does the SMLC provide a systematic method of performing software maintenance work, it produces a wealth of information that helps management assess the maintenance process to determine where the trouble spots are and to optimize both development and maintenance efforts. Information on all changes that have been made to software may help management determine whether a program should be reengineered, for example. In addition, such information helps to identify problems in the organization's software development life cycle, its programmer training methods, and in the standards the organization uses.

The key to generating such information is the maintenance work order form. Specifically, the form is used to:

- Compute a variety of maintenance cost analyses.
- Measure the number of failures per program.
- Calculate the total number of hours spent on each maintenance type.
- Compute the proportion of emergency, urgent, and routine maintenance.
- Derive the average number of changes made per program, per language, and per maintenance type.
- Develop a profile of those making most of the maintenance requests and the common problems encountered.
- Determine average number of hours spent per line of executable code to change, add, or delete such code.
- Calculate the average turnaround time per maintenance work order. This calculation entails the Mean Time To Repair.

- Build a mean time between failure (MTBF) profile on all applications. From this profile it is possible to determine those applications that are consuming the largest portion of the maintenance budget and why.

TOOLS FOR SOFTWARE MAINTENANCE

Tools that support software maintenance fall into three categories: reverse engineering, reengineering, and restructuring.

Reverse Engineering

Reverse engineering must be performed in situations in which the appropriate development techniques were not applied. Reverse engineering is a process of examining and learning more about the existing software by recreating its design. The entire system is read, including source code, screens, reports, data definitions, and Job Control Language. The results are abstractions of design specifications in the form of models such as data flow diagrams and structure charts. From these resources, systems professionals can obtain a clear view of the old system so they can analyze and evaluate its design quality and capabilities. After the system has been fully evaluated, a decision may be made to scrap it.

Unfortunately, much of the software that was developed 10 to 25 years ago was poorly designed, structured, and documented. An important and logical question is whether IS should continue to maintain this old software. Sometimes scrapping the existing software and developing new software from scratch is more effective and efficient. Reverse engineering provides enough design-level understanding to reengineer or restructure the software for easier maintenance or to give management sufficient information to support a replacement decision.

Reengineering Tools

Some software may be worth reengineering. Reengineering generally includes some form of reverse engineering to gain a better understanding of the existing system, followed by redevelopment engineering to redesign and change the quality and capability of the software. Unnormalized data is normalized, data names are standardized, and ambiguities, redundancies, anomalies, and unused code are eliminated. Inefficient code is recoded to be made efficient. Unstructured code is structured. Documentation is prepared or improved. In essence, the quality and capability of the existing software are improved. The software is then reimplemented in a new form.

Reenginneering is ideal for supporting major corrective, adaptive, perfective, and preventive maintenance projects. A substantial number of Work Order pertaining to a given system is indicative of a need to reengineer the system.

Restructuring

If the software's capability essentially meets the needs of the user, then the software is functionally sound. However, old software that is functionally sound is often structurally unsound, which makes the software difficult to understand and difficult to maintain.

The restructuring process converts unstructured spaghetti code into fully structured documented code. The restructuring (or more precisely, the structuring) of existing unstructured code is one of the simplest methods available to decrease the cost of maintenance.

Many standalone products or elements of CASE systems are available that enable existing COBOL programs to be structured automatically. These products input spaghetti code at one end and structured, documented code is produced at the other end. The resulting structured software preserves the capability of the original unstructured software and makes it easier and less costly to maintain.

EMPLOYING A CHANGE MANAGEMENT SYSTEM

Change management has become more important as the amount of software maintenance has increased. A comprehensive Change Management System (CMS) assists in controlling the maintenance resources being deployed, in developing new software, and in maintaining existing software. A CMS can be purchased for many hardware platforms for as little as $500 for a microcomputer and for more than $100,000 for a mainframe. A CMS is used to:

- Restrict access to production source and object code.
- Reduce errors and design defects that may be introduced into the production system.
- Prevent the existence of more than one version of source- and object-code programs in the Production Master File.
- Increase security and overall control of software development and maintenance activities.

A CMS is illustrated in Exhibit 57.3. Its principal components are the Librarian Function Facility, programmer workstations, the Test Master File, the Quality Assurance Master File, the production master file, the Backup Master File, and management reports and audit trails. A maintenance Work Order initiates change management activities.

Librarian Function Facility

The Library Function Facility is the heart of the CMS. It works in a manner similar to any librarian function, collecting and controlling vital documents and software.

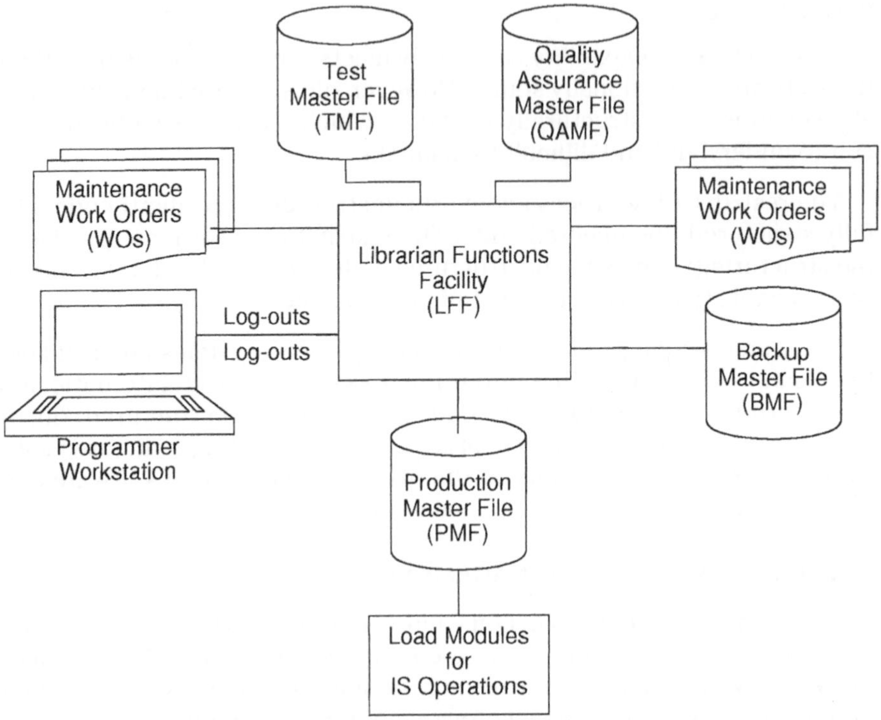

Exhibit 57.3. A Change Management System

The librarian function facility is itself a software package that centralizes, tracks, controls, and automates changes to software against an approved maintenance work order. It also controls the implementation of newly developed or acquired software. Exhibit 57.4 depicts the program promotion and release hierarchy. If a program that is already in production has to be changed, it is logged out to the test master file. If a new program is to be placed into production, it must first enter the test master file. No direct introduction of new software or changes to old software are allowed in the production master file.

The librarian function facility controls linkage between source and object code and automatically loads modules online for execution, thereby ensuring synchronization of both the source and object code. Comprehensive management reports and audit trails are available on screen or as hard copy for history, status, tracking, and performance information. All master files are backed up to safeguard the system from disasters. Programmers have online access to the CMS to augment change productivity. Programmers' access privileges are controlled by passwords or biometric control devices.

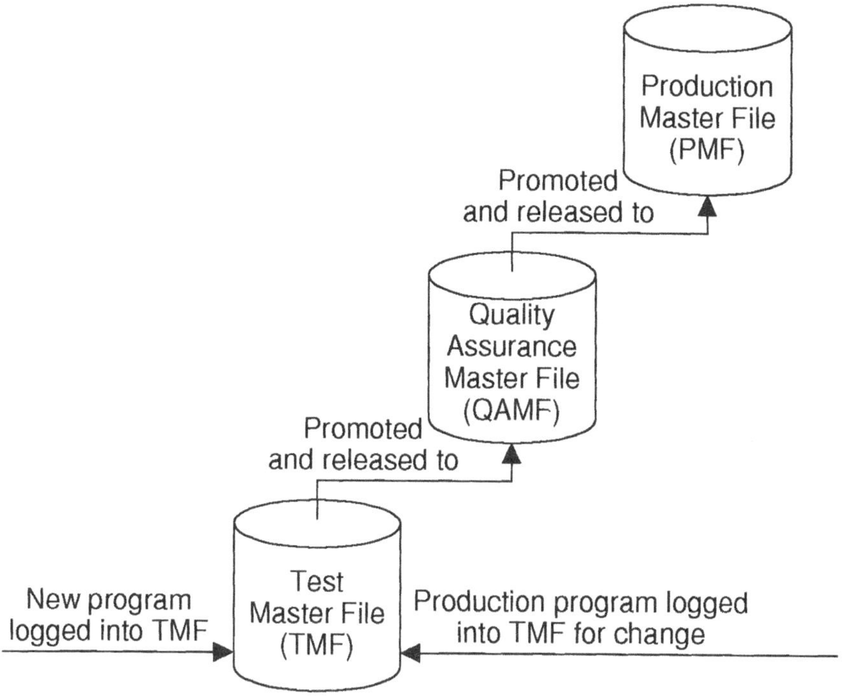

Exhibit 57.4. Software Promotion and Release Hierarchy

Programmer Workstations

The CMS acts as a single point of control, and approved work order initiate log-outs and log-ins that allow programmers to do their job at their workstations. Log-outs are done against an approved and assigned work order.

When working against a specific work order, programmers are permitted to log out as many modules as necessary to complete the assigned unit of work. Program modules outstanding to other work order are noted during the log-out process.

Log-ins are performed to promote and release a changed and tested program to the quality assurance master file and then to the Production Master File. Careful testing and walkthrough procedures are conducted before any program or program modules are promoted and released to the production master file.

Middle-of-the-night production problems generally require a maintenance programmer to be onsite or, if at home, to return to the office to correct the problem. On-call programmers with workstations installed at their homes and connected to the CMS can increase the efficiency of maintenance work.

Although this setup does not guarantee that programmers may not receive a late-night phone call, it may reduce the need for a trip to the office.

Test Master File

To change a production program, a work order must be opened and the program demoted from the Production Master File to the test master file. This operation changes the program from production status to test status. As long as the test status is maintained, the program can be changed.

A new program entering the test master file is subjected to testing procedures. If it passes these tests, it is promoted and released to the quality assurance master file. A production program that is demoted to the test master file has already been subjected to these tests, but after it is changed, it is subjected to regression testing.

Quality Assurance Master File

Some CMS employ an independent quality assurance group. This group serves as an additional control, because it reviews and tests the program independently of the maintenance programmers before the program is promoted and released to production. In addition to performing an array of tests, a chief function of the QA group is to conduct source code walkthroughs. In a source code walkthrough, the QA group reviews the actual program code to see whether it matches change requests, design specifications, and standards. Then the group simulates how such code will be processed by the computer to discover coding errors or malfunctions.

Production Master File

After a program enters the production master file, it is locked into production status and cannot be changed. With proper authorization, a program can be copied and logged into the test master file with a new name, and the copied version can be changed. This protective feature helps to ensure that production programs will not be changed inadvertently.

Backup Master File

In the event that any master files is destroyed, the CMS permits IS personnel to recover from a backup master any files or specific modules that may have been lost. Similarly, if a program placed into production fails to operate as expected, recovery is enabled by the retrieval of a previous version. Usually, a copy of the backup master file is maintained locally and another copy is stored off site in a secure location.

Management Reports and Audit Trails

Reporting features help managers to develop an optimized CMS and auditors to attest to the integrity of the CMS. Management needs information about the maintenance process so that it can evaluate and optimize maintenance activities. Audit trails help to ensure the integrity of the system.

RECOMMENDED COURSE OF ACTION

Software maintenance includes all changes made to a software product after it has been turned over to operations. Like any product, software must be changed as necessary to continue to satisfy changing user requirements. IS managers can take certain actions to make this task less expensive and time-consuming.

BUILT-IN QUALITY

Corrective maintenance is the most expensive task in information systems development, and the reason for this resource-consuming task is that the software product was not designed and developed correctly in the first place. Correcting errors and design flaws during operations is the worst kind of software maintenance. The IS manager should therefore ensure that systems developers practice Total Quality Management and follow a well-developed SDLC. A major part of the SDLC implementation phase requires stringent testing procedures and design walkthroughs. Before becoming operational, all software products should be subjected to a comprehensive testing process and pass stringent quality standards.

IS managers can learn a lot by taking notice of what is happening in world-class manufacturing. Traditional manufacturers believed that quality increased costs. Today's world-class manufacturers have learned that quality actually decreases costs. The underlying concept is to design quality in, rather than try to build (or maintain) it in. World-class manufacturers recognize that as a product moves from design to production to consumers, the more costly it is to correct errors and defects. IS managers can develop world-class information systems (and easy-to-maintain software) by emulating their counterparts in the manufacturing sector by designing quality into their products.

DEVELOPING MAINTAINABLE SOFTWARE

Generally, poorly designed software is not only expensive to maintain, but some of it is difficult or even impossible to maintain. Indeed, the high costs of software maintenance are in large part due to the need to maintain software that was developed without the use of structured methods and sound documentation procedures. Such software lacks proper modular structure and contains spaghetti code, so that it is difficult to change one part of the program without affecting other parts. As a consequence, it is hard to develop testing procedures to validate the modified program. Without comprehensive, current, and correct documentation, the maintainer may not be able to understand enough about the software to perform any maintenance. CASE products can recast a program from spaghetti and undocumented code into a structured and documented format. CASE products can reverse engineer, reengineer, or restructure old software so that it becomes much easier to maintain. IS managers should encourage the use of CASE tools if unstructured and undocumented software exists in their systems.

ORGANIZE FOR SOFTWARE MAINTENANCE

Maintenance costs are frequently increased by low morale on the part of the maintenance staff, with resultant low productivity. Usually, this unhappy and costly situation is a consequence of the lower status accorded by some organizations to maintenance work as compared with systems development. The job of software maintenance should not only be accorded high status, it should be organized properly.

IMPLEMENT A SMLC

Software development follows a software development life cycle. Because software maintenance should also follow an engineered methodology, the installation of a SMLC is strongly recommended. Besides providing an engineered approach to performing maintenance, the SMLC is instrumental in providing information that helps IS managers to analyze and optimize software maintenance.

INSTALL A CMS

To support the foregoing actions in an efficient and effective manner, a CMS should be installed. A CMS centralizes, controls, tracks, and simplifies the development and maintenance of all computing resources, especially software. Additional IS management benefits delivered by a CMS include:

- Clearer separation of responsibilities.
- Avoidance of loss of changes.
- Improvement in both development and maintenance productivity.
- Synchronization of source and object code.
- Ability to back out of changes if necessary.
- Enforcement of quality assurance standards.
- Improvement in auditing, security, and control.
- Upgraded management reporting and review.
- Improved priority setting.

Bibliography

Chapin, N. "Software Maintenance Life Cycle." *Proceedings of the Conference on Software Maintenance 1988*. Washington D.C.: Computer Society Press of the IEEE, 1988.

Chapin, N. "Changes in Change Control." *Proceedings of the Conference on Software Maintenance 1989*. Washington D.C.: Computer Society Press of the IEEE, 1989.

Hanna, M.A. "Defining the 'R' Words for Automated Maintenance." *Software Magazine*, May 1990.

Marek, B. *CA Librarian Change Control Facility: Source Management for the 1990s and Beyond.* Phoenix: Computer Associates International, Inc., March 1990.

Tayntor, C.B. "Maintenance Magic."*System Builder*, "October–November 1990.

Section XI – Checklist

1. How does your organization allocate resources to software support?
2. In your opinion, does system maintenance consume a high portion of staff time? How does this impact your responsibilities?
3. At which age would you define a legacy system? Would this classify most of your organization's systems as legacy?
4. What analysis has been performed to determine the scope of legacy applications? Does this cover multiple languages?
5. Within an existing legacy application, has there been any effort to perform portfolio analysis to determine which programs are the most difficult to maintain? Does this apply to the library of all developed programs?
6. Has your organization estimated the cost of supporting existing applications vs. cost of replacement? If not, what effort would be required to make this determination?
7. Which methods has your organization applied to evaluate the support of newer systems that were deployed in the last few years?
8. In your opinion, did the year 2000 crisis create more or less recognition for the need of software maintenance?
9. What is the ratio between support and development projects in your organization? Has anyone ever calculated this ratio before?
10. What percentage of existing software is absolutely crucial to business survival? How are these systems supported?
11. What plans, if any, does your organization have toward reengineering older applications?
12. Has conversion of older systems been successful? If so, was this due to the use of methodologies, procedures, or tools?
13. Do you favor the use of software tools for reengineering or does it seem more practical to redevelop an application as if it were new? Are there advantages to this approach?
14. What steps has your organization taken to evaluate support beyond the year 2000 date change?
15. Would you support the use of newer technology, such as the Intranet, to extend the life of older systems? If not, how would keep legacy systems functioning longer?

Section XII
Post Development Administration

The prestige of design and development activities frequently overshadows the subtle but important need of system administration. Typically, administrative tasks are neglected or ignored soon after the implementation process has ended. In turn, this can lead to long term support hardships throughout the entire application system life cycle. Development managers, in numerous IS environments, struggle with the ongoing demands of administration duties. Larger organizations are often more successful due to dedicated staff resources. But smaller environments, which are prone to hectic development schedules, are less capable of keeping up with post implementation requirements. In the latter situation, development managers should adopt practices that can minimize the overhead needed for system administration, especially in the area of data retention management.

One of the most crucial areas for system administration is in the area support services. Unfortunately the decentralization of enterprise applications due to remote and distributed access has impacted traditional support techniques. Chapter 58, "Delivering Support Services Through the World Wide Web," explores the numerous opportunities that can aid organizations in meeting support demands amidst shortages in staff and budgetary allocations. The unique characteristics of the Web have made it an ideal support tool in the last several years. It is expected that newer advancements in audio and video components of the Web will further the advantages in the support arena.

As development of applications increase, the need for adequate procedures and resources to handle the volume of stored data becomes paramount. This should embrace all types of operating environments and hardware platforms including those from mainframes, servers, and desktop workstations. Chapter 59, "File Retention and Backup," provides an overview on the fundamentals for adequate file control. Despite the obvious need for backups, many organizations do not have comprehensive backup procedures across all computing platforms. Usually, the realization of this fact comes to light only after a need for data restoration is required.

Organizations that store data in disparate repositories struggle with the variety of file structures that are used by software applications. But environments that use a formal database product may be better prepared and benefit from the inherent backup capabilities that are integrated into the product. Nevertheless, databases still need careful administration for effective recovery. Chapter 60, "Managing Database Backup and Recovery," delivers practical advice on the methods needed to maintain database integrity. These methods can even be used during the early stages of development so that preliminary data files are not lost or corrupted via software errors.

Chapter 58
Delivering Support Services through the World Wide Web

Nathan J. Muller

The traditional help desk provides network, systems, and applications support for internal corporate users. But in recent years, the trend toward corporate downsizing has expanded the help desk function to include telecommuter sites and branch and international offices — locations that often are too expensive to tie into the corporate backbone network through leased lines or switched digital services.

At the same time, customers are becoming more demanding and deluging companies of all types and sizes with requests for technical support for the hardware and software they purchase. Customers want expert assistance when they need it, regardless of business hours. This increased demand for service combined with limited budgets and staff has led companies to seek a more efficient and economical approach to delivering support to customers and internal users.

One of the ways companies extend their support operations is through the Internet, specifically, the World Wide Web (WWW). Conceived in 1990 at the European Particle Physics Laboratory in Switzerland (CERN), the Web was originally designed as a means of facilitating the distribution and access of research papers among scientists around the world. The Web has since grown to become one of the most sophisticated and popular services on the Internet, which, according to various industry estimates, now has between 20 and 30 million users worldwide.

The Web's characteristics make it particularly suited to the delivery of technical support for both internal users and customers. The Web provides intuitive, graphical navigation from any place and from any platform. Businesses that use the Web for delivering support services assert that speeding up problem resolution through the Web more than justifies the cost of setting up a Web site.

0-8493-9822-3/00/$0.00+$.50

CHARACTERISTICS OF THE WORLD WIDE WEB

The Web can best be described as a dynamic, interactive, graphically oriented, distributed, platform-independent, hypertext, client/server information system.

Dynamic Features

The WWW is dynamic because it changes daily. New Web servers are continually being added to the estimated 250,000 already online. New information is also being continually added, as are new hypertext links and innovative services — many of which are commercial.

Interactivity

The WWW is interactive because specific information can be requested through various search engines and returned moments later in the form of lists, with each item weighted according to how well it matched the search parameters. Another example of interactivity are online forms for business transactions, whereby users can select items from a catalog, fill out an order form, and send it by electronic mail.

Graphics

The WWW is graphically oriented. In fact, it was designed for the extensive use of graphics. The use of graphics not only makes the Web visually appealing but also easy to navigate. Graphical sign posts direct users to new sources of information accessed through hypertext links. More recently, sound and video capabilities have been added to the Web.

A Distributed System

The WWW is distributed, meaning that information resides on hundreds of thousands of individual Web servers around the world. If one site goes down, there is no significant impact on the Web as a whole, except that access to that site is denied. Some servers are mirrored at other sites to keep information available, even if the primary server fails.

Platform Independence

The WWW is platform independent, which means that virtually any client can access the Web , whether it is based on the Windows, OS/2, Macintosh, or Unix operating environment. This platform independence even applies to the Web servers. Although most Web servers are based on Unix, Windows NT is growing in popularity and may become the platform of choice among developers of new sites.

Hypertext Links

The WWW makes extensive use of hypertext links. A hypertext link is usually identified by an underlined word or phrase, or by a graphic symbol that points the way to other information, which may be found virtually anywhere: the same document, a different document on the same server, or another document on a different server that may be located anywhere in the world. A hypertext link does not necessarily point to text documents; it can point to maps, forms, images, sound and video clips, or applications such as electronic mail, telnet, and remote printer. Hypertext links can even point to other Internet resources such as Gopher, a menu-based system for text-only documents sites, and UseNet, topical discussion groups.

A Client/Server Network

The Web operates as a vast client/server network. The clients are the millions of individual PCs and workstations that run Web navigation software such as Netscape Navigator and Mosaic. These browsers render the text and graphics retrieved from the servers, which are coded in the HyperText Markup Language (HTML). The servers are interconnected by Internet links that run the hypertext transmission protocol (HTTP).

THE BUSINESS CASE FOR WEB-BASED SUPPORT

By publishing support information on the World Wide Web, companies can project a professional image while meeting the routine informational needs of diverse constituents at greatly reduced overhead expense. This, in turn, has strategic ramifications.

For example, an engineering department can use an internal Web server for distributing technical documentation and drawings to suppliers and customers, as well as to design consultants, anywhere in the world. This can greatly speed product development and shorten the time to market.

Companies can also use the Web server to distribute help information, drivers, software patches, and other commonly requested items to customers. This saves staff time and mailing costs while meeting the support needs of customers on a timely basis. Posting product configuration and troubleshooting advice on the Web can ease the telephone bottleneck and reduce support costs. This, in turn, increases customer satisfaction and hence customer loyalty.

Banks and other financial institutions are turning to the Web to offer a variety of customer support services. Not only can bank customers retrieve information about various services and products, in some cases they can access a range of additional services, such as applying for credit and checking account balances. In the near future, such services will be expanded to include online banking, with Web pages providing banks with an alternative to building new branches. Brokerage houses are enabling investors to track their portfolios over the Web and even trade securities in real time. The movement of banking and other financial services to the Web provides institutions with a strategic advantage, because convenience increasingly accounts for the influx of new customers.

DELIVERING WEB-BASED SUPPORT

Using the Web to Enhance Network Support

Many companies are finding that the Web is an ideal medium for enhancing systems and network support. The following are some of the routine tasks being implemented over the Web:

- LAN managers at distributed locations troubleshoot systems and network problems by accessing an HTML-coded database stored in an internal Web server. The Web server makes a valuable adjunct to the help desk, especially when corporate locations are spread across multiple time zones.
- Service requests are dispatched electronically to carriers, vendors, and third-party maintenance firms through standardized forms written in HTML.
- Remote sites that are too small to justify the expense of being tied into the corporate backbone network expedite inventory management by using HTML forms to convey, move, add, and change information to a central management console. Among other things, forms can also be used to report trouble and request technical assistance.

Remote sites too small to afford private lines or switched digital services can tie into central help desk facilities through dialup lines. All that is needed is a SLIP/PPP (Serial Line Internet Protocol/Point-to-Point Protocol) account from an Internet service provider, which can cost as little as $10 per month per user. SLIP/PPP essentially enables the TCP/IP (Transmission Control Protocol/Internet Protocol) suite to run over ordinary phone lines. Access to the Web server can be secured through user IDs, passwords, and site IDs to prevent unauthorized usage and break-ins.

Additional security can be provided by a firewall, which allows all traffic to leave the server but screens incoming traffic in ways that control various levels of access. For example, all packets directed at the firewall can be filtered to block access to unauthorized ports. Or connections can be allowed only from authorized hosts. The firewall administrator can grant or deny access from a broad level down to specific host/port combinations.

Help Desk Support for Remote Users and Customers

In keeping with the trend toward increasingly decentralized corporate operations using client/server and remote access technologies, the traditionally centralized help desk is giving way to a more distributed approach. Accordingly, new ways of delivering help desk support are being implemented.

For a long time, many companies relied on bulletin board systems (BBSs), which enable remote users and customers to dial into databases that provide answers to common problems. The big advantage of bulletin board systems is that they are available 24 hours a day and provide answers to the most frequently asked questions, thus conserving corporate resources. The disadvantage of such systems is that they are often difficult to navigate. In addition, because users typically pay long-distance phone charges while they attempt to learn arcane commands, they are reluctant to use such systems.

Internet access, on the other hand, entails only a local SLIP/PPP connection to an Internet service provider. For a flat monthly fee, users have unlimited access to a variety of services, including the World Wide Web. Unlike BBSs, the Web uses a standardized method of navigation.

Today, companies are capitalizing on the growing popularity of the Internet and are leveraging their existing Internet connections to offer support services over the Web. Although a growing number of vendors offer Web-based modules that work in conjunction with their help desk systems, support applications can easily be developed in-house with the C language, or a derivative such as Perl (Practical Extraction Report Language).

For example, a user at a branch office that is not connected to the corporate backbone network can dial into the company's Web server and fill out a standard help request form. By clicking on the form's "send" button, the completed form is processed by the server's program and sent to the help desk by E-mail. There it is logged, acknowledged, and responded to based on the reported severity of the problem. Exhibits 58.1a–1d show the scrollable online form filled out by the user. Exhibit 58.2 shows the E-mail message that arrives at the corporate help desk through the Web server.

Vendor Add-On Modules

As noted, vendors are recognizing the potential of Internet connections for augmenting help desk operations and offer add-on modules that integrate the Web with their LAN-based support products.

Problem Reporting and Resolution. Remedy Corp. of Mountain View, CA and the Molloy Group of Parsippany, NJ provide two examples of problem-reporting features.

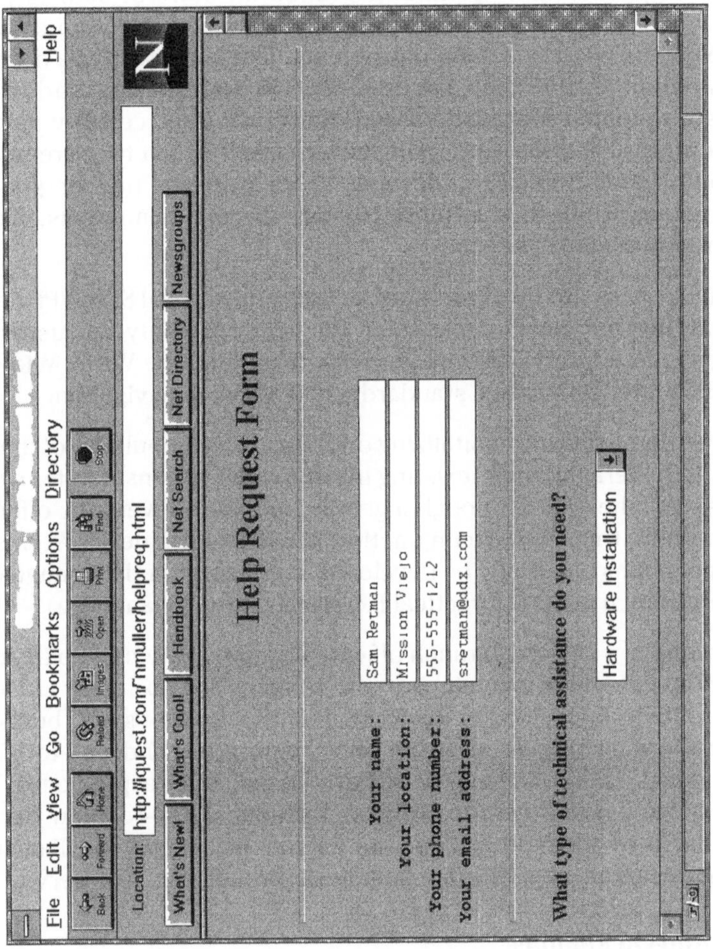

Exhibit 58.1a. Scrollable Online Help Desk Form

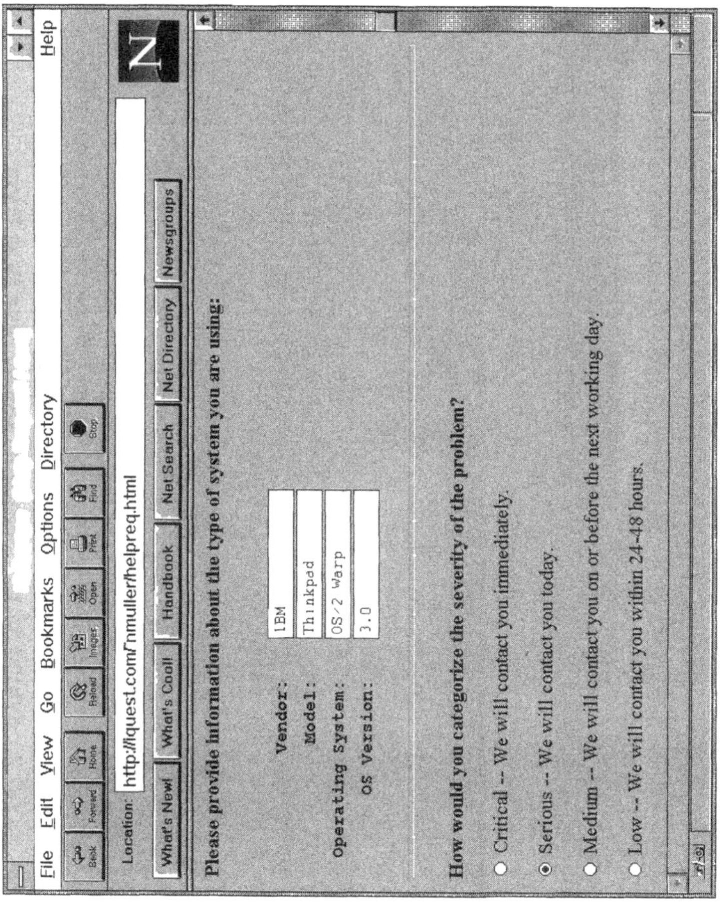

Exhibit 58.1b. Scrollable Online Help Desk Form

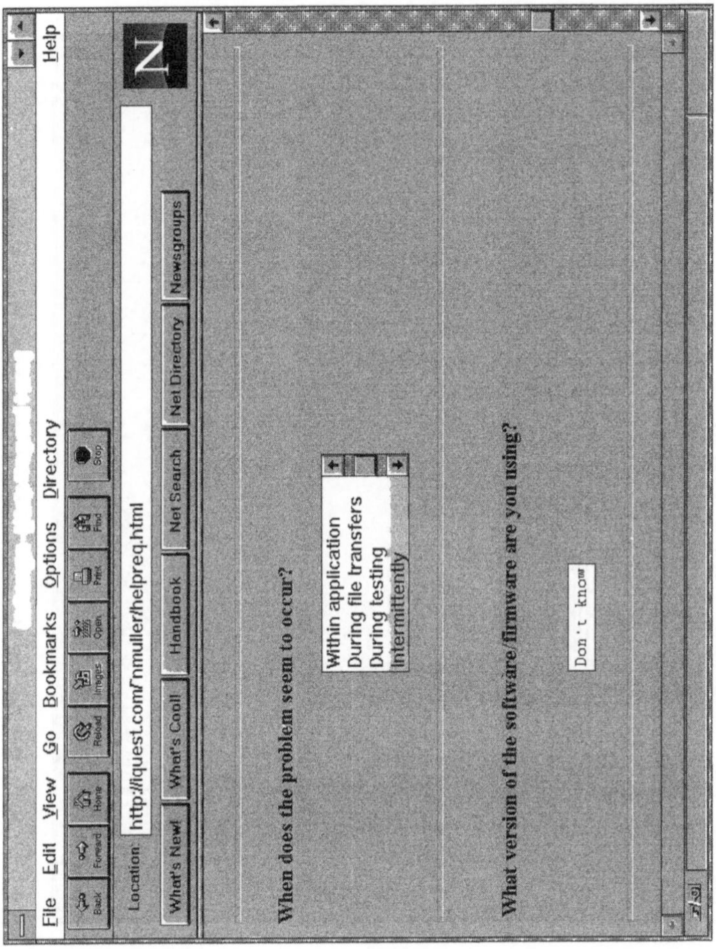

Exhibit 58.1c. Scrollable Online Help Desk Form

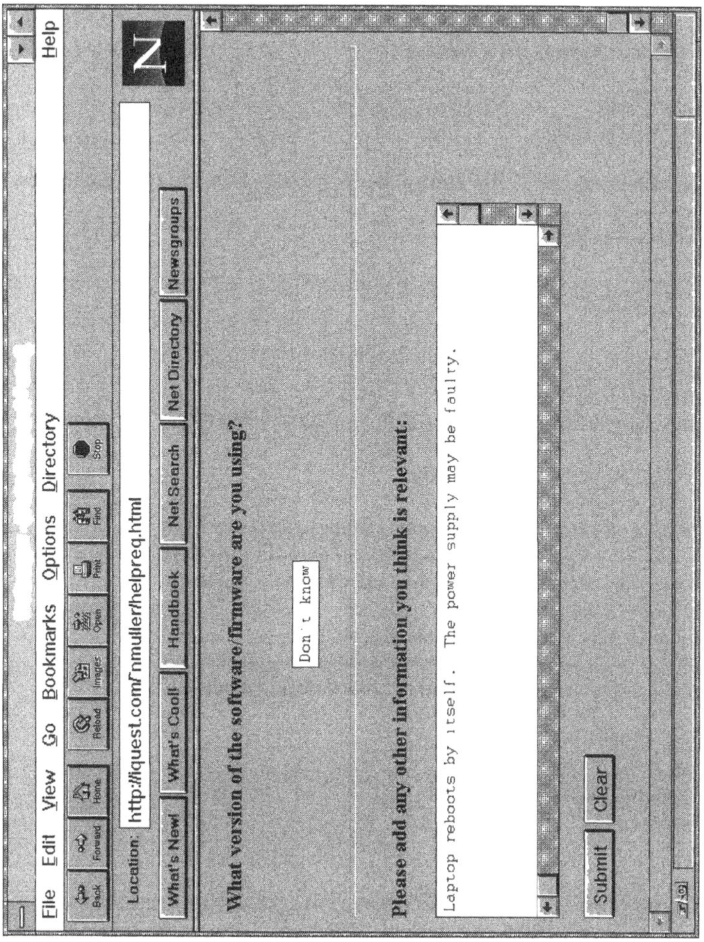

Exhibit 58.1d. Scrollable Online Help Desk Form

Exhibit 58.2. E-Mail Message Received by the Corporate Help Desk through the Web Server

Date: Thu, 7 Sep 1995 09:25:34-0500
To: nmuller@ddx.com (Help Desk)
From: Sam.Retman
Reply-to: sretman@ddx.com (Sam Retman)

This is a request for technical assistance from Sam Retman, who is reachable at sretman@ddx.com.

Sam Retman can also be reached as follows:

Location: Mission Viejo
Phone number: 555-555-1212

The kind of technical assistance Sam Retman needs is related to hardware installation.

The type of system Sam Retman has is:

IBM
thinkpad
OS/2 Warp
3.0

Sam Retman has categorized the severity of the problem as: SERIOUS

The problem seems to occur intermittently.

The version of the software/firmware Sam Retman uses is: Don't Know

---

Sam Retman believes the following additional information is relevant:

Laptop reboots by itself. The power supply may be faulty.

Here is some information about Sam Retman's machine and connections:

Server protocol: HTTP/1.0
Server port: 80
Remote host: nmuller.iquest.com
Remote IP address: 204.177.193.22

ARWeb. Remedy Corp. offers ARWeb, a program that connects its Action Request System with Web browsers. ARWeb permits browsers, such as Netscape Navigator, to function as read-only clients of the Action Request System. This gives end users the capability to submit a trouble ticket, look up a ticket, and check its resolution status. Users also have access to the AR System database of problem solutions as well as to third-party knowledge databases for more solutions.

Cognitive E-Mail. The Molloy Group allows remote users and customers to use the Internet to report problems directly to its Technical and Office Protocol (TOP) of MIND help desk software using its Cognitive E-Mail feature. Received messages are imported into TOP of MIND, and the system automatically opens a trouble ticket for each one and starts the problem diagnosis and resolution process using artificial intelligence.

Configuration Support and Troubleshooting. The Web is also being used to deliver configuration support and troubleshooting assistance.

WebManage. One innovative configuration management application from Tribe Computer Works of Alameda, CA offers routers, switches, and remote-access servers. Through firmware called WebManage, which contains an integral home page to display and configure network device settings, customers can view and interact with the devices using Netscape Navigator. Using hypertext links for quick movement between management functions and Tribe's technical support servers, WebManage allows a network manager to get immediate answers to setup or troubleshooting questions. Different views and access privileges can even be created that vary by user log-in and password.

Network Management. Some hub vendors, such as the Thomas-Conrad Corp. of Austin, TX, offer network management capabilities over the Web.

A Built-In Web Server. As part of its Simple Network Management Protocol (SNMP)-based management processor for its 100VG-AnyLAN Hub, Thomas-Conrad offers a built-in Web server. The Web server can be accessed from a LAN, or over dialup Internet connections. The user's browser software provides a graphical user interface (GUI) to configure ports, display hub status, and view statistical information. Because Internet browsing software is available on many platforms, users can benefit from WYSIWYG (what you see is what you get) management, whether they use IBM, Unix, or Macintosh-based computers. This method of support is designed for users who do not need all the management features of a full SNMP software package but who still require management capabilities delivered in a friendly manner over the network.

Customer Support. Several vendors offer support modules that allow organizations to provide customer service through the World Wide Web.

Target WebLink. Marlboro, MA-based Target Systems offers the product support module Target WebLink, which allows organizations to create a home page containing customizable incident-logging forms with direct links to a customer support center. Customers can access the forms through the support center via the Web and log incidents directly. Every aspect of the forms is customizable, including screen color, fonts, fields, and workflow rules. Companies that provide customer support worldwide can use WebLink to create multilingual forms or different forms in different languages.

ClearExpress WebSupport. Clarify, Inc., of San Jose, CA also offers a Web-based customer support solution. ClearExpress WebSupport is an extension of the company's Customer Service Management (CSM) system. It consists of two components: a data server and a set of HTML templates.

The first component, WebSupport Data Server, is tightly integrated with ClearSupport, the company's customer service and support application, which handles problem diagnostics, call handling, service contract verification, and report generation. The data server component provides a real-time, secure connection between the Web server and the server and database used by ClearSupport. Additionally, data specific to the Web interface, such as usage and traffic, is maintained for reporting purposes.

The other component, WebSupport Forms, consists of a set of preconfigured HTML templates that companies can use out-of-the-box or customize to fit their business needs. The templates include fill-in forms for new and open cases, as well as prompts to search the Clarify database.

ADAPTING TEXT DATABASES FOR WEB ACCESS

Companies that have gone to considerable time and expense to set up distributed support databases with such products as Lotus Notes and Folio Corp.'s Folio Views can now adapt them for WWW access.

InterNotes Web Publisher

InterNotes Web Publisher from Lotus Development Corp. enables users to publish their Notes applications to the Internet. Notes is a leading client/server platform for developing and deploying groupware applications that help organizations communicate, collaborate, and coordinate strategic business processes, including support operations.

Notes presents data in Forms and Views. Forms show a particular database record, and Views provide a summary of some or all of the database. Like a Web document, a Form can contain rich text and graphics, making Notes suitable as a platform for Web publishing. In addition, Notes' DocLinks icon functions exactly like a hypertext link used in a Web document.

Rather than requiring dedicated staff to convert existing documents into HTML, InterNotes Web Publisher leverages Notes' distributed authoring and management environment to automatically populate Web sites. Individual authors prepare their own information in Notes. Using Notes' replication and distributed storage model, authors from various locations contribute documents to the corporate Web server. The product's selective replication feature even allows specific portions of a database to be extracted for HTML translation and publication on the Web. InterNotes Web Publisher then automatically converts Notes databases, documents, and DocLinks into HTML so that they are accessible to popular Web browsers such as Mosaic or Netscape.

As content changes and as contributors submit new Notes material, InterNotes Web Publisher automatically updates the pages, as well as all links that refer to the new documents, without any manual intervention. Items can be programmed to show a "New" sign, or to be present on the Web site for only a specified period of time. InterNotes Web Publisher, which runs on Windows NT and OS/2 servers, also gives Notes authors more flexibility in presenting information. It allows HTML commands or whole HTML documents to be embedded in Notes documents.

Folio Corp.

Folio Corp. offers Infobase Web Server, which enables users to publish their Folio Views "infobases" on the Internet. An infobase is a repository of text, graphics, and multimedia objects. Infobases are created by the Folio Views Infobase Production Kit (IPK), which is used to structure information with such aids as embedded notes, highlighters, and hypertext links. Folio Views also features a powerful search-and-retrieve capability.

The Web server translates infobases into HTML on-the-fly for viewing with a Web browser, leaving infobases in their native format. Because there is only one copy of the infobase to update, maintenance is simplified and infobases can be authored once for distribution on CD-ROM, floppy disk, and PC LANs. When an infobase is accessed from the server, the user is presented with the infobase information screen or taken to a particular point in the infobase by a link. The buttons at the top of the screen — Document, Contents, and Query — provide navigation assistance through the infobase. The Document button takes the user directly to the body of the infobase. The Contents button displays a multilevel contents list, with each level capable of being expanded or collapsed by clicking on its associated icon. The Query button allows the user to perform key word search and retrieval. The dialog box displays a map of the results as well as the number of hits.

The Web Server, which runs on the Windows NT platform, also provides firewall security. With the firewall in place, the server allows access to only specified persons or IP addresses. Users can be restricted by password and IP address or by a complete subnet of IP address. Even users from a particular IP address or range of addresses can be specified.

CONCLUSION

Businesses are showing a clear trend toward leveraging existing Internet connections and exploiting the forms-handling capabilities of the Web to extend help desk and customer support functions worldwide. This frees staff from handling time-consuming telephone calls for routine problems and can shield them from some of the abrasiveness inherent in verbal exchanges. Delivering support electronically can also lower stress levels among support staff and permit them to devote more attention to high-priority problems.

From the buyer's perspective, the ability of vendors to provide online support services should be considered in any major purchase of systems and network components. Anything less can result in prolonged downtime, lost productivity, and hinder the ability of the organization to serve customers in a timely manner.

Chapter 59
File Retention and Backup

Bryan Wilkinson

WHEN DATA WAS STORED solely on paper, information was often duplicated and distributed to several locations. If one source of the information was destroyed, most of the data could be reconstructed from the alternative sources.

In a centralized data processing environment, an organization's current and historical data and the programs that process this data are stored on magnetic media in a central library. Although centralization offers certain advantages, it also exposes the organization to the risk of losing all its data and processing capacity in the event of a major accident. In addition, files stored on magnetic media are more susceptible to damage than are files stored on paper. For example, if a disk, reel, or cartridge is dropped, the data it stores could be destroyed; dropped papers require only resorting. In the event of fire, the glue binding ferrite particles to tapes, disks, and diskettes begins to dissolve at temperatures as low as 125° F; paper begins to burn at 451° F. Therefore, a fire-retardant vault designed for paper files provides only limited protection for magnetic media. Magnetic files are also susceptible to tape crimping or stretching, disk deformation, head crashes, viruses, and magnetic erasure.

Furthermore, when mainframes were the sole source of computer power, retention and backup procedures could be enforced. Copies of all files and programs could be conveniently kept in a central library. Copies of essential files and programs could be kept in a secure off-site location. Automated tape management systems were developed to facilitate proper file retention and backup.

Microcomputers and local area networks (LANs) have greatly complicated data storage and backup. Vital information is often stored on hard disks and diskettes that are scattered throughout an organization. The systems manager may have little or no authority or control over such distributed data. Furthermore, in environments in which data is transmitted by way of electronic data interchange, the data may reside only on magnetic media; there may be no input forms, no documentation, and no printed output. If a microcomputer's hard disk is damaged by physical accident or malicious mischief, the

0-8493-9822-3/00/$0.00+$.50

data is lost if the user has not followed proper backup procedures. If a diskette is lost or damaged through mishandling, the data is lost if no duplicates exist. This chapter explains how these problems can be minimized with proper file retention and backup procedures.

FILE BACKUP

The most common causes of file damage or destruction are operational errors, natural disasters, and sabotage. The proper backing up of files considerably lessens the adverse impact of such occurrences. The following sections discuss causes of damage and their effect on file integrity in both centralized and decentralized computing environments.

Operational Errors

In a centralized processing environment, more files are lost or damaged because of human error than for any other reason; the most common errors are probably unintentional scratches. Inadvertent scratches can occur when unlabeled tapes are being labeled, filed, pulled, and mounted. Labelling tapes does not necessarily prevent accidental scratches. Although most mainframe operating systems have an option that permits a retention date or period to be placed in the label, this capability is not always used, thereby making it impossible for the operating system to detect a tape that must not be scratched. With some operating systems, the operator can ignore the warning console message and write over a tape even when a retention period is specified in the internal label. An operator or user can also erase or incorrectly alter a file by entering a transaction that overwrites the file or by failing to save the file.

Updating the wrong generation of a master file can also destroy data. Both the operator and user are responsible for this error. The operator mounts the wrong generation of the file and ignores warning messages from the operating system; the user fails to notice the problem when reviewing the reports. If the error is not detected until after the transaction or the proper version of the master file has been scratched, it can be extremely costly and nearly impossible to correct. Additional updating problems can occur when an update period covers more than one transaction tape. A given tape can be used more than once or not at all. Without externally generated control totals, such errors are almost impossible to detect.

Unlike tape files, disk and diskette files have no automatic backup capabilities. A special operational procedure is necessary to copy the file. This problem is complicated by the update-in-place process used with disk and diskette files. If the system fails during an update, the operations manager must determine how much was accepted by the system to avoid duplicate updating. The use of a data base by several applications compounds the seriousness of losing a file.

Online systems present a special problem when input is not recorded on hard copy. If a file is accidentally destroyed, reconstruction may be impossible unless a tape or another disk copy was made during data collection. With online updating, transaction logs in the form of journal tapes can provide a valuable source of backup. Program, software, and equipment malfunctions can also destroy or alter data and therefore necessitate file reconstruction.

Another operational error is the improper handling of magnetic media. If, for example, an unprotected tape reel is grasped by the outer edge rather than at the hub, the tape can be crimped and made unreadable. Destroyed or degraded files must be restored, which requires file backup.

An automated tape management system can minimize some operational errors, especially if a computer center uses many tape files. Proper file retention and backup standards and procedures are other solutions to operational problems.

Microcomputer File Backup

An increasing amount of data is stored on microcomputers or downloaded from mainframes and then maintained on microcomputers. These computers are usually operated by people who are relatively inexperienced with data handling procedures. As a result, files have a greater chance of being lost or damaged. The systems manager should ensure that all microcomputer users know and understand the following basic precautions:

- If the microcomputer has a hard disk, the heads of the disk drive should be positioned over a nonsensitive area of the disk before the computer is moved — usually done by running a PARK routine. Many portable microcomputers also feature a headlock capability, which provides the same protection.
- If a large file is being created, it should be saved periodically during the creation process.
- Two files should not be created with the same name unless the older version is no longer desired — the new file will overwrite the old.
- File names should print in a standard location on output documents.
- Diskettes should be kept in protective envelopes and storage containers when not in use.
- No portion of the diskette's magnetic surface should be touched.
- Diskettes should not be bent or squeezed.
- Diskettes should be kept away from smoke, liquids, grease, motors,

magnets, telephones, display monitors, extreme temperatures and humidity, and direct sunlight.

- Diskettes should be removed from disk drives before the system is shut off.
- Only felt-tip pens should be used to write on 5 1/4-inch diskette labels.
- Paper clips and staples should not be used on diskettes.
- Diskettes should not be cleaned.

Natural Disasters

Operational errors usually destroy only a limited number of files; disasters can damage an entire library. Fire is the most common disaster threatening a data center. The data center environment creates its own fire hazards (e.g., high voltages and easily combustible paper dust). Fire melts or burns disk packs, diskettes, and tape cartridges and reels, as well as the glue that binds the ferrite particles to the medium. Media damaged by smoke are unreadable until cleaned. If water is used to extinguish the fire, the files must be dried before they can be used.

Microcomputers are vulnerable to such localized disasters as small fires, power surges, electrical shorts, or collapsing desks. This is reason enough for regularly backing up the hard disk by using diskettes, tape streamers, or Bernoulli boxes; by uploading to a mainframe; or by using another backup method.

Although other natural disasters — earthquakes, hurricanes, tornadoes, and floods — might not destroy the files, a medium is rendered unusable until it is cleaned, tested, and refiled. Magnetic files must be backed up and stored in a location that is not exposed to the same threat of natural disaster as is the central data library to ensure the organization's ability to recover these files in the event of a natural disaster.

Sabotage and Theft

Sabotage of files or programs can include magnetic erasure and physical abuse. In addition, programs can be altered to erase or modify files when a specified event occurs, and external tape labels can be interchanged, requiring the files to be reidentified. Anyone with physical, program, or online access can sabotage files and programs. An effective approach to protecting files from disaster and sabotage is off-site backup.

Microcomputer users should be warned about using bulletin board programs, programs obtained from friends, and programs purchased from people who do not have a well-established reputation in the computer industry. Such programs can carry viruses, worms, or Trojan horse programs that can wipe out or alter files or deplete a computer's resources. If the microcomputer is linked to a mainframe, there is the added hazard that the problem instruction set could be transmitted to the mainframe, where the problems it causes could be magnified and spread. It is recommended that someone well versed in programming review new microcomputer programs or that the programs be vetted by antiviral software before they are used.

In addition, microcomputers have increased the threat of file loss through theft. Microcomputer file libraries are usually not behind locked doors. Diskettes are easy to conceal. People steal diskettes, not only for the data on them but to use on their home computers. If the diskettes are stolen, the files are gone if no backups exist.

FILE-RETENTION REGULATIONS

The Internal Revenue Service, in Revenue Procedure 64-12, requires that adequate record retention facilities be available for storing tapes, printouts, and all applicable supporting documents. Because this procedure was issued in 1964, before the widespread use of disks, it refers only to tapes. Revenue Ruling 71-20, however, states that punched cards, magnetic tapes, disks, and other machine-sensible media must be retained for as long as their contents may be regulated by the administration of internal revenue law. If punched cards are used only as input and the information is duplicated on magnetic media, the cards need not be retained. The IRS has also developed audit programs that can be performed through the computer by using files retained on magnetic media.

There are about 3,000 federal statutes and regulations governing the retention of records. Not all the records covered by these regulations have been automated, but many have. A digest of these regulations, *Guide to Record Retention Requirements in the Code of Federal Regulations*, is available from the US Government Printing Office. These regulations can be grouped in the following categories:

- Accounting and fiscal.
- Administrative.
- Advertising.
- Corporate.
- Executive.
- Insurance.
- Legal.
- Manufacturing.
- Personnel.
- Plant and property.

- Purchasing.
- Research and development.
- Sales and marketing.
- Taxation.
- Traffic.

Although many of these records might not be automated, those that are can be retained economically on magnetic media. State-regulated organizations (e.g., banks and insurance firms) must also satisfy state file-retention requirements because audit software is used to expedite and expand state audits.

EDP AUDIT REQUIREMENTS

Electronic Data Processing (EDP) auditors must be able to verify that programs are operating properly and that magnetic file data is accurately represented by the tab listings for audit. In addition, they must confirm an organization's ability to recover from a disaster or an operational error. EDP auditors can impose retention and backup requirements on data processing by requesting that specific files — usually year-end files for important financial systems and transactions — be kept for testing.

Retention and Backup Standards

Generally, the absence of file-retention and backup standards means that the system designers probably decide which files are retained and backed up; consequently, too few or too many file generations may be retained. Each situation is costly and illustrates the need for file retention and backup standards. Standards should be established for local and disaster recovery backup and legal file-retention requirements (see Exhibit 59.1). The sources of information and approaches to file storage vary according to these requirements.

Local Recovery. The systems manager provides information about local recovery requirements. Responsibilities include detailing the types of operational errors that affect file or program integrity and documenting how and when a problem was detected and what steps were taken to restore file or program integrity. The causes and consequences of any situation in which integrity cannot be restored must be thoroughly investigated. Constraints on restoration should be listed, and steps that can simplify or improve restoration should be examined. When files are updated online or data is collected through communications networks, the individual most familiar with data

I. Purposes
   A. Retention
   B. Backup
II. Policies
   A. Existing files
   B. New systems and files
III. Standards
   A. Basic retention and backup schedules (time and location)
      1. Operating systems
      2. Software packages
      3. Application programs
      4. Master files
      5. Transaction files
      6. Work files
      7. Documentation
      a. System
      b. Program
      c. File
      8. Input documents
      9. Other material
   B. Retention and backup schedule approvals
      1. Retention
      2. Disaster backup
      3. Operational problems backup
   C. Security considerations
      1. Company private data and programs
      2. Government-classified data
      3. Customer files
   D. Use of retention periods in file header labels
   E. Storage location
      1. Backup
      2. Retention
   F. Transportation of files to and from off-site storage location
   G. Procedural Documentation
      1. For users
      2. For MIS
   H. Periodic tests of the usability of the backup and retained materials
IV. Appendix
   The appendix should provide an item-by-item schedule of all material whose retention and backup schedules differ from the basic schedule.

Exhibit 59.1. Outline for Developing Standards

communications should provide the same type of information for communications failures.

Data Restoration. Users who prepare input should be questioned about the disposition of original input documents and data transmission sheets. This information is particularly important when data is entered online with no paper documentation for backup. The data entry supervisor should be questioned to determine the cost and time required to reenter the average quantity of input for one processing cycle (i.e., one transaction file).

The programming manager should be consulted about problems associated with restoring application programs and other software files. Particular attention should be paid to the recovery of packaged programs that have been modified in-house. It is important to determine the availability of procedural documentation needed to restore the programs. The programming manager should provide the same information for the operating system and its various subroutines.

Microcomputer users should be questioned about the types of data in their files. Such data is increasingly of the type usually stored on the mainframe and centrally maintained. If there is data of this type, the problems and costs associated with its loss must be considered.

Disaster Recovery. Some of the information needed to establish disaster recovery backup standards is collected during the local recovery survey. Additional data can be obtained from reviews of a file inventory that identifies the files of each department within the organization. Department managers should review the inventory on a file-by-file basis to specify which files are vital to operations and must be reconstructed, department documents from which files can be restored, and the maximum time limit for recreating each file (assuming that the disaster occurred at the worst possible time). The systems manager should review all application programs, software packages, and operating system files. If several departments maintain organizational data bases, it may be necessary to recreate data at the data element level of the file.

Although all this information may not be needed to develop retention and backup standards, it does provide justification for developing and enforcing the standards. The information can also be used to establish backup and recovery procedures.

Legal Requirements. Retention requirements are set by the IRS, other government regulatory agencies, and departments within the organization. The controller is generally responsible for meeting the legal requirements and therefore should be consulted when it is being determined which files must be retained and for how long. The IRS recognizes that not all magnetic files can be maintained for long periods because of cost and volume and therefore has found that the appropriate method of determining record-retention needs is to evaluate each system and current retention policies. If the IRS has not reviewed organizational retention policies, the controller should ensure that such an evaluation is made. If the IRS has identified what should be retained and for how long, this information should be incorporated into the retention standards. The retained files should be periodically inventoried to confirm that the standards are being followed.

Department managers must be familiar with the other federal and state guidelines that apply to their files. In addition, record-retention requirements established by users, senior management, EDP auditing, and other departments must be enforced. Differences between the requirements specified by the users and those deemed appropriate by the auditors should be resolved.

STORAGE LOCATIONS

For efficient operation, files are usually stored in the computer room or an adjacent tape library. Microcomputer users who back up their files usually store the backups near the microcomputer. As protection against disaster, sabotage, or theft, a duplicate copy of important files should be stored off site. Various facilities can be used for this purpose:

- *Commercial off-site storage facilities.* These are useful for an organization with hundreds of files to be stored.
- *Moving and storage companies.* Several of these organizations use part of their warehouses to store magnetic files.
- *Bank safe-deposit boxes.* The size and cost of safe-deposit boxes make them appropriate for only a small number of files. Access to safe-deposit boxes may be limited to banking hours.
- *MIS facilities of another organization.* This alternative provides an environment with proper temperature and humidity controls. Unauthorized access can be prevented by keeping the files in a locked facility that can only be opened by an employee of the customer organization.
- *Remote corporate buildings.* This approach is probably the least costly of this type of facility.

Off-Site Storage Selection

Several factors should be considered during the selection of an off-site storage location:

- *Availability.* Backup files should be available 24 hours a day. Bank safe-deposit boxes present accessibility problems.
- *Access.* File access should be limited to a few employees. Individuals outside the organization should not have file access.
- *Physical security.* Fire safeguards (e.g., heat and smoke detectors and automatic fire extinguishers) that will not damage the files should be installed. The storage facility should be located and built to minimize damage from disasters. On-site and off-site facilities should not be concurrently vulnerable to the same disaster.
- *Environmental controls.* The proper temperature and humidity should be maintained continuously, including weekends and holidays.
- *Identifiability.* If a storage facility is used that is not part of the organization, there must be a method of distinguishing and identifying the material that belongs to the organization. If this is not done and the storage company declares bankruptcy, the bankruptcy court will seize and hold the files.
- *Storage requirement flexibility.* A facility should be able to meet the organization's current and future storage needs. It must be determined whether increased storage requirements will require the organization to use different locations in the building, purchase additional equipment, or pay for remodeling.
- *Cost.* This factor should be considered only after all other requirements have been satisfied. Compared with the reconstruction of files, any form of off-site storage is a less expensive alternative.

Storage Contracts

If a commercial storage facility, bank, or warehouse is selected as a storage location, the proposed lease should be reviewed by legal counsel. The lease should specify the lessor's file protection responsibilities and the resource for appropriate indemnification of file damage or loss.

If the data center of another organization is used for storage, a written agreement should identify the legal owner of the file, stipulate access rights, and define the liability of the organization providing the storage facility (or its insurer) if the files are accidentally or deliberately destroyed while on its premises. Legal counsel should review the proposed agreement to verify its appropriateness and validity. If the other organization refuses to sign an acceptable written agreement, use of the proposed facility should be approved by the senior management of the organization wishing to obtain off-site storage.

Transportation Considerations

The method of transporting files to and from the off-site storage facility should be considered carefully. Because magnetic media can be damaged by excessive heat, jarring, and mishandling, files should be packed in protective containers. Logs of all material stored off site should be maintained, and if a commercial transportation service is used, a packing slip should accompany each file.

OPERATIONAL CONSIDERATIONS

Proper off-site backup can shorten disaster recovery time and simplify the process. Because backup takes time and costs money, the frequency of backup should depend on how long the organization can continue to function without up-to-date data. In some operations, the answer may be no time. In such cases, the data must be captured simultaneously on two or more remotely located computers. If the answer is one week, weekly backup of master files and daily backup of transaction files should be adequate.

Frequency of backup depends on the type of application. For example, most manufacturing companies first used computers for financial data. In such cases, the company could manage for a week or two without the usual computer-produced reports. Now, many production applications are running so that production lines are scheduled, material is bought, and product status is determined using online automated systems. Off-site backup is often needed in these situations.

A standard approach to backup is to require a minimum of three generations of each master file, with the oldest generation being off site. Transaction tapes needed to bring the off-site version up to current status would be taken off site daily, weekly, or monthly, depending on the frequency or volatility of the update. Some organizations maintain their permanent-hold (usually year-end) tapes at the off-site location if the off-site storage location is more secure or spacious than the organization's storage area.

In a VS1 or MVS environment, the system catalog should be backed up for off-site storage. When the catalog matches the tapes at off-site storage, recovery is much easier; it is unnecessary to modify job controls to specify volume and serial numbers or absolute generations. Instead, restore jobs can refer to the relative generation number with a symbolic parameter that is easily modified.

Many data centers use reel numbers instead of labels on tapes that are managed by a tape management software package. Even when external labels are on the tapes, finding a particular tape among hundreds or even thousands can be next to impossible. Therefore, it is strongly recommended that a complete listing of tapes to be sent to off-site storage be prepared just before pickup and that the list be sent off site with the tapes. The list should include the tape volume and serial number, the date and time that it was created, and the data set names of every file on each tape. Automated tape management systems can produce such a list quickly and easily, and the list is important enough to justify the labor of producing it manually if no tape management system is in use.

SPECIAL FILE ACCESS PROBLEMS

Special file access problems complicate file retention and backup procedures. For example, if customer, classified, trade-secret, and sensitive data are processed in an online environment, a security software package must limit file access. The following sections address other access considerations for such files.

Customer Files. If an organization performs processing for other entities, it must access their files and programs. Customer agreements should be reviewed to determine the organization's contractual liability. Standards and procedures should have safeguards that minimize the possibility of lost or altered files. The customer should agree in writing to proposed backup and retention schedules.

Classified Data. Files with a government security classification must be stored and transported according to government regulations. The systems manager and EDP auditor should review these limitations to verify their enforcement.

Trade Secrets. Trade secrets are programs, formulas, and processes that give an organization a competitive edge. Methods of handling and protecting trade secrets are specified by state law and therefore vary. Several requirements, however, are basic to maintaining trade secrets:

- A trade secret and its associated material must be physically secured and designated as company confidential.
- The information cannot be published or made available to the public.
- If the material must be disclosed to someone outside the organization, this individual must be advised of the trade secret and must agree to maintain its confidentiality.
- A permanent record should be maintained of the material's location when it is not in the usual storage location.

Senior management must designate which files or programs represent trade secrets, and the systems manager and EDP auditor should ensure that an organization's retention and backup standards and practices meet state and internal requirements. The standards and practices should be reviewed with legal counsel to ensure adequate control.

Sensitive Data. Financial, payroll, and similar accounting information is generally considered confidential, with access limited to specific employees. Such data may be found on both hard disks and diskettes. If the data is on hard disk, access to that computer must be limited. If the data is also on diskette and is not encrypted, the handling and storage of the diskette (including its off-site storage) must be controlled. The systems manager must determine which files contain sensitive information, who is permitted access to each of these files, and how such access is controlled. Access control should be specified in the appropriate standards and procedures.

BACKUP USABILITY

Although the proper files may be retained and backed up, procedures must be established to maintain and test backup file usability.

One problem occurs when files that are to be retained for several years are stored on tape. Unfortunately, gravitational pull usually deforms tapes that are unused for a year or longer. A standard technique to prevent this problem is to rewind unused backup tapes every 6 to 12 months. If this practice is not being followed, the readability of the older tapes should be verified through a tape-to-print program.

If there is no standard on file retention, or if the standard is not followed, the proper versions of files, transactions, and programs may not be retained. To detect this problem, the systems manager can inventory the files at the backup location and compare this listing to the standard. A more useful but difficult approach is to use the files and programs at the backup site (instead of those at the data center) to process one or more applications. This method determines whether the standards are adequate and are being adhered to and whether operators know the procedures for using the backup material. Even if this technique fails to make these determinations, the processing pinpoints unexpected problems that could arise in an actual emergency and reemphasizes the need for workable emergency procedures.

ACTION PLAN

To ensure effective file retention and backup, the systems manager should:

- Determine file exposure.

- Determine the government record retention requirements that affect the organization.
- Compare current record retention standards with exposures and requirements.
- Identify and evaluate local recovery problems and their solutions.
- Review the organizational understanding of potential problems, proposed solutions, and legal requirements for record retention.
- Inspect and evaluate off-site storage.
- Review off-site storage agreements.
- Inspect and evaluate the facilities used to transport files to the off-site location.
- Determine special file access restrictions.
- Evaluate the usability of backup files.
- Prepare recommendations based on reviews and evaluations.

Chapter 60

Managing Database Backup and Recovery

Michael Simonyi

MANAGEMENT OF THE CORPORATE DATABASE is arguably one of the most mismanaged areas in information technology today. Database technology has evolved from historical glass house foundations of the past into the point and click implementations that come right out of the box today. Where databases and systems were once carefully designed, implemented, and deployed, they are now installed, loaded, and deployed without regard to basic effective design. This chapter addresses the concepts necessary to formulate a method to protect, back up, and in the event of failure, recover, perhaps the most important aspect of a business, its database. Without proper preparation, planning, and testing an entire database infrastructure can become the target of lost devices, indices, degraded backup mechanisms, and corrupted data.

HIGH AVAILABILITY VERSUS RECOVERABILITY

There are important differences between database availability and recoverability. Database availability can be a driving factor to recoverability, but it does not guarantee recoverability. Database availability is the measurement of production uptime and physical access to production data in a networked environment. In contrast, database recoverability refers to the ability to successfully recover a database in its entirety. Recoverability is a measurement of how accurate and lengthy the process of recovering from partial or total failure can be. The difference lies in the application of backup tools used in conjunction with high-availability tools. The redundancy of high-availability systems in an environment can directly relate to a higher grade of successful backups for the database environment as well as the supporting systems. In this chapter, a database environment is defined as the database, connecting middleware, and application front end screens. These technologies are used to complement each other to offer accuracy, reliability, and stability.

0-8493-9822-3/00/$0.00+$.50

METHODS OF DATA PROTECTION

The common methods of data production include the following: (1) Tape; (2) Mirroring (RAID 0); (3) Data Guarding (RAID 5); (4) Duplexing; (5) Partitioning; (6) Replication; and (7) Clustering. Each of these are explained further in this section.

Before investigating these different methods available for protecting a database environment, this chapter discusses the business requirements for data recoverability and availability. For example, should a database, in the event of failure, cause individuals to be placed into a life-threatening situation or force an organization into financial chaos and eventual closure? In such a case it is necessary to implement all available methods to become 100 percent fault tolerant. However, should a failure be merely an inconvenience, then a simple tape backup procedure may suffice. Most organizations seek the middle ground.

Tape Backup

Tape backup should form the foundation of a corporate backup strategy due to its ease of use and low cost. In order for the tape backup mechanism to be useful it must be well designed and tested regularly. At a minimum, backups should be performed on a daily basis and not less than weekly. If possible, the entire database(s) should be backed up on a daily basis. The database transaction logs should be backed up during and after business hours, or whenever feasible to minimize the risk of lost data.

Mirroring

Mirroring or RAID 0 provides for duplicate sets of data on two separate hard disk drives, a primary and a secondary. This is also known as a master/slave configuration. For each logical write operation there are two physical write operations to the hard disks. This scenario protects against an individual or set of drives from failure. If either the primary or secondary drive fails, the data on the surviving drive allows for system recovery. In most situations, this option is ideal for protection of the database transaction logs. However, it does not offer protection against multiple simultaneous failures.

Data Guarding

Data guarding or RAID 5 has the ability to stripe redundant data across multiple drives (minimum 3) in an array. The striping of data protects against a single drive failure in the array. When an array loses a drive, the system still functions by using the redundant data found on the surviving drives. There are two types of RAID 5 available today, namely software and hardware-based RAID 5. Hardware RAID is by choice the desired implementation method. This stems from the fact that RAID 5 was designed with drive failures in mind. Extending the tolerance level of a RAID 5 system can then be achieved by mirroring or duplexing drive arrays. This type of extension allows for whole drive arrays to fail without impacting the system

Duplexing

Duplexing is similar to mirroring except that in a duplexed configuration separate controller cards manage each drive or sets of drives. In essence, duplexing is Raid 0 with an additional layer or redundancy. The second disk controller cards removes a single point of failure that is exhibited in a standard mirroring (Raid 0) configuration.

Partitioning

Partitioning is the ability to deploy a database system across multiple servers where each server houses a different portion of the overall database. Should a server go down, only the component running on that server becomes unavailable. In this scenario the database can continue to function normally, provided applications are written to handle these types of situations. Additional protection can be achieved by employing RAID 0, 5 or duplexing to further minimize system down time.

Replication

Replication offers the ability to publish the contents (complete or portions thereof) of a database to another or multiple servers in an environment. The technique is similar to partitioning; however, to employ replication requires sophisticated application transaction logic in order to be used effectively. Replication allows for the mirroring of database transactions to be replicated in a secondary database at the central site or in a distributed location. Ideally all transactions should be processed at a central database and the transactions should be replaced to the other subscribing sites. This eliminates the difficulty that becomes inherent with transaction logic of the traditional two-phase commit that fails due to hardware failures.

Clustering

Clustering is the ability for a group of servers to share or cooperate with each other in using common resources. Clustering allows systems to monitor each other and in the event of failure, transfer processing to their counterpart. Clustering is a very reliable method for maintaining a fault-tolerant and highly available systems environment. However, vendors approach clustering differently. It is recommended that organizations examine their application architecture and processing requirements prior to selecting a clustering strategy and infrastructure.

Each of these individual methods can be used in tandem to build a graded level of fault tolerance and high availability. Again, as with any other technology, the system requirements dictate the configuration and detail that is ultimately required. In most cases the higher the required tolerance, the more methods that are included in the solution.

Batch Cycles

The size and complexity of the database environment determines the most suitable backup cycle. A small site can afford the luxury of daily full database and transaction log backups. A medium sized site must perform a mix of backups of full database and transaction log backups on daily and weekly cycles. A large site requires multiple staggered sets of backups and transaction logs on a daily basis with weekly and even monthly cycles backing up segments of the database to achieve a full database backup.

Transaction logs should be backed up at least once during the day. However, this depends on the transaction flow of the database. A low volume On Line Transaction Processing (OLTP) database may require only a single transaction log backup at the end of a business day, before or after any additional processing is enacted on the data. In the case of high-volume OLTP processing environments, the backup of the transaction log may require hourly backups. It will be necessary to gauge the transaction flow of the environment to determine the backup schedule of the transaction logs.

Sample backup schedules for small, medium and large sites are shown in the tables given in Exhibit 60.1.

With each scenario outlined above, the robustness of the hardware also impacts the backup schedule of an organization. Since most organizations cannot afford to replace hardware on an as needed basis, different backup schedules may need to be adopted over time, for different pieces of hardware.

ACCURACY OF BACKUPS

Although data backups are important, equally important is the need to determine the accuracy of the data prior to backup and the ability to guarantee the restoration of the contents of the backup into the original database or backup database system. The accuracy or consistency of the backup is paramount for recoverability. Should inconsistent data or data structures be stored onto the backup media, any attempt to restore them will most likely render the database inoperable, or worse, introduce inconsistent data into the production environment that may unknowingly place the organization at risk.

Most databases on the market today provide built-in tools that provide some level of data integrity checking that verifies that internal data structures are intact and tables, indices, and page linkage are consistent. Any warnings or errors reported for these utilities should be acted upon at

Exhibit 60.1. Sample backup schedules for small, medium, and large sites.

Schedule for a Small Site for Database Less than 10GB

Time	Mon	Tues	Wed	Thurs	Fri	Sat	Sun
12am	DB Check	DB Check	DB Check	DB Chek	DB Check	DB Check	DB Check
1am		Full DB	Full DB	Full DB	Full DB	Full DB	
5pm	Tlog	TLog	Tlog	TLog	TLog		
9pm	Purge Log	Purge Log	Purge Log	Purge Log	Purge Log		

Times noted are for clarity only

Schedule for a Medium Site for Databases greater than 10GB but less than 100GB

Time	Mon	Tues	Wed	Thurs	Fri	Sat	Sun
12am	DB Check	DB Check	DB Check	DB Check	DB Check	DB Check	DB Check
1am						Full DB	
5pm	Tlog	TLog	Tlog	TLog	TLog		
9pm	Purge Log	Purge Log	Purge Log	Purge Log	Purge Log		

Times noted are for clarity only

Schedule for a Large Site for Databases greater than 100GB

Time	Mon	Tues	Wed	Thurs	Fri	Sat	Sun
12am	DB Check	DB Check	DB Check	DB Check	DB Check	DB Check	DB Check
1am	DB Seg 1	DB Seg 2	DB Seg 3	DB Seg 4	DB Seg 5	DB Seg 6	DB Seg 7
5pm	Tlog	TLog	Tlog	TLog	TLog	TLog	TLog
9pm	Purge Log	Purge Log	Purge Log	Purge Log	Purge Log	Purge Log	Purge Log

Times noted are for clarity only

DB Seg refers to a portion or segment of the database to be backed up. Each segment or portion of the database in conjunction with the transaction logs will provide for a full database backup at any point in time.

once. Failure to act on these messages can render a database inoperable and depending when the problem surfaced cause a loss of data. The following pseudo implementation provides an approach to handling a database backup.

Generic Backup Stream

1. Perform a data integrity check on the contents of the database.
   - 1.1. Have inconsistencies been found in the database?
     - 1.1.1. Send alert to DBA and Operations staff, write events to log file.
     - 1.1.2. Halt backup stream. (Problem resolution takes place at this point.)
     - 1.1.3. Reestablish backup stream after problem has been resolved.
   - 1.2. Be sure database is free of defects.
2. Begin backup stream.
3. Verify completion status.
4. Notify operations and DBA of backup completion.

Incremental Backups

Incremental backups are something that should be performed only if it is not possible to complete a full backup during the allotted timeframe or backup window. Incremental backups extend the period of time required for restoring the contents of a database in the event of a failure. Although unavoidable in huge database environments where incremental backups are the mainstay, they should still be staggered in such environments.

Backing Up in a Distributed LAN/WAN Environment

Backing up a distributed database in the LAN/WAN environment can be a nightmarish challenge. Time zones and production uptime in differing geographical areas can affect the ability of ensuring a reliable and accurate backup. If the data volumes are small and maintainable, it will be possible to coordinate backups and replication over the WAN. Some thought should be given to using redundant WAN links so as not to affect other communications over primary WAN Links. If data volumes are of an extremely high nature or the network spans the globe, it may become practical to build a hot site for this type of environment. Whether the site is built and maintained internally or through third-party vendors is purely academic. The rationale is to provide a site for conducting business transactions should the primary production facilities fail. The site should mirror the current production facilities at all times. It can be updated by replication or by the use of tape media. Such a site should also be tested on a regular basis to ensure accuracy and guarantee the ability to continue business if failure encroaches upon the production systems (see Exhibit 60.2).

Administration Tools

As mentioned previously, most products on the market ship with some sort of administration tool sets to maintain and administer database environments. These tools can be either GUI based or Command line based, and at a minimum the following tasks should be included in the process: user management, DDL scripting, data import and export, database consistency, device management, data recovery, and security utilities. Some database vendors also provide additional utilities in the areas of Hierarchical Storage Management (HSM), Database Cluster Management, and on-line statistics monitoring tools. If a database does not provide for a specific level of administration, there are many third-party products available on the market that can complement most database environments.

Areas to Protect

There are three basic areas of a database that must be protected. The data, of course, being the blood of the system, the catalogs, being the skeleton of the system, and the transaction logs, which are the heart of a database

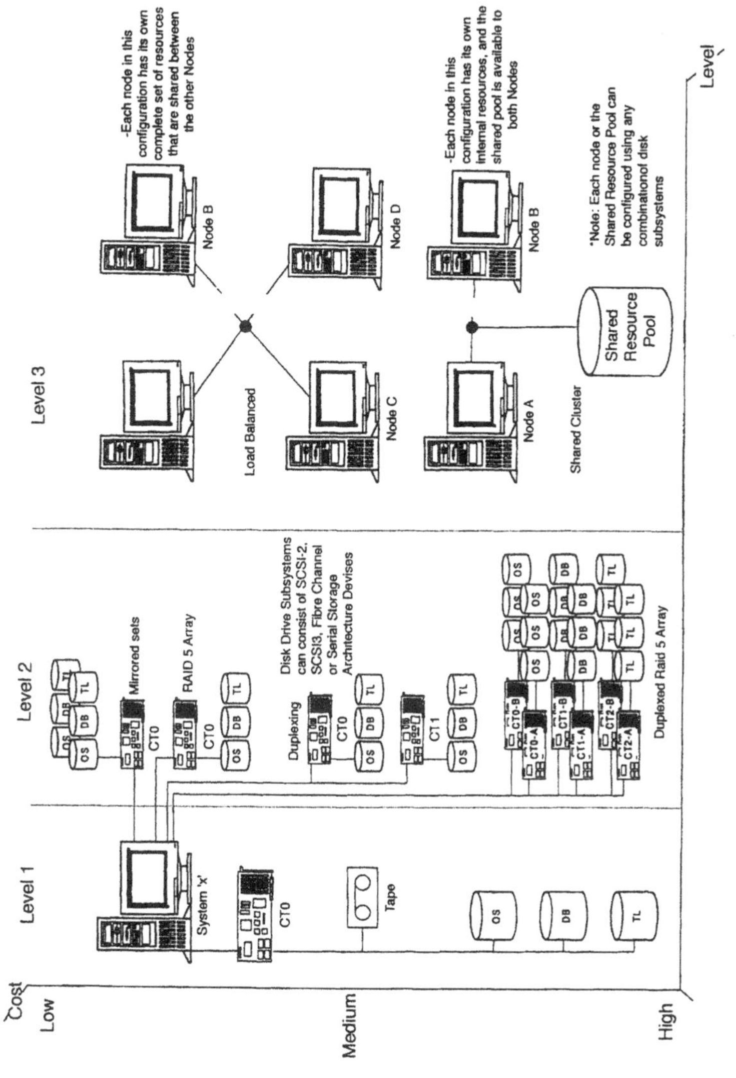

Exhibit 60.2. Types of Protection

as they detail all the events that have transpired against the data since the last full backup.

The transaction logs are considered paramount for any database system, especially after a database failure. Without the ability to maintain a readable copy of the transaction logs, any failure in the database places the data at extreme risk. For example, suppose a database is backed up fully once a week on Friday nights. During the week the transaction logs are written onto the hard disk. If the hard disk that holds the transaction log fails the following Thursday, and no prior backup of the transactions logs have taken place, the database will only be recoverable to the last point of a full backup.

The database catalog, as described above, acts as the skeleton for the database. It details the structure of the physical database. The catalogs must be rigorously maintained. Each and every change to the database modifies the catalog. The catalog has two facets, the system catalog and the user database catalog. Each has it own specialized backup requirements.

The system catalog defines the database environment, including the disk drives, database devices, configuration, logon privileges, tuning parameters, and device load points. This catalog must be backed up after every change because it affects the entire database environment. Any changes to the system catalog that are lost will seriously impair the ability to recover a database. In addition to having a backed up system catalog, a paper-based reproduction of the system catalog can be beneficial for audit purposes or if the need ever arises to restore an older database backup on a system prior to the installation of a new RAID array. As hardware is added to the system, database load points will vary. This can have undesirable effects when loading an older version of a database back onto the server.

The user database catalog on the other hand is the definition of the user database. It contains all the details regarding the tables and indexes used in the physical implementation of your database. This must be kept under strict observance. It should follow a strict change control process and must be backed up after each and every change to the database using a version control system. A failure to back up the database catalogs will result in loss of data if you are ever placed into a position of reloading the database from flat files. The database catalog, sometimes referred to as a schema, is the blueprint to your database. It is the foundation of your database. Keep it up to date and make sure you are able to retrace the path of its evolution.

The data, of course, being the lifeblood of the database and the reason for its existence, must also be safeguarded. The data should be backed up on a daily basis, if time permits, but not less than once a week. Backups should be restored from time to time to verify the validity of the backup

Exhibit 60.3. The Varying Levels of Database Recovery and Associated Costs

Method	Level	Cost	Down Time
Tape (mandatory)	Low	Low	Hours
Mirroring	Medium	Low	Minutes to hours
Duplexing	Medium	Low	Minutes to hours
Data Guarding	High	Medium	Minutes
Partitioning	Medium	High	Minutes to hours
Replication	High	High	Minutes
Clustering	Very High	Very High	Seconds to minutes
Hybrid Combinations	Extremely High	Extremely High	Seconds

and its state. There is no point in performing a backup if it is not tested periodically. What may have been restored last year may not be restorable now. Also be careful to test recoverability from tape backups.

Levels of Protection

Each of the individual methods provides a level of afforded protection. The base level of protection and last line of defense for a system failure should be a tape backup, the slowest of all methods to get the system back into operation when disaster strikes — the highest level being a hybrid system. Exhibit 60.3 demonstrates the varying levels of recovery and associated costs.

The application of each method will dictate the level of availability in the system and the degree of time required in recovering from a failure. For example, in a partitioned system the database is distributed between many separate servers. Should one of the servers go down, only a portion of the database becomes unavailable. Its cost is relatively high as there are many servers deployed and set up in a modular fashion. Each server then employs its own recovery mechanism.

In defining the level of protection to meet ones particular needs ask yourself these questions:

- Can I run the company without my database for an extended period of time?
- Do I risk my customer relationships if my database is unavailable?
- If the system becomes unavailable, is human life at risk?

If you answer yes to any of the above questions, you will need some form of high-availability solution to meet your needs. As mentioned previously, a tape backup should form the foundation of any backup strategy. Use the decision tree in Exhibit 60.4 to help guide the requirements for your backup strategy.

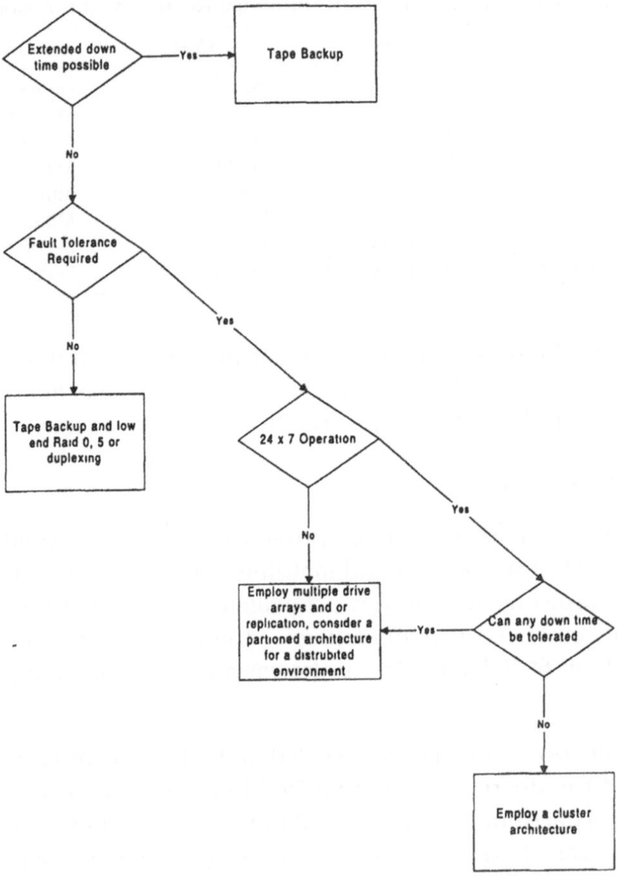

Exhibit 60.4. Decision Tree for Selecting Desired Level of Protection

Virus Protection

Although a database system is usually well protected against direct virus attacks, you should make sure that the database is well secured from the rest of your computing environment. This usually means protecting the database by placing it on a dedicated system, making sure that the only way of reaching the system is via administrative tools, the deployed middleware, or operating-system-related administrative tools.

Even with a well-secured database, you will need to take similar precautions on the front end systems as well. Virus checking utilities should be deployed at the end-user client workstations and at any point in the environment where data will be fed into the database. Of course, this depends on the types of data being stored in the database. If Binary Large Objects

(BLOBs) are allowed to be inserted into documents, applications, or images that a virus can attach to, it may be necessary to implement additional levels of virus protection.

Internet and Intranet Firewalls

Database vendors are pursuing the ability to allow corporate data to become extensible to the Web if it is not already there. Most databases provide for this by using extensions to the middleware or database interface, providing extended datatypes in the database or providing plugins to the database.

This presents the problem of how to ensure that no one can gain direct access to a corporate database. By implementing hardware/software firewall combinations and proxies, it is possible to carefully segregate the database from the publicly exposed portion of a network. This allows construction of unidirectional paths into and out of the database that cannot be compromised easily.

CONCLUSION

In my experience, there is never too much protection, only too little. Having a well-thought-out backup and recovery procedure in place will save you time, money, and embarrassment when things go wrong. All of the topics examined within the body of this chapter detail methods that can be used to safeguard corporate databases or any other system. Pick and choose the pieces that best suit your needs when building your fail-safe environment.

Section XII Checklist

1. How does your organization manage the different system administration duties? Are there dedicated staff for the various functions?
2. Which administrative tasks are more likely to suffer from incompleteness in your environment?
3. Do you feel confident that post implementation tasks receive the necessary attention for ongoing system support? If not, what steps have you taken to improve this?
4. Are system administrative projects scheduled as part of development or are these handled when time permits?
5. Is it your impression that programmers are more or less willing to complete administrative duties, such as documentation, and backup procedures? Is this due to lack of time, misunderstanding, or other factors?
6. Should specialized staff be assigned to system administration functions? Would this improve the quality and the quantity of completed projects?
7. Has system support become more demanding in your environment? If so, could this be simplified with better technology such as the Internet?
8. How prepared is your environment for a major site disaster? What about a small disaster?
9. Does your organization have an enterprise wide file recovery procedure in place? If so, has it ever been tested?
10. What changes would you implement to improve the file retention and backup of the application systems in your organization?
11. Assuming that a major disaster occurred in your environment, how much time would it take your organization to restore crucial business files?
12. How is change management handled in your environment? Are there procedures that control pre- and postimplementation changes?
13. What is the frequency of applications changes in deployed systems? Are these due to corrections or enhancements?
14. Is there a steering committee that governs the priority and authorization for system changes?
15. How are end user workstation files backed up in your environment? Is it done automatically, or voluntarily? Is it effective?

About the Editor

PAUL C. TINNIRELLO IS CHIEF INFORMATION OFFICER of a leading insurance information publishing organization and a consulting editor for Auerbach Publications. He is responsible for the development and support of financial software products in microcomputer and mainframe environments. He holds an MS in computer and information sciences as well as a BA in mathematics. Tinnirello has been a graduate and undergraduate adjunct professor at state and local colleges in New Jersey and is a founding member and past director of the Software Management Association, formerly the Software Maintenance Association. He has written and published numerous articles on the development and support process and has presented his material at various computer conferences throughout the country.

Index

B

C

D

E

J

K

L

M

P

Q

S

T

X

Y

T - #0211 - 101024 - C0 - 234/156/43 [45] - CB - 9780849398223 - Gloss Lamination